90 0752943 1

Under the wilfully archaic heading of the 'Nationalities Question' the editors have put together a resoundingly topical collection of cutting-edge essays that highlight what European integration has meant to stateless or minority nations and to the states that harbour them.

The conclusions of this volume are sober and surprising. The process of European integration may ebb and flow but the 'Nationalities Question', from Ireland to Moldova, in all its complex and variegated forms will persist long after EU budgetary and other squabbles have been resolved.

Andre Liebich, IUHEI, Switzerland

This is an exciting and innovative contribution to the study of how the process of European integration is influencing the politics of nationalism and ethnicity. The editors have composed a collection of essays that represents the best of the most recent and challenging theoretical thinking and empirical research in the study of the politics of nationalism and ethnicity in Europe. Moreover, it is one of the few books of its kind that is truly 'European' in its scope. The book is a major contribution to the literature in this field and will be required reading for academic experts, policy-makers and students alike.

James Hughes, London School of Economics, UK

European Integration and the Nationalities Question

This new and topical book examines the effect of European integration on relations between states and minority nations. The editors, picking up an older vocabulary, call this the 'nationalities question'.

The collection brings together the leading specialists in the field, and covers a wide range of cases, from Northern Ireland in the West, to Estonia and Latvia in the East, and Cyprus in the South-East. The contributors assess how European integration has affected the preparedness of states to accommodate minorities across a range of fundamental criteria, including: enhanced rights protection; autonomy; the provision of a voice for minorities in the European and international arena; and the promotion of cross-border cooperation among communities dissected by state frontiers. The comprehensive chapters stress the importance of the nationality question, and the fact that, contrary to the hopes and beliefs of many on the left and right, it is not going to go away.

Beginning with an introductory essay that summarises the impact of European integration on the nationalities question, this accessible book will be of strong interest to scholars and researchers of politics, nationalism, ethnic conflict and European studies.

John McGarry is Professor of Political Studies and Canada Research Chair in Nationalism and Democracy at Queen's University, Kingston, Canada. **Michael Keating** is Professor of Regional Studies at the European University Institute in Florence and Professor of Scottish Politics at the University of Aberdeen.

Routledge innovations in political theory

European Integration and the Nationalities Question

Edited by
John McGarry and Michael Keating

LONDON AND NEW YORK

First published 2006
by Routledge
2 Park Square, Milton Park, Abingdon, Oxon OX14 4RN

Simultaneously published in the USA and Canada
by Routledge
270 Madison Ave, New York, NY 10016

Routledge is an imprint of the Taylor & Francis Group, an informa business

© 2006 John McGarry and Michael Keating for selection and
editorial matter; individual contributors, their contributions

Typeset in Baskerville by Wearset Ltd, Boldon, Tyne and Wear
Printed and bound in Great Britain by TJI Digital, Padstow, Cornwall

British Library Cataloguing in Publication Data
A catalogue record for this book is available from the British Library

Library of Congress Cataloging in Publication Data
European integration and the nationalities question / edited by
John McGarry and Michael Keating.

p. cm. – (Routledge innovations in political theory ; 21)

Includes bibliographical references and index.

1. Minorities–European Union countries. 2. Nationalism–European
Union countries. 3. Europe–Economic integration–Social aspects. 4.
National characteristics, European. I. McGarry, John, 1957– II.
Keating, Michael, 1950– III. Series.

JN34.7.E87 2006

323.14–dc22

2005034187

ISBN10: 0-415-40100-3 (hbk)
ISBN10: 0-203-08840-9 (ebk)

ISBN13: 978-0415-40100-5 (hbk)
ISBN13: 978-0-203-08840-1 (ebk)

Contents

Illustrations

Figures

Tables

Contributors

Judy Batt is Jean Monnet Chair ad personam and Senior Research Fellow at the EU Institute for Security Studies in Paris, where she works on EU policy towards the Balkans. Her recent publications include *Region, State and Identity in Central and Eastern Europe* (2002), co-edited with Kataryna Wolczuk; and *Developments in Central and East European Politics* (3rd edn, 2003), co-edited with Stephen White and Paul Lewis.

Rainer Bauböck is senior researcher at the Institute for European Integration Research (EIF) of the Austrian Academy and president of the Austrian Association of Political Science (2003–05). His publications include *Transnational Citizenship: Membership and Rights in International Migration* (1994); *Blurred Boundaries: Migration, Ethnicity, Citizenship* (1998), co-edited with John Rundell; and *The Challenge of Diversity: Integration and Pluralism in Societies of Immigration* (1996), co-edited with Agnes Heller and Aristide Zolberg.

Sten Berglund is Professor of Political Science at Orebro University, Sweden and has published extensively on comparative post-Communist studies.

Anwen Elias is a Lecturer in European Politics at the University of Wales, Aberystwyth. She has recently completed her PhD at the EUI, Florence, on the subject of minority nationalism and European integration in Wales, Galicia and Corsica.

Montserrat Guibernau is Professor of Politics at Queen Mary, University of London. Her recent publications include *Catalan Nationalism* (2004); *Nations without States: Political Communities in a Global Age* (1999); *History and National Destiny: Ethnosymbolism and its Critics* (2004), co-edited with John Hutchinson; and *The Conditions of Diversity in Multinational Democracies* (2003), co-edited with Alain Gagnon and Francois Rocher.

Elena Jurado is an administrator in the Secretariat of the Framework Convention for the Protection of National Minorities of the Council of Europe. She has published a number of articles on European integration and minority rights in Estonia and Latvia, in such journals as *Democratization*; the *Journal of Baltic Studies*; and *Claves de Razón Práctica*.

Eve Hepburn is a researcher at the European University Institute, Florence. She is currently completing her PhD on the impact of European integration on territorial politics in Scotland, Bavaria and Sardinia.

Gurutz Jáuregui is Professor of Constitutional Law at the University of the Basque Country. He is the author of 12 books, including, in English, *The Decline of the Nation-State* (1994). He has also co-authored and edited several volumes.

Michael Keating is Professor of Regional Studies at the European University Institute in Florence and Professor of Scottish Politics at the University of Aberdeen. He has published widely on regional politics and on nationalism. Among his recent books are *Plurinational Democracy* (2001) and *The Government of Scotland* (2005).

Walter Kemp is Senior Adviser to the Secretary General of the Organisation for Security and Co-operation in Europe (OSCE). From 1999 to 2003 he was a Senior Adviser to the OSCE's High Commissioner on National Minorities. He is the author of *Nationalism and Communism in Eastern Europe and the Soviet Union: A Basic Contradiction?* (1999); and *Quiet Diplomacy in Action: the OSCE High Commissioner on National Minorities* (2001).

Charles King is Ion Ratiu Associate Professor in the School of Foreign Service at Georgetown University, Washington, DC. His books include *The Black Sea: A History* (2004); *The Moldovans: Romania, Russia, and the Politics of Culture* (2000), and, as co-editor, *Nations Abroad: Diaspora Politics and International Relations in the Former Soviet Union* (1998).

Will Kymlicka is the Canada Research Chair in Political Philosophy at Queen's University, Kingston, Canada, and a Visiting Professor in the Nationalism Studies programme at the Central European University in Budapest. His books include *Multicultural Citizenship* (1995); and *Politics in the Vernacular: Nationalism, Multiculturalism and Citizenship* (2001).

John McGarry is Professor of Political Studies and Canada Research Chair in Nationalism and Democracy at Queen's University, Kingston, Canada. His recent books include *The Northern Ireland Conflict: Consociational Engagements* (2004), co-authored with Brendan O'Leary; and *The Future of Kurdistan in Iraq* (2005), co-edited with Brendan O'Leary and Khaled Salih.

Margaret Moore is Professor of Political Studies at Queen's University, Kingston, Canada. Her recent books include *The Ethics of Nationalism* (2001); and *States, Nations and Borders: The Ethics of Making/Boundaries* (2003), co-edited with Allen Buchanan.

Neil Munro is Senior Research Fellow at the Centre for the Study of Public Policy, University of Strathclyde and co-author, with Richard Rose, of *Elections without Order: Russia's Challenge to Vladimir Putin* (2002); and *Elections and Parties in New European Democracies* (2003).

Michel Nicolas is Professor of Cultures and Regional Languages at the Université Rennes, Brittany, France. His books include *Bretagne: Un Destin Européen* (2001); and *Histoire de la Revendication Bretonne* (2006).

Richard Rose is Professor and Director of the Centre for the Study of Public Policy, University of Aberdeen and the author of many books. In 1991, he created the New European Barometer surveys to monitor the transition from Communism in Russia, Ukraine, the Balkans and what are now eight new member states of the European Union.

Gwendolyn Sasse is Senior Lecturer in Comparative European Politics in the European Institute and the Department of Government at the London School of Economics and Political Science. Her publications include *Europeanization and Regionalization in the EU's Enlargement to Central and Eastern Europe: The Myth of Conditionality* (2004), co-authored with James Hughes and Claire Gordon; and *Ethnicity and Territory in the Former Soviet Union: Regions in Conflict* (2002), co-edited with James Hughes.

Nathalie Tocci is a Marie Curie Fellow at the Robert Schuman Centre for Advanced Studies, European University Institute, Florence. Her most recent book is *EU Accession Dynamics and Conflict Resolution: Catalyzing Peace or Consolidating Partition in Cyprus?* (2004).

Stefan Wolff is Professor of Political Science at the University of Bath, England, Senior Non-resident Research Associate at the European Centre for Minority Issues in Flensburg (Germany), and editor of the journal *Ethnopolitics* (Routledge). His latest publications include *Disputed Territories: The Transnational Dynamics of Ethnic Conflict Settlement* (2002); *Peace at Last? The Impact of the Good Friday Agreement on Northern Ireland* (2002), co-edited with J. Neuheiser; and *Autonomy, Self Governance and Conflict Resolution: Innovative Approaches to Institutional Design in Divided Societies* (2005), co-edited with Marc Weller.

Acknowledgements

We would like to thank the Carnegie Corporation of New York for providing the funding which made this book possible, and all of the contributors for delivering their chapters as promised. Thanks is also due to Anna Drake, Eve Hepburn and Allison McCulloch-Kandulski for their help with myriad tasks involved in putting the book together. Finally, we are grateful to Craig Fowlie and the rest of the Routledge editorial team for their patience, encouragement and constructive advice.

1 Introduction

European integration and the nationalities question*

John McGarry, Michael Keating and Margaret Moore

This book is concerned with how the process of European integration has affected what we, picking up an older vocabulary, call the 'nationalities question'. These are both broad concepts and some definitional clarity is in order. European integration has, for our purposes, three strands. The first strand is normative, involving changed understandings of sovereignty, self-determination and rights, including the rights of individuals and minorities. These changes may affect both states and national movements directed against states. The second strand is market integration, with the free movement of goods, services, capital and labour, which has altered the relationship between the economy, the polity and the cultural community, so that they no longer need to share the same territorial boundaries. The third strand is the rise of transnational political and institutional structures, notably the European Union (EU) but including the Council of Europe, the Organization for Security and Cooperation in Europe and NATO, as well as a number of inter-state agreements such as the Schengen Agreement on border controls.[1] These are creating a new, complex and not always consistent set of transnational regimes, located above the states but also penetrating their domestic politics.

The 'nationalities' question refers to the issue of politically conscious national movements without their own state. A nationality comes in different varieties. It may exist as a minority that is wholly contained within a 'host' state, such as the Scots within the UK. It may also be a minority in one state (the 'host' state), but have ethnic kin who dominate another state (the 'kin' state). This is a classic configuration throughout Central and Eastern Europe, and examples include the Hungarians of Slovakia, Romania and Serbia; the Serbs and Croats of Bosnia-Herzegovina (and possibly, in the near future, the Serbs of Montenegro and Kosovo); and the Turks of Bulgaria (Brubaker 1996). A prominent example in Western Europe is the Irish nationalists in Northern Ireland. Nationalities may also be minorities in more than one state, and majorities in none, such as the Basques in Spain and France. Nationality movements, their preferences shaped by these political-geographic circumstances, may seek autonomy within a state; secession; autonomy combined with cross-border links

between them and their ethnic kin; or dual/multiple secessions followed
by the unification of what is seen as their national territory.

Nationalities in Europe are usefully distinguished from immigrant
communities who have recently arrived from distant countries. Unlike immigrants, such as the Turkish and Kurdish minorities in Germany, or the predominantly Arab minorities in France and Spain, nationality movements see
themselves as living on their ancestral territory, and seek some form of
collective self-government. Some communities, such as the Russians of the
Baltic Republics, bear features of both nationalities and immigrant
communities. Most Russians arrived after 1945, but they were 'settled' in
such large numbers that they are now demographically dominant in particular regions.[2] Moreover, they were settled at a time when the Baltic states were
seen, however unjustly, as part of their (Soviet, previously Tsarist) patrimony.

Nationalities can thus be considered a synonym for what others, and we
in earlier works, have called 'national minorities' or 'minority nations',
and these terms are used interchangeably throughout the chapter and
volume.[3] Many nationality movements, however, resist being identified as
'minorities', because they see this as blurring the distinction between
them and immigrants, and as not conducive to equality between them and
the state's dominant national community.[4]

We use the term nationality 'movement' frequently to underline that
these are political projects rather than primordial categories, and to avoid
the standard criticisms of constructivists. Not every cultural or ethnic
community develops a vibrant nationalist project. There are examples of
groups throughout Europe, such as the Sorbs, Wends and Frisians, that
did not develop a nationalist project either in the nineteenth century
(Hroch 1985) or more recently. Where nationalist projects develop, not
everyone from a particular cultural or ethnic community will automatically consider himself or herself as part of it. Even in Northern Ireland,
where there is a remarkable degree of coincidence between cultural
community and national community, there is a significant number of
Catholics who are not politically Irish nationalist.[5] Similarly, nationalist
projects, while invariably based predominantly on one cultural community, may have support across such communities. To accept that nationalist
movements are socially and politically constructed does not mean, as some
think, that they are superficial or unpopular, or that their aspirations do
not need to be taken seriously if justice and stability are to prevail.

This introduction indicates why the new European transnational
context is important and what kind of potential it generates for responding to national minority concerns.

The challenge posed by nationalities

The issue of the effects of transnational regimes on nationality movements
is important for a number of reasons, but one of the most crucial is that

these movements pose a significant challenge to the existing nation-state order. Minority nationalism challenges the assumed coincidence between politically significant identities and political boundaries. Since the eighteenth century, when conceptions of democracy and self-determination first entered the public realm, it was widely assumed that these identities and boundaries would coincide so that states would be nation-states. This did not necessarily mean that they would be culturally homogenous, but that, at the minimum, the territory of the state would coincide with a political identity of the people as constituting a single, sovereign nation, to which the democratic political system was, ideally, ultimately accountable. Many argued that, to achieve this, cultural difference would need to be eradicated. Jean-Jacques Rousseau, in one of the earliest discussions of the need to create a 'nation' – a people who identified with each other and with the territory or 'homeland' – thought that this required a uniform education in the history and culture of the society to inculcate the necessary feelings of social solidarity (Rousseau 1973: 149).[6] This is the basis for the 'Jacobin' theory of assimilation, which received its fullest expression in the French Third Republic and has been influential across Europe. The coercive policies to achieve linguistic and cultural homogeneity in France to create a single French nation attest to the fear and concern that cultural difference would translate into political difference; that, to achieve the national dream, and a shared political identity, cultural differences would need to be eliminated (Weber 1979).

From the nineteenth century onwards, modernist social science, with its strong teleological tendencies and normative assumptions, has been predicting that economic and social forces would secure the triumph of the nation-state and the end of the nationality question (see Keating and McGarry 2001a: 2–3). Marx and Engels famously distinguished between historical nations and nations without history, dismissing the latter as necessary casualties in the march of progress. Eventually, of course, the triumph of the proletariat would do away with all forms of nationalism (Marx and Engels 2002). Karl Deutsch, writing a century later, and representing a dominant view in American political science, argued that a modernity-induced increase in social communications among diverse communities was bound to erode differences (Deutsch 1953). In the UK, by the end of the 1980s, the Marxist, Eric Hobsbawm was convinced that the new transnational order, which was reducing the functional importance of nation-states, would put an end to all nationalisms. At the very time that the former Yugoslavia and Soviet Union were breaking apart along national lines, Hobsbawm wrote that these events, ironically, confirmed the imminent end of the nationalities question:

[T]he world history of the late twentieth and early twenty-first centuries … will see 'nation states' and 'nations' or ethnic/linguistic groups primarily as retreating before, resisting, adapting to, being absorbed or dislocated by, the new supranational restructuring of the globe ... [T]he very fact that historians are at last beginning to make some progress in the study and analysis of nations and nationalism suggests that, as so often, the phenomenon is past its peak. The owl of Minerva which brings wisdom, said Hegel, flies out at dusk. It is a good sign that it is now circling round nations and nationalism.

(Hobsbawm 1990: 182–3)

Some 'post-nationalists' have focused more narrowly on European integration, arguing that it portends the erosion of nationalism, and the creation of new overlapping and multiple forms of identity linked to an overarching Europeanness (Kearney 1997). From this perspective, the nation-state model, to which nationalists are purported to be wedded, involves assumptions of the congruence of nation and state, centralised notions of power and absolute notions of sovereignty; and this is becoming increasingly anachronistic in a world of overlapping sovereignties and identities. One version of this argument has been around at least since the inception of the European order with the Treaty of Rome, but the more explicitly post-modernist and post-colonial versions are relatively recent (McKay 1996: 46–9). The original vision underlying the European Economic Community (later the EU) was based on twin economic and political bases. Economically, the Community would foster prosperity and prevent a return to the destructive protectionism of the inter-war years. Politically, it would resolve the historic problem of the co-existence of German and French nation-states.[7] Some had even broader visions, inspired by notions of European federalism dating back as far as the Renaissance period and taken up again in the face of nineteenth-century nationalisms. Much of this was directed against state nationalism, particularly German nationalism, but Europeanist post-nationalists and post-modernists also directed it against minority nationalism (Kearney 1997; Taylor 2001: 45). Whoever the precise target, the idea was a post-national one: that the institutional structures of cooperation would lead to the transcendence of nationalism, which had wreaked such havoc on the European continent, in favour of a genuinely post-national, or European 'identity'.[8] These thinkers argued not only that minority nationalism (or nationalism) would die away, but that this was desirable.

Others have resurrected the nineteenth-century distinction between the nationality of large, established states (good) and that of stateless nations and minorities (bad) (Dahrendorf 1995). Dahrendorf claims that the large nation is needed to sustain democracy and civic values within the European market. This is part of a long tradition in which minority nations were presented as dysfunctional, atavistic, romantic carry-overs of a different and bygone world order. They were regarded as uncivilized, as vessels for ethnocentrism and illiberalism, and obstacles to social justice and solidarity. Nationalism was not only unattractive and unattainable, it was also dangerous: because there are an infinite number of potential nations; and unnecessary, because nations are not real, but the creation of states or state-aspiring nationalist intellectuals who mobilise the masses behind their projects. Nationalism was seen as producing conflict and instability, and not just the expansionist state nationalism of Nazi Germany or Milosevic's Serbia, but also the minority nationalisms of the Basque Country, Northern Ireland, and throughout the Balkans.

Such arguments are suspect on both empirical and normative grounds. Predictions that minority nationalism would fade away have, in our view, run up against observed reality. What we have seen instead throughout the world, including both parts of Europe, is the emergence or re-emergence of ethnic and nationalist politics. In Western Europe, post-Franco Spain has experienced a number of strong nationalist movements, particularly in Catalonia and the Basque Country; the UK, since the late 1960s, has had vibrant nationalist movements in Scotland and Northern Ireland and an emergent one in Wales; and Belgium has developed from a polity in which the main division was between the religious and the secular to one which is more focused on nationalism. In Eastern Europe, three pluri-national federations, the Soviet Union, Yugoslavia and Czechoslovakia, fell apart at least partly because of nationalist divisions, and there are continuing difficulties around the nationalities question in many of the successor states, including Serbia, Bosnia-Herzegovina, Slovakia, Estonia, Latvia, Moldova, Georgia, Azerbaijan and Russia. To these, can be added the question of the Turks in Bulgaria, the Kurds in Turkey, and the long-standing dispute between Turkish and Greek Cypriots in Cyprus.

These facts suggest that recent predictions that global transformations will wash away minority nationalism are as suspect as their nineteenth-century equivalents. Far from weakening minority nationalism, a number of recent changes can help account for its emergence and re-emergence in various places. First, the process of economic integration, with the increased mobility of capital, goods, services and labour, and the rise of transnational corporations has weakened the state's capacity for managing its economy through tariffs, taxes and subsidies, and has shifted power from the state to the marketplace. Minority nationalist movements are sometimes a response to this weakened state, and an attempt to forge a new collective response to economic change. Second, the lowering of international tariffs and the construction of regional economic associations, particularly the EU, have helped reduce the risks associated with independence and have heightened the popularity of nationalism in places like Scotland or Quebec. Even small countries now have easier access to global markets. The development of multilateral defence organisations, particularly NATO, has also made statehood more viable than it once was. Third, the cultural dimension of globalisation, with the development of new communications technology, increased travel, the spread of English as a *lingua franca* and increased migration flows, has posed a threat to some minority cultures, and facilitated a nationalist response. The new communications technology – satellite TV, desktop publishing and the Internet – paradoxically, has also provided tools which facilitate minority mobilisation. Finally, the spread of global norms on human rights has arguably made minorities more resistant to a subordinate status than they once were. We now live in a world where discrimination and/or alien rule is more difficult to justify. The spread of norms of self-determination, brought about first by decolonisation, and then by the emergence of multiple new states in Eastern Europe, may also have reinforced pro-independence arguments from minority nationalist leaders. As both Keating and Guibernau point out in their contributions to this volume, even the EU's enlargement process provides a fillip to minority nationalist leaders in Western Europe, because every time a small state joins the EU, it provides a reminder to sometimes larger nationalities in Western Europe that they do not have direct representation in the Council of Ministers, and that their language is not an official language of the EU (Chapters 2 and 11).

Minority nationalism is not always, as many socialists and liberals appear to think, a conservative reaction against economic change. Such change may also give rise to regional forms of cooperation and mutual defence associations, which permit and even encourage the flourishing of more local forms of identity. Whereas in the past, for example, the Scots saw the force of the argument that they had to be aligned with the British political project to survive in the imperial age, in the current context, it is possible for much smaller units to survive and do well (Keating 1996: 62–4). Minority nations are no longer as dependent on their host state, but much more dependent on international and continental regimes, like the EU. This gives them some autonomy, at least in the sense that they are able to play off these various forms of dependency against each other. Moreover, smaller units might be better positioned in these circumstances than larger units to take advantage of local expertise, to tailor their policies and programmes to highlight and reinforce their particular competitive advantage.

Nor are minority nationalist movements necessarily more illiberal and ethnocentric than their state-led counterparts, as some liberals believe (Dahrendorf 1995). Scotland, the Basque Country, Catalonia and Quebec are societies in which democratic and liberal norms are deeply entrenched and nationalists there are no less committed to democratic government and justice than the majority national communities of the state in which they are encapsulated.[9] It is not that minority or majority nations are inherently more just or more democratic or less so: it is that the question of their values is strongly related to their political traditions, and not to either their minority or majority status in the state as a whole.[10]

In addition, the minority nationalism that has been facilitated in the new transnational context of European integration is not necessarily of the hard-core, uncompromising, secessionist variety. Europeanisation has encouraged moderation so that nationalist movements may be accommodating, more willing to be satisfied with forms of autonomy and political input within the state context as long as there are possibilities to transcend this context across a range of functional and symbolic issues (Keating 1996). Evidence for this can be found in the contributions to this volume by Elias, Hepburn and Nicolas (Chapters 10, 12 and 16).

Finally, nationalities can reasonably claim that the current state system is unfair. Like majority nations, they are politically mobilised; they have a history and homeland; they seek to exercise political self-government. Increasingly, their demands have been framed in exactly the same language and with the same normative underpinnings as the claims to self-determination made by the states themselves, moving from an ethnic particularism to a broader civic nationalism, invoking liberal democratic norms and often embracing the new international order. This normative approximation might be thought to reduce the ideological distance between majorities and minorities and to some degree it has. Yet paradoxically it may make self-determination issues more difficult to resolve since they are competing on the same normative ground, with both majorities and minorities invoking the same principles to lay claims to broad powers of social regulation (Keating 2001a). Civic nationalism may represent a form of social and political progress but it does not in itself resolve the fundamental question of where authority lies.

Nationalism, then, is not just going to go away. It cannot simply be de-mobilised or de-constructed, and minority nationalism is actually more likely to thrive in the new institutional arrangements of Europe. It cannot be dismissed as inherently reactionary and alien to the emerging European value system. Nor is secession and the redrawing of boundaries the answer. States are generally reluctant to abandon territory, and secessionism, particularly if it becomes widespread, is likely to be enormously de-stabilizing. It is notoriously difficult to draw new state boundaries that satisfy everyone's national preferences. Inevitably, there will be minorities in the new state who would rather remain in the old (rump) state, minorities in the old rump state who would rather be in the new state, and minorities in both areas who would rather have their own state than either of the existing ones (McGarry 1998). Even this, moreover, assumes discrete and fixed national identities, when people often have multiple identities; that is, they identify with both the new state and the rump state, and identities are more or less fluid, depending on context, and are amenable to change in the new state configuration. In the latter case, a consensus behind independence in the secessionist region may soon be replaced by a post-independence dissensus. It is therefore of importance that we examine ways in which the concerns of national minorities can be addressed, in ways that fall short of breaking states apart.

European integration and the nationalities question: Europe's potential

The chapters in this book examine whether European integration has altered the contours of the nationalities question and helped to defuse 'the minority problem' that is endemic in nation-state systems. There are arguably four ways in which European integration has demonstrated the potential to positively impact on the nationalities question:

(i) An end to unitarism?

While Europe has not promoted a post-nationalist politics, it has, arguably, facilitated a post-sovereigntist politics conducive to the accommodation of minorities, in which the notions of the unitary nation-state, and of the international order as one between competing and discrete states, has receded. The EU is based on the idea of shared sovereignty, challenging the doctrinal basis of the traditional state. At the same time, several Western European countries have been transformed from unitary states to federal or de-centralised ones. Policy areas that are important to minority national communities have been transferred to their jurisdictional authority, going some way towards meeting the aspirations of minority nationalists for greater control over their collective life (Danspeckgruber 2002). In 1978, Spain established itself as a de-centralised state, in which the Catalan, Basque and Galician nationalities were given significant autonomy. Belgium was transformed from a unitary state into a federation of three language communities and three regions in 1992. Italy negotiated autonomy for the South Tyrolese in 1948, and extended it in 1972 and 2001. The UK created a parliament for Scotland in 1998, as well as assemblies for Northern Ireland and Wales (see, respectively, Chapters 12, 10 and 15). Even France has been prepared to extend limited autonomy to Corsica and more modest concessions to other regions (Chapter 16).

Arguably, this preparedness to de-centralise has been influenced by European integration. The kind of sovereignty-sharing among states associated with transnational institutions like the EU may have made states more prepared to devolve power downwards, including to regions controlled by minorities. The European principle of subsidiarity, in which decisions are to be made at the most de-centralised level possible, pushes in the same direction. The demonstration-effect of de-centralisation by other co-members may have been helpful. The context of membership in transnational bodies, like the EU and NATO, may also have reduced fears about the consequences of granting autonomy to minorities in the form of security threats, irredentism and distortion of markets.

(ii) The erosion of borders?

European integration is also reducing the significance of borders in a way that may facilitate the accommodation of minorities cut off from their co-nationals by state boundaries. The most obvious sense in which borders are less significant is related to the EU's common market, which has removed restrictions on the flow of capital, goods and labour, and which, within the Schengen countries, even dispenses with passport controls. Another sense is that many policy areas that were once matters of sovereign-state jurisdiction have now been transferred upwards, and are matters to be discussed at the European level, or transferred downwards, to more local levels, in accordance with the principle of subsidiarity. As Keating shows, new functional systems are being created which no longer respect state boundaries (Chapter 2). These provide minorities in control of their own regions with new opportunities to explore constituting cross-border political communities with their co-nationals, without the disruption, chaos and possible bloodshed associated with redrawing state boundaries (Miall 1992; Danspeckgruber 2002). The EU directly encourages cross-border initiatives through its INTERREG programme while the Council of Europe, through the Madrid Convention, has produced a legal instrument for establishing cross-border partnerships. The European Parliament has also encouraged inter-state and cross-border cooperation in a way that has been helpful to national minorities (Haagerup 1984).

European integration may also make states less sensitive about cross-border cooperation, including cooperation between kin-states and host-states over national minorities. It has promoted good neighbourly relations and cooperative behaviour among Western European states, including previously warring states such as Germany and France, and it has firmly embedded the principle of the territorial integrity of states. While previously, states resisted cross-border cooperation, or even autonomy for minorities, because this was thought to facilitate irredentism, this is, arguably, much less of a concern now. European integration has also, arguably, made it possible for minorities to sell such ideas to states, or to members of the state's dominant community exposed in border regions, as the cooperation can be marketed in functional rather than political terms, and as the sort of development that is not peculiar to their situation, but common throughout the EU (Alcock 2001: 177).

The most far-reaching example of cross-border and inter-state cooperation within the EU is that between the UK and the Irish Republic with respect to Northern Ireland. In 1985, through the Anglo-Irish Agreement, the British government formally allowed the Irish government a role in the governance of Northern Ireland, in order to address the aspirations of its large Irish nationalist minority. In 1998, cross-border (all-Ireland) political institutions were established, including a North–South Ministerial Council (McGarry and O'Leary 2004: 273–6). As part of the Agreement, the Irish Republic removed its constitutionally entrenched irredentist claim to Northern Ireland. Austria's accession to the EU in 1995 was immediately preceded by a new treaty with Italy and followed by an increase in cooperation in the South Tyrol.

(iii) Political space beyond the state?

Transnational organisations, and particularly the EU, have the potential to create political space to include non-state actors, such as sub-regions, including those controlled by nationalities. In the nation-state model, the only legitimate 'voice' is that of the central state, which expresses the undifferentiated will of 'the people'. This has the perverse consequence that it leads nationalities to place a high value on secession or independence. Independence is the only effective form of recognition, the only mechanism for having an international personality, of being accepted as a nation within the global family of nations. Autonomy arrangements by themselves have the drawback of having no external dimension in which the minority community can imprint its public culture on the international community; the prized aspiration for 'recognition' is not satisfied by this sort of institutional arrangement. In a regional association such as the EU, however, there is the potential for more imaginative arrangements where not only member states are represented, and have 'voice', and institutional recognition of their collective identity, but also the regions and minority national communities.[11]

(iv) An international regime of minority-rights protections?

A shortcoming of the traditional nineteenth-century state order is the presumption that the treatment of minorities is an internal matter for the states concerned. This leaves minorities open to discrimination or persecution, and bereft of external protections, giving them a strong incentive to seek their own states. As a result of European integration, and changing international norms, traditional conceptions of state sovereignty are now being questioned. Members of the Council of Europe are subject to the European Convention on Human Rights and the European Court of Human Rights. This has been used by nationalities to challenge state persecution, such as the British government's treatment of Irish nationalist detainees in Northern Ireland. The European Convention has the advantage, from the perspective of nationalities, that it is not connected, as individual state's bills of rights often are, to a nation-building project,[12] and the European Court may be seen as less partisan than state courts.

In the early 1990s, international organisations were prepared to move more in the direction of group rights, including the rights of national minorities (Chapters 3 and 4). The Council of Europe's 1992 European Charter for Regional or Minority Languages and 1995 Framework Convention on the Protection of National Minorities (FCNM) include some positive group rights, including public funding for minority elementary schools, and the right to write to public authorities in one's own language. The FCNM is a legally binding document, which has now been ratified by 34 states and signed by a further eight. Other international documents were even more radical, either endorsing territorial autonomy for minorities (the 1990 OSCE Copenhagen Declaration) or recommending that there be an internationally recognised right to it (Recommendation 1201 of the Council of Europe Parliamentary Assembly, 1993). The OSCE and the Council of Europe's initiatives have become connected to the EU (and to NATO) through the device of 'conditionality'. Since 1991, minority rights have been one of the four criteria that states must meet to join the EU. Jurado shows here how European pressures facilitated accommodation of Russian minorities in the Baltic states (Chapter 14). This is a theme also taken up in the chapter by Rose, Berglund and Munro, who argue that such accommodation, and the EU-related promise of economic prosperity, has helped to integrate politically these minorities into their respective states (Chapter 17).[13]

In addition to promoting general standards of minority rights, European organisations have been involved, in Eastern and South Eastern Europe, in what we might call, by contrast, a 'fire-engine' approach, involving conflict prevention, post-conflict mediation, reconstruction and peace-keeping. The OSCE, concerned by the violence that accompanied the break-up of the Soviet Union and Yugoslavia, established the Office of the High Commissioner on National Minorities (HCNM) in 1993. The HCNM's job has been to monitor the treatment of national minorities and to encourage states to adopt policies conducive to stable majority–minority relations. The OSCE and, to a lesser extent, the EU have engaged in conflict mediation activities throughout what King here calls the 'European periphery', from Moldova to the Caucasus (Chapter 7). They have also participated in democratic development and economic reconstruction in Kosovo and Bosnia-Herzegovina, while the EU is currently in charge of peacekeeping in Bosnia-Herzegovina. The EU, along with the UN, has been in the vanguard of finding a settlement to the dispute in Cyprus, the subject of Tocci's contribution (Chapter 18). Most radically, NATO has twice intervened militarily to bring an end to civil war and to human rights abuses, in Bosnia-Herzegovina in 1995 and in Kosovo in 1999. International organisations have played an important role in the design of post-conflict constitutions in both countries, and continue to play the dominant role in their governance. These developments, taken together, are evidence for what Gurr has described as a novel and 'emergent international regime of minority rights protection' (Gurr 2000).

In combination, these four categories – a move towards de-centralised states; the erosion of boundaries and increased inter-state cooperation over minorities; a political role for minority regions in the European (international) arena; and an internationalised rights regime – would appear to have the potential for improving minority conditions in a way that undercuts demands for statehood.

European integration and the nationalities question: Europe's limits?

On balance, our contributors show that while European integration has made a positive contribution to the nationalities question, this should not be exaggerated, and its future direction is unclear. Several note that while the concept of the discrete sovereign state may be weakening, it remains of primary importance, particularly, but not exclusively, in Eastern Europe, affecting all four of the categories we have just outlined.

(i) An end to unitarism?

While Western Europe has been moving towards de-centralisation, this has been uneven. France and Greece have largely resisted the trend towards autonomy seen elsewhere and, like others, have sought to avoid creating regional governments corresponding to historic nationalities or minorities (Chapter 16). The Spanish state under the former government of the Popular Party, was keen to ensure that de-centralisation was both moderate and symmetrical, so that it does not distinguish the claims of Spain's historic nationalities from its other regions (Chapter 11).

In Eastern Europe, the ideal of the centralised unitary state remains dominant. This is not surprising, given the recent history of the region, which saw three ex-communist pluri-national federations break apart along the lines of their internal administrative boundaries and the constant fear of irredentism fuelled by twentieth-century history. Moreover the 1992 opinion of the international Badinter Commission on the former Yugoslavia, which declared that its republics could secede but that there could be no secessions from the republics, appeared to confirm both that self-governing structures facilitated the prize of international legal recognition for secessionist regions and that unitary structures prevented it.

Kymlicka's chapter indicates, that while most Western European states have been prepared to de-centralise, they are reluctant to encourage other states to do so, either by making territorial autonomy a recognised right in international documents like the FCNM, or by making it a condition for entry into any of Europe's prestigious, political, military and diplomatic alliances (Chapter 3).[14] Despite hinting in that direction in the early 1990s, there has been a steady retreat from support for such a radical form of accommodation. Now, the OSCE's HCNM is more likely to urge non-territorial autonomy. Around 2000, ironically, EU regional development policy and advice on state restructuring shifted from promoting de-centralisation to favouring centralisation (Hughes *et al.* 2003; Keating 2003). As Batt shows, pre-EU accession steps in South Eastern Europe have had the effect of promoting centralisation (Chapter 9).

While international organisations have endorsed autonomy for nationalities in a number of areas of Eastern and South Eastern Europe, including Bosnia-Herzegovina, Kosovo and Macedonia, as well as Georgia, Moldova, Azerbaijan and Cyprus, this is because the minorities in these cases have been able to win autonomy through military rebellion, sometimes aided by kin-states. Support for autonomy in these cases, then, is not a result of some pan-European norm, but a reaction to *realpolitik*, and the threat to regional stability. In the longer term, if European integration is able to reduce fears of secession and irredentism, matters may be different.

(ii) Eroding frontiers?

Regarding the role of European integration in fostering cross-border and inter-state cooperation of the sort that benefits national minorities, McGarry shows that in the most far-reaching case of such cooperation, between the UK and Ireland, only some of this can be traced to Europe (Chapter 15). He writes that British–Irish cooperation, while facilitated by a supportive European context, was importantly influenced by the imperatives of managing an intractably violent conflict, and by the increasingly interventionist diplomacy of the US. Fundamentally, he argues that the UK was prepared to engage in such radical cooperation with the Republic of Ireland over Northern Ireland only because the British state and British public have long been prepared to abandon Northern Ireland, if it could be achieved peacefully. In support of his case, McGarry points out that nowhere else in Western Europe has there been inter-state cooperation to the extent seen over Northern Ireland. As a consequence, he cautions against over-optimism about the ability of European integration to bring about significant inter-state and cross-border cooperation in the rather unpropitious circumstances of Eastern Europe.

In Eastern Europe, the difficulty is that while none of its states wants to contract, there are some which would like to expand, or at least recover 'lost' territory. Many states in the region are new states, which have won their independence through secession, and which jealously guard their territorial integrity. Several of the others are rump-states, from which the new ones were carved out. They have not accepted their enforced downsizing, and irredentism is still popular. This is particularly true, as Batt shows, in the case of Serbia and Hungary, where the situation has been exacerbated by the fact that they have not simply lost territory but territory that, in the nationalist mythology, represents the ancestral heartland of Kosovo and Transylvania, respectively (Chapter 9).[15] Even Republika Srspka is seen by Serbian nationalists, including central figures in Serbia's governing elite, as an indispensable part of the Serbian homeland, its 'left lung'. The situation has been further exacerbated, in Serbia's case, both because the loss is so recent, and by the fact that there are so many refugees from the lost territories, who are not socially and economically integrated, but who have political clout and are ultra-nationalist. In this context, which does not exist in Western Europe, where states are older and borders more stable, it is more difficult to imagine European integration making a difference, or at least a quick difference.

However, as Wolff shows, there is at least one unambiguous example of positive cross-border and inter-state cooperation in Central and Eastern Europe: this is the case of Germany, which after reaching agreement with Eastern European states in which there are German minorities to facilitate their 'repatriation', is now channelling aid to these minorities, with the agreement of the states involved, which is aimed at protecting their culture and allowing them to remain *in situ* (Chapter 8). The secret of Germany's success has been its clear preparedness to accept its post-Second World War contraction and to forgo territorial claims on its neighbours. Unlike Hungary in recent years (Chapter 6), Germany has also sought to aid its kin-minorities through bilateralism, with the clear consent of the host-states involved, and respecting their sovereignty. The minorities involved are also relatively small in number, the vast bulk having emigrated to Germany in the early 1990s, and the states in which many of them live are not Germany's immediate neighbours. These facts, combined with Germany's respect for the state system, mean that there are few fears of irredentism, and cooperation can proceed accordingly. As Wolff notes, Germany's abandonment of irredentism and expansionism is partly a result of its acceptance of European norms on state sovereignty.

Four chapters in the collection deal, at least implicitly, with the question of what facilitates state-contraction or down-sizing mindsets (either on the part of host-states like the UK or kin-states like Hungary) and thereby cross-border and inter-state cooperation (Chapters 6, 8, 9 and 15). Together these provide us with a set of conducive conditions. The first condition is time. As Batt writes, one vital difference between Hungary and Serbia, which helps to explain the more aggressive position of the latter, is that Hungary's loss took place over 80 years ago, whereas Serbia's loss has occurred within very recent memory. Indeed, Serbia's contraction has not yet ended, as it looks set to lose Montenegro and, more importantly, Kosovo, in the near future. Down-sizing mindsets cannot be created overnight. The second condition relates to the value of the relevant territory in the nationalist mythology. Great Britain's political elite and public have been able to withdraw psychologically from Northern Ireland because they see it as part of Ireland rather than as part of Britain. Hungary and Serbia's elites are finding it more difficult to abandon Transylvania and Kosovo, as they are seen as the ancestral hearts of their people. Spain too, as Jáuregui notes, sees the Basque provinces as part of its homeland and this is reflected in its constitutional doctrine and practice (Chapter 13).

The third condition concerns military defeats or setbacks. The idea here is that down-sizing mindsets can be acquired through learning behaviour: if it becomes clear that expansionism, or retaining a particular territory, carries considerable costs, in violence and destruction, or economic loss, states may be induced to contract. German expansionism and irredentism has brought disaster to Germany twice in the past century, while peaceful cooperation has resulted in prosperity. Batt explains Hungary's increasing preparedness to accept European norms on neighbourly cooperation as a reaction to the costs that irredentism has imposed over the years, including bloody defeat and loss of territory in the Second World War. McGarry explains that Irish republicans' protracted war against the British presence in Ireland helped to inform the view of the British political elite and public that Northern Ireland is 'a place apart'. The fourth condition relates to demographic facts on the ground. Irredentist claims from host-states are, arguably, more likely if there are significant numbers of ethnic kin in the territory in question. Germany's lack of irredentism may owe something to the fact that its neighbouring states no longer contain sizeable German minorities. It may be a normatively problematic conclusion, but ethnic cleansing may weaken irredentism. The fifth condition relates to the role of minority refugees from the host-state in the kin-state's political system. One might expect that the more political clout such refugees have in the kin-state and the less integrated they are in the host-state's social and economic system, the more likely the latter is to remain irredentist. Following their loss of territory, both Germany and Serbia acquired significant numbers of displaced people from the lost territories who gained full citizenship rights. The difference is that while these displaced people gradually became socially and economically integrated into (West) Germany, this has not yet happened in Serbia. In Batt's view, the presence of Serbian refugees from Croatia, Kosovo and Bosnia-Herzegovina in Serbia is an important part of the explanation for continuing Serbian irredentism, which in turn raises obstacles to cross-border and inter-state cooperation. The sixth condition is economic performance. Hungary's fixation with its lost territories was reduced as it took solace in its relative economic prosperity within the Soviet bloc. Even more clearly, Germany's post-war *wirtschaftswunder* made it easier for it to abandon the lost territories, facilitating Willy Brandt's *Ostpolitik*, just as hard economic times in the 1920s concentrated German minds on losses at Versailles. Serbia's relative economic failure, similarly, has compounded its irredentism. Finally, politics matters, even if it is shaped by the historical, demographic and economic factors that have just been discussed. Adenauer and Brandt were more comfortable with the politics of down-sizing than Kostunica and Antall, and were capable of selling this to their followership.

The point we are making here is that the ability of European integration to facilitate cross-border and inter-state cooperation, and indeed autonomy, is a complex matter, and context-sensitive. It is not a question of simply admitting countries into the EU or any other European club, and it cannot be expected to unfold evenly across the continent. Moreover, to the extent that European integration has made a difference, it has been, as both Batt and Wolff point out, when access to the EU appears both likely and imminent.

Just as European integration has promoted centralisation rather than autonomy in some cases, it has sometimes erected new barriers between kin-states and related minorities. This is because, while the EU erodes internal boundaries, it has also strengthened boundaries between it and neighbouring states. Batt notes that Hungary's accession to the EU required it to enforce the EU's common visa regime to Romania, Ukraine and Serbia, all of which contain Hungarian minorities. This forced Hungary to renege on an obligation it made to its kin-minorities, not to hinder their access to their 'motherland', and made it 'markedly more difficult' for Hungarians in these other countries to travel to Hungary. Attempts to get round this difficulty by issuing long-term multiple entry visas, she claims, is unlikely to survive Hungary's accession to the Schengen agreement in 2006. Similarly, it is unlikely that the EU will tolerate Croatia's policy of maintaining a dual citizenship agreement with Bosnia-Herzegovina, which is aimed at eroding frontiers between the two states, in the interests of the latter's Croatian minority. Such a policy would likely fall foul of the Schengen *acquis* and perhaps EU anti-discrimination law, which prevents discrimination on the basis of ethnicity. These problems go beyond Hungary and the former Yugoslavia, to potentially effect minorities elsewhere, including Bulgaria's Turkish minority and Turkey's Kurdish minority, as well as relations between Romania and the ethnic majority in Moldova.

(iii) Political space beyond the state?

European integration has opened up political space beyond the state that nationalities can occupy. It is clear from our volume, however, that this space is restricted and that the EU and other European institutions remain largely intergovernmental in nature (see Chapters 2 and 11). Just as states control whether or not cross-border and inter-state cooperation happens, they also control Europe's political institutions and access to them. While some states, such as Belgium, give their regions input into state policy towards the EU, others, such as Spain until recently, do not. Thus, achieving a role of this sort requires victory at the state level, and there has been an understandable reluctance at the European level towards developing general approaches to this question. The Committee of the Regions gives regions some direct input into EU policy-making, but it has very weak powers, lacks resources and has been a general disappointment to its members. The Convention on the Future of Europe and the draft constitution were a missed opportunity to address the position of actors beyond the state. Some nationalist political parties, as a consequence, came away from the Convention convinced that, as its agenda was statist, statehood was necessary (Chapters 10 and 12). Others were prepared to accept it, because they continue to value European integration and what it can do for nationalities. The lack of a suitable space in Europe helps to explain the Ibarretxe Plan for the Basque Country, which is discussed by Jáuregui, in which the Basque government has reverted to the old logic of nation against state (Chapter 13).

The statist nature of the EU can also be seen from the way it treats regional languages. As Guibernau makes clear with respect to Catalan, it is not one of the EU's 20 official languages in spite of the fact that it is spoken by millions of people in three European states, is the tenth most widely spoken language in the EU, and is the official language of three European regions (Chapter 11). Maltese, by contrast, is an official EU language. Ironically, she argues, the easiest way for Catalan to become an EU official language may be for Andorra – whose official language is Catalan – to become a member of the EU. The recognition of language does not simply confer functional advantages, it is intricately connected to the self-esteem of minorities.

(iv) Assessing the international regime of minority-rights protections

Our contributors point to a number of limits to the idea of an emerging international regime of minority protection. Both Kymlicka and Baubock note that there are limits to the *sort* of rights that are being promoted (Chapters 3 and 5). These tend to be the type that are least threatening to states. The rights that are promoted in the FCNM, and by the OSCE, do indeed move beyond those included in earlier documents, such as the UN's 1966 Covenant on Civil and Political Rights (ICCPR). However, they do not deal with the central aspirations of nationalities, which include territorial autonomy, but also official language status, minority language universities and consociational-type rights to participate at the level of the central governments. While there was a tentative commitment to support for territorial autonomy for nationalities in the OSCE's Copenhagen Declaration of 1990 and in Recommendation 1201 of the Council of Europe's Parliamentary Assembly in 1993, there has been, Kymlicka argues, a marked movement away from support for it ever since. International organisations, such as the High Commissioner on National Minorities (HCNM), have appeared more interested in supporting less threatening forms of non-territorial autonomy rather than territorial autonomy, even though there is no evidence that sizeable nationalities would accept this (McGarry and Moore 2005). Ironically, the HCNM's recommendations in this respect goes against what Keating describes as a growing norm in Western Europe, the 'de-ethnicisation' of nationality movements, and an associated increased emphasis on territory as the criterion of inclusion. In Kymlicka's view, the rights that are protected are helpful for those small minorities of 5–10 per cent or less that are incapable of exercising self-government, and that are already well on the road to assimilation, such as those who live in the Czech Republic, Slovenia and Hungary, but are 'largely irrelevant' for sizeable national minorities.

There are also questions surrounding Europe's *commitment* to minority rights. There is no Western European consensus on such rights. Some states have generous provisions for minorities, while others, such as France, have been much less accommodating. This helps to explain why the thrust of Europe's efforts at minority-rights protections has been directed against states in Eastern Europe. This, in turn, has given rise to a double standard with the EU's member states pressuring candidates to embrace documents, such as the FCNM, which several of them have not accepted.[16] Western Europe's lack of consensus may also help to explain why the policy of conditionality has been inconsistently, or unwholeheart-edly, applied. While Sasse acknowledges that conditionality has produced positive results, particularly when external pressure coincides with favourable domestic circumstances, she notes that the minority-rights cri-terion 'has not been a key determinant' in the EU's assessment of appli-cant countries, and that it declined in importance towards the end of the accession process (Chapter 4). Batt explains that when in 1996 the EU decided that Slovakia and Romania would not be invited to start negotia-tions for accession, in neither case was unsatisfactory treatment of minori-ties raised as a reason for their exclusion. Romania was already adjudged to have satisfied the Copenhagen political criteria, in spite of the reserva-tions of Romania's Hungarian leaders. In Slovakia's case, the EU had con-cerns about its democratic shortcomings, but nothing specifically to do with the way in which it treated minorities (Chapter 9). Both Sasse and Batt note that when minority issues were raised by the EU in Eastern Europe, it was often the Roma that were of uppermost concerns, rather than sometimes larger minorities like the Magyars of Romania and Slova-kia or the Turks of Bulgaria. This was at least partly because of the associ-ation in Western European minds between the maltreatment of the Roma and their migration to the West: self-interest drove matters rather than a concern for minorities. It may also have been because the sort of rights that were sought by Roma were of the non-threatening sort: as a dispersed minority, the Roma do not seek territorial autonomy.[17] The Russian minorities in the Baltic states have also been a focus of attention, a result, arguably, of the need for good relations between Russia and the EU.

When the Copenhagen criteria were added to the '*acquis de l'Union*' in 1997, the criterion that minority rights be protected was left out. Similarly, the draft European Constitution incorporated the Copenhagen criteria minus minority rights. The weakness of commitment towards generalised minority protections is such that Kymlicka concludes that, having set themselves the task of protecting the rights of national minorities, Europe has now lost its nerve, and that 'the bold experiment of articulating international norms targeted at national minorities, and capable of resolving potentially violent ethnonationalist conflict, is slowly being abandoned'(Chapter 3). Baubock also believes that Europe has not been prepared to support general substantive minority rights, and is pessimistic that this will change. As a normative philosopher, he nonetheless details the principles that should inform such rights (Chapter 5).

As in the case of the other three categories of minority accommodation, the effectiveness of European support for minority group rights has been heavily context-sensitive, and the role of European integration has been facilitative rather than a sufficient or even a necessary means for minority protection. In the case of Hungary, which in the early 1990s enthusiastically endorsed the new European norms on minority-rights protection, its chief motive appears to have been to shame its neighbours into acting to protect their large Hungarian minorities. The same has been true of Austria over recent decades. It is the fact that Magyars are minorities in several states that help explain why Hungary reacted differently from Slovakia, even though both were presumably open to the influence of European norms and conditionality incentives (Chapter 4). Similarly, we can expect those parts of Europe, where memories of nationalist conflict is still raw, to be less open, *ceteris paribus*, to new norms on minority rights than areas where hostilities are a more distant memory.

As the most obvious incentive that has been brought to bear on Eastern Europe is membership of prestigious Western organisations, such as the EU and NATO, there is a question mark over what will happen to minority rights once membership has been granted. Two distinct scenarios appear possible: optimists anticipate a form of 'reverse conditionality' where pre-2004 member states come to embrace some of the policies and minority-rights documents that have been adopted by the new member states from Eastern Europe; pessimists forecast a tacit policy consensus on inaction within an enlarged EU.

The role of European institutions in 'fire-fighting' ethnic conflicts has also been less than exemplary. In some cases, the problem has been one of ineptitude. As Tocci details, EU diplomacy in Cyprus helped to *prevent* conflict resolution (Chapter 18). On one side, the Turkish Cypriots were told that they had to compromise in order to get into the EU, and they did, by endorsing the Annan plan in a referendum. The other side, Greek Cypriots, were told that Cyprus would be accepted into the EU regardless of whether or not there was an agreement. The incentive structure set by the EU was such that Greek Cypriots could plausibly conclude that their negotiating hand would be strengthened if they refused a deal now, were admitted into the EU, and acquired veto rights over Turkey's accession.

The result was that European diplomacy, instead of contributing to a settlement, increased tensions in the area. King notes that the diplomacy of European organisations has been similarly ineffective in a number of conflicts on Europe's eastern periphery, including Moldova, Georgia and Azerbaijan. Even if the violence has ebbed there, the disputes appear intractable in spite of, and sometimes because of, the best efforts of international mediators and peacekeepers (Chapter 7).

Conclusion

European integration offers a historic opportunity to reframe the old nationalities question at the level of norms, institutions and practices. Norms take a long time to change but over time ideas of Europeanism have served to inculcate democratic practice in southern and then Central and Eastern Europe. To some degree this is true of minority rights, although as our volume shows, Europe has not developed as consistent a line on this as it has towards individual rights and democratic practice. Nationalist parties have sought to use the European framework to project their demands and in the process have been Europeanised (Chapters 10, 12 and 16). There is some institutional innovation, in the form of cross-border partnerships in places like Ireland or the Tyrol for which Europe provides a context and some instruments. Practices are emerging in which nationalities issues are no longer zero-sum matters but questions of normal politics, amenable to negotiation and compromise. Europe of the 15 (the EU before 2004) showed a remarkable ability to resolve the problem of state nationalism and inter-state war, to the degree that the achievement is hardly noted any longer. It has some prospect of spreading this zone of international peace eastwards. Its record on non-state conflict is more difficult to assess in the short run, if only because conflicts that do not take place are not recorded. Compared with the inter-war experience, however, the management of nationality issues has been largely successful, with the notable exception of former Yugoslavia. Even there the prospect of membership of European institutions provides an incentive to engage in cooperative behaviour. At the same time there have been failures, and European institutions have often tried to dodge the difficult issue of minority politics, or to reduce them to matters of democracy and individual rights. European diplomacy has committed mistakes, as in the case of Cyprus. Yet the issue is not going to go away and if the European project is to continue to expand and deepen, policy-makers will need to address the nationalities question in a more thorough and explicit manner.

Part I

Theoretical and comparative approaches

2   Europe, the state and the nation

Michael Keating[1]

Introduction

A perennial feature of modern European politics is the problematic linkage of borders, political authority and national identity. For a time this was solved by the system of nation-states, in which territorial frontiers bounded a consistent set of identities and functional systems, although we know that the homogeneous nation-state was more aspiration than reality, and never applied across the entire continent. In recent years, the question has been transformed by the emergence of an overarching and multi-faceted European order above both states and nations. Some optimists see in this a means of transcending the nationalities question as we move into an era of post-nationalism, a Europe of the Regions, or a new mediaeval-ism (Tamir 1993; Kearney 1997; Murphy 1999); yet states are still very much with us. Others have seen nationalism as the product of an era of modernity now coming to an end (Hobsbawm 1990); yet nationalisms seem to have proliferated in recent decades. The perspective adopted here is less stark. The rescaling of functional systems and political author-ity are changing the meaning and scope of both state and nation, and the relationship between the two.

European integration does not do away with the nation-state but trans-forms it. Nation and nationality take on new meanings in this context, as state transformations both stimulate new minority nationalisms or the revival of old ones, and provide new means for their accommodation (Keating and McGarry 2001a). Some states and some nationality move-ments have adapted to these new opportunities better than others. There is no prospect of a Europe of the Peoples replacing the Europe of the States, but there is a new form of politics in which nationalities questions can be managed and normalised. There are four levels of adaptation, which have affected movements differentially:

- a doctrinal transformation concerning the doctrine of sovereignty; and a certain de-ethnicisation of nationalist movements;
- a change in the framework and conception of democracy and human rights, taking them out of the state framework;

- a functional transformation as the state shares authority and capacity with other levels of social regulation and collective action to make possible new forms of autonomy;
- a new opportunity structure allowing non-state entities a role in the European polity.

Rethinking sovereignty

At its simplest, Europe may provide an external support system lowering the costs of national independence. So every time the European Union (EU) admits a small new member state, minority nationalists within the existing states note the anomaly that they do not have direct representation in the decision-making instances of the Union. More interestingly, however, the European project transforms the meaning of independence itself, challenging the doctrine of unitary and exclusive state sovereignty and encouraging a legal and constitutional pluralism (Walker 1996; MacCormick 1999). The demystification of state sovereignty at the European level has led to a more general loss of ideological hegemony and opened up a discursive space for doctrines of shared sovereignty and constitutional pluralism within and across states. There are two versions of the argument. One is that sovereignty is still in principle indivisible, but that, since a number of actors at different levels are making claims to it, we have no alternative to compromise among them. Politics thus comes in where constitutional theory falls down. In an open constitutional order, we can live with many of these anomalies, and it is often preferable not to resolve them. The other version sees sovereignty not as a claim to the monopoly of authority, but rather as a claim to an element of original authority (that is not derived from a higher authority), but which recognises the existence of other sources of original authority which necessarily and inherently limit each other. This 'post-sovereignty' argument is increasingly heard among Europeanists and national minorities, although often at a rhetorical level rather than as a concrete policy proposal (Keating 2001). It allows nationalists to avoid difficult questions about defence, currencies and market access, and lets them turn the tables on defenders of the existing states, accusing them of being narrow nationalists and separatists.

Apart from providing doctrines of limited and shared sovereignty, Europe allows nationality movements to build or rebuild the nation internally by projecting it externally as part of a European family. The two levels are linked so that the European discourse becomes part of the constitutive fabric of nationalist movements themselves (McCrone 1998; Guibernau 1999; Paquin 2001). In turn, the commitment allows them to contribute to the shaping of the European polity itself, where they argue for a pluralism, diversity and constitutional asymmetry. Yet the switch is not universal or easy. It is easier for movements that have never been separatist or which have been ambivalent about their ultimate aims. It also depends on the coherence of the values of the movements with the dominant values of the European project. This was founded on the rejection of Fascism in the aftermath of the Second World War and the emphasising of democracy and tolerance. Nationalism was widely discredited and some minority nationalisms were tainted by collaboration with Nazism. Since then, the European political arena has been open to nationalist and regionalist movements that have emphasised territorial and inclusive nationalism and democracy, and not to those that cleave to ethnic exclusiveness or racism. It has thus encouraged the growth of a self-consciously 'civic' nationalism (Keating 2001).

Efforts by extreme right-wing or ethnically exclusive or racist parties to adapt to Europe have been less successful, since they violate the founding norms of the postwar European order. Adaptation is also easier for parties within the main Christian Democrat, Social Democrat or Liberal families, for whom the European model of the social market is congenial. Radical left nationalists also tend to hostility to Europe, seeing it as a capitalist club dominated by large states. At least until the 1970s, an ideological underpinning for these radical leftist parties was provided by internal colonialism – an extrapolation of the Third World struggles for liberation back to the imperial countries of Europe. Gradually this theme lost its attraction or relevance and a certain ideological shift took place, aided by the emphasis on social solidarity and cultural pluralism in the European discourse of the 1980s. In some cases, this led to a discovery of Europe and the deployment of the theme of a Europe of the Peoples as an alternative to a Europe of the States.

Nationality movements usually look back as well as forward, seeking legitimacy in a historic past that is itself continually reinvented. Yet the search for a usable past is limited by the available materials, and by their present resonance. In the nineteenth and early-twentieth centuries, nationalist movements often evoked a myth of ancient independence and precocious statehood, crushed by external repression. Many contemporary nationality movements, by contrast, have chosen to present themselves as the most European of the Europeans and have rediscovered pre-state traditions of shared sovereignty and pactism, which lend themselves to the new European dispensation (Keating 2001). Such historical revisionism has been favoured by the rediscovery of regional history (Applegate 1999) and efforts to construct a history of Europe as opposed to its states (Davies 1997). This is not always mere opportunism. Small nationalities caught between big powers naturally tend not to develop norms of absolute sovereignty and statehood, but to emphasise shared authority and subordination to overarching forms of order.

In other cases, the extant traditions are less clear or usable. Efforts to invent a past can be dismissed as fabrication or mere antiquarianism. In some cases, earlier traditions have been lost altogether or irrevocably associated with reaction and anti-modernism or imperial domination. In Central and Eastern Europe, a powerful theme after the fall of Communism was the 'return to Europe'. Yet this could be interpreted in different ways: to evoke an older Europe of diffused authority; the Europe of the States; or the modern multilevel European order evoked by minority nationalists in the West.

Democracy and rights

One of the strongest normative arguments for the nation-state is that only it can provide the common identity to underpin liberal democracy and social solidarity (Mill 1972; Miller 1995). This is deployed both against the idea of national pluralism and the idea that the EU can be democratised (Dahrendorf 1995, 2000; Smith 1995). Others have abandoned the nation-state analogy and argue that Europe can and must democratise but according to a more pluralistic and multicultural perspective. If Europe must manage with multiple *demoi* or without one at all, then the same argument can in turn be applied to multinational states within it. So there is a direct relationship between debates about democratising Europe and plurinational democracy within and across the states.

States have similarly lost their monopoly as the definers and protectors of rights, as Europe has, for the first time in modern history, separated human rights from nationality and citizenship. The European Convention for the Protection of Human Rights and Fundamental Freedoms and the European Court of Human Rights (part of the Council of Europe machinery) work with national systems of law, allowing a margin of appreciation, rather than seeking to overturn national laws or substitute its own. The European framework also enables rights discourse to be freed from nationalist or nationalising rhetoric. Thus Europe has largely escaped the problems experienced in Canada where the Charter of Rights was promoted in the early 1980s as a measure of Canadian nation-building and has consequently been widely rejected in Quebec. Human rights are not explicitly protected in the treaties of the EU but under pressure from states who have wanted to place their rights guarantees above EU law. The EU's European Court of Justice has recognised the need to incorporate both national and European charters of rights in its jurisprudence (Moravcsik 1995). The draft EU constitution includes an effort to bring these elements together by incorporating the Charter within it and adhering to the Convention.

Legal protection for the *collective* rights of minorities in Europe is, by comparison, underdeveloped. After the First World War, the minorities question in Central and Eastern Europe was addressed through bilateral and multilateral treaties, mostly on the same template but without creating any pan-European system (Capotorti 1991). Following the Second World War, the emphasis moved to individual rights, and apart from some bilateral treaty arrangements, efforts to extend rights to minorities made little progress (Hillgruber and Jestaedt 1994; Fenet 1995). The issue came back with the end of the Cold War and since then there has developed a complex net of charters, institutions and guarantees, under the auspices of the Council of Europe, the Organisation for Security and Cooperation in Europe (OSCE) and the European Union. While formally separate, these form an interlinked system, with mutual penetration and influence and a growing tendency for judgements under one to cross-reference the others (Fenet 1995).

The OSCE has been drawn into the question since the 1975 Helsinki Accords as an extension of human rights but, while it has a High Commissioner on National Minorities, it has been reluctant to be drawn into broader issues of self-determination. The Council of Europe adopted a Charter on Regional and Minority Languages in 1992 and returned to the question with the 1995 Framework Convention for the Protection of National Minorities, designed to be adopted in appropriate form by signatory states but without direct application. It does not define minorities or recognise them as collectivities, but rather addresses itself to the rights of individuals belonging to them. Membership of a minority is determined by a mixture of self-designation and objective criteria, but signatory states were allowed to designate their own minorities before ratification. Matters covered include the use of language, education, the media, public administration, commercial signs and cross-border contacts.

Some of the EU's internal market policies, in matters such as labelling, land purchase or ethnic quotas for employment can be seen as a threat to minority cultures and languages. Gradually, however, the EU has incorporated some measures for minority protection. The Maastricht Treaty had a clause in favour of cultural and regional diversity, used by the European Parliament and Commission to fund various measures, including the Bureau of Less Widely Spoken Languages in Dublin (Fenet 1995). The Parliament and the Committee of the Regions have also pressed for wider recognition of culture and language in the operation of regional policies. The EU has intervened more effectively in candidate countries, as has the Council of Europe, making treatment of minorities a condition for membership. The EU's approach has often relied on principles and processes from the Council of Europe and the OSCE, providing hard conditionality where they rely on moral force (Brusis 2003). It has pressed candidate countries to adopt the Framework Convention on National Minorities and incorporated minority protection in the Copenhagen criteria for candidate countries (Hughes and Sasse 2003).

This is a patchwork approach but, by individual initiatives linked across the various institutions, a minority-rights regime of sorts has come into being, although still dependent on state compliance (Roter 1997; Jackson Preece 1998). Priority is given to individual rights, although there is more attention on the collective means by which these rights are exercised in matters like educational provision or public services. There is a reluctance to broach broader political questions. No European regime recognises a right of self-determination for minorities, although the Council of Europe insists on the need for local self-government, and there is always explicit recognition of the integrity of states and their borders. There is a bias towards seeing Central and Eastern Europe as the seat of the problem, rather than taking a broader pan-European perspective, and West European states have jealously guarded their rights to deal with their minorities in their own way. So when the Copenhagen criteria were incorporated into the *acquis de l'Union*, the minority-rights clauses were left out, so ensuring that the old member states would not be affected by them (Hughes and Sasse 2003).

Functional transformation and territorial restructuring

There is a large literature on the end of territory (Badie 1995) or the relaxation of the constraints of space and time in the information age (Castells 1997). As the bonds of identity, function and space are severed, new forms of individual and collective enterprise should be possible. So, according to some authors, nationalities might be reconceptualised as non-spatial cultural communities and endowed with various forms of non-territorial rights (Tamir 1993). The debate about nationalities and nationalism then flows into the more general debate about multiculturalism and group rights.

Such approaches, however, wish away the nationality claim too easily. In the first place, territory is becoming more, not less, important to cultural survival in the modern world. Territory remains central to nationality claims in most cases and, far from weakening, its importance may be growing. This is because instruments like education and other public services essential to maintaining a cultural community are usually territorial, and because face-to-face communication remains important. More fundamentally, nationality claims are not merely about cultural self-expression, but about self-government and the scope and bounds of public authority. While there are examples of non-territorial means for providing specific services like education, nobody has yet devised a workable non-territorial system of general self-government for the modern world. Moreover, the de-ethnicisation of nationality movements, encouraged by the need to legitimate themselves in present-day Europe, has led to an increased emphasis on territory as the criterion of inclusion. It might at first glance appear that this should make nationality conflicts less acute, as value and cultural differences are less important or consigned to the private sphere. In some ways, however, it makes them more acute since, while cultural demands can be met through public policies, territorial or civic nationalism carries greater legitimacy and can lay claims to global social regulation. So civic nationalists can make very plausible claims to a state of their own.

On the other hand, there are, in modern Europe, alternatives to state-hood as a mechanism for achieving collective goods. The 'new regional-ism' holds out the prospect of forms of territorial autonomy and collective capacity without the need to set up a separate state. The new regionalist paradigm embraces functional change, institution-building and new ways of conceptualising territorial politics (Keating 1998). The most important strand concerns the importance of local and regional levels for economic development and change, within global and European markets (Storper 1997; Scott 1998). Much of this literature also stresses the social construc-tion of the region and the role of norms, collective identities and shared memories in facilitating social cooperation and change (Keating *et al.* 2003). The key powers are no longer those held by the classic state, such as tariff policy or even macroeconomic powers, but rather supply-side factors that stimulate entrepreneurship and adaptation. Many of these powers, including education, training, infrastructure and planning, are held by sub-state governments.

Regionalism has also involved institution-building in state and civil society. States have devolved to their constituent territories to varying degrees, both to accommodate autonomist demands and for reasons of functional efficacy. Interest groups and other elements of civil society have adapted, to consolidate the territory as a social, economic and political system. Regions are increasingly competing with each other for invest-ment, technology and markets, within European and global spaces. It is not surprising then, that stateless nations have often emerged as sites of such region-building, with nation-building elites committed to new regionalist theories about the ability of small units to compete in Euro-pean space autonomously. Territorially integrated nations and nationali-ties may thus gain a substantial degree of functional autonomy within the new regional political economy. Identity and culture, previously seen as an obstacle to modernisation, may be assets in the new development para-digm. This is not because territories now projected as nations have any natural coincidence between territory, identity and functional systems, but because the evolution of the Western European state and transnational order has encouraged stateless nation- and region-builders to construct new systems of action. Yet this, too, is less a universal trend than a variable, presenting opportunities for accommodation in some places but not in others. So it may be difficult to apply the territorial solution in Central and Eastern Europe, as recommended by Kymlicka (2001a), where the nationalities have not undergone the same process of territorial consolidation.

Territory and nationality do not coincide where more than one group shares the same territory; where one group straddles two territories; and in combinations of these. The old nation-state model is very uncompro-mising on the issue of borders. They are fixed and, at least in the ideal type, encompass all identities, governing institutions and functional systems. Modern understandings of space in political geography, however, allow a more open conception of the region, with less rigidly defined boundaries and complex identities (Paasi 2002; Batt 2003). One territory blends into the next and functional systems, while still territorial, may not all have exactly the same boundaries. This allows for partially territorialised solutions, in which territories are open rather than closed and their citizens can profess different degrees of identity with it. We may thus see a more open-ended regionalism, in which a territory may be a homeland for a nationality group, providing symbolic recognition and some public goods, while containing pressures to move state borders. A nationality can thus have a territorial base without either monopolising this territory or being confined to it.

There is no consensus on what to call these new territorial systems of action or on what the political implications are. Allen Scott (1998) writes of 'regional directorates' and Ohmae (1995) of a 'regional state', which looks like a neo-liberal regime rather than a state. The term is taken up by Thomas Courchene (2001) and by Alain G. Gagnon (2001), who see the regional state as a way out of the Quebec dilemma between federalism and independence. Georg Jellinek (1981) in the nineteenth century wrote of fragments of state, entities that have some but not all of the characteristics of statehood. We seem, once again, to have reached the limits of our terminological range in trying to grasp the new phenomena.

Territorial opportunity structures

The emerging European order is complex and multilayered, with a range of continental bodies, not all of which have the same territorial coverage. There is the EU, the Council of Europe, the Organisation for Security and Cooperation in Europe and a range of interstate and inter-regional bodies. Although the European theme first entered the discourse of minority nationalists between the two world wars with visions of a European federation of nations, the European Economic Community attracted little enthusiasm among the minorities, who tended to see it as remote, bureaucratic and unsympathetic to nationality claims. During the 1980s and 1990s, however, institutional incentives emerged for minority parties to enter the European political game (Lynch 1996; De Winter 1998; De Winter and Gomez-Reino 2002). Direct elections to the European Parliament from 1979 encouraged minorities to organise, and in 1981 the European Free Alliance was created, linking minority and nationalist parties and creating a forum for dialogue and debate about building a new Europe. The 1980s also saw a deepening of European integration and extension of Community competences into new areas, together with a strengthening of its supranational aspects and an institutionalisation of the regional level.

In the late 1980s and early 1990s there was a flurry of interest in the Europe of the Regions, a vaguely-specified order in which regions would be recognised as a third level of government alongside states and the EU itself (Bullman 1994). Regions and stateless nations were too hetero-geneous ever to fit into such a scheme and in practice it evolved into a series of opportunities to intervene in EU policy making, either by direct links to Brussels or via the member states. Nationalities may be able to adapt themselves to these regional opportunity structures, and to ally themselves to 'non-national' and powerful regions; at the same time it gives further incentives to territorialise nationality claims. A clause in the 1992 Treaty on European Union allows regional ministers to represent member states in the Council of Ministers where domestic law permits. This is applied in Germany, Austria, Belgium and the UK, in different ways. So, while European 'high' policy making remains largely intergov-ernmental, there are mechanisms for regions to act, provided they first achieve victory in domestic constitutional arenas.

A lot of attention has been given to the Structural Funds as a means of giving regions access to Brussels, a partnership with the Commission, and a source of funding independent of member states. In practice, this field is intergovernmental and regions have no means of getting money directly from Brussels. The Funds are, rather, an arena for symbolic politics, in which regional politicians can claim to have established a funding link to Brussels, while the EU can claim credit for looking after vulnerable regions. In this way, they have helped bring Europeanism and regionalist and minority claims further together.

A more direct form of access is the Committee of the Regions. This has proved a disappointment to regionalists and minority nationalists because of its weak powers and lack of resources, and because it represents all levels of sub-member state government equally. Frustrated at having to share a place with municipal governments, the strong regions, stateless nations and feder-ated units launched an initiative for the 'Regions with Legislative Powers', or 'Constitutional Regions', to gain recognition in the European constitution. Although these do not always correspond to cultural or national regions or minorities, there is enough of an overlap to make common cause. While they have as yet achieved few concrete results, they have created another discur-sive space in which dialogue and exchange takes place about the building of Europe. Such dialogue is also pursued by the many regional offices in Brus-sels, which have become part of the policy community and an important link in the exchange of ideas and policy initiatives. Another arena is the Council of Europe, whose Committee of Regional and Local Authorities has been divided into two chambers, for the regions and the municipalities. This has produced a European Charter of Local Self Government and a draft Euro-pean Charter of Regional Self Government.

An important opportunity lies in the transformation of borders. Borders remain important as expressions of state sovereignty and are for the first time generally uncontested; but they are losing their functional significance. These twin changes have encouraged new forms of cross-border penetration and cooperation, which are no longer automatically seen as threats to the state. As empirical studies have shown, identities in border regions are typically complex, with individuals identifying both with their respective states and with a transborder nationality or ethnic group, defying a simple geographical definition of identity (Sahlins 1989; Fure 1997; Kaplan 2000; Bray 2002). Permeable borders allow a renegotiation of these and the emergence of new forms of layered identity. On a more concrete level, there is scope for cross-border functional cooperation on economic, environmental and cultural matters, allowing more expression for the new regionalism. The Council of Europe produced the Madrid Convention which provides a legal instrument for cross-border partnership. The EU has a substantial programme of cross-border partnerships under the INTER-REG initiative, which by the end of the 1990s was active across every border within the EU and with the candidate countries as well. Experience of cross-border partnership has been mixed, since differences in legal systems and political incentives, together with the tendency of regions and localities to be in competition for investment, have often stymied genuine partnership (Scott 1999). The effects on identity are also subtle. There are few instances of border communities on abandoning their state identities to find a common ethnic or national one. Cooperation has, however, helped redefine borders as complex zones in which multiple identities can be expressed and negotiated.

The constitution of Europe

Much has been written about multilevel governance in Europe, about pluralism and the complexity of policy-making structures. Yet without a constitution, it is feared, Europe lacks a clear normative basis and becomes merely an arena for group competition. This applies equally to the nationalities question, where we are witnessing a plethora of claims to self-determination, historic and present rights and a variety of sovereigntist and post-sovereignty claims. Such a complex normative order requires a new form of constitutional thinking, adapted to a world in which the old triad of nation, territory and sovereignty can no longer be taken for granted.

This would require a European constitution that was strong enough to provide an overarching framework, but flexible enough to allow diversity within it. A European 'state' could no more solve the question than could the old nation-state. At the other extreme, Europe as a mere holding company, a market order, or a convenience for externalising difficult problems, would not sustain the common values and constitutional order in which pluralism is possible. The Convention on the Future of Europe was intended precisely to fill this gap and there has been an intense debate on what the future polity should look like. The national/regional question was not a priority in the Convention, which was not tasked with proposing a new statute for nations and national minorities. Nor could it challenge the sovereignty of states and their authority head-on. On the contrary, the debates followed a logic in which authority is divided in complex ways between European and state-level institutions. Yet the various visions of Europe on offer provide more, or less, space for the accommodation of nationalities in the interstices of the state system (Jáuregui 1997). An intergovernmental Europe based on the existing states clearly offers least scope for stateless nationalities. An integrated but centralised and uniform Europe would offer little more. So regions and nationalities have pressed for an integrated Europe but one that is decentralised and pluralist. In this way, the pro-Europeanism of the national minorities and stateless nations can serve as a means to legitimise the European project itself by linking it to local mobilisation and identity. Rather than Europe seeking its own separate *demos*, therefore, it can be the framework for multiple *demoi*, themselves constitutive, along with the state, of a larger political community. Such a dispensation is closer to the idea of pluralistic federalism (Caminal 2002) than the classical uniform federalism of the US model.

The clarification and demarcation of roles and responsibilities undertaken by the Convention, however, threatens to reduce the space available for regions and nationalities to those specified in the new constitution. Indeed, the very process of constitution-making may reduce those areas of uncertainty in which new forms of authority might be negotiated, and Europe could end up as an obstacle to new forms of accommodation. In the last major treaty revision, at Maastricht, opportunities were created which member states could use at their discretion (discussed above). In the present constitutional round, there seems less willingness to allow such differentiation. The majority in the Convention and in the Committee of the Regions even refused to distinguish between federated units and devolved national parliaments on the one hand, and municipal government on the other. More radical proposals did not even reach the agenda. These included the idea that it be possible to divide a member state's vote in the Council of Ministers; a chamber of the nationalities for stateless nations and minorities; and a provision for 'internal enlargement' in which stateless nations could become full members of the EU. Another suggestion expanded on the Lamassoure proposal, whereby regions could become partners of the Union, to provide for them to become 'associated states', a half-way house to independence. Yet the original Lamassoure idea, which was already a long way from this, was further diluted to a form of administrative decentralisation. The EU has been reluctant to allow states to differentiate internally in their application of EU directives the way they are allowed in many cases to differentiate between themselves, although some progress is being made here. The numerous exceptions in the existing treaties to accommodate regions are not to be generalised. Even the proposal to recognise a category of regions with legislative powers fell victim to a combination of those who considered that all regions were the same and those who thought that they were so different that they were impossible to categorise. As a result, the draft constitution divided the stateless nationalist movements. While some supported it on the basis of their visceral Europeanism, others complained of its statist bias. Some voices argued that, since the constitution entrenches the states, they should revert to a policy of independent statehood.

Conclusion

European integration has thus modified both aspects of the old nationalities question, changing both the nation and the state, while creating a new level of political accommodation above both. The mystique of the old state form has been broken and its regulatory claims challenged. Europe has created a new discursive space for forms of post-sovereignty theory and claims, some of which have historical resonance. Nationalities movements have tended, in varying degrees according to the local circumstances, to adopt a post-sovereign stance; to express a civic, inclusive form of nationalism; and to emphasise their territorial basis. While this has in some circumstances encouraged them to make the next step towards statehood (as has also happened in Quebec), others have seen in the European framework an alternative to this. States have also been transformed. Europe, by externalising common functions and individual rights, permits a greater asymmetry within states and some have responded to this. Others, however, have reacted to the loss of authority upwards and downwards by insisting on their sovereign prerogatives; this has particularly affected the states of Central and Eastern Europe, which have just regained their sovereignty.

European organisations provide opportunities for non-state actors to intervene, gain recognition, build systems of action and secure protection. On the other hand, the concrete opportunities are limited and rather disparate. Europe encourages diversity and provides spaces for non-state actors, but many of its institutional and policy initiatives assume a homogeneous sub-state level of authority and identity (Closa 2002). So far, a gradual evolution has allowed Europe and the nationalities to adapt together, exploring new forms of political order. Formulas such as the 'regional state', 'fragment of state' or 'incomplete state' have been criticised for their implication that they are somehow unfinished, but this very characteristic marks the evolution of Europe itself. An open and loose form of constitutionalism would allow this process to continue, making adjustments where necessary. An effort to close the process or to fix the status, categories and competences of Europe, member states and nationalities and regions, would risk recreating the type of misfit that has caused such problems in the past.

3   The evolving basis of European norms of minority rights

Rights to culture, participation and autonomy

Will Kymlicka

The last 15 years has seen an explosion of efforts to develop international norms of minority rights, both at the global level and at regional levels. Globally, the UN adopted a declaration on the Rights of Persons Belonging to National or Ethnic, Religious and Linguistic Minorities in 1992, and is debating a Draft Declaration on the Rights of Indigenous Peoples. Other international organisations, such as the International Labour Organisation and the World Bank, have also developed norms on minority rights. Declarations have also been drafted by organisations at the regional level, such as the Organization of American States and the Council of Europe.

These developments offer the promise of protecting some of the most vulnerable groups in the modern world from serious injustices. Ethnic minorities have not fared well under the Westphalian system of sovereign 'nation-states'. Various policies of assimilation and exclusion have been directed at minorities in the name of constructing homogenous nation-states, and the international community has historically turned a blind eye to these injustices. Today, however, there is a growing commitment to remedy this situation, and it is increasingly accepted that the treatment of minorities is a matter of legitimate international concern and monitoring. At a minimum, these evolving norms set limits on the means that states can use to pursue their visions of national homogenisation. But they also, implicitly at least, offer a competing vision of the state, one which views diversity as an enduring reality and defining feature of the polity, and which views tolerance as a core value.

Viewed in this light, the trend towards codifying international norms of minority rights is surely a desirable and progressive one. And yet it raises a number of moral dilemmas and ambiguities. These emerging norms are uneven in their coverage, in part because of the way they have been shaped by larger geopolitical considerations, and in part because we simply lack the conceptual vocabulary to define these norms in a consistent and principled way.

In this chapter, I want to explore some of these dilemmas through a close examination of recent attempts to codify the 'rights of national minorities' in Europe. As I hope to show, the European experience provides a fascinating, if flawed, experiment in developing international norms of minority rights, one with lessons for other contexts.

The drive to internationalise minority rights in post-communist Europe

The story begins with the collapse of communism in Central and Eastern Europe in 1989, which was accompanied by a number of violent ethnic conflicts. In retrospect, these violent conflicts have largely been confined to the Caucuses and the Balkans. But this was not clear at the time. In the early 1990s, many commentators feared that ethnic tensions would spiral out of control in wide swaths of post-communist Europe. For example, predictions of civil war between the Slovak majority and Hungarian minority in Slovakia, or between the Estonian majority and Russian minority in Estonia, were not uncommon. Overly-optimistic predictions about the rapid replacement of communism with liberal democracy were supplanted with overly-pessimistic predictions about the replacement of communism with ethnic war.[1]

Faced with these potentially dire trends, the Western democracies in the early 1990s felt they had to do something. And they decided, in effect, to 'internationalise' the treatment of national minorities in post-communist Europe.[2] They declared, in the words of the Organisation for Security and Cooperation in Europe in 1990, that the status and treatment of national minorities 'are matters of legitimate international concern, and consequently do not constitute exclusively an internal affair of the respective State'.

The international community often makes pious declarations of its concern for the rights and well-being of peoples around the world, without ever really intending to do much about it. But in this case, the West backed up its words with actions. The most important and tangible action was the decision by the European Union (EU) and NATO in December 1991 to make minority rights one of the four criteria that candidate countries had to meet in order to become members of these organisations. Since most post-communist countries viewed membership in the EU and NATO as pivotal to their future prosperity and security, any 'recommendations' that the West might make regarding minority rights were taken very seriously. As a result, minority rights moved to the centre of post-communist political life, a core component of the process of 'rejoining Europe'.

Having decided in 1990–91 that the treatment of minorities in post-communist Europe was a matter of legitimate international concern, the next step was to create institutional mechanisms that could monitor how post-communist countries were treating their minorities. Since 1991, therefore, various international bodies have been created with the mandate of monitoring the treatment of minorities, and of recommending changes needed to live up to European standards of minority rights. A crucial step here was the formation of the Office of the High Commission on National Minorities of the Organisation for Security and Cooperation in Europe (HCNM-OSCE) in 1993, linked to OSCE mission offices in several post-communist countries. Another important step occurred at the Council of Europe, which set up a number of advisory bodies and reporting mechanisms as part of its Framework Convention on the Protection of National Minorities (FCNM) in 1995. The EU and NATO themselves did not create new monitoring bodies specifically focused on minority rights,[3] but they have made clear that they support the work of the HCNM-OSCE and the Council of Europe, and expect post-communist countries to cooperate with them, as a condition of accession.

In short, Western states have made a serious commitment to internationalising minority rights, embedded not only in formal declarations but also in a dense web of European institutions. It is an interesting question how and why this commitment emerged. After all, the EU had shown very little interest in the question of minority rights prior to 1989, and had deliberately avoided including any reference to minority rights in its own internal principles. Nor have Western countries traditionally shown much interest in protecting minorities elsewhere around the world. On the contrary, Western states have often propped up governments in Africa, Asia or Latin America that were known to be oppressive to their minorities, even to the point of selling military equipment with the knowledge that it would be used against minority groups (e.g. selling arms to Indonesia to suppress minorities in Aceh and East Timor, or to Guatemala to suppress the Maya). So why did the West suddenly become a champion of minorities in post-communist Europe?

I think there were a number of reasons. One factor was humanitarian concern to stop the suffering of minorities facing persecution, mob violence and ethnic cleansing. But humanitarian concern is rarely enough, on its own, to mobilise Western governments. A more self-interested reason was the belief that escalating ethnic violence would generate large-scale refugee movements into Western Europe, as indeed happened from Kosovo and Bosnia. Also, ethnic civil wars often create pockets of lawlessness which become havens for the smuggling of arms and drugs, or for other forms of criminality and extremism.

Another reason, more diffuse, was the sense in the West that the ability of post-communist countries to manage their ethnic diversity was a test of their overall political maturity, and hence of their readiness to 'rejoin Europe'. As the General Secretary of the Council of Europe put it, respect for minorities is a fundamental measure of a country's 'moral progress' (Burgess 1999). The ability of a country to get its deficits under 3 per cent of GDP (one of the other accession criteria) may be important from an economic point of view, but does not tell us much about whether the country will 'fit' into European traditions and institutions.

In short, for a complex mixture of humanitarian, self-interested, and ideological reasons, minority rights have become 'internationalised' in Europe. Acceptance of the international monitoring and enforcement of these norms has become a test of a country's readiness for Europe. Meeting international norms of minority rights is seen as proof that a country has left behind its 'ancient ethnic hatreds' and 'tribal nationalisms', and is able to join a 'modern' liberal and cosmopolitan Europe.

The sources of international minority-rights norms

Between 1990 and 1993, then, a rapid consensus developed amongst all the major Western organisations that the treatment of national minorities by post-communist countries should be a matter of international concern, and that there should be international mechanisms to monitor a country's compliance with international norms of minority rights.

The precise details of how these various international organisations operate – their standards, monitoring functions, reporting procedures and enforcement mechanisms – have been described elsewhere (e.g. MRG 1999; Pentassuglia 2003). And while many of these institutions are still relatively new, there have been some attempts to evaluate the effectiveness of particular mechanisms in protecting minorities and preventing or reducing ethnic violence in post-communist Europe (e.g. Alfredsson and Turk 1993; Packer 1996, 2000; Cohen 1998; Gal 1999; Zaagman 1999).

What has not been well-studied, however, is the underlying normative bases of these international declarations. The very project of internationalising minority rights implies that there are certain shared 'international norms' (or at least 'European standards') regarding the rights of national minorities – i.e. some degree of normative consensus on the legitimate claims and rightful entitlements of minority groups. In reality, there was no such consensus in 1990. There were no formal pan-European declarations or conventions enumerating the rights of national minorities, and no common vocabulary or normative framework for discussing the issue.

Indeed, the very term 'minority rights' or 'rights of national minorities' was largely unknown in the West. Western countries differ greatly in how they talk about issues of accommodating diversity. For example, some countries (such as France, Greece, Turkey) simply deny that they have 'minorities'.[4] Other countries acknowledge that they have 'minorities' but differ about what sorts of groups this term applies to. In some countries (e.g. the UK), the term 'minorities' generally refers to post-war migrant groups, typically from the Caribbean or Southern Asia, not to the historic Welsh or Scottish groups. In other Western countries (as in most of post-communist Europe), it is the opposite: 'minorities' typically refers to historic groups (like the Slovenes in Austria), not to post-war migrants (like the Turks in Austria), who are instead described as 'foreigners'.

So the term 'minority' has different connotations across the West. In any event, in none of these countries was there widespread reference to general principles about 'the rights of national minorities'. Consider debates about Scots in the UK, or about Catalans in Spain, or about Slovenes in Austria. These debates were not phrased in the form:

- all national minorities have a right to X;
- Scots/Catalans/Slovenes are a national minority;
- therefore Scots/Catalans/Slovenes have a right to X.

Claims of particular national groups are not deduced from some broader principle or theory about what 'national minorities' as a category have 'rights' to. Instead, the rights of particular groups are debated in terms of historic settlements, built up over time, by which various accommodations have been reached between different communities.

In fact, to my knowledge, the term 'national minority' had no legal status or meaning in any Western country prior to the adoption of the Framework Convention in 1995. No legislation in any Western country specified which groups were 'national minorities', and which rights flowed from having this status. No Western country had an 'Office of National Minorities', or a 'Law on National Minorities'.

In short, there was no Western discourse of 'the rights of national minorities' prior to 1990, either within particular countries or across Europe as a whole. If you asked citizens or elites in Western Europe what were 'the rights of national minorities', you would probably get a blank stare. So the decision to internationalise state–minority relations through the articulation of 'European standards of the rights of national minorities' was, in a sense, a remarkable decision. It is not surprising that Western governments wanted to 'do something' about ethnic conflict in post-communist Europe, but it is surprising that they chose do so in an idiom or vocabulary that is essentially foreign to the Western experience. As Chandler notes, Western countries were determined to develop European standards as a way of monitoring post-communist countries, but they 'had no conception of how to apply such policies in relation to their own minorities' (Chandler 1999: 66).

How then were 'European standards' of minority rights formulated? Observers with a long memory recalled that this question had been tackled earlier, at the last major period of imperial breakdown after the First World War, resulting in the 'minority protection scheme' of the League of Nations. A mini-industry has arisen examining that older scheme, and trying to learn lessons from its successes and failures for contemporary European debates (e.g. Burns 1996; Cornwall 1996; Sharp 1996; Kovacs 2003).

However, the minority protection scheme of the League of Nations was particularistic, not generalised. It involved multilateral treaties guaranteeing particular rights for particular minorities in particular (defeated) countries, while leaving many other minorities unprotected. It did not attempt to articulate general standards or international norms that all national minorities would be able to claim. That indeed was one reason why the idea of minority rights fell out of favour and largely disappeared from the post-war international law context, replaced with a new focus on human rights.

However, the idea of minority rights did not entirely disappear from international law. It retained a foothold in Article 27 of the UN's 1966 International Covenant on Civil and Political Rights (ICCPR), which states that:

> In those States in which ethnic, religious or linguistic minorities exist, persons belonging to such minorities shall not be denied the right, in community with the other members of their group, to enjoy their own culture, to profess and practise their own religion, or to use their own language.

For all intents and purposes, this was the only example of an international norm of minority rights that was available in 1990, and so it inevitably provided the background for attempts to define European norms.

While Article 27 provided a starting point, it was widely viewed as insufficient, for two reasons. First, the right to 'enjoy one's culture' as originally formulated included only negative rights of non-interference, rather than positive rights to assistance, funding, autonomy or official language status. In effect, it simply reaffirms that members of minorities must be free to exercise their standard rights of freedom of speech, association, assembly, and conscience.[5]

These minimal guarantees, while vital, are inadequate to address the issues underlying violent ethnic conflicts in post-communist Europe. These conflicts centred on various positive claims, such as the right to use a minority language in courts or local administration; the funding of minority schools, universities and media; the extent of local or regional autonomy; the guaranteeing of political representation for minorities; or the prohibition on settlement policies designed to swamp minorities in their historic homelands with settlers from the dominant group. Article 27 has nothing to say about such claims. It protects certain civil rights relating to cultural expression, but it does not prohibit states from rescinding funding to minority-language schools and universities, abolishing local autonomy, gerrymandering electoral rules or constituency boundaries, or encouraging settlers to swamp minority homelands. None of these policies, which can be catastrophic for national minorities, and which often lead to violent conflict, violate the rights to cultural expression and association protected in Article 27.[6] If European standards were to be useful in resolving such conflicts, they would have to address claims for positive minority rights.

Article 27 has a second limitation. It applies to all types of ethnocultural minorities, no matter how large or small, recent or historic, territorially concentrated or dispersed. Indeed, the UN Human Rights Committee has declared that Article 27 applies even to visitors within a country! Article 27, in other words, can be seen as a truly *universal* cultural right – a right that can be claimed by any individual, and carried with her as she moves around the world.

This commitment to identifying universal cultural rights limits the sorts of minority rights that can be recognised. In particular, it precludes claims that flow from facts of historic settlement or territorial concentration. Since Article 27 articulates a universal and portable cultural right that applies to all individuals, even migrants and visitors, it does not articulate rights that are tied to the fact that a group is living on, what it views as, its historic homeland. Yet it is precisely claims relating to residence on a historic homeland that are at stake in all of the violent ethnic conflicts in post-communist Europe – e.g. in Bosnia, Kosovo, Macedonia, Georgia, Chechnya, Ngorno-Karabakh. Indeed, homeland claims are at the heart of most violent ethnic conflicts in the West (e.g. the Basque Country, Cyprus, Corsica, Northern Ireland). In all of these cases, minorities claim the right to govern themselves in what they view as their historic homeland, including the right to use their language in public institutions within their traditional territory, and to have their language, history and culture celebrated in the public sphere (e.g. in the naming of streets, the choice of holidays and state symbols). None of these claims can plausibly be seen as universal or portable – they only apply to particular sorts of minorities with a particular sort of history and territory. In short, these are all cases of ethnonational (or ethnonationalist) conflict, revolving around competing claims to nationhood and national territory.

If European standards were to be useful in resolving conflicts in post-communist Europe, they would need to go beyond universal minority rights and articulate *targeted* minority rights, focused on the specific types of ethnonational groups involved in these conflicts. As a result, the new European norms that have emerged since 1990 are all targeted at so-called 'national' minorities. Whereas Article 27 lumps together 'national, ethnic, religious and linguistic' minorities, the Council of Europe's Framework Convention refers only to 'national minorities', and the OSCE High Commissioner focuses solely on 'national minorities'. While there is no universally agreed-upon definition of 'national minorities', the term usually refers to historically-settled minorities, living on or near what they view as their national homeland. These are the sorts of groups involved in the violent and destabilising ethnic conflicts that generated the call for European norms in the first place. Most European countries have explicitly stated that immigrant groups are therefore not national minorities.

This commitment to developing targeted norms for 'national' minorities was courageous. No other international body has attempted to formulate such norms. Several international organisations have targeted minority rights for other types of minority groups. For example, the United Nations, the International Labour Organisation, and the Organization of American States have all developed targeted norms regarding indigenous peoples. Some of these organisations have also formulated norms targeted at migrants.[7] However, no one had previously attempted to formulate international norms directed at 'national minorities'.

This is a puzzling omission. If one thinks about the sorts of state–minority relations with the greatest potential for large-scale harm, injustice and violence, one could argue that they typically involve national minorities. While both indigenous peoples and migrants are vulnerable groups in need of international protection, most of the violent and destabilising ethnic conflict around the world involves conflicts between states and homeland ethnonationalist groups (e.g. Kashmir, Kurdistan, Tamil Eelam, Aceh, Tigray). As Walker Connor notes, the phenomenon of minority nationalism is a truly universal one. The countries affected by it

> are to be found in Africa (for example, Ethiopia), Asia (Sri Lanka), Eastern Europe (Romania), Western Europe (France), North America (Guatemala), South America (Guyana), and Oceania (New Zealand). The list includes countries that are old (United Kingdom) as well as new (Bangladesh), large (Indonesia) as well as small (Fiji), rich (Canada) as well as poor (Pakistan), authoritarian (Sudan) as well as democratic (Belgium), Marxist–Leninist (China) as well as militantly anti-Marxist (Turkey). The list also includes countries which are Buddhist (Burma), Christian (Spain), Moslem (Iran), Hindu (India), and Judaic (Israel).
>
> (Connor 1999: 163–4)

In this light, developing international norms that address the difficult challenges raised by such ethnonational groups is a central task for the theory and practice of minority rights around the world. The European experiment in defining these norms, therefore, is of pivotal significance.

Unfortunately, having set themselves this courageous task, I believe that European organisations then lost their nerve. The new norms that have been developed by the Council of Europe and the OSCE do not in fact address the distinctive challenges raised by national minorities. The Council of Europe's FCNM and the OSCE's recommendations do move beyond Article 27 by explicitly including certain modest positive rights, such as public funding of minority elementary schools, the right to spell one's surname in accordance with one's own language, and the right to submit documents to public authorities in the minority language. These changes are significant, but they remain essentially versions of the idea of a 'right to enjoy one's culture'. As such, they do not address the distinctive characteristics and aspirations of national minorities – that is, their sense of nationhood and claims to a national homeland. What such groups typically seek is not just the right as individuals to join with other individuals in enacting particular cultural practices, but the right as a national community to govern themselves on their homeland, and to use their self-governing powers to express and celebrate their language, history and culture in public space and public institutions.

The FCNM and OSCE recommendations are strangely silent on all of the central claims at stake in the post-communist ethnic conflicts. They do not discuss how to resolve (often competing) claims relating to territory and self-government, or how to assign official language status. Nor do they provide any guarantees that minorities can pursue higher-level education or professional accomplishment in their own language. States can fully respect these new standards and yet centralise power in such a way that all decisions are made in forums controlled by the dominant national group. They can also organise higher education, professional accreditation and political offices so that members of minorities must either linguistically assimilate in order to achieve professional success and political power, or migrate to their kin-state. (This is often referred to as the 'decapitation' of minority groups: forcing potential elites from minority communities to leave their community to achieve higher education or professional success.) Given that these norms do not preclude state policies aimed at the disempowering and decapitation of minorities, they are widely criticised by minority leaders and commentators as 'paternalism and tokenism' (Wheatley 1997: 40).[8]

The resulting framework of minority-rights norms is both ineffective and unstable. It is ineffective because these norms do not solve the problems they were intended to address. Recall that the original point of developing these norms was to deal with violent ethnic conflicts in post-communist Europe, such as in Kosovo, Bosnia, Croatia, Macedonia, Georgia, Azerbaijan, Moldova and Chechnya. None of these conflicts revolved around the right of individuals to join with others to enjoy their culture. The violation of such rights was not the cause of violent conflict, and respect for such rights would not resolve the conflicts. The same is true about the other major cases where European organisations feared potential violence, such as the Hungarian minorities in Romania and Slovakia, or the Russian minority in Ukraine.

In all of these cases, the issues in dispute are not covered by the FCNM or the OSCE recommendations. These are conflicts involving large, territorially concentrated groups who have manifested the capacity and the aspiration to govern themselves and to administer their own public institutions in their own language, and who typically have possessed some form of self-government and official language status in the past. They have mobilised for territorial autonomy, official language status, minority-language universities, and consociational power-sharing. None of these groups would be satisfied with the meagre rights guaranteed by the FCNM and OSCE recommendations.

The fact that these national minorities are not satisfied with these provisions is sometimes taken as evidence of the illiberalism of their political culture, or the radicalism of their leadership. But it is worth noting that no sizeable politically mobilised national minority in the West would be satisfied either. No one can seriously suppose that national minorities in Catalonia, Flanders, Quebec, Bern, South Tyrol, Åland Islands or Puerto Rico would be satisfied simply with minority elementary schools but not mother-tongue universities, or bilingual street signs but not official language status, or local administration but not regional autonomy.

This is not to say that there are no contexts in post-communist Europe where current FCNM or OSCE norms would provide a realistic basis for state–minority relations. I think they will work well in those countries which are essentially ethnically homogenous – where the dominant group forms 90–95 per cent of the population – and where the remaining ethnic groups are small, dispersed and already on the road to assimilation. This is the situation, for example, in the Czech Republic, Slovenia and Hungary. None of the minorities in these countries are in fact capable of exercising regional autonomy, or of sustaining a high degree of institutional completeness (e.g. of sustaining their own universities), and most already show high levels of linguistic assimilation. For these groups, the FCNM/OSCE norms provide all that they could ask for. They allow such small and half-assimilated minorities to negotiate their integration into the dominant society with a certain amount of dignity and security. Similarly, the FCNM/OSCE norms will likely be satisfactory to small, dispersed and partly assimilated minorities in other post-communist countries, such as the Vlach in Macedonia, or the Armenians in Romania.

The problem, of course, is that these minorities were not (and are not) the ones involved in serious ethnic conflict. The problem of ethnic violence and potentially destabilising ethnic conflict in post-communist Europe is almost exclusively confined to groups that are capable of exercising self-government and of sustaining their own public institutions, and which therefore contest with the state for control over public institutions.[9] And for these groups, the FCNM and OSCE norms are largely irrelevant. If the goal is to effectively deal with the problem of potentially destabilising ethnic conflict, then we need norms that actually address the source of these conflicts. And any norms that start from an Article 27-style 'right to enjoy one's culture' are unlikely to do that.[10]

The current framework of minority rights is not only politically ineffective, it is also conceptually unstable. The only groups that are currently protected by these European norms are 'national minorities', but since the actual rights being codified are not based on claims of historic settlement and territorial concentration, there is no reason why they should not apply to immigrant groups as well. And indeed we see a movement within both the Council of Europe and the OSCE to redefine the category of 'national minorities' to include immigrants.[11] This would be a move back to the original Article 27 model that attempts to articulate universal cultural rights applicable to all minorities, new or old, large or small, dispersed or concentrated.

Many commentators assume that redefining the category of 'national minorities' to include immigrants is a progressive step: the more groups that are protected, the better. Moreover, immigrants today in Europe are clearly a vulnerable group in need of international protection from hostile national governments. Since it is unlikely that EU states will adopt any declarations aimed at the protection of immigrants,[12] the only realistic way to achieve this protection is by fitting immigrants under some pre-existing scheme of minority protection, which in the European context means sliding them under the umbrella of 'national minorities'.

While this extension is progressive in some respects, giving protection to groups that would not otherwise be protected, we must also recognise that it is potentially regressive in other respects. If the category of 'national minorities' is redefined in this way, it will make it even less likely that these norms will develop in a way that grapples with the distinctive claims of historic/territorial minorities. The bold experiment of articulating international norms targeted at national minorities, and capable of resolving potentially violent ethnonationalist conflict, is slowly being abandoned.[13]

The self-government alternative?

Was there a viable alternative? Is it possible to formulate norms that can provide a principled basis for responding to the claims of ethnonational groups? Some commentators have argued that the most promising alternative lies elsewhere in international law – namely, in the principle that all 'peoples' have a right to 'self-determination'. This principle of self-determination dates back to the founding Charter of the United Nations, and is reaffirmed in Article 1 of the 1966 International Covenant on Civil and Political Rights.[14] It is therefore a long-standing norm within international law, although it has not traditionally been applied to national minorities. According to some commentators, however, a suitably revised interpretation of the principle of self-determination can and should be applied to national minorities, and would provide a principled basis for addressing their claims.

It is generally accepted that the right to self-determination in Article 1 *as traditionally interpreted* cannot simply be extended to national minorities, since it is typically understood to include the right to form one's own state. Precisely for this reason, its scope has traditionally been drastically restricted in international law. It has been limited by what is called the 'saltwater thesis'. Although the Article says that 'all peoples' have the right of self-determination, in fact the only 'peoples' who have been able to assert this right are those subject to colonisation from overseas. National minorities within a territorially contiguous state have not been recognised as separate 'peoples' with their own right of self-determination, no matter how culturally or historically distinct they have been. Groups like the Scots or Kurds may think of themselves as distinct 'peoples', and most historians and social scientists may accept this label, but the international community has not recognised them as such, for fear that this would entail granting them a right to form an independent state.

However, if we adopt a more modest interpretation of the right to self-determination, one that is consistent with the territorial integrity of states, it may be possible to extend its scope to include national minorities. This is the goal of various models of 'internal self-determination'. According to these models, national minorities, as distinct 'peoples' or 'nations' living on their historic homelands, have the right to some form of self-determination within the boundaries of the larger state, typically through some form of territorial autonomy (hereafter TA). Many commentators have argued that it is morally arbitrary to accord self-determination to overseas peoples while denying it to internal peoples. Both have a sense of distinct nationhood and a desire for self-government, and both have typically been subject to conquest, involuntary incorporation and historic discrimination. A morally consistent approach to self-determination would, therefore, recognise its applicability to internal national minorities (and indigenous peoples), at least in the form of a right to territorial autonomy (Moore 2001).

Throughout the early 1990s, many intellectuals and political organisations representing national minorities pushed for international recognition of such a right to internal self-determination. And, for a brief period from 1990 to 1993, there was some indication that this campaign might be successful. For example, the very first statement by a European organisation on minority rights after the collapse of communism – the initial 1990 OSCE Copenhagen declaration – went out of its way to endorse territorial autonomy (Article 35):

> The participating States note the efforts undertaken to protect and create conditions for the promotion of the ethnic, cultural, linguistic and religious identity of certain national minorities by establishing, as one of the possible means to achieve these aims, appropriate local or autonomous administrations corresponding to the specific historical and territorial circumstances of such minorities and in accordance with the policies of the State concerned.

This paragraph does not recognise a 'right' to TA, but recommends it as a good way of accommodating national minorities.

An even stronger endorsement of TA came in 1993, in Recommendation 1201 of the Council of Europe Parliamentary Assembly. It contains a clause (Article 11) stating that in the regions where they are a majority, the persons belonging to a national minority shall have the right to have at their disposal appropriate local or autonomous authorities or to have a special status, matching this specific historical and territorial situation and in accordance with the domestic legislation of the State.

Unlike the OSCE Copenhagen declaration, this Recommendation recognises TA as a 'right'. Of course, parliamentary recommendations are just that: a recommendation, not a legally binding document. But still this shows that in the early 1990s, there was movement in the direction of endorsing a general principle that justice required some or other effective mechanism for sharing power between majority and national minorities, specifically mentioning TA as one such mechanism.

Many national minority organisations in post-communist Europe viewed the passage of Recommendation 1201 as a great victory. Ethnic Hungarian organisations in particular viewed it as evidence that Europe would support their claims for TA in Slovakia, Romania and Serbia. They assumed this Recommendation would play a central role in the Council of Europe's FCNM which was being drafted at the same time, and that complying with this Recommendation would be required for candidate countries to join the EU.

This expectation was bolstered by the fact that internal self-determination for national minorities has clearly become the general trend within the West itself. The practice of TA for sizeable, territorially concentrated national minorities has become virtually universal in the West. Indeed, one of the most striking developments in ethnic relations in the Western democracies over the past century has been the trend towards creating political sub-units in which national minorities form a local majority, and in which their language is recognised as an official language, at least within their self-governing region, and perhaps throughout the country as a whole. At the beginning of the twentieth century, only Switzerland and Canada had adopted this combination of territorial autonomy and official language status for sub-state national groups. Since then, however, virtually all Western democracies that contain sizeable sub-state nationalist movements have moved in this direction. The list includes the adoption of autonomy for the Swedish-speaking Åland Islands in Finland after the First World War; autonomy for South Tyrol in Italy, and for Puerto Rico in the US, after the Second World War; federal autonomy for Catalonia and the Basque Country in Spain in the 1970s; for Flanders in Belgium in the 1980s; and most recently for Scotland and Wales in the 1990s.

If we restrict our focus to sizeable and territorially concentrated national minorities, this trend is now essentially universal in the West. All groups over 250,000 that have demonstrated a desire for TA now have it in the West, as well as many smaller groups (such as the German minority in Belgium).[15] The largest group that has mobilised for autonomy without

success are the Corsicans in France (175,000 people). But even here, legislation was recently adopted to accord autonomy to Corsica, and it was only
a ruling of the Constitutional Court that prevented its implementation. So
France too, I think, will soon join the bandwagon.

Moreover, while the shift to territorial autonomy was originally controversial in each of the countries that adopted it, it has quickly become
a deeply-entrenched part of political life in these countries. It is incon-
ceivable that Spain or Belgium or Canada, for example, could revert to a
unitary and monolingual state. And no one is campaigning for such a
reversal. Indeed, no Western democracy that has adopted territorial
autonomy and official bilingualism has reversed this decision. This is
evidence, I think, that this model for accommodating sizeable/
concentrated national minorities has been very successful in terms of
liberal-democratic values of peace, prosperity, individual rights and
democracy.[16]

In short, if there is such a thing as a 'European standard' for dealing
with mobilised national minorities, some form of internal autonomy
would appear to be it. This is the model Western democracies today use to
deal with the phenomenon of sub-state nationalist groups, and national
minorities in post-communist Europe had reason to hope that it would be
established as a norm for their countries as well.

Of course, the fact that internal autonomy has become the norm in
practice in the West does not mean that it can be codified as a general
norm in international law. It is not clear how such a norm of internal self-
determination could be formulated in a generalised way. However, it is
worth noting that this very issue has been debated in a closely related
context of international law: namely, the rights of indigenous peoples.
The UN's Draft Declaration on the Rights of Indigenous Peoples, submitted in 1993, has several articles affirming the principle of internal self-
determination, including:

> Article 3: Indigenous peoples have the right of self-determination. By
> virtue of that right, they freely determine their political status and
> freely pursue their economic, social and cultural development.
> Article 15: [Indigenous peoples] have the right to establish and
> control their educational systems and institutions providing education
> in their own languages, in a manner appropriate to their cultural
> methods of teaching and learning.
> Article 26: Indigenous peoples have the right to own, develop, control
> and use the lands and territories ... which they have traditionally
> owned or otherwise occupied or used. This includes the right to the
> full recognition of their laws, traditions and customs, land-tenure
> systems and institutions for the development and management of
> resources...
> Article 31: Indigenous peoples, as a specific form of exercising their

right to self-determination, have the right to autonomy or self-government in matters relating to their internal affairs...

Article 33: Indigenous peoples have the right to promote, develop and maintain their institutional structures and their distinctive juridical customs, traditions, procedures and practices, in accordance with internationally recognized human rights standards.

This draft declaration is still a draft, and hence not binding international law (Anaya 1996). But the basic idea that indigenous peoples have a right to internal self-determination is now widely endorsed throughout the international community, and is reflected in other recent international declarations on indigenous rights, including by the Organization of American States and the International Labour Organisation.

This shows that there is no inherent reason why international law cannot accept the idea of internal self-determination. The status of national minorities in post-communist Europe is not identical to that of indigenous peoples in the Americas or Asia. But there are some important similarities in both history and aspirations, and many of the standard arguments for recognising a right of internal self-determination for indigenous peoples also apply to national minorities.[17]

So there were several reasons why national minorities in post-communist states could reasonably hope that some form of internal self-government would be codified as part of the 'European standards' for the treatment of national minorities. This approach is in fact the norm within Western Europe today; it has been recognised as a valid principle in international law with respect to indigenous peoples; it can be seen as a more consistent application of the idea of the self-determination of peoples, avoiding the arbitrariness of the traditional 'salt-water' interpretation; and it was endorsed in important statements by European organisations, including the OSCE in 1990 and the Council of Europe Parliamentary Assembly in 1993.

However, as it turns out, the Assembly's Recommendation 1201 reflects the high-water mark of support for TA within European organisations. Since then, there has been a marked movement away from support for TA. As we have seen, the Framework Convention, adopted just two years after Recommendation 1201, avoids any reference to TA. Not only is TA not recognised as a 'right', it is not even mentioned as a recommended practice. Nor does TA appear in any subsequent declaration or recommendation of European organisations, such as the series of The Hague, Oslo and Lund Recommendations adopted by the OSCE from 1996 to 1999,[18] or the new constitution of the EU.[19] And the European Commission for Democracy through Law has ruled that national minorities do not have rights of self-determination, even in the form of internal self-determination (European Commission for Democracy through Law 1996). For all intents and purposes, ideas of internal self-determination have disappeared from the debate about 'European standards' on minority rights.

There are a number of reasons for this. For one thing, the idea of autonomy faced intense opposition from post-communist states. They feared that recognising any idea of internal self-determination or minority autonomy would be destabilising. Governments feared that granting TA to some groups would lead to problems of both 'escalation' and 'proliferation' (Offe 1998, 2001). The former fear is that groups granted internal self-determination will then escalate their demands into full-blown secession. The latter fear is that if internal self-determination is offered to one highly vocal or mobilised group, then other groups, previously quiescent, will come out of the woodwork and demand their own autonomy.

Of course, the same two fears of escalation and proliferation were present in the West as well, and yet Western states have nonetheless proceeded with internal autonomy. Fears of escalation and proliferation have turned out to be exaggerated, at least in the Western context.[20] However, these fears are exacerbated in many post-communist countries by the fact that national minorities often share a common ethnic or national identity with a neighbouring state, which they may therefore view as their 'kin-state' or 'mother-country' (such as ethnic Hungarian minorities in Slovakia vis-à-vis Hungary; ethnic Russian minorities in the Baltics vis-à-vis Russia). In such cases, the fear of escalation is not so much that minorities will become secessionist, but rather that they will become irredentist – i.e. that they serve as a fifth-column, supporting efforts by their neighbouring kin-state to take over part or all of the country.[21]

More generally, the very idea of recognising minorities as 'nations within', possessed of their own inherent rights to self-government, challenges the ideology of most post-communist states. These states aspire to be seen as unified nation-states, premised on a singular conception of popular sovereignty, rather than as unions or federations of two or more peoples.[22]

For a variety of reasons, then, claims to internal self-determination have been bitterly resisted in post-communist Europe. As the OSCE High Commissioner on National Minorities has noted, claims to TA meet 'maximal resistance' on the part of states in the region. Any attempt by Western organisations to push such models would therefore require maximum pressure, and would make relations between East and West much more conflictual and costly. Hence, in the High Commissioner's judgement, it is more 'pragmatic' to focus on modest forms of minority rights, such as those guaranteed in the FCNM (van der Stoel 1999: 111).

Moreover, there was also strong opposition to the idea of entrenching a right to TA for minorities *in the West*, and to the idea that there would be international monitoring of how Western states treated their minorities. France, Greece and Turkey have traditionally opposed the very idea of self-government rights for national minorities, and indeed deny the very existence of national minorities (Dimitras 2004). And even those Western countries that accept the principle do not necessarily want *their* laws and policies regarding national minorities subject to international monitoring. This is true, for example, of Switzerland and the United States (Chandler 1999: 66–8; Ford 1999: 49). The treatment of national minorities in various Western countries remains a politically sensitive topic, and many countries do not want their majority–minority settlements, often the result of long and painful negotiation processes, re-opened by international monitoring agencies. In short, while they were willing to insist that post-communist states be monitored for their treatment of minorities, they do not want their own treatment of minorities examined.

Given these obstacles, it is not surprising that efforts to codify a right to autonomy or internal self-determination for national minorities have failed. While the international community has shown some willingness to consider this idea in the case of indigenous peoples, it has proven too controversial in the case of national minorities.

From minority rights to geopolitical security?

It seems then that neither of the two approaches to building European standards of national minority rights – whether based on a right to enjoy one's culture or a right to self-determination – has succeeded in developing meaningful and effective international norms. Even though the right to enjoy one's culture is now being interpreted in a strengthened form compared to its original formulation in Article 27 of the ICCPR, it is still too weak to actually resolve the sources of ethnic conflict. And even though self-determination is now being pursued in a weakened form compared to its original formulation in Article 1 of the ICCPR, it is still too strong for many countries to accept.

If neither of these options is feasible and effective, what are the alternatives? One option is to abandon the idea of developing European norms on minority rights. After all, the EU and NATO survived and flourished for many years without paying any attention to minority rights.[23] Why not reconsider the decision to make minority rights one of the foundational values of the European order?

Indeed, one could argue that the original decision in the early 1990s to develop such norms was based on a mistaken prediction about the likelihood that ethnic conflict would spiral out of control. It has since become clear that ethnic violence is a localised phenomenon in post-communist Europe, and that the prospects for violence in countries like Slovakia or Estonia are virtually nil for the foreseeable future. So perhaps it is unnecessary to monitor whether these countries are treating their minorities in accordance with (so-called) European norms.

To be sure, Western observers might not approve of some of the policies that these countries would adopt if left to their own devices. But it is unlikely that these policies would lead to violence and instability. Some of these countries might experiment with heavy-handed assimilationist policies, but if so, these policies would almost certainly fail, and in the end a domestic consensus would emerge on a more liberal policy. This, of course, is what happened in the West, and there is no reason to assume it would not or could not happen in the East. Moreover, liberal policies are more likely to be perceived as legitimate, and hence to be stable, if they emerge from these sorts of domestic processes, rather than being imposed from without.

For these reasons, some commentators have suggested that we stop pressuring post-communist countries to comply with international norms on minority rights.[24] This would not necessarily preclude all forms of Western intervention. As I noted earlier, ethnic conflicts can undermine regional peace and stability. Violence, massive refugee flows and arms-smuggling can spill over into neighbouring countries, and destabilise entire regions. The international community has a right to protect itself against such potentially destabilising ethnic conflicts in post-communist Europe.

However, insofar as *security* is the real motivation for Western intervention, then presumably state–minority relations should be monitored, not for their compliance with international norms, but for their potential threats to regional peace and security. Monitoring should aim to identify those cases in which the status and treatment of minorities might lead to these sorts of spillover effects.

And indeed European organisations have been engaged in this sort of security monitoring. In addition to the monitoring of compliance with international norms, European organisations have also been engaged in a parallel process of monitoring countries for their potential threats to regional security. This parallel process has largely been organised through the OSCE, including the office of the High Commissioner on National Minorities. Indeed, the High Commissioner's mandate is explicitly defined as part of the OSCE's 'security' basket, and his task is to provide early warnings about potential threats to security, and to make recommendations that would defuse these threats (Estebanez 1997; van der Stoel 1999). And behind the OSCE, of course, lies NATO, with its security mandate, and its power to intervene militarily if necessary, as we saw in Bosnia and Kosovo.

In short, we have two parallel processes of 'internationalising' state–minority relations: one process monitors post-communist states for their compliance with general norms of minority rights (what we can call the 'legal rights track'); and a second process monitors post-communist states for their potential threats to regional stability (the 'security track').[25]

The existence of this parallel security track means that even if compliance with international norms was no longer monitored, Western states could still intervene based on considerations of regional security where there are identifiable spillover risks. In fact, this security track has always been more important than the legal rights track in determining actual intervention in post-communist states. The most important and well-known cases of Western intervention on minority issues in post-communist states have worked through the security track. These interventions have been based on calculations about how to restore security, not on how to uphold universal norms such as the FCNM.

Consider the way Western organisations have intervened in the major cases of ethnic violence in post-communist Europe, e.g. in Moldova, Georgia, Azerbaijan, Kosovo, Bosnia and Macedonia. In each of these cases, Western organisations have pushed post-communist states to go far beyond the requirements of the FCNM. They have pushed states to accept either some form of territorial autonomy (in Moldova, Georgia, Azerbaijan, Kosovo) and/or some form of consociational power-sharing and official language status (in Macedonia and Bosnia).

In short, in the contexts where Western organisations really have faced destabilising ethnic conflict, they have immediately recognised that the FCNM is of little use in resolving the actual conflicts, and that some form of power-sharing is required. The precise form of this power-sharing is determined by a range of contextual factors, not least the actual military balance of power amongst the contending factions. Since the motivation for Western intervention is to protect regional security, it is necessary that the West's recommendations be based on an accurate assessment of the actual threat potential raised by the various actors.

Since the security track has done much of the real work in enabling and guiding Western policies towards post-communist Europe, why do we need the legal rights track? If there is no feasible way to ground effective international norms of minority rights on either a right to enjoy one's culture or a right to self-determination, why not just give up on the idea of a legal rights track, while preserving the capacity to intervene in post-communist Europe based on considerations of security?

I suspect that there are some leaders of Western organisations who regret having established the legal rights track in 1990, and who might now wish to retreat from it.[26] However, I doubt this is possible. As I mentioned earlier, ideas of minority rights have now become institutionalised at several different levels in Europe, and would be difficult to dislodge.

Moreover, the security track may not work without an underlying legal rights track. On its own, the security track has a perverse tendency to reward state intransigence and minority belligerence. It gives the state an incentive to invent or exaggerate rumours of kin-state manipulation of the minority, so as to reinforce their claim that the minority is disloyal and that extending minority rights would jeopardise the security of the state. It also gives the minority an incentive to threaten violence or simply to seize power, since this is the only way its grievances will reach the attention of the international organisations monitoring security threats. Merely being treated unjustly is not enough to attract Western attention within the security track, unless it is backed up with a credible threat to be able to destabilise governments and regions.[27]

For example, consider the OSCE's approach to TA. As we have seen, after its initial recommendation of TA in 1990, the OSCE has shifted towards discouraging TA, and has actively counselled various minorities to give up their autonomy claims, including the Hungarians in Slovakia. But the OSCE has supported autonomy in several other countries, including Ukraine (for Crimea), Moldova (for Gaugazia and TransDneister), Georgia (for Abkhazia and Ossetia), Azerbaijan (for Ngorno-Karabakh) and Serbia (for Kosovo). What explains this variation? The OSCE says that the latter cases are 'exceptional' or 'atypical' (Zaagman 1999: 253 n84; Thio 2003: 132), but so far as I can tell, the only way in which they are exceptional is that minorities seized power illegally and extra-constitutionally, without the consent of the state.[28] Where minorities have seized power in this way, the state can only revoke autonomy by sending in the army and starting a civil war. For obvious reasons, the OSCE discourages this military option, and recommends instead that states should negotiate autonomy with the minority, and accept some form of federalism or consociationalism that provides after-the-fact legal recognition for the reality on the ground. Hence the HCNM recommended that it would be dangerous for Ukraine to try to abolish the autonomy that ethnic Russians in Crimea (illegally) established (van der Stoel 1999: 26).

By contrast, wherever a minority has pursued TA through peaceful and democratic means, within the rule of law, the OSCE has opposed it, on the grounds that it would increase tensions. According to the HCNM, given the pervasive fears in post-communist Europe about minority disloyalty and secession, any talk about creating new TA arrangements is bound to increase tensions, particularly if the minority claiming TA borders on a kin-state. Hence the HCNM's recommendation that Hungarians in Slovakia do not push for TA, given Slovak fears about irredentism (van der Stoel 1999: 25).

In short, the security approach rewards intransigence on the part of both sides. If minorities seize power, the OSCE rewards it by putting pressure on the state to accept an 'exceptional' form of autonomy; if the majority refuses to even discuss autonomy proposals from a peaceful and law-abiding minority, the OSCE rewards it by putting pressure on minorities to be more 'pragmatic'. This is perverse from the point of view of justice, but it seems to be the inevitable logic of the security-based approach. From a security perspective, it may indeed be correct that granting TA to a law-abiding minority increases tensions; while supporting TA after it has been seized by a belligerent minority decreases tensions.

Insofar as this is the logic of the security approach, it has the paradoxical effect of undermining security. Long-term security requires that both states and minorities moderate their claims, accept democratic negotiations and seek fair accommodations. In short, long-term security requires that state–minority relations be guided by some conception of justice and rights, not just by power-politics. And this, of course, is what the legal rights track was supposed to be promoting, and why it must supplement the security track.

The right to effective participation

We seem to be caught in a bind. European organisations have made an irreversible commitment to developing international legal norms regarding national minorities. However, existing attempts to develop such norms have been either too strong (if based on norms of self-determination) or too weak (if based on a right to enjoy one's culture). Is there some third approach that can provide a more principled guide for regulating the sort of claims that actually underlie ethnic conflict in post-communist Europe?

One option that seems to be gaining strength is to invoke the principle that the members of national minorities have a right to 'effective participation' in public affairs, particularly in matters affecting them. This idea of 'effective participation' was already present in the original 1990 Copenhagen Declaration. Indeed it was on the basis of this principle that the Declaration recommended TA. Minority autonomy was advocated as a good vehicle for achieving effective participation. More recent declarations have dropped the reference to internal autonomy, but retain the commitment to effective participation.[29] Indeed, references to effective participation are becoming more prominent. For example, it is the central topic of the most recent set of OSCE Recommendations (the Lund Recommendations on Effective Participation of National Minorities, adopted in 1999).

This idea of a right to effective participation is attractive for a number of reasons. For one thing, it sounds admirably democratic. Moreover, it avoids the tokenist connotations of a right to 'enjoy one's culture'. It recognises that minorities want not only to speak their languages or profess their religions in private life, but also want to participate as equals in public life. A right to effective participation recognises this political dimension of minority aspirations, while avoiding the 'dangerous' and 'radical' ideas of national self-determination (Kemp 2002).

From the perspective of normative theory, this approach has the added advantage of avoiding the danger of 'essentializing' groups. Both the 'right to enjoy one's culture' and the 'right to self-determination' seem to rest on assumptions about the inherent character of national minorities: the former implies that such groups have a shared and distinctive 'culture' that they seek to preserve, the latter implies that they have a shared and distinctive 'national identity' that they seek to advance through self-government. Yet we know that such groups are not internally homogenous. Members of the group are likely to disagree over the sorts of cultural traditions they wish to maintain, and the extent to which they wish to remain culturally distinct from the larger society. Similarly, they are likely to disagree over the nature of their 'national identity', or the sort of self-government needed to protect it. For the international community to endorse a 'right to culture' or a 'right to self-determination' appears to prejudge these internal debates, siding with those who argue for greater cultural distinctiveness and/or greater national autonomy, as if 'culture' or 'nationhood' were somehow essential and indisputable characteristics of these groups, rather than contested claims. This sort of concern has been invoked by postmodernists and critical theorists as a grounds for rejecting the constitutionalisation of substantive group rights, and endorsing instead purely procedural minority rights, such as guarantees of participation and consultation (e.g. Benhabib 2002; Fraser 2003: 82). These procedural rights avoid making substantive assumptions about the distinctiveness of a group's culture or the boundedness of its identity. A right to effective participation allows members of a group to advance claims of culture and nationhood, but requires that these claims be vindicated through deliberative democratic processes, rather than pre-approved by international law.

The main reason why effective participation has become so popular, however, is that it is vague, subject to multiple and conflicting interpretations, and so can be endorsed by people with very different conceptions of state–minority relations. In this sense, the apparent consensus on the importance of effective participation hides, or postpones, deep disagreements on what this actually means.

On the most minimal reading, the right to effective participation simply means that the members of national minorities should not face discrimination in the exercise of their standard political rights to vote, engage in advocacy and run for office. This minimalist reading is invoked to push Estonia and Latvia to grant citizenship to their ethnic Russians, and to enable them to vote and run for office even if they lack full fluency in the titular language.

On a somewhat more robust reading, effective participation requires not just that members of minorities can vote or run for office, but that they actually achieve some degree of *representation* in the legislature. This may not require that minorities be represented precisely in proportion to their share of the overall population, but serious under-representation would be viewed as a concern. This reading is invoked to prohibit attempts by states to gerrymander the boundaries of electoral districts so as to make it more difficult to elect minority representatives. It can also be invoked to prohibit attempts by states to revise the threshold needed for minority political parties to gain seats in PR electoral systems.

In Poland, for example, the German minority regularly elects deputies to parliament because it is exempted from the usual 5 per cent threshold rule. A similar policy benefits the Danish minority party in Germany. By contrast, Greece raised its electoral threshold precisely to prevent the possibility of Turkish MPs being elected (MRG 1997: 157). This sort of manipulation might well be prohibited in the future.

But neither of these two readings – focusing on the non-discriminatory exercise of political rights and equitable representation – really gets us to the heart of the problem in most cases of serious ethnic conflict. Even when minorities are able to participate without discrimination, and even when they are represented in rough proportion to their population, they may still be permanent losers in the democratic process. This is particularly true in contexts where the dominant group views the minority as potentially disloyal, and so votes as a bloc against any policies that empower minorities. (Consider the near-universal opposition within Slovakia to autonomy for the Hungarian-dominant regions, or the opposition within Macedonia to recognising Albanian as an official language.) In these contexts, it may not matter whether minorities exercise their vote, or elect MPs in accordance with their numbers: they will still be outvoted by members of the dominant group. The eventual decision will be the same whether minorities participate in the decision or not.

Taken literally, the term 'effective participation' would seem to preclude this situation of national minorities being permanent political minorities. After all, 'effective' participation implies that participation should have an effect – i.e. that participation changes the outcome. The only way to ensure that participation by minorities is effective in this sense within divided societies is to adopt counter-majoritarian rules that require some form of power-sharing. This may take the form of internal autonomy or of consociational guarantees of a coalition government.

We can call this the maximalist reading of a 'right to effective participation' – one that requires counter-majoritarian forms of federal or consociational power-sharing. This is obviously the interpretation that many minority organisations endorse. But it is strongly resisted by most states, East and West, for precisely the same reason that earlier references to internal self-determination were resisted (fears of escalation, proliferation, irredentism). Having successfully blocked the move to codify a right to internal autonomy, states are not going to accept an interpretation of effective participation that provides a back-door for autonomy. Agreement on a right to effective participation was possible precisely because it was seen as an alternative to, not a vehicle for, minority self-government. The interpretation of effective participation is therefore likely to remain focused at the level of non-discrimination and equitable representation – i.e. at a level which does not address the actual sources of ethnic conflict.

There is one potential exception to this generalisation. European organisations may adopt a maximalist interpretation of effective participation *where forms of power-sharing already exist.* It is widely recognised that attempts by states to abolish pre-existing forms of minority autonomy are a recipe for disaster (e.g. Kosovo, Ngorno-Karabakh, Ossetia). European organisations would therefore like to find a basis in international law to prevent states from revoking pre-existing forms of minority autonomy. The norm of effective participation is a plausible candidate: attempts to revoke pre-existing autonomy regimes can be seen as a deliberate attempt to disempower minorities, and hence a denial of their right to effective participation.

This idea that effective participation protects pre-existing forms of autonomy and power-sharing has been developed by some commentators,[30] and has implicitly been invoked by the OSCE itself, when justifying its recommendations for TA and consociationalism in countries like Georgia and Moldova. I said earlier that these power-sharing recommendations emerged out of the 'security track', rather than from any reading of international legal norms. But Western organisations have been keen to show that these recommendations were not just a case of rewarding belligerent minorities, and that there is a normative basis for their recommendations. The claim that abolishing pre-existing forms of power-sharing erodes effective participation provides a principled basis for their recommendations.

The difficulty, of course, is to explain why it is only *pre-existing* forms of TA that protect effective participation. If TA is needed to ensure the effective participation of Abkhazians in Georgia, or Armenians in Azerbaijan, why is it not also needed for Hungarians in Slovakia or Albanians in Macedonia? If abolishing pre-existing autonomy disempowers minorities, why are minorities, whose claims to autonomy were never accepted, also not disempowered? (Conversely, if power-sharing institutions are not needed to ensure the effective participation of the Hungarians in Slovakia, why are they needed for Armenians in Ngorno-Karabakh, or Russians in Crimea?)

There seems to be no principled basis for privileging those minorities that happen to have acquired or seized autonomy at some point in the past. The differential treatment of minority claims to autonomy can only be explained as a concession to realpolitik. From a prudential point of view, it is simply much more dangerous to take away pre-existing autonomies from minorities who have fought in the past to acquire it than to refuse to grant new autonomies to minorities who have not shown the willingness to use violence in their pursuit of autonomy.

In short, interpretations of 'effective participation' that privilege pre-existing autonomy suffer from the same flaw as the security track: i.e. they reward belligerent minorities while penalising peaceful and law-abiding minorities. Like the security track, the 'effective participation' approach, as it is currently being developed, is calibrated to match the threat potential of the contending parties. Those minorities with a capacity and willingness to destabilise governments and regions can acquire and maintain serious forms of power-sharing in the name of effective participation; those minorities who have renounced threats of violence do not.

This suggests that the effective participation approach replicates rather than resolves the problems we identified with the other approaches. If effective participation is interpreted maximally to entail power-sharing, then it is too strong to be acceptable to states, and will be rejected for the same reason that the internal self-determination approach was rejected. If effective interpretation is interpreted minimally to cover only non-discrimination and equitable representation, then it is too weak to actually resolve serious cases of ethnic conflict, and will be ineffective for the same reasons that the right to culture approach was ineffective. And if we examine how the idea of effective participation has actually been invoked in cases of conflict, we will see that, like the security track, it is based on power politics, not general principles.

We can make the same point another way. When we talk about effective participation, we need to ask 'participation in what'? From the point of view of most post-communist states, the members of national minorities should be able to effectively participate in the institutions of a unitary nation-state with a single official language. From the point of view of many minority organisations, the members of national minorities should be able to effectively participate in the institutions of a multilingual, multination federal state. These different conceptions of the nature of the state generate very different conceptions of what is required for effective participation within the state. Commentators sometimes write as if the principle of effective participation can be invoked to resolve these conflicts between states and minorities over the nature of the state, but in fact we need first to resolve the question of the nature of the state before we can even apply the principle of effective participation. And to date, that basic conflict over the nature of the state has been resolved in post-communist Europe by force, not principles. Where minorities have seized autonomy, effective participation is interpreted as supporting federal and/or consociational power-sharing within a multilingual, multination state. Where minorities have not used force, effective participation is interpreted as requiring only non-discriminatory participation and equitable representation within a unitary, monolingual state.

Advocates of the idea of effective participation suggest that it can provide a principled formula for resolving deep conflicts over the nature of the state. It seems to me, however, that the idea of effective participation presupposes that this issue has already been resolved, and is therefore either too strong (if it presupposes that states have accepted the idea of internal self-determination within a multination state) or too weak (if it presupposes that minorities have accepted the idea of a unitary and monolingual state).[31]

Notwithstanding these limitations, it seems clear that European organisations now view the idea of effective participation as the most promising avenue for the ongoing development of international norms on minority rights. So we are almost certain to see new, and perhaps more successful, interpretations emerging in the future.

For example, some commentators have suggested that the Advisory Committee which monitors compliance with the FCNM can and should adopt a norm of 'progressive implementation'. According to this norm, countries would be expected and required to fulfil progressively stronger interpretations of the various FCNM provisions. What counts as adequately fulfilling the FCNM's norms regarding language rights or effective participation today will not be sufficient five years from now. Each time a state submits a report to the Committee, it will be asked 'What have you done for minorities *lately*?' The idea is not simply to prevent countries from back-sliding (the non-retrogression clause I mentioned earlier), but also to progressively raise the bar in terms of what is required to meet the FCNM norms.[32]

There is no doubt that the Advisory Committee has done some innovative thinking along these lines, aided by the fact that it is composed of independent experts rather than state representatives (Hofmann 2002a). If my analysis is correct, however, there are likely to be limits on the extent to which the independent experts on the Advisory Committee will be able to ratchet up the requirements of the FCNM. In particular, I doubt that official language status or TA will come to be seen as requirements of the FCNM, except where minorities have shown a willingness and capacity to undermine stability and security. At the end of the day, the Advisory Committee is only advisory: its recommendations must be approved by states. I suspect that any attempt at raising the bar to include TA and official language status will be rejected by states for the same reason that previous attempts to codify such rights have failed.

Conclusion

I have argued that attempts to develop international norms of national minority rights in Europe since 1990 have run into a series of dilemmas. Appeals to a right to internal self-determination have proven too controversial; appeals to a right to enjoy one's culture have proven too weak; and appeals to a right to effective participation have proven too vague to actually address any of the conflicts in post-communist Europe that generated the call for the 'internationalisation' of minority issues in the first place. As a result, the European experiment in formulating the rights of national minorities remains a fascinating but flawed attempt to grapple with one of the most urgent issues of the twenty-first century. Despite the extraordinary efforts made to codify a set of principles and norms, most ethnopolitical conflicts in Europe are still being resolved on the basis of bargaining power, threat potential and force, not considerations of justice or international law.

Part of the explanation for this is simply that considerations of realpolitik have trumped arguments of justice: attempts to develop a morally consistent approach to minority rights have run up against the self-interest and security fears of states. But that is not the whole story. There have also been genuinely conceptual difficulties. Effective norms seem to require a degree of 'targeting' of minority rights, connecting different categories of rights to different categories of groups. But any such targeting is intensely controversial, and immediately raises fears of arbitrariness, under- and over-inclusion, and essentialism. This is particularly true of the attempt to specify the rights of 'national minorities'. The decision by European organisations in 1990 to single out this category of group for legal protection was bold, and potentially of global relevance. However, little progress has been made in developing a consensus on the validity of the category or of the sorts of rights attached to it. While progress is continuing in international settings on codifying the rights of other types of groups, such as indigenous peoples and migrants, it remains very unclear whether the European experiment of elaborating norms for national minorities will endure, let alone be repeated in other contexts. The flurry of activity around international norms of national minority rights in Europe in the early 1990s may prove to be a temporary and passing phase.

If so, I think this would be regrettable, although the consequences are unlikely to be catastrophic, at least in the European context. As I noted earlier, the initial impulse to develop these norms was an unduly pessimistic view about the likelihood of ethnic violence in post-communist Europe. If violence is unlikely, then why not let countries come to their own settlements on ethnic issues, at their own speed? After all, it took Western countries many decades to work out their current accommodations with national minorities, and the success of these accommodations is arguably due to the fact that they were the result of gradual domestic negotiations, rather than being imposed through external pressure.

Actually, international pressure did play an important and beneficial role in several Western cases, although this is often forgotten. For example, the autonomy arrangement for the Åland Islands was an externally-determined solution under the League of Nations, which has nonetheless worked very well. Germany's accession to NATO in 1955 was conditional on its working out a reciprocal minority-rights agreement with Denmark, an agreement which is now seen as a model of how kin-states can work constructively through bilateral relations to help minorities in neighbouring states. There was strong international pressure on Italy to accord autonomy to South Tyrol in 1972, which today is seen as a exemplar of successful accommodation. In all of these cases, a certain degree of international pressure was needed to initiate settlements,[33] although they have become domestically self-sustaining, and indeed have often been enhanced or expanded as a result of domestic procedures.[34]

So it would be inaccurate to suggest that Western states have 'naturally' or inevitably gravitated towards fair accommodation of national minorities without international pressure. In fact, some combination of international pressure and/or domestic violence was present at one point or another in most Western cases of autonomy.[35] Given this history, it seems naïve to assume that countries in Eastern and Central Europe (or elsewhere in the world) will inevitably and peacefully move towards significant minority rights through their own domestic democratic processes. As in the West, some extra-parliamentary push – whether it is international pressure and/or domestic violence – may be needed for post-communist countries to seriously consider federal or consociational power-sharing. However, the goal of any international pressure should be to start a process that becomes domestically self-sustaining (and, ideally, domestically self-improving).

In that sense, perhaps the international community should limit its role in post-communist Europe to ensuring that there is the minimum level of respect for human rights and political freedom needed to create a democratic space for states and minorities to slowly work out their own accommodations. The increasing prominence of the idea of 'effective participation' may reflect the belief that Western intervention should be aimed at creating the conditions for post-communist societies to work out their own account of minority rights through peaceful and democratic deliberations, rather than seeking to impose some canonical set of internationally-defined minority rights.

This may be the direction we are headed in. And perhaps this is the most we can reasonably expect. Attempts to formulate general principles of international law to resolve deep conflicts over autonomy, power-sharing and language rights may simply be unrealistic.[36] Over time, we might hope and expect post-communist countries to follow the Western trend towards multilingual, multinational states, but it is unnecessary, and perhaps counter-productive, to try to jump-start this process through the codification and imposition of international norms of substantive minority rights.

However, if this is indeed the direction we are headed in, it is important that the minimal standards being demanded of post-communist states be presented as precisely *minimum* standards. A serious problem we confront at the moment, I believe, is that many actors view the FCNM and other international norms, not as a minimum floor from which minority rights should be domestically negotiated, but rather as a maximal ceiling, beyond which minorities must not seek to go.

There is in fact a concerted effort by most post-communist states to present the FCNM and OSCE recommendations as the outside limits of legitimate minority mobilisation. Any minority leader or organisation that asks for something beyond what these documents provide is immediately labelled as a 'radical'. These minimal international standards are not being treated as the preconditions needed to democratically negotiate the forms of power-sharing and self-government appropriate to each country, but rather are viewed as eliminating the need to adopt, or even to debate, forms of power-sharing and self-government. When minority organisations raise questions about substantive minority rights, post-communist states respond 'We meet all international standards', as if that foreclosed the question of how states should treat their minorities. The claim that 'we meet all international standards' has in fact become a mantra amongst post-communist states, taking the place of any substantive debate about how to actually respond to minority claims regarding powers, rights and status.

Sadly, I believe that the international community is often complicit in this effort to treat international norms as a maximal ceiling rather than a minimal floor, and to stigmatise minority leaders who dare to ask for the sorts of substantive minority rights enjoyed by most sizeable national minorities in the West.[37] If it proves impossible to codify substantive minority rights in international law, we must at least be clear that the meagre provisions currently codified in European instruments are the starting point for democratic debate, not the end point.

4 National minorities and EU enlargement

External or domestic incentives for accommodation?

Gwendolyn Sasse

Introduction[1]

The first Copenhagen criterion of 1993 spells out the political conditions for EU membership. It includes a reference to 'the respect for and protection of national minorities'. In theory, the political conditions have to be met before the EU opens accession negotiations with a candidate country. In practice, the European Commission has continued to monitor and criticise compliance with the political criteria, in particular the minority condition, throughout the negotiation process. Ultimately, the minority criterion has not been a key determinant in the EU's assessment of an applicant country, and the EU's leverage in this policy area had to be limited once the political conditions were officially considered as being 'fulfilled' and the accession negotiations got underway. The ambiguity of the minority criterion was further enhanced by the fact that the EU has promoted norms which lack a basis in EU law and do not directly translate into the *acquis communautaire*.[2] The gradual development of an EU 'rights agenda' had stayed clear of an explicit endorsement of minority rights and opened up only indirect avenues for the discussion and promotion of these rights. The Treaty of Maastricht (1992) entrenched specific provisions on fundamental rights and a vague Community commitment to 'national and regional diversity' within the member states (then Articles F TEU and 128 TEC).[3] Through the European Convention for the Protection of Human Rights and Fundamental Freedoms and the European Court of Human Rights, a direct link was established between EU membership and membership of the Council of Europe. In addition to the 'burgeoning jurisprudence' in the European Court of Human Rights (Gilbert 2002), the European Parliament has performed a showcase role for the EU, in particular during the early 1990s, by passing numerous resolutions on human rights and minority protection, thereby reinforcing the discourse swell on minority rights.

The EU's external relations have provided the key momentum for the internalisation of an explicit commitment to human rights and a greater awareness of minority issues. Human and minority rights map an area in which external relations have pushed for a (partial) rethinking of the EU's internal values, objectives and policies. The nexus between human rights and conditionality had been an integral part of the EU's external relations since the Luxembourg European Council of 1991.[4] The EU's eastward enlargement increasingly blurred the distinction between the EU's internal policy and external relations, and an extension of this type of normative conditionality appears to have been a logical step in the EU's adaptation to a new political environment. The emphasis on minority rights in addition to human rights, however, cannot fully be explained by this logic. It was the post-Cold War, post-imperial and post-communist political environment that highlighted the salience of minority issues and the potential for ethno-regional conflict amidst multi-facetted transition processes. A mixture of humanitarian, and 'hard' and 'soft' security concerns informed the push for a greater internationalisation of minority rights in the early 1990s. Minority issues have a significant historical resonance in Central and Eastern Europe (CEE). The experience of genocide, expulsion, coercion or accommodation is intrinsic to the emergence and development of many of the states in the region. After 1989, most of the post-communist countries prioritised the strengthening of central state capacity and the position of the titular nationality, thereby running the risk of discriminating against, alienating and politicising minority groups. The violent disintegration of former Yugoslavia and a number of intractable post-Soviet conflicts, as well as a perception of further conflict potential in view of sizeable minorities in many East European countries (in Latvia the titular nationality accounts for only 58.2 per cent of the population; while countries like Slovakia, Romania and Bulgaria have to accommodate politically organised Hungarian and Turkish minorities of 7 to 10 per cent), informed the EU's approach.

The EU's political conditions for accession took shape against the background of a widening pan-European normative and institutional framework. In turn, EU conditionality has increased the visibility and political salience of minority issues in the candidate countries of CEE. The nexus between democracy and human rights had always been at the core of the Council of Europe's self-definition and membership criteria. The quick engagement of the Council of Europe in CEE – Hungary became a member as early as 1990, followed by the Czech Republic and Poland in 1991 – turned it into an institutional stepping stone towards the EU, and the EU's first Copenhagen criterion bears the imprint of the rather amorphous democratic conditionality of the Council of Europe.[5] The CSCE/OSCE process from 1990 onwards provided a further normative source of inspiration for the EU through its link between conflict-prevention and minority issues.[6] The CSCE Paris Charter of 1990 stipulated that 'peace, justice, stability and democracy, require that the ethnic, cultural, linguistic and religious identity of national minorities be protected and conditions for the promotion of that identity be created'.[7] The OSCE

General Recommendations of 1996, 1998 and 1999 on education rights, linguistic rights and effective participation, respectively, attempted to define a European standard of minority protection. While the EU borrowed the link between democracy and human (and later minority) rights from the Council of Europe, the CSCE/OSCE provided the EU with the security-based rationale for minority protection, a combination that resonated strongly with the member states in the early 1990s.

In the absence of a 'clean' methodological take on conditionality and its presupposed causal effects,[8] the analysis presented in this chapter will proceed in two steps. First, the EU's minority criterion will be 'unpacked' both in terms of its inherent dilemmas and the way in which the EU translated it into an institutional process. Where has the EU leverage been anchored and how has it been communicated during the accession process? A closer look at the EU's monitoring mechanism, including the Commission's Regular Reports and perceptions from within the Commission shortly before the Commission turnover and the dissolution of Directorate General (DG) Enlargement,[9] highlight the scope and limits of EU conditionality in the area of minority rights. Second, this chapter will locate the EU's minority criterion in the domestic political context of three accession countries (Hungary, Slovakia, Romania) in order to determine the balance between internal and external incentives for policy change.

Minority rights: a challenge for conditionality and Europeanisation

Conditionality is widely seen as a primary means of 'democracy promotion' and 'Europeanisation' in CEE. The clear incentive structure for the candidate states and the power asymmetry characterising the interaction between the EU and the accession countries underpin the scope for the EU to shape the design of structures and policy processes in the accession countries. As yet few studies have systematically analysed the impact of conditionality on specific policy areas or countries. The issue of minority rights is a test for the very notion of conditionality. A consensus on norms and rules and their transmission within the EU and beyond, clear benchmarks and enforcement mechanisms ensuring credibility, consistency and continuity over time are at the centre of a meaningful definition of conditionality. The political Copenhagen criterion generally, but in particular the reference to national minorities, defies these basic principles of conditionality. 'Europeanisation' has been defined as 'ways of doing things' which are first defined and consolidated in the making of EU decisions and then incorporated into 'the logic of domestic discourse, identities, political structures and public policies' (Radaelli 2000: 3). The issue of minority rights does not easily fit these conceptual boundaries either. Can the EU have an impact on minority issues without an internal consensus on the norms and practices in this field? The Treaty of Amsterdam (TEU) of 1997 illustrates the underlying ambiguity: it incorporated all of the values set out by the EU in the first Copenhagen criterion in Article 6(1) as 'liberty, democracy, respect for human rights and fundamental freedoms and the rule of law', but expressly excluded 'respect for and protection of minorities'. That Article 6(1) draws on the Copenhagen criteria is specifically alluded to in Article 49, which specifies that the principles laid out in Article 6(1) are preconditions for any state applying for EU membership.[10] This inconsistency was addressed in a footnote in the Commission's Regular Reports of 2002. It states that 'the political criteria defined at Copenhagen have been essentially enshrined as a constitutional principle in the Treaty on the European Union'.[11] The wording falls short of an explicit endorsement of the minority criterion, but it suggests that minority protection is subsumed under Article 6(1).

The minority 'condition' faced several compliance problems during the accession process: first, it lacked a firm foundation in EU law and concise benchmarks. The practices of the current member states range from elaborate constitutional and legal means for minority protection and political participation to constitutional unitarism and the outright denial that national minorities exist. Second, minority rights have never been an internal EU political priority. Third, the question of what constitutes a 'national minority' and the nature of minority rights are deeply disputed in international politics and law. Moreover, the minority criterion did not figure prominently in the EU's pre-accession funding. PHARE has been the main instrument for the design and delivery of EU policy in CEE. Established as early as 1989, the programme was reoriented to address the accession priorities set by the EU in 1997. PHARE did not have a separate budget line for assistance in the policy area of minority protection, and the most closely related activity heading 'civil society and democratisation' accounted for only about 1 per cent of the total PHARE funds distributed.[12]

The EU's monitoring exercise

The Commission's annual Regular Reports, following on from the Opinions of 1997 and the Accession Partnerships, have been the EU's key instrument to monitor and evaluate the candidates' progress towards accession.[13] The Reports have a formulaic structure, which broadly follows the Copenhagen criteria and thereby permits cross-country comparisons. The political Copenhagen criterion rests on generic concepts, such as 'democracy', the 'rule of law' and 'the respect for and the protection of national minorities', and, therefore, leaves a wide scope for interpretation. Moreover, it was not based on the *acquis* as such. The Commission had to find a different way to operationalise the political criteria. In the case of the minority criterion it based its monitoring exercise on a set of values and non-EU documents, namely the European Convention on Human Rights (which by now has become part of the *acquis*), the major OSCE documents of the early 1990s and the UN Declarations. Though not a source of inspiration and legitimacy at the outset of the accession process, over time the FCNM of 1995 became the Commission's primary instrument for translating the minority criterion into practice.[14] The Regular Reports frequently reminded the candidate states to sign and ratify the FCNM – despite the fact that several EU member states, such as Belgium, France, Greece, Luxembourg and the Netherlands, have not done so.

The Reports are a compendium of results compiled from a variety of sources, for example the candidate countries, the Council of Europe, the OSCE, International Financial Institutions and NGOs, as well as 'assessments made by member states'. It is difficult to measure the relative weight of these inputs and to assess the process by which they were filtered and evaluated, but it is clear that in the area of minority issues the Council of Europe and the OSCE were privileged sources of information. During the drafting stage, the Commission also scheduled a regular annual briefing session in Brussels with the Council of Europe (including the Chairman of the Advisory Committee) and the OSCE (including the Director of the Office of the High Commissioner on National Minorities).[15] Due to the more specific political agenda of NGOs, the Commission had no official 'privileged relations' with any one of them, although groups like Transparency International or Human Rights Watch were regularly consulted. As a Commission official closely involved in the drafting process put it, 'we were dependent on solid information which had to be used in a careful manner. We used as many different sources as possible, provided we could double-check them'.[16] Issues were left out when 'hard' evidence was unavailable: 'If a country had proven the Commission wrong on a single issue, the whole exercise would have suffered tremendously.'[17]

The whole monitoring process, including cooperation between the Country Desks in DG Enlargement and the relevant line DGs, was overseen by a Horizontal Co-ordination Unit within DG Enlargement (about 25 people). Each year this Unit produced a manual listing the issues to be addressed by the Country Desks[18] and streamlined the draft reports in terms of substance and language in order to ensure consistency and comparability within and across reports. As one official pointed out, 'There has been a tendency for country teams to go native, both in terms of overly positive or negative assessments. It was our job to maintain the balance.'[19] A colleague from the same unit detected 'a tendency to tone down or neutralise the language, while not dropping issues completely'.[20] Amidst a continuous flow of information from different organisations, monthly updates and a draft report from the EU delegations in the candidate countries, contributions by the candidate countries' governments and the bullet-point reminder provided by the Horizontal Co-ordination Unit marked the starting point for each annual report. Over time, previous reports became a further point of reference, in particular their 'set phrases, such as the references to international or European standards'.[21] The Commission officials involved in the actual drafting of the Reports generally emphasised that they did not feel bound or restricted by the previous reports or the Horizontal Unit's guidance when producing their first draft. Nevertheless, some admitted that over time the submissions by the EU delegations became 'relatively complete' and 'provided the jargon'.[22] The in-house drafting usually began around the end of June once all the different submissions had been received and the meetings with other international organisations had been held. Over the summer, the relevant line DGs and the Country Desks were involved in the revising of the drafts overseen by the Horizontal Unit. The texts were generally ready for consultation with the Legal Service in September. A briefing with high-level civil servants from the candidate countries preceded the official release of the Regular Reports in October or November. For the first-wave accession countries, the Commission issued Comprehensive Monitoring Reports in the autumn of 2003, which dropped the political section and focused solely on the *acquis*. Minority-related issues were mentioned in the context of non-discrimination under Chapter 13 (Social Policy), thereby reflecting a wider institutional development: over time the line DGs had started to build more direct contacts with the candidate countries. Gradually, the emphasis moved away from DG Enlargement, and DG Justice and Home Affairs, DG Employment and DG Regional Policy emerged as the Commission's focal points for minority-related issues.

The characteristics of the reports

A comparative study of the Regular Reports 1998–2002 reveals their three key characteristics with regard to the minority criterion: a hierarchy of minority issues, ad hocism and inconsistencies resulting from the lack of clear benchmarks and a dilemma of implementation. Although most of the ten candidate countries of CEE have significant minority populations, only two minority groups are consistently stressed in the Regular Reports: the Russophone minority in Estonia and Latvia, and the Roma minorities of Bulgaria, the Czech Republic, Hungary, Romania and Slovakia. In the first Reports on Bulgaria, Hungary, Romania and Slovakia, for example, the Roma are the only minority issue commented on at all, despite the fact that there are numerically greater minority groups in these countries. This 'hierarchy' of minority issues reflects the EU's interest in good relations with its most powerful neighbour and energy supplier – Russia – and its own soft security concerns linked to migration. Furthermore, a non-territorialised, internally diverse and marginalised minority like the Roma, is a politically less sensitive group to focus on, compared with territorialised and politically mobilised minorities, such as the Hungarians in Slovakia and Romania or the Turks in Bulgaria. Undoubtedly, the Roma face severe problems of systematic discrimination, political and social exclusion, segregation and poverty, but this is by no means a unique feature of the candidate countries (Guglielmo 2004).

In essence, the Reports are a patchwork of formulaic codes encapsulating 'progress' on the road to membership. The general commitment of the candidate countries to improve minority protection is taken at face value and described positively as 'continuing commitment to the protection of minority rights', 'a number of positive developments', 'significant progress', 'considerable efforts', 'considerable progress', 'consolidating and deepening (...) the respect for and protection of minorities'.[23] Some candidate countries earn generic praise, for example through the statement that minorities are 'well integrated into Hungarian society' or that Hungary has a 'well-developed institutional framework protecting the interests of its minorities and promoting their cultural and educational autonomy'.[24] The Regular Reports are designed in a way that renders them a cumulative success story for each candidate country. The Regular Reports illustrate the EU's difficulties in measuring progress in the absence of clear benchmarks in the field of minority rights. The Reports track the adoption and amendment of laws on citizenship, naturalisation, language and elections, the establishment of institutions that manage minority issues within the executive or legislative structures, and the launch of government programmes to address minority needs. Trends are evaluated by numerical benchmarks, such as the number of minority members obtaining citizenship, the number of requests for naturalisation, the pass rate for language or citizenship tests, the number of schools or classes taught in the state or minority languages, the number of teachers trained to teach in the state or minority languages and the extent of media broadcasting in minority languages.

The Reports make frequent general references to 'international standards' or 'European standards' and cross-reference the recommendations, activities and documents of the Council of Europe and the OSCE. This practice is most evident in the cases of Latvia and Estonia, where the Europe Agreements included a reference to the need to comply 'inter alia with the undertakings made within the context of the Conference on Security and Cooperation in Europe (CSCE) and the Organisation for Security and Cooperation in Europe (OSCE) – the rule of law and human rights, including the rights of persons belonging to minorities'.[25] The 1998 Report on Latvia, for example, states that the Commission based its evaluations of Latvia's citizenship and naturalisation policies on the extent to which they complied with OSCE recommendations.[26] The Reports indicate that the EU has also relied on the OSCE (and presumably the Council of Europe) for basic data collection.

Ad hocism and the borrowing of different external 'standards' have given rise to ambiguity and internal inconsistencies. The 1999 Report on Latvia asserts that: 'Latvia now fulfils all recommendations expressed by the OSCE in the area of naturalisation and citizenship'.[27] Yet, fresh concerns over the linguistic rights of the Russophone minority are expressed in the 2001 Report on Latvia, which broadly refers to the 'joint efforts' of the EU, the OSCE and the Council of Europe to establish guidelines for the new language law.[28] The 2002 Reports on Estonia and Latvia report that the OSCE mission in these states closed in late 2001,[29] including the official OSCE reasons for this decision, while also highlighting the EU's continued concerns. Latvia was urged to ratify the FCNM and noted EU and OSCE concerns regarding the naturalisation and effective political participation of minorities in the context of restrictive language laws, including a reference to the 2002 ruling of the European Court of Human Rights against Latvia's narrow application of the language proficiency criterion in the national parliament. Despite the inherent contradiction, the 2002 Report concluded that 'the country has made considerable progress in further consolidating and deepening [. . .] respect for and protection of minorities'.[30]

The overall assessment of the Roma issue, in particular, hovers uncomfortably between the realisation that the socio-economic and political situation of the Roma has not improved and policy activism, as reflected in the detailed lists of new activities and programmes targeting the needs of the Roma.[31] The fact that the Regular Reports harshly criticise the treatment of the Roma in the candidate countries, which are generally recognised as continuing 'to fulfil the political Copenhagen criteria', underlines that minority issues were not the EU's priority during the accession process. As a Commission official in DG Enlargement put it:

> There has been a constant inherent tension between the fulfilment of the political criteria and the criticism of the Roma treatment. We also lack benchmarks to determine when the issue would be considered sufficiently 'resolved'. As long as the situation wasn't getting any worse, we tried to be as consistent as possible by focusing on the direction of policy-making.[32]

Throughout the accession process, the Commission's emphasis has shifted gradually from the adoption of the *acquis* towards issues of 'capacity' and implementation. However, the Regular Reports demonstrate that the Commission is less equipped to monitor and follow-up on problems of implementation. In the area of minority policies these problems are dealt with in general terms, listing the lack of funding, weak administrative capacity, understaffing and the low levels of public awareness in the candidate countries as the main shortcomings. The 'gap between policy formulation and implementation' is addressed most explicitly with reference to the Roma, for example in the Reports on Slovakia in 2000 and 2001.[33] Similarly, the potential implications of weak policy implementation are referred to most explicitly in the 2002 Report on Bulgaria, which obliquely notes that there are 'signs of increased tension between the Roma and ethnic Bulgarians'.[34] At times, the EU and the candidate countries appear to be acting out a charade on Roma policy. For example, the 1999 Report on Bulgaria states:

> Significant progress was achieved concerning further integration of Roma through the adoption of a Framework Programme for 'Full Integration of the Roma Population into the Bulgarian Society' and establishment of relevant institutions at central and regional level.[35]

By what measure this formal adoption of a programme marks 'significant progress' is not clear, and two years later, little of this programme had been implemented (Rangelov 2001). Moreover, EU-inspired policies can also have some counterproductive effects. In 2001 Romania adopted a package of policies targeting the Roma for which it gained praise in the Regular Report 2002. In Romania's 2003 Report, the Commission notes progress, but also an overall 'uneven' implementation of the Roma Strategy of 2001.[36] The package included the appointment of advisers who would advise the regional prefects on Roma-related issues. Though formally implemented, this measure has done little to change perceptions or policy outcomes. It has, however, separated 'Roma issues' from mainstream policy-making, reinforces marginalisation and contributes to a growing frustration among the office holders, Roma activists and the wider Roma community (Pogány 2003).

Views from 'inside': the perceptions of policy-makers

Judging from the author's interviews in the Commission,[37] the notion of a double standard now occupies a prominent position in the perceptions of policy-makers currently or previously involved in the EU's monitoring of minority rights in the accession countries. Not all of them accepted that such a double standard exists, but even those who argued against its existence or relevance brought up the issue without being prompted to do so, thereby illustrating an acute awareness of the grey zone in which the Commission has had to define the parameters of its monitoring exercise. There was widespread normative agreement that a double standard should not guide EU policy: 'there shouldn't be any double standards, in particular as the Commission doesn't have any competence in the area of minority rights'. Commission officials involved in the drafting of the Reports have been aware of an inherent 'consistency problem', in particular in the sections which were not explicitly based on the *acquis*. Some of them pointed out that 'the links as well as the distinctions between the political criteria and the other criteria were not always clear'. An awareness of the notion of a double standard is also reflected in 'the political decision not to comment on the political criteria any more in the 2003

Comprehensive Monitoring Report'. The Commission decided that it was against the logic of the accession process to monitor the political criteria again at the very end of the process, although some officials inside DG Enlargement had argued in favour of the inclusion of a political assessment in the final round of monitoring.

In the words of one Commission official, 'the Regular Reports marked the key moment in the accession process each year. They were carefully worded, and they were carefully studied.' In this context a Commission official admitted that 'the strange wording tends to reflect political compromises'. In contrast to other Commission documents, DG Enlargement had a monopoly over the drafting process, thereby turning the Reports into 'political documents of the Commissioner for Enlargement'. The Reports reflect the fact that, ultimately, 'the Commissioner had no interest in creating new obstacles, given that his main goal was to see the negotiations through to the end'.[38] Despite diverging views on the objectivity of the Reports, there was widespread agreement among Commission officials that their quality had improved over time, and that the 2003 Reports for Bulgaria, Romania and Turkey, as well as the Comprehensive Monitoring Reports, signalled an improvement in the structure, content and use of the monitoring exercise.

In the view of some Commission officials involved in the monitoring, the Regular Reports have increased the political relevance of the political criteria for the EU itself. As one Commission official from DG Justice and Home Affairs put it:

> In many old member states, minorities have been a taboo. Now the Commission has given the issue a new emphasis, and at least we now recognise the need to address these issues.

From here the official jumped to a very optimistic conclusion:

> The new member states will maintain this emphasis and help to overcome the fears of some old member states. Their fears to open up a Pandora's box of territorial and economic demands, for example by ratifying the FCNM, are bound to fade with the progress of European integration. France's position will not be tenable for much longer, and Greece will follow.[39]

This rosy post-enlargement scenario did not resonate with the majority of the Commission officials interviewed by the author. Most of them simply referred to the fact that the process of European integration would have to take over from where the EU's monitoring had left off. The view prevailed that the enlargement process had not had a 'spill-over effect' on the discussion about minority issues inside the Union. The Commission officials simply spoke of a temporal coincidence between the enlargement process, the EU's push for more comprehensive anti-discrimination legislation and the establishment of the Network of Independent Experts, which is funded by the Commission and began monitoring fundamental rights in the member states in 2002.

Beyond some defensive and vociferous statements about the 'success' of the EU's monitoring exercise, its actual impact has been described rather realistically in Commission circles. 'In general', one official said, 'the Regular Reports were good for the EU to establish the candidates' strengths and weaknesses, and they were good for the candidate countries because governments and civil society could refer to them to facilitate domestic policy changes.'[40] Another official described the impact of the Regular Reports as twofold:

> their most immediate impact has been on legislation, but they have also influenced the mentality and public debate in each country. They have helped to redraw the line of political correctness, for example with regard to statements about the Roma. Implementation, however, has only begun, and the momentum has to be kept alive.

Last but not least, the impact of the EU's monitoring exercise might be best understood as having a 'lock-in effect' and reinforcing existing trends. In the words of one Commission official, 'we help them do what they are already doing anyway'. This balance and interaction between domestic and external incentives for policy change requires closer attention.

Domestic vs. external incentives for minority policies

The exact relationship between domestic political incentives and EU conditionality in the area of minority protection is difficult to pin down, and the interlocking conditions and recommendations of institutions like the EU, the OSCE and the Council of Europe make it impossible to disentangle their respective effects. Nevertheless, the timing of certain decisions, for example the adoption of international instruments or legislation and the domestic political context of individual candidate countries, provide insights into the effectiveness of EU conditionality and, more specifically, the conditions facilitating or limiting the EU's impact.

Given the EU's frequent references to external 'standards' of minority protection, in particular the FCNM, the ratification of this document by the candidate countries provides for a rough correlation between enlargement conditionality and a degree of commitment to minority policy in CEE. All ten candidate countries of CEE signed the FCNM. Almost all of them signed up shortly after the document was opened for signature on 1 February 1995, though the process of ratification and implementation took longer. Only Latvia had still not ratified the document when joining the EU. The early commitment of the candidate countries to the FCNM contrasts with some of the old EU member states that have still not ratified it.[41] Among the countries of CEE, Bulgaria, Estonia, Poland and Slovenia added special declarations to the FCNM, a practice fairly evenly spread among EU member states and candidate countries. The Bulgarian declaration, for example, cautiously refers to 'the policy of protection of human rights and tolerance to persons belonging to minorities' and stipulates that the ratification and implementation of the Framework Convention do not imply 'any right to engage in any activity violating the territorial integrity and sovereignty of the unitary Bulgarian state, its internal and international security'.[42] Estonia's declaration is concerned with specifying its own legal definition of 'national minorities', who are stated to be

> citizens of Estonia who reside on the territory of Estonia; maintain long-standing, firm and lasting ties with Estonia; are distinct from Estonians on the basis of their ethnic, cultural, religious or linguistic characteristics; and are motivated by a concern to preserve together their cultural traditions, their religion or their language which constitute the basis of their common identity.[43]

Similarly, Poland's declaration affirms that it recognises as national minorities only those residing in the Republic of Poland who are Polish citizens. It also includes a reference to international agreements protecting 'national minorities in Poland and minorities or groups of Poles in other States'.[44] Slovenia's declaration limits its definition of national minorities to 'the autochthonous Italian and Hungarian national minorities', but also states that the provisions also apply to 'the members of the Roma community, who live in the Republic of Slovenia', while excluding its numerically largest minority group, the Croatians.[45]

The Council of Europe's European Charter for Regional or Minority Languages (ECRML) was opened for signature as early as November 1992. It proved more controversial among candidate countries (and member states), not least because of the specific obligations it imposes on the signatories, such as the establishment of a committee monitoring compliance. The Regular Reports record the ratification of the Charter by individual countries, but they do not use it as a standard point of reference comparable to the FCNM. By the end of March 2004 only three of the ten CEE candidates (Hungary, Slovakia, Slovenia) had ratified it.[46] All three countries ratified in the latter stages of the enlargement process, between 1998 and 2002, but they added specific, and rather complex declarations to it which tend to add to the ambiguity in defining the differences between a regional and a national language. Slovenia's Declaration states that only the Hungarian and Italian languages 'are considered as regional or minority languages'.[47] It also limits the number of provisions applied to the above-mentioned languages. Slovakia's Declaration confers the status of regional or minority language to Bulgarian, Croatian, Czech, German, Hungarian, Polish, Roma, Ruthenian and Ukrainian. However, it also establishes a hierarchy of languages according to which Hungarian, followed by Ukrainian and Ruthenian, enjoy more far-reaching rights, for example the availability of pre-school education in a particular language as opposed to the right to apply for this type of education. The Slovakian Declaration also stipulates that it defines the ECRML's term 'territory in which the regional or minority language is used' as that provided for by Slovak law as those 'municipalities in which the citizens of the Slovak Republic belonging to national minorities form at least 20% of the population'.[48]

In conjunction with the ratification of international instruments of minority protection, EU conditionality has also contributed to the salience of minority rights on the domestic political agendas in CEE,[49] but a range of factors, such as the size of the minority, its location, resources and degree of political mobilisation, the relations between majority and minority groups, the involvement of kin-states, the constitutional design of the new regime and its transition path, has interacted with external conditionality and produced varied policy outcomes. Hungary, Slovakia and Romania are instructive cases to demonstrate some of these similarities and differences.

Hungary: minority protection as a national interest

Several countries legislated for minority protection, or were in the final stages of doing so, prior to the Copenhagen criteria. Some of these were inclusive measures, providing for autonomy arrangements and privileged quotas of representation in national parliaments. Hungary passed a law 'On The Rights of National and Ethnic Minorities' in 1993 that granted collective rights and cultural autonomy to 13 recognised minorities.[50] This law built on Article 68 in the Hungarian constitution of 1990, which had anchored the protection of 'national and ethnic minorities' as well as their collective participation in public life and representation through local and national government organisations. Most of Hungary's minorities are quite small and not politically mobilised. They had little impact on the 1993 Act. Instead, the historical resonance of the Treaty of Trianon (1920), which left large Hungarian territorialised minorities in neighbouring states (Slovakia, Romania, Serbia, Ukraine), has underpinned the political will in favour of minority protection.[51]

While the endogenous incentives for a far-reaching minority-rights regime are easy to trace in the case of Hungary, the effects are more difficult to assess. In terms of intra-state relations, Hungary's policies have both encouraged bilateral agreements and provoked concern and angry responses from political groups in neighbouring countries. Even the 1993 law itself contained a dual agenda: the active strengthening of the cultural and linguistic identity of Hungary's minorities was bound to exert explicit and implicit pressure on the governments and minorities in neighbouring states. The implementation of the 1993 Act indicates further peculiarities: local governments receive payments to offset the costs of minority education, thereby creating an incentive to inflate the number of children requiring education in their own language. According to Hungarian government statistics of 1998, almost 45,000 primary-school children were enrolled in German-minority programmes, although the last census recorded only about 8,000 Germans living in Hungary.[52]

Local minority self-governments have mushroomed as a result of the simple procedure by which they are set up.[53] By 1999 there were already more than 1,400 registered across the country, half of which are Roma councils, followed by German councils as the second most represented group.[54] The local councils, in turn, elect the national council. The councils are supposed to have extensive consent and consultation rights with regard to laws impacting on minority issues, such as culture, education and the media. While there is evidence of such consultation between the national councils and the Hungarian parliament, the involvement at local level seems to be minimal. The main function of the councils, therefore, is to promote minority culture, but the limited funding at local level has curbed their potential. While the national minority governments receive state funding according to the size of the minority, the local governments all receive a small flat sum. There is also evidence of local governments trying to shift responsibility for minority issues to the minority councils, especially in the case of the Roma. The election of the minority self-government councils takes place alongside the national elections in a two-ballot system. Anybody can vote for the members of self-governments irrespective of his/her nationality. The only restriction is that a vote can only be cast for one of the self-governments. It is hard to track voting patterns in these elections, as the voters' nationality is not registered, but the emergence of a Serbian nationalist on a Croatian council or the popularity of German councils, which are associated with external funding and travel opportunities, suggest a range of voting motivations.[55] The minority groups, in turn, are interested in high voter turnout to boost their national-level funding.

Most importantly, the progressive 1993 law represents only one of several elements of Hungary's minority policy. The highly controversial Hungarian 'Status Law' of 2001, giving rights and entitlements to Hungarians living in other countries, brings the primary rationale behind the 1993 Act to a logical conclusion, but can hardly be seen to contribute to the consolidation of good-neighbourly relations and stability within neighbouring states.[56] The case of Hungary demonstrates the overarching significance of domestic incentives for minority protection, the ambiguity and practical difficulties attached to the implementation of collective rights and a certain corrective effect of EU conditionality on potentially destabilising policies like the 'Status Law'. In the context of the discussions about the Status Law, the Council of Europe's Venice Commission did not per se rule out co-ethnic socioeconomic entitlements, provided they are available to other foreign citizens. The European Commission's emphasis on the Schengen Agreement, the exclusion of Austria from Hungary's Law and the repeated references to the need to amend the Law to comply with EC law signalled the limited scope of the law after Hungary's accession to the EU.[57] The Commission reproduced the wording of the recommendations of the Venice Commission in its Reports, but restricted itself to urging Hungary to complete agreements with Romania and Slovakia on the implementation of the Law. Behind the scenes the Commission, including the Legal Service, commented in detail on the Law and recommended changes which were not taken up by the Fidesz government, illustrating once again the lack of EU competence in this area and the importance of domestic political constellations. The EU, the OSCE and the Council of Europe paved the way for a new round of bilateral treaties under a new Hungarian government. The Romanian–Hungarian Agreement of September 2003 and the Slovak–Hungarian Agreement of December 2003 effectively reduced the original law to a mutual declaration of support for cultural and linguistic activities for the Hungarians in Romania and Slovakia and the Romanians and Slovaks in Hungary.

Slovakia and Romania: regime change through minority participation

The presence of sizeable, politically mobilised Hungarian minorities in Slovakia and Romania allows for a comparison of their interaction with the respective majorities and sheds light on the dynamics between endogenous political developments and external interests and incentives – here represented by the Hungarian government and various European organisations. In Slovakia, four Hungarian parties emerged in the early transition phase, illustrating that the Hungarian minority did not represent a unified political force. A first ethnically inclusive government, involving a Hungarian party, collapsed quickly. The emergence of the sovereignty issue on the political agenda 'ethnicised' statehood and the political process as a whole. The Slovak majority and the Hungarian minority favoured a common state with the Czechs, but the distance between the Slovak political elite and the Hungarian minority grew, especially when the Movement for a Democratic Slovakia (HZDS) formed a coalition with the Slovak National Party in 1992 (Csergö 2002: 4–5).

Romania adopted provisions for minority representation in parliament. The 1992 election law enables minority organisations to field candidates on the same basis as political parties, and guarantees a seat in parliament for a minority failing to cross the 3 per cent threshold on the condition that they receive more than 5 per cent of the average vote needed to elect one representative.[58] This provision was not the result of active minority campaigning, but an early signal to the West and the EU – preceding the Copenhagen criteria – that the Romanian government protects its minorities. The law was also a good-will gesture to smaller minorities, but it failed to address the most pressing minority issues concerning the Hungarians and the Roma. The fact that representatives of the state-funded minority organisations – the state funds one organisation per minority – dominate among the minority deputies in parliament, and the low rates of ethnic voting of medium-sized minorities compared with a proliferation of very small minorities, demonstrate the pitfalls of a policy which looks progressive at first glance.[59]

In Romania a single Hungarian party, the Democratic Alliance of Hungarians in Romania, emerged as early as 1989, but it combined within its own ranks a range of different viewpoints. Iliescu's National Front initially proclaimed a commitment to collective minority rights in return for the Hungarian party's support, but Iliescu – like Meciar – polarised ethnopolitical differences in their attempt to build nation-states. Iliescu's regime lasted from 1990–96, while Meciar stayed in power during 1992–98. In both cases Hungarian minority parties were represented in parliament, questioning their respective governments' policies, especially institutional safeguards for minority representation, language and regional administration. In Romania, the Hungarian party countered the increasing centralisation and restrictive language legislation with calls for territorial autonomy. While national territorial autonomy did not emerge as the Hungarian parties' priority in Slovakia, they went on a collision course with Meciar's plan to redraw regional administrative boundaries so as to break up the relatively compact Hungarian settlements.

The Hungarian minority elites formed part of the political opposition in both countries, but the majority–minority ethnic division did not become the only or predominant cleavage structure. Instead, three clusters of parties representing 'majority nationalist, majority moderate and minority pluralist perspectives' on state-building crystallised (Csergö 2002: 13). Gradually, the Hungarian parties increased their cooperation with the Slovak and Romanian opposition parties, although these attempts were initially overshadowed by frictions. In 1994 the Slovak-Hungarian opposition managed to topple the Meciar government in a vote of no-confidence, but already six months later the HZDS was re-elected and, under Meciar's leadership, managed to divide and suppress the opposition forces. Thus, the friendship treaty with Hungary, which clearly ruled out autonomy rights for minorities, was signed in 1995 and a number of laws were passed with the full or at least partial support of the Slovak opposition: the State Language Act of 1995, making Slovak the only official language; the act on the redrawing of the territorial administrative boundaries in 1996, trying to minimise the political strength of the

Hungarian minority in areas where it constituted a numerical majority; amendments to the act on school administration, limiting the authority of local communities over schools; and a law on the elevation of a national Slovak organisation (*Matica slovenská*) to the highest national cultural, social and scientific organisation (Csergö 2002: 17–18). On the basis of the political Copenhagen criterion, Slovakia was excluded from the first wave of candidates at the Luxembourg Council in 1997 and was sharply criticised in the Report of 1998.[60]

The Hungarian parties' demands for regional self-government proved the biggest stumbling bloc for the cooperation between Hungarian and Slovak opposition parties. Over time the Hungarian parties switched to an emphasis on decentralisation and local government, thus allowing for a narrowing of the political divide within the opposition. The electoral law of 1998 led to the consolidation of one moderate Slovak opposition party (Slovak Democratic Coalition) and the Hungarian Coalition, made up of three Hungarian parties. In Romania, the Hungarian party and the Romanian political opposition encountered similar differences in defining more coherent positions and reaching a compromise. Shared conceptions regarding the nature of the post-communist state and its relationship with other European democracies were at the heart of the political coalitions toppling Iliescu in 1996 and Meciar in 1998. In Romania the resulting coalition governments struggled for a political compromise on amending restrictive laws on language use, education and administration and managed to forge a consensus in the end.[61] The regime change in Slovakia marked the beginning of a new state policy on minorities, which quickly became an integral part of the attempt of Dzurinda's government to speed up economic reforms and integrate into Western security and political and economic structures. In a direct response to the earlier criticisms of the EU and the OSCE High Commissioner on National Minorities, it prioritised the adoption of a new language law in advance of the Commission meeting of July 1999, which was scheduled to review Slovakia's accession prospects.[62] The new language law came to symbolise the regime change and placed Slovakia in the first wave of the candidate countries. The language law allows the use of minority languages in local public administration subject to a minority population threshold of 20 per cent in a given area.[63] The Commission's 1999 Report declared that the requisite 'significant progress' in this policy area had been delivered, despite the fact that the final text of the law was adopted without the support of the governing Hungarian parties. Though no longer a priority of the EU, definitional ambiguities in the text and a problem of legal precedence with regard to the more restrictive provisions of the constitution of 1992 further overshadowed the implementation of the law.[64] In its Opinion on Slovakia of 22 September 2000, the Advisory Committee on the FCNM noted on the one hand that the implementation of the 1995 State Language Law 'has not, to date, had a widespread negative impact on minority languages', while stressing on the other hand 'that the State Language Law is lacking in clarity' and could at the very least 'produce a 'chilling effect' extending to legitimate activities of minorities'. It asked for the relationship between the Law on the Use of National Minority Languages of 1999 and the State Language Law to be clarified.[65]

Slovakia and Romania are instructive cases in several respects: first, they demonstrate how the incentive of EU membership, tied to a bundle of political criteria, can help to galvanise domestic political forces in favour of a democratic regime change. In both cases, minority parties, which already existed as organised opposition forces, played a crucial and active role in this process. Furthermore, the EU's critique of the 1995 Slovak language law is a rare example of an explicit EU stance on a specific piece of minority-sensitive legislation. Second, the predominant political conflicts in Romania and Slovakia did not hinge on ethnic divisions. In the early transition period the main political majority embarked on centralised nation-state building. The Hungarian parties fairly consistently represented the ethnic and political minority in opposition to the ruling party. Over time they built a joint electoral platform with the moderate Slovak and Romanian forces, thereby cutting across ethnic divisions and forging a new political majority. These coalitions proved essential for state consolidation and democratisation. Third, the EU contributed to the creation of the domestic political space for minority participation and inclusive governments, but it did not intervene in the internal disputes over the appropriate institutional responses to minority demands, as seen in the case of the new Slovak language law of 1999. The democratisation and Europeanisation processes neither put an end to the domestic disputes over minority issues, nor did they guarantee a smooth political and economic reform process, as the case of Romania demonstrates.

Conclusion

The empirical evidence suggests that, on balance, international actors and a vaguely defined European norm framed debates and perceptions in CEE and affected the timing and nature of specific pieces of legislation, while the domestic political constellations and pressures ultimately had a more significant effect on the institutional and policy outcomes. The EU has had an impact if its vague conditions in the field of minority protection have fitted the domestic political agenda and could be empowered by it, in particular during the early stages of the accession process. EU conditionality in the area of minority protection is best understood as the cumulative effect of different international institutions. The actual policy leverage of the EU in minority protection has been anchored in the instruments and recommendations of the Council of Europe and the OSCE, and a range of other actors, including NGOs, have translated them into the domestic political context. The changes to the citizenship and naturalisation provisions in Estonia and Latvia in particular, demonstrate to what extent the EU has drawn on the recommendations of the OSCE, especially the High Commissioner on National Minorities and the Council of Europe. The policy domain of minority protection not only questions the notion of EU conditionality per se and widens the notion of 'Europeanisation' by highlighting the need to investigate the links (and gaps) between different international institutions and tools; it also decouples ethnic minorities and majorities from political minorities and majorities in the study of transition politics.

The decision calculus of the ruling elites in the candidate countries over whether to comply with EU conditionality has been shaped not only by their perceptions of how a particular decision may affect the accession process of their country, but also by the degree of domestic mobilisation among majority or minority groups, the elites' definition of 'national interests' and personal concerns about power and political risks. EU conditionality has anchored minority protection in the political agenda of the candidate states, but the EU had little to offer in terms of substantive guidance, as the lack of benchmarks, inconsistencies and the limited scope for follow-up on implementation in the Regular Reports demonstrate. The Hungarian case illustrates best how the domestic political will in favour of minority protection is critically shaped by national interests, namely the concern for the sizeable Hungarian minorities located in neighbouring countries. Here the EU has acted as one of the brakes on the controversial Hungarian Status Law. In general, it is easier to trace the EU's impact on specific laws or regulations. The adoption of Slovakia's language law of July 1999 is one of the best examples of a close link to the EU accession process, as reflected in the Regular Reports. The cases of Slovakia and Romania confirm that the EU's political leverage is greatest in the early phase of the accession process. In the presence of organised minority interests, the EU has helped to legitimise these actors in the domestic political scene by encouraging power-sharing through formal and informal domestic coalitions. Inclusive government and participation have de facto been the EU norm vis-à-vis candidates with politically mobilised minority groups.

The EU's normative overstretch has anchored the value and objective of minority protection in the 'EU speak', which, in turn, could be a first step towards internalisation, institutional change and modified political behaviour. It is too early to predict the outcome of the interaction between West and East European models of minority protection in the post-enlargement period. Rather than reinforcing the distinction between new and old member states, the issue of minority rights cuts across geographical and historical boundaries. Two major scenarios are feasible: on the one hand a form of 'reverse conditionality', emanating from the new member states, could infuse the EU with a new commitment to minority rights; on the other hand, a new tacit policy consensus on inaction may emerge within an enlarged EU. In the new member states, a contraction in this domain could have a more immediate destabilising effect on polity and society. For the time being, a combination of both scenarios appears to be the most likely outcome. As long as the EU remains committed to further enlargement – to include Bulgaria, Romania, Turkey, Croatia and other South East European states – the 'respect for and protection of national minorities' will remain an integral part of the rhetoric of accession. In the case of Croatia, which gained candidate status in June 2004, the Copenhagen criteria were supplemented by the Stabilisation and Association Process of 1997 to include, *inter alia,* full cooperation with the International Criminal Tribunal for the former Yugoslavia, 'real opportunities for displaced persons', the return of refugees to their places of origin, non-discrimination and good-neighbourly relations.[66] Though unlikely to become an internal EU policy priority, this 'minority momentum' tied to future enlargement may promote awareness inside the EU and bolster the profile of related instruments, most importantly the FCNM and its complex and dynamic monitoring mechanism.

The Race Discrimination Directive 2000/43/EC, once fully transposed into domestic legislation in all member states, legally embeds the norm of 'equal treatment between persons irrespective of racial or ethnic origin'.[67] It arguably represents the EU's furthest reaching 'constitutional resource' for minority-sensitive policies.[68] A couple of initiatives point to the continued relevance of the monitoring of rights inside the EU. The Network of Independent Experts, which was set up upon a request by the European Parliament in connection with Article 7 TEU and is funded by the Commission, marks a step in this direction. Its task is to monitor fundamental rights in the member states, and its first two reports adopt a wide definition of fundamental rights, explicitly including minority issues.[69] However, these annual reports of independent experts will only have political clout if they become mandatory items on the agenda of all the main EU institutions. Moreover, the redesign of the remit of the European Centre on Racism and Xenophobia is currently under discussion.[70] The widening of the remit to include a human rights dimension could allow for more systematic minority-relevant research.

Despite the link between the EU's eastward enlargement and the ongoing constitution-making process at the European level, minority rights did not emerge as a prominent issue during the Convention on the Future of Europe. The resulting Draft Constitutional Treaty was void of any mention of minorities. Article 2 of the Draft Constitutional Treaty concealed the ambiguity surrounding the EU's internal values and its conditions for membership, as the wording no longer copied the language of the first Copenhagen criterion.[71] During the Intergovernmental Conference, which initially failed to generate an agreement, Hungary took a lead in a last-minute attempt to enshrine explicit minority rights in the final version, and the final amendments, tabled by the Italian Presidency, included a prominent reference to the 'respect for human rights, including the rights of persons belonging to minority groups'.[72] When the negotiations resumed, this amendment remained uncontroversial and now forms part of Article I-2 of the Constitutional Treaty for Europe of 18 June 2004.[73] In the final text 'the rights of persons belonging to minorities' are clearly characterised as a sub-category of human rights, and an explicit reference to 'national' minorities is missing. Nevertheless, political and societal actors are bound to legitimise their demands with a reference to the newly declared 'values' of the EU, and the new treaty formulation establishes greater coherence with the political Copenhagen criterion. Article 21 of the Charter of Fundamental Rights, now incorporated as Part 2 in the Constitutional Treaty, explicitly singles out 'membership of a national minority' among the grounds of discrimination to be prohibited. Together with the related Article 22, stipulating the Union's respect for 'cultural, religious and linguistic diversity', it would apply to any action of the EU institutions and the member states when implementing EU law if the Charter becomes legally binding.

5 Autonomy, power-sharing and common citizenship

Principles for accommodating national minorities in Europe

Rainer Bauböck

National minority rights in Europe

How do democratic states respond to minority claims for self-government and how should they respond? In recent years a number of comparative and normative analyses have addressed these questions. Most cases discussed in this literature are Western European countries. The most frequently analysed ones are the Spanish *Estado de las autonomías*, the Belgian transition from consociation within a unitary constitution to multilingual federation, and devolution in the UK. Switzerland is a more ambiguous case since it is not obvious that its language communities have developed distinct national identities characterised by a desire for self-government. What these cases have in common is that multinational and multilingual arrangements are a constitutional feature of the larger polity itself so that it may be regarded as a composite entity consisting of several autonomous and culturally distinct subunits. Outside Europe, Canada and India are the only two long-term stable democracies that can be described in this way.

Among the pre-2004 member states of the European Union (EU) there are several countries that grant special autonomy to small and culturally distinct minorities concentrated in a peripheral part of the state territory. Strong forms of political autonomy exist in Italy for the German and Ladino-speaking population of South Tyrol/Alto Adige (and a weaker autonomy status for francophone citizens in the Aosta Valley), in Denmark for the Faeroes and Greenland, and in Finland for the Swedish-speaking Åland Islands. In France, legislation that would have established autonomy for Corsica failed to win a majority in a referendum on 6 July 2003. Most of the other old EU member states grant special minority rights or political status to various ethnolinguistic groups whom they recognise as 'autochthonous' without, however, devolving substantial political powers to institutions of minority self-government.

None of the ten new member states, and none of the accession candidates for 2007, is currently a multinational democracy, nor do any of them recognise strong political autonomy for a national minority. Cyprus would have become a multinational democracy of the Belgium or Swiss type, had the Greek population in the South not rejected the UN plan for reunification in a referendum on 24 April 2004. Yet in several of the East and Central European countries there are territorially concentrated, culturally distinct and politically organised minorities that could very well qualify for minority self-government. These new member states had been monitored for their compliance with the minority-rights clause of the 1993 Copenhagen criteria for EU membership and most have passed minority-rights legislation that is quite generous compared to general West European standards. However, wherever minority nationalist politicians have raised demands for territorial autonomy, they have met fierce resistance.

Reasons for this discrepancy between West and East Central European approaches to minority self-government have been analysed very well in a book edited by Kymlicka and Opalski (2001), and in several contributions to the present volume. In my chapter I will not be concerned with explaining this difference. Instead, I will discuss the three basic ingredients of successful multinational federations: (1) comprehensive political autonomy for the minority nation; (2) a system of power-sharing and federal representation that integrates the minority as a distinct polity into central state government; and (3) a common democratic and multicultural citizenship for all citizens of the wider polity. I will discuss each of these elements and how they could be interpreted, modified and weighed against each other. My conclusion is that there is not one best way of combining the three elements but that they still should be affirmed as basic principles in a common European minority-rights regime.

Political autonomy

Self-government is the most important demand raised by national minorities. Some authors distinguish between, on the one hand, stateless nations (Keating 1997) or nations without states (Guibernau 1999) and, on the other hand, national minorities. Whereas the former have no independent national 'homeland', the latter are seen as linked to an external kin-state where their national identity is established as a dominant one. A more precise classification could distinguish four types according to whether a national identity is state-based or without the institutional support of an independent state and whether its claim to self-government is confined within a state or straddles its borders to include territories and populations in other countries. We can then classify French nationalism as internal and state-supported, Scottish nationalism as internal and stateless, Basque nationalism as transborder and stateless and Hungarian nationalism (in its relation to Hungarian minorities in Romania and Slovakia) as transborder and state-supported.[1]

These distinctions are important for analytical and comparative purposes, yet we still need to clarify how to define a national minority. In the academic literature there are two quite different interpretations of what the term 'minority' refers to: the smaller part of a nation that lies outside its state territory, or a distinct national group in a subordinate position within the state where it lives.[2] For my present purposes, the latter definition is the appropriate one. Political autonomy claims emerge from attempts to oppose a minority nation-building project to a dominant one within a state. Normative justifications for such rival nation-building do not depend on whether or not this group enjoys the support of an external kin-state. As I will argue below, there is also a normative trade-off between the two goals of extra-territorial inclusion in a homeland polity and self-government in the minority's territory. The stronger the political autonomy a minority enjoys within a federal arrangement, the weaker are its claims to external protection from a kin-state. I will therefore use the term national minority as a generic concept applying to non-dominant groups within a state that strive for self-government. This includes stateless nations as well as those with links to external kin-states. One implication of this definition is that a national group would cease to be a minority not only when it forms a demographic majority in a state of its own, but also when it is no longer subordinate but fully recognised as a constituent people within a multinational state.

The desire for national self-government distinguishes minority nationalism from the broader phenomenon of multiculturalism. Multiculturalism is about religious, ethnic and cultural minority claims for protection against discrimination, for special exemptions, symbolic recognition, material support or special representation. National minority demands, however, aim at redrawing international or internal state borders so that the group in question can set up its own independent state, join a neighbouring kin-state, or achieve political autonomy within a distinct part of the present state territory. It is important to understand the genuinely political nature of such projects. If the goal of nationalist struggle were merely to protect a distinct language or culture, then a generous public recognition of such diversity, e.g. through official multilingualism in public institutions combined with regional education systems in the minority language, might suffice to demobilise a national identity. However, in nationalist mobilisations, cultural preservation serves more often as a means for marking the boundaries of a national territory and population, whereas political power exercised through autonomous institutions of government is the ultimate goal.

Political autonomy is often regarded as 'internal self-determination' and distinguished from 'external self-determination'. The latter is regarded as a property of independent states or of peoples with a right to change international borders through decolonisation, secession or unification with another state. I believe that this terminology, too, is misleading and inappropriate for a normative theory of multinational federalism. Self-determination in international law refers to the right of peoples to determine their own political status. If this right is interpreted as including a right to secede, it clashes with the equally strong right of existing states to territorial integrity. In order to reconcile the two conflicting principles, the notion of peoples has been narrowly restricted to, on the one hand, total populations of existing states and, on the other hand, colonial peoples whose challenges to international borders were accepted as legitimate in the post-1945 period (Cassese 1995).

From a normative perspective this current consensus in the international community is quite arbitrary, but it is hard to challenge as long as we define self-determination as a natural right of peoples. The only consistent alternative is a libertarian theory of self-determination, as worked out by Harry Beran (1984, 1998) and David Gauthier (1994). This perspective can do without a definition of peoples because it regards legitimate states as voluntary territorial associations of individuals and defends a unilateral right to secede for any regional majority. As Allen Buchanan (1997, 2003) has pointed out, this approach is not only incompatible with current principles of international law, but also with domestic concerns of social justice and democratic stability. I have argued elsewhere that in order to solve the conceptual conundrums of self-determination we need to reverse the normative order of rights in international law. Instead of regarding self-determination as the basic principle and self-government as a derivate aspect of 'internal self-determination', one should consider self-government as the primary right and self-determination as a derivative and remedial right in exceptional cases where self-government rights have been persistently violated and cannot be restored by other means (Bauböck 2004a).

There is another reason why 'internal self-determination' is a misleading terminology for political autonomy rights. 'Self-determination' is a procedural notion that allocates to the community concerned the decision-making power concerning its status, whereas 'self-government' is a substantive notion whose emphasis is on political institutions that allow the community to collectively shape its own future. Saying that a national minority enjoys a right of internal self-determination suggests that it is entirely up to the group to choose its own political status within the polity. Yet, in contrast with external secession, which separates populations previously united within a state, political autonomy preserves the institutions of a central government, a common constitution and shared citizenship. Sub-state self-government requires institutionalised cooperation and ongoing consent regarding the status and the division of powers between the autonomous group and the central state government. Working out these political arrangements is therefore a matter for joint decision-making rather than for unilateral self-determination.

A remedial theory of self-determination may nevertheless justify internal self-determination in the procedural sense for colonised and indigenous peoples who have historically been excluded from equal citizenship within the polity. If such groups neither have the capacity nor the desire to establish independent states, they may exercise self-determination rights internally by opting for a special autonomy status that will often be regulated outside the general constitutional framework. The status of aboriginal first nations in North America or of territories like Puerto Rico can be described in this way. Such postcolonial constellations should be distinguished from multinational ones, where rival nation-building projects have been pursued within a common territory and have resulted in the inclusion of minorities as integral parts of a dominant conception of nationhood. In these latter constellations, minority claims for political autonomy involve a demand for transforming a mononational conception of the larger polity into a multinational one in which the minority is recognised as a constitutive partner of a federal contract. For this very reason its self-government rights must not be seen as grounded in a right to internal self-determination that can be exercised by the minority unilaterally.

While internal self-determination may thus be too strong a claim for constituent national minorities, what international law has to offer is definitely too weak. The most advanced document in this area so far is the 1999 Lund Recommendations on the Effective Participation of National Minorities in Public Life initiated by the OSCE High Commissioner on National Minorities. These recommendations combine two prongs: 'participation in governance of the State as a whole, and self-governance over certain local or internal affairs' (Foundation 1999: 6). The section on self-governance contains both non-territorial and territorial devolution and the indicative list of powers that can be devolved includes education, culture, use of minority language, environment, local planning, natural resources, economic development, local policing functions, and housing, health, and other social services. This is a very useful, although of course non-binding, document. Yet its main concern is to promote self-government and power-sharing as potentially useful instruments for conflict prevention and resolution and not as minority rights properly speaking. It is therefore left to state governments whether or not they consider these instruments as appropriate for accommodating a minority in their territory. Some international lawyers suggest that effective participation implies also a prohibition of dismantling already established institutions of minority self-government.[3] However, as Kymlicka points out in his contribution to this volume, this norm would only protect pre-existing forms of territorial self-government but not legitimate aspirations of minorities whose autonomy claims have never been recognised by a central government.

This leads me to conclude that within a normative theory of multinational democracy, political autonomy for national minorities should be stronger than the OSCE conception of self-governance and effective participation, but weaker than a right to internal or external self-determination.

In multinational states, self-government should be regarded as a very basic and general right that can be exercised simultaneously by the total population of democratic states and by distinct national minorities nested within that population. Mutual acceptance of such nested self-government by historic national majorities and minorities is the first and most important normative ingredient of stable multinational arrangements.

Power-sharing

The second basic element of multinational democracy is a system of power-sharing that gives minorities a stake and voice in the government of the encompassing polity. Will Kymlicka and other political philosophers who start from liberal justifications of minority rights tend to emphasise self-government at the expense of power-sharing, whereas theorists who are mainly concerned with democratic stability in deeply divided societies reverse this emphasis. According to Arend Lijphart, the basic feature of power-sharing (also called consociational) democracy in divided societies is representation and cooperation of all significant segments in central political decision-making. Lijphart does list autonomy for constituent groups as another primary characteristic of power-sharing democracy. Such groups enjoy delegated authority for internal decision-making on matters that concern only the group. But the essential integrative mechanism is joint decision-making in all matters of common concern (Lijphart 1977; 1995: 856). This emphasis is underlined by the two secondary characteristics of consociational democracy: proportional representation of constituent groups in central state institutions and minority veto in joint decisions.

Power-sharing arrangements are in fact quite different in federal democracies and in consociational democracies divided by religious affiliations or political ideologies. Only in the former do constituent units enjoy constitutional autonomy and legislative powers. Federalism, in Daniel Elazar's definition, involves a combination of self-rule and shared rule that amounts to divided sovereignty (Elazar 1987: 5, 12). Both the autonomy of constituent units and their representation in federal government must therefore be entrenched in a written constitution guarded by a supreme court and the powers of delegated, as well as, joint decision-making are not merely executive, but also legislative ones. By contrast, consociational arrangements in the Dutch and Austrian cases meant that the religious pillars or political camps of a divided civil society were represented in government directly through political parties and indirectly through institutionalised consultation of corporate interest organisations (trades unions, employer and farmer associations). The most important power-sharing institution in consociational democracy is a grand coalition cabinet, whereas the most important such institution in a federal constitution is a second chamber of parliament.

In a federal system there are always two dimensions of power-sharing: a horizontal one that refers primarily to the representation of constituent units in federal government,[4] and a vertical dimension along which political powers are allocated between federal and constituent governments. This vertical division of powers can result in strictly separate policy competencies or in 'cooperative federalism' in which provincial and federal administrations have joint responsibilities in making and implementing laws. Dual federalism in the US illustrates the extreme case of a non-cooperative vertical division of powers (Friedrich 1968). In multinational democracies where boundaries between federal units represent a major cleavage in society, introducing elements of German-style cooperative federalism may help to strengthen cohesion.

Not all multinational democracies, however, are constitutional federations. While granting substantial autonomy to distinct substate political communities that have emerged from rival projects of nation-building is a defining characteristic of such polities,[5] not all among them involve these communities fully into a federal system of power-sharing. In the UK, the main obstacles are the doctrine of parliamentary sovereignty, the absence of a regional chamber and of a written constitution. In Spain the second chamber does not primarily represent the provinces or autonomous communities and the main integrative mechanism has been the central governments' reliance on regional nationalist parties for mustering parliamentary majorities (Requejo 2001: 120). Since this mode of political integration depends on election results, this is a very fragile and non-institutionalised arrangement that can be characterised as a deficiency of the power-sharing dimension in Spain's multinational democracy. Belgium has gradually moved from a unitary consociational democracy to a fully federal constitution. Here, the diagnosis is the opposite one. Integration through power-sharing has been weakened by allocating so many powers to constituent units that there is little left for joint decision-making in central government. The most important factor of political disintegration in Belgium is, however, not a matter of constitutional design but the legacy of consociationalism: a nearly complete division of the party system along linguistic lines, which minimises the articulation of cross-cutting cleavages in Belgian politics and creates strong incentives for politicians to support ever more devolution (Peeters 1994; Fitzmaurice 1999).

A robust form of power-sharing is an essential corollary of self-government in multinational democracies that recognise national minorities as constitutive parts of a composite polity. It is not equally required in special autonomy arrangements for groups that have been historically excluded from the polity and enjoy a measure of internal self-determination. In multinational federations, self-government and federal representation are complementary elements that can be simultaneously strengthened or weakened. In contrast, special autonomy arrangements are characterised by a trade-off between these two elements. Daniel Elazar has coined the term 'federacy' for the latter constellation in which 'a larger power and a smaller polity are linked asymmetrically in a federal relationship whereby the latter has greater autonomy than other segments of the former and, in return, has a smaller role in the governance of the larger power' (Elazar 1987: 7).

The importance of power-sharing for cohesion in multinational federations has been emphasised by Brendan O'Leary. He suggests a general law that 'a stable democratic majoritarian federation, federal or multinational, must have a *Staatsvolk*, a national or ethnic people, who are demographically and electorally dominant … and who will be the co-founders of the federation' (O'Leary 2001: 284–5).

> [W]here there is no *Staatsvolk*, or where the *Staatsvolk's* position is precarious, a stable federation requires (at least some) consociational rather than majoritarian institutions if it is to survive.
>
> (O'Leary 2001: 291)

O'Leary draws this conclusion from a comparative analysis of multinational federations. I suggest that normative considerations lead to a similar, although not identical, conjecture: stable and fair multinational arrangements can be achieved either through recognising self-governing minorities as partners in a foundational contract that constitutes the polity as a multinational democracy, or through a special contract that establishes autonomy for a minority outside the general constitutional framework. In the former case, but not in the latter, even a demographically dominant *Staatsvolk* must agree to extensive power-sharing with national minorities in central government. Exclusive majority control over central government institutions undermines the minority's identification with the larger polity. Although comprehensive political autonomy is normatively sufficient to defeat a national minority's claim to external self-determination, it is not sufficient for the stability of a multinational federation in which the minority claims constitutive status.

The institutional choice between federacy arrangements and multinational federation will be largely determined by demographic, geographic and historical circumstances. If national minorities are numerically small, concentrated in peripheral or off-shore territories, and have neither been accepted, nor see themselves, as co-founders of the larger state, a highly asymmetric federacy arrangement may be stable because it is acceptable to both sides. This seems to be generally true for the Faeroes and Åland Islands or for South Tyrol/Alto Adige. For the autonomous Flemish, Catalan, Basque, Galician, Scottish and Welsh regions, however, providing them with stakes in the central government through federal power-sharing arrangements may be the key to long-term stability of multinational democracy in Belgium, Spain and the UK.

Democratic citizenship

As I have pointed out above, self-government is not merely a right of national minorities but also a feature of every encompassing democratic polity. Citizenship at the level of the larger state should therefore not merely be regarded as a formal status of nationality that establishes a legal relation between individuals and states, but also as a bundle of individual rights and obligations and a democratic system of direct representation and accountability in which every citizen counts equally.

It is this element that distinguishes federal from confederal arrangements. Confederation is often defined as a federation with a weak central government. However, as the Belgium case demonstrates, this may be a derivative rather than a defining characteristic. From a democratic perspective the most important difference is between confederal institutions in which only the governments of constitutive units are represented and federal governments in which citizens are directly represented alongside the constitutive units. Democratic federation of the latter type was the revolutionary invention of the 1787 US Constitution, whereas the Articles of Confederation adopted in 1777, as well as earlier political theories such as Johannes Althusius' *Politica* of 1603 (Althusius 1995) had envisaged multilevel systems in which governments at an encompassing level were exclusively composed of representatives of lower-level governments. A democratic federation can therefore be defined as a triple system of representation in which governments of constituent units represent their respective citizens, and federal government represents the citizens as well as the constituent units of the federal polity.

The importance of democratic citizenship for stable multinational democracies can be seen when considering its relation with self-government, with power-sharing and with external kin-states.

Citizenship and minority self-government

Democratic representation in a federal polity amounts to vertical dual citizenship because individuals are both members of a constituent polity and of the encompassing one. Not all federal constitutions recognise this by establishing a formal status of provincial citizenship. Yet if we define substantive citizenship as a status of full and equal membership in a self-governing polity, then every robust sub-state autonomy in a democratic state generates nested dual citizenship. This view raises, but leaves unanswered, a problem that has plagued most multinational federations: Which of the two citizenships takes priority? This question can be split into three quite different ones: (1) Which membership is primary and which is derivative in the acquisition of citizenship status?; (2) Which membership takes priority in conflicts between citizenship rights and duties attached to the different levels?; and (3) Which citizenship expresses the stronger identity? My tentative answers are that (1) generally federal acquisition should dominate provincial one; (2) a federal constitution should regulate conflicts over rights and duties without giving general priority to one level; and (3) federal citizenship must be compatible with opposite rankings between nested identities among national majorities and minorities.

Nested citizenship implies the simple rule that all citizens of a constituent unit must also be citizens of the federation, and all citizens of the federation must be citizens of one constituent unit. This rule makes it logically impossible that all polities at various levels in a nested democracy could exercise self-determination rights in matters of citizenship, as sovereign states do when they claim a right to determine under their own laws who will be their citizens.[6] One of the two levels must yield to this prerogative. With regard to acquisition of formal citizenship through birth, residence or naturalisation, there seem to be only two contemporary exceptions to the rule that it is the encompassing level that takes priority. These are Switzerland and the European Union.[7] In both cases, citizenship is acquired at a lower level – in Switzerland in the municipality under cantonal law, in the EU in a member state – and federal citizenship is derived from this decision. The difference between the two cases is that Switzerland has a federal law on nationality that lays down the basic rules within which the cantons can adopt their own policies, whereas the EU has no competency to interfere with, or to harmonise, its member states' nationality laws.

The EU is a supranational polity that is neither adequately described as a confederation nor as a federal state. The derivation of Union citizenship from member-state citizenship is, in my view, a specificity of supranational democracy that would be problematic for multinational federal states but is adequate for the EU. This does not, however, justify full sovereignty of member states with regard to citizenship policies. Even if it is derivative of member-state nationality, Union citizenship is a bundle of uniform individual rights valid throughout the Union. Prudential as well as normative reasons suggest a need for harmonising the rules of acquisition and loss. On the one hand, member states must be interested in preventing each other from turning persons into Union citizens that they would not have admitted to their own citizenship. On the other hand, standards of equal treatment and non-discrimination should not only apply to the Union's present citizens but also to its future ones. Gross differences in access to EU citizenship for immigrants in different countries undermines the idea and significance of a common European citizenship. Since the Tampere European Council of October 1999, the Commission has made cautious moves towards putting naturalisation policies on the European agenda (Bauböck 2004c).

Examining more closely citizenship policies in other federal democracies we find that, in contrast with North America, European federal provinces often enjoy delegated powers and administrative discretion in the implementation of federal nationality laws, and use these in a way that produces substantially different naturalisation rates in different parts of the country.[8] Such powers could also be used by provincial governments controlled by national minorities for preferential naturalisation of immigrants who share an ethnic identity or speak the language of a national minority. If one accepts normative arguments that long-term immigrants have a moral right to full citizenship (Walzer 1983; Carens 1989; Bauböck 1994), then such selective naturalisation would be more problematic than immigration policies that allow national minority governments to introduce their cultural preferences.[9]

With regard to the second question, of which level takes priority in defining citizenship rights and obligations, I suggest a more open-ended answer. In all federal systems, constituent units have final decision-making powers in some policy matters. This implies that constituent level citizenship has supremacy with regard to rights and obligations in fully devolved policy areas. Nevertheless, in any multilevel system there are potential conflicts between citizenship at different levels. What is needed in order to resolve these conflicts, and to ensure coherence in the general system of rights and obligations, is a federal bill of rights that must be respected by all levels of government and a supreme court that interprets these common rights as well as the vertical division of powers. The court's task is not to ensure the supremacy of federal legislation over the provincial one, but to prevent the intrusion of each level of government into the domain of the other level.

Constraints on diversity in order to ensure the coherence of citizenship throughout the federal polity are least plausible with regard to its identity dimension. In multinational polities there is an unavoidable asymmetry of national identities. Historically dominant groups tend to associate their national identity with the larger polity and generally include the minority as a subgroup within that state-nation. The minority is not seen as a separate nation but as a culturally distinct part of the larger population, and a province where it forms a majority is regarded as a part of the state territory with no claim to special status and powers. The opposite view is to regard the minority as inassimilable and therefore excluded from the dominant nation. This attitude, which has historically prevailed towards indigenous peoples, enslaved populations, Jews or Roma, is normatively indefensible. In contrast, a national majority identity that includes the minority as an integral part of its imagined political community is not only defensible but may also be essential for maintaining stable multinational democracies.

Politically mobilised national minorities, however, consider themselves a polity apart and often rank their minority identity above their association with the larger state. These asymmetric identity constellations raise a problem for David Miller's idea that stable multinational democracies are held together through a shared sense of nested nationality (Miller 2000:

chap. 8). Miller expects minorities to accept that the larger polity is not merely a multinational state but a nation in its own right and that they fully share in this larger national identity. The political implication is that it would be wrong for Scots, Québécois, Catalans or Flemish to secede because this move would misinterpret their historic identities that make them an integral part of a nested nation. This solution for identity conflicts is, however, obviously biased in favour of national majorities and cannot offer an equilibrium solution in contexts of rival nation-building projects. It seems more appropriate and realistic to expect that national identities will not merely remain asymmetrical, but in a certain sense irreconcilable even in stable, peaceful and prosperous multinational democracies. Instead of pushing national minorities to see themselves as parts of a nation whose historical dominance has turned them into minorities, federal citizenship should be regarded as a supplementary and thin identity that is shared across persistently rival national identities, and can thus be disconnected from its historic association with a dominant project of nation-building.

Citizenship and power-sharing arrangements

The relation between a common citizenship and power-sharing in multinational democracies is equally complex and fraught with conflict. In such polities, citizenship at the federal level is necessarily differentiated rather than homogenous and this may generate tensions with the basic principle of equal respect and concern for all citizens. There is, for example, the question of official languages. If citizens have the right to communicate with public authorities in any of several official languages, this supports a corresponding requirement of individual multilingualism for civil servants in public administrations. Often this condition means greater job opportunities and representation for historically subordinate groups that had to learn the dominant language in addition to their mother tongue. Such side-effects may be justified as a compensation for other minority disadvantages.[10]

A more controversial question concerns equality of representation in a federal chamber. If each federal province has an equal number of seats (as in the US Senate), then this implies greater representation and weight in joint decisions for citizens in the less populous provinces. For some critics of American federalism this amounts to a violation of the 'one person one vote' principle (Stepan 2001: chap. 15; Dahl 2001: 17–18, 46–54). I believe that this critique is overstated and not consistent with the idea that democratic federation requires a balance between the three legs of triple representation sketched above. When Stepan describes disproportional representation of units in a federal chamber as a 'demos-constraining' feature of federal systems, he considers only the federal people as a demos. If we regard instead a federation as consisting of multiple and nested demoi, then strictly proportional representation of all federal provinces could be similarly described as constraining the demoi of the smaller units by diminishing their weight as partners in the federal agreement. Avoiding unequal representation of citizens in a federal chamber can still count as an argument in favour of proportional representation of units according to population size.[11] Federal power-sharing in multinational polities may, however, require some overrepresentation of national minority units to counterbalance the greater size, and often also greater number, of provinces that represent historic majorities.

A more serious concern about equality of citizenship arises in the case of federacies that are not overrepresented, but underrepresented in federal government. The best known examples are the non-incorporated territories of the US, among them the Marianas Islands and Puerto Rico, whose inhabitants are US citizens but cannot vote in presidential elections and have merely non-voting representatives in Congress. This contrasts with the situation of the French DOM/TOM (*départments et territoires d'outre mer*) whose citizens enjoy full voting rights in French parliamentary and presidential elections.

My general point here is that in multinational democracies the idea that the encompassing federal demos should prevail in determining the formula for federal representation ought to be rejected because it privileges a dominant majority's conception of national identity. Instead, the proper allocation of seats must be worked out by balancing a vertical structure of nested demoi with a horizontal one of constitutive nationalities.

Citizenship relations with external kin-states

National minorities with external kin-states may also try to establish links of citizenship with these countries. In Europe, this concern has been particularly strong in Hungary, which sees itself as a protector of about three million ethnic Hungarians living in neighbouring countries. In 2001 Hungary adopted the so-called 'Status Law', which introduced a Hungarian certificate for members of these minorities that allows them to claim specific benefits in Hungary. At the point of writing, a referendum initiative has been launched by the World Federation of Hungarians abroad that requests a Hungarian law to enable these 'certified Hungarians' in neighbouring countries to claim Hungarian citizenship in addition to a Romanian, Slovakian or Serbian one.[12] Much less attention has been paid to a similar move by Germany, which distributed German passports to ethnic Germans in the Silesia region of Poland in the early 1990s (Münz and Ohliger 1998: 166–7).

Dual citizenship that links a minority to an external kin-state ought to be assessed differently in different contexts. For migrants who have multiple social ties in source countries and host-states, it is entirely compatible with a democratic stakeholder principle and with legitimate interests of states that entertain friendly relations with each other (Faist 2001; Bauböck 2003; Hailbronner and Martin 2003). Dual citizenship may also be acceptable for historic ethnic minorities who define themselves as a diaspora oriented towards an external homeland and do not aim for self-government in the state where they live. Finally, access to the citizenship of an external kin-state may in some cases be a useful instrument for protecting a national minority from oppression by offering its members an escape route of emigration.

However, transnational multiple citizenship of this kind should not be combined with nested dual citizenship in a federal arrangement that grants national minorities comprehensive self-government. An international law perspective is not sufficient for arguing this objection, since dual nationality itself does not provide the kin-state government with a formal legal title to engage in remote control of the external minority's autonomous institutions. Yet in a broader sense, citizenship is not merely a formal relation between individuals and states, but signifies membership in self-governing political communities. A minority's claim to autonomy is compatible with the self-government of a larger multinational polity in which it forms a constitutive community and participates in federal power-sharing. It is not compatible with being simultaneously involved in a nation's self-government across international borders. Dual citizenship for autonomous national minorities would indirectly acknowledge this latter claim and would thereby undermine the integrity of nested self-government in the multinational polity.[13]

These are grounds for rejecting dual nationality for autonomous minorities even in contexts where their host-states have no reason to fear that kin-states will use it as an instrument for revisionist and irredentist policies.[14] Hungarians in Romania or Slovakia and other minorities in similar constellations would therefore have to choose between either regarding themselves as diaspora citizens affiliated to a larger ethnic nation or claiming territorial autonomy and a transformation of the country where they have lived for many generations into multinational democracies.

Towards a European minority-rights regime?

The main benefits of European integration for national minorities have so far been of the spill-over type. The EU has provided an external environment that has facilitated recognition and accommodation of minority claims in member states, even without admitting these claims explicitly onto the European political agenda. The pooling of state sovereignty has undermined the claims of dominant national traditions to exclusive cultural hegemony, and free movement within the Union has allowed minorities to connect more easily with ethnic-kin populations across borders (Keating 2001a: chap. 5). Some minorities, such as the Catalans and Basques, are clearly not satisfied with this and strive for direct representation within Union institutions. So far, neither the principle of subsidiarity nor the rather weak Committee of the Regions have done much to extend multilevel democracy in the Union to sub-state levels (Ibid.). The great variety of federal or unitary constitutions, and the different kinds of minority claims, would also make very problematic any general formula for regional representation in the government of the Union.

What is, however, both possible and important is that the Union takes a principled stance on the accommodation of national minority claims not only outside its borders but also inside. In contrast with the weak powers of international institutions such as the UN, the Council of Europe, or the OSCE, an EU minority-rights regime would be less dependent on state consensus and therefore less vulnerable to government refusal of recognising minority rights, or sometimes even the very existence of minorities. European law has supremacy over national law and direct effect within the member states, and the European Court of Justice has played a pivotal role in reinterpreting provisions for market integration as rights of European citizens. The potential benefits of a supranational minority-rights regime are thus considerable, not only for minorities within the member states, but also for developing new standards in international law. While there is little reason to expect that such a regime will become part of European law in the short term, the kind of normative arguments I have suggested above could be used to demonstrate the desirability and feasibility of such a regime. In the European context one may also be reasonably optimistic that such normative considerations may in the longer run converge with prudential interests to resolve nationality conflicts that threaten to undermine the political stability of certain member states and often also affect relations with neighbouring countries.

Comparing the different responses to national minority claims for self-government leads me to conclude that in polities shaped by rival projects of nation-building, multinational federal democracy is normatively preferable to alternative arrangements. This arrangement is characterised by a balance between the three pillars of minority political autonomy, power-sharing in central government institutions and a democratic citizenship that provides all members of the polity with equal rights and a basis for a shared political identity. Since multinational democracies of this kind entrench national identities through drawing borders of constituent units, through devolution of political powers to these units' governments, and through federal representation of these units in central government, there is no prospect that such polities will eventually overcome their national cleavages and turn into mononational democracies. Those who would like to disconnect citizenship from national identities are likely to criticise multinational federal arrangements for this reason. However, mononational democracies do not necessarily provide a better environment for achieving this goal, since their institutions are just as much involved in fostering national identities for their citizens as are minority polities within a multinational federation.

The specific danger in multinational democracies is not so much excessive nationalism, but their greater potential for 'state failure' through territorial disintegration. Will Kymlicka has called this the 'paradox of multination federalism: while it provides national minorities with a workable alternative to secession, it also helps to make secession a more realistic alternative to federalism' (Kymlicka 2001c: 118). The paradox is real, but putting greater emphasis on power-sharing and common citizenship might explain the surprising stability of democratic multinational federations in Canada, India and Western Europe.

There are, however, particular circumstances that explain why the three pillars are not equally strong in all institutional arrangements for accommodating minority self-government. Consociational arrangements are characterised by the absence of legislative autonomy for the segments of a power-sharing democracy; federacy is marked by a lack of representation of autonomous units in the power-sharing institutions of countrywide government; and weakening the common citizenship transforms a multinational federation into a confederation. Contextual arguments can justify such solutions that deviate from the democratic federation model. Consociational democracy is an important, although generally transitory, solution for reuniting a polity deeply divided along non-territorial cleavages. Federacy is generally an adequate solution for postcolonial constellations in which a national or indigenous minority is not regarded, nor regards itself, as constitutive within a larger polity from which it has been historically excluded. And confederation may be a lesser evil in situations where territorial separation can no longer be avoided or has already been implemented.

How could these very general findings become politically relevant for the European Union? Addressing conflicts over minority self-government in its member states may eventually become unavoidable for the institutions of the Union. The need for shared principles in this area is even greater after 1 May 2004. First, all potential candidate states for the next rounds of EU enlargement, i.e. Romania, Bulgaria, Croatia and Turkey, have substantial national minorities and the Copenhagen criterion of minority protection is likely to play an important role during negotiations. Second, the new member states that have joined in 2004 will no longer accept double standards that Western states have imposed on candidates for accession without enforcing them among the EU-15 or incorporating them in the draft Constitutional Treaty. Third, the kind of minority rights that have been promoted by the EU, the Council of Europe and the OSCE are very important but also insufficient since they do not address claims for comprehensive political autonomy by territorially concentrated stateless nations and national minorities that have not been recognised by central governments. Fourth, apart from the Cyprus conflict there are at the time of writing several other unresolved ones in old and new member states, including the failure to implement the Good Friday Agreement in Northern Ireland, the recent initiative for a referendum on sovereignty in the Basque provinces of Spain, the unresolved status of Corsica, and autonomy demands among Hungarian minorities in Slovakia and Romania. Moreover, nobody can be sure that apparently stable settlements in some other conflicts will not again be upset by nationalist mobilisations among regional minorities or dominant majorities. Fifth, in Central and Eastern Europe many minorities have external kin-states that will act to protect their minorities abroad if the international community fails to do so. Such external minority protection by kin-states is, however, a major source of international conflict in the area. A European minority-rights regime would not only provide minorities with alternative sources of external support but would also protect more effectively minorities without kin-states, such as the Roma.

I am not optimistic that the example of successful federal arrangements in West European multinational democracies might suffice to generate a broader endorsement for a basic right of minority self-government, which can and must be modified in specific circumstances. But I do think that there are good normative reasons for endorsing such a principle and that reasonable fears that this would endanger the security of multinational states that are not yet fully consolidated democracies can be allayed by combining this principle with an equally strong endorsement for power-sharing arrangements and for building a shared democratic citizenship.

A final argument for endorsing principles of multinational democracy within the member states is that the Union itself can be interpreted as an arrangement of this kind. I have suggested above that by introducing a common citizenship the Union has taken a step beyond confederation. At the same time, the rule that this citizenship is derived from member-state nationality, and complements the latter without replacing it, indicates a strongly multinational conception of the European polity. Another illustration of this feature is the EU's language regime. Turning all official languages of member states into official languages of the Union requires a costly regime of translation and interpretation services. If the EU were an international organisation there would be little difficulty in adopting a small number of official and working languages (as the Council of Europe or the OSCE do). And if it were a federal state, it would have to develop a language regime that might resemble the Indian one, with one or two federal languages combined with the establishment of different official languages in the member states and some protection for regional minority languages (Laitin 2001). The fact that even adding nine new languages through the recent EU enlargement has not triggered moves towards a consolidated federal-language regime demonstrates that the Union is neither an international organisation nor a federal state, but a supra-national and multinational federation.

Paradoxically, however, the multinational features of the Union may be the greatest obstacle for developing common European principles of multinational democracy. As long as the Union is only committed to respecting the national identities of its member states,[15] but not those of national minorities, there is little hope that it will insist on applying multinational principles that underpin European integration also to the states of which it is composed.

6 Kin-states protecting national minorities

Positive trend or dangerous precedent?

Walter Kemp

The enlargement of the European Union (EU) has led to a new space within Europe where borders are more porous and sovereignty less rigid. Within the EU, nations that straddle frontiers are less divided than in the past. But does this change the rules when it comes to the protection of persons belonging to national minorities? As borders within the EU become less relevant, can so-called 'kin-states' play a more active role in the support of so-called 'kin' who live in neighbouring states? The debate over the Act on Hungarians Living in Neighbouring Countries (also known as the 'Status' or 'Preference' Law), which was adopted in June 2001, is a fascinating case study of how a transforming Europe is trying to come to terms with kin-states, minorities, borders and sovereignty.

Defenders of the Act argued that it was an innovative form of supporting 'kin' in neighbouring states – a welcome example of cross-border cooperation in a post-modern Europe where frontiers are losing their significance. Opponents called it unlawful interference in the sovereign jurisdiction of the state, discriminatory, and a reversion to the nineteenth-century ideal of the nation-state. So was the Status Law a positive trend or a dangerous precedent? And what are the implications for inter-ethnic and bilateral relations in Europe? What lessons, particularly relevant to the transformation of the EU, can be learned concerning citizenship, minority protection and sovereignty in a new Europe?

This issue has plagued Europe in the past. For example, Hitler's claim of kinship ties to Germans in Poland and Czechoslovakia was a catalyst for the outbreak of the Second World War. Ethnic conflict in the Balkans in the 1990s was fuelled by kin-states and their defence of so-called blood brothers. Kin-related conflicts, although not always violent, rage on. The role of kin-states and minorities have complicated relations between Romania and Moldova, Italy and Austria over South Tyrol and Turkey and Greece over Cyprus. Russia's role as a kin-state has affected its relations with new EU members Latvia and Estonia. In short, the seemingly old-fashioned notions of nationhood based on blood and belonging, and the right of the motherland to protect its kin, are alive and well and complicating bilateral relations in and around the European Union. An examination of the debate over the Hungarian Status Law provides an example of how such issues affect domestic policy, bilateral relations, regional cooperation and European institutions.

An unexpected extra-territorial *fait accompli*

In early 2001, few people's thoughts were focused on Hungary's relations with its neighbours. It was assumed that Hungary, a NATO member since 1999, was well on the way to EU accession, together with its neighbours Slovenia and Slovakia. Bilateral relations between Hungary and Romania, and Hungary and Slovakia, were good. So too were relations, in Romania, between the Hungarian Democratic Federation of Romania (UDMR) and the governing Social Democratic Party (PSD) – who had agreed to a protocol on cooperation – and, in Slovakia, between the Hungarian Coalition Party (SMK) and the four other parties which made up the government coalition. Since the mid 1990s, the Romanian and Slovak governments had taken gradual but significant steps in adopting legislation and projects to protect and promote the Hungarian communities living in their respective countries. In Serbia, Hungarians enjoyed considerable self-government, held leading positions in local and regional government, and the leader of the Alliance of Vojvodina Hungarians, Jozsef Kasza, was Deputy Prime Minister. Quarrels about Hungarian minorities seemed to be giving way to common aspirations for economic cooperation, good-neighbourly relations, and European integration. Drafts of the Act on Hungarians Living in Neighbouring Countries therefore generated little interest either within states in the region, or among European intergovernmental organisations. It was assumed that Hungary had put to rest any minority-related disagreements through the bilateral treaties of the mid 1990s.

The Status Law was the idea of some Hungarians abroad. It appears to stem from a proposal for quasi-citizenship designed to accommodate the desire of some Hungarians abroad to have dual citizenship, so as not to be left outside of the Schengen zone when Hungary joined the EU. The drafters of the Law tried to temper some of the more radical ideas, the result being what they perceived as a harmless recognition of the status quo.

According to the Law, adopted on 10 June 2001, the aim is, *inter alia*, for the Parliament 'to comply with its responsibility for Hungarians living abroad and to promote the preservation and development of their manifold relations with Hungary',[1] and to 'ensure that Hungarians living in neighbouring countries form part of the Hungarian nation as a whole to promote and preserve their well-being and awareness of national identity within their home country'.[2] The idea was to support Hungarians living in other countries in their communities, thereby protecting and promoting their culture and discouraging brain-drain, particularly after Hungary joined the European Union. It was, in effect, a type of transborder cultural extra-territoriality designed to discourage emigration while preventing assimilation.

The assistance foreseen in the Law would be provided to those who, on the basis of a recommendation from an 'organisation representing the Hungarian national community in the country concerned', would be certified as being of 'Hungarian nationality'[3] and issued with a Certificate of Hungarian Nationality.

The principle of the Law was more significant than the actual benefits or assistance that it provided. In the field of culture, persons falling within the scope of the Law would be entitled, in Hungary, to rights identical to those of Hungarian citizens, for example use of public cultural institutions, access to cultural goods, access to state-run public libraries, the possibility to become a member of the Hungarian Academy of Sciences, be awarded distinctions and prizes of the Republic of Hungary as well as eligibility for state scholarships. Modest assistance was also foreseen for travel benefits, and public service media in Hungary were encouraged to transmit information on Hungary and the Hungarian 'nation' to Hungarians abroad. No big deal.

More controversial was employment, social assistance and education. Article 15 stated that persons falling within the scope of the Act could be employed on the territory of Hungary. Persons who took up such employment would then pay, unless otherwise provided for by international agreement, for health insurance and a pension contribution and then be eligible for social security provisions and health services in the Republic of Hungary – hardly a way of discouraging emigration. It was also stated that students registered at public education institutions in neighbouring countries pursuing their studies in Hungarian could receive benefits, as could ethnic Hungarian teachers. Assistance would be channelled through 'public benefit organisations'.

The latter provisions were unprecedented. What Hungary did within its own jurisdiction was its own concern. But how it sought to assist 'kin' who are citizens of neighbouring countries outside its sovereign jurisdiction was a different story, and one which would become the focus of a protracted debate within Hungary, among Hungarians abroad and between Hungary and its neighbours.

Hungary ran into problems early on. The first indication was that, despite the Law's title, Austria was not included among the countries where the Law would have effects. Despite imaginative explanations by the Hungarian government, the real reason seems to be that the European Commission made it clear to the Hungarian government that any reference to Austria would be unacceptable because EU law forbids discrimination on the basis of nationality. The decision to delete Austria from the list of countries where the Law applied may have solved a short-term problem with the EU, but it proved to be a weak link later on. As Slovenia and

Slovakia moved closer to EU accession, they argued for the same legal treatment as Austria. Furthermore, the exclusion of Austria strengthened the case of those who portrayed the law as an attempt to roll back the Trianon Treaty of 1920 under which Hungary lost 60 per cent of its population and 70 per cent of its territory.

Romania and Slovakia, which have the biggest Hungarian communities and the most turbulent history with Hungary, were the most upset by the Law. They did not like what they perceived as Hungary's unilateral approach, or the fact that Hungary had not used existing agreements and mechanisms (like the Joint Committees created as a result of the bilateral treaties) in order to discuss the issue before it became law. They felt that they had been presented with a *fait accompli* and were now being told that it would be implemented on their territory. On 22 June, President Illiescu said that, in light of the Hungarian government's decision, he hoped it would not be necessary to suspend the basic treaty.[4] A week later he called the Law 'diversionist, provocative, anti-democratic and discriminatory' (RFE/RL 2001a). Foreign Minister Mircea Geoana characterised the Law as 'anachronistic and non-European' and said that it would not be applied in Romania (Ibid.). Prime Minister Adrian Nastase was particularly perturbed by the Law's labour provisions and said that 'Romania is no colony from which Hungary can recruit a workforce' (RFE/RL 2001b). The Slovak government suggested that Hungary's approach 'disturbed' good-neighbourly relations and regretted that better use had not been made of existing bilateral mechanisms.[5] Hungary described these public statements as 'incomprehensible and disproportionate'.[6]

The other effected states were either supportive or passive. On 10 July 2001 Hungarian and Croatian representatives declared that 'the Act on Hungarians Living in Neighbouring Countries has a favourable impact on regional stability, it promotes the preservation of the identity of Hungarians living in Croatia and their continued residence in [sic] their native soil'.[7] Croatia, perhaps, valued good relations with Hungary more than a row over limited benefits for a relatively small Hungarian community. The new government in Serbia and Montenegro also gave cautious support, more interested, no doubt, in repairing relations with an important European-oriented neighbour than with rocking the boat on this issue (BBC Monitoring Service 2001a). Serbia and Croatia may have also regarded the Law as a potentially useful precedent for supporting 'their' kin in neighbouring states. For its part, Ukraine was relatively quiet on the issue (Deutsche Presse Agentur 2001).[8] Slovenia, by Hungary's own admission, was never consulted.[9]

Internationalising the issue

On 21 June, Prime Minister Nastase requested the (Council of Europe's) European Commission for Democracy through Law, also known as the

Venice Commission, to examine the compatibility of the Status Law with European standards and the norms and principles of contemporary public international law. Wanting to avoid stigmatisation, on 2 July Foreign Minister Janos Martonyi of Hungary – arguing that the Hungarian case was not unique – requested that the Venice Commission carry out a broader comparative study of the recent tendencies of European legislation and practice concerning the preferential treatment of national minorities by their kin-state. A working group was formed and agreed to present a report in the autumn. The Parliamentary Assembly of the Council of Europe (PACE) also decided to study the situation.

The European Commission watched from a distance. While it urged Romania to tone down its rhetoric, it did not say much about the substance of the law. On 26 June, the Commissioner responsible for enlargement, Guenther Verheugen, said that he thought that the Law did not contradict the EU's association agreements, but his team would need time to review the details further to see if it was fully in line with EU law.

A positive trend?

The Venice Commission issued its 'Report on the Preferential Treatment of National Minorities by Their Kin-State' on 22 October 2001. It underlined the importance of an adequate and effective protection of national minorities as an integral part of the protection of human rights and fundamental freedoms and as an important part of promoting stability, democratic security and peace in Europe (European Commission for Democracy through Law 2001). It highlighted the full implementation of international agreements as a priority for all member states of the Council of Europe. In a controversial *non-sequitur* that followed, the report stated:

> Against this background, the emerging of new and original forms of minority protection, particularly by the kin-States, constitutes a positive trend insofar as they can contribute to the realisation of this goal.
>
> (Ibid.)

Nevertheless, a few paragraphs later the report qualified this statement by saying that, in the Commission's opinion, 'the possibility of States to adopt unilateral measures on the protection of their kin-minorities, irrespective of whether they live in neighbouring or in other countries, is conditional upon the respect of the following principles: 'a) territorial sovereignty of States; b) *pacta sunt servanda* [treaties must be respected and performed in good faith]; c) friendly relations amongst States, and d) the respect of human rights and fundamental freedoms, in particular the prohibition of discrimination' (Ibid.).

These limitations were expanded upon in some detail. For example, the report noted that 'a State can legitimately issue laws or regulations concerning foreign citizens without seeking the prior consent of the relevant States of citizenship, as long as the effects of these laws or regulations are to take place within its borders only'. But when the law specifically aims at deploying its effects on foreign citizens in a foreign country, 'it is not conceivable, in fact, that the home-State of the individuals concerned should not have a word to say on the matter' (Ibid.: 13). A nuance was made concerning fields like culture and education. Here, according to the report, 'if there exists an international custom, the consent of the home-State can be presumed and kin-States may take unilateral administrative or legislative measures' (Ibid.). That said, 'in the absence of a permissive rule to the contrary – either an international custom or convention – a State cannot exercise its powers, in any form, on the territory of other States' (Ibid.). Furthermore, if there is an international custom or convention, for example a bilateral treaty already in force, then (bearing in mind the principle that *pacta sunt servanda*) legislation or regulations on the preferential treatment of kin-minorities should not duplicate these existing instruments, unless 'the home-State concerned had been consulted and had approved of this step or had implicitly – but unambiguously – accepted it, by not raising objections' (Ibid.: 15). It also noted that 'in case of disputes on the implementation or interpretation of bilateral treaties, all the existing procedures for settling the dispute must be used in good faith, and such unilateral measures can only be taken by the kin-State if and after these procedures prove ineffective' (Ibid.: 17).

The report also underlined the importance of good-neighbourly relations. It reminded readers that friendly inter-state relations are 'unanimously considered as a precondition for peace and stability in Europe' (Ibid.: 15). Therefore, 'States should abstain from taking unilateral measures, which would risk compromising the climate of co-operation with other States' (Ibid.). In that respect, it warned against the proposed 'Hungarian certificate' creating a political bond between the holder and the kin-state, or being used as a substitute for an identity document issued by the authorities of the home-state (Ibid.).

On the issue of discrimination, the Venice Commission said that benefits relating to culture and education would be permissible if the differential treatment they engender can be justified by the legitimate aim of fostering cultural links between the minority and the kin-state (Ibid.: 17). It rather vaguely noted that 'preferential treatment can not be granted in fields other than education and culture, save in exceptional cases and if shown to pursue a legitimate aim and be proportionate to that aim' (Ibid.: 18).

The Venice Commission report was a rather damning indictment of the Act on Hungarians Living in Neighbouring Countries. Slovakia and Romania claimed victory. Remarkably, the Hungarians said that it vindicated their position. The Foreign Ministry seized on the reference to the Law as 'a positive trend'.[10] Foreign Ministry State Secretary Zsolt Nemeth's interpretation was that the Venice Commission did not conclude that the

Law should be amended. It was therefore time for the Slovak and Romanian governments to come back to the negotiating table 'to conduct consultations on the nitty-gritty of the instructions concerning its implementation' (BBC Monitoring Service 2001b). Furthermore, Nemeth said that the Venice Commission report constituted a new international standard for minority protection, enabling the Hungarian Status Law to have an impact on debates about the future of Europe (Perry 2001). Foreign Minister Martonyi (not a member of the ruling Fidesz party) was more circumspect and suggested that the necessary 'adjustments' would be made to address the points raised by the Venice Commission.

A dangerous precedent

The OSCE High Commissioner on National Minorities, Rolf Ekeus, profoundly disagreed. On 26 October he issued a statement entitled 'Sovereignty, responsibility, and national minorities' (Ekeus 2001). In it, he stressed the importance of minorities having their rights protected and being integrated within the societies where they live. He stated unequivocally: 'Protection of minority rights is the obligation of the State where the minority resides.' He warned that 'History shows that when States take unilateral steps on the basis of national kinship to protect national minorities living outside of the jurisdiction of the State, this sometimes leads to tensions and frictions, even violent conflict.' He noted that he is obliged by his mandate 'to focus special attention on situations where similar steps, without the consent of the State of residence, are contemplated'.

He went on to stress the importance of the international legal regime that has been developed since the Second World War, following the principle that protection of human rights and fundamental freedoms, including for persons belonging to national minorities, 'Is the responsibility of the State having jurisdiction with regard to the persons concerned'. This, as he said, 'is not only a cornerstone of contemporary international law and requisite for peace, it is necessary for good governance, particularly in multi-ethnic States.'

Because nations and states seldom overlap, national groups are often divided by borders. Ekeus noted that

> although a State with a titular majority population may have an interest in persons of the same ethnicity living abroad, this does not entitle or imply, in any way, a right under international law to exercise jurisdiction over these persons. At the same time it does not preclude a State from granting certain preferences within its jurisdiction, on a non-discriminatory basis. Nor does it preclude persons belonging to a national minority from maintaining unimpeded contacts across frontiers with citizens of other States with whom they share common ethnic or national origins.

In short, one may have an interest in one's kin abroad and be interested in offering them support. The issue is not if one can do this, it is how. After all, as Ekeus pointed out, 'it is a basic principle of international law that the State can act only within its jurisdiction which extends to its territory and citizenry'. It is up to the state where the minorities live to protect and promote the individuals and groups concerned. This can be augmented by bilateral arrangements within the context of multilateral norms.

The Hungarians were wrong-footed and upset. They felt that they had been blind-sided in a way that was uncharacteristic of the High Commissioner's style of quiet and cooperative diplomacy, and they were concerned that the statement would make the already stubborn Romanians and Slovaks even more intransigent. Nevertheless, Ekeus had no regrets. While being concerned about falling out with the Hungarian government, he felt that it was important to come out strongly in defence of international standards. Indeed, his statement became a reference – particularly for opponents of the law – for the duration of the discussion on kin-states and minority protection.

Countdown to implementation

Prospects for bilateral agreements seemed remote. On the one hand, the international community (particularly the Venice Commission and the OSCE High Commissioner on National Minorities) had raised significant doubts about the Law. This vindicated the argument of Romania and Slovakia that the Law was fundamentally flawed and needed a major overhaul, if it was to be implemented at all. On the other hand, the Hungarian government did not seem willing (or sufficiently pressured) to amend the Law and only wanted to discuss its implementation. While the EU and the OSCE urged the parties to resolve the issues bilaterally, the parties themselves had different interpretations of what this meant. For the Romanians and Slovaks, it meant Hungary should listen to their concerns and make the necessary changes (preferably in the Law itself). For the Hungarians, it meant that the Romanians and Slovaks should stop obstructing agreement on the Law and be specific as to which aspects of its implementation they felt were discriminatory and extra-territorial.

The Hungarian government argued that there was enough room for manoeuvre through the implementation decrees to satisfy the points made by neighbouring states and European intergovernmental bodies. The European Commission seemed to indicate that it could live with this approach. In its regular report on Hungary, issued on 13 November 2001, it paid particular attention to Article 27 (2), emphasising that, as noted in that article, 'the Law will need to be aligned with the *acquis* at the latest upon accession, since it is currently not in line with the principle of non-discrimination laid down in the Treaty (Articles 6, 7, 12 and 13)'. The report also urged further bilateral discussions in order for Hungary to reach agreement with its neighbours as regards future implementing legislation.[11] The view that the problems with the Law could be ironed out through implementation was echoed by Commissioner Verheugen who quipped that 'the proof of the pudding is in the eating'.

This was not much comfort to the neighbouring states. They argued that if this was a framework law, where were the implementation decrees? And if these decrees were so important, why were they not incorporated into the Law itself? Besides, what was the big hurry with implementation of the Law by 1 January 2002? If the key to the effectiveness of the Law was its implementation, and implementation of the Law was to occur, in part, in neighbouring states, would it not be correct (bearing in mind the lack of transparency in drafting the Law in the first place and the points made by the Venice Commission and HCNM) to consult with the states concerned? The Slovak and Romanian governments also stressed to the international community that this was not strictly a bilateral issue between Hungary and some of its neighbours; this was an issue of precedent with serious implications for international law, minority protection and inter-state relations.

The Romanians did not want to be guinea pigs for an unprecedented law that was not in line with international standards:

> For us it is quite clear that these rights granted on ethnic grounds are nowhere to be found in the European standards for minority protection ... If Europe wants to go for [new rules], that is okay for us, we will not oppose them. However, this law will act as a precedent for the Albanians living abroad, as well as for Russians living in the Baltic states. We can not create an island of certain rules.
>
> (*Nine O'clock* 2001)

The Slovaks took the position that since the Law was a violation of international legal norms like sovereignty, equality and respect for jurisdiction of independent states, it would not be a party to its implementation. They expressed concern about institutionalised bonds between Hungary and its kin abroad. They had concerns about how benefits would be distributed (according to Slovak law) and how Hungarian certificates would be handed out. They felt that this was unilateral interference in their jurisdiction. Furthermore, they felt that the law was discriminatory and created a double standard based on ethnicity. This was particularly acute in the case of support for education. They argued that handing out cash to parents who sent their children to Hungarian language schools in Slovakia amounted to a bribe and/or ethnically-based social assistance. They also asked why the mechanisms created by the Treaty on Good Neighbourly and Friendly Cooperation of 1995[12] had not been used more effectively in explaining the Law in the first place, or indeed why the

Treaty had not been used as a basis for expanding support for Hungarians in Slovakia. Either the Status Law should be brought in line with international law, or Slovakia – like Austria – should be excluded from the states where it applies. Failing that, the Slovak government would simply refuse to allow for the implementation of the Law within its jurisdiction.

Time was running out. The Law was due to be implemented on 1 January 2002. There was still no resolution on implementation of the Law, and few implementation decrees. Therefore, it was not clear how the Hungarian government would implement the Law in neighbouring states. How far would neighbouring states go to protect their sovereignty, and what would be the consequences? Romania warned that it would take 'all necessary measures at international and domestic level in order to prevent the occurrence of negative consequences generated by the implementation of the Law'.[13] Slovakia threatened counter-veiling legislation.

In a meeting with Foreign Minister Martonyi at the OSCE Ministerial Council in Bucharest on 1 December 2001, High Commissioner Ekeus recommended that the Hungarian government get rid of the extra-territorial and discriminatory aspects of the Law, and focus (or restrict) the benefits foreseen in the Law to culture (in the broadest sense). That way the Hungarian government and Hungarians abroad would be satisfied that the cultural bonds between them would be strengthened, Hungary's neighbours would not be annoyed, and no bad precedent would be set. As a face-saving measure, Hungarian certificates could be issued early in the new year. While these were being produced, details could be worked out concerning what benefits cardholders would be entitled to and how they would receive them.

A deal with the Romanians

On 22 December in Budapest, the Romanian and Hungarian governments agreed to a Memorandum of Understanding (MoU) 'concerning the Law on Hungarians Living in Neighbouring Countries and issues of bilateral co-operation'. The Romanian government secured agreement on most points which it had objected to. It won assurances that all Romanian citizens, regardless of ethnic origin, would enjoy the same conditions and treatment in the field of employment on the basis of a work permit on the territory of the Republic of Hungary. The parties also agreed to review an agreement on seasonal workers. Romanian citizens of non-ethnic Hungarian identity (i.e. spouses) would not enjoy any benefits under the Status Law.[14] Some clarity was given about the issuing and content of certificates, for example that the benefit cards would only be issued in Hungary. Most significantly, the agreement included a commitment by the Hungarian government to 'initiate the review and necessary amendments' of the Law within six months after the signature of the Memorandum of Understanding.[15] This was the first public commitment by the Hungarian government to amend the Law.

The MoU did not solve all problems between Romania and Hungary but it was, in the words of Romanian Foreign Minister Geoana, 'a temporary solution in order to avoid the predictable tensions related to the moment of 1 January 2002'.[16] However, it was, as Geoana said, no substitute for the suspension of the implementation of the Law or its amendment. That was still the aim.[17] Until then, 'as an international agreement which prevails upon domestic legal norms, the Memorandum has the advantage to inactivate the unacceptable provisions of the Law'.[18] This was a win–win situation for the Romanians. They had secured a deal on employment and a commitment by the Hungarian government to revise the Law within six months. As far as the Hungarians were concerned, they had silenced their toughest critic and could go ahead with implementation of the Law. Furthermore, the two states had demonstrated that they could resolve a thorny issue bilaterally and that disagreement over the Status Law would not stand in the way of strategic and economic cooperation.

Trouble with the Slovaks

No similar deal was struck with the Slovaks. As a result, the Slovaks found themselves isolated – which had perhaps been the Hungarian strategy all along. However, the Hungarian government knew that it could not unilaterally implement the Status Law in Slovakia without the Slovak government's understanding, which did not seem likely. Some sort of agreement needed to be reached, but how?

Already strained relations were made worse by the issuance of Hungarian certificates in early 2002. The certificates looked like passports of the Hungarian nation. They were green, passport-sized booklets with the crown of Saint Stephen on the cover. In case there was any doubt about the symbolism of the crown (in a country that is a republic and not a monarchy), the booklet included a reference to the Constitution of 1989 that says, 'The Republic of Hungary bears a sense of responsibility for the fate of Hungarians living outside its borders and shall promote and foster their relations with Hungary.' The booklet included pages for travel benefits, student benefits, teacher benefits and employment benefits. In short, they included elements that had nothing to do with support for culture, the symbolism was blatantly nationalistic, and the format and content implied a political bond between the state of Hungary and the certificate holders, which the Venice Commission had warned against. For all these reasons, some neighbouring states and international organisations were alarmed while some Hungarians abroad hailed the certificates as an important recognition of kinship among members of the Hungarian nation.

On 7 February the Slovak National Council (Parliament) issued a statement (supported by 112 of the 129 MPs) in which Members of Parliament expressed their belief that the Act on Hungarians Living in Neighbouring Countries, by its purpose of extra-territoriality and by asserting the principle of one-sidedness at supporting the citizens of neighbouring countries claiming Hungarian nationality, interferes with the exclusive territorial and personal jurisdiction of the Slovak Republic and seeks to create a precedent in a sphere of exclusive scope of activities of a sovereign state.[19]

The Parliament considered this a 'violation of international law and interference with the integrity of the intrastate legal order of the Slovak Republic' and said that it 'does not agree with the implementation or the effects of this act on the territory of the Slovak Republic'.[20]

Still, Slovakia could not categorically reject any support from Hungary because it has bilateral and international obligations that foresee the possibility of support from Hungary to Hungarians living in Slovakia. Article 18 of the Framework Convention for the Protection of National Minorities, for example, encourages parties to conclude agreements with, *inter alia*, neighbouring states in order to ensure the protection of persons belonging to national minorities concerned and to take measures to encourage transfrontier cooperation. Counter-measures aimed at ethnic Hungarians living in Slovakia could have opened Slovakia to criticism of discrimination, and could have led to social instability not to mention the possible collapse of the Slovak government.

In Budapest, Prime Minister Viktor Orban's pre-election rhetoric added more fuel to the fire. On 13 February he made a less than subtle reference to the fact that Slovakia's decision to join NATO would have to be debated and approved by the Hungarian Parliament (CTK 2002). Orban's public statements, generously described by *The Economist* as 'breezy nationalism' (*The Economist* 2002), included a reference to Transylvania as part of Hungary's 'living space in the Carpathian Basin' (BBC Monitoring Service 2002), a pledge to re-open the debate on the Benes decrees, and a refusal to rule out governing with the support of the far-right MIEP. He also used the Status Law as an example of his party's dedication to defending the interests of the Hungarian nation, and suggested that those parties who criticised the Law were not true patriots.

But if the Status Law was regarded as a means of improving Fidesz's chances of being re-elected, it failed. While Fidesz won 48.6 per cent of the vote on 21 April and took 188 seats, the Socialists, with 46.1 per cent and 178 seats, were able to come to power with the support of the (liberal) Alliance of Free Democrats (SZDSZ) who won 19 seats and therefore held the balance of power.

New government, same problem

The Socialists had voted for the Status Law in 2001, but had criticised the MoU with Romania. The SZDSZ had been the only party to express serious reservations about the Law in 2001, and now called for changes to bring it in line with international standards. The new Foreign Minister Laszlo Kovacs – who had been instrumental in concluding bilateral treaties with Slovakia and Romania in the mid 1990s – said that the law would be amended according to four principles or guidelines: the original intention of the Act will be retained; amendments will have the support of Hungarians abroad; the legitimate concerns of neighbouring states will be addressed; and the Act will be brought in line with international stand-ards.[21] This was a tall order and, in the eyes of many, virtually impossible because of the contradictory objectives.

The Socialists were not the only ones in a tight spot. Representatives of Hungarians in neighbouring countries, particularly in Slovakia and Romania, were in a lose–lose situation. The Status Law strained their rela-tions with Budapest, if Budapest did not deliver, and strained their rela-tions with their government allies (in the case of Romania)[22] and coalition partners (in the case of Slovakia) if the extra-territorial and discriminatory aspects were not resolved. Furthermore, representatives of Hungarian minorities, particularly in Slovakia and Romania, had difficulty explaining to their constituencies that benefits which would be available pursuant to the law were relatively minor; hard-liners had played up the merits of the Status Law out of proportion. As the leader of the UDMR, Bela Marko, explained to the OSCE High Commissioner, people on both sides of the argument were making a mountain out of a mole hill: 'my constituents think that they will actually be getting a great deal when in fact the bene-fits are limited. And the opponents of the law also think that the law will deliver a great deal when in fact it is mostly symbolic.'

A blueprint for compromise

Some signs of improvement were evident in the summer of 2002. Prime Ministers Nastase and Medygessy met on 6 July in Cluj-Napoca and developed a good rapport (aided by Medygessy's ability to speak Roman-ian, having been raised in Transylvania). Medygessy publicly announced that amendment of the Preference Law (as the Socialists liked to call it) would be on the agenda for the autumn session of Parliament. On 17 July the Hungarian Standing Committee (MAERT) – representing Hungarians abroad – also agreed to amend the Law.

The OSCE High Commissioner on National Minorities hoped that the summer could be used to hammer out a compromise. He was aware of the strains on all sides, and the danger of waiting too long for a satisfactory resolution. As it became evident that the Hungarians had no blueprint for amending the law, he tried to spur them into action. Ekeus invited the Hungarian government to send a group of experts to confidential, expert-level consultations in the coastal resort of Noordwijk in the Netherlands on 26 and 27 August 2002. Here a draft revision of the Law was hammered out that was, in the interpretation of the High Commissioner's experts, in line with minimum international standards. As the High Commissioner said in a letter to Foreign Minister Kovacs, dated 28 August 2002, the main intention of the changes was 'to allay concerns about extra-territoriality and discrimination and to clarify the limitations of benefits and assistance to ethnic Hungarians who are the intended beneficiaries.' For example, in line with recommendations of the Venice Commission, explicit reference was made to respect for the territorial sovereignty of states, *pacta sunt servanda*, friendly relations amongst states, and respect of human rights and fundamental freedoms, in particular the prohibition of discrimination.[23] Elsewhere, language was either added or deleted to limit the scope of the Law to support for culture (language and education). In order to overcome the issue of discrimination, the suggestion was made to give support to institutions rather than individuals. The High Commissioner's legal team insisted that benefits be solely given on the basis of maintaining cultural links with Hungary. Provisions relating to social and economic support were dropped. Recommendations were also made to eliminate any discrimination on the basis of ethnicity. Language relating to the issuing of Hungarian certificates was simplified.

Stepping up the pressure

In late October 2002 a new draft was finally made public. Since it took into account many of the recommendations made at Noordwijk, the Hungarians looked for the High Commissioner's blessing as well as his support in explaining the amendments to neighbouring states. This was not forthcoming. On 7 November 2002, Ekeus sent a letter to Foreign Minister Kovacs in which he noted that while the latest draft showed some progress, the proposed revisions did not go far enough. He cautioned that 'there remain some further steps to be taken to bring the Act into full conformity with international law and to allay the legitimate concerns of neighbouring States some of which persist due to existing uncertainty in the Act'. He also implied that while he understood the need for flexibility – taking into account the number of divergent interests that the Hungarian government had to balance – basic principles of international law are non-negotiable:

> While prospective amendments, including those that I have recommended, may not completely satisfy the points made by neighbouring States, they should not go below minimum standards.[24]

With the EU Copenhagen Summit around the corner, Commissioner Verheugen became increasingly concerned about how this quarrel could affect EU-accession. While the EU did not want to be overly critical of Hungary, it did not want to inherit an unresolved dispute between two new members.

The pressure was building on Hungary. Kovacs personally became more involved in seeking a resolution. Winning over Fidesz, and getting the same type of support for the amendments as there had been for the original Law, was virtually impossible because the domestic political scene was so polarised. Fidesz accused the government of being the 'hangman of the Status Law' (RFE/RL 2003), failing to protect the interests of the Hungarian nation, and selling out Hungarians abroad. Criticism from the World Federation of Hungarians was also shrill.

A key consideration was to win over representatives of Hungarians living in neighbouring countries to the possibility of further amendments. This was done, with some cajoling, through a meeting of MAERT experts on 17 November (although they warned that if some conditions were not met, they reserved the right to revisit the issue[25]). The Hungarian negotiators were now more or less clear on what they had to do to get the support of European institutions (even if they were not there yet), they had a conditional blessing from Hungarians abroad, and they could interpret the revised Law in such a way that it still supported Hungarians abroad. The challenge now was to convince the neighbours, particularly Slovakia and Romania.

Things did not go well. On 26 November Prime Ministers Dzurinda and Medgyessy met in Budapest. Dzurinda stuck to his guns saying 'Slovakia rejects the Status Law, despite the amendments made to it'. Medgyessy said that for the Slovaks

> the only acceptable solution would be to abolish the status law altogether. I, naturally, can not volunteer to do this; the status law has been adopted by the Hungarian parliament. So, one must accept that we cannot progress in this respect.
>
> (Hungarian Radio 2002)

Dzurinda subsequently warned that the implementation of the Law would be blocked 'by all possible means' and that 'not one forint' would be spent in Slovakia. Needless to say, Medgyessy and Kovacs were exasperated. One may speculate that Dzurinda was buoyed by his unexpected re-election, the prospect of joining NATO, the increasingly likely accession of Slovakia to the EU at the same time as Hungary, and the support for this position from European institutions on the issue. But his absolute intransigence risked painting Slovakia into a corner. By saying that he would reject the Law, even if it were amended, he did not leave the Hungarians or himself much room for manoeuvre.

Status Law fatigue

In December 2002 further amendments were made to the Law and this time it looked as if the international community was content. On 20

January 2003, Verheugen wrote to Kovacs saying that 'the new proposal seems to constitute a substantial improvement over earlier versions'. He was particularly pleased to see that 'you have taken into account my earlier observations and that the language and the declared purpose of the law have changed significantly, thus giving no scope for queries'. This almost unequivocal support was an overwhelming endorsement as far as the Hungarian government was concerned. Still, Verheugen conditioned his support by saying that

> taking into account that the implementing rules to the law are not yet available, I am sure you will understand that I must reserve my final position until I have also seen the implementing legislation.

Furthermore, he reminded Foreign Minister Kovacs that

> the agreement of your neighbouring countries would be needed on the extra-territorial application of the law in conformity with the principles embedded in your new proposal, in particular those cited in Section 2(2), such as the principle of territorial sovereignty of states, friendly relations, etc. I trust that you will be able [to] come to such an agreement in the near future.[26]

This was echoed by a letter from Ekeus to Kovacs, dated 23 January, in which the High Commissioner praised the Hungarian government for proposed modifications 'which I believe take into account the essential concerns and recommendations which I previously conveyed to you'.[27] But this was not *carte blanche* support. Ekeus noted that

> with respect to the implementation of the revised Act, I observe that much will depend upon the specific content of implementing legislation and, as foreseen and necessary, agreement with your neighbouring States. In this connection, I trust that this will be achieved in full conformity with the principles contained in Section 2(2) of the revised Act.[28]

Securing written endorsements of Verheugen and Ekeus was regarded as a major coup by the Hungarian diplomats involved. Now they could claim that the Law lived up to international standards, thereby silencing the main criticism of their neighbours.

Amending the Law

On 28 May 2003, the Hungarian government felt that it had done enough to accommodate all concerns and, after final consultations with MAERT, brought the amendments to Parliament. Slovakia and Romania were again offended, saying that they only found out about the changes through the media. The Slovak government sent an official note to the Hungarian government on 29 May saying that the draft had been submitted to Parliament 'without acquainting the Government of the Slovak Republic with the text of the bill'.[29] By doing so, 'the Government of Hungary annulled the space for seeking a solution based on agreement of both Governments'.[30] Furthermore, the Slovaks reiterated their view that the Act on Hungarians Living in Neighbouring Countries 'cannot have any effects on the sovereign territory of the Slovak Republic without the consent of the competent constitutional authorities of the Slovak Republic'.[31] Despite these reservations, and complaints by Fidesz that amendments to the law had completely undone its original purpose and substance, the amendments were adopted on 23 June 2003, two years after the adoption of the original Law.

On 25 June, at long last, the Parliamentary Assembly of the Council of Europe adopted its report on the preferential treatment of national minorities by the kin-state. While welcoming, in principle, assistance given by kin-states to kin-minorities in other states in order to help these kin-minorities preserve their cultural, linguistic and ethnic identity, the Assembly stressed that

> such kin-states must be careful that the form and substance of the assistance given is also accepted by the states of which the members of the kin-minorities are citizens, and to which the basic rules contained in the Framework Convention on National Minorities are applicable.[32]

It repeated the main points made by the Venice Commission and the HCNM. Interestingly, the Assembly noted that 'up to now there is no common European legal definition of the concept of the "nation"'.[33] As if to demonstrate the type of problems that this can create, it referred to 'Magyars' rather than Hungarians to make a distinction between people identifying themselves as part of the Hungarian nation (the Hungarian 'national' cultural and linguistic community) as distinct from Hungarian citizens.[34]

The Assembly concluded that some issues, like the scope of potential beneficiaries and the role played by minority organisations in implementing the Law 'could possibly have been accepted or modified had they been preceded by bilateral discussions and agreements, such as the MoU between Hungary and Romania'.[35] While noting with satisfaction the amendments made by the Parliament of Hungary on 23 June, 'thus responding in part to the critical comments that have been made', the PACE said that the amendments were not based on bilateral agreements with the neighbouring countries concerned.[36] It therefore urged the government and parliament of Hungary

to find ways to make further amendments to the law of 19 June 2001
... in such a way that it is based on bilateral discussions and agreements with the neighbouring countries and meets the proposals of
the Venice Commission and the criticism of the existing law by the
OSCE HCNM and by the Parliamentary Assembly itself.[37]

This was a non-starter as far as the Hungarians were concerned. There was
no way that they were going to further amend the Law. Rather, they
sought to come to agreements with their neighbours on ways to implement the amended Law.

While the Romanian government was satisfied that the amended
version of the Law took into account many of its concerns, it wanted to
fine tune some elements concerning the Law's implementation in
Romania. In effect, it wanted an updated version of the Nastase–Orban
agreement to reflect the updated version of the Law. Negotiations on an
agreement began in July in the Joint Inter-Governmental Romanian–
Hungarian Commission. A bilateral agreement was reached in August
which was signed by Prime Ministers Nastase and Medgyessy on 23 September in Bucharest. This enabled the implementation of the Status Law
in Romania. Nastase described it as 'a battle for Europe that we have won
together'.[38]

The Slovaks felt that, again, the Romanians had sold out on their position of principle. As far as they were concerned, they would not enter into
a similar agreement that referred explicitly to implementation of the
Status Law. But they had no objection to signing a bilateral agreement on
improving cooperation in the field of education and culture. After long
negotiations, mainly through a joint commission of experts, an intergovernmental agreement between Hungary and Slovakia on mutual support
of national minorities in the field of education and culture was agreed on
7 December 2003.

By the end of 2003 major disagreements over the Act on Hungarians
Living in Neighbouring Countries were finally resolved. But while that
may have been the end of a long and complex political and diplomatic
process that provoked an intense debate about kin-states, minorities and
bilateral relations, it was not the end of the story. Indeed, it now looks as if
new chapters are being opened.

Conclusion: kinship and citizenship

The Act on Hungarians Living in Neighbouring Countries, as it has been
amended, is no longer a dangerous precedent, but it is hardly a positive
trend either. While most of the extra-territorial and discriminatory elements have been removed, a precedent has been set and it will be interesting to see if and how it is followed. Romania – of all countries – has tried
to enact similar legislation! Speaking to representatives of the Romanian

diaspora on 9 August 2003, Prime Minister Nastase (arch critic of the Status Law for two years) said 'whether we like it or not, the most efficient, the most advanced, and the most dynamic model is the Hungarian model'. The consequences of this decision on Romania's relations with Vlachs and, in particular, 'kin' in Moldova should be interesting to see.

This is uncharted territory. The Venice Commission report was some help, but when it comes to relations between 'mother' states and their kin, the Hungarian case is a rare contemporary example for which there has been only limited legal and political guidance. As Brigid Fowler points out, on the Status Law issue, 'Europe' (whether it be the EU, the OSCE or the Council of Europe) was appealed to for adjudication, but ' "Europe" finds that its own principles on the issue are far from clear' (Fowler 2002: 9; Malinverni 2002: 313–17). Does this mean that when it came to advising and cautioning the Hungarian government, European institutions were making it up as they went along? No, for although the extent of kin-state support may not be clear, international law is unambiguous about what is *not* allowed, and this was reflected in the OSCE High Commissioner's statement of 26 October 2001, the Venice Commission's report and the view of the EU. To summarise, protection of minorities rights is the obligation of the state where the minority resides. Although a state with a titular majority population may have an interest or 'concern' in persons of the same ethnicity living abroad, this does not entitle or imply, in any way, a right under international law to exercise jurisdiction over these persons. At the same time, it does not preclude a state from granting certain preferences within its jurisdiction, on a non-discriminatory basis. Nor does it preclude persons belonging to a national minority from maintaining unimpeded contacts across frontiers with citizens of other states with whom they share common ethnic or national origins. Any support from the kin-state should be provided in a way consistent with the laws of the states concerned, in the spirit of bilateral treaties and in line with international law, in particular the principles of the territorial integrity of states, *pacta sunt servanda* and friendly relations amongst states. Furthermore, the assistance should be offered with the aim to promote intercultural tolerance, dialogue and cultural pluralism.

A lesson to all is the importance of states in protecting and promoting minorities within their sovereign jurisdiction. The point should not only be made by governments in reaction to 'interference' from kin-states. If host-states did more to protect and promote minorities, the complaints of kin-states would ring hollow. The necessary steps should be taken within multiethnic societies to guarantee equality of opportunity, protection of minority rights and languages and ensure the effective participation of minorities in public life. Otherwise, ethno-cultural bonds – kinship – will trump citizenship. If minorities feel that state structures, laws and institutions are stacked against them and in favour of the titular majority they will feel that ethnic ties offer more than a social contract. This will accentuate their sense of ethnic uniqueness and defensiveness vis-à-vis fellow citizens from the majority population. If this leads to closer links with a kin-state, it may strengthen schisms in society even more and generate tendencies of either assimilation or isolation, even separation.

Hungary argued that it needed a Status Law to protect Hungarians against possible assimilation. This was a veiled critique of ethno-cultural majoritarianism. But instead of trying to work harder with the states concerned to develop minority rights and opportunities by strengthening civil society, the Hungarian model replicates the very ethno-cultural majoritarianism that it sought to protect its minorities against. This is a slippery slope towards the nation-state and pan-national movements of the nineteenth century. If one wanted to go down this road, one could outsource responsibility for protection of minority culture to the kin-state. But this is disintegrative, suggests that the host-state does not see the merit in protecting cultural diversity, and could lead to a deepening of concerns about the loyalty and integration of minorities and the role of the kin-state. In short, one should move away from ethnicity and nationalism as politically mobilising principles, both domestically and in terms of the kin-state paradigm.

That is not to say that there is no scope for support from neighbouring states that share the same national culture as people on the other side of the border. As Rainer Hofman[39] points out,

> it seems indeed possible that kin-states, by broadcasting programmes dealing with issues of particular interest to persons belonging to certain national minorities abroad, or by providing text-books and scholarships as well as sending (and financing) qualified teachers, or by financially supporting cultural and other activities such as the production of print and audio-visual media and the activities of libraries, theatres, and editing houses, or even contributing to the costs of running educational institutions such as private kindergartens and schools, might contribute to the protection and promotion of the distinct identity of persons belonging to national minorities and, thus, assist the state primarily responsible in the fulfilment of this task.
>
> (Hofman 2002: 257)

The challenge is to do this in a way that does not raise security concerns. Kin-state relations with minorities usually provoke arguments with the host-state over history, borders, loyalty and the danger of external interference or the threat of a fifth column. This is fertile ground for populists and nationalists on all sides. One way of de-securitising such situations is to ensure that there is no discrimination on the basis of ethnicity. If one promotes culture to all who are interested (like the Goethe Institute or the British Council), as opposed to only for people of one's kin, then one will avoid discrimination and build wider appreciation for one's cultural heritage.

Another key consideration is transparency and cooperation. There should be no unilateral steps from the kin-state and any initiatives should be properly discussed with all those concerned. This should be feasible in the context of bilateral agreements, and modalities could be worked out in joint commissions and other meetings of experts that include representatives of the minority concerned. In most cases, at least in Central and Eastern Europe, these frameworks and mechanisms already exist. The Status Law debate shows what happens when they are not properly or sufficiently used. Many problems could probably have been avoided if bilateral discussions had been more frequent and meaningful before the Status Law was presented to Parliament. Another lesson is that minorities need to be involved in bilateral discussions that affect them. The minority has the most to gain from outside assistance and the most to lose if it is improperly handled. It understands best its needs and interests, and the possibilities and limitations of fulfilling them in relation to both the kin-state and its own state authorities.

The debate over the Act on Hungarians Living in Neighbouring Countries should be a wake-up call to the EU. If part of the European transformation process will be the erosion of borders, and if one accepts that states and nations seldom overlap, then weakening state sovereignty (within a supra-state entity that encourages diversity) may cause some to seek to strengthen national unity. If, in the past, ethno-cultural union was hindered by borders and borders are now losing their significance, then – goes the argument – European Union facilitates national union. Is this indeed the path the EU wants to follow?

In retrospect, we can thank Hungary for bringing to the surface an issue that had always been there, but had not received much attention from legal experts and intergovernmental organisations. We are now better aware of the legal framework and the possibilities and limitations of support by kin-states. If handled well, bilateral cooperation over minority support can be a source of improving the position of minorities. If handled badly it can strain inter-ethnic and bilateral relations. These are lessons worth learning because this issue will no doubt recur in the process of European transformation with implications for intra-EU cooperation and relations between EU states and their neighbours.

7 Minorities, violence and statehood on the European periphery

Charles King

The widespread belief in a resurgence of something called 'ethnic conflict' in the 1990s was in large part a function of timing and geography. Conflicts that had long been labelled 'ideological' during the cold war contained clear 'ethnic' components, but they had taken place in far-away lands, not on Europe's doorstep. The end of superpower competition and the rise of social violence in Europe gave a new hue to what had been a familiar form of warfare in other parts of the world. That was the essential message of Boutros Boutros-Ghali's famous promise in 1993, during a speech in Sarajevo, to give besieged Bosnians a list of places in the world where people had it far worse than they. The remark was ill-considered, but the facts spoke for themselves.

In fact, in global terms, the former communist lands of Europe and Eurasia have been remarkably peaceful places. Beginning in the late 1980s, several violent conflicts raged across Eastern Europe and Eurasia: in the former Yugoslavia, Moldova, Georgia, Azerbaijan, the north Caucasus republics of the Russian Federation and Tajikistan. Yet compared to the number of potential disputes over borders, resources and identities, that number is probably far less than might have been predicted. 'Historical enemies' did not necessarily take up arms; long-standing territorial disputes did not necessarily lead to bloodshed. Moreover, most of the armed conflicts that did take place involved relatively few casualties, at least when compared to conflicts in other parts of the world. To make a macabre comparison, the total number of people killed in all the post-communist wars was, in round figures, about the same as the number killed during the same period in Sudan. It was about half the number killed in only 100 days in Rwanda in 1994.

Regardless of the relative scale of human suffering, the post-communist wars were highly complex affairs, involving an array of different actors and affecting the interests of major global and regional powers, from the European Union (EU) to Russia and the United States. They all sprang from a complicated mix of ethnic grievances, disputes over territory and struggles for power among old and new elites, all within the context of political transformation, ideological change, economic transition and state collapse. They were also wrapped up in basic questions of legitimacy: Who was to be the spokesperson for old nations and new states? Which claims to independence were justified and which spurious? What forms of self-determination – from local autonomy to outright independence – would the international community recognise as appropriate for one minority group but deny to another? With the exception of the second Chechen war, which began in 1999, the military side of most of the conflicts had ended by the late 1990s. Full-blown peacekeeping and state-building missions had been launched in Bosnia, Kosovo and Macedonia under the aegis of the United Nations, NATO and the EU. Negotiating forums had been established under the UN and the Organisation for Security and Cooperation in Europe for disputes in the former Soviet Union: in Transnistria, Abkhazia, South Ossetia and Nagorno-Karabakh.

In none of these areas, however, has a real resolution yet been achieved. The Bosnian central government is remarkably weak, held hostage to the local interests of canton-level governments and the Republika Srpska, as well as to the powerful vice-regal fiat of the international community's High Representative. In Kosovo, the 'final status' of the province – independence, autonomy or a three-state federal solution with Serbia and Montenegro – is rarely even discussed by international representatives. In Macedonia, the price of relative peace has been the central government's surrender of control over much of the western part of the country to local Albanian authorities. And in the Eurasian conflict zones, from Transnistria to Karabakh, functionally independent but unrecognised states have grown up over the last decade or more; one has its own currency, three have their own postal systems, all have their own foreign policies, economies, parliaments, presidents and armies. The results of the post-communist wars have been a combination of weak international protectorates, relatively powerful unrecognised states, and rather dysfunctional recognised ones.

The dynamics of war and postwar negotiations in each of these disputes are in many ways unique. The reasons for the violence, the kinds of outcome acceptable to the belligerents, and the form of future statehood palatable to external mediators differ in each instance. The geopolitical context is also distinct; wars that arose in 'geographical Europe' – Bosnia, Kosovo, Macedonia – have received much greater attention from Euro-Atlantic institutions than those farther to the east, in Moldova or the Caucasus. Still, there is a common feature to all of these disputes. In each, the rhetoric of ethnic confrontation and minority rights covers up the basic conundrum that has prevented these conflicts from moving towards a final resolution: the fact that no party with decision-making power is sufficiently hurt by the status quo that it has an incentive to push forward with a real settlement. Or to put the argument less charitably, plenty of individuals on all sides benefit from the current state of affairs to such a degree that a lack of resolution – and the profound weakness of legitimate state institutions that results – is preferable to a stable, defined final status. In some instances, the very nature of the mediation process has contributed to maintaining things as they are.

Mediators such as the OSCE and the UN, and to a lesser degree the EU, continue to insist that negotiations and peacekeeping operations are mainly meant to facilitate the rebuilding of single states on the ruins of those destroyed by war. But the reality on the ground is rather different. After years of surreptitious state-building in the former conflict areas, peace negotiations today are not so much about trying to bring together two (or more) parties in a civil war as about trying to merge functionally separate states and societies. The longer decisions about basic questions of sovereignty are put off, the harder it will be to imagine a political future for all former belligerents within the boundaries of existing, internationally recognised states. Postponing resolution is, however, not a neutral outcome; beneath the veneer of peace negotiations, in more and less overt ways, the groups normally labelled 'secessionists' have gone about creating something like states of their own. Maps of Eastern Europe and Eurasia that show clear lines of sovereignty and treat all recognised states as equal players in the international system are thus remarkably inaccurate in their representation of the reality of recent state-building across the wider Southeastern Europe, from the Balkans to the Caucasus.

This chapter examines the relationship between the de facto states of Eastern Europe and Eurasia and broader questions of political violence, ethnicity, international legitimacy, and the role of external mediators. The first section below outlines some of the key pillars that have sustained the intractable status quo into which many of the disputes have lapsed in the past 15 years or so. (The discussion does not consider Montenegro and Chechnya, although both exhibit some of the characteristics of the conflicts examined here. The Montenegro dispute has so far not led to violence, while the second Chechen war continues as a low-level guerrilla conflict. The dynamics of international mediation and state-building analysed here are thus rather different.) The second section focuses particularly on four conflicts in Eurasia: Abkhazia, South Ossetia, Transnistria and Nagorno-Karabakh. The third section examines the role of outside interests and mediators, especially the Russian Federation and key international organisations such as the OSCE and UN. The EU has only recently begun to take an active interest in the post-Soviet conflict zones, and its corporate involvement in these disputes is of little significance compared to the long-term involvement of other international bodies and individual states, such as the US and Russia. The final section offers some conclusions about how to understand the relationship between violence and minorities issues on Europe's eastern periphery within the context of EU enlargement.

State-making and the structure of violence

Each of the major East European and Eurasian wars had similar mid-range causes.[1] Conflicts usually involved an ethnic minority which was distinct from the majority population in the country or republic as a whole, and which had enjoyed a relatively privileged position during the communist period. Lines of dispute also usually ran along the borders of ethnically defined administrative subunits. Indeed, the greatest predictor of the likelihood of armed conflict in the immediate post-communist period was whether an ethnic minority enjoyed some form of territorial autonomy before the communist regime began to weaken. Those that did were far more likely to have at their disposal institutional resources that could engender social mobilisation and even collective violence. (Mobilisation outside existing institutional structures was rare; where it did occur – as among the Serbs of Bosnia and the Krajina, or the Slavs of Transnistria – it was facilitated by direct assistance from external powers, in these cases Serbia and the Russian Federation.) Ethnic minorities that controlled existing territorial subunits were also more likely to be seen by central governments as an existential threat. That, in turn, meant that governments were more likely to use force early on against these minorities than against minorities that did not control a defined piece of territory (Bunce 1999; Beissinger 2002). The post-communist cases thus support Phil Roeder's finding that, over the last two centuries, nearly all secessionist movements arise on the basis of territorial subunits, something that Roeder calls a 'segment state' (Roeder 2004). Without a segment state, minorities rarely have sufficient mobilisational resources to launch a successful secession; with a segment state, the success of a secessionist movement, once launched, is almost guaranteed.

The real puzzle about the post-communist wars is not why they arose. In a context of sudden regime change and radical economic transformation, some violence was probably inevitable. Rather, the striking thing is how long disputes have wound on even after the fighting stopped – despite the best efforts of international mediators, peacekeepers and even virtual international protectorates. Several small-scale wars were waged in the period from 1988 through to the early 2000s, and the destruction was considerable: entire cities virtually destroyed, hundreds of thousands of refugees and internally displaced persons (IDPs), tens of thousands dead. The depth of inter-ethnic animosity wrought by the violence is still evident. Armenians in Karabakh fear a renewal of war by the government of Azerbaijan, a Turkic state that is often compared in the rhetoric of Armenian politicians with the Ottoman empire, perpetrator of the Armenian Genocide of 1915. Abkhaz and South Ossetians in Georgia remember the rhetoric of the early 1990s, when ethnic minorities were treated as unwelcome guests by a Georgian government that seemed to be striving for ethnic purity. Renewed communal violence, as in Kosovo in the spring of 2004, is a constant threat.

This mutual enmity, perhaps predating the outbreak of violence but in any case exacerbated by it, is clearly a major brake on settlement. The fact that some of the elites who had a hand in making the wars are still in office is also partly to blame. However, the chief obstacle has been the fact that, beneath these unresolved grievances, political elites in the secessionist areas have gone about the process of building states – in some instances, states that function about as well as the recognised countries of which they are still nominally constituents. All of the post-communist wars took place within nominally federal systems, and from the point of view of secessionist leaders, from Kosovo to Karabakh, the fate of their territories is simply part of the process of sorting out the successors to the communist world's failed federations. Today, the conflict zones of Eastern Europe and Eurasia are not so much 'stalled' or 'frozen' ethnic conflicts as they are examples of a process known in other parts of Europe from the late Middle Ages forward: the creation of new states out of the crucible of war.

These conflicts are 'unresolved' only in the sense that the international community is unprepared to recognise the outcome of the military confrontations of the 1990s. In all of the East European and Eurasian wars, there were rather clear military winners. In most instances, the recognised states were defeated by a combination of secessionists and some outside power – from NATO in the case of the Kosovar Albanians to the Russian Federation in the case of the Abkhaz. (These two cases, although vastly different from the perspective of Washington and Prishtina, are fundamentally similar from the perspective of Moscow and Sukhum.) But the fact that these military victories have not been transformed into clear political ones is no more than a function of the orientation of the international community. There was a clear 'right to self-determination' at work in the 1990s, but that right applied only to secessionist movements that arose within the highest-level administrative subunit of existing communist federations. For less well-endowed minorities – those that lived within 'autonomous republics' or 'autonomous regions' rather than simply 'republics', or that had no existing territorial status at all – outside powers were generally unwilling to support or recognise de facto separation.

All of this points to the central irony of the post-communist wars. In every instance in which a 'rebel' or 'secessionist' group won on the battlefield – Kosovo, Transnistria, Abkhazia, South Ossetia and Nagorno-Karabakh – full victory has been blocked by the international community's unwillingness to add the imprimatur of political legitimacy to the military outcome. (We could also add to this list Republika Srpska, which might well have turned out like Transnistria or Abkhazia had it not been for US assistance to Bosnia and Croatia in the spring and summer of 1995.) Being a military winner has usually meant ending up as a political loser. The basic political aim that brought 'rebels' onto the battlefield (the de jure creation of a country called Kosovo or Nagorno-Karabakh, say) has not been attained, despite its de facto achievement through military means.

The cynicism that such an outcome has engendered among both political winners and losers is hard to overestimate. Recognised governments are wary of granting significant territorial autonomy to minorities for fear that such a scheme is merely the first step towards full independence. Unrecognised 'rebels' are reluctant to settle for autonomy, in any case, since they have already proven their ability to fulfil one of the base-level requirements of statehood: ability to exercise sovereign control over a defined piece of real estate. The post-communist world thus has a clear 'stateness' problem, but not quite in the sense that Juan Linz and Alfred Stepan intended (Linz and Stepan 1996). The recognised countries have too little stateness simply because the unrecognised ones have managed to garner too much. All of these dynamics can be seen most clearly in the four Eurasian conflicts that raged in the early 1990s and have today settled into a state of limbo between war-fighting and international recognition.

States and non-states in Eurasia

From the late 1980s through the mid 1990s, four major secessionist conflicts erupted in the former Soviet Union. Each was associated with the demand for independence by the inhabitants of a distinct territory. They were also often associated with self-determination for a distinct minority population, even in instances in which the minority population did not form a clear majority or even plurality within the territory concerned. In all of these conflicts – over the Nagorno-Karabakh region of Azerbaijan, the Abkhazia and South Ossetia regions of Georgia, and the Transnistria region of Moldova – ceasefires had been signed by the middle of the 1990s. So far, however, very little real progress has been made on deciding the final status of the secessionist areas, despite the active engagement of the UN, OSCE and foreign governments, including the Russian Federation.

How have peace negotiations managed to languish for more than a decade? Certainly, the depth of animosity and mistrust created by the wars themselves is in part to blame. Thousands of dead, now memorialised on both sides as either freedom fighters or patriotic defenders of territorial integrity; hundreds of thousands of refugees and IDPs; towns and villages left in ruins – all have played a role in deepening the dividing lines of language and culture along which the conflicts originally erupted. However, the outcome of the secessionist disputes is best seen not as an instance of 'stalled' or 'frozen' conflict, but as a case of rival projects of underground state-making within the context of already weak recognised states.

Sizeable portions of Azerbaijan, Georgia and Moldova – the secessionist regions themselves – remain outside central control. Nagorno-Karabakh and the occupied zone around it are 14 per cent of Azerbaijan's territory; Transnistria is 12 per cent of Moldova's; Abkhazia and South Ossetia together are 17 per cent of Georgia's. Even beyond the unrecognised republics, there are many parts of the country where the central government's writ does not run. This chronic state weakness is of clear benefit to the secessionist governments. Taxes can be avoided. Lucrative imports can be brought in for resale or trans-shipment. The degree to which the secessionists have been able to benefit from the weak states differs, however.

The least successful has been Nagorno-Karabakh. Its population, estimated at around 150,000, survives mainly on the basis of subsistence farming or resale of consumer goods imported from Iran and Armenia. Swaths of towns and villages remain in ruins. Removal of the thousands of mines laid during the conflict has progressed with international assistance, but the fear of unexploded ordnance continues to restrict agricultural production. Despite these difficulties, local authorities have been able to construct something resembling a state, with its own police, army, judicial system and foreign ministry (whose representatives regularly visit the United States on fundraising visits among the Armenian diaspora).

Abkhazia and South Ossetia have fared slightly better. Both were reasonably important regions of Georgia during the Soviet period, boasting impressive tourist facilities, mining complexes, and light industry. Now, however, few enterprises function, since the outflow of refugees and IDPs more than halved the populations, which now stand at under 200,000 in Abkhazia and perhaps 80,000 in South Ossetia. (There has been no publication of census data or systematic population estimates since 1989.) The local economy is centred on other pursuits. In Abkhazia, export of fruits and nuts remains an important source of revenue. Trade in scrap metal, both from dysfunctional industries as well as from power lines, is also important – even though it has destroyed what little industry and power distribution capacity the region has left. In South Ossetia, geography has been the local government's chief asset. Lying across a major north–south artery linking Georgia with the Russian Federation, the republic has been able to extract considerable revenue in the form of transit taxes, particularly on goods passing through the Roki Tunnel through the Caucasus Mountains.

Transnistria's economic position is probably better than that of any of the unrecognised states. Transnistria was the mainstay of Moldovan industry during the Soviet period, with heavy machine industries and power-generating plants concentrated there. A high-quality rolled steel facility in northern Transnistria was the pride of Soviet Moldovan industry, and it has continued to function under Transnistrian control. Given the dire state of Moldova's own economy, Transnistria looks rather better in some areas. In every major field except consumer goods, the secessionist region has been a net 'exporter' to the rest of Moldova.[2]

Central authorities frequently complain about the economic benefits that accrue to the secessionist governments. But those benefits also flow to the institutions and individuals ostensibly responsible for resolving the conflicts. The links between corrupt central governments and the secessionist regions, especially in Georgia and Moldova, have further imperilled already weak state structures while enriching those who claim to be looking after state interests. For example, the illegal trade with Russia benefits people in both South Ossetia and Georgia proper. The South Ossetian government receives money from transit taxes – that is, from the Georgian perspective, smuggling; in turn, Georgian authorities, especially the police and interior ministry, are able to take a cut by exacting fines from truck drivers who carry the transited goods onto Georgian-controlled highways. It is partly for these reasons that relations between the two sides have actually been rather cordial. The South Ossetian president openly supported Eduard Shevardnadze in his campaign for Georgian president in early 2000 – even though Shevardnadze was technically running for office in what the South Ossetians considered a foreign state. Cooperation between the two sides was explicitly recognised by the new president, Mikheil Saakashvili, who succeeded Shevardnadze in early 2004: one of his early moves was to close down the market selling illegal goods that had passed through the Roki Tunnel.

The unrecognised states, beyond benefiting from the weakness of the recognised ones, have also worked to foster a sense of loyalty and identity among their small populations. (The total population of all the Eurasian secessionist zones is probably under one million.) New national festivals have been inaugurated. History curricula have been redesigned to highlight the citizens of the secessionist regions as the indigenous inhabitants of their territory. Local intellectuals have also worked, as far as possible, to discover cultural or historical heroes around which semi-official cults could be built, and previous experiences of statehood, no matter how short-lived, have been marshalled to serve the cause. The wars of the 1990s are also now treated as hallowed struggles against external aggression. Children who were not even born when the national movements began in the late 1980s are now adolescents, and they have spent the last decade reading of the sacrifices of their parents and siblings in the liberation struggles of the past.[3]

Of course, no one has a monopoly on uncritical patriotism. There are equally tendentious versions of history and recent politics in textbooks published by the ministries of education of Azerbaijan, Georgia and Moldova. But in both the recognised and the unrecognised states, the result of ten years of such propagandising has been the creation of populations that will not easily shed the version of the truth that they have invested so much in defending. Those whose job it is to create and propagate these ideologies – university professors, academicians, school teachers, even writers and poets – have a huge personal incentive to continue doing so. Since many have progressed in their careers precisely because they came to control a set of cultural institutions divorced from the recognised central governments (a local polytechnic that overnight became a 'national university', for instance), they are loath to make any move that would undercut the advantages that they derive from existence inside a functionally separate state.

The role of external mediators

Negotiations under the aegis of multilateral organisations have been ongoing since the mid 1990s. In Azerbaijan, the OSCE-sponsored Minsk Group has provided good offices and a mechanism for negotiations since 1992. In Moldova an OSCE mission has been active since 1993 and has sponsored numerous rounds of negotiations. In Georgia a UN observer mission, UNOMIG, was deployed in 1993 to provide a basis for negotiations on Abkhazia's future and to monitor the peacekeeping operation conducted by Russian forces (nominally under the control of the Commonwealth of Independent States) in the Georgian–Abkhaz security zone. In South Ossetia, Russian peacekeepers have been in place since the end of the war, and negotiations on South Ossetia's final status have continued apace, involving Russia, North Ossetia and the OSCE as mediators.

The multiple rounds of negotiations, both during and after the fighting, have often seemed endless. Consider the example of Karabakh, the longest-running dispute in the former Soviet Union. In the late 1980s, the Gorbachev administration used appeals to socialist brotherhood and the Soviet army to restore order, both to little avail. Boris Yeltsin and Nursultan Nazarbaev, the president of Kazakhstan, brokered an agreement on territorial autonomy for Karabakh within Azerbaijan in September 1991, but the agreement was scuppered when an aircraft carrying Russian and Azerbaijani officials was shot down over Karabakh. The OSCE began its own mediation track in 1992, leading to an unsuccessful draft peace accord in 1993. The same year, the UN Security Council passed three resolutions demanding the withdrawal of Armenian and Karabakh forces from Azerbaijani territory. In May 1994 the Russian Federation finally managed to secure a full ceasefire agreement, the Bishkek protocol. Russia attempted unsuccessfully to broker a final settlement, and the peace process was put under the sole aegis of the OSCE's Minsk Group (so called because the final peace conference was to take place in Minsk, Belarus), co-chaired by France, Russia and the United States. However, the Minsk process has long been primarily a form of shuttle diplomacy, since the parties to the conflict have rarely been able to meet. It was not until 1999 that the Armenian and Azerbaijani presidents announced their willingness to join in serious face-to-face talks, which culminated in a cordial meeting in Key West, Florida, in April 2001. Since then, however, the situation has returned to deadlock. The Armenian and Azerbaijani sides, in fact, have radically different views on what happened at Key West. The former contend that a land-for-peace deal was put on the table, via which Azerbaijan would relinquish control over Karabakh; the latter contends that no such thing was ever discussed. A similar litany of meetings postponed and agreements variably interpreted characterises the other conflicts as well.

There are four broad obstacles that have prevented international organisations from making real progress towards a final settlement – and each is likely to remain in place even as European institutions begin to take a more active role. First is the overwhelming interest of a neighbouring power, the Russian Federation, in how the disputes are eventually resolved. At the beginning of the wars, Soviet (later Russian) troops were either stationed on the ground in the conflict zones (Abkhazia, Transnistria) or were implicated in providing weapons and personnel to secessionist forces (Nagorno-Karabakh, South Ossetia). Later, Russia provided peacekeeping troops and served as an informal guarantor of the interests of the secessionist powers in ongoing talks. The official Russian history of the Eurasian wars argues that the government had a largely pacifying role in each of the conflicts (Zolotarev 2000: chap. 8). However, Russian assistance was a major component in the early stages of state-building. In Moldova, Russian Federation troops were the main source and conduit of weapons and personnel to the Transnistrians, including highly trained senior officers. There were no troops in Azerbaijan after mid 1993, but Russian troops in neighbouring Armenia aided both Armenian government troops as well as Karabakh secessionists during the war. Leakage of weapons and soldiers from the Russian base in Abkhazia, along with the arrival of freelance fighters from the Russian north Caucasus republics, was critical to Abkhaz success against the rag-tag Georgian army.[4] As of late 2004, Russian troops remained stationed in both Georgia and Moldova against the wishes of the recognised governments, while separate Russian peacekeepers were on the ground in Abkhazia, South Ossetia and Transnistria. Russian advisers were known to be active in Karabakh. No proposed settlement, however promoted by the international community, can ignore the power of Russian interests on the ground.

Second, for all the decision-making elites concerned, there are some benefits to continued 'dialogue' but no costs to non-implementation of agreements. The belligerents have been favourably disposed to negotiate, even if scheduled sessions are routinely postponed or cancelled, largely because they understand that they will thereby remain within the good graces of the facilitating parties – and receive development assistance and other rewards for staying in the game. But never have talks produced more than an agreement to continue talking. At a minimum, there is no disincentive to continue meeting; at a maximum, the belligerents get the best of both worlds: the continued approbation of the international community for their 'willingness to maintain dialogue' while continuing to reap the rewards of stalemate. Precisely because the current situation is less bad than potential alternatives – the escalation to full-scale war, for example – no international mediator has ever attempted to pressure either the central governments or the unrecognised states into making a binding agreement and then sticking with it.

Third, there is a persistent dilemma at the heart of the conflicts concerning the relationship between individual citizens and their governments. In instances in which there is a mobilised group with clear interests in resolving the conflict, they have little access to political power; and in cases in which citizens have access to political power, there is no mobilised group with an interest in resolving the conflict. In Azerbaijan and Georgia, the existence of substantial IDP populations, who have spent years in squalid 'temporary' housing, should have produced a powerful domestic lobby for the resolution of the conflict. Indeed, in Azerbaijan more than half the total population views the Karabakh conflict as the most serious problem facing the country (Ismailzade 2002). But in neither case have the governments – both of which have regularly falsified elections – felt a serious need to be responsive to the interests of their electorates, including the IDPs. The exact opposite situation obtains in Moldova. There, the record on responsiveness has been relatively better, but there is no vocal and organised constituency that might press the government to settle the secessionist dispute. When asked to name the most important problem facing Moldova, only 3 per cent of Moldovans name the Transnistrian problem; only 18 per cent put it among the top three problems. (By contrast, 75 per cent name economic development, and 41 per cent said the fight against corruption.[5]) People have gone about their lives on the assumption that Transnistria is simply no longer a part of their country. In all three disputes, the effect is the same: no real domestic pressure on governments to change the status quo.

Fourth, at times the actions of international negotiators have inadvertently bolstered the statehood of the secessionist regions. The criticism that outside negotiators automatically legitimise belligerents by the very act of speaking with them is a mantra often repeated in civil wars, usually by governments reluctant to engage in dialogue with insurgents. That, however, is not the real issue in the Eurasian conflicts. There, international organisations have actually gone much further, working with and through the institutions of the unrecognised states or otherwise pursuing policies that strengthened their statehood. To a certain extent, the very idea of peace negotiations has entailed some recognition of the legitimacy of those institutions. The secessionists, after all, were the military victors and could dictate the basic terms of the talks – at a minimum, some form of 'substantial autonomy' within the confines of the internationally recognised states that would allow their institutions (particularly, their armies) to remain in place.

But in more subtle ways, the policies of external actors have raised to the level of a 'state' the very congeries of institutions that negotiators have continued to label no more than the germ of a future 'autonomous' area inside Azerbaijan, Georgia or Moldova. In Karabakh the difficulty of cross-ing the front line between Karabakhtsi and Azerbaijani forces (and the excellent road link to Armenia, constructed with assistance from ethnic Armenians abroad) has meant that humanitarian and development pro-grammes, including those sponsored by the US government, are managed from Armenia, not from Azerbaijan.[6] In Moldova, the OSCE urged the Moldovans to sign an accord in 1997 that committed both sides to exist-ence within a 'common state', a form of language that the Transnistrians now interpret as Moldovan acquiescence to no more than a loose confed-eration – and a form of wording that was also proposed by the Minsk Group in Karabakh in 1998 before being rejected by the Azerbaijani side. In Abkhazia, international relief agencies remain an important part of the local economy, injecting around four to five million dollars into the economy each year through rents and payment of local staff.[7] Of course, there is no insidious plot on the part of the OSCE or the UN to bolster the stateness of the unrecognised governments, although more than a few Azerbaijani, Moldovan and Georgian conspiracy theorists insist there is. Rather, in a context in which there are already functional but unrecog-nised state institutions in place, outside mediators have had little choice but to work with and through them.

Russia has long insisted that the existence of the secessionists is a fait accompli and that any final settlement will have to square the circle by somehow affirming the territorial integrity of the existing states while also providing for something close to independence – 'maximum autonomy' or 'confederation' – for the unrecognised ones. Since 1999, there has been a clear change in Russian policy in each of these conflicts. The OSCE Istanbul summit, which committed Russia to withdrawing from Moldova and Georgia, also signalled a major new willingness to see the conflicts resolved. International negotiators report that Russian represen-tatives seem far more willing to support resolution rather than look to gain some particular advantage. The problem remains, however, that Russian policy has always been made in the plural; the presidency, indi-vidual ministries and the State Duma pursue their own policies with little regard for the actions of other Russian actors. The administration of President Vladimir Putin does seem to have moderated its views on the strategic usefulness of the unrecognised entities, but there is still little reason to believe that Russia will accept anything short of major autonomy for the secessionist zones as part of a final settlement. That outcome, while allowing the international community to claim that the conflicts had at last been resolved, would probably do little more than legitimise the status quo – one in which outsiders have very little influence at all on democracy, human rights and crime in the unrecognised states.[8]

The European dimension of the Eurasian conflicts

Even though Eurasia's secessionist conflicts have taken place on the periphery of Europe, they now have a clear European dimension. All of the recognised states involved are members of the Council of Europe; they regularly appeal to the Council and the Parliamentary Assembly for moral support and for analysis of the legal dimensions of proposed settlements. Within the next decade, Moldova will lie on the eastern edge of the EU, which should make the Transnistrian conundrum of considerable interest in Brussels. Azerbaijan and Georgia lie farther afield, but European policy-makers are beginning to take all of these conflicts seriously. European institutions and think tanks have begun to provide analysis on Moldova and the south Caucasus; conferences and multi-track dialogues have proliferated as part of the EU's embrace of its interests in and obligations towards the wider 'European neighbourhood'.

EU officials have often stated that the chief responsibility for conflict resolution in this region lies with the OSCE (Verheugen 2003). But so far, most forms of external involvement, by whatever organisation, have been rather naïve (Merlin 2002; van Meurs 2004). Throughout the 1990s, leaders of the recognised and unrecognised states were invited to conferences on minority rights, federalism and similar themes; they were taken to view examples of European regions where creative constitutional engineering had allowed minorities to live in peace amid culturally distinct populations. The OSCE proposed various schemes for protecting minority rights while maintaining the territorial integrity of the recognised states. It was only at the very end of the decade that international mediators began to understand that no one had much of an interest in seeing the conflicts resolved, on any of the belligerent sides, and that the status quo was in fact of considerable benefit to many players – from corrupt customs officials to business leaders to the presidents of both recognised and unrecognised regimes. A greater appreciation for the power of vested interests led to the imposition of a visa ban on Transnistrian leaders by the EU and the United States in 2003. That is a remarkable change: from touring South Tyrol and the Åland Islands in the early 1990s to being treated as international pariahs ten years later. But it is a far more hard-nosed understanding of the real dynamics of deadlock in each of these conflicts (van Meurs 2004).

The benefits that individuals have derived from deadlock are relative, of course. Azerbaijan, Georgia and Moldova, three of the poorest states in the former Soviet Union and, at best, on an uncertain path towards democracy, would profit immensely from stable governance in a unified and peaceful state. A 2000 World Bank study concluded that Azerbaijan could wipe away a quarter of its trade deficit by resolving the dispute over Karabakh, simply because of increased exports and transport savings.[9] The problem is that the benefits of settlement are long term and diffuse, while the benefits of the status quo are short term and targeted. What may be good for the country as a whole demands an extraordinarily high degree of selflessness and patriotism on the part of those who have profited – literally – from the unsettled nature of the disputes over the last ten years or more.

In the unrecognised states, throughout all levels of the administration and society, there are plenty of disincentives to settle for less than the de jure independence that was won de facto on the battlefield several years ago. In the recognised ones, no political faction is likely to agree to a settlement that will diminish the power and profits that they have spent the last decade learning to acquire through the status quo. Given the right mix of incentives – the structure of the local economy, the views of regional powers, the policies of external mediators – deadlock can become its own kind of equilibrium. And until at least one of these factors begins to change, it is difficult to see how any of the major actors in Eurasia's conflict-ridden states and their unrecognised 'rebel' regions will find settlement a preferable option to intractability.

As Europe begins to take a greater interest in the Eurasian conflict zones, EU institutions will have to face exactly the same kinds of dilemmas already encountered in Bosnia, Kosovo and elsewhere. From the perspective of the 'secessionist' states, the ongoing disputes are simply another round in the sorting out of borders and identities that attended the collapse of the socialist federations. They have to do with basic questions of which new states are meant to succeed the old Soviet order and where the boundaries of those new entities should lie. It was no more than the fiat of the international community that determined that places called Azerbaijan or Georgia should exist and that their boundaries should be those of the internal administrative divisions of the communist-era states of which they were once a part. There was, of course, no objective reason why any of this should have worked out as it did. None of these countries could lay claim to a clear 'historical right' to independence that would obviously trump the right of any other cultural group; few showed themselves particularly committed to minority rights or democratic governance after they were recognised as sovereign.

The 'secessionists', however, defeated the recognised governments by force of arms. They have voted for independence in referenda. They have built functioning state institutions and local economies. They have held numerous rounds of elections for public office. Some, such as Abkhazia and Transnistria, have even developed local democratic opposition movements; others, such as South Ossetia, have replaced a head of state in a generally fair election (which has never happened, in fact, in Georgia or Azerbaijan). It is in this context that outside mediators have tried to persuade the 'secessionists' that the states they have built are wholly illegitimate and that their rightful place is within the confines of three states whose flags fly at the UN but have not flown over the 'rebel' territories for more than ten years. That may be a workable strategy in places such as Cyprus and Kosovo, where the short- and medium-term incentives of membership in, and closer relations with, the EU can be a powerful tool with which to break deadlocked negotiations. Even then, as Cyprus has shown, the carrot of EU membership, when decoupled from competent diplomacy, is no guarantee that the sides will reach an agreement. Yet in regions located on the European periphery, with few prospects of EU membership over the coming decades, if ever, it is difficult to see how the language of minority rights, negotiated settlements and the stability of European borders can produce a viable peace. So far, it has mainly produced a deep cynicism about minorities, negotiated settlements and Europe itself.

8 The impact of post-communist regime change and European integration on ethnic minorities

The 'special' case of ethnic Germans in Eastern Europe*

Stefan Wolff

Introduction

The collapse of communism in Central and Eastern Europe and the Soviet Union in the late 1980s and early 1990s brought with it a fundamental reshaping of social, political and economic conditions in the countries of this region. These changes also manifested themselves dramatically in a recalibration of the relationships between ethnic minorities and the titular majorities of the countries concerned. Breaking free from Soviet and communist domination, minority and majority communities reclaimed and asserted their ethnic identities and sought to establish conditions conducive to the expression, preservation and development of such identities. While the liberalisation of political systems across the region provided some of the impetus for this, it failed initially to create a situation characterised by recognition and tolerance of the wide spectrum of distinct ethnic identities and an acceptance that states must respect the rights of all their citizens to identify with a particular ethnic community without fear of discrimination. Institutional uncertainty and instability, combined with the negative consequences of economic reforms and the budgetary constraints it placed on the governments of the transition countries, exacerbated sometimes pre-existing ethnic tensions. The dynamics ensuing from this, at times deliberately stirred up by political entrepreneurs seeking to maximise electoral support, led to a significant increase in the number of inter-ethnic conflicts in Central and Eastern Europe and the former Soviet Union.

Faced with grave threats to security and stability, international organisations like the Organisation for Security and Cooperation in Europe (OSCE), the Council of Europe (CoE) and the European Union (EU), as well as individual member states of these organisations, took a very active interest in developments in the region and sought to influence, through different incentives and pressures, the way in which states and ethnic groups managed their relations with one another. The very obvious advantages of closer political and economic relations with the EU in particular proved a powerful incentive and provided the organisation with significant leverage. Countries that had been given a clear European perspective of association and future membership were subjected to rigorous monitoring of their minority policies and had to comply with standards and criteria set or accepted by the EU (Wolff 2002b, 2004a; Hughes and Sasse 2003).[1]

This underlines a recent trend to the effect that ethnopolitics is no longer just a dimension of the domestic affairs of the states concerned, but increasingly contingent on a complex and dynamic interplay of various internal and external factors (Brubaker 1996; Smith 2002; Wolff 2004a). The impact of European integration, however, cannot be understood in isolation. The situation of ethnic minorities, and the nature of ethnopolitics more generally in Central and Eastern Europe and the former Soviet Union, must be viewed in the context of both historical legacies and the transition process that the countries in the region have undergone since the end of communism. For an examination of what exactly the impact of domestic and international forces on ethnopolitics in Central and Eastern Europe and the former Soviet Union has been since 1990, the case of ethnic German minorities in these countries is particularly instructive. It exemplifies the impact of both internal and external factors, and the interplay between them, on the situation of ethnic minorities in transition countries. By including both countries with and without a clear perspective of EU membership the significance of the latter can be determined with a greater degree of certainty. This means that my examination of the situation of ethnic German minorities will also consider countries in Central and Eastern Europe and the former Soviet Union which were not part of the 2004 accession round.

The chapter is structured as follows. I begin by outlining the analytical framework that will guide the subsequent examination of my empirical material. Grouping my cases into two different geographical categories, I first examine in broad terms the situation of ethnic Germans in the successor states of the Soviet Union and then turn to three more in-depth case studies of German minorities, namely in Poland, Hungary and Romania. In a concluding section I attempt to summarise and systematise these developments and their causes and consequences with a particular emphasis on the significance of EU enlargement.

An analytical framework for assessing the impact of transition and enlargement on the situation of ethnic German minorities in Central and Eastern Europe and the former Soviet Union

Domestic factors

Demographics

The number of distinct ethnic groups, their size and territorial concentration are very important factors in determining the nature and conduct of ethnopolitics. If groups are large and/or live in compact areas, it is easier for them to preserve and develop their identities as community structures are more likely to be fully developed and groups' languages, often a key element in their identities, can play a role in a variety of public and private social situations ranging from professional contexts to communication with public authorities, the delivery of services, education and a range of electronic and print media. Even more so, if territorial compactness of ethnic groups combines with administrative devolution, including autonomy and federal arrangements, promoting and facilitating identities other than those of a country's titular nation or majority is normally less contested and achievable at reasonable cost. As compactness of ethnic groups, however, cannot always be equated with ethnic homogeneity of a particular territory, inter-ethnic relations will continue to matter. Historically grown settlement patterns hardly ever coincide with ethnic borders. Thus, the promotion of minority identities in some geographic areas sometimes comes to be perceived as discrimination by members of the titular nation or other ethnic groups with a different identity who happen to be in a local minority in a particular area.

Historical legacies

Given the symbolic importance of identity, it comes as little surprise that history, and the various interpretations it is given by different groups, plays a major role in shaping ethnopolitics and the prospects of peaceful and culturally enriching ethnic diversity. What Michael E. Brown refers to as 'problematic group histories' (Brown 2001: 5) is particularly apparent in the relations between ethnic Germans and other ethnic groups in the countries of Central and Eastern Europe and the former Soviet Union. A long history of conquest, colonisation and empire had, for centuries, made ethnic Germans dominant over local minorities across the vast Habsburg and German empires and given them privileged status in the Tsarist empire. This began to change gradually in the nineteenth century, but the position of ethnic Germans was fundamentally changed for the worse only after the First World War and the territorial revisions across Europe that followed it. In more recent history, the most influential factor in terms of inter-group relations was the Second World War. The occupation regimes installed by Nazi Germany, often with the active support of local ethnic Germans, across the countries of Central and Eastern Europe and parts of the former Soviet Union during the Second World War, made ethnic Germans in these countries the subject of retribution and discrimination after 1945 and well beyond the immediate post-war period (Wolff 2001, 2000b, 2000c; Wolff and Cordell 2003; Cordell and Wolff 2005).

The political system

A number of more general aspects of the political system in a particular country also affect the nature of ethnopolitics. They include answers to questions about whether the system of government is democratic and whether the state is organised according to federal or unitary principles. While democracy is normatively and pragmatically preferable to any other form of government, in itself it does not guarantee acknowledgement of, respect for, or active promotion of ethnic diversity (Kymlicka 1995; May 2001, 2003; Kymlicka and Grin 2003; Kymlicka and Patten 2003). On the other hand, the absence of democratic institutions is not synonymous with a lack of consideration for ethnic diversity. The multinational empires of the recent and not so recent past – Soviet Union, Yugoslavia, Austria–Hungary – were well aware of the importance of at least tolerating such diversity, if for no other reason than the avoidance of conflict.

Federal or quasi-federal arrangements intuitively seem to favour better prospects of ethnic diversity,[2] yet much depends on the way in which the boundaries between different entities are drawn and whether demographic factors favour ethnic minorities within such systems of territorial organisation. As I will show below, German minorities in Central and Eastern Europe and the former Soviet Union do not benefit from any specific federal or quasi-federal arrangements, but their territorial concentration in Poland, for example, and the fact that in the Russian Federation two German rayons were established in western Siberia has created somewhat improved conditions.

A last point that is worth making in relation to the impact of the political environment on ethnopolitics is about the role of individuals within the institutions concerned in formulating, implementing and assessing relevant policies. Effective policies for the preservation and promotion of ethnic diversity will always have to be multi-faceted and to occur at multiple levels within the administrative structure of a given polity. For example, constitutional provisions often require implementation legislation, policies have to be properly funded, officials from the institutions of central government down to local government need to be aware of relevant regulations, they may need training, and apart from skills and resources they have to have the will to implement standards and legislation. Obstruction by officials at local level and more generally prejudice against population groups that are to be the beneficiaries of specific policies aimed at creating conditions conducive to the expression, preservation and development of their distinct identity as part of an effort to protect and promote ethnic diversity are often the main obstacles to translating (good) political intentions at the central government level into meaningful practice across all levels of government. While economic and financial constraints may limit what can be done at any one time, they often serve as excuses where political will is lacking.

Ethnopolitics at the domestic level is thus a complex and multi-dimensional process. It is played out within and between different majority and minority groups and their individual members, it involves institutions and the individuals working within them, it includes most elements of more general minority–majority relationships, it is shaped by demographic realities, it is dependent on economic and financial resources, and it is influenced by different perceptions and interpretations of history and what is seen as their policy relevance for the present day. Despite this complexity, many Central and Eastern European countries and some of the successor states of the Soviet Union have achieved quite remarkable results in their efforts to protect and promote ethnic diversity. One reason for this is that many aspects of ethnic diversity have significance beyond the national level – be it for reasons of security and stability, as is the case in some ethnic conflicts with a strong ethnopolitical dimension, or be it for reasons that issues related to ethnic diversity are often seen as manifestations of wider human and minority-rights concerns, two areas in which international and European norms and standards have developed quite rapidly over the past ten to 15 years (Henrard 2000, 2001, 2003).

External factors

In his analysis of EU-induced changes in the minority policies of Poland, the Czech Republic and Hungary, Vermeersch (2003: 24) has argued that

> there is not a very strong connection between European pressure and policy change on minorities in Central and Eastern Europe except when it concerns issues that are important . . . for the individual candidate state or when these are security priorities for individual EU member countries.

This latter point is of particular relevance also for the following case study of German minorities: an assessment of the factors conditioning their situation since 1989/90 also has to take account of the nature and impact of bilateral relations between the relevant host-states and the Federal Republic of Germany (Wolff 2000a, 2002a; Heintze 2000, 2004). The international dynamics of ethnopolitics in Central and Eastern Europe and the former Soviet Union are thus primarily played out at two levels – that of regional organisations and that of bilateral relations. Both are often connected closely to one another, with membership in regional organisations in many ways shaping the interest and opportunity structures of states that also engage with one another at a bilateral level.

Regional organisations

Over the past decade and a half, European organisations have become an important forum for ethnic minorities across the continent to articulate their demands. This has been a result of the securitisation of minority–majority relations in the post-Cold War period (Buzan and Wæver 2003). One result of this has been that regional organisations have actively promoted and supported the implementation of European and international minority-rights standards in the countries of Central and Eastern Europe and the former Soviet Union, albeit with mixed records of success. For example, the EU has taken a strong stance towards the rights and protection of ethnic minorities in the candidate countries of the 2004 accession wave, and which it continues to take in the accession negotiations with Bulgaria, Croatia, Romania and Turkey. Other organisations, such as the OSCE and the CoE, have also had a significant influence on the way in which the prospects for the peaceful and democratic management of ethnic diversity have developed. While their activities have been mostly limited to the formerly communist countries of Central and Eastern Europe and the former Soviet Union and have led to frequent allegations of double standards in relation to minority policies in East and West, the achievements of the EU, CoE and OSCE in effecting positive change, or at least commitment to change, in the management of ethnic diversity in Central and Eastern Europe and the former Soviet Union are, in my view, significant and should not be belittled.

The Copenhagen Criteria, adopted by the EU, to which countries must adhere if they wish to join the organisation, explicitly require respect for human rights, the rule of law and the protection of minorities. Thus, ethnopolitics and the rights and status of ethnic minorities in the candidate countries have been a major issue in the accession process.[3] Apart from its own accession criteria, the EU was also able to exercise its influence more indirectly through the relevant processes and institutions within the CoE (Framework Convention for the Protection of National Minorities, European Charter for Regional or Minority Languages) and the OSCE (Oslo Recommendations on the Linguistic Rights of National Minorities and the institution of the High Commissioner on National Minorities) (Kemp 2001; Hanson 2002; Packer 2003). Quite clearly, membership in CoE and OSCE, and to a lesser degree accession to and ratification of the two CoE documents mentioned above, is seen as an implicit pre-condition for EU membership, especially for those countries which had, during their post-1990 transition process to democracy and a market economy, suffered from different incidents of inter-ethnic conflict. This is underlined by the fact that of all the ten accession countries[4] and the four candidate countries,[5] nine have signed and four ratified the Charter (a legally binding document), while all but one (Turkey) have signed and all but two (Turkey and Latvia) have ratified the Framework Convention (a legally non-binding document).

While the argument that international organisations act as pull factors in 'encouraging' the implementation of certain norms and standards of human and minority rights is slightly weaker with regard to the Charter (only four ratifications with Estonia and Latvia absent from the signatories), the story of the Framework Convention is very different with only two countries who have not ratified it. While both documents leave significant loopholes for states whose commitment to actual implementation of either of the two documents is lacking compared to their enthusiasm to sign and ratify them, the Council of Europe has established an important monitoring mechanism around the Charter and the Framework Convention that allows for continued involvement of the organisation, even if it has no real enforcement powers to follow up on any of its findings in the monitoring process. The EU's ability to affect changes in minority policy in Central and Eastern Europe thus was much helped by the promise of better relations between the countries in the region and the EU, all the way up to full membership. This facilitating factor, however, has not fully or not at all been present in the former Soviet Union, thereby limiting the direct positive effects of enlargement on the conduct of ethnopolitics in this region mainly to the Baltic states.

Bilateral relations

Apart from the general concern for human and minority rights, security and stability that drives the involvement of international organisations in ethnopolitical issues in countries in Central and Eastern Europe and the former Soviet Union, there is another group of external actors that has been historically prone to engage in more or less direct interference in actual or potential conflicts in other states. This group of actors consists of so-called kin-states, i.e. states whose titular nation has an ethnic bond with population groups in other (mostly neighbouring) states. As such relationships were often the result of border changes after wars, they have, historically, often given rise to territorial disputes, most vividly illustrated by the 1938 Munich Agreement which meant to 'rectify' some of the territorial losses incurred by Germany after the First World War. This territorial revisionism was disguised by concern for co-ethnic groups living abroad and framed in the language of linguistic, cultural and/or educational rights.

The post-Cold War period has seen no real resurgence of any territorial disputes, but old and new kin-states have continued to engage with their neighbours over issues of minority rights. Almost immediately after the collapse of communism, Germany concluded a range of treaties with states in Central and Eastern Europe, which, among other things, provided a framework for the rights of ethnic German minorities in these countries and for German government support programmes (Heintze 2000, 2004; Wolff 2000a). All the treaties that were signed[6] included provisions according to which the contracting parties recognise existing international boundaries as inviolable, respect each other's territorial integrity and sovereignty and commit themselves to ensuring that minorities were free to preserve, express and develop their distinct ethnic identities.

Despite the conclusion of such treaties in the early 1990s, bilateral relations between Germany and host-states of ethnic German minorities in Central and Eastern Europe and the former Soviet Union have not been free from tensions. The ups and downs in bilateral relations between Germany on the one hand and Poland and Czechoslovakia on the other, to name just one example, can be explained in the context of the domestic and foreign policy considerations states make (Wolff 2002a; Cordell and Wolff 2005). Governments have to take into account national sentiments towards minorities and their kin-states, which are often based on the historical experience of the majority population. They need to factor in the effects of their policies vis-à-vis one kin-state on their relations with other such and third states and international organisations, as well as on ethnic relations in their own territory and in a wider regional context. Finally, there are issues of resources: for instance, how far a government can go in its commitment to implement minority rights, or alternatively, for how long it can sustain a policy of internal repression and external confrontation. The recent trend towards the pursuit of cooperation has its source to a significant degree in the influence exercised by international organisations. In connection with the greater openness of societies in Central and Eastern Europe, their desire for integration into Western structures, and the resulting greater leverage of international organisations using incentives and pressures, have created a situation in which bilateral relations between sovereign states have become much more dependent on an international context in which other state and supra-state actors have priorities of their own. In addition, developments in international law and within international organisations have contributed to the elevation of minority issues above the level of domestic and bilateral affairs. While this affirms earlier observations about the significance of the international dimension of ethnopolitics, it does not simultaneously mean that its bilateral aspect has become less important; it simply places it into a broader context (Smith 2002).

Weighing the importance of different factors

The previous two sections have presented a multitude of factors that, in one way or another, can be said to have shaped post-Cold War minority policy in Central and Eastern Europe and the former Soviet Union. It would be empirically incorrect and theoretically unsatisfactory to assign them all equal importance in this process. Thus, two further questions arise from the theoretical framework presented so far: which factors are more important within each category – domestic and external – and which of the two categories bears greater importance in determining the nature and quality of minority governance in a given country.

To begin with the first question, I identified three different domestic factors – historical legacies, demographics and the political system. While none of them can be seen in isolation from the other, I take the political system, and especially the role of elites in it, to be the overriding domestic factor in shaping minority policy. The way in which history is being used or abused for political purposes is a deliberate choice. While some historical legacies are more difficult to overcome, especially if negative perceptions of minorities have been built on them for decades, as has been the case with German minorities in Poland and the former Soviet Union, conscious efforts at reconciliation are at the very least able to limit the negative repercussions of this.[7] Similarly, demographic conditions that are less than favourable, such as an over-aged or scattered minority population, do not preclude the implementation of a meaningful minority-rights policy. They may limit their impact and require the adoption of some measures rather than others, but do not determine the general direction of minority policy in a particular country.[8]

As for external factors – regional organisations and bilateral relations – the question to ask is not merely about the relative importance of the two. The number of international organisations operating in the region and the similarity, if not identity, in the aims they pursue with regard to inter-ethnic relations makes it more difficult to judge the precise impact of each individual organisation. While it is often obvious which particular instrument of external intervention brought about a specific outcome (e.g. advice given by the OSCE High Commissioner on National Minorities, implementation of the CoE's Framework Convention or its Charter for Regional or Minority Languages), this in itself does not fully explain the rationale of a particular country in adhering to specific demands made by external actors. The reason for this is that compliance with OSCE and CoE standards is, as mentioned above, often seen as a necessary measure for improving relations with the EU. Consequently, gauging the impact of European integration on the situation of ethnic minorities is less possible regarding the precise impact of each individual organisation. However, I will show to what extent the 'EU factor' is crucial in determining the overall impact of European integration.

Bilateral relations, or the so-called kin-state factor, cannot be seen in isolation from regional organisations either. In the German case, but also in relation to other kin-states, such as Hungary or Russia, a kin-state's integration into regional organisations is a significant factor in shaping the range of policy options available. German policy makers have for decades been socialised into a specific normative context that determines what kind of policies are appropriate vis-à-vis the countries of Central and Eastern Europe and the former Soviet Union given the historic legacies of bilateral relations. German integration into the EU and its predecessor organisations in particular, but also Germany's role in the broader European integration process more generally, have shaped, and been shaped by, similar normative determinants of foreign policy in the domestic context. This is particularly the case for the constitutive role that Germany's *Ostpolitik* played in making the original CSCE process possible that led to the 1975 Helsinki Final Act.

By its very nature, therefore, bilateral relations establish important connections between domestic and external factors and highlight that none of the factors discussed can be seen in isolation. Yet at the same time this analysis also points to a certain hierarchy among external factors and by extension between external and domestic ones. Thus, regional organisations are the more important among external factors, even though important 'feedback loops' exist between them and bilateral relations. Overall, however, domestic conditions in the political systems of the countries of Central and Eastern Europe and the former Soviet Union are more significant than external factors, precisely because international enforcement mechanisms are still weak and minority governance is, despite the existence of international standards, still primarily a matter of domestic legislation and policy implementation. Of course, the latter can be triggered by external pressure, especially if it coincides with domestic foreign policy priorities such as EU accession, and assisted from the outside with advice and financial aid, but in the absence of a domestic environment susceptible to this kind of external intervention, little can be done by external actors.[9]

Ethnic Germans in Central and Eastern Europe and the former Soviet Union since 1990

The former Soviet Union

Apart from Russia, ethnic Germans live in the three Baltic Republics, in Ukraine, in the four Central Asian successor states of the former Soviet Union and in Georgia.

The numerically smallest groups live in Estonia (1,800), Latvia (4,000) and Lithuania (8,000).[10] In terms of their origin, they come from diverse backgrounds, comprising remaining members of the historic German population in the Baltics, some several thousand Memel Germans, and ethnic Germans from Russia who migrated to the Baltic Republics in the Soviet era. The latter group faced severe difficulties in obtaining citizenship rights in Estonia and Latvia in the 1990s. This, however, was not a specifically anti-German policy by the governments of these two countries, but a consequence of the discriminatory citizenship policy, which was primarily aimed at the sizeable non-indigenous Russian population. More recently, the German government's commissioner for German minorities, Jochen Welt, noted that the support given by the governments of the Baltic states had been a crucial factor for the success of the cultural revival of the small German communities there (Welt 1999a). In Georgia, a similarly small group of only some two thousand ethnic Germans is still resident. Apart from their larger size, the single most significant difference between the German minorities in the Baltics and in Georgia, on the one hand, and those in Central Asia, on the other, is the fact that most ethnic Germans from Kazakhstan (almost 700,000 in 1993), Kyrgyzstan (about 60,000 in 1993), Tajikistan (around 30,000 in 1993) and Uzbekistan (approximately 40,000 in 1993) resolved to leave their host-states very early in the transition process, because they continued to be denied the essential conditions to preserve their identity or were discriminated against because of their previously close affiliation with ethnic Russians or because of their Christian rather than Muslim religion. Another reason, particularly in Tajikistan, was the civil war of the 1990s. The origins of Germans in these newly independent states lie in the deportations from the European parts of the Soviet Union after the German attack in 1941. Only in Kyrgyzstan and Kazakhstan had there already been German colonies as early as the nineteenth century. Even though the favoured destination of most émigrés remains Germany, a growing number of them settle temporarily or permanently in ethnic German settlements in Russia, especially in the two German rayons of Asowo and Halbstadt in western Siberia.

In all these countries on the territory of the former Soviet Union, perhaps with the exception of Ukraine (where, supported by the German federal government and within the framework of a 1996 agreement between the two countries, the 40,000 strong German minority in Ukraine is seeking to restore its traditional settlement areas), the future for the continued existence of German communities is rather bleak. Either the degree of assimilation has already progressed irreversibly or the conditions for a sustained recovery of the minority, including the rebuilding of viable community structures, are simply not there because of a lack of government commitment to promote minority rights, insufficient support from Germany, popular resentment against ethnic Germans, or the small number of the remaining members of the minority group. There is, however, a slim chance that the situation in Kazakhstan will change for the better. The minority there is much bigger and makes up about 6 per cent of the total population of the country. Its age structure is well balanced and community structures are generally functioning. Even more importantly, there is an effort on the part of the Kazakh government to provide for conditions that would make it possible for members of the minority to remain in the country and be able to express, preserve, and develop their distinct ethno-cultural identity. The Kazakh Decree on Independence guaranteed the equal rights of all citizens regardless of their ethnic and/or linguistic origin as one of the basic principles by which the country's future policy would be guided. This has been a remarkable departure from the often repressive and discriminating policy of the Soviet era. Since the German minority as a whole is valued for its professional and labour skills, and the mass emigration of the early 1990s had a negative impact on the economy, ethnic Germans are encouraged to stay in the country. Support from Germany has been forthcoming, and an inter-governmental conference, including minority representatives, has been in operation since 1992. By 1997, some moderate success in slowing down emigration had been achieved. Nevertheless, severe problems remain. One is the degree of Russification of the minority that had already progressed very far before the collapse of the Soviet Union. This is unlikely to change in the near future as part of the internal migration pattern of ethnic Germans is their increasing urbanisation, i.e. a move away from the relatively secluded rural environment in which the restoration of functioning community structures would have been somewhat easier. Another is that the economy of the country as a whole has been in permanent crisis since the early 1990s. Similar progress has been made in Kyrgyzstan where about 15,000 ethnic Germans remain. A bilateral commission has been meeting annually since 1997, and the German government has sponsored a range of programmes and projects aimed at improving the German minority's living conditions (Welt 2002b).

In both countries, desperate material conditions are the main problem facing ethnic Germans. Humanitarian aid programmes, sponsored by the German government, seek to alleviate the lack of basic elements of human life, such as food, medication and clothing and so on (Infodienst Deutsche Aussiedler 2000). The most complex situation has probably evolved in relation to ethnic Germans living in the Russian Federation. Deportation and decades of repression and finally emigration have resulted in the steady decline of the minority and its increasing assimilation. This process continues despite significant efforts by the German government to improve the living conditions of the minority in Russia. Aid programmes in the areas of German language education, economic recovery, and culture have been put in place to slow down the process of assimilation and emigration. The success of these programmes, however, also depends on the will of the minority to consolidate itself and survive ultimately as a distinct ethno-cultural group in Russia. Clearly, the political and economic situation in Russia also has significant bearing on whether ethnic Germans will see their future there or in Germany. While German government programmes in support of ethnic German communities in Russia amount to several million euros each year, the balance sheet of these aid programmes has been mixed. In the early to mid 1990s, largescale projects aimed at creating housing and employment opportunities did not fully live up to expectations (Welt 1999b). Since the late 1990s, the focus has shifted to smaller and more targeted measures in specific areas, such as training and qualification, twinning arrangements between German towns and districts and areas in Russia with a significant ethnic German presence, and seed funding for small- and medium-sized enterprises (Welt 2000c). Another key area of support is the cultural work of German minority communities. Several so-called meeting centres (*Begegnungsstätten*), funded by the German government, provide focal points for language training and cultural activities, enabling members of German communities to express, preserve and develop these aspects of their identity (Infodienst Deutsche Aussiedler 2001). While the Russian government offers some limited support for these activities and is generally favourably disposed towards facilitating the success of German government programmes (Welt 2000b), the wider problems of the Russian transition process, politically as well as economically, also affect the opportunities of ethnic Germans in the country to work towards conditions in which their identity and livelihood would be more secure and their future more certain.

What becomes clear from this overview is that, with the exception of the three Baltic Republics, EU leverage to shape the minority policies of the successor states of the Soviet Union has at best been marginal due to the fact that none of the countries in question have any perspective of membership in the organisation. Notwithstanding existing political and economic relations between the EU and individual successor states, there is no measurable impact of the EU on minority policy. The impact of other regional organisations such as the OSCE and the CoE has also been limited, even though there has been significant engagement of the OSCE in the Caucasus and of the CoE in Ukraine/Crimea, for example. Thus, in contrast to the majority of countries in Central and Eastern Europe, Germany played individually a much more significant role in influencing the situation of ethnic German minorities in the former Soviet Union. In the frequent absence of general legislative frameworks of minority rights, or at least of their meaningful implementation, the German government nevertheless managed to negotiate specific treaties and agreements that related exclusively to resident German minorities. In the Baltic Republics, where the influence of the EU and the OSCE High Commissioner on National Minorities was more pronounced (Hansson 2002; Smith 2003), the German government also engaged with the respective governments on a bilateral basis and negotiated relevant agreements to benefit the few remaining members of the German minorities in the three countries. Paradoxically, in all the countries of the former Soviet Union, ethnic Germans at the same time benefit and suffer from the fact that they are no longer seen as significant players or major security concerns. This, combined with the perceived economic advantages resulting from accommodating policy objectives of the German governments, makes it easier for the latter to engage constructively with the governments of the host-states, but also positions issues concerning the situation of ethnic Germans in these countries very low on their host-states' domestic policy agenda. In contrast to the situation of numerically more significant minorities, such as the Russians in all the former Union Republics, or minorities that are considered a security concern, especially in the Caucasus and Central Asia, ethnic Germans remain mostly on the margins of policy debates. The re-securitisation of minority policies in the wake of the terrorist attacks on the USA on 11 September 2001, and the subsequent US-led war on terrorism in particular in Central Asia, does not bode well for the future of German minorities either: the failure to establish and implement a robust framework of minority-rights policies and to pursue a course of determined democratisation in the early days of the transition process cannot but have negative consequences for all minorities whether they are implicated in terrorist activities or not. Thus, without significant external influence, domestic conditions resulting from political and economic reforms that can at best be described as incomplete, remain the key determinants of the situation of ethnic German minorities in those countries of the former Soviet Union that have no prospect of EU accession.

Central and Eastern Europe

The situation of ethnic German minorities in Central and Eastern Europe also differs significantly from country to country. Leaving aside the political uncertainties of the former Yugoslavia where ethnic Germans number only a few thousand, and the Czech and Slovak Republics where also only a few and mostly assimilated ethnic Germans remain (Wolff 2001, 2002a; Cordell and Wolff 2005), the external and internal factors that shape the situations of the minorities in Hungary, Poland and Romania are very different.

The German minority in Hungary

In the 1991 census, just under 900,000 people in Hungary declared their nationality or ethnic identity as other than Hungarian, thus giving minorities a total share of just under 9 per cent of Hungary's ten million population. The most numerous among them were Roma, followed by Germans and Slovaks. Smaller minority groups include Jews, Croats and Romanians, as well as Greeks, Serbs, Slovenes, Armenians and Bulgarians.

After 1945, as in Poland and Romania, the German minority, which can trace its earliest origins to migration and colonisation in the thirteenth century, was held collectively responsible for Nazi atrocities in Hungary during the Second World War. Approximately 200,000 of its members were expelled to the American and Soviet occupation zones immediately after the war before the Allies put a stop to the expulsions. Between 1950 and the early 1990s, another 20,000 ethnic Germans emigrated to the Federal Republic. Preliminary results from the most recent Hungarian census of February 2001 indicate that 62,233 individuals declared themselves to be of German nationality. This number in fact represents an increase of over 100 per cent since the census of 1991, when only 30,824 declared themselves to be German. This data indicates that an identity shift has occurred among some Hungarian citizens. Of those who claimed German nationality in 2001, only 33,792 stated that German was their mother tongue. As there is no evidence that self-declaration of German ethnicity would open a Pandora's Box of discriminatory practices, these figures can be assumed to reflect fairly accurately the actual number of ethnic Germans in the country.

The overall decline in numbers of the German minority in post-1945 Hungary had a significant impact upon the ability of remaining members of the German minority to express, preserve and develop their identity, especially as vital community structures had been destroyed. Even in communities where today more than half of the population is ethnically German, the German language is rarely used regularly in public life, although, for example efforts to re-initiate religious services in German have met with some success in several settlements during recent years.

From the 1980s onwards, changes towards a more liberal minority policy began to take effect when the communist regime began to open up and gradually transform itself. Today, Hungary has an extensive network of legislation regulating the situation of ethnic minorities in the country. The constitution recognises national and ethnic minorities as integral parts of society and obliges the state to protect them and to ensure their collective participation in public life. The state is also required to create conditions within which minorities can foster their culture, use their mother tongues, and provide school instruction in native languages. The state guarantees the right of minorities to use their names in their own language. The Law on the Rights of National and Ethnic Minorities of 1993 provides a complex system of general regulations, individual and group rights, local and national minority self-government and cultural autonomy, and – with regard to the private and semi-public spheres – sanctions the unrestricted use of minority languages.[11] The provisions of this law are backed up by according regulations in the Law on Public Education (1993), in the National Curriculum (1994), in laws regulating the procedures of civil and criminal law, and in laws on the conduct of local authorities. Closely modelled on the bilateral treaty between Germany and Poland, that between Hungary and the Federal Republic of 1992 makes explicit and far-reaching provisions for the protection of the German minority in Hungary, including the possibility of support from Germany. A similar agreement exists between Hungary and Austria.

Within the public education system, the German minority has its own educational structure, comprising native language schools, bilingual schools and so-called language training schools, where efforts are made to teach part of the curriculum in German. The German minority maintains its own native language libraries with the support of public libraries of the local community governments. School libraries of educational institutions participating in minority education stock literary and non-literary works in German. Native language education of students from the German minority is provided, among others, by 140 to 150 visiting teachers. For the second half of the 1990s, total student numbers at pre-school and primary school level were just above 50,000. Most of them, however, went to language training schools, with the smallest number attending native language schools (below 1,000). Despite improvements in the provision of school facilities, textbooks, native language teachers, etc., the language skills of most of the younger members of the minority are significantly below those of older generations, particularly because of the functionality of Hungarian in daily life and the attractiveness of English. The lack of situations in which German remains used and useful thus decreases constantly, and the language therefore continues to lose its appeal. The Hungarian government makes available about €150,000 worth of extra funds annually for cultural and educational programmes and there is significant support from Germany and Austria.

The cultural life of the German minority is organised at local and national level by private associations and the minority self-government.[12] These private associations include the Association of German Writers and Artists in Hungary, founded in 1990, the German Theatre at Szekszárd, founded in 1986, the German Nationality Museum, founded in 1972, the Alliance of School Societies of Germans in Hungary, the Saint Gellért Catholic Association, founded in 1991, and the National Council of German Song, Music and Dance Groups, founded in 1996, which acts as an umbrella for almost 400 member organisations. Hungarian Television has broadcast programmes in German since 1978. Since 1998 programmes in German are broadcast daily for 90 minutes at regional level and for 30 minutes at national level, totalling 840 minutes of weekly programming time. This marks considerable progress from the previous situation before when there was only a half-hour programme every two weeks (Nelde 2000: 126). The German weekly *Neue Zeitung* receives annual subsidies of approximately €100,000, and the German national self-government council in Budapest publishes its own periodicals.

Cross-border cooperation functions well and is encouraged. The two primary legal instruments for bilateral German–Hungarian cooperation are the 'Treaty between the Republic of Hungary and Federal Republic of Germany on Friendly Cooperation and Partnership in Europe' and the 'Joint Declaration by the Government of the Republic of Hungary and the Government of the Federal Republic of Germany on Assistance for the German Minority in Hungary and on the Teaching of German as a Foreign Language', both of which were signed in 1992. In addition, there are numerous twinning arrangements with villages or towns in Germany and Austria, and the National Self-Government of German Hungarians has also established ties with German minorities elsewhere, including with Germans from Denmark and South Tyrol. In the context of existing bilateral treaties and agreements, Germany and Austria support the professional and linguistic training of teachers, provide funding for schools, offer assistance for curriculum development, school book design and production, and supply scholarships for secondary, college and university education and scientific exchange programmes. Funds are also made available for libraries and the German Theatre in Szekszárd. Some 165 local self-administration offices, set up by the German minority under the provisions of the 1993 Law on the Rights of National and Ethnic Minorities, have been furnished and equipped with German assistance.

The German minority in Poland

Only approximately 2 per cent of Poland's population of over 38 million are members of an indigenous ethnic minority. Poland is thus ethnically highly homogeneous with the largest minority groups being the Ukrainians, Germans and Belarusians. Other minorities include Roma, Jews, Rusyns, Lithuanians and Slovaks.

Ethnic Germans in Poland, whose origins as a national minority in the country primarily date back to the territorial revisions after the First and Second World Wars (when large parts of formerly German territory were annexed to Poland), have only since 1989 been a recognised national minority. Prior to the census of 2002, it was widely accepted that up to 500,000 Polish citizens consider themselves as ethnically German. However, as the census results confirm, this was a significant overestimation – only 152,000 people made a claim to an ethnic German identity. Many members of this community simultaneously regard themselves as ethnically Polish, or have a primary regional identity, such as Silesian. Ethnic Germans in Poland are territorially concentrated in the Opole Voivodship, where the German language is still used in everyday life, especially in the south and east of the Voivodship. There are also small and declining German communities in parts of the Silesian Voivodship and the Warmia-Masuria Voivodship. Apart form the apparent identity shift in the 1990s and the post-war expulsions of some eight million ethnic Germans from the territory of today's Republic of Poland, between 1950 and 1992 another one and a half million ethnic Germans left the country and emigrated to the Federal Republic in reaction to the severe level of discrimination and the perpetually dire economic situation that they had faced during the era of communist rule.

Since the end of communism in Poland, the situation of national minorities, and in particular that of ethnic Germans, has much improved. Legal provisions that relate to minority languages and their users in Poland are laid down, among others in the country's constitution of 1997, the Law on Radio and Television (1992), and the Law on the Educational System (1991). Article 27 of the constitution stipulates that 'Polish shall be the official language in the Republic of Poland. This provision shall not infringe upon national minority rights resulting from ratified international agreements.' Article 35, para. 1, further states that the 'Republic of Poland shall ensure Polish citizens belonging to national or ethnic minorities the freedom to maintain and develop their own language, to maintain customs and traditions, and to develop their own culture', while para. 2 lays down that '[n]ational and ethnic minorities shall have the right to establish educational and cultural institutions, institutions designed to protect religious identity, as well as to participate in the resolution of matters connected with their cultural identity'. Another part of the reason for the marked improvement since 1989 can be located within the extensive legal framework for cooperation between Poland and Germany in the fields of education and culture. The major legal instruments include the Treaty between the Republic of Poland and the Federal Republic of Germany on Neighbourliness and Friendly Cooperation (1991), the Agreement between the Government of the Republic of Poland and the Government of the Federal Republic of Germany on Polish and German Youth Cooperation (1991), the Agreement between the Government of the Republic of Poland and the Government of the Federal Republic of Germany on the Establishment and Operation of the Representative Office of the German Academic Exchange Service (1997) and the Agreement between the Government of the Republic of Poland and the Government of the Federal Republic of Germany on Cultural Cooperation (1997).

These treaties and agreements indicate only to a limited extent the nature of bilateral relations between Germany and Poland which, much more so than in the cases of Hungary and Romania, are overshadowed by events of the Second World War and its aftermath – primarily the excessively brutal German occupation regime, the expulsion of almost ten million ethnic Germans from Poland and the lack of legal (albeit not political) clarity as to the German–Polish border. Yet, politicians on both sides recognised that this complex and difficult legacy required extra efforts at reconciliation, and German–Polish accomplishments in this respect are, if anything, only second to those achieved in German–French relations after 1945. In December 1970, German Chancellor Willy Brandt made a historic and unprecedented gesture during his visit to Warsaw to sign the second of the so-called *Ostverträge*: during a commemorative act for the victims of the uprising in the Warsaw ghetto in August 1944 he fell to his knees as a sign of apology for what Germans had done to Poland during the Second World War. Some 24 years later, in August 1994 on the occasion of the fiftieth anniversary of the Warsaw uprising, German Federal President Roman Herzog in a speech in Warsaw also apologised for German actions during the war and expressed Germany's unconditional and strong support for Poland's accession to NATO and the EU. Another ten years later, German Chancellor Gerhard Schröder paid respect to the heroism of those that had participated in the Warsaw uprising and to the contribution they had made to liberate Europe from the Nazis. And two weeks later, during a ceremony commemorating the beginning of the Second World War in the western Polish town of Wielun, Polish President Aleksandar Kwasniewski praised the reconciliation achieved between Poland and Germany over the past several decades, acknowledging the efforts undertaken by both countries to overcome mistrust and prejudice.

The reconciliation achieved at the highest political levels has, over the past 15 years, also been matched to a considerable extent with the improvement of the situation of the ethnic German minority in Poland, which was only officially recognised by the Polish government in 1989. On the basis of national legislation and agreements with Germany, funding for the minority in the areas of education and culture comes from both Polish and German sources. The German government has provided staff support to improve the quality of German language teaching in Poland. The number of teachers sent to Poland has increased from just one in 1989 to over one hundred by 1994, and has remained at that level. In addition, four federal government-sponsored experts on German language teaching have been working in Poland since 1994; the German Academic Exchange Service funds 26 lecturers at Polish universities, and is in the process of establishing a new German–Polish research institute in Wrocław, with the collaboration of the local university. In addition, the Goethe Institute has supplied eight lecturers for the further training of Polish teachers in German. However, the chronic lack of German-language teachers in German minority schools remains the most important and yet unresolved problem. Very few qualified German school teachers are prepared to relocate to Poland even on a temporary basis. Since 1993, members of the German minority in Poland have had access to a special grant programme to study in Germany for a period of up to 12 months. The federal government also provides partial funding for TV and radio broadcasts and print media for the German minority, and supplies German newspapers and magazines to the cultural organisations of the minority. While the German minority in Poland remains one of the two priority groups supported by the German government, the majority of the funds in the approximately €40 million budget for German minorities in Central and Eastern Europe is assigned to projects in the former Soviet Union, especially in Russia and Kazakhstan. However, declining financial support from Germany is partly compensated by the Polish government, which contributes about half of all funding for minorities available to the German minority.[13]

Members of the minority have access to educational institutions where German is either taught as a second language or is the medium of instruction. As Polish law requires a minimum of seven students in each class, requests that such a provision be made available, in effect access to German-language teaching, is largely restricted to the Opole Voivodship. As of January 2003, German was the main language of instruction in 182 primary schools and 34 grammar schools in the Opole Voivodship. The Voivodship also created two bilingual primary schools. A further four grammar schools provided bilingual classes. In addition, German-language lectures are delivered at Opole Polytechnic, and a number of colleges offer teacher-training courses in German as a foreign language. Elsewhere in Poland primary and secondary German-language education barely exists outside of a few large cities. Students graduating from all such establishments are guaranteed full and equal access to universities. All Polish universities have departments of German philology.

The German minority in Poland has four print media – the weekly *Schlesisches Wochenblatt*, as well as one monthly, one bi-monthly and one quarterly magazine. One regional TV station (in the Opole Voivodship) broadcasts a regular, albeit short programme in German, while a number of others have programmes in Polish aimed at the German minority. Radio Opole broadcasts three times a week in German and bilingually in German and Polish, and four other radio stations have weekly programmes in German.

There are no restrictions on cross-border cooperation, the framework for which is covered by the bilateral treaties and agreements between Germany and Poland. In addition, some members of the German minority have benefited from the establishment of the Praded/Pradziad Euroregion in 1997, which straddles the border between Poland and the Czech Republic. These measures came too late to arrest the decline of the German population and language in the Silesian, and especially the Warmia-Masuria, Voivodships. There is, however, every sign that in the Opole Voivodship the policy of linguistic regeneration has succeeded in increasing the number of people with a working knowledge of the language. Any increase in German national consciousness is, as much as anything else, the unintended consequence of the botched 're-Polonisation' campaign, and the superior economic performance of the Federal Republic in comparison to Poland.

The German minority in Romania

According to the 1992 census, Romania comprises 16 national minorities within a total population of almost 23 million people, the largest of them being the Hungarian minority, followed by the Roma and German communities. The 1992 census recorded 120,000 ethnic Germans living in the country. However, due to further emigration since then, the current size of the German minority in Romania is estimated by the German government to be around 80,000 (Welt 2002a).[14] Although scattered over the Romanian Banat area and Transylvania, there remain a large number of predominantly German settlements in which German is widely and commonly used.

With about 220,000 ethnic Germans left in 1989, many of them in their historic settlements and maintaining functioning community structures (including educational facilities teaching German as a mother tongue), the future of the minority in Romania seemed secure. However, the violent toppling of the communist regime in 1989/90 and the subsequent upheavals during the early period of Romania's transition to democracy led about two-thirds of the pre-1989 members of the minority to emigrate to Germany. A change in government in 1996 enabled Romania to make significant progress in adopting laws and policies aimed at establishing and implementing regulations of minority protection. Several articles in the constitution provide the wider legal framework for this. Article 6 establishes 'the right of persons belonging to national minorities, to the preservation, development and expression of their ethnic, cultural, linguistic and religious identity' even though it denies a right to positive discrimination for members of national minorities on the basis of 'the principles of equality and non-discrimination in relation to the other Romanian citizens'. Article 32 guarantees the 'right of persons belonging to national minorities to learn their mother tongue, and their right to be educated in this language', while Article 59 ensures that 'organizations of citizens belonging to national minorities, which fail to obtain the number of votes for representation in Parliament, have the right to one Deputy seat each', thus securing representation of all recognised national minorities in the national parliament. Article 127 declares that Romanian citizens 'belonging to national minorities ... have the right to take cognizance of all acts and files of the case, to speak before the Court and formulate conclusions, through an interpreter...'. In addition to these constitutional provisions, there are a number of other bills and regulations pertaining to minority protection in Romania, in particular in relation to media and education. A bilateral treaty between Germany and Romania was concluded in 1992, followed by agreements on cultural cooperation (1995) and school cooperation (1996). These have been the basis for strong and positive relations between the two countries, which have also benefited the situation of the German minority in Romania.

In the area of education, members of the German minority have access to the whole range of educational institutions existing in Romania, including those that have been specifically established to cater for the needs of mother-tongue education in German. In an effort to create an adequate education system for its national minorities, the Romanian government has made provisions for the opening of multicultural schools that have classes for children of the German minority (and/or other national minorities) in addition to classes for Romanian children. In 1997–98, there were a total of 286 such institutions that catered for around 20,000 pupils in Bucharest, as well as in eight counties with areas of significant German settlement. In 1998, a teacher-training college was established in Sibiu with financial and personnel support from Germany, and in 1999 the University of Bucharest, in collaboration with the Goethe Institute, launched a course for the training of primary-school teachers of German. Babes-Bloyai University offers 12 subjects for study in German (including history, applied modern languages, physics, mathematics, biology, chemistry, geography, philosophy, the arts). The University College of Bistrica runs a course in tourism management and German. In 2000, preparations were finalised for the establishment of a multicultural German–Hungarian–Ukrainian university in Transylvania. A total of over 400 teachers at primary and secondary level provide instruction in German as a mother tongue, while an additional 60, co-sponsored by the German government, work in teacher training.

The German minority still has a rich cultural life, even though some of the most impressive and long-standing traditions have significantly declined, including an independent German literary tradition from which such important German contemporary writers as Herta Müller and Richard Wagner originated. Four German cultural centres exist in Iais, Cluj, Sibiu and Timisoara, providing a varied programme of activities and access to resources, such as newspapers, books and films in German. A strong tradition in the area of print and electronic media also continues: several local German newspapers and radio stations exist in areas of minority settlements. In addition, two nationwide cultural magazines are published in German, co-financed by the Romanian government. A total of 24 hours and 40 minutes per week of TV broadcasts by state television are specifically aimed at the German minority; in addition, there is a weekly two-hour German-language broadcast on national television, as well as 45 minutes per week of German-language programming on TV Cluj-Napoca, which reaches ten districts in the northwest and west of Transylvania. This is complemented by approximately 14 hours of German-language local radio programming per week.

The German government has helped the German minority in Romania extensively in the preservation of its cultural traditions. Between 1990 and 2000, it provided a total of approximately €90 million of funds in support of the German minority in Romania. Increasing rapidly in the first half of the 1990s, funding remained relatively stable until 2000, when the federal government decided that the German minority in Romania was no longer a funding priority. Nevertheless, funding continues, especially in the education and cultural sectors, albeit it at more modest levels. Equally important at the bilateral level, regular meetings of the German–Romanian government commission established under the 1992 treaty have ensured that the Romanian government was involved in and informed about German support programmes for the minority. The commission also provided an important platform for the German government to lobby its Romanian counterpart on specific issues. One recent example of the success of this strategy are changes introduced by the Romanian government to the land and property restitution decree which make ethnic Germans eligible to apply for restitution of land and property taken away from them after the Second World War (Welt 2002a).

Conclusion: the double-edged sword of post-communist transition and European integration

Across Central and Eastern Europe and the former Soviet Union, the situation of ethnic German minorities has fundamentally changed over the past decade and a half. This change has manifested itself in two distinct, and contradictory, developments – a dramatic decrease in numbers, second only to the post-war expulsions, and a significant improvement in the overall conditions under which members of the minorities can express, preserve and develop their ethnic (German) identities, especially in Central and Eastern Europe. Both patterns of change are connected with the social, economic and political transition processes that began across the region in the late 1980s, early 1990s after the collapse of communism and with the effects (or lack thereof) of European integration.

Liberalisation in Central and Eastern Europe and the former Soviet Union, the political and economic instability that it brought with it in the first half of the decade in particular, the liberal immigration law that Germany applied to members of ethnic German minorities, and uncertainties about their future that many ethnic Germans felt against the background of historical experiences all led, in different ways, to just under three million ethnic Germans from Central and Eastern Europe and the former Soviet Union leaving their homes for Germany between 1987 and 2002. In the former Soviet Union, the main push-factors for emigration clearly were the desperate economic situation in most of the successor states and the political instability that accompanied the transition process, as well as a clearer, and above all positive perspective for the future. In Central and Eastern Europe, the most dramatic decrease in numbers affected the ethnic German communities in Romania and Poland. In the former, a strong German identity, the political upheavals during and after the overthrow of the Ceausescu regime and the economic crisis that the country had been living through for most of the 1980s prompted many ethnic Germans to leave as soon as the opportunity arose. Their emigration was also facilitated by the fact that a sizeable Romanian-German community already existed in Germany which was willing and able to help new arrivals integrate quickly in the Federal Republic. This was also a factor in emigration from Poland, but here, additionally, decades of repression and assimilation pressures contributed to the desire of many ethnic Germans to leave the country for what most of them still considered their 'real' homeland – Germany. In contrast, the ethnic German community in Hungary has seen very little emigration since the late 1980s: only about 6,000 have left for Germany since 1987. The reason for this is first of all the very high levels of integration, and to some extent assimilation, of the German minority in the country, but also because the Hungarian transition process happened without any major political unrest and that standards of living in Hungary, already among the highest in the former eastern bloc, improved further as a result of the country's economic transformation.

By 1993, when German immigration and citizenship law changed, putting the burden of proof of discrimination on ethnic grounds on ethnic Germans in Central and Eastern Europe rather than taking discrimination as a given consequence of the Second World War, most of those who had wanted to come to Germany had already done so. For both Poland and Romania the numbers of ethnic German emigrants dropped significantly in 1993 – to about one-third of the year before. Simultaneously, funding for German government programmes aimed at supporting ethnic Germans in their home countries, rather than facilitating their emigration, increased and legal and policy frameworks for minority politics began to change across the region. This happened at different speeds and with different amounts of pressures and incentives from international organisations (primarily OSCE and CoE at this stage), but by the end of the decade, much more favourable legal and policy frameworks regarding language use, educational opportunities and cross-border cooperation were in place, which, combined with the continued support from public and private initiatives in Germany, have contributed to the improvement of living conditions for ethnic German minorities, including their opportunities to express, preserve and develop their identities.

The remaining members of German minorities in Central and Eastern Europe and the three Baltic Republics also benefited from the enlargement process of the EU. In anticipation of impending EU accession negotiations, and partly in response to demands made by the EU in its so-called Copenhagen criteria and in the regular progress reports on their implementation, more liberal legal and policy frameworks and more proactive measures by the states concerned for the protection and promotion of ethnic diversity (although not primarily aimed at German minorities *per se*) have created better conditions under which ethnopolitics is now conducted. However, what needs to be borne in mind is that in Hungary, for example, such changes occurred relatively early on in the transition process, whereas in other countries, such as Poland and the Baltic Republics, changes were left until quite late in the 1990s and early 2000s. Romania, whose accession to the EU is not envisaged prior to 2007, has implemented significant changes to its minority policy since 1996. These policy changes and their timing are only in part a result of the pressure of the EU and other international organisations; they can often also be explained by changes in the domestic balance of power. The defeat of the ex-communists in Romania in 1996 contributed as much to the *possibility* of change in this country as did increasing pressure by the EU and other external actors (OSCE, CoE, Russia) in the case of Estonia. Thus, differences between countries that joined the EU in 2004 and Romania, as a candidate for 2007 accession, are differences of degree rather than general policy direction. A comparison between countries with a clear EU membership perspective, i.e. 2004 accession and 2007 candidate countries, and those without it, i.e. the successor states of the Soviet Union (minus the three Baltic Republics) indicates that the 'EU factor' indeed seems to be significant in the sense that its presence has generally led to a more permissive legislative and policy framework in the area of minority governance.

More specifically with regard to the situation of the ethnic German minorities in the region, not all problems that have been identified since 1990 are solved, or are actually solvable given the small and decreasing size of German communities, budgetary constraints in their host-states and in the Federal Republic, and the fact that inter-ethnic relations remain a sensitive field of domestic (and in the specific case of German minorities, bilateral) politics. Nevertheless, it remains an obvious fact that German minorities have overall benefited from the political and economic reforms of the transition process and the opportunities that it brought for them and for increased involvement of the German government, as well as from the impending EU enlargement process in those countries where this is relevant.

This generally positive verdict for Central and Eastern Europe has to be qualified for those ethnic Germans living in any of the successor states of the Soviet Union (except for the Baltic Republics). What has improved here is less the legal and policy frameworks of minority protection, and more the opportunities for members of the minority communities to emigrate to Germany and to benefit from direct support of the German government as long as they still live in their current home countries. Compared to Central and Eastern Europe, this is clearly a lesser achievement, but it is an achievement nonetheless that has its source in the transition process that began in these countries in the early 1990s. However, the same transition process must also be 'credited' with exacerbating some of the push factors of emigration – political instability, economic crisis and worsening inter-ethnic relations can all be directly traced to the dynamics ensuing from mostly incomplete transformations of formerly communist societies into either thinly disguised authoritarian states or at best semi-democracies. The reason for this, in my view, at least partially lies in the fact that none of these countries has a clear perspective of, or indeed interest in, membership of the EU. The lack of leverage that the EU therefore has over the transition processes in these countries has, among other things, meant that there were few if any incentives for political leaders to improve their countries' track records in human and minority-rights policies. Without the threat of the EU withholding the benefits of membership, the impact of other regional organisations has also been more limited. While this can only be part of a far more complex explanation, it is striking how much more developed the legal and policy frameworks are in the countries of Central and Eastern Europe and the three Baltic Republics. Hungary may be the only one of the countries examined here that has a specific minority law, but all of the accession and candidate countries have explicit legislation on minority languages, education and cultural rights as detailed above. This legislation either presents a significant departure from the communist era (as in Poland and Hungary) or is the result of substantial revisions of existing laws (as in Romania and the Baltic Republics). While implementation has, and will probably always lag behind the passage of legislation, significant funds have been committed by governments for this purpose, often with funding from the EU as part of the accession partnerships. In addition, membership of the EU (or the promise thereof as in the case of Romania) has the further advantage of consolidating the legal and policy changes of the 1990s and early 2000s and extending enforceable EU standards of human rights to the accession countries. These factors are missing in countries without the prospect of EU membership and weaken both the incentives for relevant policy change and its entrenchment.

Speaking of a double-edged sword of transition and enlargement thus means to recognise that minorities are among the most vulnerable groups during times of dramatic social, economic and political change. In the case of ethnic Germans, this (perceived) vulnerability is perhaps best measured in the levels of emigration from most countries in Central and Eastern Europe and the former Soviet Union in the early years of the transition processes there. With international pressures and incentives limited in most of the successor states of the former Soviet Union, the dynamics of the transition process seem to have had more negative consequences overall for the German minorities there. These have been mitigated, to some extent, by the fact that the German government has facilitated the emigration of ethnic Germans from these countries and continues to support those that remain there. This is a unique feature of the particular case of German minorities, and it can therefore not be generalised to the situation of any other minority community in the region, with the exception perhaps of the sizeable Russian minority populations, as well as, with some qualifications, the Hungarian minority communities in Central and Eastern Europe. From this perspective, the double-edged sword of transition processes also means that they can fail, be aborted or remain incomplete – in all of which cases minority communities are less likely to reap any benefits from them, and in fact are likely to be worse off.

This is particularly obvious in those countries without the perspective of EU membership, i.e. the non-Baltic successor states of the former Soviet Union, where the situation of ethnic Germans (and that of other minorities) has, if anything, improved less. While this must not be equated with conclusive proof of the overwhelming significance and impact of EU enlargement, it strongly suggests that this process at least creates a context in which governments are more likely to pursue constructive and positive minority policies, and in which these become more acceptable among the wider population. The commitment to EU membership on the part of political elites and the broad public support that this policy, at least initially, received among large sections of the population in the relevant countries, has also made political leaders and their constituencies more susceptible to demands for meaningful minority-rights legislation and its implementation, regardless of whether this came in the (vague) form of the Copenhagen criteria or in the (more concrete) shape of advice offered by the OSCE High Commissioner on National Minorities or initiatives by the CoE.

Without prejudging further research, the case of ethnic Germans in Central and Eastern Europe and the former Soviet Union also suggests that the presence and engagement of a kin-state can have a positive impact on the situation of minorities in particular countries even where there is no EU membership prospect. The case of German minorities shows clearly that a kin-state's 'external minority policy', if embedded in the wider OSCE, CoE and EU processes of engagement with countries in the region, can make a positive contribution to the situation of a particular ethnic group. This also indicates that, apart from regional and international organisations, traditional 'triadic' patterns of ethnopolitics as examined by Brubaker (1996) continue to remain politically relevant. Yet, this positive German experience cannot be so easily generalised, as the political fall-out from the so-called Hungarian Status Law of 2001 indicates (see Kemp's chapter in this volume). Apart from historical explanations pointing to policy learning in Germany (from the disastrous consequences of the inter-war and war periods), the explanation for the more constructive and accommodating approach taken by Germany since the end of the Cold War may also lie in the nature and degree of Germany's integration in Europe. German policy makers had, for a long period of time, been socialised as to what the appropriate course of action was for German policy vis-à-vis the countries of Central and Eastern Europe and the former Soviet Union both from a domestic and external perspective.[15] Thus, their main concern was to continue the reconciliation process that had begun in the late 1960s and to encourage and support regime change in Central and Eastern Europe and the former Soviet Union. Obviously, ethnic German minorities were a significant factor in both. In particular,

German minorities were seen as important bridges between the Federal Republic and their host-countries. In turn, countries like Poland and Romania, where the minority was more of a domestic 'issue', saw it as important to make conciliatory gestures towards the minority and allow the German government to increase its support for ethnic Germans, considering this approach as an important element of improving their relations with the EU where Germany remained a significant player and advocate of enlargement. In relation to countries where EU membership is not an issue, German involvement was nevertheless welcomed, in particular as it often happened in the much larger context of bilateral political and, above all, economic and trade relations. Notwithstanding the different outcomes of German external minority policy in the 1990s, Germany's long-standing socialisation in the European and EU context provided a significant part of the environment in which kin-state support for national minorities became less threatening for the host-state, and rather than threatening bilateral relations, has contributed to their stabilisation and improvement since 1989/90. The very fact that Germany could economically afford the levels of financial and other support for ethnic Germans in Central and Eastern Europe and the former Soviet Union at a level that does not only benefit members of the minorities but comes as part and parcel of the Federal Republic's support of the transition process in the former communist bloc is perhaps obvious, but no less significant, especially when compared to other kin-states with substantial external minorities in the regions, such as Albania, Serbia, Russia, Ukraine and Belarus among others.

Notwithstanding the individual conclusions drawn above in relation to the particular factors that have influenced the situation of ethnic German minorities in Central and Eastern Europe and the former Soviet Union since the end of communism, the changes that had an impact on ethnic German minorities examined in this chapter can only be explained comprehensively in the context of the post-communist transition process and the impact (or lack thereof) of European integration – especially EU enlargement – and the influence these processes had on the dynamic relationship between domestic and external factors.

The impact of post-communist transition has had obvious consequences for the development of the political systems in the countries in question, making them more liberal in those cases where there was an additional impact of international organisation involvement, especially of the EU. This in turn has improved legal and policy frameworks for minority policies, especially in the countries of Central and Eastern Europe and the Baltic Republics. By the same token, even where political liberalisation was more limited, such as in the non-Baltic successor states of the former Soviet Union, transition processes have at least provided the context for, if not indirectly encouraged, the substantial degree of emigration of ethnic Germans in the post-1989/90 period. This is also true for two of the three

Central and Eastern European countries studied in greater depth – Poland and Romania.

The comparison with Hungary, where such emigration was by and large absent, highlights that similar historical experiences of German minorities of expulsion, discrimination and/or forced assimilation, which are clearly facilitating factors in the emigration process, do not inevitably lead to emigration once the opportunity to do so arises. Historical legacies must be put in a contemporary context to understand their significance. Economically and politically, the living conditions of ethnic Germans in Hungary were significantly better than anywhere else in Central and Eastern Europe and the former Soviet Union, while at the same time, and partly as a consequence of this, the degree of integration and assimilation of members of the minority was also higher. In addition, Hungary's early adoption and implementation of relevant minority-friendly legislation contributed to a sense among many minority members that emigration to Germany was neither necessary nor desirable.

The demographic changes, however, were not only facilitated by these domestic factors, but also by the particularly liberal immigration regime that Germany operated for ethnic Germans from Central and Eastern Europe until 1993 and continues to operate, albeit with some modifications, for those from the former Soviet Union until 2010. The consequences of these domestically and bilaterally induced emigration patterns, in turn, have clearly limited the impact of subsequent improvements in the living conditions of German minorities, be they caused by changes in the legal and/or policy frameworks or by greater involvement of the German government. Where minority groups are greatly decimated in size, no longer settle in contiguous territories or are over-aged, their future as functioning communities is inevitably bleak, regardless of the support they receive from their own government, the German government or from the involvement of international organisations.

Demographic factors to one side, the political system is crucial in its own right when it comes to assessing the relative weight that domestic and external factors have in shaping the situation of ethnic minorities in a given country. The defeat of the ex-communists in Romania in 1996 made it possible for external pressure to work more effectively and to ensure that Romania makes rapid progress in passing legislation aimed at the protection of ethnic minorities.[16] The point here is less about the political background of a specific government (after all, Hungary has had, and has at present, a government led by ex-communists, and Poland has had both an ex-communist president and government), and more about the degree to which governments are susceptible to external pressure, the extent to which they have a pro-European integration orientation that is supported by their constituents, and about the skill with which they can combine domestic reform efforts with external reform pressures. In other words, external pressure is only likely to succeed if it meets with a domestic environment that shares a similar basic policy orientation. In such cases, external pressure can play a key facilitating role in supporting the drafting and implementation of more permissive minority legislation and policy frameworks, such as in Poland, Hungary, Lithuania and Romania; and it can be used by domestic policy elites to justify changes in minority governance regimes by presenting them as necessary trade-offs in the European integration process, and more especially as the price necessary to ensure EU membership, as was the case in Latvia and Estonia. In the case of ethnic German minorities in Central and Eastern Europe and the former Soviet Union, and by extension in other cases of minorities with pro-active kin-states, such as ethnic Hungarians or Russians, the bilateral dimension is an additional, specific factor that needs to be added to the equation. Firmly embedded in the European integration process, German external minority policy made significant contributions to shaping the environment in which host-states adopted more minority-friendly policies. This impact was, however, more limited where it occurred outside the process of EU enlargement.

The case of the German minorities in Central and Eastern Europe and the former Soviet Union is, for historical and contemporary reasons, unique. While, on one level, it exemplifies many of the dynamics of the impact of the post-communist transition process and EU enlargement (or lack thereof) on the ethnopolitics in the former communist countries in the region, it also has a number of very specific variables that make generalisations more difficult. Keeping this general caution in mind, if an overall verdict of the impact of the transition process, increased bilateral engagement and (the prospect of) EU enlargement on the situation of ethnic minorities in general and of the German minorities in particular is possible, it would have to be that only where the three dimensions of post-communist transition, European integration with a clear perspective of future EU membership and increased bilateral engagement have occurred in parallel, their impact has unreservedly been positive for ethnic German minorities in their host-countries. This, in turn, suggests the centrality of the promise of EU membership in this process both as direct and indirect factors in the development of minority governance, yet it also underlines that it must not be seen as an overwhelmingly important factor in its own right nor be taken out of context of the transition process and the broader framework of European integration.

9 Cross-border minorities and European integration in Southeastern Europe

The Hungarians and Serbs compared

Judy Batt

Introduction

The collapse of communism delivered a profound shock to the foundations of statehood throughout Eastern, Central and Southeastern Europe, opening up questions of national identity and state borders. All three of the communist multinational federal states collapsed, changing what had formerly been internal administrative borders into the international borders of new 'nation-states' based more or less explicitly on the claim of the ethnic majority to 'self-determination'. The question of the rights of minorities inevitably appeared again on the European security agenda, especially where newly formed minorities looked to their ethnic 'motherland' for support. Autonomist movements of Russians and Russian-speakers, backed more or less openly by Russia, challenged the integrity and security of the Baltic Republics and other new states formed on former Soviet territory. The break-up of Yugoslavia led to a series of exceptionally brutal ethnic wars over the borders of the states that emerged from the defunct federation. Even where borders were not in question, the fragile new democratic order offered opportunities for minorities to air long-suppressed grievances and stake their claims for enhanced political rights, including in some cases territorial autonomy. When such minorities received backing from a neighbouring ethnic 'kin-state', as was the case with Hungary and the Hungarian minorities, the prospect of renewed ethnic conflict engulfing the whole of the European Union's post-communist neighbourhood set alarm bells ringing.

Upon the collapse of communism, the European Union (EU) had begun to define a more ambitious role for itself as the pivot of order and stability in the 'new Europe', yet its efforts in the early 1990s to avert crises in the disintegrating Yugoslavia were dismally ineffective. Then the French-initiated idea of a 'Stability Pact' for the Central and Eastern European countries sought to promote bilateral agreements among the countries of the region, including mutual recognition of borders and rights of minorities. This was met with a certain scepticism in the countries concerned, which wanted EU membership and suspected this was merely a delaying tactic on the part of the member states. But by 1993, the EU member states had come to accept that EU enlargement was the key to a durable resolution of the problems of stability and security in Central and Eastern Europe.

There were powerful reasons to believe that inclusion of these countries in the processes of deepening European integration would break up the dynamic of cross-border ethnic conflict. First, the EU would set new political conditions for candidates, which would provide decisive political and economic incentives for candidate states to moderate their behaviour towards their minorities and towards their neighbours in order to reap the rewards of EU membership. The 'Copenhagen criteria' set out in 1993 thus included reference to 'respect for and protection of minorities'. It was also expected that general processes of 'Europeanisation' would temper the aggressive territoriality of national identities by promoting reconciliation among states, following the pattern of post-Second World War Western Europe – the example of Franco–German reconciliation was often singled out as especially instructive. This would greatly ease the situation of cross-border minorities, who could be reassured that host-states would cease to see them as a threat, and would not impede their contacts with their ethnic 'motherland'.

Moreover, preparation for EU accession would deeply penetrate processes of institutional reform in the candidates, anchoring fragile democratic structures and providing important guarantees for minorities and opportunities for their full participation in political life. Rapid socio-economic modernisation in the context of EU accession would also have an impact on minority issues by deflecting popular energies away from identity politics into more 'rational' channels, including the pursuit of improved living standards and socioeconomic welfare.

In this chapter I assess the impact of the prospect of EU integration on two of the most important cross-border minority problems of post-communist Europe, those involving the Hungarians and the Serbs. These two nations share the predicament of being divided by state borders that they find hard to accept as legitimate. The borders, resulting from their respective defeats in war, are a constant reminder of national humiliation, and are widely regarded as unjust because they leave large parts of the nation (more than 20 per cent in the case of ethnic Hungarians, about a third of ethnic Serbs) living as more or less insecure and aggrieved minorities in neighbouring states. Moreover, for each nation the lost territories include regions – Transylvania and Kosovo – that play a central role in their national foundation myths as 'heartlands' of national identity. The predicament of national division is thus the key factor in keeping strong ethno-nationalist sentiment alive in the domestic politics of both states.

Hungary's 'national trauma' is of course a long-running saga, dating back to the 1920 Treaty of Trianon, which partitioned off the Kingdom of

Hungary after the collapse of the Habsburg Empire at the end of the First World War. The Hungarians thus spent most of the twentieth century struggling to come to terms with the result. The collapse of communism in 1989 was accompanied in Hungary with renewed popular interest in the fate of the Hungarian minorities beyond its borders, and renewed tensions with neighbours. Nevertheless, these tensions were managed much more successfully than in the past, and substantial progress was achieved in integrating the Hungarian minorities into their host-states. To what extent can this be attributed to the benign workings of EU integration on Hungary and its neighbours during the 1990s?

Since the end of the wars in the former Yugoslavia, and the demise in 2000 of the Tudjman regime in Croatia and the Milosevic regime in Serbia, the EU has committed itself to integrating the successor states of the former Yugoslavia into the EU. The Thessaloniki European Council in July 2003 declared that: 'The future of the Balkans is in the European Union'. The aim, clearly, is to repeat the 'success story' of the 1990s in Central Europe in the much more precarious circumstances of the post-war Balkans. This will be a major test of the proposal that EU integration is the key to solving ethnic conflict. To what extent can the 'EU perspective' induce the Serbs, arguably the major 'losers' from the dissolution of Yugoslavia, to come to terms with their lot as a divided nation? In contrast to the Hungarian case, the Serbs' 'national trauma' is still very recent, very raw, and indeed, still unfinished, insofar as the question of Kosovo remains open. Although Milosevic is now removed from the scene, the Serbian 'national question' has not yet been conclusively resolved and still looms ominously over the fledgling Serbian democracy, and hence over the stability of the volatile Balkans region.

The national question and the promise of European integration

The Hungarians

Hungary's present-day borders result from the Treaty of Trianon of 1920, which reduced the territory of the former Kingdom of Hungary by more than two-thirds, leaving about 7.4 million Hungarians in Hungary (along with nearly 600,000 non-Hungarians). About 2.75 million Hungarians then found themselves under the rule of the neighbouring states of Czechoslovakia, Romania and the Kingdom of Serbs, Croats and Slovenes (later Yugoslavia). Hungarians almost unanimously regarded the Treaty as an unjust and punitive 'dictat' imposed by the victorious Great Powers. Among its new neighbours, only Czechoslovakia took seriously its international commitments to respect minority rights. Inter-war politics in Hungary was thus driven by the goal of revising the borders and regaining as much as possible of the 'lost' territory and kinsfolk. This led it into an ill-fated alliance with the Axis Powers, who supported Hungary's re-annexation of Hungarian-inhabited territory in southern and eastern Slovakia, northern Transylvania and northern Serbia in 1939–40. When Hungary ended the Second World War once again on the losing side, all those territories were restored to the neighbouring states (except Trans-carpathia, which was ceded by Czechoslovakia to the Soviet Union to become part of Ukraine).

In the communist period, the 'national question' was rigorously suppressed in Hungary in the interests of 'socialist internationalism' – solidarity with its neighbours now also under Soviet-backed communist control. Despite this purported 'fraternal' alliance, contacts between the minorities and their 'motherland' were tightly restricted by the neighbouring states, and minority educational and cultural facilities were reined back and placed under close political supervision. While Hungarians in Tito's Yugoslavia (not part of the Soviet bloc) fared rather well – indeed better in economic terms and in access to the West than their compatriots in Hungary – in Slovakia, Soviet Ukraine and especially Ceausescu's Romania, Hungarians felt at best marginalised and at worst directly threatened by the local national-communist regimes.

In the last decade of communist rule, the condition of the minorities beyond the borders gradually crept back onto the public agenda in Hungary, and research on the 'national question' in public opinion became possible as the political regime loosened up. In the 1980s, the sociologist Gyorgy Csepeli found from his surveys that only 1 per cent fully accepted the territorial arrangement defined by the Trianon Treaty, and concluded: 'We have no reason to believe that this proportion will ever increase. We cannot forget our traumas, nor should we. We must learn to live with those traumas' (Csepeli 1997: 198). The rising salience of the 'national question' in Hungary in the years immediately preceding and following the collapse of communism in 1989 was not only due to the fact that it became possible to speak openly about the minorities' difficulties, but also because waves of Hungarian emigrants began arriving from Romania, Ukraine and Serbia, fleeing discrimination, repression, economic destitution and – in the case of Yugoslavia – war. Their stories were regularly and openly aired in the Hungarian media.

About 2.8 million Hungarians still now live in neighbouring countries, while the population of Hungary itself is about 10.2 million (see Table 9.1). The largest Hungarian minority contingent is in Romania (around 1.6 million), about half of whom live concentrated in two counties in the centre of the country, Covasna and Harghita, at the southeast edge of the former Hungarian territory of Transylvania, where they constitute over 70 per cent of the local population. The rest are more scattered throughout western Transylvania and Banat in the south west, with significant concentrations in some major towns such as Cluj, Oradea and Timisoara. Other significant Hungarian minority populations live in Slovakia, Serbia and

Table 9.1 Hungarians in neighbouring countries

Country	Total	Percentage	Year
Romania	1,624,959	7.1	1992
Slovakia	520,528	9.7	2001
Serbia	345,376	3.9	1991
Ukraine	163,111	0.3	2001
Croatia	15,595	0.37	2001
Slovenia	6,200	0.3	2002
Austria	40,583	–	2001

Source: Government of Hungary Office for Hungarians Abroad website, citing national census data (www.htmh.hu).

Ukraine, for the most part clustered along the borders of these states with Hungary. All of these territories were affected by their annexation to Hungary during the Second World War and the subsequent territorial reversals, which in all cases heightened ethnic tensions between the Hungarians and the respective local majority populations of these states. Thus when in 1990 the newly elected Prime Minister of Hungary, Jozsef Antall, declared that he regarded himself as 'in spirit the Prime Minister of 15 million Hungarians', the vehement reaction in the neighbouring countries demonstrated that local memories of the wartime events were still very much alive, and that nationalist politicians in the capitals of these states would not hesitate to exploit them.

In Hungary itself, the sense of historical injustice done to the nation remains strong: a poll in 1995 found that 80 per cent in Hungary regarded the 1920 territorial partition as unfair (Csepeli 1998: 151). However, just as significant is the rather sober attitude of public opinion about what could or should be done about it. By this time, 49 per cent accepted that the borders were permanent and unchangeable, and only 5 per cent believed that the use of force could bring about a rectification of the borders in Hungary's favour. This left about one-third of respondents continuing vaguely to hope that somehow the borders could be changed without recourse to force. This illusion was no doubt briefly nurtured in the early 1990s by peaceful border changes elsewhere in Europe, with the unification of the two German states and the 'velvet divorce' in Czechoslovakia. But a quite contrary message was delivered by the outbreak of the wars in Yugoslavia, which forcefully reminded the Hungarians of the wholly unacceptable costs implied by any lingering revisionist aspirations.

By the mid 1990s, the prospect of European integration (and also NATO membership) had also entered into Hungarian calculations of their national self-interest. Hungary had good reason to be optimistic about its chances of EU accession among the 'front-runners', and preparation for accession rapidly became the key priority of Hungarian domestic and foreign policy. Like all of the other post-communist states in Central and Eastern Europe, Hungary grasped the offer of EU membership as the ultimate 'prize', ending an unhappy twentieth century of chronic insecurity, vulnerability to Great Power politics, subjugation first to Nazism then Soviet communism, and political and economic marginalisation.

But for Hungary, EU integration also presented a special challenge: that of redefining the 'national question'. There is no doubt that the EU perspective had a moderating influence on Hungarian governments' behaviour towards neighbouring states hosting Hungarian minorities. The connection appears clearly in post-1989 Hungarian foreign policy, where cross-party elite consensus was rapidly formed and sustained around a foreign policy comprising a 'holy trinity' of objectives: securing rapid 'Euro-Atlantic' (both EU and NATO) integration, working towards the best possible relations with neighbouring countries, and promoting the rights of the Hungarian minorities in their homelands.

All three objectives were seen as mutually interconnected and self-reinforcing, and of equal importance to the national interest. The assumption was that there could not and would not be any trade-offs between them, and that EU integration of Hungary and all its neighbours would, in effect, bring about 'virtual unification' of the nation, not by changing state borders but by rendering them permeable, and eventually irrelevant. This vision of 'Europe' as a 'common roof' under which all Hungarians could shelter together is no doubt one of the reasons why even fervent nationalists in Hungary have supported European integration. Strong nationalist sentiment thus did not contradict strong commitment to 'Europeanisation'. Throughout the EU accession process, public opinion in Hungary was consistently the most favourable towards EU integration of any of the 2004 accession candidates. The referendum on accession in April 2003 produced a vote of 84 per cent in favour (albeit on a low turnout of 45 per cent).

However, we should note the extent to which the ground was already prepared in Hungary for a recalibration of national priorities well before the EU prospect appeared on the horizon. This will be an important element of comparison with the Serbian case, for, as noted in the introduction, Hungary has been struggling with the predicament of national partition for the best part of a very difficult century. It is not merely the lapse of time that is significant, but also the changes that took place in Hungarian society and political outlook. First of all, Hungary suffered repeated catastrophic defeats. Its attempt to revise the Trianon borders during the Second World War led to defeat, not only reversing the wartime territorial gains, but opening the way to an even greater national catastrophe – Soviet occupation. Hungary's wartime alliance with the Axis Powers meant that, in Soviet eyes, Hungarians were an enemy 'fascist' nation: Hungary itself was subject to punitive reparations, and in no position to defend the rights of Hungarian minorities against its vengeful neighbours. The Soviets played the same 'divide and rule' game with the

Central and East European nations as the Habsburgs had, but this time, the Hungarians were much weaker.

Then came the 1956 Revolution in Hungary. This was a national revolution, but in a liberal and democratic idiom, directed against communism. The question of Hungary's borders and the rights of the Hungarian minorities were not on the agenda in Budapest – but the neighbouring countries used the Revolution as an opportunity to further tighten restrictions on the minorities. The defeat of the Revolution, and deep disappointment at the failure of expected help from the West to materialise (the Suez crisis diverting Western attention at a crucial moment) only confirmed for Hungarians that they were completely powerless: small, poor and entirely lacking in friends. The impact of these traumatic experiences was decisive: the heroic-romantic national self-image was radically tempered by pessimistic and fatalistic realism. The best example of this was the way in which Hungarians would thereafter refer obliquely to 'geopolitical realities' to explain why traditional national goals could no longer be pursued – or at least, not by traditional means.

After 1956, the Hungarians of Hungary found an unexpected means of at least partially salvaging national self-respect. Under the Kadar regime, from the early 1960s, Hungary embarked on a course of economic reform that involved substantial decentralisation, and limited market mechanisms to replace traditional Soviet-style central planning. The first results were clear in the increasing prosperity of the Hungarian rural population, followed later by small independent businesses that sprang up in the towns and cities in a flourishing 'grey economy' – not legalised, but tolerated by the regime which saw the benefits of diverting Hungarian energies away from high politics into economic self-interest. At the same time, the regime opened up trade with the West, which gradually led to increased contacts over wider fields. Huge borrowing from the West in the 1970s allowed Hungarian socialist industrial giants to sail through the stormy waters of the decade without restructuring and the attendant social unrest that afflicted much of Western Europe. A more relaxed political regime accompanied these changes in which communist 'dogmatism' was officially decried as an 'ideological deviation' at least as dangerous as the 'revisionist heresy' that meanwhile had broken out in Czechoslovakia in the late 1960s. The 1968 Warsaw Pact invasion of Czechoslovakia was a salutary reminder to Hungary's small dissident intellectual community of the need for self-censorship in the given 'geopolitical realities' of Central Europe.

None of this was very glorious, but Hungarians learnt to congratulate themselves at least on their pragmatism – not a quality traditionally associated with their national culture – and the skilful way they (and their government) negotiated a space for themselves in an otherwise stifling Soviet bloc. In the new folk wisdom, Hungarians self-identified as 'the sort of people who go into a revolving door behind you but come out in front', which made their country into the 'the jolliest barracks in the Soviet camp'. More seriously, the economic prosperity – however illusory – brought about a modernised, consumption-oriented society with a generously funded welfare state. By the 1980s, Hungarians felt they had a lot more than chains to lose if they were to repeat the quixotic national uprisings of their past – not only their material prosperity, but the increasing attention that the West was paying to their country as an outpost of 'liberal' reform-communism.

This latter factor became increasingly important for Hungary in the 1970s and 1980s. First, Hungarian national identity was increasingly bound up with the state's distinctive reformist policies, which, although inconsistent and only partially effective, received flattering Western commentary and won Hungary some high-profile visits from Western politicians. This confirmed a sense among Hungarians of being more 'advanced' and closer to the 'European' way of life than their neighbours. Moreover, Hungarians found that their good reputation in the West could be put to use in multilateral international fora to raise their concerns about minority rights in neighbouring countries. A notable example was the 'Helsinki process' which established the Council for Security and Cooperation in Europe (CSCE). In the Helsinki Final Act, all signatories signed up to the principle of the inviolability of borders in Europe, which thus committed Hungary to respect the territorial status quo. But the Act also included important commitments to human rights, including minority rights. Hungary was quick to see the uses of CSCE gatherings to attack Romania's treatment of the Hungarian minority under Ceausescu. No doubt this experience was formative in shaping Hungary's future strategy on the minorities question.

Hungarians of course felt for their less fortunate ethnic kin beyond the borders, and helped family members struggling beyond the borders. But it was symptomatic of the change that had occurred in Hungary that in the late 1980s, public opinion surveys showed rising concern, even resentment, at the potential costs to the state of caring for Hungarian emigrants and refugees arriving just at the time that the economic bubble burst. While one anthropologist found that Hungarians regarded the minorities beyond the borders as the 'best' Hungarians, the truest exemplars of the national spirit (Paladi-Kovacs 1996), they clearly preferred them to stay where they were, rather than competing for jobs and welfare benefits in the 'motherland' itself.

Thus by 1989, Hungarians in Hungary had already come a long way towards redefining their 'national question', first, by accepting the permanence of borders and working through multilateral institutions, supported by powerful European states, to change their neighbours' behaviour towards Hungarian minorities; and second, by reorienting their 'national' goals to include the achievement of Western European standards of consumption and welfare in Hungary. Thus the offer of EU membership in the 1990s did not so much represent a radical break in strategy, but a confirmation and culmination of several decades of learning experiences.

But how far would EU integration in practice fulfil Hungarian expectations of a smooth and painless solution to the 'national question'? Two major problems appeared in the 1990s: first, EU enlargement would take place in successive 'waves'; and second, EU standards of minority rights proved to be ambiguous, and fell short of what the Hungarians felt appropriate for their minorities. In 1996, the EU decided that Slovakia and Romania (along with some other candidates) would not be invited to start negotiations for accession. In neither case was unsatisfactory treatment of the Hungarian minorities raised by the EU as a reason for their exclusion from the planned 'first wave' of enlargement. Romania was deemed to meet the Copenhagen political criteria. A party of the Hungarian minority, formed in 1989, had been participating successfully in elections. Thus key outstanding minority issues in Hungarian eyes were passed over (we shall return to these in the final section). In the case of Slovakia, shortcomings in the functioning of its democratic institutions and rule of law were identified, but again, the Hungarian minority's position was not singled out as of special concern. In both countries, where minority issues were noted, it was the plight of the Roma, rather than the Hungarians, that gave cause for concern – but that was also an issue on which the European Commission required further action from Hungary too.

This was a set-back for Hungary, which had also in the meantime run into an unexpected lack of sympathy in many West European states for its insistence that minority rights should be defined collectively, and include the right to territorial autonomy where minorities lived compactly. Hungary's efforts to block the accession of Slovakia and Romania to the Council of Europe on grounds of unsatisfactory treatment of the Hungarian minorities in fact tended to undermine its position, and made it look like a 'trouble-maker' in the eyes of West European states that had strong reservations about collective 'ethnic rights'.

More worrying still was the prospect that Hungary's accession to the EU in advance of some of its neighbours would require it to enforce the EU common visa regime, which until 2000 applied to Romania, and which had to be applied by Hungary to Ukraine and Yugoslavia (later Serbia-Montenegro) from 2003. In fact, this required Hungary to backtrack on the obligation it took when it joined the Council of Europe, namely, not to impede minorities' free access to their motherland. The Hungarian minorities in the latter two countries face considerable uncertainty about their prospects of joining Hungary under the 'common European roof'. The EU officially regards the question of Ukraine's eventual membership as 'open', but for the foreseeable future it is not on the agenda. Serbia, along with the rest of the western Balkans, does have the prospect of EU membership, but it seems likely to continue for some time to struggle with the profound political instability that has so far greatly delayed the opening of negotiations on a Stabilisation and Association Agreement, the first step towards EU accession.

Travel to Hungary for citizens of Ukraine and Serbia, and thus the ability of the Hungarian minorities to maintain their links with the 'motherland', has become markedly more difficult after many years of rather free access. Even throughout the decade of sanctions on Serbia, Hungary (alone among Western countries) kept a visa-free regime for citizens of the rump Yugoslav federation (Serbia and Montenegro), mainly out of concern for the plight of the Hungarian minority. For the present, Hungary has implemented the visa regime vis-à-vis both countries in a flexible way, including free-of-charge, long-term multiple-entry visas, in exchange for which both Serbia-Montenegro and Ukraine have maintained a visa-free regime for citizens of Hungary. But this is a temporary measure, which will become problematic for Hungary to sustain after it accedes fully to the Schengen zone (at least after 2006), because its EU partners are unlikely to accept Hungary's current flexible visa regime towards these two countries.

Thus borders continue to pose problems for Hungarians, despite, and even to some extent because of, Hungary's European integration. We shall return to consider how this has obliged Hungary to adapt its strategy for the minorities in a later section. But first, we will turn to the predicament of the Serbs of former Yugoslavia.

The Serbs

The Serbs are now in rather the same position as were the Hungarians after 1920, having just emerged from war to find themselves divided by new borders that leave a very large proportion of the nation living in varying conditions of insecurity outside the territory currently under Serbian government control.

Table 9.2 Serbian minorities in neighbouring countries

Country	Total	Percentage	Year
Hungary	5,000 (estimated)	0.05	2001
Croatia	201,631	4.54	2001
Slovenia	38,964	1.98	2002
Macedonia	35,939	1.78	2002
Bosnia-Herzegovina	1,366,104	31.21	1991 (no newer census yet)
Bosnia-Herzegovina (without Republika Srpska)	105,091 (estimated)	4.52	2003
Romania	22,561	0.10	2002

Source: National census data; UN.

Croatia

In 1995, Croatian government forces drove most – some 370,000 – of the troublesome Serbian minority out of the country by force, thus re-establishing its control over the secessionist regions of Krajina and Slavonia. The Serb minority in Croatia has as a result been reduced from 12 per cent to 4.5 per cent of the population, and the Croatian government shows rather weak commitment to refugee returns. Despite this being a condition of Croatia's further integration into the EU, the country was accepted as a candidate in April 2004, and will open accession negotiations in 2005. Croatia's case was much helped by the free participation of the Serb minority parties in political life, including participation in government after 2003 (Vlahutin 2004).

Bosnia-Herzegovina (BiH)

In BiH, the Serbs are mainly grouped into one of the two tenuous self-governing entities (Republika Srpska), but others form a significant minority in the other (Bosnian-Croatian Federation). BiH is an international protectorate headed by a 'double-hatted' UN/EU Special Representative with the extensive powers to overrule elected bodies and remove elected politicians from office. BiH is seeking a Stabilisation and Association Agreement with the EU, but this will require the transfer of many powers currently exercised by the two entities to central government institutions. Serbs fear that this will eventually require a revision of the 1995 Dayton Agreement, which ended the war in BiH, and open the way for dismantling Republika Srpska, which they would resist (Knaus and Cox 2004).

Kosovo

An estimated 130,000 Serbs still live in Kosovo, whose population is probably more than 90 per cent Albanian. Since 1999, Kosovo has been an international protectorate established by UN Security Council Resolution 1244. This also recognised the territorial integrity of the rump Yugoslavia, of which Kosovo remains formally part, but in practice the province is governed wholly independently of Belgrade. About one-third of Kosovar Serbs live as a concentrated local majority in the northwest corner (in Northern Mitrovica and surrounding municipalities) where they militantly resist the control of the Kosovo governing institutions, while two-thirds live in scattered settlements, highly exposed among the (for the most part) hostile Albanian majority. UNMIK, the international authority, and NATO's KFOR, have proved quite unable to protect the Serbs' and other minorities' basic security – about 4,000 of them were driven out of the province by an outburst of mass violence on the part of the Albanians in March 2004. Kosovo Serbs remain not only formally citizens of Serbia-Montenegro, and continue to vote in Serbian elections, but for many practical purposes they remain dependent on Belgrade, which continues to fund health, education and welfare services and to provide top-up salaries to public-sector employees to induce them to remain (ICG 2002).

As a result of the wars of the 1990s, there are still about 280,000 refugees from former Yugoslav states living in Serbia-Montenegro (180,000 from Croatia, 100,000 from BiH) and an uncertain number – estimates vary from 65,000 to 220,000 – of internally displaced persons (IDPs) from Kosovo (ESI 2004). Most of these are ethnic Serbs, and they are concentrated mainly in southern Serbia and in the northern province of Vojvodina. Despite the fact that the flow of refugees from Croatia and BiH was largely the product of Milosevic's disastrous policies, most of these refugees were for many years denied Serbian citizenship. According to the law of 2002, Serbian citizenship was open only to registered residents of Serbia as of that date – the aim being to ensure the eventual return of refugees to their republic of origin. This legislation was only changed in 2002, leaving large numbers of people who had no wish to return in a distressing state of limbo. The post-Milosevic government now has a 'National Strategy' for integrating refugees who choose to remain permanently in Serbia (ECRE 2002). Not surprisingly, the former refugees and IDPs, as well as the Serbs remaining in Kosovo, are a reliable source of electoral support for extremist nationalists still propounding a 'Greater Serbian' ideology.

As we saw above, in Hungary at the end of the communist period, public opinion polls found that many Hungarians were still not fully reconciled psychologically to the given territorial borders. But very few seriously believed that they could be changed. In Serbia, however, the borders remain an open question, not just because of the psychological attitudes of the majority of Serbs, who have not yet had time to adjust to the fact of their defeat, but because that defeat has not yet produced a definitive, internationally sanctioned answer to key questions about Serbia's borders. This keeps territorial revisionism alive in Serbia and among Serbian minorities beyond its borders. Two outstanding issues remain unresolved: the 'final status' of Kosovo; and the fate of the Serbia-Montenegro Union (SMU), which recast the rump Yugoslav federation as a loose-knit and barely functional union of two equal partners.

The question of Kosovo's final status is now in the hands of the international community, as any change in the 1999 arrangement will require a new UN Security Council Resolution 1244. There is no agreement either among the key international players or the parties concerned as to what that final status should be. The March 2004 events alerted the international community to the fragility of the situation, and there is a growing sense that the prolonged uncertainty over final status is contributing to deterioration rather than reconciliation and stabilisation (Glenny 2004;

ICG 2004). The Albanian majority clearly will accept no alternative short of independent statehood, and many Western experts accept this as the most viable way forward. Western governments are extremely cautious about this for a variety of reasons. There is little confidence in the Kosovar Albanian elites to exercise democratic self-government, reverse the penetration of the province by organised crime, and respect the minority rights of the non-Albanians. The majority of Kosovar Serbs appear intransigently opposed to Kosovo independence, and seek reintegration into Serbia. Kosovo independence would entail redrawing the borders of a sovereign state (SMU), with acutely destabilising potential effects for Macedonia (where an armed attempt at secession by local minority Albanians was only narrowly thwarted in 2001), and BiH, where many Serbs still hope that Republika Srpska will unite with Serbia one day. Moreover, Russia and China would almost certainly use their Security Council vetoes to block any move that appeared to set a precedent for the secessionist movements they face on their own territory.

A key consideration is, of course, the position of Serbia, as no change in the status of Kosovo is possible without its assent. For Serbia, Kosovo presents a wrenching problem: a chronically underdeveloped and still economically hopeless patch of land overwhelmingly inhabited by Albanians with a visceral hatred of Serbs and long-established skills of thwarting any attempt by outsiders to govern them – and yet a place elevated in Serbian national mythology to the status of inalienable heartland of Serbian history and identity. The advent of democratic government in Serbia after the fall of Milosevic in autumn 2000 has seen little change in Serbia's official position, that Kosovo is an alienable part of Serbia. There are three reasons for this. First, leading figures in the democratic opposition to Milosevic were in fact nationalists who broadly supported his 'Greater Serbia' goals, and opposed him as a 'communist' who had betrayed those goals by his failure to achieve them (Dragovic 2004). The most prominent of such figures are Vojislav Kostunica (President of rump Yugoslavia 2000–03 and Prime Minister of Serbia since December 2003) and Vuk Draskovic (SMU Foreign Minister since 2004). Other leading democratic politicians, such as Zoran Djindjic (Serbian Prime Minister until his assassination in March 2003), have shown signs of a pragmatic approach, waiting for an opportune moment to 'tell Serbs what they already know' – that Kosovo is lost, and that the interests of the 7.5 million Serbs in Serbia would be better served by recognising that and focussing instead on rapid integration of Serbia into the EU. However, such pragmatic figures have been acutely aware of the political risks of openly confronting Serbian voters with that choice, and the EU itself has not explicitly included resolution of the Kosovo issue on the list of conditions that Serbia has to meet to become an EU candidate. In the meantime, however, the continuing strength of the Serbian Radical Party, an extreme nationalist party that won the largest share of the votes in the December 2003 parliamentary elections and that was a strong runner-up in the June 2004 presidential election in Serbia, makes it extremely hard for Serbian pragmatic democrats to take the political risk of posing the choice of 'Kosovo or Europe' before Serbian voters.

The second uncertainty surrounding Serbia's own 'final status' arises from the precariousness of the 'state union' with Montenegro, launched in 2003 largely at the behest of the EU but since then proving a hindrance rather than a help to Serbia's European integration. Serbia traditionally had close and amicable relations with the Montenegrin republic, which remained with Serbia in the rump Yugoslav federation. But during the Milosevic years, Montenegro distanced itself from Serbia and developed independently close relations with the West in the interests of avoiding the impact of Western sanctions. After the fall of Milosevic, the Montenegrin government made clear its determination to continue that course, and proposed to call a referendum on independence in 2002. This was greeted with alarm in Brussels, and the EU's High Representative for CFSP, Javier Solana, stepped in to broker a new State Union of Serbia and Montenegro between the two very reluctant partners.

Solana's primary concern was to avert conflict within Montenegro between supporters of independence – at most a bare majority, and showing a tendency to decline after 2000 – and opponents, including not only minorities of Albanians and Slav Muslims, but also growing numbers of Montenegrins who insist on the primacy of their Serbian national identity. Serbia, on the other hand, would probably quite happily have seen Montenegro secede. Many Serbs seem to feel quite ready to dump a partner who poses no threat to them, is poorer and thus unable to pay its way in the union, and whose elite is highly unpredictable, with unsavoury connections to local organised crime. Despite the huge disparity in population size (about 650,000 in Montenegro to about 7.5 million in Serbia without Kosovo), the union accords Montenegro full equality with Serbia in decision-making, a further source of Serbian misgivings (for arguments in favour and against the Union, see van Meurs 2002; and ICG 2003a).

However, the union is likely to be only a temporary arrangement, as the Belgrade agreement of 2002 included – at Montenegrin insistence – the right of either republic to hold a referendum on independence after three years. This uncertainty has been a disincentive to both sides to make significant concessions in the interests of consolidating the union – but that is exactly what the EU required of them, arguing that a Stabilisation and Association Agreement (SAA) could only be negotiated with the State Union, not with each partner separately. But the powers of the component republics are such that most of the technical economic issues that form the bulk of an SAA are in their hands, not the union's. The two republics use different currencies (Montenegro having abandoned the Yugoslav dinar for the euro in the 1990s), and have widely divergent tariffs. The union is not a single market. Divergent economic interests, and lack of political commitment to the union, meant that progress towards an SAA became irretrievably bogged down, confirming the view of sceptics in both republics who agreed at least on one point – that each would advance faster towards European integration on their own. After much delay, the EU recognised the reality in October 2004 and modified its approach, so that a 'twin-track' procedure is to be adopted for the SAA, in which those issues that are in republican competence will be negotiated separately, and then brought together with the mainly political, human and minority-rights provisions that are within the union's competence in a single SAA. It remains to be seen how far this complex procedure will get before 2006, the date at which the present separatist Montenegrin government is still committed to holding an independence referendum. This leaves Serbia still in a position of uncertainty as to its final state borders, while also opening the prospect of yet another cross-border Serbian minority, the some 30 per cent of the population of Montenegro who regard themselves as Serbs.

These unresolved border questions are already enough to place huge obstacles in the way of Serbs seeing European integration as a ready recipe for resolving their 'national question'. But EU conditionality also poses a further, acute and direct challenge to Serbian national sensitivities: cooperation with the International Criminal Tribunal for the former Yugoslavia (ICTY). The first dramatic step towards compliance was the extradition of Milosevic in April 2001, but since then, the process has stalled. This issue exposed a deep division in the tenuous coalition government between conservative/liberal nationalists insisting on Serbia's sovereign right to judge past leaders in its own courts, and pragmatic 'modernisers' prioritising the restoration of ties with the West. The 'modernisers', mainly the Democratic Party (DS) formerly led by Zoran Djindjic, have clearly felt boxed in by the strength of unrequited nationalist sentiment in public opinion, and suffered a huge blow with the assassination of Djindjic on March 2003, which was probably connected with his plans for further extraditions. The conservative nationalists of the Democratic Party of Serbia (DSS), led by Kostunica, are challenged by the resurgence on the extreme right of the SRS (led by an indicted war criminal now in detention in the Hague). In any case, Kostunica is extremely reluctant to acknowledge what is at stake, namely, Serbia's prospects for European integration. The DSS has failed to grasp the challenge of transforming the Serbian 'national question' along the lines pursued by nationalists in Hungary, namely, by recalibrating the 'national' and 'European' elements of Serbian identity. Instead the Serbs have been allowed to wallow in an overwhelming sense of victimisation that perpetuates the tendency to see 'Europe' as a continuing threat to their national interests. Public opinion polls show that about 60 per cent oppose any extraditions to the Hague – the primary precondition set by the EU before an SAA can be concluded.

In any case, the incentive effect of the prospect of EU membership is much weaker for Serbia today than it was for Hungary after 1989 because of its parlous economic condition. Yugoslavia in 1989 was arguably as promising a candidate as Hungary or Poland for EU integration, with the advantages of even closer economic and cultural ties with the West, large numbers of migrant workers living in Western Europe, and a cohort of managers and professionals with experience relevant for accelerated economic transition. These advantages were squandered in the decade of war, which, far from seeing a 'return to Europe' along with other post-communist countries, saw the progressive isolation of Serbia from Europe under international economic embargo and eventually NATO bombardment. While post-Milosevic governments have made commendable progress in economic reform, there is no doubt that reforms could have gone even faster had it not been for the political instability of the country. Moreover, foreign investors – absolutely crucial to economic recovery – have been put off by political instability both inside the country and in the Balkans region as a whole due to the unresolved issues of borders and statehood, as well as by the endemic corruption inherited from the Milosevic-era war economy, which is proving hard to dislodge (Altmann 2004). Public opinion in Serbia in fact strongly supports the country's integration with the EU: polls show that about 80 per cent in favour (BBC Monitoring 31 March 2004; Marten Board International, July 2004). But there is deep apprehension about the coming economic transition, which will no doubt see socio-economic conditions still further deteriorating. The estimated GDP of SMU in 2003 was less than half the 1989 level. Officially registered unemployment is about 30 per cent. Poverty is widespread, and the state budget is overstretched. Very few see EU integration as a key priority for the country, no doubt because they simply do not believe it will happen for many years.

Thus while Hungary was ready and willing to recast its 'national question' in a European context after 1989, the attractive power of the 'European perspective' has not yet become strong or credible enough to provoke a decisive change in the way the Serbs frame their national objectives. The pattern established under Milosevic of pitting the Serbian nation against the rest of Europe and the world has not yet been broken.

Cross-border minority rights and regional stability

In practice, EU member states' policies for their minorities vary widely. While some, such as France and Greece, have reservations about recognising ethnic minorities as a legal category at all, others implement special provisions in education, culture and even territorial self-government for specific groups. Most such provisions thus imply recognition that minority rights have a collective dimension, even if the idea of 'collective rights' is not part of official discourse. Thus in practice, if not always in theory, EU member states' policies contain both 'civic' and 'ethnic' elements. But when monitoring the practices of candidates for accession, there seems to be a distinct nervousness about 'ethnic' approaches. This is in part to be explained by the lack of serious debate among existing member states about minority rights prior to 1989, when this was regarded as a purely internal matter for states. Many were thus caught off-guard by discovering the extent of divergence across Europe, and the lack of a clear common formula for the 'European standards' to which candidates were now required to conform.

This left the EU (and also the Council of Europe) in some confusion when it came to arbitrating between the conflicting interpretations of minority rights embraced by Central and East European candidate states and their minorities. Even where candidate states shared the broad goals of 'Europeanisation', minority rights could remain a source of tension, as was the case particularly between Hungary and its neighbours, where cross-border minorities were involved. Here, the key to preventing an escalation of tension was not EU minority-rights conditionality, but EU pressure on both states, in the interest of their respective accession prospects, to compromise in the interest of regional stability. When it came to the Balkans, therefore, 'regional cooperation' was elevated into an additional explicit condition for would-be candidates to fulfil.

Hungarian and Serbian approaches to minority rights tend towards 'ethnic' and 'collectivist' definitions of minority rights. Conforming rigorously with a purely 'civic' paradigm of statehood and rights would imply simply disavowing any special interest in co-ethnics beyond the borders – a political, and for most, a moral impossibility. While neither Hungary nor Serbia is defined constitutionally as an ethnic nation-state, this is not because the ethnic principle is rejected, but precisely because the current state borders do not encompass the whole Hungarian or Serb nation. In 1989, Hungary inserted into its constitution a clause (Article 6(3)) claiming a special interest in co-ethnics abroad: 'The Republic of Hungary recognises its responsibilities towards Hungarians living outside the borders of the country and shall assist them in fostering their relations to Hungary.' A similar (long-standing) clause was retained in the revised 1990 Serbian constitution (Article 72), stating that: 'The Republic of Serbia shall maintain relations with the Serbs living outside the Republic of Serbia in order to preserve their national and cultural-historical identity.'

As Walter Kemp's chapter in this volume shows, the Hungarian 'Status Law' (Act on Hungarians living in Neighbouring Countries), passed on 19 June 2001, provoked fierce controversy between Hungary and its neighbours. At the root of the controversy was the Hungarian ambition to 'transcend' the limits of the nation-state by attributing quasi-citizenship rights to ethnic Hungarian citizens of neighbouring countries. This was justified by a vision of 'Europe' drawn from post-modernist literature, and tapping into fashionable intellectual preoccupations with the 'demise of the nation-state', the 'end of territoriality' and 'transnational citizenship' in a 'Europe without borders' (Fowler 2002). As the then Hungarian Foreign Minister, Janos Martonyi, put it:

> In the future it won't be the territorially defined state that determines everything. Its role will remain important, but alongside it national communities, for example, will also strengthen. For me, in the future there won't be minorities, only communities. And I believe that our continent will become a community of communities.
>
> (quoted in Fowler 2002: 5)

This not surprisingly provoked vehement reaction on the part of Hungary's neighbours, who immediately read it as barely-disguised traditional Hungarian territorial revisionism. Romanian and Slovak counterattacks focussed on the unacceptably 'ethnic' basis of the Hungarian approach, and laid claim to a more conventional understanding of 'Europe', designed to win wide support among West Europeans, that emphasised the enduring place in an integrated Europe of the liberal-democratic nation-state, based on individual citizenship rights. This coincided with the view of the EU's lawyers, who insisted that the law could not be applied to any EU member state, insofar as its provisions could be construed as discriminating between EU citizens on ethnic grounds, which contravenes the Maastricht Treaty. Moreover, the EU made it very clear that the Schengen *acquis* could not accommodate Hungary's aspiration to maintain visa-free access for Hungarian minorities to Hungary.

Investigating the controversy, the Council of Europe's Venice Commission discovered that the Hungarians were not alone in this respect: many other post-communist constitutions – including those of Romania and Slovakia – committed states to take some form of interest in non-citizen co-ethnics abroad (Venice Commission 2001), and concluded that this was neither a new phenomenon nor necessarily undesirable in principle. What mattered was how such commitments were implemented. Hungary was found wanting in its unilateral approach that had neglected the normal bilateral inter-state channels of consultation and agreement, and in assigning responsibility for issuing the special identity cards for Hungarian minorities to non-state actors in the neighbouring countries, rather than to Hungarian consulates.

Hungary was therefore obliged to introduce modifications in full cooperation with its neighbours, regarded by the law's more radical proponents as a humiliating climbdown that rendered the law virtually useless. Thus, with Slovakia's and Slovenia's EU accession, the law has ceased to apply to those countries' Hungarian minorities in line with Hungary's commitment to EU anti-discrimination principles. The same will follow in the cases of Romania and Croatia. As for the Hungarian minorities in

Serbia and Ukraine, the law was a big disappointment from the start because it failed to offer them any privileged exemption from the EU visa regime, which is what they most wanted.

Serbia has long had a 'diaspora policy', developed well before Milosevic came on the scene. Yugoslav governments have traditionally accepted a responsibility for the diaspora, given that country's history of mass (economic) emigration, as a means of tapping into the advantages to be gained from maintaining contacts with wealthy and successful entrepreneurs in North America and Western Europe (many of whom are not Yugoslav citizens), and sustaining the loyalty of the army of migrant workers (with Yugoslav citizenship) in Western Europe whose remittances helped keep the country afloat during the 1970s and 1980s. Relations with such groups (particularly the first) became severely strained under Milosevic. After he was ousted, a Council for the Diaspora was revived under the Djindjic government, but disbanded (for reasons I have yet to ascertain) in 2002 (limited information is available on the SMU Ministry of Foreign Affairs website). The new Serbian government under Kostunica has now established a Ministry for the Diaspora, under the leadership of Vojislav Vukcevic, the former chairman of the disbanded Council for the Diaspora, and a naturalised Serb refugee of the early 1990s from Croatia.

The Ministry has yet to be allocated premises in Belgrade, and still has no web-site nor other means of public communication. From recent Serbian press interviews, it appears that the Ministry's remit will now be extended to the Serbs in neighbouring countries, the former Yugoslav republics. This is likely to be problematic, certainly in the eyes of the international community. In a recent interview, Vukcevic was described as the 'Minister for Good Will' (*Politika,* 15 March 2004). He will have his work cut out to live up to that. One issue he wishes to pursue is securing agreements on dual citizenship with neighbouring countries like BiH and Croatia. Neither Croatia nor BiH is likely to accept dual citizenship with Serbia after their recent experience of Serbian armed separatism and lingering mistrust (especially in BiH) of Serb loyalty to their new states.

In fact, Serbia's relations with Croatia have been steadily improving for several years. From the point of view of both Serbia and Croatia's Serbian minority, EU conditionality is here working in their favour, insofar as Croatia's aspirations to EU accession have modified its behaviour. The Croatian nationalist party (HDZ) has, since the demise of wartime President Tudjman, undergone significant internal reform and, having returned to power in 2003, has made strenuous efforts to reach out to the Serbs and has brought Serbian minority representatives into the government (Vlahutin 2004). The major obstacle in relations between the two countries is the issue of the return of refugees and their property rights. Evidence of more serious effort on Croatia's part to resolve this issue is being demanded by the EU as a key condition of its accession. But the EU will not look with favour on Serbian efforts to secure a dual citizenship

arrangement with Croatia. Croatia already has a dual citizenship agreement with BiH, which is likely to cause problems in future for Croatia's
EU accession negotiations. This has led to a large proportion of Bosnian
Croats – one of the three constituent peoples of that precarious quasi-state
– taking out Croatian citizenship. It is not clear that the EU can accommodate this fact when Croatia comes to implementing the Schengen *acquis*,
as well as EU anti-discrimination law, since it would allow ethnic Croats
who have the benefit of Croatian passports to evade the EU visa regime
that applies to BiH citizens.

BiH is most unlikely to extend the dual citizenship arrangement it has
with Croatia to Serbia because relations between the two countries are far
more sensitive. Although Serbia (as part of the then Yugoslav federation)
recognised BiH statehood as part of the Dayton Agreement of 1995,
signed by Milosevic, post-Milosevic nationalist politicians have not helped
to rebuild trust. Major responsibility for this lies not only with the SRS,
which continues to hark back to the 'Greater Serbia' project, but also with
Vojislav Kostunica, who replaced Milosevic as President of Yugoslavia in
2000, and now, as leader of the DSS, is Prime Minister of Serbia.

The ambiguities of Kostunica's position are particularly apparent on the
question of relations with BiH. On the one hand, his party (DSS) is committed to the 'consistent implementation' of the Dayton Agreement, which
looks encouraging from the point of view of Serbia's compliance with the
EU's regional stability conditionality. The section of his party's programme
dedicated to 'National Policy' declares its commitment to the maintenance
of the existing borders in the region, and 'resolutely opposes any renewal of
a [Yugoslav-type] state or the eventual creation of a community of states
with the neighbouring peoples' (see DSS website). But all this is couched in
the language of defending the Serbian national interest and strengthening
Serbian statehood – and in particular, keeping Kosovo as part of Serbia –
rather than that of commitment to rebuilding the region in line with the
logic and practical demands of preparing for European integration.

What the DSS finds most valuable in the Dayton Agreement is precisely
what the international community has found its most troublesome aspect
– the formal recognition of Republika Srpska as one of the two constituent entities of the BiH state. Not only was this created by violent
ethnic warfare, but remains governed by a deeply entrenched, corrupt
and criminalised elite who have obstructed the project of building a functional Bosnian state promoted by the successive High Representatives of
the international community who retain ultimate powers of government
(ICG 2003b; Knaus and Cox 2004). Dayton also provided for the right of
the entities to develop 'special relationships' with neighbouring countries.
In March 2001, Republika Srpska duly signed an agreement with the then
Yugoslavia proclaiming their 'special relationship' (although the practical
substance of this remains obscure). Shortly afterwards, in July 2001, Kostunica's party, the DSS, concluded a 'Protocol on Cooperation' with the

Bosnian Serb nationalist party, the SDS, founded by the fugitive indicted war criminal Radovan Karadjic (see DSS website). These moves indicate that Kostunica has not abandoned the commitment to Republika Srpska as an organic part of the 'Serbian nation' that he expressed in the 1990s:

> Only with the continued survival of Republika Srpska will Serbia continue to have two lungs. Without the western lands [i.e. territories in BiH], Serbia would become an invalid, with only one lung
>
> (quoted in Cigar 2001: 25)

In this context, dual citizenship between Serbia and BiH has obviously threatening implications for the latter acutely fragile state. This is aggravated in light of recent moves, promoted by Mr Vukcevic, the Serbian Minister for the Diaspora, to further develop Serbian electoral law to allow Serbian citizens resident abroad to exercise their right to vote in Serbian elections without returning home (*BETA online*, 2 April 2004). This right has hitherto only been exercised by Serbs living in Western Europe (very few of whom have shown any interest in it). But if it were extended to Serbs with dual citizenship living in BiH, the implications would be much more far-reaching. What would happen if Bosnian Serbs decided to turn out *en masse* to vote for deputies in the Serbian parliament, or the President of Serbia, while boycotting BiH elections? This is by no means an improbable scenario, and has already happened in Kosovo.

Conclusions

European integration has not proved an unambiguous benefit for the Hungarians in their pursuit of rights for the Hungarian minorities beyond the borders. The Schengen *acquis* proved an immovable obstacle to the hoped-for 'melting away' of borders, as long as neighbouring states were left outside the magic circle of the enlarged EU. In striving to overcome borders, Hungarians discovered that the 'nation-state' could not so easily be wished away. European integration in fact presupposes the existence of states. While these states must demonstrate 'respect for and protection of the rights of minorities', the Hungarians were frustrated to find that their European partners and neighbours did not interpret this in the same way as themselves. The requirement that any state wishing to join in the process of European integration conform with the imperative of regional stability reconfirmed the primacy of states over minorities, and host-states over kin-states. Thus trade-offs between the elements of the Hungarian foreign policy 'triad' were found, after all, to be unavoidable: they could not continue to pursue their goal of strengthening the national bond between Hungarians irrespective of borders without jeopardising their relations with their neighbours; and as they could not secure enough support for that model among other European states, they risked their wider 'Euro-Atlantic' integration prospects. In the end, Hungary chose European integration because it had developed a parallel, state-centred sense of its 'national interest' focussed on material prosperity, social welfare, and its international reputation as a reliable 'European'. But the sense of having 'lost' on the national question lingers on.

The Serbs today are only just at the beginning – if even that – of the process of coming to terms with the borders bequeathed to them by the utter failure of the 'Greater Serbia' project launched by Milosevic in the 1990s. Their nationalism has yet to undergo the liberal metamorphosis that has taken place in Hungary. The attractive power of 'Europe' is much weaker, and on certain key issues – especially cooperation with the ICTY and the resolution of Kosovo's 'final status' – they are still likely to find themselves pitted against Europe, the EU and the international community. The Serbs will no doubt prove less graceful losers than the Hungarians.

Part II

Case studies

10 From 'full national status' to 'independence' in Europe

The case of Plaid Cymru – the Party of Wales

Anwen Elias

Introduction[1]

Since the late 1980s, Plaid Cymru has proposed the notion of 'full national status for Wales within the European Union' (Plaid Cymru 1989) as an expression of its constitutional aims for Welsh self-government, according to which Wales would take its place in Europe alongside other small nations such as Luxembourg, Denmark and Belgium. In September 2003, however, the party's Annual Conference voted to modify this expression in favour of 'independence in Europe'. Such a move may seem surprising when the following two observations are taken into account. In the first place, Plaid Cymru has, since it was established in the mid 1920s, persistently rejected the nineteenth-century vocabulary of sovereign statehood as the expression of its constitutional aims, preferring to use terms such as 'freedom' and 'autonomy' as more appropriate representations of its long-term aspirations for the Welsh nation (Christiansen 1998: 130–2). Second, this move seems out of sync with the similarly 'post-sovereigntist' formulations adopted by other minority nationalist parties in Western Europe, constitutional alternatives which appear propitious in a European context where traditional structures of political authority are being undermined (Keating 2001b).

This chapter will argue, however, that rather than signalling a radical new departure in Plaid Cymru's attitude towards European integration, 'independence' is the latest attempt by the party to reconcile a normative project for the recognition of the 'nationalities question' (Keating 2004a) on the supranational level, with the more problematic reality of a European polity in which the role for these historic nations is not clear. Building upon a deeply rooted ideological commitment to an international context for Welsh self-determination, Plaid Cymru has fashioned a European discourse which, by the 1990s, established an intrinsic link between the two processes of self-determination and European integration. In order to understand the trajectory of this discourse, however, it is necessary to examine the changing political and institutional contexts in which it has been forged. Of interest in this respect are developments on the

Welsh and British levels, as much as on the European one. As such, it will be argued that changes in Plaid Cymru's European discourse over time reflects the emergence and closure of different political opportunity structures in different political spheres, and the responses made by the party to these opportunities. Finally, it will be suggested that, contrary to what the slogan 'independence in Europe' has suggested to many commentators, Plaid Cymru's conceptualisation does not necessarily equate to sovereign statehood, and as such, the terminological change in describing the party's long-term constitutional objective does not betray the party's post-sovereigntist legacy. On the contrary, it represents the most recent attempt by a party committed in principle to Welsh self-government in a European framework to reconcile the challenges of being a non-state actor in a state-dominated political world without actually having to become a state itself.

The historical and ideological origins of Plaid Cymru

Plaid Cymru was established in 1925 in response to the rapidly changing socioeconomic, political, cultural and religious conditions in Wales in the immediate post-First World War period (Morgan 1981: chap. 7), as an expression of rising fears over the future of the Welsh culture, language and way of life. To this extent, Plaid Cymru's early years were dominated by cultural and linguistic considerations, couched in the conservative Catholicism of its leader at the time, the poet and prominent cultural figure Saunders Lewis.[2]

While the relative importance of this cultural dimension was to wax and wane over time, to these core values a more socioeconomic project was gradually elaborated. While it took until 1981 for the party to officially include the word 'socialism' in the party's aims, Plaid Cymru has always been inspired by socialist principles to a greater or lesser degree, albeit an interpretation which rejects the centralisation of economic control in the hands of the state, in favour of a social model inspired by the twin themes of decentralisation and cooperation. The continuity of this line of thinking can be traced from the early thinking of D.J. Davies in the 1930s, to the economic strategies proposed by Plaid's newly active research group at the end of the 1960s (Wigley 1992), to the party's most recent policy proposals. A second ideological tenet is that of environmentalism. If much of the nationalist mobilisation in the inter-war period was inspired by a strong, if romantic, attachment to the land of Wales, over time this would be re-fashioned into a more tangible ecological dimension in Plaid's ideology. The 'greening' of Plaid Cymru during the 1980s and 1990s saw this strand of policy become intrinsically linked to the notion of economic responsibility for the Welsh environment (McAllister 2001: 179).

Finally, and most importantly for the interest of this chapter, Plaid Cymru's political and constitutional project has historically espoused a conceptualisation of the self-determination of the Welsh nation which has been both post-sovereigntist and internationalist in character. It has been post-sovereigntist in as much as – as suggested above – Plaid Cymru has traditionally rejected the language of classic statehood and independence as the ultimate aims of Welsh nationalism in favour of alternative constitutional options which fall short of these modern legal and political configurations, although it has not always been clear what 'freedom' or 'autonomy' for Wales would mean in practice. These constitutional proposals have also been internationalist in their linking of Welsh self-determination to a broader international framework within which a self-determined Wales would take its place alongside other similar historical and cultural entities. For Saunders Lewis, Wales' cultural, socioeconomic and environmental predilections were placed, not in a British, but a European historical context. His definition of Wales as an old European nation harked back to the Middle Ages, in which no European country was independent or free, but where the authority of the Church respected and guaranteed cultural diversity. The subsequent growth of statist nationalism, with its corresponding pressures for cultural, linguistic and institutional homogeneity, undermined this 'unity in diversity'. According to Lewis, therefore, the only hope for Welsh nationalism was to go back to the principle of the Middle Ages, in which self-government for Wales would be achieved within an overarching European framework of authority. In this respect, Plaid Cymru welcomed the League of Nations as a basis for a new and united Europe which would achieve just that.

This early 'internationalism' is vital for understanding Plaid Cymru's nationalist project and, more specifically, its response to European integration. Historically, this influence has translated into successive attempts to situate Welsh nationalism in a broader political and historical context and has provided an important reference of legitimation for the party in its pursuit of self-determination. While Plaid's early aspirations for European cooperation were undermined by the political conflicts and failures of the European state system in the 1930s and 1940s, an alternative agenda of cooperative small-nation politics had become deeply ingrained in Plaid Cymru's political thinking, and would re-emerge in Plaid's responses to the development of European integration in later years (Lynch 1996: 57). However, the precise form that these responses would take would depart markedly from Saunders Lewis' archaic Catholic ideal, and would be conditioned not only by the enduring historical influences of the party's social and economic ideological profile as outlined above, but also the more immediate effects of the changing political situation in which Plaid Cymru was to find itself, both on the domestic and supranational levels.

From pressure group to political party – 1945–79

In the post-war period, however, Plaid's preoccupation was more with domestic organisation than with supranational posturing. Under Gwynfor Evans' leadership (1945–81), the party concentrated on the pragmatic challenges of internal organisation and electoral advancement, although its impact on the Welsh political stage remained marginal until the mid 1960s (Butt Philip 1975: 104–23). While the party may have been aware of the advances in European cooperation and the potential impact on Welsh issues (Lynch 1996: 58–9), it had no official policy on Europe, and Plaid's day-to-day attentions were firmly focused closer to home. Its constitutional proposals were still presented in essentially domestic terms – a Welsh government within a British federation, complemented by an internal market for the British Isles, with authority for certain issues (defence, macroeconomic policy) residing with the British state (Wigley 1993: 14).

The 1960s and 1970s, however, was a period of profound change for Plaid Cymru, both in terms of internal programmatic and organisational changes that the party undertook, and its placement within the Welsh and British political system in relation to other political parties. In the first place, the electoral strategy undertaken by the party leadership depended on developing a more conventional political profile which would present Plaid Cymru as a more acceptable and responsible political option for the Welsh electorate. While such a programmatic shift was not unopposed by party traditionalists, a split was avoided by the creation, in 1962, of a separate Welsh Language Society. This effectively served as a division of labour, enabling Plaid to distance itself from the image of being a radical Welsh language pressure group and brand itself as a more inclusive nationalist political party with a broad socioeconomic programme for Wales. This strategic choice was rewarded with a series of electoral successes in general and local elections in the 1970s.[3] Choosing to go down the electoral avenue, however, presented a new set of challenges for a small party with limited financial resources, and the question of the most appropriate institutional sphere in which to compete electorally (Westminster vs. local government) dominated internal party debates during these years of transition. It will be argued below that the opening up of new political and institutional opportunities on the supranational level in the late 1970s provided a new set of options for the party to consider in attempting to resolve these strategic dilemmas, new opportunity structures which would play a role in encouraging and confirming the party's changing attitude towards Europe during the 1980s and 1990s.

Second, by the end of the 1970s, two issues had emerged on the political agenda that were to dominate British politics for the decade to come, and which were to be decisive in defining the politics of Welsh nationalism for much longer: UK membership of the European Economic Community (EEC) and devolution for Scotland and Wales. The way that

Plaid Cymru responded to these two issues, and its failure in both cases to mobilise popular support for its political programme, set the scene for a period of profound reflection in the 1980s which not only saw Plaid Cymru revive Saunders Lewis' idea of a European dimension to Welsh nationalism, but the very aim of self-government for Wales would become intrinsically associated with the process of European polity formation.

Plaid Cymru and European integration up to 1979

On its third attempt, the UK finally acceded to the club of European member states in 1973. This decision fuelled a highly contentious and deeply divisive debate within British political parties which was to constitute a new issue cleavage within the political system. For Plaid Cymru, UK accession to the European Community raised a specific set of concerns about the potential impact of integration on the Welsh economy, still largely dominated by heavy industries such as coal and steel and plagued by high levels of unemployment (Morgan 1981: 336).

Pushed to take a position on the European dimension by the 1975 Referendum on continued UK membership of the EEC, the party's stance was both complex and ambiguous. Plaid Cymru's slogan for its referendum campaign – 'Europe, YES; EEC, NO' – represented an attempt to reconcile fundamentally opposed ideological tendencies within the party. On the one hand, the EEC as it had evolved up to that point was conceived as being highly unsatisfactory. Two strands of opposition can be distinguished. A first rejects European integration on the political grounds that the lack of representation for Wales within the centralised and state-dominated European institutions was incompatible with the stated aims of Welsh self-government. Membership of the EEC represented yet another layer of remote, bureaucratic and undemocratic government which would not only add nothing to the prospects of Welsh self-determination, but would effectively move in the opposite direction (Turner 1998: 75). A second, more virulent, basis of opposition takes issue with the economic principles underlying the EEC, a critique taken up by the left-wing of the party and which was to prove the more enduring tenet of Plaid's anti-integrationist rhetoric. For these 'anti-marketeers' (Wigley 1992: 323), the EEC was a 'capitalist club' whose common market would leave Wales economically isolated on the periphery of Europe. Echoing the pronouncements of the British Labour Left more generally, the EEC was therefore incompatible with the socialist underpinnings of Plaid's basic ideology which emphasised local democracy, social justice and communitarianism. Furthermore, Wales would only enter the free market when it could negotiate its own terms – in other words when it had achieved self-government – at which time, a re-negotiation of the Rome Treaty would be a priority (Mathews 1971).

On the other hand, however, and as this last observation suggests, there was a simultaneous hankering for independent membership for Wales if the conditions were right, as expressed by a reluctance to dismiss the European project outright and a commitment to European union in principle. Plaid Cymru's preference, in other words, was for some kind of Europe, but not this kind of Europe, although nothing more concrete was offered as an alternative beyond the frequent invocations of the romantic 'internationalism' first elucidated by Saunders Lewis in the 1920s and 1930s.

It should be noted that a third strand of opinion within Plaid Cymru at this time, albeit wholly marginalised, recognised from the outset the political potential that European integration presented for Wales. Dafydd Wigley, long inspired by the political writings of the Austrian Leopold Kohr on European federalism and decentralisation, recalls the contradictions in Plaid's arguments at the time (Wigley 1992: 308–12). Not only was Wales a long way from achieving the self-government they made the precondition of any possible Welsh membership of the EEC, but European integration was also a reality ignored at the party's peril, and any hope of reforming the European project along more amenable lines could only be done from within the EEC. However, the dismissal of these arguments designated Wigley to the political sidelines, at least in so far as the European debate at the time was concerned. However, as is argued below, the eventual success of the Yes vote in the referendum,[4] subsequently interpreted as a rejection of Plaid Cymru's two-pronged approach to European affairs, provided the conditions for this pro-European minority to advance anew their alternative European agenda.

Devolution in the 1970s and the defeat of Welsh nationalism

The issue of devolution for Scotland and Wales was first mooted in the late 1960s, when the unexpected success of Welsh and Scottish nationalists in a series of Westminster by-elections (Wigley 1992: 73–83) pushed Harold Wilson's Labour Government to set up a Commission of Inquiry into the relationship between Westminster and the nations and regions of the UK. Widely viewed as a tactic for stalling the political momentum of the nationalists, the question of devolution did not, however, go away. In the October 1974 British General Election, the Labour Government returned to power with a slim majority of only three seats, leaving the Scottish Nationalist Party and Plaid Cymru (with 11 and three seats, respectively) to hold the sway of power. The bargaining leverage accorded to the nationalists led to significant concessions from the government on the issue of constitutional reform, and paved the way for the 1979 referendum on devolution for Scotland and Wales.

Far from delivering the constitutional reform that the advocates of Welsh devolution had hoped for, the results of the referendum were disastrous for Plaid Cymru for several reasons. First, the unequivocal rejection of devolution by the Welsh electorate also equated to the rejection of the political project that Plaid Cymru had made its own, one which presented devolution as the first step to Welsh self-determination. The devolution proposals put to the vote on 1 March of that year were rejected by an over-whelming 79.74 per cent of those who voted in Wales, on a turnout of 58.8 per cent.[5] Second, and most damagingly, Plaid Cymru's credibility had been greatly compromised by the campaign in the run-up to the referen-dum. The party's decision to support the plans for devolution even though they fell far short of what they had called for, contrasted with opposition on the part of a significant number of Labour MPs to their own govern-ment's proposals. As a result, Plaid Cymru was put in the bizarre position of advocating legislation that the governing party itself was deeply divided over (Wigley 1992: 319). By being too closely identified in the eyes of the electorate with devolution and the incumbent administration, a vote for Plaid Cymru was also a vote of sanction for the deeply unpopular Wilson government. Finally, and in an affirmation of the strategic use of the refer-endum vote as a rejection of Labour policies, the landslide win of Thatcher's Conservative Party in the General Election a few months later sounded the death knell to any hopes that Plaid Cymru had of keeping the devolution issue on the British political agenda for years to come.

From 'anti-EEC' to 'full national status in Europe'

> There can be no doubt that many of our present problems as a party can be traced back directly to 1979, the year that witnessed the disap-pearance of Devolution and the beginning of the reign of Thatch-erism in Britain . . . The devolution vote put an end to the relevance which Plaid's political programme may have had, placing the party on the fringes of Welsh politics. Similarly, the Tory Party's complete dom-inance at Westminster also served to castrate the party in the very field it had chosen to take the path of freedom.
>
> (Jones 1985: A80)

Plaid Cymru in the early 1980s, therefore, was a party in considerable turmoil, its political project having been undermined by the 1975 and 1979 referendums on EEC membership and Welsh devolution, respec-tively, and its relevancy for the future of Welsh politics seriously ques-tioned in light of the electoral whitewash that was the 1979 General Election. Plaid Cymru was rendered a party devoid of purpose or strategy, relegated to the margins of the political system. In such unfavourable con-ditions, Plaid Cymru had little choice except to reflect deeply on its *raison d'être*, to attempt to understand the reasons for its successive failures over recent years, and to seek a way out of the political wilderness and reinstate itself as the only party of Welsh self-government.

However, if domestic political conditions provided the catalyst for such a re-evaluation, developments on the supranational level would provide a new framework within which this process would take place. What began as an attempt to re-align itself vis-à-vis an unsympathetic domestic political arena by a party whose sphere of reference was, up to that point, essentially British, culminates by the mid 1990s in a party ideologically committed to the European polity as the only context in which a self-governing and autonomous Welsh nation could be achieved. By providing an alternative political arena when the domestic one is firmly closed off, Europe allows Plaid Cymru to 'rebuild the nation internally by projecting it externally as part of a European family' (Keating 2004b: 3). The next section will return to this theme of the new European political opportunity structure and how Plaid Cymru sought to take advantage of it to resolve the internal crisis that arose out of British political developments at the end of the 1970s. Suffice it here to give an overview of the main developments in this evolving European discourse during the 1980s and 1990s.

In the immediate aftermath of 1979, it would seem, at least on the level of political rhetoric, that little has changed. An internal inquiry set up to consider the position of the party at the beginning of the 1980s notes on the issue of European integration that 'it will be necessary to determine whether we should seek to amend and improve the structure and functioning of the EEC (as well as fighting for proper representation for Wales) or whether we should promote the collapse of the EEC' (Plaid Cymru 1981: 9). However, these alternatives were largely academic; the internal political turmoil within the party at the time provided the conditions for the Left to tighten its grip on the party machinery, and their preference for the latter option showed continuity with their opposition to the EEC in 1975. Under the sway of the radical so-called 'National Left', a political programme inspired by the principles of 'democratic socialism' did not tire of pointing out the ills of European economic integration, encompassing the discriminatory effects of the CAP, the undermining of the Welsh coal and steel industry, and the detrimental social effects of rising unemployment. Plaid Cymru's manifesto for the 1979 European Parliamentary elections was largely consistent with the tone and content of the party's rhetoric four years earlier, and combined a lambasting of the economic free-trade model of integration with the idealism of a 'Europe of the peoples based on free and equal nations co-operating within a loose confederation' (Plaid Cymru 1979). The fact that the issue of Europe was not discussed at all at the party's Annual Conferences in 1981 and 1982 suggests that, at least for the time being, this was a subject not up for discussion.

And yet, behind the scenes, changes were afoot that were to gradually steer the party towards a more favourable stance on the European issue. For example, Turner (1998: 109–10) notes that by 1978, Gwynfor Evans had already accepted the realities of British membership of the EEC and that Plaid Cymru's priority should be to campaign for better representation for Wales within the European institutions. Moreover, the election of

Dafydd Wigley as Plaid Cymru's president in 1981 boosted the confidence of the pro-European minority within the party, which gradually took on the arguments of the radical Left at a time when the latter's appeal was being undermined by the collapse of the Left more generally within the British political sphere. As a result of the tension between these two tendencies, the European question was one of the most hotly debated issues at the party's 1983 Annual Conference, in response to a motion put forward by the National Executive which would re-affirm the party's opposition to Wales' incorporation within the EEC as part of the British state, but which called for a new relationship between the nations and regions of Europe (*Welsh Nation* 1983: 1). In the face of considerable opposition from the membership, the compromise eventually reached was essentially a repackaging of existing policy, which condemned the institutional and economic failures of the EEC whilst calling for better Welsh representation within the European institutions (Lynch 1996: 73). Interestingly, however, the party's manifesto for the 1984 European Parliamentary elections (Plaid Cymru 1984) was more constructive in tone and content than either the 1983 conference motion or the 1979 European Parliament electoral manifesto, advocating a strong voice for Wales in Europe alongside other small nations and historic regions. The party's eventual pro-EEC stance was thus the outcome of an elite-driven process which, by the end of the 1980s, would be distilled down to, and be endorsed by, the party faithful.

As will be illustrated in greater detail below, the results of the 1984 European elections were to prove decisive in confirming the direction of the party's changing attitudes vis-à-vis Europe, and constituted the breakthrough of ideas long mooted by the likes of Dafydd Wigley, into the mainstream of the party's thinking. The party's Annual Conference in 1988 endorsed, for the first time, a motion supporting the Single European Act and calling for reform from within, rather than withdrawal. At the 1989 European Parliamentary elections, the party campaigned under the slogan 'A Voice for Wales in Europe', and even appeared as 'Plaid Cymru – Wales in Europe' on the ballot paper. The party's Annual Conference in 1990 gave unanimous support for a new constitutional blueprint spelling out how a self-governing Wales would take its place in a wider European Community, and laid down the constitutional principles which would constitute Plaid's European policy until the end of the 1990s. 'Full national status for Wales within the European Union (EU)' would mean, in the short term, giving Wales 15 MEPs and direct representation in the Council of Ministers. In the longer term, a European Confederation would emerge from the twin processes of the transfer of competences upwards to the European polity and downwards to the historical nations and regions which already existed below the state level in most European countries, thus creating a two-tier polity in which the autonomy of the constituent units would be constitutionally guaranteed. The Committee of the Regions would evolve into a Senate of the Nations and Regions to be a second chamber of the European Parliament, and would be composed of representatives of national and regional parliaments. Moreover, the powers of the Council of Ministers would be transferred to the European Parliament and Senate, which together would make European law.

In summary, therefore, 'full national status for Wales within the European Union' represented Plaid's answer to the question of Welsh self-government and how to achieve it, and in the political climate of the time, seemed to offer a feasible way forward for a small nation seeking to establish itself as an autonomous political actor on the European political scene. It is inspired by the party's awareness of the clearly regionalist momentum that European integration seemed to be mounting at the time, with the creation of the Committee of the Regions and the increases in European Regional Funds seemingly giving substance to calls for a 'Europe of the Regions'. The adoption of the terminology of 'full national status' as opposed to outright independence for Wales in Europe, reflects this regionalist dynamic, in as much as it seeks to put forward an alternative model of organising political authority and decision-making which does not depend on classic models of statehood. Given what has been said above of Plaid Cymru's historical ideological preference for post-sovereigntist conceptualisations of Welsh self-determination, the appeal of this European discourse is clear to see. 'Full national status', according to Plaid Cymru's understanding, represents a qualitatively different kind of political organisation and representation which is an alternative to, rather than simply falling short of, full statehood. In the details of Plaid Cymru's proposals for arriving at this non-state based European Confederation, it is difficult to see in which ways 'full national status' differs pragmatically from the rights that would be accorded to an independent state, in other words being a member state of the EU, and this semantic vagueness would return to haunt the party in later years. Nevertheless, in the mid 1990s, this constitutional formulation represented Plaid Cymru's aspirations for a future European and regional constitutional order which appeared to hold the potential for Wales to accede to the responsibilities of statehood without having to become an independent state.

If these are the key turning points in the development of Plaid's European discourse, what are its defining features? Two things are important to note in this respect. In the first place, on the rhetorical level, the attraction of Europe is unequivocally as an alternative to, rather than co-existing with, the British state; indeed, Europe is precisely a way of circumventing the constraining framework of the latter, with the corollary that the supranational level is both more receptive to, and considerate of, arguments for Welsh political, economic and cultural specificity. In this spirit, the party's electoral propaganda for the 1989 elections makes no bones about the fact that Plaid Cymru's aim is to replace the idea of 'Britishness' with 'Europeanness' as the broader context for Welsh identity, and this within the framework of a 'Europe of the Peoples' where values dear to Plaid Cymru –

local democracy, social justice and 'community socialism' (McAllister 2001: 171) – are better safeguarded than within the framework of the British state. Indeed, and on the evidence of the comparable cases of other small nations and historic regions in Europe, a self-governed Wales in Europe appears not as utopian but, on the contrary, demonstrably preferable to the current situation (Christiansen 1998: 130). Moreover, the fact that Plaid Cymru's new European sentiments echo the aspirations of other like-minded political actors within the European political space reinforces and legitimises this discourse, and provides the basis for a common platform for promoting nationalist concerns within the supranational sphere.

Second, and especially during the 1990s, there is an attempt by the party to refine these new ideas by going beyond the political rhetoric and symbolism of Europe as an abstract normative construction (Hermant 1992: 3), to consider the pragmatic implications of this new constitutional project for the Welsh nationalist project. There are three dimensions to such an endeavour, which consider the programmatic, strategic and political implications of 'full national status in Europe' respectively. Thus, a programmatic linkage is established between Plaid's socioeconomic policy priorities and the supranational context through a policy division of labour which argues that while some policy areas, such as the environment and international peace and security, are by their very nature better dealt with on a supranational level, other policy areas which are domestic in their scope (housing, education and health and social services) would remain on the 'national' level, but nevertheless considered against the backdrop of European developments.

Similarly, from a strategic perspective, the new institutional opportunities created on the supranational level, in stark contrast to the lack of such opportunities on the domestic level, prompted a comprehensive review of the party's political action plan. The emergent strategy emphasised three fronts on which the party should concentrate its political and electoral activities in order to present anew its policy on self-government. These included (1) capitalising on the unique context provided by European elections for setting out Plaid's role as an international voice for Wales; (2) the development of an 'all-Wales' party which appeals to an electorate beyond the party's traditional Welsh-speaking heartlands; and (3) the mobilisation of a broader coalition of social forces around the idea of autonomy, by making contacts with other political forces (Lynch 1995). As such, the European sphere is accorded a central position in the party's comprehensive strategic thinking and is no longer simply a five yearly electoral cycle which periodically demands the party's attention.

Finally, and perhaps most strikingly, the rhetorical and strategic opportunities identified at the supranational level provide the impetus for a far-reaching ideological re-evaluation of Plaid Cymru's constitutional aims. Whereas these had largely been ignored since the 1950s, the debates that took place within the party during the 1990s attempted, not only in adopting these out-dated references to reflect a changed reality, but proposed a programme of political and constitutional reform within the European framework in which the latter is conceived as the basic constitutive element of the nationalist project. By the mid 1990s, these ideas took the shape of a two-phase process, the first corresponding to the devolution of a range of powers to a law-making Welsh Parliament, and the second seeing the transfer of all remaining Westminster competencies (apart from those already transferred to Brussels) to a fully self-governing Wales. When this second stage would be completed,

> Wales would . . . no longer send MPs to Westminster nor would it have a Secretary of State. There would then be a full seat for Wales in the European Council of Ministers . . . Wales would also have its own Commissioner in Brussels. Eventually we would want to see the diminishing and eclipse of the Council of Ministers, with its replacement coming by way of a second chamber in the European Parliament – a Chamber of the regions and nations.

In other words, 'a system of full self-government within the European Union' (Plaid Cymru 1995).

If this evolution from Plaid Cymru's virulent anti-EEC stance at the beginning of the 1980s to its Euro-enthusiasm by the mid 1990s is striking in terms of the changing content of the party's European discourse, it should also be said, however, that unlike the experience of other statewide political parties in Wales, this evolution was relatively undramatic, with individuals coming to their own decisions in their own time. For Dr Phil Williams, an influential intellectual figure within the party, the introduction of direct elections to the European Parliament, the positive experiences of the Irish in negotiating better deals from the CAP than was the case for Wales, and the opportunities of attracting foreign investment to Wales, provided evidence that there was no longer an alternative to campaigning for Welsh interests within the EEC (Turner 1998: 113–14). Dafydd Elis Thomas, doyen of the radical Left in the early 1980s and party president from 1984 to 1991, attributed his change of attitude during the 1983 General Election campaign to a tactical move destined to differentiate Plaid Cymru from the Labour Party, who was campaigning for withdrawal from the EEC at the time, as well as by an increasing awareness of Wales' disadvantageous economic situation vis-à-vis other European regions (Turner 1998: 115).

The testimony of these two leading opponents to EEC turned zealous Europhiles, returns to a theme already introduced in passing above, namely that of developments on the supranational level as an important background to, and influence on, Plaid Cymru's re-evaluation of European integration since the 1970s. It is to a further consideration of these developments on the European level that this chapter will now turn.

Developments in European integration: a new opportunity structure

If the EEC to which Plaid Cymru objected so strongly in the 1970s was essentially an economic project grounded in the principles of a common market and a free-trade model of competition, the EU has developed into a transnational regime explicitly committed to political as well as economic integration, developments which have gone some way towards assuaging the nationalist aspirations of actors like Plaid Cymru. These developments have assumed a variety of forms. Legally, the entrenchment of the 'subsidiarity' principle in European Community law provides the basis, at least according to one interpretation, for a reinforcement of the regional level as appropriate for certain areas of decision-making, while the evolution of a pan-European rights regime, divorced from national citizenship, acknowledges issues such as the collective rights of minorities and cultural and linguistic diversity (Keating 2001a: 143–7). Functionally, the redistribution of certain policy competencies from the state domain to the European institutions has overlapped with Plaid Cymru's own policy priorities, for example environmental protection and peace and security. This policy overlap has been exploited by the party as evidence of the common political interest between itself and Europe, and has been used to reinforce the idea of the functional division of labour between Wales and Europe alluded to above. Symbolically, a 'Europe of the Peoples' may be a slogan, but it represents an important discursive turn because it shows that other ways of realising nationhood can at least be imagined (Keating 2001a: 137) and constitutes a basis for uniting different actors with common interests to mobilise for the future regionalisation of the European polity (see below).

Institutionally, the supranational level allows Plaid Cymru to project itself as a political actor in the new European order. In the sphere of Welsh politics, Wales' receipt of EU structural funds provides a good example of how Plaid Cymru has sought to exploit European avenues to reinforce its own political position vis-à-vis other state-wide political parties in Wales. As well as providing an important financial resource, the politics surrounding the administration of these funds have provided a political platform for Plaid Cymru to flaunt its direct contacts with European Commission officials, usually with the effect of putting to shame the Government's own failures in this area. One interviewee recalls how, upon the introduction of the European Milk Quota regime in the UK in the early 1980s and its damaging repercussions for the Welsh dairy industry, Plaid Cymru organised a deputation to Brussels to meet with the responsible European Commissioner and give voice to the grievances of Welsh farmers. The fact that a Commission official subsequently visited Wales and declared publicly that at no point had the impact on Welsh agriculture been raised by the Thatcher government in the preceding negotiations, represented a huge political coup for the party, one which it is claimed translated into notable numeric gains in subsequent elections.

Directly on the European level, even though the Committee of the Regions did not prove to be the harbinger of a regional Europe that Plaid Cymru had hoped for, the European Parliament provides a second forum where non-government parties can achieve representation of their interests within the EU. Even though Plaid Cymru voted against the introduction of direct elections to the European Parliament in 1977 on the grounds that the body constituted nothing more than a 'democratic charade',[6] the European Parliament has provided a fruitful new arena for mobilising around the themes of cultural and linguistic diversity and the rights of the small nations and regions of Europe. The ways in which this is so is worth examining in greater detail.

European parliamentary elections

As with many other minority nationalist parties (Raunio 2003), Plaid Cymru boasts a pattern of better-than-average results in European elections (see Table 10.1), historically performing better than in state-wide General Elections (see Figure 10.1). Most importantly, however, at a time in the late 1970s and early 1980s when the party suffered a profound identity crisis, the political effect of such positive results cannot be underestimated. The results of the 1979 European Parliamentary elections were to be as decisive as they were unexpected: Plaid Cymru polled 11.7 per cent of the Welsh vote, compared to 8.1 per cent in the General Election a few months earlier, and its best ever electoral performance at the time. In the words of one senior Plaid Cymru member,[7] 'the loss of the 1975 referendum, losing ground in the 1979 UK General Election, but making significant gains in the European elections had an important psychological effect on Plaid', and forced people to reflect seriously on the implications of these different experiences.

A similar electoral pattern reproduced in June 1984 served to reinforce the gradual evolution of a more positive European discourse which had begun to emerge since the end of the 1970s. As Dafydd Wigley recalls in his autobiography, 'we succeeded in destroying the misconception that had poisoned the mindset of Plaid for over twenty years, that is that the European Community was a threat to our nationalist aspirations. Things changed in light of the 1984 election' (Wigley 1992: 327). Indeed, if European elections up to this point had the effect of vindicating the opportunities on the supranational level, once the party had committed itself to this route, European elections became a platform from which to project the party's new image, a unique opportunity for situating Wales directly in its international context; 'the European campaign has a very important political and ideological significance for Plaid in that it relates Wales directly to the international level outside the British State' (Thomas 1989: E14). To

Table 10.1 European election results for Wales, 1979–2004

Party	1979		1984		1989		1994		1999		2004	
	%	Seats	%	Seats	%	Seats	%	Seats	%	Seats	%	Seats
Labour	41.5	3	44.5	3	48.9	4	55.9	4	31.9	2	32.5	2
Conservatives	36.6	1	25.4	1	23.4	0	14.6	0	22.8	1	19.4	1
Liberal Democrats	9.6	0	17.4	0	3.6	0	8.7	0	8.2	0	10.5	0
Plaid Cymru	11.7	0	12.2	0	12.9	0	17.1	0	29.6	2	17.4	1
Others	0.6	0	0.6	0	11.2	0	3.7	0	7.5	0	20.2	0
Total	100	4	100	4	100	4	100	4	100	5	100	4

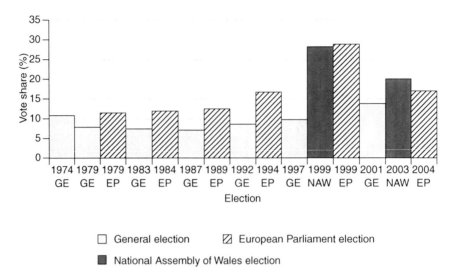

Figure 10.1 Plaid Cymru results in General, European and National Assembly of Wales elections (1974–2004).

heighten this effect, the selection of senior party members, including party presidents, as candidates was a tactic both for emphasising the importance of the European dimension to Plaid's political project, and guaranteeing the high-profile media coverage that would achieve such an effect.[8]

Two additional observations should be made on the data shown in Table 10.1 on Plaid Cymru's performance in European elections. First, the fact that the party did not return an MEP to Strasbourg until 1999, despite commanding an increasing percentage of the vote since 1979, can be attributed to the disproportional effects of the first-past-the-post electoral system operational for most of these contests. The change of system in June 1999 to one of proportional representation thus removed a major structural obstacle for Welsh nationalist representation within the European Parliament. Plaid Cymru's chances were further improved in 1999 by the creation of a fifth European constituency in Wales. In the event, Plaid Cymru's first ever MEPs were elected by 29.6 per cent of the Welsh vote, only a few points behind the Labour Party. The elimination of this fifth constituency in 2004 would reinstate this disadvantage for Plaid Cymru, who lost its second MEP. Second, however, the loss of this second European representative cannot only be attributed to the decrease in the number of constituencies. Figure 10.1 illustrates a clear decline in the party's vote percentage in 2004, a change in fortunes which had been anticipated by a similar electoral downturn in the National Assembly elections in the previous year. Explaining this decline will be the subject of the final section of this chapter.

Momentarily putting aside the 2004 electoral downturn, how can Plaid Cymru's positive electoral performance up until 1999 be accounted for? If the added political exposure and degree of electoral success can explain the strategic importance assigned by Plaid Cymru to European Parliamentary elections, understanding the causes of this success in the first place is less straight forward. On the one hand, and as suggested by the notion of 'second-order elections', voters may find it easier to vote for Plaid Cymru in European elections because they are not voting for a government, and therefore there is less at stake. This logic has been used to explain the general trend for small and non-governmental parties to do better at European parliamentary elections than in other types of elections, especially national legislative elections (Raunio 2003).

On the other hand, however, Plaid Cymru itself proposes a second explanation of the party's success which relates to the greater ease with which Plaid can get its message across in European elections. It is argued that the fact that the European Parliament is not only external to the domestic political sphere, but also operates according to a different logic to that which drives British political competition, means that European elections will be less conditioned by Westminster rhetoric and conventional determinants of voter choice. In such a situation, Plaid Cymru, as the only party in Wales with a programme anchored in the representation of Welsh interests in Brussels, is recognised as the most favourable political option. In brief, European elections provide a much more amenable context for Plaid Cymru to get its message across than is the case in other domestic elections.

However appealing this argument may be, the degree to which it holds up to empirical scrutiny is debatable. A considerable scholarship has argued precisely the opposite, that European elections are often viewed by both domestic political parties and the electorate as a mid-term evaluation of the incumbent government's performance, rather than an expression of preferences for European-level representation. Paradoxically, the example of Plaid Cymru's experiences in the 1989 European elections would also seem to support this counter argument. Contrary to the party's high expectations for winning the North Wales constituency and considerably improving its performance in the other three Welsh seats, the eventual failure to do so, and an electoral return considerably below the 20 per cent of the Welsh vote that had been forecast, reflects the effects of domestic political competition on voter preferences. An internal post-election post-mortem notes that all opposition parties presented themselves on a ticket of opposition to the Conservative government. The late come back of Labour and the unprecedented success of the Green Party – the latter perceived as directly competing for the nationalist vote – was thus a protest vote against the dominant political agenda of the Thatcher government. Furthermore, the party notes that the tendency of national media to prefer these domestic dynamics reinforced the 'domesticisation' of the European electoral campaign and eventual outcome (Keelan 1989: A96).

In spite of the pragmatic difficulties of separating domestic political dynamics from European ones, however, there is little doubt that Plaid Cymru's approach to European elections, and the EU generally, has been strongly motivated by the belief that a distinctly European political sphere necessitates new kinds of political coalitions adapted to these new conditions. In as much, the party's desire to maximise its political visibility on the supranational level and give added political weight and legitimacy to the Wales–European linkage, has led it to engage in various pan-European initiatives alongside other minority nationalist and regionalist parties. The increasingly institutionalised cooperation of these like-minded actors directly on the supranational level provides an important resource not only for representing these shared interests coherently within the European institutions, but also to propose an alternative view of Europe which embodies the historical, territorial, cultural and political claims of its component parties.

Transnational links on the supranational level

The first such endeavour undertaken by Plaid Cymru was the Bureau of Unrepresented Nations, which became operational in 1975 and brought together Plaid Cymru, the Breton and Alsace nationalist movements, and the *Partido Nacionalista Vasco* (the Basque Nationalist Party). Through the establishment of an office in Brussels, the aims of the organisation were threefold: to publicise the policies of the four movements, to act as a pressure group on European institutions, and finally to gather information on the impact of EEC legislation on the social and economic life of the members.[9] From the perspective of Plaid Cymru's two-pronged strategy vis-à-vis European affairs during this period, it made political sense to try to complement opposition to the EEC in its economic guise, with a more constructive alternative to the status quo, thus giving its argument more political credibility than simply opposition for opposition's sake. In this way, Plaid Cymru was very quick to recognise the added legitimacy that could be brought to their argument by taking it directly to the European level, and pointing to the support from other movements as evidence of the broader appeal of Plaid's stance.

Having said this, it must also be noted that the Bureau of Unrepresented Nations was somewhat of a non-starter, and by 1980 the initiative had dwindled due to a combination of lack of financial resources and administrative infrastructure, and a lack of political will. Nevertheless, the political logic that inspired this association would subsequently be given a new channel of expression through the European Free Alliance (EFA). Plaid Cymru obtained observer status within the association in 1981, and subsequently became a full member in 1984; Plaid Cymru's MEPs sit within the EFA group in the European Parliament.

In its earliest years, the EFA represented a forum for listening to the experiences of other small nations in Europe, of learning about the possibilities for Wales in the European Community and the European Parliament, and of discovering a unity of approaches which confirmed the legitimacy of Plaid's own gradual re-assessment of its attitudes towards European integration since the end of the 1970s. Pragmatically, this process of mutual learning took the form of visits to the European Parliament, the putting down of parliamentary questions by EFA MEPs on behalf of Plaid Cymru, and generally sharing information about different national situations and fortunes. As the EFA itself matured and developed a clearer political role as an organ for representing the interests of the small nations and regions of Europe, so Plaid Cymru's relationship to it also evolved to be one of reciprocal political cooperation and policy development, with Jill Evans as Plaid's long-term representative within the EFA playing a major role in nurturing and exploiting this link to its full potential.[10] Logistical and financial support for European electoral campaigns, common manifestos and an evolving institutional and strategic capacity on the European level, provided the practical and moral support for Plaid's rhetorical discourse, and a mechanism for translating these political aspirations into a supranational context. Without its own direct presence in the Parliament until 1999, the EFA acted as a spokesperson for Welsh interests within this sphere; with the election of two Plaid MEPs in 1999, the EFA provided a ready-made structure within which these representatives, already well acquainted with the practices of this institution, could be effortlessly integrated.

'Independence in Europe' – a new departure?

If 'full national status within the EU' seemed to offer the best way forward for Welsh self-government in the mid 1990s, this notion also became highly contested, first by external political and media observers, and later by an increasing number of people within the party itself. The deeply ambiguous nature of this terminology, not least the implication that giving Wales a political status equal to that of other small member states within the EU implied, to all effects and purposes, Welsh statehood, was an easy target for Plaid Cymru's political competitors, who denounced the fancy terminology as a ruse to detract attention from the party's true separatist aspirations. Such was the implication of Lembit Opik MP's ten-point 'IQ test' (independence question) for Plaid Cymru, consisting of a series of questions on how existing British and European institutions would be affected by Plaid's constitutional project.[11] Similar pressure for constitutional clarifications from the media in the run up to the May 1999 Welsh Assembly elections, led Dafydd Wigley to claim that 'Plaid Cymru has never – ever – stood for independence as our constitutional objective' (Wigley 2001: 130).

If this idea became increasingly difficult to defend against a deeply hostile domestic audience, an increasing awareness on the part of Plaid Cymru's keenest EU-watchers that the trajectory of European integration had shifted back in favour of member-state dominance, confirmed the inadequacy of the 'full national status' formulation. The failure of the Committee of the Regions, the limited reform of the European Parliament in the Amsterdam and Nice Treaties, and the successive refusal of national governments to give up their veto rights in certain areas of policy-making, are all cited as evidence of the dwindling political force of the regionalist momentum that inspired Plaid Cymru's European discourse in the 1990s. Most recently, the limited success of the EFA in getting the interests of their constituents inscribed in the constitutional debate (Mac-Cormick 2003), seems to confirm that not only has the march towards a Europe of the Regions stalled, but that it is even going into reverse: 'In the European Constitution, it's clear that this, far from being a Europe of the Regions, is still a Europe of the Nation-states ... In a way, we're back in the same place as we were in the 1980s'.[12]

It is against this background that Plaid Cymru's recent decision to adopt the terminology of 'independence in Europe' must be understood. While unease over constitutional terminology was already being expressed prior to 1999, the political and institutional developments that came with Welsh devolution at the end of the 1990s provided the catalyst for a rethinking of the party's European discourse. The creation of the National Assembly of Wales constitutes a new centre of gravity for all political parties in Wales; state-wide parties are forced to discuss regional issues, produce regional solutions and establish regional institutions, and their programmes have been given a 'Welsh face'. More specifically, Labour, the Liberal Democrats and the Conservative Party have taken on the nationalist challenge by re-positioning themselves within the political space that Plaid Cymru could previously stake out as its own. After replacing Alun Michael as the leader of Welsh Labour in February 2000, one of the first things Rhodri Morgan oversaw was the re-branding of the Labour Party in Wales under the slogan 'Welsh Labour: The True Party of Wales', a move clearly aimed at taking on the challenge posed by Plaid Cymru.

Faced with the challenges of adapting to this new political state of affairs in post-devolution Wales, unable to hide behind the loose rhetoric of 'self-government', and forced to re-position itself within this new political space in such a way that makes it distinctive from its political opponents, a clarification of the party's long-term political aim became even more urgent (Jones 2000) and a priority of the new party leadership under Ieuan Wyn Jones. At the party's 2001 Annual Conference, a motion which acknowledged that only 'full member-state status of the European Union is most likely to advance [Wales's] national interest' was approved, although the retention of the label 'full national status' won out over 'independence'. Nevertheless, the decisive decision had been taken to acknowledge for the first time in the party's history that member-state status, and not full national status, would be the party's long-term goal. It was only a matter of time before the 'i' word was to become the official policy of the party, a decision taken in the 2003 Plaid Cymru conference.

In summary, if Europe in the 1980s seemed to offer Plaid Cymru a way to circumvent the state, by the end of the 1990s, the realities of being a political actor trying to reconcile the different dynamics of European, British and Welsh politics has revealed the inadequacy of 'full national status' as a constitutional option for Wales in Europe. Faced with the closure of political options in the British political climate in the 1980s, an emerging European opportunity structure was seized upon by Plaid Cymru as offering a viable alternative to Welsh self-determination within a British legal framework. Twenty years later, new developments in both the domestic and European political spheres have necessitated a re-evaluation of Plaid Cymru's constitutional project to take these developments into account. The slogan 'independence in Europe' tries to do so in two ways: (1) by acknowledging that the regionalist aspirations of the 1980s no longer ring true with the state-dominated nature of the European polity; and (2) by responding to the increased pressures of party competition in post-devolution Wales to clarify the party's long-term aims for the country.

Most interestingly, however, is Plaid Cymru's strenuous rejection of claims that independence equates to the creation of a Welsh state and outright separation from the UK.[13] In keeping with its historical rejection of the concept of the state as a nineteenth-century construct which has little continued relevance in the twenty-first century, the party's conceptualisation of 'independence' seems to imply the assumption of all the tasks traditionally associated with statehood but which, within the European framework, does not require the final step of formal state status. As such, the EU continues to provide an alternative solution for organising political authority which allows nations and regions to participate alongside member states on an equal legal footing without the formal trappings of sovereignty ascribed to such a status historically. For Plaid Cymru, therefore, independence does not equate to renouncing the post-sovereigntist legacy that has informed its European discourse up to this time. Neither does a change in terminology to describe its constitutional aims equate to a substantive change in policy, which remains consistent with the European model set out in the mid 1990s: 'An independent Wales would be on an equal footing with other small countries – with more seats in the European Parliament, full voting rights in the Council of Ministers and representation in the Commission. Independence would overcome the difficulty of the Member States' reluctance to devolve power to the regions' (Plaid Cymru 2004).

And yet, it is by no means clear that this semantic switch will be enough in itself to resolve the debates around the ultimate aims and future fortunes of Welsh nationalism. The fact that the adoption of 'independence in Europe' in 2003 was achieved by a large conference majority should not hide the fact that this shift provoked, and continues to provoke, an increasingly hostile polemic within the party on its future direction and strategy and, accordingly, the final goals of Welsh nationalism. Paradoxically, this most recent radicalisation in the party's European discourse comes at a time when the dynamic of Welsh politics is pushing Plaid Cymru in the opposite direction, namely that of the moderate centre ground. More specifically, for the first time, via the National Assembly of Wales, Plaid Cymru has a realistic prospect of concrete political responsibilities which the European level, for all its rhetorical and institutional opportunities, cannot offer. As a party whose *raison d'être* is based on achieving political change via democratic institutional means, the Assembly represents a new focus in the party's policy-making and political activity, with precisely the aim of developing a project for Welsh society which will convince the electorate of the party's governing credentials.

However, despite the party's overwhelming performance in the first Assembly elections in 1999 and the consequently high expectations for the legislature to come, the party's experience of the first term of Assembly politics brought a whole range of unforeseen challenges in adapting to its numerically significant position. Internal tensions over strategy, policy, and organisation resulted in a period of unstable leadership and unclear political direction, factors which have contributed to the tarnishing of the party's credibility and which may help to explain the party's poor performance in the 2003 Assembly elections and the 2004 European elections (Elias 2004). With regard to the European dimension of interest here, a new tension has emerged around the notion of 'independence in Europe' which continues to split the party in two with no signs of being resolved. On the one hand, more moderate supporters of pursuing a governing strategy through the structures of the Assembly have criticised the idea of independence as overly-radical and out-of-touch with the reality that is facing Wales in the twenty-first century.[14] On the other hand, a radical faction to the left of the party links the adoption of the independence slogan to a need for a more confrontational strategy within the Assembly, as part of a general shift in the systemic role of Plaid Cymru from that of a party of potential government to one more akin to a pressure group. In conclusion, it is arguable that the most recent evolution in Plaid Cymru's European discourse can be attributed as much to the dynamics of domestic politics as it can to European influences, and reflects the more fundamental challenges that face the party over its future role and political project. It remains unclear how these challenges will be overcome.

Conclusion

While the internationalism of Plaid Cymru's founding fathers has always been present in Plaid Cymru's political development, the degree to which this influence shaped the party's political programme, and the concrete form given to this normative ideal, has changed significantly as the party has evolved. Since the late 1970s, the distinctly European guise given to this internationalism reflects the changing domestic and supranational context in which Plaid Cymru has successively found itself, and to which it has sought to adjust and respond. At a time of political crisis at home, European integration was opening up a new arena for the articulation of nationalist demands. However, the contingency of this process brings its own set of problems; developments which at one time seemed to point towards the regionalisation and federalisation of Europe now point the other way, towards the entrenchment of state interests at the expense of the 'national' level. Just as 'full national status' seemed like the best option for Wales in the 1990s, so 'independence in Europe' now seems to offer the best way forward.

In the fluidity and ambiguity of Plaid Cymru's constitutional formulations, Christiansen (1998: 131) recognises an 'acknowledgement that such an ambiguous programme must be part of (post-)modern nationalism'. Certainly, processes such as European integration have put into question traditional configurations of political authority, and constitutional formulations which seek alternative models for structuring political action and fulfilling functional obligations are responding to such developments. However, this chapter has tried to show that there is also a fundamental paradox in the relationship between minority nationalism and European integration. At the same time as transnational integration creates new opportunities for a politics of nationalism, the example of Plaid Cymru shows the limits of such an argument, and the degree to which such actors remain constrained to operate within political arenas where state-inspired logics continue to predominate. For minority nationalist parties situated at the interstices of domestic party politics and supranational opportunity structures, the dilemma is that of trying to reconcile the irreconcilable, not wanting to become a state while still aspiring to do what states do. If 'independence in Europe' is Plaid Cymru's latest attempt at trying to resolve this tension, it certainly will not be its last.

11 Nations without states in the EU

The Catalan case

Montserrat Guibernau

Introduction

The aim of this chapter is to consider the current status of Catalonia within the European Union (EU) in light of the 2004 enlargement and the draft European Constitution. Taking the Catalan case as a point of reference, it is argued that nations without states ('regions' in EU terminology) have not obtained the recognition they sought during the European Convention. As a result, they are not recognised as political actors within the draft Constitution, which EU member states began their efforts to formally sanction through their parliaments or by referendum in 2005.

The chapter is divided into four sections. First, it offers a succinct overview of how Catalan political parties, the Spanish state and the EU define Catalonia. Second, it outlines the relationship between Catalonia and Spain during Francoism and the transition to democracy up to the present. Third, it examines the position of Catalonia within the EU after its May 2004 enlargement. The discussion concludes by defining cosmopolitan Catalanism as a way forward for a nation without its own state such as Catalonia, which is caught up between the desire for cultural and economic development, the wish to strengthen its long-term democratic tradition, and the will to overcome a long-standing recognition-deficit that is rooted in the denial of the Spanish state to acknowledge its multinational character.

Defining Catalonia

The main political parties of Catalan origin (CiU – Convergence and Union; PSC or the Socialist Party of Catalonia federated with the PSOE or Spanish Socialist Workers Party – PSC-PSOE; ICV – Initiative for Catalonia-Greens; and ERC – Catalan Republican Left) define Catalonia as a nation. However, Catalonia is not recognised as such within Spain where it has the status of autonomous community – one of 17 established at the dawn of Spain's transition to democracy. The 1978 Constitution declares itself 'based upon the indissoluble unity of the Spanish Nation, the common and indivisible *patria* of all Spaniards, and recognises and guarantees the right to autonomy of the nationalities and regions forming it and solidarity between all of them' (Article 2).

Within the EU, Catalonia is defined as a region. It is not a European electoral constituency and lacks direct access to EU decision-making institutions. At EU level, delegates of the Spanish government represent the Catalans. Catalonia has its own delegates within the Committee of the Regions, however this is merely an advisory body with no decision-making powers, formed by representatives from regions as well as cities. Furthermore, it is worth bearing in mind that the EU only recognises nation-states and regions within its territory, and that the term 'region' includes administrative, economic and geographic regions as well as regions with an historical basis and a well-defined cultural identity.

From Francoism to democracy: Catalonia and Spain

The advent of democracy marked the transition from a clandestine Catalanism of resistance to a Catalanism in favour of restoring Catalonia's rights within the framework of the Constitution (1978) and the Statute of Autonomy (1979). During the transition to democracy and up to the present, the Spanish government has adopted different attitudes towards both Catalanism and Catalonia. Without going into detail, it is possible to distinguish five historical periods.

1   *Recognition.* After the death of General Franco (1975) and the decision to proceed with the democratic reform of the Spanish state (1976), the political forces in Spain considered it necessary to grant some kind of political recognition of Catalan specificity, which was defended by a powerful social movement of a democratic and nationalist nature. The re-establishment of the *Generalitat* (Autonomous Government) of Catalonia, the return of its president in exile, Josep Tarradellas, in 1977, and the subsequent ratification of a new Statute of Autonomy (1979) signalled the transition to democracy.
2   *Disenchantment.* Many Catalans were progressively disappointed by insufficient autonomous funding and a slow and costly process of transferring powers from the central government to the autonomous institutions, accentuated as a result of the attempted *coup d'état* in February 1981.
3   *Bargaining time.* The period of governments with absolute majorities in the Spanish parliament ended, and suddenly, in this new political context, the votes of the Catalan nationalist coalition *Convergència i Unió* (CiU) became 'useful' for the central governments, first the PSOE (1993–96) and later the *Partido Popular* (PP) (1996–2000). The CiU nationalists obtained certain 'concessions' in return for their contribution to the governing of Spain, and Catalan autonomy benefited from this.

4   *Against national diversity*: Since March 2000, the majority government
    of the PP has no longer required the support of the CiU, or of any
    other political party, to govern. When the CiU's support was needed
    in Madrid, the PP adopted a sympathetic attitude vis-à-vis Catalan
    claims. Soon after the 2000 election, however, sympathy and under-
    standing were replaced by a neo-centralist political discourse charged
    with conservative overtones. During its mandate, the PP was dismissive
    of claims for greater autonomy for the historical nationalities and
    adopted an arrogant attitude towards former political allies.
5   *The beginning of a new era*: Radical political change was initiated after
    the Catalan election on 16 November 2003 when the new PSC(PSC-
    PSOE)-ERC-ICV government, under the leadership of Pasqual Mara-
    gall, ended 23 years of CiU government in the Generalitat.[1]

On 11 March 2004, just three days before the Spanish General Election, a terrorist attack in Madrid killed almost 200 people and left more
than 1,000 injured. Immediately, the PP government accused ETA of
being responsible for the attack, and delayed revealing information that
pointed to Al Qaeda. The PP government also underrated two Al Qaeda
messages acknowledging responsibility for the massacre. Many Spaniards
felt misled and saw the attack as a consequence of Spain's involvement in
the invasion of Iraq. On 14 March, against all predictions, the PSOE, led
by José Luís Rodriguez Zapatero, obtained a narrow victory in the Spanish
General Election.

Zapatero's unexpected election as Prime Minister of Spain raised great
expectations among Spaniards wishing for a change from the increasingly
autocratic and conservative PP. In Catalonia the demands for greater autonomy, which are defended by the new coalition government, are no
longer faced with a hostile PP. On the contrary, their fellow socialists hold
power at all levels: autonomous government, diputació of Barcelona,
Barcelona city council as well as the central government in Madrid. Such a
strong concentration of power is totally unprecedented in Catalonia's
history.

Zapatero has promised a more sympathetic approach to Catalan
demands for greater devolution including a new Statute of Autonomy and
a better financial arrangement to alleviate the considerable imbalance
between Catalonia's contribution to the Spanish coffers and the revenue it
receives in return. It is still premature to predict whether Catalan aspirations, as specified in the 'Agreement for a Catalanist and Left of Centre
Government at the Generalitat of Catalonia' subscribed to by the three
political parties forming Catalonia's coalition government on 14 December 2003, will be met by the new Zapatero government. Very influential
sectors in the PSOE and the PP, now the main opposition party, are
hostile to granting further powers to the autonomous communities. In
particular, they oppose any initiatives leading to a differential treatment

between historical nationalities such as Catalonia, the Basque Country and Galicia, and the rest. Curiously, the majority of the PSOE and the PP, representing the left and right of the political spectrum, share an outright opposition to acknowledging the multinational character of Spain, and instead insist on a unitary view of the country.

Catalonia in the EU

The EU was created to fulfil the needs of some European nation-states devastated by two world wars (i.e. Germany, Belgium, France, Holland, Italy and Luxembourg). These founding members, in addition to those who have joined the EU during its successive enlargements, determine the functioning of the EU and set its priorities, objectives and budget. The EU is a political institution run according to the intergovernmentalist principle: the pre-eminence of states as dominant political actors, which seek to expand their collective power in order to accomplish actions that they would be unable to perform individually.

Catalonia is an EU region, which lacks the status of a European electoral constituency. The Catalan language, despite being known by millions of Europeans living within the territories of three member states (Spain, France and Italy), has the status of 'regional language' within the EU. The A3–169/90 EU Parliament Resolution concerning community languages acknowledges the significance of Catalan as a European millennial language employed at all levels of education and in the media. A language enjoying a significant cultural and literary production, which is official and employed by the majority of the population within a territory comprising more than ten million people is, however, not granted official status within the EU. Furthermore, being the official language of three EU regions with legislative powers has no relevance when considering the status of Catalan within the EU. Ironically, an easier route for Catalan to become an EU official language may depend on whether Andorra – whose official language is Catalan – joins the EU.

Following the May 2004 enlargement, the EU has a total of 25 members, including ten new nation-states: Cyprus, Czech Republic, Estonia, Hungary, Latvia, Lithuania, Malta, Poland, Slovakia and Slovenia. After enlargement, EU cultural and linguistic diversity has increased considerably. At present there are 11 official languages in the EU (Danish, Dutch, English, Finnish, French, German, Greek, Italian, Portuguese, Spanish and Swedish). With enlargement, a further nine languages have been added (Czech, Estonian, Hungarian, Latvian, Lithuanian, Maltese, Polish, Slovak and Slovene). However, in spite of being the tenth most spoken language within the new EU, Catalan will not have the status of EU official language. This reflects a stark contrast between the expectations and demands of the Catalan people, who are traditionally strongly pro-European, and the statist nature of the EU, which disregards most demands for cultural, linguistic and political recognition advanced by nations without states such as Catalonia.

At present, the greatest dilemma faced by many Catalans – who are used to turning to Europe as a model of democracy, progressivism, cultural and artistic movements and socio-economic progress – is whether they can vote 'no' to the EU Constitution while maintaining a strong commitment to Europe or whether, on the other hand, they should say 'yes' to a Constitution that does not satisfy their aspirations.

Demands for the recognition of Catalonia as a nation and for Catalan as an EU official language are present in the programmes of the main political parties of Catalan origin. They can be found in documents such as the 'Declaration of Barcelona' signed by the CiU, the PNV (Basque Nationalist Party) and the BNG (Galician Nationalist Bloc) in 1998; the 'Self-Government Report' elaborated by the ICV, ERC and the PSC (PSC-PSOE) in 2001; and the 'Catalonia with no limits report' prepared by the CiU in 2002. Recognition of the Catalan nation was also one of the key demands of the Catalan Convention for the Future of the EU,[2] which was presented to the Convention chaired by Valéry Giscard d'Estaing in 2003.

In my view, the relationship between Catalonia and the EU is defined by the lack of recognition received by Catalonia, a situation stemming from the status of Catalonia and the Catalan language within Spain. Catalonia's status in the EU can only be modified if the Spanish government decides to do so; for this reason, in the first instance, the debate and negotiations to attain Catalonia's recognition in the EU ought to take place between the Catalan and Spanish governments. Catalonia is not considered a nation within the EU, as Scotland or Wales are, simply because Catalonia is not defined as such within Spain, in spite of widespread agreement among all the political parties of Catalan origin.

The schism between Catalonia's aspirations and its current status has to be dealt with by the Spanish government. It is not the responsibility of the EU to redress Catalonia's situation, but Spain's, since the EU strictly acknowledges and follows its member states' advice on matters considered as internal to them. It lies with the Spanish government to propose to the EU Council of Ministers the acceptance of Catalan as an official language. Similarly, any decision to define Catalonia as a European electoral region, or to give Catalan representatives access to the EU decision-making bodies, fully depends on the Spanish state which, so far, has exhibited a strong centralist outlook that denies what other EU countries with a longer standing democratic and decentralised tradition have already implemented, for instance the UK and Belgium.

The case of Catalonia shows that the role and status of nations without states in the EU depends on the will of the state within which they are included. This confirms the strong intergovernmentalist leanings of the EU, a feature which in itself does not help to alleviate the so-called EU democratic deficit. If only nation-states have a voice in the EU, then peoples, regions, national and ethnic minorities are excluded and depend on the will of the particular nation-state within which they are included.

The marginalisation of 'regions' in the Convention and the draft EU Constitution

The regional movement seeks to reverse, or at least alleviate, the peripheral role of regions within the EU, as a supranational institution founded and governed by nation-states. Hence, regions that are already peripheral within their own nation-states feel even more remote from the EU core. At the same time, relatively powerful regions enjoying self-determination within their own nation-states find themselves in a weak position within the EU due to their lack of direct representation in EU institutions. The Convention for the Future of the EU chaired by Valéry Giscard d'Estaing received numerous demands from regional bodies and movements throughout Europe in favour of regional representation within EU institutions. For instance, the citizens of 75 EU regions already enjoying devolved legislative powers, which comprise 56.3 per cent of the EU's total population, demanded the recognition of their legislative and administrative relevance as well as their contribution to democracy in terms of subsidiarity and the functioning of the EU. This was met with no success (Kant 1996: 3).[3]

Previously, the Declaration signed by leaders of the constitutional regions of Bavaria, Catalonia, Scotland, Flanders, North Rhine-Westphalia, Salzburg and Wallonia on 5 July 2001 was also ignored. The signatories of this Declaration highlighted the consequential effects of further EU integration for the devolved powers enjoyed by the regions they represented. They also pointed to the critical role of regions in the implementation of EU legislation, whilst emphasising their lack of representation in the EU. They requested the direct involvement of regions in the preparatory work leading to the 2004 Intergovernmental Conference (IGC) where enlargement and a new draft Constitution were to be agreed. They also suggested that the role and status of regions in the EU should be considered and strengthened according to the subsidiarity principle.[4] It should be noted that EU regions were not allowed to send their own delegates to the Convention preparing the IGC and, in the end, only the representatives of six regions were allowed to attend as observers.

Within the EU, the demands of the regional movement are opposed by influential sectors representing a statist vision of Europe in line with the intergovernmentalist principle that continues to prevail in the draft Constitution. For instance, speaking at a meeting with the presidents of European regions with legislative powers (or 'constitutional regions') in 2002, Romano Prodi, then President of the EU Commission, acknowledged the significance of regions and local government for the development of the European project (Prodi 2002). At the same time, however, he requested the EU not to interfere in the relationship between member states and their regions and not to establish a uniform EU norm in dealing with regions.

A further example concerns the document submitted to the Convention on 28 August 2002 by the Italian MEP Giorgio Napolitano (PSE), then president of the Commission for Constitutional Affairs in the European Parliament. Here, Napolitano acknowledged the role of regions, but argued against the right of peoples to self-determination and a possible institutionalisation of the most powerful regions to the detriment of others, while defending the need to maintain the merely consultative role of the Committee of the Regions.

For a cosmopolitan Catalanism

The challenges faced by Catalan society are by no means exhausted by those mentioned above, but, in my view, it is important to set up some limits and to prioritise those questions which require more urgent and continuous attention. The proposals to overcome these challenges are also limited, although each of them can be divided into different parts and requires a thorough development of all the aspects involved.

First, I argue that a cross-party agreement involving the main political forces with a Catalanist tradition is essential to promote a common project for Catalonia. In my view, it is immoral for them to place particular party interests above the general interests of the Catalan society they seek to represent. This cross-party agreement would have to cover at least the following aspects:

- Proposals for a sufficient and fair funding budget for Catalonia.
- Recognition of Catalonia's status as a nation. This should be reflected in the Spanish Constitution and in the Statute of Autonomy.
- Greater devolved powers for Catalonia within the framework of a Spain that defines itself as plurinational, plurilingual and pluricultural.
- Acceptance of Catalonia as a European electoral district, and of the right and duty of Catalan government representatives to participate in EU decision-making bodies, whenever matters directly concerning Catalonia are to be discussed.
- Agreement for the promotion of Catalan culture and language in Catalonia, Spain and the EU, using all available resources to do so at the regional, national and European levels.

Second, there is a need to construct what I refer to as a 'cosmopolitan Catalanism'. It is not a contradiction to speak of cosmopolitan nationalism, although it is perhaps necessary to explain its meaning. We should be aware that cosmopolitanism – that is, world citizenship free from national prejudices – could only occur under the following conditions (Kant 1996: 326ff):

a   The establishment of democratic constitutions in all nation-states as a guarantee of respect for freedom, equality before the law and national, ethnic, cultural and gender diversity (Held 2003).

b   The predominance of democracy as the principle governing international relations, which must involve a relationship of equality between nations. This should also include the establishment of an 'International Civic Constitution' to regulate international relations and disputes, coupled with a democratic 'International Court of Justice', which should not remain in the hands of the economically and politically strongest countries. The key objective of this Court would be to prevent war. In my view, such an institution would require its own army to enforce its resolutions. It would have to be financed by the nation-states, which would contribute in proportion to their resources. No state government would have the power to interrupt or to reduce their contribution to the maintenance of the 'International Court of Justice' (Held 2003: 523).

c   The enactment of a 'cosmopolitan law', emanating from the International Civic Constitution, which would provide for what Immanuel Kant called 'universal hospitality', that is the right of any foreigner – not a citizen of the specific state – to be treated without hostility in the country of arrival, supposing that he or she behaves peacefully (Kant 1996: 326).

To exercise cosmopolitanism, the above three conditions should be complied with, since their fulfilment would be sufficient to eradicate the discrimination, repression and attempted annihilation suffered by some nations and ethnic groups. It is not ethically sound to demand that a nation engaged in a struggle for its own cultural and political survival declare itself 'cosmopolitan' (*kosmos polites*), simply because to be able to do so, this nation should be free, and freedom is not available to it while there are states that threaten or deny its own right to exist and to form a part of this 'cosmos'. But, what all nation-states and nations without states should be encouraged to do is to contribute to the development of conditions which would favour the emergence of cosmopolitanism, and this is why Catalanism must become cosmopolitan. Although cosmopolitanism can be branded utopian, I am convinced that the political agenda for the future of Catalonia should include not only specific policy aspects but also the commitment to cosmopolitan ideals and values capable of informing political action.

Democratic nationalism is legitimate. It defends the right of nations to exist and to develop whilst recognising and respecting internal diversity. It rejects the territorial expansion of nations and shows a commitment to the construction of a democratic society, egalitarian and free, where individuals could fulfil their potential and contribute to building a strong and cohesive community with a shared identity and a cosmopolitan outlook. Only by being committed to these principles can democratic nationalism become cosmopolitan. For instance, Durkheim (1973: 101) is not clear about what attitude individuals should adopt in facing patriotism (he does not employ the term nationalism). He argues: 'to what extent should we desire this other kind of society [the human patrie]? Should we try to bring it about, to hasten its coming or, indeed, should we jealously maintain the independence of the present home-country to which we belong at all costs?' This dichotomy is partially solved by Durkheim's identification of what he calls the 'national ideal' with the 'human ideal'. He argues that each state becomes an organ of the 'human ideal' in so far as it assumes that its main task is not to expand by extending its borders, but to increase the level of its members' morality. Therefore, societies should place their pride in becoming the best organised, having the best moral constitution, rather than in being the biggest or richest of all societies.

In this respect, Catalan society and in particular its institutions, its politicians, intellectuals and businessmen and women have a moral duty to work towards the construction of a democratic, open country, and to promote the civic values that favour social cohesion and harmony. A cosmopolitan Catalanism needs to take the country forward and contribute to the social well-being of the citizens through efficiency, responsibility and transparent management, and also by endorsing ethical values promoting the development of Catalan society as a whole. Catalanism should not be a *modus vivendi*, an excuse for political inaction, or a reason to maintain or generate social inequalities, but rather a progressive ideology, a tool for the social integration and the cultural, ethical and political regeneration of the country.

12 Scottish autonomy and European integration

The response of Scotland's political parties

Eve Hepburn

Introduction

The issue of constitutional change has never been far off the top of the agenda for Scotland's political parties since the late 1980s. One could go further and argue that the pursuit and accommodation of autonomy has been the stuff of Scottish politics for most of the twentieth century. However, what makes the last 20 years interesting – apart from the devolution settlement – is how the issue of European integration has become entwined in debates about Scottish self-determination. The processes of decentralisation and supranational integration have created a new political playing field in which parties compete not only on the class dimension, but also on the territorial and European dimensions. The last two issues have never been the exclusive domain of the pro-European, pro-independence Scottish National Party (SNP). Instead, parties of every political creed have become involved in issues of territorial autonomy, and have articulated separate visions of the Europe that Scotland should play a role in, whether that be a Confederal Europe, a Europe of the Regions or a Socialist Peoples' Europe, for example. The diversity of party responses to European integration counters the assumption that minority nations tend to act as homogenous blocs. Rather, the Scottish case mirrors the experience of other nations such as Brittany, Catalonia and the Basque Country, in which parties compete in their representation of national identity and interests, many of them expanding their constitutional goals to include Europe.

In the last decade, every one of Scotland's major political parties has declared itself to constitute *the* national party of Scotland. The SNP monopoly over national identity politics in the 1960s and 1970s (Mitchell 1996) has given way to a complexity of political actors, motives, bargains and rivalry which determine the ever-changing 'national question'. The Scottish Labour Party, Scottish Conservative and Unionist Party, Scottish Liberal Democrats, and smaller parties such as the Socialists have proclaimed themselves to be the true representatives of the Scottish people, offering a range of constitutional proposals including sovereign statehood, regional autonomy, decentralisation and federalism. Civil society groups and cross-party initiatives have also actively campaigned for self-determination, of which the Scottish Constitutional Convention – paving the way for devolution in the 1990s – is the most famous. The involvement of Scotland's political organisations in issues of autonomy reflects an important territorial dimension to Scottish politics. But what is more pertinent to this discussion is how nationalism has acquired a distinctively European flavour. Since the late 1980s, the deepening of European integration has provided a new set of reference points for political debate, whilst parties have re-aligned themselves to take advantage of opportunities in Europe for advancing their political projects. The SNP policy of 'independence-in-Europe' has met calls from all political parties claiming to be the true 'voice' of Scotland in Europe.

This chapter examines how Scottish parties have re-positioned themselves in response to European integration, and how this has affected their rhetoric, policies and strategies. The discussion is arranged in a loosely chronological order. It begins with an analysis of how Scotland's parties responded to UK entry of the European Community, moves on to examine the pressures for constitutional change in Scotland in the period between the first and second devolution referendums, and then demonstrates how these two issues – Europe and Scottish autonomy – were linked by political parties at the time of the acceleration of European integration. Finally, the chapter considers how the achievement of devolution has led to different types of demands from Scottish parties. In order to analyse the underlying causal mechanisms informing the relationship of Scotland's political parties to Europe, the following questions will be tackled throughout this chapter: What are the factors influencing change in party attitudes? Was a pro-European switch for some parties driven by domestic issues or by European developments? Have the parties really become 'Europeanised' or is Europe only a tactical issue? And what advantages does Europe hold for Scotland's political parties?

The European Community: UK entry and Scotland's response

British entry to the European Community (EC) in 1973 caused as much political discord in Scotland as it did in the rest of the UK. However, the discussion of 'costs' and 'benefits' of EC membership took a somewhat different hue north of the border. It has been noted by Bennie *et al.* (1997) that Scots were decidedly critical of the EC before and after joining, despite voting positively during the referendum on continued UK membership of the EC in 1975 (but less so than England and Wales by about 10 per cent). What made the issue distinctive north of the border in the 1970s was the fear that Scotland would be further removed from the new economic and political centres and that Scotland's fisheries, agriculture and traditional industries would be threatened by the common market. Therefore the Conservative government's principal argument in favour of EC membership – that the UK would recover its prosperity (during the decline of the Empire) through increased trade – had less resonance in Scotland than in the rest of the UK. The Conservative Party itself had suffered a consistent decline of support in Scotland since the late 1950s, which made its policies a more difficult 'sell' there. Instead, the Scottish electorate's cautious approach to Europe was better captured by left-wing parties. The Labour Party and the SNP consistently argued against EC membership at the time of entry, and both radically altered their positions the following decade. To what extent the Scottish electorate also altered its attitude to Europe will be discussed later.

During the 1970s, the Scottish Council of the Labour Party viewed the EC as a 'capitalist club' that threatened its programmes for nationalisation and the welfare state. Labour had vehemently rejected the neo-liberal free-market Europe that the Tories had painted a picture of in the lead up to EC entry. To that end, members of the Labour Party in Scotland voted against continued EC membership during their March 1975 party conference, even though the UK Labour Party had overcome its divisions by supporting the Callaghan government's referendum campaign (Butler and Kitzinger 1996). Yet a number of factors led to a change in policy in the 1980s. These included the conversion of the trade unions to a more pro-European position, public support in favour of EC membership and the need to take a proactive role in determining European affairs in order to avoid the creation of a 'Fortress Europe' that the single market may herald. David Martin MEP (former leader of the UK Labour Group in the European Parliament) made a strong association between constitutional change in Scotland and Europe by arguing that an 'enlarged democratic Europe of the Regions' would connect 'devolved economic and democratic structures at national and regional level [to] a more democratic European Community' (Martin 1988: 83). Labour's 'about-turn' on Europe would become intricately linked to its re-commitment to constitutional change in the UK, and in particular Scottish devolution.

The SNP was, during the post-war era, highly suspicious of European integration. The EC was viewed as centralist and elitist, and it was unclear to the party how Scottish interests would be represented if the EC operated on an intergovernmental basis – with the UK government taking important decisions over Scottish affairs. During the 1975 referendum, the SNP campaigned on the theme 'No voice, no entry', hoping that Scotland would distinguish itself from the rest of the UK by voting against the EC. However, the party misjudged the mood of Scottish public opinion (which at the beginning of the year had favoured the SNP's position) and when 61.7 per cent of the Scots population turned out to vote 'Yes' by 58.4 per cent, the SNP had to re-think its position. The change in attitude was assisted by the election of Winifred Ewing to the European Parliament in

1979, who obtained publicity for the SNP and its defence of Scottish interests in Europe, and whose 'political activities imported a more positive European dimension into the party' (Lynch 1996: 37). Another influential proponent of European integration came in the form of Jim Sillars, a former Labour politician who in 1975 had formed a short-lived socialist-nationalist breakaway group. Sillars was the first to advocate the benefits of independent Scottish membership of the EC and upon joining the SNP was instrumental in developing the party's 'independence-in-Europe' platform (Drucker 1977; Lynch 2002).

As for Scotland's other main parties, the Liberal Democrats were enthusiastic advocates of European integration. They had supported applications for membership of the European Coal and Steel Community in 1951, the European Economic Community and Euratom in 1957 and the attempts of both Labour and Conservative governments to join the EC in the 1960s and 1970s. During the 1975 referendum, the LibDems campaigned for a 'Yes' vote, however they did not fall in with the Conservative line: 'Although Liberals have all along supported European economic integration, they have always laid the greatest stress on the need for a political union' (Liberal Party 1975). In contrast, the Scottish Conservative and Unionist Party (SCUP) was openly hostile to the idea of closer political integration, though they were not immune to the benefits that a deregulated economic Europe would bring. It was solely upon this basis that the Tories supported the 1975 referendum. However, with Thatcher's election as leader of the UK Conservative Party in 1975, and Prime Minister in 1979, the Tories pursued a more pugnacious approach to Europe. The party's aversion to political reform in Europe was matched by its opposition to constitutional reform in the UK, an issue which came to a head during the referendum on devolution in Scotland and Wales in 1979.

Pressures for constitutional reform

In the period between the two devolution referendums of 1979 and 1997, the relevance of Europe to the constitutional debate in Scotland increased considerably. At the domestic level, a number of developments in Scottish and UK politics pushed the issue of Europe to the forefront of party agendas, whilst certain advances in European integration were looked upon favourably by those seeking constitutional change in Scotland. At a time when Thatcher's Britain held little attraction for Scottish political elites, Europe was beginning to look like a more agreeable system of shared sovereignty for Scotland. The re-election of the Conservatives in 1987 and 1992 (despite Scotland voting Labour) augmented pressures for a Scottish Parliament with strong European relations to protect it from future 'English' governments. According to Brown *et al.* (1998: 23), 'it is this European dimension ... that ensures that the campaign for a Scottish Parliament has a recurrent tendency to keep coming back on the agenda'.

Given the distrust of both the Labour Party and SNP towards Europe as we saw previously, it is not surprising that there was no major political force that had linked Scottish self-determination to the European context during the first referendum on devolution in 1979 (Cabrol 2001). This referendum had been introduced by Wilson's Labour Government as a tool to beat down the SNP, which had won 11 seats during the October 1974 General Election. At the time, most political parties perceived European integration as a process detrimental to devolution, whereby Scotland would have less access to institutional channels of representation in Brussels than Westminster. Thus, debates on constitutional change in 1979 were articulated solely within the UK context. On the 'Yes' side, the separate campaigns and inter-party wrangling between the SNP, Labour and the Liberal Democrats compared unfavourably with the sleek and simple 'No' campaign of the Conservatives. In the end, most Scots *did* vote for constitutional change, but failed to surpass the 40 per cent rule: 32.9 per cent voted 'Yes' whilst 30.8 per cent voted 'No' with a 63.9 per cent turnout (Harvie 1998: 164).[1] The result was an enormous blow to the home rule movement, as well as to the Labour government, which later saw a vote of no-confidence and the subsequent election of Thatcher's Conservatives.

Whilst the debate on Scotland's constitutional future was understandably subdued in the years following the referendum defeat, developments in Europe began to make headlines in Scotland in the run-up to the Single European Act (SEA) of 1987. For most Scots, the EC was seen primarily as a source of funds (Bennie *et al.* 1997: 13). The SEA had important consequences for the economy, as it was believed that Scotland would be the recipient of large amounts of structural funds. However, the year 1987 may be remembered in Scotland for a different reason. The ratification of the SEA coincided with the re-election of Thatcher's Conservatives in spite of the Scottish electorate voting in 50 Labour MPs (out of a total of 72). Thatcher's already considerable unpopularity in Scotland was augmented with her test introduction of the poll tax north of the border in 1990, inciting various forms of civil and political disobedience (Barker 1992). The poll tax debacle indicated to Scots that the Tories were an 'English' party insensitive to Scottish needs, a view compounded by the Party's consistent rejection of constitutional change. In response, Scottish political elites decided to take matters into their own hands. The Campaign for a Scottish Assembly – a cross-party pressure group established in 1980 – appointed a Constitutional Steering Committee in 1988. This body issued a *Claim of Right* for Scotland, invoking popular sovereignty in the demand for self-government (Edwards 1988). The Committee also recommended the creation of a Scottish Constitutional Convention, whose aim was to translate widespread support for devolution into concrete proposals for legislation that could be adopted by a sympathetic incoming government.

The founding membership of the Convention in 1989 included representatives from the Labour Party, the Scottish Liberal Democrats, the Social Democratic Party (now defunct), the Cooperative Party, the Communist Party, the Scottish Green Party and the Orkney and Shetland Movement.[2] The Conservative Party refused to join. The SNP left the Convention almost immediately on the grounds that it had become an instrument of Labour and the LibDems, which caused internal divisions and public criticism. Some members left, whilst others such as Neil Mac-Cormick defied the SNP leadership by engaging in cross-party negotiations, thereby providing an important bridge between different demands for constitutional change. The Convention produced two reports – *Towards Scotland's Parliament* (1990) and *Scotland's Parliament, Scotland's Right* (1995) – to which Labour and the LibDems committed themselves in their 1997 election manifestos. In the latter document, the Convention attached 'great importance . . . to Scotland's dynamic and developing relationships with the institutions of the European Union' and drew up proposals for a Scottish Parliament's relations with Europe. Not only was it understood that many of Edinburgh's competences would fall under EU legislation and directives, but the Convention also had lofty hopes of seeing Scotland act on an international stage, a desire that was shared by Scotland's opposition parties.

Scottish devolution in a European context

In the years leading up to devolution, the European context was put forward by parties seeking constitutional change as an alternative (multi-national) framework in which Scottish self-determination could be realised. Of the three parties advocating various forms of autonomy – the Scottish LibDems, Labour and SNP – only the former had a consistent line on Europe. Nevertheless, there appeared to be an overall shift in favour of using the European dimension to advance Scottish claims in the 1990s. According to Brown *et al.* (1998), this was because of the constitutional and social-welfare ramifications of European integration in Scotland. Europe altered the debate on the nature of Scotland's place within the UK, and the social welfare policies that the EC had begun developing were looked upon favourably by the Scottish public. During this period, only the Tories resisted the linkages being developed between constitutional change and European integration. The Conservatives, who had once been the most pro-European party in the UK, became the most Europhobic (Evans 2003). Their refusal to sign the Council of Europe's Charter of Local Self-Government in 1985 and the Maastricht Treaty's Social Chapter in 1992 demonstrated their hostility to all social and political dimensions of European integration later extolled by Labour and the SNP. Non-economic integration was perceived as a threat to British sovereignty, which was made clear in Thatcher's 'Bruges speech' of 1988.

However, this message did not have the same political impact in Scotland, whose sovereignty was already shared with the UK.

Once the SNP and Labour both switched sides to a comfortably pro-European stance in the late 1980s, joining the solidly Europhile Liberal Democrats, Scottish parties had a field day parodying the 'little Englander' mentality of the Tories' Europhobia, and playing on the commonly-held perception that Scotland is a more pro-European nation. Instead, Europe was put forward as an alternative to Thatcher's free-market ideology (despite Thatcher herself arguing that the single market was the only worthwhile development in Europe), and a new arena for developing the social-democratic project that the Tory government had tried to bring to an end. The re-positioning of parties in response to Europe underlines the radically differing views of what European integration means. One of the most critical points of interpretation was that, for Scotland's opposition parties, it offered a way out of the constitutional stalemate which the Tories signalled. Although there was a general perception that Europe heralded the possibility of constitutional reform, there was contestation amongst parties as to the nature of such reform, whether it be for the purposes of federalising, decentralising or separating the constituent parts of the UK.

To take the parties individually, the Scottish Labour Party (SLP) became a committed supporter of a 'Europe of the Regions', whereby the party was able to link domestic arguments in favour of devolution with the provisions for subsidiarity as laid out in the Maastricht Treaty. The late UK Labour leader John Smith stated in 1992 that regional government was increasing in power and influence in Europe, and Scotland – like the German Länder – should have its share of it (*The Herald*, 24 October 1992).[3] In 1995 another prominent Scottish and Labour politician, Robin Cook, argued in favour of a Europe of the Regions, which he defined as 'the development of common policies at a European level that are matched by devolution of decision-making to regions of Europe' (*The Herald*, 4 August 1995). The notion of subsidiarity became central to Labour's rhetoric of Scottish self-determination. It was linked to the need for a Scottish Parliament which could participate in European decision-making.[4] For instance, the SLP in its 1997 campaign manifesto promised that Scotland would have direct access to the Council of Ministers (which was later reneged on), a high proportion of representatives in the CoR, the creation of offices in Brussels and a Scottish Minister of European Affairs. One could argue that these proposals were formulated to defuse support for the SNP, and to demonstrate how influential Scotland could be without having to go the separatist way. Yet in reality, it appears that Scottish Labour and the SNP were moving over the same terrain, with each proposing similar strategies for enhancing Scotland's voice in Europe, for protecting its economic interests and establishing links with other stateless nations.

Scottish Labour were not the only ones trumpeting the virtues of a Scottish place in a decentralised Europe. Although the Scottish Liberal Democrats (SLD) ideally envisaged the creation of a federal Europe, a policy 'based upon decades of commitment to European integration and a realistic assessment that subsidiarity is the way forward for Europe as well as for Scotland',[5] they also advocated a Europe of the Regions. Since the 1990s, the LibDems have associated decentralisation of UK structures with European subsidiarity, in many ways mirroring Labour's attempts to counter the SNP's vision of Scotland in Europe. This policy makes sense given that the SLD acted in coalition with Labour in the Constitutional Convention, and later in the Scottish Parliament. Also, the notion of a Federal Europe, which receives little sympathy in Scottish or British politics, has tended to be a liability in elections. Recently, the party has omitted the word 'federalism' from their manifestos, replacing it with the terms 'decentralisation' and 'subsidiarity'. Support for a 'Europe of the Regions' is more palatable to the Scottish electorate, even if it has been for the SLD simply another way of saying that Europe should develop along federal lines.

The SNP adopted a policy of 'independence-in-Europe' in 1988, for which the justifications appear to be largely pragmatic: the European context would provide economic and security safeguards and dispel voters' fears of 'going it alone'. Such an arrangement would entail the creation of a European confederation, i.e. an association of member states which pool sovereignty in certain areas but do not surrender total control to an authoritative body. Yet despite aiming for a confederal Europe with power concentrated at the member-state level, the SNP during the 1990s became active in debates about the regionalisation of Europe. For example, the party supported the creation of a Committee of the Regions, an issue that split the SNP when its leaders made a secret 'deal' with the Conservative government to win more Scottish seats (*The Scotsman*, 9 April 1993). The inconsistency in using opportunities for regional engagement in Europe to advance Scotland's claim to autonomy, whilst aiming to achieve membership of a confederal Europe in which regions have little power, is indicative of a fault line that has run through the party since the merger between the pro-home rule Scottish Party with the pro-independence National Party in Scotland to form the SNP in 1934. This is referred to as the division between 'fundamentalists' and 'gradualists'. The former see independence as a zero-sum game and argue that devolution undermines the momentum for independent statehood. A small section of this group also denounces EU membership, somewhat similar to Scottish Socialist and Green Parties (see below). The gradualists, on the other hand, see sovereign statehood arriving in stages, and seek to use devolution as a 'stepping stone' to independence. The strategies of this section of the party are uncannily similar to those of Labour devolutionists. Despite different end goals, both parties wish to gradually expand the powers of the Scottish Parliament in its European relations. Fortunately for the SNP, the gradualist section of the Party prevailed over the hardliners during the second referendum on devolution.

Following the electoral victory of the Labour Party in 1997, a white paper was drawn up and an Act passed to organise referenda on Assemblies in Scotland and Wales. The legislation introduced by Labour was directly based on the Constitutional Convention's proposals. The Labour Party, SLD and SNP led the Scotland FORward's campaign to achieve a Yes–Yes vote in July. Unlike the first devolution referendum, the group was able to create a unified campaign despite Labour's jeering that devolution would 'kill the SNP stone dead', and the SNP's retaliation that devolution would lead to independence. In contrast, the 'No' camp was almost invisible. The Conservative Party was isolated in the Scottish political arena in its continuing hostility to home rule, and dispirited following its electoral defeat and loss of all parliamentary representation in Scotland. The results of the referendum in Scotland exceeded many expectations: 74.3 per cent were in favour of a Scottish parliament and 63.5 per cent thought the parliament should have tax-raising powers. Even though the poll was slightly lower than in 1979, the result definitively demonstrated the 'settled will' of the Scottish people.[6]

The UK Government quickly passed the relevant acts to establish devolved assemblies for Scotland, Wales and Northern Ireland. The Scotland Bill was far more extensive than that proposed in 1979. Foreign affairs, defence and social security were powers retained by Westminster, whilst Edinburgh's 129 MSPs were given the power to legislate in an extensive range of domestic policies including education, economic development, health, housing, law, home affairs and local government; and the ability to vary taxation. There was one issue, however, which was interpreted ambiguously: Edinburgh's relationship with Europe. Even though relations with the EU are officially 'reserved' to Westminster, the UK Government has acknowledged that the Scottish Executive and Parliament should have an 'important role' concerning EU affairs. In order to clarify its position, the Scottish Executive outlined an EU strategy to promote Scottish interests in Europe, maximise influence with the UK Government on EU issues, and enhance the profile of Scotland in Europe (Scottish Executive 2004: 1–2). This begs the question of how far Holyrood's remit may be extended before Scotland stands in violation of the Treaty of Union. It also casts doubt on any sharp distinction between the actual practise of devolution and that of an independent Scotland. As the most important legislative decisions are made in Brussels, with national and regional parliaments implementing social policy, would it really make a difference whether Scotland is with or without its own state?

A Scottish Parliament with a European agenda?

With the arrival of devolution in Scotland, political parties have been faced with a new set of challenges, problems and opportunities. The Scottish branches of unionist parties have since 1999 been operating in a peculiarly Scottish context. Devolution has been met with calls for greater organisational autonomy of Scottish branches of statewide parties to fight for exclusively Scottish interests. The system of proportional representation (PR) has opened up spaces for small parties to have their say and articulate different visions of Scottish self-determination. The experience of living in a coalition has resulted in a new politics of compromise and cooperation that differs markedly from the clashes at Westminster. The Scottish Executive and Parliament have been putting out 'feelers' to discover how far their mandate travels. Importantly, the territorial transformation of power has meant that there have been different types of demands from Scottish parties. Following devolution, the Scottish Parliament has been used as a vehicle to further Scottish interests, and most parties have argued for greater Scottish autonomy from Westminster and increased Scottish influence in Brussels. This is, perhaps, with the exception of the SLP, which is set on defending the current form of the devolution settlement against the SNP, LibDems, Conservatives, Greens and Socialists.

Since taking office, the SLP has become active in the practice of subnational 'paradiplomacy' (Aldecoa and Keating 1999). The first years of devolution saw the establishment of a regional office in Brussels (Scotland House), cooperation agreements with Catalonia, Tuscany, North-Rhein Westphalia and Bavaria, the creation of a Nordic–Scottish Action Plan, joint projects with German Länder, and active participation in the Council of Local and Regional Authorities in Europe (CLRAE), and the European Group of Regions with Legislative Powers (REGLEG). Within Parliament, a European and External Relations Committee was established to scrutinise EU legislation and 'ensure that the Executive's handling of EU issues will not be neglected' (Wright 2000: 140). Therefore, although the Labour government is at pains to emphasise that EU policy is a reserved matter, the Scottish Executive has been encouraged to become involved in EU matters that impact devolved areas, and to create links with other European regions. The main goals of the Executive in Europe, set out in their European Strategy (2004), are 'to position Scotland as one of the leading legislative regions in the EU' and 'to bring effective influence to bear on the UK Government, EU member states, regions and institutions on EU policies affecting Scotland'. The document bears a strong resemblance to Labour's strategy in Europe, which combines distinctive Scottish representation with 'the punch that comes from being part of a big player' in the UK.

Despite being elevated to the official Opposition in the Scottish Parliament, the devolution settlement has put the SNP into a somewhat awkward position. It has necessitated a change in strategy for achieving the goal of independence in Europe and has reinforced divisions between gradualists and fundamentalists. For instance, the SNP has been supportive of the Executive's efforts to expand Scotland's European activities; it just wants to take these activities further, for example by creating the post of a Scottish Minister of European Affairs. But it is unclear whether this means that the SNP could live with increasing the powers of a devolved Parliament, or if it considers these moves useless in the absence of an independent Scottish seat at the European Council of Ministers. Moreover, former leader John Swinney's decision to oppose the European constitution (*The Scotsman*, 22 April 2004) raises the question of how 'Europeanised' the SNP really is, and whether commitment to Europe is simply a tactical issue. This is not the first time the SNP has suffered splits over Europe. In 1990 a section of the fundamentalist wing launched the group Sovereignty '90, arguing that for Scotland to be independent, it had to be free from Brussels as well as London (Macwhirter 1992). Worryingly for the gradualist leadership of the SNP, this argument receives sympathy amongst its voters, who are in fact less Europhile than the voters of the other main parties (De Winter 2001). So although the EU may have solved some of the SNP's initial problems, it has also re-introduced them. The SNP is now in the position of having to reconcile its pro-European rhetoric with a mixed bag of European policies that both commend the idea of European integration and denounce certain aspects of it, whilst having to develop strategies to win over its relatively Eurosceptical electorate. The inherent contradictions of the independence-in-Europe platform, and the internal divisions (and external confusion) that it produces, are never far from the surface.

The SNP's fundamentalist wing is not the only pro-independence political grouping in the Scottish Parliament suspicious of Europe. With the introduction of proportional representation, Scottish politics has enjoyed a greater pluralism of political opinions. In the 1999 elections, the Scottish Greens and Scottish Socialist Party (SSP) both succeeded in electing their leaders to Holyrood (Robin Harper and Tommy Sheridan became the first Green and Socialist Parliamentarians in the UK respectively), and a further six MSPs for the Greens and five for the SSP were elected in the 2003 elections. Although small, these parties have been extremely vocal in the Parliament, raising a number of new issues and articulating different positions on Scotland's constitutional question.

The main goal of the SSP is to create an independent socialist Scottish republic that would 'stand up to the economic power of the multinationals and political power of Washington, London and Brussels' (Scottish Socialist Party 2003). A socialist state operating on the principles of public ownership would not seek a place within the free market EU. Independence in Europe is viewed as contradictory by the Socialists as it entails the transferral of rule over Scottish affairs from Westminster to Brussels, as opposed to 'genuine' self-rule. Furthermore, the EU itself represents a 'semi-despotic and undemocratic' set of institutions that operates behind closed doors to impose neo-liberal policies on the citizens of Europe (Scottish Socialist Party 2003). Of particular concern to the SSP is the lack of European-wide social rights to off-set the disequilibrium created by free market economics. The SSP has, however, taken advantage of some opportunities in Europe. In 2001 the Party became a founding member of the European Anti-Capitalist Left (EACL) which seeks to lobby the EU on the draft constitution, not least because it makes 'it difficult for small states, like Catalonia and Scotland, to increase the powers devolved to them'.[7] The Scottish Socialists have also become active in the European Social Forum, which has staged demonstrations against global capitalism. Of interest here, the SSP co-sponsored a workshop during the Florence 2002 demonstration with the Basque socialist group Zutik, entitled 'Globalisation and the right to National Self-Determination'. It appears that the SSP is echoing the SNP's tactics by forging alliances with like-minded territorial parties in Europe that are sympathetic to the main goals of independence and socialism.

The Scottish Green Party also supports the goal of Scottish statehood without subscribing to an 'independence-in-Europe' policy line. The party is critical of the EU's failure to meet pressing environmental problems, and reservations have been made about the democratic nature of EU structures. Alternatively, the Greens propose an independent Scotland where competitive growth is replaced by self-sufficient regional economies and public utilities would fall under 'locally accountable democratic structures'. Unlike the other two independence parties, the Greens are predominantly gradualists. 'Devolution of power is a process. The next stage is for the Scottish Parliament to have greater control over its finances and increased powers in areas such as energy, transport, health and consumer affairs' (Scottish Green Party 2003). In 2003 attempts were made to capitalise on the existence of three independence-seeking parties in the Scottish Parliament. The Socialists proposed the creation of an 'independence convention', imitating the 1990s Constitutional Convention, which would exist as an umbrella grouping for the sovereigntist parties. This idea was rejected by both the Greens and Swinney's leadership, although the SNP leadership bid of Alex Salmond and Nicola Sturgeon (2004) indicated some sympathy for a pro-independence grouping. If the three parties are able to cooperate on 'the dream that is shared by Mr Sheridan and by the Green Party and by every member of the SNP, of an independent, free Scotland',[8] Europe will certainly become a major point of debate.

Last but not least, the Scottish Tories have undergone a minor transformation since entering the Scottish Parliament. There have been significant policy divergences from the main branch, such as resistance to university tuition fees and support for free personal care for the elderly, leading to quarrels with London. Furthermore, there is a vocal section of the Party in Scotland demanding increased powers for the Scottish Parliament, including full tax and spending powers. Plans for fiscal autonomy are part of a broader argument for federalising the UK, whereby the House of Lords might be converted into a chamber to negotiate the affairs between different units in a federal system.[9] Some sections of the party have also argued for stronger links to Brussels and Scottish Ministerial representation in Europe for policy areas important to the territory, such as agriculture and fishing. The party's approach to Europe is a decentralising one, with support for subsidiarity tempered by strident calls for maintaining the primacy of the nation-state. These policies mark a major change in the party's position on Europe and Scottish autonomy, and it is clear that the Scottish Tories have since devolution become more responsive to Scottish interests.

It is now possible to say that all the parties in Scotland have pursued strategies designed to maximise Scotland's influence, achieve recognition of its distinctiveness and increase the Parliament's ability to act on domestic and European matters. Europe has become the litmus test for proving devotion to Scottish interests. However, the pro-European consensus of Scotland's parties has not transferred as easily into public attitudes towards European integration. Although surveys have indicated that Scottish attitudes to the EU have been slightly more positive than the rest of Britain since 1992, it is also true that all parts of Britain – including Scotland – have become more hostile to the EU since the Maastricht Treaty was signed (British Election Survey 1997; British Social Attitudes Survey 2001). Scottish public opinion still remains less Europhile than that of its political elites, particularly in outlying rural regions where Scots are greatly in favour of reducing the EU's powers (Scottish Election Survey 1997). The SNP's efforts to remove EU control over fishing from the list of exclusive competences in the Draft Treaty of the European Constitution is a strategy designed to assuage these voters. However, whether or not voters will accept, or even understand, the SNP's mixed message that 'removing fishing as an exclusive competence … is a pro-European position to take' remains to be seen.[10] So far, Scottish public opinion has decided that the Scottish Parliament and the EU should be the bodies tackling social reform (Brown *et al.* 1998), and this supports some of the territorial and pro-European strategies of political parties. But until the public begins making the same connections as political elites between European integration and constitutional reform, the growing European orientation of Scottish politicians will not translate into strong electoral support.

Conclusions

Scottish responses to Europe have been unique due to the constitutional implications of Europe linked to the Scottish territorial dimension. At earlier times during the European integration process, many Scottish parties viewed Europe more as a hindrance than an opportunity. Scotland, it was thought, could have been further peripheralised from the central areas of decision-making, thereby making Scottish administrators and representatives doubly distant from Brussels and London. This view began to change at the end of the 1980s due to a combination of domestic factors and the heightened importance of the social and regional dimensions of integration. As a result, Europe became associated with the protection of regional interests and social rights, two issues of great importance to the Scottish public and its political elites. The EU became attractive to parties seeking constitutional reform, such as Labour and the Liberals who, in their support of devolution, viewed subsidiarity as a vital aspect of increased Scottish autonomy, and the pro-independence parties such as the SNP who proposed the EU as an alternative framework for security and trading opportunities that could replace the 'external' structure of the UK. Even smaller parties such as the Greens and SSP, as well as the Scottish Conservatives, admit that there are some issues which necessitate greater access to decision-making in Europe.

However, this does not imply that there is now a fixed and straightforward pro-European consensus amongst Scotland's parties. The discussion has indicated that the re-alignment of parties on Europe has inevitably left behind a number of contradictions in their policy and strategies, particularly for Labour and the Scottish Nationalists. The protectionist rhetoric of the SNP's 2004 European Election manifesto, Scottish Labour's strategy to hide behind London when pressed on the issue of the European Constitution, in addition to the Scottish Green and Socialist Parties' vehement criticism of the EU's lack of accountability are all reminiscent of the antipathy directed towards the European ideal in the 1970s. This illustrates that parties are likely to continue re-positioning themselves with regard to European issues if it suits their political projects and, because of this, Europe is now a critical space in which the territorial dimension of Scottish party politics is being played out.

13 Basque nationalism

Sovereignty, independence and European integration[1]

Gurutz Jáuregui

Introduction

The Basque Country is a collectivity that throughout its history has maintained it own distinct personality, traditions and institutions. During the last two centuries its relationship to the Spanish state has been conflictual, and since the beginning of the liberal state in the nineteenth century there has been a constant struggle between state policies of integration and Basque resistance. This resistance has been led by various political forces, including 'foralists', autonomists and nationalists, but since the end of the nineteenth century it has been dominated by nationalism. It is therefore necessary to begin by noting some of the fundamental features of Basque nationalism, especially as compared with Spain's other important minority nationalism, the Catalan. This will enable us to understand the important differences in their strategies up to the present (Conversi 1997).

Historically, Catalonia has been a *terra de pas* (land of passage). In contrast, Euskadi (the Basque Country) has demonstrated a historical isolationist tendency as exemplified in the *fueros* by the concept of universal nobility and purity of blood. While Catalonia has recognised a *jus soli*, and has been open to people from outside, the *jus sanguinis* reigned in the Basque Country. The Basque language is another force for isolation. While Catalan is a romance language, easily learned, Euskera represents a barrier to people from other parts of Spain. From its origins, Catalan nationalism was linked to the industrial revolution, and provided an alternative path to modernisation against a backward Spanish state. By contrast, Basque nationalism, at least initially, represented the old precapitalist society threatened by the rise of industrial society. This further encouraged the isolationist tendency. In consequence, the two nationalisms had a different character from the start.

Basque nationalism made its *raison d'être* a fundamental opposition between the Basque and the Spanish, presenting Euskadi as 'occupied' by a foreign state (Jáuregui 1981, 2000). Signs of this occupation, according to the nationalists, were the marginalisation of the language, the progressive displacement of native elites and the massive immigration of workers from elsewhere in Spain. It followed from this analysis that the only valid strategy was the expulsion of the 'occupier', the rejection of everything Spanish, the maintenance of Basque purity, and the rejection of participation in Spanish political life. A Basque political force must be constituted with the overriding objective of Basque independence. This resulted in a profoundly ethnic and radically separatist nationalism. In Catalonia, by contrast, there emerged a civic nationalism based on self-identification and sociocultural integration, compatible in general with remaining part of Spain (Keating 1996).

By the second decade of the twentieth century, the Basque's radically anti-Spanish nationalism and refusal to participate in the Spanish state was modified considerably as the need to accommodate political networks within Basque society gradually encouraged a more pragmatic strategy. Yet this pragmatism constantly encountered opposition from the more intransigent sectors of the movement, which insisted on their ideological legitimacy. Thus was born a contradiction between ideological purity and strategic realism that has marked Basque nationalism to the present day, provoking a series of schisms in the movement: Aberri in 1921, *Jagi-Jagi* from 1931 and, most notably, ETA from 1959. All of these considered the mainstream Basque Nationalist Party (*Partido Nacionalista Vasco*–PNV) to have betrayed its principles. The same tensions exist within the PNV, which, maintaining its roots in the defence of Basque national identity, has oscillated in its strategies depending on external circumstances and the balance of forces within the party (De Pablo *et al.* 2001). Sometimes the pendulum has swung towards autonomy within Spain, at other times to independence, but most of the time the party has maintained a calculated ambivalence, allowing it to defend both autonomy and self-determination, sometimes simultaneously. The maintenance of this ambiguity has continued to provoke important internal conflicts in the PNV during the 30 years since the arrival of democracy in 1975. The most relevant was the 1986 split resulting in the birth of a new political party: Eusko Alkartasuna (EA), promoter of a more radical and independence-oriented nationalism, albeit not as marked as ETA's.

In this chapter the following issues will be analysed: (1) the practical manifestation of this ambiguity since the Constitution of 1978 and particularly since the approval of the Basque Statute of Autonomy; (2) the projects to reform the Constitution and the Basque Statute of Autonomy proposed by the Basque Government through the Ibarretxe Proposal; and (3) the influence of European integration on the evolution of traditional Basque nationalist claims.

Basque nationalism and the Constitution of 1978: the statute of autonomy

The biggest transformation experienced by Basque nationalism occurred in 1959 with the birth of ETA. For the first time, the PNV, a party of the moderate centre-right and committed to peaceful and democratic means, ceased to be the only significant representative of Basque nationalism and instead faced a radical organisation committed to armed struggle. Franco's death in 1975 and Spain's transition to democracy confirmed the distance between the PNV and ETA. The latter made the original theses of Basque nationalism its own, refusing any connection with the Spanish state or participation in Spanish politics, and demanding that the PNV join in a nationalist front for an independent state. ETA and the groups that support it (notably *Herri Batasuna*–HB) have maintained this rigid position ever since, unmodified by the Constitution of 1978, the Basque Statute of Autonomy of 1979, or the entry of Spain into the European Community in 1986. The PNV, by contrast, rejected ETA's proposal and decided, after the death of Franco, on a pragmatic strategy based on accepting the legitimacy of the Spanish state. This did not imply a rejection of its ideological principles. The PNV's participation in Spanish politics was purely instrumental and conditional on the recognition by the Spanish state of a distinct Basque national and political identity and the transfer of powers necessary to develop it. This calculated ambiguity allowed the party to press for autonomy in the short term but a broader right of self-determination in the long term.

The ambiguity was reflected in the Constitution and the Basque Statute of Autonomy, notably in two aspects. The first is the terminology of nationhood, where the PNV pressed for recognition of Basque nationality. Article 2 of the Constitution recognises plurinationality in an ambivalent way by guaranteeing autonomy to the *nationalities* and regions, but only within the indissoluble unity of the Spanish *nation*. This did not satisfy Basque nationalists, since it implies a hierarchical relation in which the Basque *nationality* is a mere component of the Spanish *nation*.

The second issue concerns historic rights. For centuries the Basque Country had a distinct political and juridical regime within Spain, rooted in the *fueros* or traditional laws. These were undermined in various stages during the nineteenth century, with the Basque Country's incorporation into a unitary state, and their restoration was a long-standing demand. The 1978 Constitution expressly recognised these historic rights and committed the state to respect and develop them, but then subordinated them to the Constitution by stating that their updating would proceed within its provisions. This ambivalent formula gave Basque autonomy its own legitimacy and a set of political powers greater than those enjoyed by other autonomous communities, but only within the constraints of the Spanish Constitution. From a pragmatic point of view, the PNV was satisfied with these provisions but, ideologically, could not accept Spanish sovereignty. So instead, it adopted a hybrid position, neither approving nor rejecting the Constitution, but abstaining in the parliamentary vote and referendum.

On the other hand, the PNV did accept the Basque Statute of Autonomy, since this included a clause recognising that acceptance of the statute 'did not imply a renunciation by the Basque Country of the rights that it would possess by virtue of its history.' This left open the possibility of a future exercise of the right of self-determination.

In the 25 years since the approval of the Spanish Constitution (1978) and the Basque Statute of Autonomy (1979), the autonomous system has had two positive effects. In the first place, it has defused many of the problems that have historically plagued the relationship between the Basque Country and Spain, proving an effective instrument in the recovery of Basque identity. Euskadi has gained political organs (including a government and parliament) with ample competences to develop its own policies, within the limits of the Spanish Constitution. It has its own public administration with a decision-making capacity, and a powerful financial base. The basis has also been laid for a recovery of Euskera.

In the second place, autonomy has allowed the conflicts to be resituated in their proper dimensions. So some problems traditionally considered to arise from the 'conflict between Euskadi and Spain' have been revealed as not exclusively external, but also rooted within Basque society itself. After a century in which the Basque Country, and in particular Basque nationalism, has blamed many of its problems on external agents, Basque society is now obliged to confront its own internal difficulties.

Although the internal and external dimensions of the conflict are connected, they are distinct issues. So while the internal problems are fundamentally, although not exclusively, social or pre-political, external problems stem from the relationship with the political system established in the Spanish Constitution. Internally, Basque society is divided almost evenly into two sectors, the nationalist and non-nationalist, and it remains fractured, conflictual and tense. Externally, the autonomous system has not achieved its main aim, which is a definitive resolution of the age-old conflict between Spain and the Basque Country. Proof of this is the continued lack of confidence in, or rejection of, the present system by an important part of Basque society (Jáuregui 1996).

Nationalism has traditionally been linked to a concrete idea, that the construction of a nation leads necessarily to the creation of an independent state. Basque nationalism, as we have seen, is no exception. The Spanish Constitution, on the other hand, whilst providing for ample autonomy, also lays down the indissoluble unity of Spain, implying the impossibility of secession. It does not permit the exercise of the right of self-determination in its classic sense. This is the core of the 'Basque problem'. Yet the treatment of this problem by both Basque nationalists and the Spanish state shows the prevalence of theory and rhetoric rooted in the nineteenth century over the realities of the twenty-first century, of form over substance and of solemn declarations over practical objectives.

In the new century, it seems necessary to demystify old political concepts, notably those of state, nation and nationalism. Old scholastic myths like those that, from the Spanish state, speak of the 'indissoluble unity of the Spanish Nation, common and indivisible fatherland of all Spaniards' and, from the Basque nationalists, talk of inalienable and untouchable rights, lie in contrast with the present process of globalisation and European integration. Nations are social realities and as such are contingent phenomena, subject to many factors, circumstances and events. It is enough to look at history to see the fall of great empires or, in recent years, the collapse of a world political order that appeared destined to last indefinitely. The ability of nations to survive does not depend on formal grandiloquent declarations but on the adaptability of their peoples at concrete historic moments.

The nation-state, particularly in Europe, is going through a fundamental transformation in which it is progressively losing power to supranational structures. The Basque problem could lose much of its virulence if seen in this light. It is in this context, then, that the accommodation of Euskadi in Spain should be placed. As noted earlier, Spain is a state in which several nations co-exist, but neither the constitution, nor the implementation of the autonomy provisions over the years have favoured the effective consolidation of this plurinationality. Article 2 rhetorically recognises the existence of nationalities, but in practice this recognition is diluted by blurring the distinction between nationalities and regions in the neutral, technical term 'autonomous communities'. The Autonomous Community of the Basque Country still has a level of autonomy notably inferior to that which could be permitted within the constitution. Finally, measures have not been developed for the integration and participation of the Basque Country in the institutions of the Spanish state or, at another level (as will be discussed further below) – the European Union (EU). All this has provoked dissatisfaction within Basque nationalism in recent years.

The Ibarretxe Proposal: the status of free association

Echoing this dissatisfaction, the Lehendakari (President) of the Basque government, Juan José Ibarretxe, presented a proposal in the Basque Parliament in September 2002. This provided for a 'new political pact with the state' to reconcile 'our self-government framework to the desires of the majority of present-day Basque society'. He sketched out the bases for the proposal and announced the formal opening of a process for producing the draft of a new statute, which would be negotiated with the state, culminating in ratification by referendum. The draft was formally presented to the Basque parliament in October 2003.[2] Both the initial speech and the October draft provoked a great polemic, as they directly affected the content of the Spanish Constitution, proposing a profound change in the system of autonomous government. Instead of devolution, it proposed, at least as far as the Basque Country was concerned, not merely a federal but a confederal system. The formal text referred to 'a new model of relationship to the Spanish state, based on free association and compatible with the development of a compound, plurinational and asymmetrical state'.

Regarding the content, it is necessary to distinguish two elements within Ibarretxe's proposal. On the one hand, there are the fundamental principles, laid out in the preamble and first section. On the other hand, there is the substantive content of the proposal, contained in the remaining articles. These two aspects reflect, once again, the historic ambiguity of Basque nationalism, caught between immutable ideological principles and a more flexible practice. The most controversial aspects of the proposal are not its substantive content, but the principles underlying it, notably:

1   The Basque Country constitutes a people with its own identity among the peoples of Europe, with its own distinct, historical, social and cultural patrimony 'situated geographically in seven territories which at present have three distinct forms of political-legal status in two states (the Basque Autonomous Community and the Foral Community of Navarre in Spain, and Lapurdi, Behe Nafarroa and Zuberoa in France)'.

2   The Basque people has the right to decide its own future, 'in conformity with the right of self-determination of peoples, internationally recognised, among other places, in the International Pact on Civil and Political Rights, and in the International Pact on Economic, Social and Cultural Rights'.

3   The acceptance of the regime of free association 'does not entail the renunciation of the historic rights of the Basque people, which can be recuperated at any moment by the exercise of its own democratic will'.

It is from these principles that conflicts have arisen over questions of sovereignty and self-determination. These will be discussed further below, but first we will briefly examine the substantive content.

Contrary to the views of most critics, the Ibarretxe Proposal is not, at least formally, a plan for independence or secession in the classic sense. It does not, in other words, propose the establishment of an independent Basque state, but rather, in its own words, a 'specific regime for a political relationship with the Spanish state based on free association, in mutual respect and recognition'. This model is founded on the right of Basque citizens to freely decide the type of relation they wish to maintain with the state and the need to secure a process of negotiation between it and the Basque Country in order to realise, by agreement, the democratic will of Basque society. To this end, Ibarretxe proposed the creation of a Bilateral Commission with equal representation from the state and the Basque Country, charged with establishing mechanisms for consultation, information and cooperation so as to harmonise their actions and pre-empt confrontations. Conflicts that did arise would be resolved by a special chamber of the Spanish Constitutional Court composed of six judges, three to be chosen by the Constitutional Court itself, and three by the Basque Parliament among Basque jurists.

On the other hand, the proposal recognises the Spanish Supreme Court as the superior judicial organ responsible for the unification of juridical doctrine and the resolution of conflicts between Basque and Spanish courts. On the political side, it allows the state to maintain a series of important competences, notably on Spanish nationality; the right to asylum; defence and armed forces; production, trade and use of arms and explosives; the monetary system; customs and tariffs; the merchant marine; and international relations (with the exceptions discussed below).

So the material content of the Ibarretxe Proposal establishes a very high level of political autonomy, clearly above that normally found in federal systems, but it does not amount to independence. For example, as we will discuss later, it does not provide, in relations with international institutions or the EU, a status comparable with that of member states, since the Basque presence in Europe would still operate through the Spanish state. It is, rather, a form of free association somewhere between federalism and confederation.

The question of sovereignty

The Lehendakari alludes, in his proposal, to an 'original sovereignty (of the Basque people) recognised in the entrenchment and updating of our pre-existing historic rights, explicitly repeated in the Constitution'. This, at first sight, contradicts Article 1.2 of the Spanish Constitution, according to which 'national sovereignty rests with the Spanish people'.

The present international political-juridical order is indeed based on the division of the world into sovereign states, each of which exercises exclusive sovereign power over a given territory, defined by frontiers and boundaries. The state is above all other power-holders within its territory, becoming within its territory a 'supreme, exclusive, irresistible and substantive power, the 'supreme creator of norms' with 'the monopoly of power and legitimate physical coercion, the *ultima ratio* of power' (Heller 1985).

Nevertheless, this notion of exclusive and hermetically sealed sovereignty has always been more myth than reality. Few states, even in the nation-state's heyday, exercised this sort of sovereignty in practice. Nowadays, globalisation is undermining the foundations which have sustained the classic theory of the state. A glance at the effective functioning of states is enough to show how obsolete this theory is, with the progressive disappearance of those elements that Heller characterised in 1934 as intrinsic to the state: territorial centralisation; effective monopoly of power; or subjection of all powers to that of the state (Heller 1985). Instead, we see, at the internal and international levels, centrifugal processes, producing a dispersion of powers and competences among different groups and institutions. The result is that the classic principle of sovereignty is profoundly broken and it is difficult to identify any real example of singular sovereignty. Borders are penetrable and lose their significance when non-state actors can communicate across space. The state has ceased to be a unitary actor, and has instead become one framework, and not the only one, in which political differences are negotiated and resolved (MacCormick 1999; Keating 2001a).

This does not mean that states will disappear, merely that they are subject to fundamental structural changes. This is visible in a particular form in Europe, through the process of European integration. The integrative myth of the nation-state has traditionally defined itself by three classic dogmas of the supremacy, the indivisibility and the unity of the state. In the application of these principles, the state and the law have been permanently united, with law as the emanation of national sovereignty. No law other than state law was recognised and international law itself was accepted only in so far as it was legitimated by the state.

These principles are undermined by European integration (Jáuregui 1997). In place of a coincidence between a sovereign entity and an exclusive territory, there has arisen a multinational political system, geographically open and constantly expanding. In place of single and indivisible sovereignty, there is shared sovereignty. Alongside state law there are European norms of equivalent status and, in many instances, regional or devolved laws. In addition, there is an international law derived from juridically valid agreements among inter-regional, transfrontier and other entities. The idea of a State of Law, understood as the ultimate abstraction of power, is still valid and continues to exist, but this State of Law does not rest exclusively on the idea of the nation-state. The mutual interaction among European law, state law, regional law and international law is such that power and sovereignty are shared among the various instances depending on the competences assigned to each. The nation-state has ceased to the sole means for legitimating and applying the State of Law, as is shown by the presence of the Court of Justice of the European Community, or even the European Court of Human Rights.

If it is obvious that globalisation and European integration have opened such profound breaches in the classical conception of sovereignty, it is difficult to defend the concept, at least in the sense upheld by the

Spanish Constitution or the proposal of the Lehendakari. Can we really sustain the idea that the only depositories of sovereignty are states, or continue talking of indivisible and original sovereignties? If not, then to which bodies other than the state can we attribute which types of sovereignty?

These changes affect both aspects of sovereignty, the constituted power and the constituent power. European integration has not only reshaped the constitutional order but, in so far as the state renounces its exclusive sovereignty, the Constitution ceases to be the unique source of authority (Hesse 1996). The same is true, *a fortiori*, for Basque original sovereignty as defended by the Lehendakari. To date, however, the process of European integration has not totally invalidated the Constitution as a norm creating or constituting the state. It is well known that the European treaties emanate or derive from the constitutions of the member states so that sovereignty remains rooted in these constitutions. Indeed the relation between the constitutional order and European integration is set to be the decisive question in the constitutional order in the next few years. A united Europe cannot be created against the states or against the regions, or outside of them, but must emerge from the varied, complex and rich social and cultural texture of the various collectivities that make up European society.

A European constitution does not imply the disappearance of the constitutions of the nation-states but rather a radical transformation of their content. A complex and open society such as that of present-day Europe needs an open and complex concept of sovereignty, based on the principle of subsidiarity and permitting a division not only of competences but also of sovereignty among the various levels and institutions. A new model should combine the positive elements of both federal and confederal ideas at European level, without doing away with states altogether (Archibugi and Held 1995). As MacCormick (1993) indicates, this involves a pluralist concept of law that permits the overlapping and interaction of diverse legal systems without assuming any hierarchy or subordination among them, or in relation to other systems. As Hart (1995) has noted, there are many forms and degrees of dependence and independence. While the word 'state' does suggest some measure of autonomy, it does not necessarily follow that this autonomy is unlimited, or can only be limited by a certain type of obligation. Both Article 1.2 of the Spanish Constitution and the proposal of the Lehendakari rest on a classic, monist conception of sovereignty and this renders them necessarily antagonistic. This antagonism, however, can be overcome if the principle of sovereignty is understood in a more limited and pluralistic sense.

The Spanish Constitution and the right to self-determination

Similar questions are raised by the right of self-determination of the Basque people. The Constitution permits a considerable degree of autonomy but not territorial separation, and the Ibarretxe proposition makes no reference to secession or the creation of a Basque state. Rather it suggests 'a new form of relationship with the Spanish state on the basis of a new status of free association'. So we must ask whether this is compatible with the constitutional text. Among other juridical documents, the Lehendakari refers to the right of self-determination on the basis of the International Agreements on Civil and Political Rights and on Economic, Social and Cultural Rights respectively, approved by the United Nations in 1966. Article 1 of both agreements stipulates that 'all peoples have the right of free determination' and continues that 'the contracting states to these agreements promote the exercise of free determination and respect this right in conformity with the terms of the United Nations Charter'.

The content of this right was later filled out by the Declaration on the Principles of International Law with reference to the Relations of Friendship and Cooperation among States, of 24 October 1970. In this it was stipulated that the establishment of a sovereign and independent state, free association with, or integration in, an independent state, or any other form of free status determined by the people were the ways of realising the right of self-determination. The same declaration, however, rejected any right of secession from an existing state and condemned all action aimed at the partial or total disruption of the national unity or territorial integrity of any state or country.

Subsequently, both the UN through various resolutions and the International Court of Justice (for example in its rulings of the Western Sahara in 1971 and 1975) have specified more precisely the premises according to which the right of self-determination could be invoked to demand separation from an existing state and the proclamation of sovereignty. These are: colonial territories; countries that were illegally occupied since 1945, so violating Article 2.4 of the United Nations Charter; and a distinct territory within a sovereign state, whose government violates the principle of equality of laws and the self-determination of peoples by excluding the members of the majority ethnic group within the territory from representation in government on the basis of one person one vote. None of these seem applicable to the Basque case.

The same line of reasoning was taken by the Canadian Supreme Court in its famous judgement of 1998 on the secession of Quebec. This established a distinction between the right of self-determination in the international and in the domestic legal context. From the point of view of international law, the court recalled that the right of peoples to determine their own status is so well recognised that it can be considered a general principle of international law. This does not, however, confer the right of secession, since international law, while not explicitly denying this right, does in general favour the principle of territorial integrity of existing states. It allows secession only under certain specified circumstances as noted above. Thus international law allows the democratic state to combat, by all legitimate and democratic methods, an attempt at secession by one of its component territories.

The fact that international law does not permit the secession of territories does not, however, prevent peoples who are not colonised from demanding and even obtaining this right. If a territory shows a clear and determined will to separate, this gives it legitimacy to sustain its secessionist demands and by the same token imposes on the state the obligation to take into consideration and respect the democratic will. If the right of secession is carried through, then international law limits itself to recognising the existence of a new state, as has happened recently in Eastern Europe or, earlier, in the case of Algeria despite the solemn affirmation of the unity and indivisibility of the republic enshrined in the French constitution. This means that, in democratic states, both the demand for self-determination and its negation by the state must be regulated in accordance with the norms of domestic law.

What is the situation with regard to Spanish domestic law? If the Basque Autonomous Community seeks to obtain the right of self-determination outside the constitutional process, this would not be legal or legitimate. On the other hand, an action by the Spanish state to impede the Basque Country, outside the juridical order, from exercising its right to self-determination could provide the motive and basis for the exercise of a unilateral right of secession. For this reason, it is necessary to think of how self-determination could be exercised within domestic law. Is this possible or necessary and what are the conditions?

On 15 February 1990, the Basque Parliament approved a declaration asserting that 'the Basque people has the right to self-determination and this right rests on the authority of its citizens to decide freely and democratically on its own political, economic and social status, either within its own framework or, wholly or partly, sharing its sovereignty with other peoples.' It continued, 'the Statute of Autonomy, resulting from a pact freely endorsed by the Basque citizenry, constitutes a point of encounter for its majority will and the framework with which the society has endowed itself at a given historical moment to accede to self-government and, in consequence, is the legitimate expression of the will of the Basque people. Therefore the devolution process and the deepening of self-government through the full and sincere development of the whole content of the Statute represents for Basque citizens a valid framework for the progressive resolution of the problems of Basque society and for the national construction of Euskadi'.

This text contains the three basic premises on which, in my opinion, the exercise of the right of self-determination must rest, namely:

1   that it is the Basque Country, and concretely the Basque Autonomous Community, that advances the right to determine its own future;
2   that the decision belongs not to the *ethnos* but to the *demos*, that is to

each and every citizen who, in accordance with the Statute of Autonomy, enjoys the condition of Basques;

3   that the decision must be taken in accordance with the existing legal procedures which means, following the line of the Supreme Court of Canada, it must be negotiated with the state.

With respect to the first premise, the proposal of the Lehendakari, following the criteria laid out in the Statute, uses two terms or concepts of the Basque people. On the one hand there is the 'Basque People' understood as a geographical, historical, social and cultural reality, covering the territories of Álava, Bizkaia, Gipuzcoa, Navarra, Lapurdi, Zuberoa and Benefarroa, in three jurisdictions and two states. On the other hand, there is the Basque Autonomous Community understood as a legal entity covering the historic territories of Álava, Bizkaia and Gipuzcoa. The 'Basque People' in the larger sense cannot be the holder of the right to self-determination, for several reasons.

1   It constitutes a geographical, historical, social and cultural reality but lacks a legal personality.
2   It goes beyond the Spanish state and it is difficult to see how the citizens in France could exercise a right of self-determination in a Spanish framework.
3   Of the two territories within Spain, the Lehendakari represents only the Autonomous Community of the Basque Country and not Navarre, so that only the former could be the subject of self-determination. Indeed Ibarretxe himself implicitly recognised this when he indicated that 'from the Basque Autonomous Community, and within the limits of decision-making which we have as an integral part of the Basque People, we wish to articulate our right to decide our own future'.

The second premise is closely linked to the first. It is clear that, in the Ibarretxe Proposal, the holders of the right of self-determination are the citizens of the Autonomous Community of the Basque Country, that is all individuals who, in accordance with the terms of the Statute of Autonomy, enjoy the political condition of Basques.

It is the third premise that, in my opinion, poses most constitutional and legal problems. The Lehendakari proclaims the intention to 'express our right to decide our own future through the recognition of the full capacity to engage in democratic consultation via referendum'. The problem is to know whether the Basque institutions are permitted under the Spanish Constitution to promote this type of initiative. They can certainly, according to the literal text of the Constitution, take an initiative to propose a constitutional reform, but they have no competence to submit this to a referendum. On the other hand, while they may not have the positive right to hold a referendum, the Constitution does not expressly prohibit it, and the Statute of Autonomy does provide that the Basque government, by delegation from the state, may stage a referendum on the Statute itself. This could be extended to any sort of referendum or popular consultation relative to Basque autonomy. So a flexible interpretation of the Constitution could indeed permit a referendum.

This is in effect what the Canadian Supreme Court did in its famous ruling on the secession of Quebec, considering that, in such a sensitive and important question, it could not confine itself to a narrow reading of the Constitution. Given the limitations of the constitutional text itself, it insisted that the legitimacy and even the legality of Quebec secession would need to be considered in relation to certain fundamental principles of the Constitution, rather than just the normal provisions for constitutional reform. 'The principles', it noted, 'are not simply descriptive; they are invested with a powerful normative force and are binding both on the courts and governments' (para. 54). The thesis expressed in this ruling is, I believe, applicable to the Basque case. Two principles should underpin the legitimacy of the Basque institutions to hold a referendum on the right of self-determination: the *democratic* principle, and the *federal* principle.

Holding a referendum constitutes the direct expression of the democratic will of a people, in this case the citizens of the Autonomous Community of the Basque Country. If the representative institutions of this people show a clear desire to hold such a referendum, then the *democratic* principle recognised in the Constitution requires that it should go ahead, in order to determine the democratic will of the citizens. The central government has the capacity to permit and help organise such a referendum, in pursuance of the democratic principle.

The ruling of the Canadian court is also relevant to the application of the principle of *federalism*. It declared that 'the legitimate attempt, by a participant in the Confederation, to modify the Constitution has as a corollary the obligation on the other parties to come to the negotiating table' (para. 8). This obligation applies even if the modification involves the secession of a province: 'the clearly expressed rejection by the people of Quebec of the existing constitutional order would confer legitimacy on the secessionist demands and impose on the other provinces and the federal government the obligation to take into consideration and respect this expression of the democratic will, committing themselves to negotiations and carrying them forward in conformity with the underlying constitutional principles' (para. 8).

Is this applicable to the Spanish case? Certainly, the position of the autonomous communities in the Spanish system is not one of original power since they have obtained autonomy through decentralisation and not through the integration of formerly independent states. However, as many authors have noted, the degree of vertical division of power in present-day Spain is clearly of a federal nature and the mechanisms regulating relations between the state and the autonomous communities are also characteristically federal. In addition, there is the recognition in the Basque case of the historic rights, which give the Basque autonomous system the characteristics of a pact, notably in the additional protocol to the Statute of Autonomy, according to which 'the acceptance of the autonomous regime by this Statute does not imply the renunciation by the Basque people of the rights which they could have enjoyed in virtue of their history, which may be updated according to the principles established by law'.

From all this emerges, as in the case of Canada, a need to reject both extreme positions: on the one hand, the idea that the expression of a right to self-determination on the part of the Basque Autonomous Community imposes no obligation on the state; on the other, the idea that the secession of the Basque Country constitutes an absolute right. Instead, we must seek an intermediate solution seeking to reconcile the diverse rights and obligations of the two main legitimate parties, the Basque Autonomous Community and the Spanish state. Negotiation between the two, as indicated by the Canadian Supreme Court, is not merely a political obligation, but a constitutional one.

The attitude adopted towards Basque autonomy in general, and specially towards the Ibarretxe Proposal by the former Spanish government of the Partido Popular (PP) was very clear. The PP considers that the Basque Statute of Autonomy must be kept in its present terms, and consequently is against its modification. Therefore, the PP also rejects the Ibarretxe Proposal and even denies the legitimacy of the Lehendakari to propose it.

The aspiration of José-Maria Aznar's Government was to avoid Ibarretxe's proposal being put to debate at the Basque Parliament. Therefore, in November 2003, he presented a claim to the Constitutional Court, alleging it to be unconstitutional in both its content and form. According to the Spanish legislation, the proposal had to be paralysed until the above-mentioned Court decided what to do about it. In April 2004, the Court dictated a resolution in which it said that the Spanish democratic system could not avoid the proposal being put to debate at the Basque Parliament. It will only be possible to decide whether or not it is contrary to the Constitution, once this has been definitely approved by the Basque Parliament.

The Constitutional Court's decision and the completely unexpected victory of the Socialist Party (PSOE) at the general election in March 2004, have placed the Ibarretxe Proposal, once more, among the priorities of the political agenda, not only in the Basque Country, but also in all Spain. The new PSOE government is in favour of a general revision of the Spanish autonomous system and considers it necessary to reform and deepen the extent of the Basque Statute of Autonomy. Nevertheless, it rejects the Ibarretxe Proposal based both in reasons of form and content.

From a formal perspective, the PSOE considers that the Lehendakari has the legitimacy to propose such a proposal, but has no competence to call for a referendum of the Basque citizens. It also considers that its content is contrary to the Spanish Constitution. The acceptance of the Ibarretxe Proposal requires a reform of the Spanish Constitution, a question that cannot only be decided by Basque citizens, but by the whole of the Spanish citizenry.

Sovereignty, self-determination and the European Constitution

As mentioned above, both the Spanish Constitution and the proposal of the Lehendakari rest on a classic conception of sovereignty and self-determination and this renders them necessarily antagonistic. This antagonism, however, could, theoretically, be overcome by the process of European integration. Therefore, we should analyse the extent to which the process of European integration and most of all the recently adopted European Constitution may be able to overcome the classical conceptions of sovereignty and self-determination and to what extent this integration process is changing the objectives and strategies of Basque nationalism.

Surprising though it may seem, despite its isolationist character, Basque nationalism has held throughout its history a clearly international and most of all, pro-European vocation. This vocation has been consistent since 1895, the year of birth of the PNV, and has been theoretically defended by all nationalist parties and groups, with different intensities. In general, the moderate parties – especially the PNV – have maintained a more pro-European position compared with the radical groups. For example, ETA, except during its first years of existence, has traditionally moved in an ambiguous and contradictory position, manifested in a theoretical admission of the idea of Europe, whilst radically rejecting the European integration process itself.

The reasons for this apparent underlying contradiction in the Basque nationalism are diverse and it is impossible to explain them in detail here. It should nevertheless be underlined, that the leitmotiv for the generalised admission of the idea of Europe is really quite simple. Basque nationalism has always considered that the integration, in general of the states, and particularly of Spain in the EU, would provoke the weakening of the national states and would therefore simplify the strengthening and recognition of the Basque nation by the international and European community.

The PNV has always actively supported the EU. During the 1920s, it welcomed with enthusiasm the rise of the Movement for a Pan-European Union founded by Koudenhove-Kalergi and also, the 'Project for a EU' prepared by the French Minister for External affairs, Aristide Bertrand. In the 1930s, its pro-European vocation was strongly confirmed through its active participation in the diverse Congresses for European Nationalities organised between 1929 and 1935. The leitmotiv during the election campaign of 1933 was Euskadi–Europa. The Basque government, elected in 1936, opened several official delegations in Paris, London and Brussels (Ugalde 1996). The Europeanism of the PNV, and therefore the Basque government, reached its culminating point after the end of the Second World War. It was one of the founding parties of the European Movement Council, and the Spanish Federal Council for the European Movement was even constituted in 1949, in the seat of the Basque government in exile in Paris (Azaola 1995).

After the restoration of democracy in Spain and its entry to the EU, both the PNV and the Basque government[3] have maintained a very intense European activity during these last 25 years. After the accession of Spain to the EU, a Basque delegation in Brussels was established. Meanwhile, it has a leading role in the Committee of the Regions, the Assembly of European Regions and the Congress of Local and Regional Authorities of the Council of Europe (De Castro and Ugalde 2004).

The pro-European position traditionally defended by the nationalist parties, and especially the PNV, has been directed towards the recognition by Europe of the Basque claims. In this sense, the objective pursued by the nationalist parties has been oriented towards the creation of a 'Europe of Peoples' as an alternative to the 'Europe of States', understanding by peoples, a distinguishable human collectivity, named nation, nationality or ethnie. In short, Basque nationalist parties want to see a Europe that is able to recognise the Basque nation. However, the EU proposes, mainly after the Treaty of Maastricht, a 'Europe of Regions', not as an alternative to the Europe of the States, but as a complementary reality, always in subordination to states.

The Basque government is perfectly conscious of the relevance of international relations and, most of all, of the European integration process in the present globalised world. Therefore, the Ibarretxe Proposal gives great importance to these two matters. In international affairs, the following is proposed:

- a right for Basque institutions to develop outside the territory; activities necessary for the defence and promotion of the interests of Basque citizens, with the corresponding right to sign agreements and conventions with international bodies;
- the right to have a presence in international organisations concerned with language, culture, peace, human rights and other matters;
- participation by Basque institutions in the Spanish delegations negotiating international treaties that affect the Basque Country as well as their implementation;
- a requirement that for international treaties that affect the powers of the Basque Country, approval of the Basque government should be required.

For the EU, the following are proposed:

1 guaranteed access to the European Court of Justice for the Basque institutions;
2 the right of the Basque Country to promote cross-border and interregional cooperation within the EU;
3 The creation by the Spanish government of the necessary channels for active participation by the Basque government in the decision-making process in matters within its competence, such as programming and spending of EU funds;
4 the right to be part of the Spanish delegation in the European Council of Ministers.

The permanent ambiguity, the constant fluctuation between autonomy and independence maintained by Basque nationalism, and more precisely by the PNV, throughout its history, has been determined in great measure by the response of the Spanish state to nationalist demands. During historical moments in which the Spanish state has been more flexible, Basque nationalism has moved towards more autonomist positions. On the contrary, the defence of stiff and unyielding positions by the state has strengthened pro-independence lines.

Nationalists consider that, after 25 years, the Constitution and the Basque Statute of Autonomy have not satisfied their ambitions and that the political praxis throughout these years has diminished and drained away Basque autonomy. Therefore, they demand a new agreement with the Spanish state. The Ibarretxe Proposal, an obviously radical proposal that aspires to surpass autonomy without reaching independence, constitutes an expression of this radicalisation, and the progressive reinforcement of pro-independence sectors over autonomist sectors in the Basque nationalist movement.

It is therefore surprising that the Ibarretxe Proposal defends, as far as international relations and Europe are concerned, very moderate positions, that have little or nothing to do with the demands of an independent Basque state with member-state status in the EU. The two nationalist parties in the Basque Government still support in their respective political programmes the strategic objective of a much more direct presence of the Basque Country in Europe. On the one side, for the PNV, the objective is materialised in the demand for a special status of Constitutional Region for the Basque Country. On the other side, EA directly establishes the need to create an independent Basque state inside the EU as a final objective. Nevertheless, beyond sovereignty and self-determination demands, the Ibarretxe Proposal has opted for a pragmatic line.

ETA and HB, from their side, reject the Ibarretxe Proposal because they judge it as too moderate. Instead, they demand (not as a long-term objective, but as a *sine qua non* condition) the recognition by the EU of the Basque state comprising the seven Basque territories located both in Spain and France.

Moderate nationalism, especially that of the PNV, has always hoped that Europe would grant the national recognition of the Basque Country that Spain has denied. PNV has traditionally held great confidence in the idea that the European integration process would provide an adequate adaptation of the Basque Country in Spain and Europe. This might explain its main interest in participating in the integration process and why the Basque government has opted for a pragmatic and moderated relationship with Europe. PNV, and to a lesser extent EA, had expected that the draft European Constitution would gather in a suitable manner the recognition of national entities such as the Basque one. Both the PNV and the Basque government have actively and intensively taken part in the discussions of the European Convention, mainly but not exclusively through the Committee of the Regions.

The EU has traditionally maintained that regional matters and the consequent participation of regions in European affairs are not a European subject but an internal matter for states. Contrary to this position, the regions – among them especially the Basque Country – have tried to apply the regional question as a substantive and specific reality to the whole of the European project. As a consequence, these regions have sought to have this reality reflected properly in the Constitutional text. For this reason they defended the establishment of the status of Partner Region of the Union, to be applied to regions like the Basque Country, which would imply certain participation and consultative rights in community policies by having representation in the Committee of the Regions and even the right to raise conflicts of competences against acts of the Union.

Nevertheless, and despite some minor progress, the European constitutional text retains the thesis that the regional question is an internal matter for member states. Instead of transcending national states, the draft European Constitution opted towards a strengthening of their position. Because of this, the final draft of the Constitutional text has disappointed the hopes of Basque nationalists. The Spanish President, Rodríguez Zapatero announced that a referendum on the European Constitution would take place in February 2005. EA, ETA and Herri Batasuna have announced their vote against the approval of the Constitution. The PNV has announced that although its vote will not be negative, its position is not favourable, meaning that it will probably abstain from voting in the referendum. As we can see, the absence of solutions by the EU to the regional question plays in favour of the radicalisation of the nationalists' thesis.

Despite the general rejection of the Ibarretxe Proposal, the PSOE seems ready to promote greater participation of the Autonomous

Communities in Europe, and in this sense does not frontally oppose the proposals presented by Ibarretxe concerning European affairs. On the other hand, the PP rejects the possibility for a greater role of the regions in the EU. The events to take place during 2005, especially the referendum on the European Constitution, seem to be crucial; they will give us a clearer idea of the future.

14 Liberalising Estonia's citizenship policy

The role of the European Union, the Organisation for Security Cooperation in Europe and the Council of Europe

*Elena Jurado**

On 26 February 1992, less than six months since the proclamation of Estonian independence and the dissolution of the Soviet Union, a Resolution on Citizenship was passed in Estonia, creating considerable uncertainty for the country's large Russian-speaking population.[1] The Resolution denied automatic citizenship to any person living in Estonia who had not been an Estonian citizen (or a direct descendant of an Estonian citizen) prior to 1940, when the territory of Estonia was brought under Soviet control. The vast majority of Estonia's Russian-speakers, who had either been born in or had moved to Estonia in the Soviet era, were transformed overnight into aliens. Estonian politicians denied charges of discrimination by appealing to the principle of 'legal continuity': the aim of the Resolution, they argued, was to reconstruct the citizenry of pre-war Estonia, the existence of which had been 'illegally terminated' by the Soviet 'annexation' of 1940. Anyone who entered Estonia in the Soviet period was therefore an immigrant and should apply for naturalisation accordingly. However, by imposing Estonian language requirements on the process of naturalisation, the new legislation denied Russian-speakers, whose knowledge of Estonian was minimal, the chance to become citizens for many years to come. In 1989, only 13.7 per cent of the Russian-speaking population deemed themselves fluent in Estonian.[2]

Loud protests from the Russian Federation and mounting unrest in Estonia itself led the wider international community to become actively involved. In 1993 a number of international institutions began issuing recommendations regarding concrete changes to Estonian legislation based on existing European standards of minority protection. To the relief of the international community, the Estonian government's response was positive. Legislation was gradually modified to encourage the integration

* The views expressed in this chapter are those of the author and not those of the COE.

of Russian-speakers, including measures to facilitate their naturalisation. In this chapter, I provide an account of the gradual liberalisation of Estonia's citizenship policy, focusing on the role of three European institutions: the European Union (EU), the Organisation for Security and Cooperation in Europe (OSCE) and the Council of Europe (COE). The analysis centres on their efforts to ensure Estonian compliance with emergent European norms on citizenship, which call on states to facilitate naturalisation to immigrants living permanently within their borders.[3]

The citizenship question is not the only aspect of Estonia's minority policy that European institutions tried to influence. Other aspects included the availability of mother-tongue education for Russian-speakers, Estonian regulations for issuing residence permits, and Estonian efforts to regulate language use in both private and public-sector employment. I have chosen to focus on the citizenship question for three main reasons. First, the citizenship policies of states have crucial implications for the survival of minority cultures: the more restrictive a state's rules for granting citizenship, the less willing it will be to tolerate cultural diversity amongst its permanent population. Second, access to citizenship is crucial for individuals belonging to minorities to participate fully in public life. This is certainly the case in Estonia, where the Constitution, promulgated on 28 July 1992, explicitly restricts three political rights to Estonian citizens: the right to be a member of a political party, the right to stand for local, parliamentary or presidential elections and the right to vote in parliamentary elections (Arjupin 2000). Whatever other rights the Russian-speaking population may enjoy, therefore, without access to citizenship they will remain excluded from Estonia's democratic process. Finally, Estonian resistance to outside interference was particularly stubborn in the field of citizenship. It took considerably longer for the government to make concessions in this field than in other areas.[4] The citizenship question therefore represents a 'hard case' for assessing the efforts of European institutions to influence Estonia's minority policy.

Numerous authors have argued in different works that European institutions have had a liberalising effect on Estonian (and Latvian) citizenship and other minority-relevant legislation.[5] Few efforts have been made, however, to explore the mechanisms that enabled European institutions to exert their influence. Those who have probed this question argue that the successful diplomacy of European institutions owes everything to Estonia's desire to join the EU. In the view of these authors, the OSCE and COE played only a secondary role: staffed with minority-rights experts but lacking their own economic and military power, they provided the standards of minority protection that resource-rich institutions, like the EU, proceeded to enforce (Barrington 1999: 21; Pettai 2000a: 282; Gelazis 2003: 58). In this chapter I question the overwhelming importance that tends to be given to the EU, at the expense of the OSCE and COE, in the process of ensuring Estonian compliance. By proceeding unquestioningly from rationalist assumptions about the behaviour of states, the existing literature privileges certain processes over others. I try to reduce this problem by considering alternative assumptions about why Estonia might have complied with European norms in the area of citizenship. I conclude that mechanisms other than material incentives were important as well, in particular the use of dialogue by OSCE and COE representatives in their efforts to change the way Estonian decision-makers *think* about minorities.

The chapter proceeds as follows. In the first part, I identify the mechanisms at the disposal of the EU, OSCE and COE for promoting compliance with Europe's minority-rights regime, including its subset of norms on citizenship. The aim is to highlight the operational differences between the three European institutions and to examine the diverse theoretical assumptions that inform their activities. In the second section, I turn to Estonia's relations with the EU, OSCE and COE. I use the insights developed in the first part of the chapter to analyse the reasons that drove Estonian decision-makers to gradually comply with the recommendations of the European institutions. In the third section, I conclude by summarising my findings on Estonia and considering their implications for the broader practice of Europe's minority-rights regime.

The agents of Europe's minority-rights regime

It was only in the early 1990s, following the outbreak of ethnic-based conflict in Yugoslavia, that West European governments became convinced of the security implications of human rights violations, including the rights of individuals belonging to minorities. They responded by devising a new European minority-rights regime based on multicultural principles, which Central and East European governments were expected to fulfil. Rather than merely proscribe racial or ethnic discrimination, Europe's new minority-rights regime called upon states to foster cultural pluralism within their borders by creating the conditions for members of minorities to participate in society on the basis of their mother tongue and cultural particularities. Efforts were made to codify these standards in European law, most notably through the elaboration of a Framework Convention for the Protection of National Minorities, which contains a comprehensive list of programmatic norms for the protection of national minorities (Benôit-Rohmer 1996).

Eager to minimise infringements on their own sovereignty, West European governments sought various formulae to focus the new regime's attention on the countries of Eastern Europe. One formula reached was the distinction between 'indigenous minorities', which were recognised as having valid claims to cultural autonomy, and 'immigrant minorities', which did not.[6] This distinction complicated the emergence of European norms on immigrant naturalisation, even though, as mentioned earlier, the citizenship policies of states have crucial implications for the survival of minority cultures. Thus, in spite of its important standard-setting role in other areas of minority protection, the Framework Convention contains not a single provision on citizenship. Nevertheless, whilst states still reserve the right to regulate their own naturalisation procedures, a set of European norms has slowly and rather cautiously started to emerge in this area.

This process began in 1992, when the participating states of the OSCE (CSCE at the time) declared that 'everyone [has] the right to a nationality' (CSCE 1992). Even if individuals were not granted the right to a *specific* nationality, with this declaration European states accepted the duty to take measures, in cooperation with other states, to minimise cases of statelessness. The Council of Europe went even further. In 1997 it opened for signature a new European Convention on Nationality, which proclaimed the duty of states to tolerate dual nationality, to require less stringent language requirements for naturalisation, and to confer automatic citizenship to children born on the territory of a state who would otherwise be stateless (Council of Europe 1997). To date, the Convention on Nationality has been signed by 25 states (with 12 ratifications), suggesting that the norms it enshrines are beginning to gain wider acceptance.[7] Finnemore and Sikkink offer the useful image of a norm 'life cycle' to explain that norms command different levels of acceptance at different points in time. Emergent norms may be accepted only by a handful of states until 'norm entrepreneurs' (often international organisations but also non-governmental organisations) succeed in persuading a critical mass of states of their validity (Finnemore and Sikkink 1998: 895). In the remainder of this section I identify the mechanisms developed in the framework of the EU, OSCE and COE for this very purpose.

The EU

The EU only began to take an active interest in minority protection during the 1990s. From the start, its vast economic resources were taken as the basis for exerting pressure on states. A strategy of conditionality was developed whereby trade, aid and (in some cases) membership are linked to compliance with European minority-rights standards. This approach is informed by rationalist assumptions about the motivations of states. According to rationalists, states are unitary actors that seek to maximise a given set of interests in an uncertain and competitive environment. By assuming that state interests remain consistent and stable over time, rationalists argue that ensuring compliance amongst norm-violating states requires manipulating the costs and benefits that states face in pursuing alternative courses of action. States must be offered material rewards that exceed the costs of compliance or they must be deprived of material resources needed for their survival. Hence, the EU's privileged position; its impressive economic resources give it enormous political leverage over states that are dependent on aid, trade or economic cooperation.[8]

The OSCE

The main instrument created in the framework of the OSCE for promoting compliance with Europe's minority-rights regime is the Office of the High Commissioner on National Minorities (HCNM). The HCNM relies on what could be characterised as a *security dialogue* in his efforts to influence the minority policies of states. Through behind-the-scenes, diplomatic discussions, the HCNM attempts to persuade national decision-makers that respecting the rights of minority cultures would advance the security of their states. This approach is consistent with cognitivist theories of compliance. In the cognitivist paradigm, the utility-maximising behaviour of states is constrained by the subjective perceptions and beliefs of individual decision-makers. Whilst recognising that beliefs are often resistant to change, cognitivists argue that decision-makers are capable of adapting their beliefs in the light of new information, a process they refer to as 'learning'. Learning is said to be more likely in the presence of a crisis that calls for immediate reconsideration of traditional beliefs. In these situations decision-makers become responsive to the ideas of 'epistemic communities' – external advisers with recognised expertise in a given issue area. By pooling the expertise of Max van der Stoel and later Rolf Ekéus, renowned for their competence in security issues, the HCNM is arguably in a strong position to persuade decision-makers, confronted with security challenges, about the importance of minority protection for the maintenance of peace and stability.[9]

The COE

The COE's approach to promoting compliance with European minority-rights norms is influenced by the organisation's traditional legal and ethical orientation. Its main mechanisms involve immersing states in a discursive environment that attaches moral censure to their failure to live up to COE standards – that is, praising states for norm-consistent behaviour and censuring or 'shaming' them for deviation. This didactic process is maintained in various forums at once. The most public and well known is the chamber of the COE Parliamentary Assembly (PACE), where member-state delegations debate each others' behaviour on the basis of reports written by Special Rapporteurs. The second main forum for COE discussions is the confidential, intergovernmental committee system attached to the COE secretariat. These committees are in charge of drafting new conventions and providing legal advice to governments whose policies are considered problematic in the light of existing conventions. The COE's approach is consistent with constructivist propositions about state behaviour. Constructivists drop the rationality premise altogether, arguing that governments (like individuals) are role-players whose actions are driven by a desire to affirm their identities as members of a society. Identity-driven behaviour contains an important moral or ethical component: actors behave in a particular way not out of conscious choice, but because the behaviour in question is deemed good and appropriate by the society to which they belong.[10]

Estonia's evolving citizenship policy

It is possible to distinguish four phases in the development of Estonia's citizenship policy since 1991, each denoting an increasing degree of compliance with the recommendations issued by the EU, OSCE and COE. Before proceeding to analyse this evolution, it should be noted that whilst the three European institutions expressed concern about the exclusionary nature of Estonia's citizenship policy, at no point did they criticise the decision to treat the Russian-speaking population as immigrants with no *automatic* right to citizenship. In part this acceptance reflected the uneasiness of West European governments, whose own non-recognition of Soviet rule over the Baltic states during the Cold War bound them to acknowledge the Estonian argument of 'legal continuity' (Visek 1997: 326–31). Instead of rejecting this argument, the EU, OSCE and COE proceeded to criticise Estonia in more subtle ways, above all by noting that Estonia's naturalisation procedures were out of step with European norms.

Phase 1: disregarding European norms, 1991–94

By June 1993, only 12,000 out of nearly 500,000 Russian-speakers had obtained Estonian citizenship as a result of the controversial provisions established in the Resolution on Citizenship of 26 February 1992. If the purpose of the Resolution was to create such a hostile environment for Russian-speakers that they would voluntarily choose to leave Estonia, the strategy was only a partial success. Estonia experienced high levels of emigration during 1992 and 1993 (each year, nearly 20,000 Russian-speakers left Estonia). Soon, however, the rate of 'return migration' began to decline, so that by 1995 it became clear that the great majority of Russian-speakers intended to stay in Estonia. The Resolution on Citizenship therefore landed the Estonian government with an enormous 'foreign' population consisting mainly of stateless individuals (over 300,000) but also a large group that opted for Russian citizenship while refusing to leave the country (over 75,000) (Barrington 1995).

The EU (European Community at the time) seemed to react very quickly to the Resolution's large-scale disenfranchisement of Russian-speakers. In 1992, it made a series of aid and loan agreements conditional on the improvement of Estonia's citizenship record (Jurado 2003: 144). Nevertheless, in spite of mounting unrest in Estonia throughout 1993, not a single suspension clause attached to the agreements was activated. The COE also failed to use the mechanisms at its disposal to influence the situation. Estonia's early bid to join the organisation gave the COE the rare opportunity to demand changes to Estonian citizenship legislation in exchange for membership. PACE Rapporteurs were sent to Tallinn to formulate opinions on Estonia's preparedness to join the COE just months after Estonia's Citizenship Resolution was passed. Their reports, however, were surprisingly favourable to Estonia (Bindig 1993; Bratinka 1993). Thus, ironically, during the period when the COE had most leverage over Estonian policy by virtue of its right to block Estonian accession, it voiced hardly any criticism at all.

Only the OSCE (CSCE at the time) endeavoured to use the chief mechanism at its disposal – the office of the HCNM – to exert pressure on Estonia. In April 1993, the HCNM issued two recommendations regarding specific changes to Estonia's naturalisation policy: that the elderly and the disabled be waived from the naturalisation tests altogether, and that children born in Estonia be given facilitated access to citizenship, particularly those born to parents who held no citizenship at all (HCNM 1993). However, the government of Estonia chose to disregard these recommendations. On 23 March 1993, Estonian decision-makers feigned obeisance to European norms by amending the Resolution on Citizenship to allow citizenship to be passed along the female line of descent as well as along the male line. However, this did nothing to improve the Russian-speaking population's opportunities for acquiring Estonian naturalisation.

Estonian domestic politics and relations with the Russian Federation were arguably too conflictual during the early 1990s for European institutions relying on dialogue to exert any influence. Estonia's first parliamentary elections since the restoration of independence, held on 20 September 1992, brought into power a coalition of right-of-centre nationalist parties committed to reasserting Estonia's cultural, economic and political independence after more than 50 years of Soviet occupation.[11] As one observer argued, by presenting Russian-speakers as a threat to the survival of the Estonian language and culture, Estonia's new government could justify denying automatic citizenship, and thus voting rights, to Estonia's Russian-speaking population, the natural constituency of left-wing parties (Kask 1994: 379–91). The atmosphere of mutual suspicion was aggravated when Russia began to use the problems facing Estonia's Russian-speaking population to put pressure on Estonia for concessions in other areas, the most contentious being the withdrawal of Soviet-era troops from Estonian soil and the delimitation of the Russian–Estonian border (Zhuryari *et al.* 1994: 119).

Further evidence of Estonia's disregard for European norms at this stage can be gleaned from analysis of the parliamentary debates held in 1993 to discuss the establishment of language requirements for citizenship. Proposals to grant citizenship to the elderly and invalid through a simplified language test were defeated by a resounding majority. This majority voiced security concerns in defence of their position, where security (from Russia) was defined in exclusionary, ethnocentric terms. For them, Soviet-era immigrants were a Russian 'fifth column', whose presence in Estonia not only 'threatened the survival of the Estonian language' but also the future of Estonian democracy and independence: only by learning Estonian could Soviet-era immigrants 'prove' their loyalty and 'earn' their right to participate in Estonian affairs. The small minority who supported the language waivers couched their positions in ethnocentric terms as well, confirming that only this type of reasoning was acceptable at the time.[12] As one supporter of the proposals put it, since the elderly and invalid 'are already completely beyond the life of society', their influence on Estonian public affairs, even with citizenship and voting rights, would be negligible (*Riigikogu* debate 1993a, 1993b).

Phase 2: tactical concessions, 1995–96

The first cracks in the government's exclusionary approach began to appear in 1995, following an important EU offer of financial assistance. The EU made this assistance conditional on Estonia setting up a nation-wide language-training programme to assist potential naturalisation applicants by subsidising Estonian language classes, training qualified Estonian language teachers and preparing effective language-teaching material. Estonia responded quickly to the offer, announcing in mid 1995 its decision to set up a Language Strategy Centre with precisely this purpose.[13] The timing of Estonia's announcement seems consistent with rationalist propositions about compliance, which assume state preferences remain stable and, therefore, that material incentives are needed to influence the behaviour of states. The HCNM had been calling for this type of initiative since 1993, to no avail (HCNM 1994). It would appear, then, that EU conditionality changed Estonian decision-makers' calculations of the gains to be made from heeding the HCNM's advice.

Numerous factors facilitated the success of EU conditionality on this occasion, including worsening Estonian–Russian relations and the birth pangs of Estonian market reforms. With violent conflict erupting in several ex-Soviet states, developing a more interventionist stance towards the 'near abroad' became a priority for Russian policy-makers, who began accusing Estonia and other former Soviet republics of 'violating the rights of Russian-speakers' and 'pursuing a system of apartheid' (Vorontsov 1994: 2). Fear of Russia made Estonian decision-makers receptive to the demands of resource-rich institutions like the EU, which, it was felt, could provide Estonia with a measure of security against Russia. Moreover, with the social costs of Estonia's radical economic reforms becoming ever more apparent, the government of Estonia was desperate for aid, loans and opportunities for trade.

In spite of the apparent success of EU conditionality, the newly established Language Training Centre took three years to produce an action programme, suggesting that Estonia was in no hurry to improve the language abilities of Russian-speakers. Indeed, 1995 saw a considerable *drop* in Estonia's annual naturalisation rate, from 22,370 in 1994 to 16,674.[14] The tactical nature of the Estonian government's concessions was highlighted further when, in 1995, a new Citizenship Law was enacted that brought even stricter naturalisation criteria into existence.[15] Whilst declaring their desire to 'integrate' the Russian-speaking population in discussions with EU observers, Estonian government representatives defended the new Citizenship Law before parliament using the same exclusionary arguments based on ethnocentric definitions of national security. As Mart Nutt, member of the governing coalition and author of the bill, explained to the Estonian parliament: 'the most important influence on our decision [to introduce more stringent naturalisation criteria] is Russia itself . . . By offering Russian citizenship to former Soviet citizens, Russia is trying to encourage people living in the *near abroad* to be simultaneously Russian citizens and citizens of Estonia, Latvia, Lithuania or some other state. It is of course not necessary to explain the long-term purpose of this policy' (*Riigikogu* debate 1995).

Phase 3: cultural assimilation, 1997–98

A third phase in Estonia's citizenship policy began between 1997 and 1998, when opportunities for learning Estonian finally began to increase for Estonia's Russian-speaking population. The Language Strategy Centre finally published its language-training programme, which included measures to finance the publication of teaching material and provide financial support to Estonian language-course providers. This included a special fund to reimburse 50–100 per cent of the fees of students enrolled in language courses who successfully passed the citizenship language test (Report 2000). These steps demonstrated the government's unprecedented willingness to integrate the Russian-speaking population. This was to be done, however, by improving the Estonian language skills of Russian-speakers rather than by removing or reducing the requirements needed for naturalisation. As such, even if Estonia's citizenship policy was becoming more inclusive, it was still at odds with the multicultural emphasis of Europe's minority-rights regime, which calls on governments to tolerate cultural diversity amongst their citizens.

What role did Europe's three institutions play in Estonia's decision to adopt a policy of integration, albeit one based on cultural assimilation? Between 1995 and 1997, the EU, OSCE and COE used all available channels to remind Estonia's government of its minority-rights obligations. For the OSCE, these channels involved visits by the HCNM, complemented now by the activity reports of the OSCE Permanent Mission in Estonia. In January 1997, the Parliamentary Assembly of the COE made the implementation of Estonia's planned language-training programme a condition for lifting the special monitoring procedure applied to new members (PACE 1997). In July 1997, the European Commission published its first official opinion on Estonia's EU membership bid ('*Agenda 2000*'), which identified the need to provide Russian-speakers with greater language training opportunities. With EU heads of state scheduled to decide by the end of the year which candidate states should be invited to start membership negotiations, the period between the publication of *Agenda 2000* and December 1997 was one of frenetic activity for the Estonian government, which threw itself into a massive public-relations campaign to impress its candidacy upon the EU.

Rationalist scholars point to this critical period in EU–Estonia relations to explain Estonia's willingness to make concessions (Kionka 2000: 325–36). The inauguration of Estonia's language-training programme in early 1998 no doubt helped to place Estonia within the 'fast-track' group for EU accession. However, a closer look at Estonia's policy-making process suggests that EU conditionality was not the only factor at work. That autumn, amendments were made to Estonia's Aliens Law that gave holders of temporary residence permits the right to obtain permanent residence two years earlier than previously established. As permanent residence in Estonia is a necessary (albeit insufficient) condition for naturalisation, the decision to increase the number of permanent residence holders had important ramifications for Estonia's citizenship policy. A new 'security logic', resembling the dialogue on minority protection of the OSCE, emerged in the speeches of government representatives who defended the bill. Interior Minister Robert Lepikson argued that the amendments were necessary 'in order to avoid conflict' between Estonian government officials and the increasingly disaffected Russian-speaking population (*Riigikogu* debate 1997). This form of argumentation reversed the logic used by government representatives in previous parliamentary debates, where excluding Russian-speakers from participating in society was deemed the most effective way to maximise Estonian security. It suggests that persuasion by the HCNM, and other OSCE representatives, was proving effective at this time.

Domestic political developments help explain why, by 1997, the government of Estonia began to respond to the OSCE's comprehensive security model, and not only to the offer of EU material rewards. Parliamentary elections held on 5 March 1995 brought a new coalition of left-of-centre parties into government.[16] Although they had pledged to continue the previous government's policy towards minorities, their period in office was marked by great instability. In one of Prime Minister Mart Siimann's government reshuffles, Andra Veidemann was invited to become Minister without portfolio on Population and Ethnic Affairs. Under Veidemann's initiative, a special government commission was set up in 1997 to draft proposals for integrating Estonia's minorities. The vague content of the commission's early proposals about 'integration' has been noted by various observers (Pettai 2000b: 13; Vetik, undated: 24). This vagueness reflected the commission's uncertainty about how to proceed with minority integration and created a demand for European minority-rights expertise. Another notable result of the March 1995 elections was the election of six Russian-speaking deputies. Numerically too weak to contribute directly to policy-making, the Russian-speaking deputies became useful allies of the EU, OSCE and COE, providing a new channel for European ideas to penetrate Estonian political debate.

Whereas domestic political developments help explain why Estonian decision-makers became more open to European ideas by 1997, it is still not clear why they began to express the security-based arguments of the OSCE rather than ethical concerns about minorities voiced by the COE. In order to explain this we must turn to Estonia's on-going security concerns. In spite of the departure of Soviet/Russian troops by 1995, Russia continued to represent a security problem for Estonian decision-makers, not least because Russian politicians continued to cite ethnic discrimination in Estonia as a means of blocking agreement on the Russian–Estonian border issue (*BNS*, 20 December 1996). By 1997, Estonian decision-makers faced two competing conceptions of how best to manage the Russian threat: their original conception, based on antagonism towards Russia and the exclusion of the Russian-speakers from society; and the conception promoted by the OSCE, based on cooperation with Russia and the integration of ethnic minorities. In keeping with cognitivist propositions, the HCNM's ability to frame compliance with European norms in terms of security (a pressing problem facing Estonia) facilitated a conceptual change on the part of Estonian decision-makers, who replaced their original, antagonistic approach to security with the comprehensive security model advanced by the OSCE.

Phase 4: towards multiculturalism? Since 1999

On 12 July 1999 the Estonian parliament passed an amendment to the Citizenship Law of Estonia that drew a great deal of applause from the international community. The amendment allowed children under the age of 15, born in Estonia after 26 February 1992, whose parents were stateless and had resided in Estonia for at least five years, to obtain citizenship (upon their parents' request) without any examinations at all (Poleshchuk 2004: 17). This amendment represented a bigger concession to European citizenship norms than any measure taken so far by Estonian authorities. By allowing Russian-speaking children to acquire citizenship without examinations, rather than only assisting naturalisation applicants via language training, the government of Estonia demonstrated its readiness to tolerate a degree of cultural pluralism amongst its citizenry. The amendment brought Estonia closer to the European Convention on Nationality, which explicitly calls on governments to offer facilitated naturalisation to children born on the territory of their states who do not acquire at birth another nationality.[17]

A superficial reading of Estonia's relations with Europe's three main institutions suggests, once again, that conditionality played a significant role. The HCNM had advised Estonia to take precisely this step as early as April 1993. The COE offered the same advice from 1997, when the European Convention on Nationality, drawn up by COE experts, was opened for signature. In May 1997, the HCNM decided to re-issue his earlier recommendation regarding the naturalisation of stateless children (HCNM 1997). The timing was important: with Estonia's membership bid being considered by the EU, the HCNM was hoping to ride on the coat-tails of the EU accession process. His strategy proved successful. In July 1997 the EU published *Agenda 2000*, listing the need for Estonia to 'facilitate the naturalisation process' as a short-term priority, although it did not specify how this priority should be met. Five months later the government of Estonia announced that it had handed a bill proposing facilitated naturalisation for stateless children to the Estonian parliament. Within weeks of this announcement, the EU invited Estonia to begin membership negotiations.

There is little doubt that the government's decision was influenced by the prospect of EU membership. However, a closer look at Estonia's policy-making process suggests that other considerations were also at play. Although Foreign Minister Raul Mälk cited Estonia's EU membership bid during his defence of the bill before parliament, he also emphasised the need to affirm Estonia's membership in a community of law-abiding states: 'Estonia remains the only European state that does not recognise that stateless children legally residing in a state have a right to citizenship by means of a simplified procedure.' Mälk's repeated references to the practice of other European states suggest that Estonian decision-makers were driven not only by considerations of material gain, but also by the desire to affirm Estonia's 'European identity'. This does not mean that Estonian government officials had abandoned concern for the Estonian language: even Mälk, the bill's main defendant, described the naturalisation of Russian-speaking children as 'a first step towards their integration', to be supplemented by 'our educational system and cultural life'. Nevertheless, a degree of cultural pluralism was no longer deemed incompatible with Estonia's national identity.[18]

This development suggests that, in keeping with constructivist propositions, the ethical dialogue of the COE, based on presenting officials with new understandings of 'appropriate' behaviour, had started to influence the calculations of Estonian decision-makers. Other developments in Estonian citizenship policy provide further evidence of this trend. In the year 2000, a new language test for citizenship was issued that was considerably easier than the previous one.[19] The new test was the result of a long-standing cooperation programme between Estonia and the COE that was designed, amongst other things, to harmonise Estonian examination techniques with the standards established by the Association of Language Testers in Europe (ALTE).[20] Then, on 30 June 2000, Estonia's Citizenship Law was amended again, this time to lower the naturalisation fee and to allow disabled persons to apply for naturalisation without the need to pass any examinations, a move that was expected to affect 30,000 people (Minelres 2000). Both moves went beyond EU requirements for membership, suggesting that facilitating the naturalisation of Russian-speakers was no longer seen as an external imposition but rather as the rightful duty of the Estonian government.[21]

Conclusions

Given the continuing existence of a large 'stateless' population in Estonia – at the end of 2003, the government identified 162,890 people (representing about 12 per cent of the total population) as 'aliens with undetermined citizenship'[22] – it would be easy to conclude that little has changed in Estonia since 1992. It is true that the basic principle of Estonian citizenship policy remains in place: citizenship is still conferred automatically only to descendants of Estonia's pre-1940 citizenry. Nevertheless, as I have argued in this chapter, Estonia's approach to naturalisation has experienced considerable change. After an initial exclusionary phase, the Estonian government began to encourage the naturalisation of Russian-speakers, first through assimilative means (inaugurating a nation-wide language training programme) and later on a more multicultural basis (lowering and in some cases removing the naturalisation requirements for certain groups of Russian-speakers). I have argued that European institutions played a salient role in Estonia's policy transformation, with the EU, OSCE and COE each exerting greater influence at different stages.

Given the complex constellation of domestic and international factors that affects decision-making in different countries, only tentative conclusions can be drawn from the case of Estonia for the broader practice of Europe's minority-rights regime. Developing firmer conclusions would require analysing EU, OSCE and COE efforts to ensure compliance with minority-rights standards in other European states, ideally, states which have differences and commonalities along a range of variables. Notwithstanding this complexity, Estonia's example offers some tentative suggestions about the strengths and weaknesses of the EU, OSCE and COE in the area of minority protection. If these suggestions are supported by further empirical investigations, they should enable us to improve the performance of Europe's minority-rights regime by allowing each European institution to play up its strengths and reduce wasteful overlap of activities.

The case of Estonia suggests that the participation of all three institutions in Europe's minority-rights regime is necessary, but that each can best contribute in a particular way and perhaps could even intensify its activities at different stages. Given the abundant material resources at its disposal, the EU is best placed to act at the beginning of the compliance process: only the EU has the means to apply positive or negative sanctions upon a state that is marginalising members of ethnic minorities. These sanctions are necessary to encourage national decision-makers to embark on reform. However, we have also seen that material incentives on their own cannot guarantee that the reforms will produce a noticeable improvement in the situation of minority groups. (Estonia's Language Strategy Centre, set up in 1995 in response to EU conditionality, had little impact on the lives of Estonia's Russian-speaking population during the first three years of its existence.) In order to ensure that meaningful reforms are implemented, European institutions must engage in a carefully devised dialogue on minority protection, which is where the strength of the OSCE and COE lies.

In countries where ethnic minorities harbour political, economic or cultural grievances, political elites representing the majority population will tend to regard the minorities, rightly or wrongly, as constituting security threats – either because they are seen as being disloyal to the state or because they are perceived to have the support of an external and irredentist homeland. This means that once the EU has opened the door to policy reform in a country, the OSCE is best positioned to take over. The security-based arguments of OSCE representatives, particularly the HCNM, will resonate more strongly with existing concerns in the target state than the ethical arguments of the COE. The OSCE, however, must be aware of the limits of its influence. Whilst the HCNM successfully persuaded Estonian decision-makers that security requires integrating rather than excluding minorities, Estonia's citizenship policy remained assimilative in nature until Estonian decision-makers began to 'desecuritise' their thinking about minorities.[23] As Will Kymlicka has argued, by maintaining that minority protection is necessary for reasons of security rather than for reasons of justice, the OSCE encourages states to continue thinking about minorities in strategic terms (Kymlicka 2001b: 369–87). Indeed, the 'securitisation' of minority issues may delay, or even prevent, the transformation of national identities – a necessary step for states to begin to shift their minority policies in a more multicultural direction.

Once states have achieved a satisfactory degree of internal and external stability – e.g. by signing border treaties with their neighbours, by consolidating their democratic institutions and/or by joining multilateral security institutions – the OSCE should reduce its presence and hand over responsibility to the COE, which uses arguments based on considerations of justice rather than security to persuade decision-makers to comply with European minority-rights norms. With the gradual consolidation of a 'democratic peace' in Eastern Europe, it is therefore conceivable that the COE will become the most important player in Europe's minority-rights regime. In this scenario, the EU and OSCE would only intervene in the minority policies of European states if relations between minority and majority groups threaten to collapse into violence. A precondition for such a division of labour, however, is that European governments and populations alike perceive the differences between the three institutions. It is not sufficient to declare, as EU Heads of State have done in the Treaty Establishing a European Constitution, that the EU 'shall establish all appropriate forms of cooperation' with the OSCE and the COE (as well as other international institutions).[24] It is also necessary to clarify why such cooperation is necessary, and what it will entail.

Estonia's example holds out promise for the practice of Europe's minority-rights regime in other East European countries, particularly in those whose governments are eager for economic assistance and international legitimisation of their democratic credentials. However, the results are less encouraging for the economic powerhouses of Western Europe – France, Germany, Spain, to name but a few – home to ethnic minorities with long-standing links to their respective states, as well as to increasing numbers of immigrant communities. West European governments have fewer, if any, economic incentives for complying with European standards of minority protection. The tendency of European institutions to focus on East and Central Europe, moreover, means that politicians in Western Europe have less frequent contact with European discourses on minority rights as well. This double standard may eventually threaten the progress achieved so far in countries like Estonia, which attained the goal of EU accession in May 2004. Unless efforts are made to inject greater equality into Europe's minority-rights regime, it may become difficult to prevent politicians in the EU's ten new member states from questioning their commitment to minority protection.

15 Europe's limits

European integration and conflict management in Northern Ireland

John McGarry

The Northern Ireland conflict has both internal and inter-state dimensions. On the one hand, Northern Ireland is divided between Irish nationalists and British unionists. On the other, its conflict spills over state frontiers, encompassing not just the United Kingdom (UK), but also the Republic of Ireland.

There is a view that European integration has impacted positively on both of these dimensions, or has the potential to do so. For over 40 years, Irish nationalists have maintained that European integration would solve the problem of internal divisions by reconciling unionists to a united Ireland. A smaller number of unionists have argued that European integration would reconcile Irish nationalists to the Union. More recently, some have argued that European integration is eroding both of Northern Ireland's 'ethno-sectarian' identities, and is creating space for post-nationalist identities and a post-sovereigntist politics based either on a 'post-nationalist' Ireland or on Northern Ireland as a European region.

Others believe that European integration has promoted better relations between the UK and Ireland. In this view, the strong cooperation between the British and Irish governments, manifested in the Anglo-Irish Agreement of 1985 and the Good Friday Agreement of 1998, is linked to their co-membership of the European Union (EU), and to a weakening in the concept of sovereignty that has accompanied European integration.

Whether or not European integration has had these benign effects on Northern Ireland is an interesting question in its own right. However, its relevance extends well beyond the UK and Ireland. There are several sites in Europe, both within the EU and among candidate countries, that experience the same kind of internal and inter-state tensions that are associated with Northern Ireland's conflict. Much of Eastern Europe in particular, including Hungary, Slovakia, Romania, Macedonia, Bulgaria, Serbia, Bosnia, Estonia and Latvia, is affected by the same triadic nexus of homeland state, national minority and kin-state (Brubaker 1996). If European integration can benignly impact on Northern Ireland's conflict, might it not similarly impact on conflicts in other parts, and future parts, of the EU?

In this chapter, I assess the effects of European integration on inter-ethnic relations within Northern Ireland, and on relations between the governments of the UK and Republic of Ireland. The chapter concludes with a discussion of the relevance of this experience for Europe's other conflict zones.

European integration and relations within Northern Ireland

There is a long tradition in Ireland of hoping that European integration will erode one or both of Northern Ireland's antagonistic unionist and nationalist identities. Most unionists have been sceptical about this (McGarry 2001a: 305). However, since the debates on entry into the European Economic Community (EEC) in the early 1960s, some unionists have argued that European integration, with its benefits of labour mobility, common European citizenship and limited cross-border cooperation between adjacent parts of different states, has the potential to reconcile Irish nationalists to the Union. Some even claimed that it was a mechanism for undoing the rupture caused by the 'secession' of Ireland from the UK in 1921 (Cadogan Group 1992; Kennedy 1994: 186; Dixon 2000: 182–3). More recently, a unionist academic claimed that the EU is a positive influence because it is based on cooperation among sovereign states, which are obliged to respect each others' boundaries (Alcock 2001). From this perspective, European integration has the potential to weaken Irish nationalism in Northern Ireland by undermining irredentist support from the Irish republic.[1]

Since the 1950s, Irish nationalists have commonly portrayed economic integration as facilitating unionist support for a united Ireland. The thinking was first outlined by future Taoiseach Liam Cosgrave in a speech to Dail Eireann in 1954. It played an important part in convincing Taoiseach Sean Lemass to abandon attempts at autarky in the Irish Republic, to sign a free-trade treaty with the UK, and, in 1965, to meet with Terence O'Neill, Northern Ireland's prime minister, to improve economic cooperation (Lyne 1990). In a referendum on the UK's membership of the EEC in 1975, many nationalists in Northern Ireland voted 'yes', because they thought it would weaken the border and bring a united Ireland closer. From the nationalist perspective, Ireland's position on the periphery of an increasingly integrated Europe has made it more worthwhile for both parts of the island to cooperate in all island political institutions.[2] When, in the early 1990s, the Chair of the Northern Ireland Institute of Directors proposed an integrated 'island economy' in the context of the single market, a nationalist newspaper (the *Irish News*) lauded the plan as 'paving the way for unity' (Anderson and Shuttleworth 1992: 18). Nationalists also point to the way in which Northern Ireland's MEPs work together in Brussels as evidence that they are latently co-nationals. A Cambridge economist, Bob Rowthorn, has argued that closer economic cooperation between Northern Ireland and the Irish Republic in the context of the EU will lead unionists to shift their loyalties from London to Dublin (Rowthorn 1993). An Israeli political sociologist, Sammy Smooha, who has examined Northern Ireland from a comparative perspective, claimed recently that the option of a united Ireland would be less and less resisted by unionists as Ireland, a member of the prospering EU, comes to enjoy economic growth, expands its welfare services and secularises (Smooha 2001: 328–30).

A third group of 'post-nationalists' takes the view that European integration will erode both of Northern Ireland's rival identities. The new Northern Irish person, apparently, will have multiple, fluid and positive identities that are tied to Northern Ireland as a modern European region, a 'postnationalist Ireland' or a 'civic nationalist' Ireland in which the current 'sectarian' versions of unionism and nationalism are a thing of the past (Meehan 1992; Delanty 1996; Kearney 1997; Kearney and Wilson 1997; Taylor 2001). Kearney and Wilson envisage Europe evolving into a federation of regions, including Northern Ireland, which will foster allegiances 'both more universal and more particular than the traditional nation-states' (Kearney and Wilson 1997: 790). Delanty writes that 'European integration offers Northern Ireland an opportunity to build up a new democratic culture capable of embracing the two traditions in the province . . . [and] to cultivate a new post-national and pluralist identity as a European region' (Delanty 1996: 127–8).[3] McCall claims that European integration has the potential to erode unionism and nationalism in Northern Ireland, particularly in the absence of sectarian violence (McCall 1998: 408).

Some post-nationalists argue that European integration is already beginning to produce these desired results. Elizabeth Meehan wrote in 1992, the year of the Maastricht Treaty, that

> a new kind of citizenship is emerging [in Northern Ireland] that is neither national nor cosmopolitan but which is multiple in enabling the various identities that we all possess to be expressed, and our rights and duties exercised, through an increasingly complex configuration of common institutions, states, national and transnational interest groups and voluntary associations, local or provincial authorities, regions and alliances of regions.
>
> (cited in Kearney 1997: 84)

Rupert Taylor wrote in 2001 that there 'has been an erosion of ethnonationalism on both sides, a fading of Orange and Green, in favour of a commonality around the need for genuine structures of democracy and justice' (Taylor 2001: 45). Both Meehan and Taylor believe that European integration, in addition to promoting emergent post-nationalist identities, has facilitated new 'post-sovereigntist' mindsets that may have helped make possible the compromises in the Good Friday Agreement.[4]

Dissolving nationalisms?

The most charitable response to these arguments is that there is little evidence that European integration has had any identity-transforming effects, and little evidence that it looks likely to do so in the foreseeable future.

If any of the accounts referred to above were correct, we would expect to see it registered in electoral politics, in transfers of support from unionist to nationalist parties or vice versa, or in a shift of support from radical unionist and nationalist parties to more moderate unionist and nationalist parties, or in a transfer of support from ethnonational parties to parties outside the ethnonational blocs. Electoral behaviour over the past 35 years shows no such trend. While the Irish nationalist bloc's share of the vote has increased significantly, from 24.1 per cent in 1973, to an average of 32.5 per cent between 1982 and 1989 and 41.7 per cent between 1997 and 2004, the increase is not a result of unionists converting to nationalism. Rather, it is a result of Sinn Fein's decision to participate in electoral politics after 1982, a corresponding increase in turnout from the Catholic ethnonational bloc, and an increase in that group's share in the population – the result of a higher birth-rate and disproportionate emigration among unionists (O'Leary and McGarry 1996: 192; O'Leary and Evans 1997). The unwillingness of unionist voters to switch support to nationalists parties or vice-versa is also confirmed by opinion surveys and voting transfers in those elections in Northern Ireland that are based on the single transferable vote.[5] Within the two blocs, there has been a movement not towards more moderate parties but towards more radical parties. In the nationalist bloc, Sinn Fein has increased its share of the vote from an average of 37.3 per cent in its first five elections between 1982 and 1987 to 52.3 per cent in its last five campaigns (1999–2004). Since the Westminster election of 2001, it has been the most popular nationalist party in Northern Ireland.[6]

The UUP's share of the unionist vote has gone down in each election that has been held since 1998, while the usually more hardline DUP's share has increased. In the two most recent elections, the Assembly elections of November 2003 and the European elections of June 2004, the DUP emerged as the largest unionist party. Parties outside the two ethnonational blocs have never done well in Northern Ireland's elections, but they are doing worse than they used to. The most important of these, the Alliance Party of Northern Ireland, averaged 8.4 per cent of the vote in its first five election campaigns (1973–75), but only 4.6 per cent in its last five election campaigns (1998–2003). It did not even put up a candidate in the 2004 elections to the European parliament. While parties from the two ethnonational blocs won an average of 82 per cent of the vote in elections between 1973 and 1975, they received an average of 90.6 per cent in elections between 1996 and 1999, and 92.2 per cent in elections between 2000 and 2004. Non-ethnonational parties do poorly in all types of election, including those that are based on PR-STV – an electoral system that provides more openings for small and new parties than its main alternative, the single-member plurality (SMP) system.

The standard response of post-nationalists to such electoral data is that it detracts from evidence of growing post-national activity outside conventional politics. They claim that the preoccupation of political parties with constitutional issues has alienated significant numbers of people, who have instead channelled their energies into non-governmental organisations in what is called 'civil society' (Pollack 1993: 90).[7] It is here, in organisations like the EU-sponsored partnership programmes, the Corrymeela Centre and All Children Together, that evidence for the transcendence of ethnonational identities is supposedly to be found.

One problem with this argument is that survey data also consistently shows that Northern Ireland is divided into two ethnonational blocs (McGarry and O'Leary 2004: 302–3). It is also not clear that Northern Ireland's people are 'alienated' from participation in conventional politics. If electoral turnout is used as a way of measuring alienation, Northern Ireland's electorate appears less alienated than Great Britain's. Turnout in local government and European elections in Northern Ireland is usually much higher than in the rest of the UK, despite the fact that Northern Ireland's local governments have fewer powers than Great Britain's, and that Northern Ireland has more elections.[8] Turnout in elections to the Northern Ireland Forum in 1996 (64.7 per cent) and Assembly in 1998 (68.6 per cent) was higher than in the 1999 elections to the Scottish Parliament (59 per cent) and Welsh Assembly (45 per cent). Only in elections to the Westminster Parliament is turnout traditionally lower in Northern Ireland (67.4 per cent in 1997 and 69.8 per cent in 1992) than in Great Britain (71.4 and 77.9 per cent, respectively) (Butler and Kavanagh 1992, 1997). Some of the variance here can be explained by the fact that elections to Westminster, unlike other elections in Northern Ireland, take place under the SMP electoral system. Given the absence of swing voters in Northern Ireland, the SMP makes results fairly predictable, which can dampen enthusiasm for voting. Nor is there clear evidence that Northern Ireland's electorate has become less participatory over time: while there has been some drop-off in local government turnout over the past quarter-century, participation in European, Westminster and Assembly or Forum elections has remained reasonably constant.[9]

Even if we focus on 'civil society' organisations, as post-nationalists suggest, it is not always clear that they are above the ethnonational fray. The two most popular mass organisations, the Orange Order and Gaelic Athletic Association, are partisan unionist and nationalist, respectively. Shane O'Neill observes that even Northern Ireland's politically active feminists, and activists from its gay and lesbian communities, seek to be recognised as one or other of the two national communities, with most of them 'freely [acknowledging] the political primacy of the national struggle' (O'Neill 1999: 6). Many of the organisations in civil society that are committed to peace and conflict resolution understand that this will require the accommodation rather than the transcendence of nationalism and unionism. As Feargal Cochrane, the author of the most comprehensive study of these organisations, has pointed out,

> While some [peace and conflict resolution organisations] are working to erode the traditional political identities represented by unionism and nationalism, just as many (if not more) are committed to accommodating these alternative identities and establishing mechanisms that will allow them to coexist peacefully.
>
> (Cochrane 2001: 153)

This evidence suggests that Northern Ireland's elected political leaders are reasonably representative of its population. It also suggests, contrary to the advice that is tendered by many post-nationalists, that there is no democratic alternative, in the short to medium term, to designing institutions that accommodate these politicians. Of course, such institutions should also be constructed in ways that do not privilege particular identities and that allow the emergence of new identities should these become popular (McGarry and O'Leary 2004: 32–6).

Is Northern Ireland's agreement evidence of post-sovereigntist thinking?[10]

The achievement of the Good Friday Agreement does appear to indicate the presence of *post-sovereigntist* thinking in Northern Ireland. After all, in the Agreement, political parties in both blocs took major steps back from traditional positions on exclusive (British or Irish) state sovereignty.

On the nationalist side, Sinn Fein had traditionally argued that a British declaration of intent to withdraw was a pre-requisite for a settlement, but in the Agreement it accepted that a united Ireland required the consent of a majority in Northern Ireland. It agreed for the first time to participate in the Northern Ireland Assembly. It did not vocally object to the Irish government's proposal in the Agreement, subsequently ratified in a referendum, to remove its irredentist claim to Northern Ireland. All of these steps provoked criticism from republican dissidents that it was endorsing partition. Unionists who accepted the Agreement not only endorsed the participation of nationalists within a power-sharing government in Northern Ireland, but a North–South Ministerial Council and a number of all-Ireland 'implementation bodies' to administer various areas of public policy. They also accepted a role for the Irish republic in the affairs of Northern Ireland, and agreed that Northern Ireland could unite with the Irish republic, as soon as a majority within Northern Ireland consented.

It is at least as sensible, however, to see these steps as signalling a compromise between rival sovereigntist projects, than as proof that the first preferences of either group have changed. The Agreement is, in my view, more of a 'modus vivendi' than a shared consensus on the way forward. Nationalists embraced the Agreement overwhelmingly, even though it involved compromises on traditional demands, because it represented a significant advance from a unionist status quo. Nor was the Agreement considered a final settlement of the Irish question. Rather, for the nationalist politicians who accepted it, including the Irish prime minister and the leaders of the SDLP and Sinn Fein, the Agreement kept open, or opened wider, the path to a united Ireland. Indeed, in the weeks and months after the Agreement, both Bertie Ahern and Gerry Adams claimed there would be a united Ireland in their lifetime.[11]

Around half of the unionist community rejected the Agreement outright, both in the referendum of May 1998 and in the elections to the new Northern Ireland Assembly held in June 1998, largely because they shared Ahern and Adams's analysis that the Agreement weakened the UK's sovereignty.[12] This opposition has since grown. The unionist politicians who accepted the Agreement did so in the face of considerable pressure from the British and Irish governments. London and Dublin had laid out the framework for what a settlement should contain in early 1995 and made it clear to unionists, particularly after Labour won office with a massive majority in May 1997, that the alternative to agreement was not the largely unionist status quo of direct rule from London, but the deepening of Anglo-Irish cooperation over Northern Ireland and the implementation of a range of reforms, including a reformed police and a new equality agenda. Unionists were offered the choice of participating in these reforms, or alienating the British public and watching them being implemented anyway. By itself, however, this pressure was insufficient, particularly to ensure grass-roots unionist support. There was also enough balance in the Agreement to allow pro-Agreement unionist politicians to market it as securing and even strengthening the Union.[13] Pro-Agreement unionist politicians were able to argue that they had secured the removal of the Irish Republic's irredentist claim to Northern Ireland; a stipulation that Northern Ireland could only become part of a united Ireland if a majority of its people consented; North–South institutions that were much narrower in scope than nationalists had wanted, and that were accountable to, and interdependent with, the Northern Ireland Assembly; and the creation of new British–Irish, or east–west, institutions that could be seen as counter-balancing the North–South institutions

Pro-Agreement unionists did use the example of the EU, with its various examples of cross-border cooperation, to argue for the acceptance of the cross-border aspects of the Good Friday Agreement. However, their arguments were based on sovereigntist, rather than post-sovereigntist, thinking. Paul Bew, a unionist academic and key adviser to unionist leader David Trimble, helpfully pointed out that cross-border cooperation occurred throughout the EU *without threatening state sovereignty*, and was a small price to pay – a 'fig leaf' as he described it – to win nationalist approval for the principle of majority consent. Bew and two of his colleagues, Henry Patterson and Paul Teague, argued in 1997 that

> the history of the EU suggests that despite all the integration that has taken place, member states remain stubbornly intact as political, economic and social units. The lesson for unionists is that economic cooperation does not necessarily mean that Northern Ireland's position within the UK or the Protestant identity will be compromised to any great extent.
>
> (Bew *et al.* 1997: 196)

Another pro-Agreement unionist academic, Antony Alcock, who was a member of the UUP negotiating team and one of Northern Ireland's leading experts on the EU, pointed out on several occasions that the EU entrenched mutual respect for the territorial sovereignty of states, and facilitated cross-border cooperation only within this context (Alcock 2001).

European integration and relations between the British and Irish states

The view that European integration has improved relations between the British and Irish states has more substance than the view that it has improved inter-ethnic relations in Northern Ireland. It has substantial academic support, including from scholars who do not agree on much else (see Kennedy 1994; Ruane and Todd 1996: 280–1, 284; Meehan 2000: 86–7; Jakobsson Hatay 2001; McGarry 2001a: 312–13).

The evidence for a positive EU impact on British–Irish relations is circumstantial. Relations between the two states were far less friendly before and shortly after both joined the EEC in 1973, than they have been since. In 1972, just after British paratroopers shot dead 14 civilians in Derry, Irish police stood by and watched the British Embassy in Dublin being burned by a mob. The Irish government took the British government to the European Court in the 1970s, accusing it of torture, while Irish politicians commonly ascribed the root of the conflict in Northern Ireland to partition and the British presence. Yet by the 1980s, the two states were cooperating closely over Northern Ireland, with the British government agreeing, in the Anglo-Irish Agreement of 1985, to give Dublin a say in its running. Since 1985, the two governments have carefully choreographed their approach to Northern Ireland, making clear that it is a joint approach. The Anglo-Irish Agreement was followed in December 1993 by the Joint Declaration for Peace, which set out the two government's joint position on the way forward. In the Declaration, the British government indicated its commitment to 'working together with the Irish government' to achieve agreement in Northern Ireland (McGarry and O'Leary 1995: 409). In 1995, the two governments released the Framework Documents, which provided details on the institutional arrangements that they envisaged for Northern Ireland and between Northern Ireland and the Republic. Both the Joint Declaration and the Framework Documents anticipated important parts of the Good Friday Agreement, which was not just an agreement among Northern Ireland's political parties, but an international treaty between London and Dublin. The governments have continued to cooperate closely since the Agreement, with only the occasional oblique disagreement between them, as when British Secretary of State Mandelson suspended the Northern Ireland Assembly in 2000. Indeed, 'bi-partisanship', the term that has been used to describe the avoidance of disagreement over Northern Ireland by Britain's two main political parties, now applies at least as well to the approach of the two governments.

It is likely that Ireland's membership of the EU, which brought representation on a number of important bodies and veto power on the Council of Ministers, has led Britain to take it more seriously than in the past.[14] As *The Economist* put it, the 'shared membership of the European Union gives Britain and Ireland sufficiently comparable status to dissolve the mutual chippiness of the past' (*The Economist* 28 November 1998).[15] European integration may also have contributed to British–Irish cooperation, by developing precedents of sovereignty-pooling. Having transferred some aspects of its sovereignty to Brussels, the UK may have become less resistant to sharing sovereignty with Dublin, just as it was later to devolve power to Scotland, Wales and Northern Ireland. In the Joint Declaration of 1993, just after the single economic market came into existence, and a year after the Maastricht Treaty was signed, the two governments stated that European integration required not just Anglo-Irish but also north–south cooperation: 'the development of Europe will, of itself, require new approaches to serve interests common to both parts of the island of Ireland, and to Ireland and the United Kingdom as partners in the European Union' (cited in McGarry and O'Leary 1995: 409). It is thus possible to see the north–south and east–west institutions that were established in the Good Friday Agreement as linked to European integration. Dublin's decision, as part of the Agreement, to recommend in a referendum the removal of its constitutional claim to Northern Ireland also made sense in a EU context, as such a claim was anomalous within the EU's borders.

However, while the role that the EU has played in facilitating British–Irish cooperation should be acknowledged, it should also be placed in perspective. It is hardly 'impossible' to explain Dublin and London's cooperation over Northern Ireland without reference to European integration, as two academics have claimed (Kennedy 1994: 177; Lacaita 2004: 1).[16] At least three other important factors counted.

First, there is the influence of the United States. As early as 1977, President Carter took the unprecedented step of indicating that the internal politics of Northern Ireland was a legitimate concern of American foreign policy, and expressed support for a peaceful settlement that involved the Irish government (O'Leary and McGarry 1996: 214). Ronald Reagan himself helped persuade Margaret Thatcher to sign the Anglo-Irish Agreement, and the American view carried at least as much weight with her as the EU's (Guelke 1988: 147; Wilson 1997: 23). Each time Thatcher visited the United States before 1985, the issue of Northern Ireland was raised, often by President Reagan himself. Reagan continued a promise made by Carter to provide aid in the event of a settlement, and praised the report of the New Ireland Forum, a document on the way forward produced by Ireland's main constitutional nationalist parties. The report recommended three options, the least radical of which was that Northern Ireland should be jointly governed by the UK and Irish Republic. American intervention in the Northern Ireland conflict increased dramatically under the Clinton Administration (McGarry and O'Leary 2004: 316). This American intervention helped to bolster the position of the Irish government in negotiations with Britain. It also helped to increase republicans' confidence about the utility of political negotiations.[17]

Second, Anglo-Irish cooperation and the innovative institutional arrangements accepted by London in 1985 and 1998 was also a response to the imperatives of conflict management. This is what Brendan O'Leary has called 'slow learning' on the part of the British state (O'Leary 1997). The 1970s and early 1980s were, after all, associated not merely with Ireland and Britain's joint membership of the EU – they were also years of abject failure in the British government's management of the Northern Ireland conflict. After the collapse of the short-lived Sunningdale Agreement of 1973, London was incapable of restoring devolution to Northern Ireland on an agreed basis, not least because unionists were not interested in power-sharing. London's management of the security situation was also bungled. Its policies of Ulsterisation, criminalisation and normalisation failed to suppress the armed threat from republicans (O'Leary and McGarry 1996: 202–9). Its botched handling of the hunger strikes of 1980–81, which was greeted triumphantly by Tory right-wingers, had the effect of paving the way for the emergence of Sinn Fein as a potent electoral force, which threatened the constitutional nationalists of the SDLP (O'Leary and McGarry 1996: 205–6). Anglo-Irish cooperation was, arguably, more directly shaped by the necessity of confronting this threat than by European integration. The Anglo-Irish Agreement of 1985 was aimed, importantly, at improving security cooperation between the two states. By conceding a role for the Irish Republic in the governance of Northern Ireland, Britain could also be seen as bolstering the position of constitutional nationalists in their struggle with Sinn Fein. By making it clear that Dublin would continue to play a wide-ranging role in the governance of Northern Ireland until there was agreed devolution, the two governments could also put pressure on unionists to agree to power-sharing.

The remainder of this chapter focuses on a third supplementary explanation for Anglo-Irish cooperation. This explanation emphasises a state-contraction mentality among British elites that long precedes European integration. From this perspective, Britain's preparedness to pool sovereignty over Northern Ireland is intricately related to a view among significant sections of its public and policy-making elite that the people of Northern Ireland are Irish, and that Northern Ireland is a 'foreign place', properly part of Ireland, rather than part of Britain. It is seen as a piece of 'unfinished business' from Britain's withdrawal from most of Ireland in 1921, and from its overseas empire after 1945.[18]

The evidence that the British consider Northern Ireland to be expendable comes from government policy, from the utterances of leading policy-makers, and from survey opinion. Nearly a century before Britain joined the EU, the British government sought to give Home Rule to Ireland, although Home Rule fell short of independence. It was prevented from doing so on three occasions – 1886, 1893 and 1912 – by a coalition of Ulster unionists and opposition Conservatives. While London allowed what became Northern Ireland to stay part of the UK in 1921, it did not integrate it into the British state. Rather it insisted on insulating the new region from British political life through the creation of a devolved parliament in Belfast. A convention developed at Westminster that Northern Irish questions were properly matters for the Northern Ireland parliament, which meant that Westminster spent an average of two hours per year on Northern Ireland between partition and the outbreak of violence in the late 1960s (O'Leary and McGarry 1996: 143). In both the Government of Ireland Act of 1920, and the Anglo-Irish Treaty of 1921, London envisaged the eventual re-unification of Ireland – albeit within the 'Empire' – providing that the Northern Ireland Parliament consented. It made provision for a Council of Ireland, a body that was similar to, though not identical with, the North–South Ministerial Council agreed to in 1998.

British control over Northern Ireland continued to remain negotiable after 1921. Churchill considered offering Irish unification in 1940 if the Irish government was prepared to enter the war on the side of the allies, or allow Britain to cooperate in securing Eire's security 'against the fate which had overcome neutral Norway, Holland, Belgium, Denmark and Luxembourg' (McGarry and O'Leary 1995: 432, n. 83). Eire's neutrality during the war produced an upswing in unionist sentiment in Britain. However, the Ireland Act of 1949 continued to express a degree of ambivalence about the retention of Northern Ireland as it reiterated that Northern Ireland would not 'cease to be part of His Majesty's dominions and of the United Kingdom *without the consent of the Northern Ireland parliament*'. This was in spite of the fact that by the time of the Atlantic Charter of 1941, the UK and US governments thought self-determination rights should be limited to those who had been 'forcibly deprived of them'.[19]

After 1921, the two major British political parties, Labour and the Conservatives, which contested elections throughout Great Britain, refused to organise or contest elections in Northern Ireland, although there was a half-hearted attempt at organisation by the Conservatives in the 1980s. The refusal gave rise to a strange claim by unionists that the actions of these private organisations infringed upon their rights to equal citizenship within the UK (Roberts 1990). After conflict broke out in the late 1960s, and even after Stormont was abolished in 1972, the government continued to treat Northern Ireland as a place apart. It was given its own Secretary of State, who, unlike his/her Scottish and Welsh counterparts, was never from the region or elected by the people there. Irish nationalists commonly refer to the Secretary of State as a 'pro-consul'. The Prevention of Terrorism Act of 1974 included 'internal' exclusion causes that allowed the government to prevent UK citizens from Northern Ireland from travelling to Great Britain, supposedly part of the same state. Even when Anglo-Irish relations were at their supposed nadir in 1972, and before Britain and Ireland had joined the EEC, the British Conservative government allowed a 'border poll' on whether Northern Ireland should remain within the UK.[20] The UK government also convened meetings with the Irish government on the question of Northern Ireland. In the Sunningdale Agreement of 1973, London again underlined its support for a Council of Ireland linking Northern Ireland with the Irish Republic, and confirmed the 'right' of Northern Ireland to leave the UK.

The UK's preparedness to cooperate with Ireland over Northern Ireland occurred notwithstanding the fact that the Irish constitution of 1937 contained a clear irredentist claim to Northern Ireland, part of the UK. Article 2 of the constitution read:

> The national territory consists of the whole island of Ireland, its islands and the territorial seas.

While Article 3 read:

> Pending the re-integration of the national territory and without prejudice to the right of Parliament and government established by this Constitution to exercise jurisdiction of the whole of that territory, the laws enacted by that Parliament should have the like area and extent of application as the laws of Saorstat Eireann and the like extra-territorial effect.

In keeping with this claim, the Irish state extended full citizenship rights to everyone born in Northern Ireland.[21] Many of Northern Ireland's nationalist community carry Irish, not UK passports. Residents of Northern

Ireland have been appointed to the Senate, the upper house of the Irish legislature, and the current, directly elected, Irish President is a resident of Northern Ireland. Unionists in Northern Ireland have been outraged by the Republic's irredentism, and have habitually blamed the conflict on it, and demanded that it be withdrawn (McGarry and O'Leary 1995: chap. 2). However, the claim does not appear to have upset elites in Great Britain. On the contrary, after 1981, one of Britain's two major parties – Labour – officially committed itself to seek the unification of Ireland by consent. The other – the Conservatives – were not committed supporters of Irish unification, but every Conservative party leader and prime minister from 1970 to 1997 (Edward Heath, Margaret Thatcher and John Major), was prepared to sign agreements, discussed above, that recognised the interests of the Republic in Northern Ireland and that permitted Irish unification with the consent of a majority within Northern Ireland.

Regular statements and slips of the tongue by British leaders confirm that they view Northern Ireland as a foreign place. In 1967, before conflict broke out, the *Irish Times* reported UK prime minister, Harold Wilson, as saying 'The question of unity . . . was a problem for the people of Ireland to solve, and nobody would be happier than the British people if the Irish could find a solution' (cited in Dixon 2000: 180). British (Conservative) Home Secretary, Reginald Maudling, when commenting on the failure of the Stormont parliament in the early 1970s, said that it showed the Westminster constitution 'was not easily exportable'. The British (Labour) Secretary of State for Northern Ireland (1974–76), Merlyn Rees, appeared to believe that only Belfast belonged to the Union; 'I felt in Northern Ireland that the moment you left Belfast you were in Ireland' (cited in McGarry and O'Leary 1995: 113). In 1969, British (Labour) Home Secretary, Jim Callaghan, who presided over the sending of troops to Northern Ireland, compared it to Cyprus, suggesting that it was much easier to get involved in such conflicts than to get out of them. In the mid 1990s, (Conservative) Home Secretary Douglas Hurd sounded a similar note to EU foreign ministers: 'they should avoid military intervention in Bosnia lest they end up with a protracted commitment like the British government's in Northern Ireland' (cited in McGarry and O'Leary 1995: 312–13). He was suggesting, without seeming to notice, that intervention by outside states in another country was similar to the British government's 'intervention' in part of its own state. In 1990, Conservative Secretary of State for Northern Ireland, Peter Brooke, commenting on the question of negotiating with the IRA, said that past British governments had recognised and negotiated with terrorists in Cyprus (Speech to Conservative Association, November 1990). He added that 'it is not the aspiration to a sovereign, united Ireland, against which we set our face, but its violent expression' (cited in McGarry and O'Leary 1995: 48).

More generally, every British government's self-perception of its role in Northern Ireland is as an outside and impartial arbiter, holding the ring between warring natives. This does not mean that integrationism has never been considered. Ireland's neutrality in the Second World War strengthened integrationist sentiment, and it was also popular in the late 1970s under both Labour and Conservative governments (O'Leary 1997; McGarry and O'Leary 2004: 194–216). Margaret Thatcher once famously declared, in stark contrast to the views expressed above, that 'Northern Ireland was as British as Finchley', her suburban London constituency, although her own memoirs suggest that she didn't really believe it (Thatcher 1993: 383–7). Nor did many others. The Irish republican intellectual, Anthony McIntyre, wrote that it appeared as daft as John Cleese's observation that his grandfather had died 'fighting to keep China British' (McIntyre 1998).

These views of leading policy-makers are fully shared by the British public. As Brendan O'Leary and I show in *Explaining Northern Ireland*, since pollsters began to measure these sentiments there has been a preponderant plurality, and usually a majority, of the (Great) British public who favour troop withdrawal from Northern Ireland *and* the departure of Northern Ireland from the UK. In a 1994 Gallup poll conducted for Britain's most pro-union newspaper, the *Daily Telegraph*, nearly half of the 'Great' British (44 per cent) regarded events in Northern Ireland as occurring mainly 'in another country' and a mere 12 per cent could be described as being in any sense 'strong unionists' (McGarry and O'Leary 1995: 114). For the future of Northern Ireland, the most favoured option in Great Britain is most often a united Ireland. Perhaps most suggestively of all, in a survey published in another pro-union newspaper, the *Sunday Times*, in 1981, 63 per cent said that if a referendum was held on whether Northern Ireland should remain part of the UK, they would vote for its expulsion.[22] Doubtless, these opinions can be linked to the conflict, but they are also part of a historical process of state contraction that can be traced back to the mid-nineteenth century (Lustick 1993).

The Anglo-Irish Agreement of 1985, which gave the Irish government a role in Northern Ireland's affairs, and reiterated the view that Northern Ireland could join the Irish Republic if a majority wanted, can be seen as indicating continuity with earlier policies and as consistent with long-held elite and popular views, rather than as a radical new direction brought about by cooperation and post-sovereigntist thinking within the EU. Peter Brooke's official statement in November 1990 that the British government 'had no selfish strategic or economic interest in Northern Ireland', can also be seen as part of a historic pattern, rather than inextricably linked to the end of the Cold War, as argued by Cox (1997). The same can be said of the Joint Declaration of 1993, in which the British government not only reiterated Northern Ireland's right to join the Irish Republic, but accepted that the 'Irish people' as a whole enjoyed the right of self-determination, as long as that right was exercised by concurrent majorities within Northern Ireland and the Irish republic.[23] The Good Friday

Agreement again reiterated the right of Northern Ireland to join a united Ireland, confirmed Dublin's right to be involved in matters of governance in Northern Ireland that had not been devolved, and provided for north–south political institutions along the lines that were envisaged in 1921 and briefly implemented at Sunningdale in 1973. As Seamus Mallon of the SDLP put it, in a putdown to republicans who had waged a 25-year war in which thousands were killed, the Agreement was 'Sunningdale for slow learners'.[24] However, as the details of the Anglo-Irish Treaty of 1921 suggest, Sinn Fein may have been even slower in its learning than Mallon thought.

No group is more aware of the Great British view that Northern Ireland is expendable than Northern Ireland's unionists. This explains the comments of the fabled Orangewoman of Sandy Row who complained to a TV reporter 'Hey Mister, we're British, and that's something you British had better remember' (McGarry and O'Leary 1995: 112). As the loyalist paramilitary force, the UVF, echoed more recently, in a way that may not have been altogether helpful for its case, 'They [the British government] have no right to say they want rid of us because the people of Ulster are as British as the people of Gibraltar . . . or wherever' (*News Letter* 2004: 5).[25]

These non-EU based explanations for British–Irish cooperation are related. US intervention in the affairs of its closest ally was predicated not just (and not mainly) on the view among Irish Americans that Northern Ireland was a colony, but also on an awareness that British elites accepted this view, at least tacitly.[26] Similarly, Britain's decision to cooperate with Dublin to manage the conflict was shaped, not by the requirements of conflict management alone, but also by its pre-existing views on Northern Ireland. Had the British recognised Northern Ireland as an integral part of their state, it is unlikely that it would have responded to a minority rebellion by inviting a neighbouring state to play a role in the region's governance. The conflict did, however, play an important role in confirming to the British that Northern Ireland was 'a place apart' (Murphy 1979).

Northern Ireland as a model for the rest of Europe?

This analysis has implications for the several 'Northern Irelands' that exist in other parts of the EU, and in those countries in Eastern Europe that may soon join the EU. If European integration was importantly responsible for Anglo-Irish cooperation and for the far-reaching institutional arrangements that this gave rise to, then we should expect to see similar cooperation and inter-state institutional arrangements in other parts of the EU. We do not. Italy has granted autonomy to the German-speaking region of South Tyrol, and its preparedness to do so may have been helped by Austrian and Italian cooperation within the EU context. But Italy has not recognised the right of South Tyrol's people to self-determination, and it has not invited the government of Austria to have a role in the governance of South Tyrol. On the contrary, South Tyrol is seen as part of Italy, and it was Austria's recognition of that fact that facilitated Italy's accommodation of the South Tyrolese (Alcock 2001). France and Spain show no inclination to create Good Friday Agreement-type cross-border institutions in the Basque Country. The Spanish regime, as Jáuregui argues in this volume, is also unwilling to recognise a Basque right to self-determination, even though there would be very little prospect of a vote in favour of secession if it did. The Basque nationalists of ETA like to compare the Basque Country to Northern Ireland and themselves to the IRA. Keating has argued that Basque nationalists followed the Northern Ireland peace process closely, and that it was not a coincidence that ETA called a ceasefire after the signing of the Good Friday Agreement in 1998 (Keating 2001c: 200–1). The difference is that Spanish elites generally do not accept the analogy and take a different view of the Basque Country than the British government takes of Northern Ireland (see *The Times* August 24 2002). For Madrid, Northern Ireland is different from the Basque Country because the former is a colony, properly part of Ireland, while the latter is an integral part of Spain. Rather than accommodate Basque nationalists and ETA along the lines of the Good Friday Agreement, the Spanish government of Aznar favoured a security approach, particularly in the aftermath of 11 September 2001. This is one reason why the IRA's ceasefire continues while ETA's has been broken.[27]

The prospects for Good Friday Agreement-type structures among the Eastern European states that have joined, or will soon join, the EU should be considered at least as remote. Having just won independence, virtually all Eastern European states jealously guard their territorial integrity and champion a traditional view of state sovereignty. This helps to explain why they, unlike most Western European states, have been strongly opposed to autonomy for minority regions.[28] The fear is that this will facilitate the loss of territory through secession. Many of them have preferred to get rid of minorities, or to disenfranchise them, than to surrender territory. 'Host' states in Eastern Europe have shown little inclination to cooperate with 'kin' states in the management of national minorities. When Hungary proposed giving documents that looked like passports to Hungarian speakers in Slovakia and Romania, it led to an uproar from both governments (see Kemp's chapter in this volume). Contrast this with the British state's preparedness to cooperate closely with the Irish Republic, in spite of the latter's practice of extending real passports to the people of Northern Ireland, never mind its constitutional claim to sovereignty over Northern Ireland. The EU may facilitate more cooperation between neighbouring states in Eastern Europe if it convinces host-states that this involves no threat to their territorial integrity, but this level of cooperation is likely to fall far short of that achieved by the UK and Ireland.

Conclusion

In this chapter, I have argued that European integration has not led in Northern Ireland to the emergence of a transcendent Irish or British identity, or to multiple and fluid post-national identities, and looks unlikely to do so for the foreseeable future. Rather, the region remains fundamentally polarised between unionist and nationalist ethnonational blocs, as it has been since the late nineteenth century. This should hardly be surprising. While Northern Ireland has been part of the EEC/EC/EU for over 30 years, it has also been a site for much of this period of violent and polarising ethnonational conflict. The resilience of the rival ethnonational communities leaves little alternative, if there is to be peace and justice, to political institutions that accommodate these communities. Ideally, these institutions should avoid privileging and entrenching such identities, and should leave open the development of alternative forms of identity. For those other parts of Europe which have also experienced ethnonational polarisation and inter-ethnic violence, the evidence from Northern Ireland suggests that we should scale back expectations of the EU's identity-transforming capacities.

European integration has improved relations between the British and Irish states, and this cooperation has facilitated an institutional framework appropriate to the management of the Northern Ireland conflict. Anglo-Irish cooperation, however, did not flow from European integration alone. It is also a result of positive US involvement in the region, and of learned conflict management, the eventual discovery that the conflict could not be properly dealt with without inter-state cooperation. Finally, it is a legacy of a long-term process of UK state-contraction that has more to do with decolonisation than with European integration. European integration, the chapter suggests, is worrying to unionists not so much because it has given rise to post-sovereigntist thinking among British elites, but because it has reinforced a long-standing, though uneven, predisposition on the part of British elites to right-size their state. The British should be seen, from this perspective, as more post-imperialist than EU-induced post-sovereigntist.

The chapter helps to explain why Northern Ireland is the only part of the EU where two states have engaged in such radical cooperation. Its extent follows from the fact that Northern Ireland is the only part of any state in the EU that is considered expendable by state elites and most of the state's citizens. We should doubt, therefore, the ability of European integration to promote the sort of far-reaching inter-state cooperation that has marked the UK and Ireland's management of the Northern Ireland conflict.

16 Breton identity highlighted by European integration

Michel Nicolas

At the end of the Second World War, the European states undertook the reconstruction of Europe on the basis of a federal project, whilst accepting a reduction in their sovereignty. However, the states do not embody the full European reality. Indeed, the regions have emerged as essential participants in the evolution of Europe. In addition to their economic and administrative functions, many of the regions appear to be historically formed entities, and places of great interdependence and collective identity.

Brittany, like regions such as Alsace, Corsica, the Basque Country and Catalonia (to mention only those in a French context), belongs to these ethnocultural minorities, which have consistently demanded the recognition of their identity. This is illustrated by the presence of both objective and subjective elements: a long historical record, original cultural practices and, in the majority of cases, distinctive linguistic practices. Furthermore, we can observe the presence of cultural organisations and specific political parties in the form of cultural or political 'movements' working for the promotion of local social practices and cultural traditions. The political translation of this movement is expressed in the demand for more autonomy.

France is one of the European countries where the ethnocultural minorities are the most numerous and active. All have given rise, at one time or another in their history, to political movements with more or less radical claims. France is also the country which, during the last two centuries, has put into place a highly developed system to integrate, and even to assimilate, populations. At an institutional level, this system relies on administrative centralisation. At a linguistic level, it has established discriminatory measures designed to eliminate languages other than French, which are forced upon the population. This language, taught under constraint, is accompanied by the teaching of an official historiography focused mainly on the different stages of the construction of the French state, and the overshadowing and distortion of the individual history of the regions. In addition to 200 years of repressive linguistic policy, a revision of the Constitution, adopted in June 1992, declared: 'The language of the Republic is French'.

The majority of the European Union (EU) member states have reached a peaceful agreement on the question of regional identities through either a federal or a neo-federal model. Such a system prevails in Germany and Austria as well as in Belgium and, in a more specific form, in Spain, Italy and the United Kingdom.

Within such a framework, inspired by Community logic, Brittany could have a chance to witness the recognition of its individuality. At present, Europe is in the process of forging a framework and arousing dynamics resulting in the reactivation of local and particularistic characteristics. Moreover, Brittany is in a position to take advantage of European integration in the mid and long term, as it fulfils the conditions required for integrating the institutional system within which its specific characteristics can be taken into consideration and promoted. Moreover, Europe gives Brittany the means to overcome the procedures still prevalent in the French 'Hexagon', and offers an alternative institutional framework to the French state. Finally, it generates a system to legitimise identity.

A way to overcome French cumbersome procedures

Developments in Europe offer Brittany new political, economic and cultural opportunities. If, within the French framework, the region of Brittany is considered to be a periphery, at a territorial level it paradoxically appears to be at the heart of Europe, for both the general public and political actors.

The restored spatial identity of Brittany

A major element of the 'Breton question' is that of territory. To evoke Brittany requires recalling the Duchy of Brittany (see Figure 16.1), whose formation took place over ten centuries ago, and whose capital was located at Nantes. Suppressed in 1789, Brittany was divided the following year into five *départements*. It has never been reconstituted at the administrative level. Successive regional reforms have indeed created an entity with the name 'Brittany' by regrouping four of these *départements*, but the 'Loire-Atlantique' *département* is excluded from this group, thus excluding Nantes, the former capital of the Duchy. The separation of Nantes from the administrative region of Brittany undermines the historical dimension of Breton identity, and at the same time deprives Brittany of 20 per cent of its land, one million inhabitants, and important economic activities, in particular a major port around Nantes and Saint Nazaire[1] that would help to open up the region. For this reason, demands in favour of the administrative reunification of Brittany have been made since the 1960s onwards, when the reforms concerning the final partition of the region were adopted. At present, the most active movement is the Committee for the Administrative Unity of Brittany (CAUB). Created in 1981, the movement

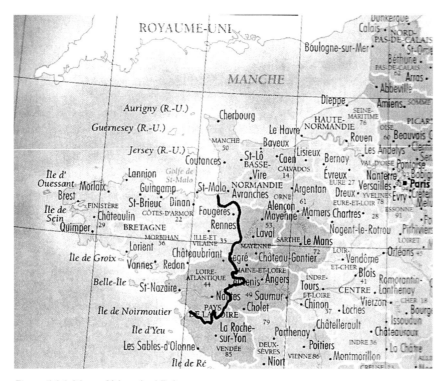

Figure 16.1 Map of historical Brittany.

was renamed 'Brittany Reunified' in February 2004. However, efforts in favour of reunification are still unsuccessful. The French authorities remain insensitive to these efforts, despite the fact that numerous petitions and opinion polls indicate a strong public sentiment in favour of this reunification.[2]

Yet there is one important element that makes the French administrative culture and the division of the regions anachronistic: the growing economic involvement of Brittany in Europe means that the majority of Breton goods are now being exported to Europe. European economic development is increasingly becoming a continental phenomenon, reinforced by the creation of new markets and the integration of states predominantly located in the East. As a result, western peripheral regions could find themselves threatened by a form of marginalisation. Bearing this in mind, Brittany would be considered a 'land's end', on the periphery of the continent, even though the main question for the region lies in its opening up to economic markets and being linked to a 'useful Europe' which is becoming more and more continental. This challenge is also faced by many areas in Europe, which could again find themselves 'adrift'.

The EU is therefore concerned with the development of the Atlantic shoreline. Brittany can play a central role in this area, which extends from northern Scotland to southern Portugal, as it is unavoidable for all maritime and land routes.

Such a scenario again highlights the maritime vocation of the Breton entity. In this way, the issues of the new economic order could benefit from the reunification of the administrative region of Brittany with the major maritime towns of Nantes and Saint-Nazaire. The economy thus contributes to the restoration of a traditional and historical relationship. What the French state rejects, and what the rivalry between Rennes and Nantes blocked at one stage, the economy henceforth compels: a Breton entity, reunified within a 'Euro-region'.

Moreover, the support given by Europe to such cooperation between the regions is not new. In 1973, the Conference of Peripheral Maritime Regions[3] was created and its headquarters located in Rennes. Its aim is to assert the role of the maritime regions at the front of the 'useful' industrial Europe. The need to create internal specialisations led to the creation of an 'Atlantic Commission', under the leadership of the presidents of the 'Brittany' and 'Pays de Loire' regions. It proposes to find a solution to their specific difficulties through a form of 'Atlantic regionalism'. The project found its solution in 1989 in Faro, South Portugal: since then a programme of interregional cooperation, better known as the 'Atlantic Arc' (see Figure 16.2), has been launched.

This programme of cooperation is basically economic. It is focused notably on the fishing industries, tourism and transportation, but it also favours the bringing together of all of the Celtic regions, an idea which, until now, has been thwarted by state nationalism. Effectively, the cultural factor accompanies the economic initiatives. Through the Atlantic Arc, a whole 'Inter-Celtic' network finds itself revived. Brittany can thus recover that part of its identity linked with this traditional cultural group, which had been overshadowed by Brittany's incorporation into the French state.

According to historical records, Brittany has maintained close relations with Cornwall, Devon, Wales and Ireland through immigration during the fourth, fifth and sixth centuries, and cultural links have continued throughout the centuries. Europe reactivates this unrecognised aspect of Breton identity. This may explain the high number of twinnings of towns in Brittany to those in other Celtic countries (notably Wales and Ireland). Finally, the success of the Inter-Celtic Festival of Lorient cannot go unmentioned. Since 1971 it has been an important cultural meeting point for these regions and also for Galicia, notably represented by the singer Carlos Nuñes.

Breton opinion in a preferential relationship with Europe

Since 1989, the French regions have been subject to annual opinion polls carried out by the Political Inter-regional Observatory (PIO).[4] Financed by

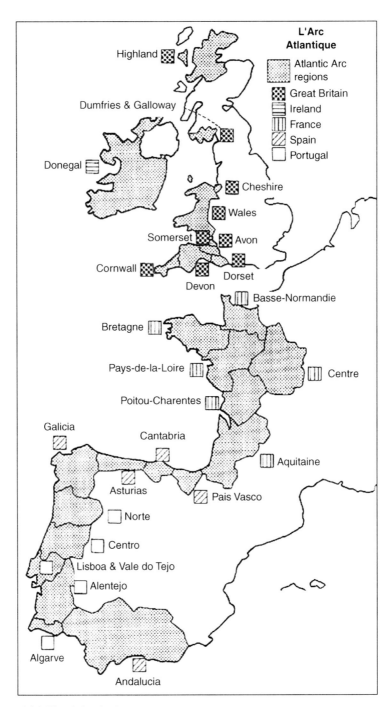

Figure 16.2 The Atlantic Arc.

the regions, these enquiries offer a two-fold interest: they evaluate the criteria through which the populations identify themselves, and provide quantified figures of public opinion vis-à-vis the regional level.

It appears undeniable that Breton public opinion holds a strong attachment to the region. For example, in 1992 a PIO enquiry identified which factors aroused the strongest identification among the participants: France, the *département*, or the town. The result of the enquiry established that 22 per cent of the people surveyed stated they felt as if they belonged 'above all' to Brittany and the report concluded that: 'It is in Brittany that regional identity is the strongest.' The figures for 1997 confirm this phenomenon: 62 per cent of Bretons stated that they felt loyal to their region (the French average being only 53 per cent). As for the image of the region, 61 per cent of respondents stated that Brittany was 'a place of history and culture' (compared with the French average of 44 per cent). Brittany therefore has the richest 'image' in terms of identity, which has been chosen as a priority by the people. Finally, it is interesting to note that Breton public opinion is favourable to new advances in regionalisation and decentralisation: 62 per cent compared with the French national average of 56 per cent.

This public opinion on regional identity is closely related with the interest shown in Europe, as mentioned by the PIO director Elisabeth Dupoirier:

> The support for regionalisation is the same. 80% of the people who state that they are 'completely in favour of' the region are also in favour of the principle of the European construction and this level of support for Europe decreases steadily with the decreasing support for the region.[5]

This analysis is confirmed by a study carried out by the PIO in September 2003 and published in 2004.

> The PIO study was carried out in Brittany, 8–11 September 2003. Unlike other regions, Brittany has not experienced a significant drop in optimism towards the future. Apart from the trust in the future of France, which is becoming increasingly reduced, the other indicators of trust remain at the same level as in 2002. Optimism regarding a regional future remains high. Three quarters of the Bretons share this view. Trust in the future of Europe was not hindered by the forthcoming enlargement of the European Union to the East and the announcement of European institutional reforms. Trust continues to be expressed by more than half of its inhabitants. Besides, those who feel European citizens are more numerous this year. The feeling of European citizenship has increased by 10 points over the last 10 years.[6]

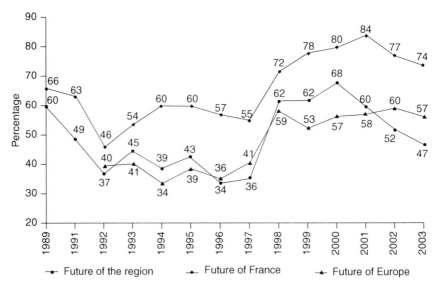

Figure 16.3 Optimism regarding the future of the region, of France and of Europe.

It is as if Brittany's relationship with Europe is offered as an alternative to the traditional, central–peripheral relationship prevailing within the French nation-state. Besides, electoral enquiries confirm the particular sensitivity of Breton public opinion to the European construction. In this regard, the most symbolic poll is the 1992 referendum on the ratification of the Maastricht Treaty. At the French level, the YES option obtained only 51 per cent of the votes. Alsace (65 per cent YES) and Brittany (59.1 per cent YES) have thus played a decisive role in the decision-making process. This poll gave Brittany a chance to clearly stand out from the 'West', where its specific identity is very often eluded in order to deprive it from its particular identity. The 'Large West'[7] ('Grand Ouest') only totalled 50.7 per cent in favour. As a result, this poll will allow the clear identification of Breton opinion inside this artificial regrouping of *départements*, which completely eludes the historical reality.

In this manner, Brittany appears as a periphery that is paradoxically at the very heart of Europe. The results of this poll give rise to a testimony: Brittany does not form that 'Land's End', that cul-de-sac at the far edge of the continent, well away from the main exchanges accompanying European integration, as clichés so complacently describe. The massive YES in favour of Europe reminds us that Brittany has a rich history in which maritime commerce, especially with European countries, was a determining element in its prosperity between the fifteenth and the eighteenth centuries. Brittany's historical tradition is one of strong relationships with Europe and the world. This poll also plays an enlightening role regarding the historical boundaries of Brittany. The Loire-Atlantique *département* voted in line with the Breton entity, thus distinguishing itself from the *départements* of the region called 'Pays de Loire', to which it has been mistakenly attached.

Results of the referendum on the Maastricht Treaty, September 1992

More generally, European elections reveal the minority nature of the anti-European vote in Brittany (see Figure 16.4). When considering the European elections of 1999, the lists of 'sovereigntists' added up to only 20.9 per cent of the total vote. The pro-European vote is expressed in the political formations explicitly calling for European federalism and in the parties that have held power over the last decades, and who were thus indirectly involved in the construction of Europe. At this poll in 1999, the pro-European lists, whatever their political colour, added up to 64.2 per cent of the vote. This is one percentage point more than in Alsace, which is reputed to be very European, and 9.1 points higher than the French average (55.1 per cent).

Europe binding new political alliances

Europe offers to Brittany the opportunity to expand its borders further than the narrow French enclosure. Now located at the heart of doctrinal developments, Europe is inspiring original alliances, and provides unexpected openings.

Europe at the heart of the doctrinal developments of the Breton movement

The concern for Europe is not new in the Breton movement (called *Emsav* in Breton), which has always been influenced by the federalist doctrine. In 1929, Maurice Duhamel, a member of the Breton Autonomy Party, published his book *The Breton Question in a European Context*, revealing a surprisingly modern outlook. Notably, he developed the idea that the awakening of nationalities foreshadows the redrawing of state borders and that the future will be a 'federation of nations and not of states'.

The organisations of the Breton movement have constantly adopted pro-European positions, as a strategy to bypass and move beyond the nation-state concept, and as a tactical opportunity to make alliances with other states and to ensure their international influence. This has notably been the case for the Movement for the Organisation of Brittany (MOB), the first autonomous post-war party created in 1957, and the author of the slogan 'We want the Breton apartment in the French block of the European district' (*Nous voulons l'appartement Bretagne dans l'immeuble France du quartier Europe*).

In 1964, a split occurred within the MOB, resulting in the creation of the Breton Democratic Union (UDB–Union Démocratique Bretonne)

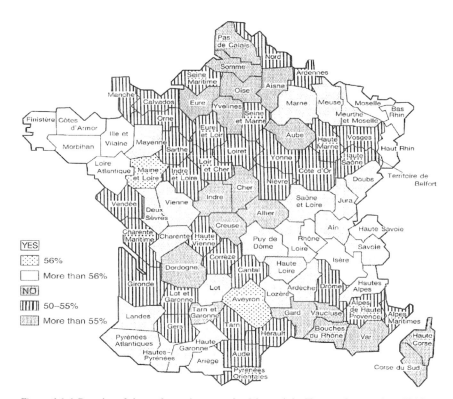

Figure 16.4 Results of the referendum on the Maastricht Treaty, September 1992.

which has since constituted the main autonomous and federalist political force in Brittany. Right from its creation, this new force stated in its charter that 'the federalist integration of the European populations is necessary to their full development'. Meanwhile, the UDB became involved in the socialist project and adopted a critical position on the European construction, which it considered to be predominantly capitalist. As a result, it expressed reservations about the European Community up until the early 1980s.

In the course of the 1980s, as Europe became more attractive to the Left, the UDB fell in with the 'Euro-optimist' side. At that time, Brittany was showing the first positive effects of the regional policies, notably with the measures implemented by the European Regional Development Fund. Changes occurring in the Common Agricultural Policy were also of considerable importance to Brittany, where agriculture is a major concern. The first measures of the Common Agricultural Policy – which encouraged the concentration of farms and concomitant disappearance of thousands of jobs, an increase in the disparity of revenues, increasing level of debt for many farms, etc. – had serious consequences in Brittany.

However, since the 1990s, a new system of benefits and subsidies has compensated for the difficulties resulting from the previous measures.

Besides, the European Parliament and the Council of Europe (CoE) took several initiatives that prompted the states to take regional languages and cultures into consideration. The European election of 1989 was held in this context. The powerful attraction aroused by Europe at that time in *Emsav* circles accompanied the new strategies aimed at reaching a goal uncompromisingly opposed by the nation-state. While in power, the Right had not conceded anything in the cultural or institutional fields. The Paris centralists and Jacobin Left has been just as disappointing. It is no surprise then that Europe, as a consequence, appears as an alternative answer to regional questions. At the same time, from 1986 onwards, the regions became local authorities in full working order: the very frail 'autonomy' given to Brittany in this context appears to be more advantageous when considered from the point of view of Europe.

Leaving aside theories about Brittany being 'overexploited' and 'colonised', the Breton movement relies on the fact that Brittany can pride itself on appreciable economic development, which is curbed by the manner in which the nation-state functions. The question is therefore to adopt these new perspectives of economic development, and to compete with other regions at the European level. In this way, Europe has considerably helped modify the evolution of the BDU, the main party of the Breton movement, which appeared in the wake of the anti-colonial struggles. This approach offers an opportunity to create new openings and new alliances.

New openings and new alliances

In France, a traditionally centralist country, the idea of regional autonomy has never been taken into consideration by the larger political parties, except in the framework of very limited powers according to a 'decentralisation' plan (granting selective powers to local authorities). But these steps are always twinned with new prerogatives granted to the Prefects, the irremovable local representatives of central power. So is it for all the reforms, whether they are inspired by right-wing parties or left-wing parties. Only the Socialist Party would have been in a position to further improvements in this matter, but the rifts between 'Jacobins' and 'decentralisers' have always resulted in holding up any such initiative. This is why members of the regionalist movement must rely only on themselves and take great care to remain united at the European level.

An official office for 'Stateless European Nations' was created in Brussels in 1975. Following this, a meeting was held in Brussels in January 1981, which was initiated by the 'Independent Group' of the European Parliament formed after the 1979 European election. That meeting brought together ten autonomous parties around the formula of 'stateless peoples, autonomy, regionalism and self-determination in Europe'. The

European Free Alliance (EFA), representing the 'Stateless Peoples of Western Europe', was born.[8] In addition, the regional movement has asserted itself in cooperation with other political forces such as the ecologists, as much at the French level as at the European, which has resulted in deep electoral collaboration. In this regard, the European election of 1989 has created a shift of policy.

Initially, the Breton movement had contemplated joining the EFA list under the leadership of a Corsican, Max Simeoni. But that list had little chance of exceeding 5 per cent of the votes – a necessary condition for getting representatives elected. Negotiations took place with the main ecological French political force at that time, the Greens, under the leadership of Antoine Waechter. An ecological and regionalist list entitled 'For ecology, the Europe of peoples and regions' was presented on which Max Simeoni featured third on the list. Following the election, and on the basis of an agreement between the Green Party and the EFA, those who had been elected split into two groups: this is how the 'Arc en Ciel' (Rainbow) group, initiated by the European Free Alliance, was born.

After his election as a Member of the European Parliament, Max Simeoni chose Christian Guyonvarc'h, responsible for European affairs in the DBU, as a parliamentary assistant. The DBU and, in fact, the whole Breton movement thus found themselves well placed in Strasbourg for a period of five years with access to useful information, the ability to collaborate with organisations of a similar nature and to pass on all proposals.

Another federation of nationalist movements, of a more radical leaning, was also created: the Conference of Stateless Nations of Western Europe. Without questioning the opportunities offered by European institutions, this movement focuses on the struggle for national liberation; its strategy is aimed at promoting self-determination. This is why the Emgann Party, in favour of the independence of Brittany, jointly with a dozen other groups, co-organised the Conference. The constitutive meeting was held in Barcelona in December 1985.[9] Soon after, the DBU, covering both regionalist and federalist tendencies, joined the Conference, which then became the Confederation of Stateless Nations of Europe.

All this collaboration had major consequences in Brittany. It strongly influenced the composition of the electoral lists of 'Breton People, People of Europe' common to Breton political parties at the regional elections in 1992. In the same way, DBU and the Green Party presented a joint list in the regional election of March 2004 and obtained 9.7 per cent of the vote. Thus, Europe, as a mobilising myth, has inspired numerous political and institutional projects.

The offer of an institutional alternative

In the French context, Brittany does not benefit from any recognition, either in relation to its place in history, as mentioned previously, or as a minority. As a result, it cannot claim to exercise prerogatives other than the limited powers currently bestowed on it by the government. On the other hand, Europe, whether through the EU or the CoE, offers it a real status at all levels.

Going beyond the authoritative management of the state

If the 1990s experienced a return to the issue of identity through a highly dynamic neo-Bretonism, it also aroused an unquestionable 'eurotropism'. Two ballots strongly contributed to renewing the debate on Europe: the European Parliament election in 1989 and the referendum on the ratification of the Maastricht Treaty. The reality of Europe had become more tangible in the eyes of the public. Up to that time, the European idea had deliberately been overshadowed, if not evaded, by a political class and the upper echelons of the civil service who were suspicious of a largely uncontrollable rival in Brussels. The progress of European integration reinforced this political aspect, affecting the state in its function as a unique decision-making authority. Furthermore, some concrete facts, such as the aid brought to the regions by structural funds, had, at that time, given reality to something which, until then, seemed to belong to the distant future.

Following the example of other regions, Brittany also benefited from its eligibility for European aid. This was the case for the fundamental question of the regeneration of regions affected by industrial decline as well as the aid for economic diversification in rural areas. As an example, the 'Morgane' programme, initially designed for central Brittany, has been later expanded to several coastal areas, reaching more than 30 per cent of the population. Through the development of the territory, there is also the search to increase the attractiveness of the town centres of the development projects, promote Brittany's cultural heritage and tourism and also to protect the environment and quality of life.

Even though one may disapprove of the lack of dynamism in European policy led by Brittany (presided by Jacobin Gaullists from 1986 to 2004: Yvon Bourges, followed by Josselin De Rohan), Europe nevertheless offers the region an unexpected opportunity to shake off the yoke of the French nation-state in the long term. Moreover, although the Breton public has little information about the functioning of European institutions, it is discovering its other component, that is the CoE, and its efforts to preserve and promote regional languages and cultures. The general context of questioning the nation-state is helpful, opportunities offered can be seized and any new possibilities of solidarity detected.

A realistic Europe of the regions

The administrative reform adopted in France in 1982 gives the regions very small prerogatives and a very modest budget.[10] The French regions thus appear as minors compared to their counterparts in federal states.

On the other hand, at the European level, the regions have the possibility of a real promotion of their status, including at the institutional level. For several decades, they have undertaken the creation of close links within the increasingly tight European network. Decisions have been taken spontaneously or at an institutional level. A promising initiative has been the creation, in January 1985, of the Council of European Regions, which later became the Assembly of European Regions (AER). One of its priorities is the defence of the principle of subsidiarity. Its project appears to be highly political, anticipating the functioning of a sort of European federalism of regions.

All the initiatives of regional associations provide a consultation on decisions taken at an institutional level by the EU or CoE. In the 1970s in particular, the EU tried hard to bring the regions in as partners in the European construction. As it was concerned about preserving and reinforcing social and economic cohesion, the EU deliberately implemented its regional policies since the regions are deemed to be closely linked to them. How else could norms or community aid be forced upon regional authorities, if they were not already involved in decision-making?

Moreover, the European Union considers the regions to be endowed with a real democratic legitimacy. As a result, their participation is logically required in the elaboration, application and control of EU standards which concern them. The reinforcement of such a role is also linked to the strategy of the EU to ensure its own legitimacy. The privileged position granted to the regions should, in effect, contribute to making up for some democratic deficit by offering citizens greater participation. Finally, the institutional situation of the regions relates to a global strategy of the political construction of Europe and European federalism. However, some states, including France, rise up against such a perspective and this is one of the reasons why the European Constitutional Convention has disappointed the regionalists.

On the other hand, it is undoubtedly the CoE which has opened itself up most widely to a regional institutional presence, even as early as 1975 with the Conference of Local and Regional Governments of Europe, which in January 1994 became the Committee of Local and Regional Governments of Europe. This Committee is split into a Chamber of Local Governments on one side and a Chamber of Regional Governments on the other. This allows the latter, where most of the regions of the member states of the CoE are represented, to play a role in foreshadowing a Senate of the Regions, where Brittany will most definitely have its place.

Progress of federalism

During the 1990s, some events occurred in Europe that gave rise to a double territorial movement that sought independence in the East and increased autonomy in the West. Since the collapse of the Soviet empire, an ever-increasing number of territories have become independent and situations of exacerbated nationalism have sometimes arisen in these areas. But the Breton movement has drawn its inspiration from the positive 'civic' models. This has been the case for the Baltic states since the start of the 1990s. Then in 1992 Slovenia, in the former Yugoslavia, acquired its freedom and the Czechs and the Slovaks separated by mutual consent. Many small republics appeared at the frontier of the EU before joining it in 2004. This gives substance to the idea that small states with small populations can become independent after more or less long periods of subjugation or forced coalition. The parties of the Breton movement unanimously greeted these events as positive, and saw them as justifying their arguments and demands. This situation also revived a tradition of comparing Brittany with other small European states of roughly equivalent geographical importance.[11] The viability of these small states, and what they offer as models of democracy and examples of economic prosperity, are to be praised.

From another viewpoint, strengthened autonomous powers are a new element to be considered in the West. The federal evolution of certain EU states is a good sign. As well as Belgium, which became a federal state in 1993, it is gratifying to note that Italy and Spain are implementing the reforms they have committed themselves to.

However, it is unquestionably the referendums organised in the United Kingdom in September 1997, which opened up the most interesting perspectives for the Breton movement. They effectively show that a state can carry out important administrative and legislative reforms in a democratic manner based on the wishes of the population: a good lesson for a country such as France, where all the decisions are issued from Paris. Moreover, the fact that the referendums concern two Celtic countries is regarded as a definite advantage to those in the Breton movement.

Finally, it appears that the majority of EU states have agreed to grant some autonomous management to intra-state territories by way of institutional processes, thus excluding all violence. Why should that which is becoming legitimate and operational elsewhere not have any validity in France and especially in Brittany? The events in Europe add further weight to the arguments of the various protagonists of the Breton movement.

The production of a system of identity legitimacy

The Breton cultural movement has led to an asymmetrical battle against the French state, which is cautious in the new rights that it accords the movement. At the European level, Brittany can rely on favourable measures, which are hindered by the French state.

A Europe of minorities still virtual, but a source of hope

The status of 'minority' that is granted to the region gives it a certain type of recognition and a right to protection. This recognition is not only valid with regard to the internal sovereignty of the state, but also with regard to the international society, which is expected to take an interest in the existence of the minority. The status of minority seems to bring together all of the objective and subjective elements relating to 'identity'. It requires specific treatment through an appropriate policy and the creation of a system of 'positive discrimination'. In France, such recognition for the regions appears to be an unattainable dream. The principle of the nation-state lies in contrast with the recognition of every minority within the Republic. France recognises individual prerogatives for its citizens, but denies all rights to any collective identity. Only these collective identities are not recognised and they are also subjected to negative discrimination. This is how the recognition of a 'Corsican people' by the Parliament was hastily rejected by the Constitutional Council. Generally, the French state is very circumspect as soon as the notion of 'minority' surfaces in international conventions. France refused to sign Article 27 of the Act relating to Civil Rights and Policies adopted by the General Assembly of the UN in 1966. That article states:

> In the States where ethnic, linguistic and religious minorities exist, the persons belonging to these minorities should not be deprived of the right to their own cultural life, their own religion and use their own language with other members of their group.

In the same way, France has not ratified Article 30 of the International Convention of the UN concerning the rights of children, which stipulates that they should be given the right to receive education in their mother tongue: for it would then have been necessary to recognise the principle of teaching regional languages, notably the Breton language.

In the European context, however, many regions can claim minority status, which is envied by those who do not have it, as it guarantees certain rights and the protection of identities. At the moment, two main institutions are concerned with minorities: the EU and the CoE. The EU treats the question of minorities in terms of cultural minorisation. Admittedly, many commissions tackle the question of cultural diversity inside the EU, in terms close to those usually used to define minorities. However, for reasons of realpolitik, the EU does not allow itself to cross the line of that which would be unacceptable for certain states such as France. Therefore it takes great care not to overstep the line of 'minority languages and cultures'.

What about the CoE? From its origins, its strategy is to promote a pan-European policy. It is the source of several initiatives, notably the Framework Convention on the Protection of National Minorities adopted on 10 November 1994. Brittany is concerned with all of these arrangements and aspires to see them applied in Brittany, should France ratify them. However, the recognition of Brittany as a minority remains uncertain given the functioning of the nation-state in France.

On the other hand, Brittany is far from benefiting from the status of a culturally eligible entity in France, in the same way as other similar regions in Europe. On the contrary, the logic of the nation-state has always been to level the differences within its territory. The few favourable arrangements that have been reached have actually been wrested from states, which are not very well disposed in this matter.

Brittany's situation appears to present quite another issue in the context of Europe. The EU displays real voluntarism in favour of cultural minorities, since being associated with an image of a 'Europe of Merchants' would not be suitable. In this light, culture, in the widest sense of the term, is considered to be a cohesive element for Europe. It appears necessary to face the facts. *Culture as a whole* is made up of *different cultures.* However, each state produces its own cultural policy, developing and promoting prestigious places where capital cities have ritually had a central role. This phenomenon is typically French. This is why, as it is scarcely able to interfere in the political culture of a member state, the EU has chosen another terrain, less ambitious, less spectacular and less prestigious: that of regional cultures.

The first EU initiative commenced in the 1980s, when the European Parliament approved, on 16 October 1981, a resolution on the 'Community Charter of Languages and Regional Cultures' and on a 'Charter of Rights of Ethnic Minorities'. Regarding the agreements of Maastricht in 1992, they reaffirmed this principle that: 'The Community contributes to the blooming of the culture of Member States with respect to their national and regional diversity'.

However, the CoE, in drafting a 'European Charter of regional or minority languages' undoubtedly demonstrates itself to be the more active organisation in the defence and promotion of minority cultures. This Charter was adopted by the Council of Ministers of Europe on 29 June 1992, and represents the culmination of resolutions previously approved by the CoE. The aim is to safeguard and promote minority languages by highlighting the value of interculturalism and bilingualism. The basic idea is that the liberty of speaking a regional language in private or public life should be recognised as constituting an inalienable human right. This text offers a comprehensive framework that urges all states to eliminate all discrimination in the use of minority languages and to facilitate their usage in public life. The need to ensure that they are taught at all levels is particularly emphasised. Obviously, the Charter does not apply to the states that have not ratified it – and this is the case of France. The French government agreed to sign the Charter on 7 May 1999, but the Constitutional Council declared that the Charter could not be ratified for constitutional reasons.

Ultimately, even if cultural associations have once again returned to their function of protest, the Breton language can find support in a Europe that is protective of minority cultures, and cultural circles in Brittany are continually calling for the ratification of a charter that would strengthen their legitimacy.

A new momentum for culture

If Breton culture and language are still thriving, it must be noted that it is mainly due to the dynamism of associations. State help remains very limited and cautious. The cultural militants have had to fight strongly to obtain the creation of Breton diplomas at university, for example, or for favourable arrangements on public financing of the *Diwan*[12] schools still confronted with very serious difficulties, notably financial. Due to pressure, the state agreed to ensure a certain amount of teaching of Breton at schools, but the subsidies remain very limited and, by all estimates, derisory in comparison with what a real linguistic policy should look like.

The regional institution of Brittany was originally intended to take Breton culture and language into account. This direction was adopted in 1977. At the time, a Charter was signed, that combined financial efforts of the state and local authorities, both regional and departmental. As a result the Cultural Council of Brittany (which groups together almost all of the cultural associations of Brittany) and the Cultural Institute of Brittany were created. Nevertheless, the state's financial commitments towards Brittany remain extremely modest.

The emergence of Europe as a new interlocutor, if not as a new partner, thus offers an advantageous context. Regions such as Brittany are hardly in a position to assert themselves at an international level. They have little capacity to act and make their needs and projects known. Often isolated from each other, they find it almost impossible to insist upon their common interests or maintain relations of cooperation and coordination for shared actions or initiatives. In this respect, Europe plays a key role in offering a framework for minorities to network. The minorities can participate in these actions and benefit from initiatives, information and innovations that go beyond state borders and the usual institutional obstacles.

At the same time, it is perhaps the support brought by Europe which is as interesting as the network itself. To give but one example, the European Bureau of Lesser Used Languages,[13] created in 1982, has played an interesting and sometimes leading role in the cultural coordination of numerous initiatives concerning the preservation of European cultural diversity. All associations stemming from issues of minority rights and protection thus function in a narrow symbiosis – nothing important concerning a minority can be produced in Europe without being known about by others. Brittany actively participates in this network.

Conclusion

If federalism is on the move in Europe, it is still unacceptable to France for historical reasons. At the start of the French Revolution, two institutional notions clashed: the federalised state vs. the centralised state. The latter was imposed by the Jacobins in order to establish the revolution from Paris. The Jacobins triumphed, but the 'Franco-French' debate on this question has never really ended. The heirs to this institutional concept have maintained the pressure. Struggles for identity are still not recognised and no concessions are made either to language or to regional culture, except in a parsimonious way, and all forms of official minority recognition are refused.

However, federalism is no longer a utopian dream. It arouses great hope by offering a suitable alternative to the traditional rivalries that this part of the world has witnessed. At the same time, it generates tension among the most conservative, combined with an obsolete centralism and archaic phobia of 'centrifugal tendencies'. This appears to be the case in France, where all sorts of technostructures slow down initiatives which could indeed call into question the privileges attached to the exercise of power in Paris. Despite rearguard opposition, federalism constitutes the active principle and driving force of the European construction. Many states, and not only the smaller ones, have also adopted its principles of organisation. This institutional system appears to be the most satisfactory method to negotiate centre–periphery relations. It is also the best way to take the personality of regions with a strong identity into account and to respect their identities. It is one of the permanent debates to which the Breton movement bears witness.

Given this perspective, an event took place on 20 March 2004, which will undoubtedly overhaul the future of Breton identity and the position of Brittany in Europe as well. For the first time, the regional poll elected a left-wing majority, which is favourable both to the institutional reunifica-tion of Brittany and to applying a real language policy. The regional council of Brittany unanimously adopted a motion relating to linguistic policy on the 19 December 2004, which was inspired by the minority lan-guage debates of the CoE and the European charter on regions. Within this new left-wing majority, there are councillors who support increased autonomy and a European federalism of regions. One of them was appointed Vice-President for European and International affairs in the regional executive body. The result will undoubtedly be a new and closer relationship between Brittany and Europe.

The idea that the 'defence of the individual' is the highest form of liberty has existed for a long time. This ideal, which still applies only to a small part of mankind, remains absolutely unchanged. However, it is not possible to separate the abstract individual from the historical and cultural background to which he identifies himself. This is what explains the demands proposed by a region such as Brittany. The new federalist trend in Europe allows the region to bypass the nation-state and have reasonable hope for the future of its identity.

17 Baltic identities and interests in a European setting

A bottom-up perspective

Richard Rose, Sten Berglund and Neil Munro[1]

Among the 25 member countries of the European Union (EU), the Baltic states are exceptional because they are officially nation-states with a multi-national population. Estonia, Latvia and Lithuania achieved independence as nation-states after the First World War, and each made its distinctive Baltic language the state language. As a consequence of the Second World War, the Soviet Union absorbed the three states as Soviet republics; Russian became the official language; and the three republics became bi-national. After regaining independence, each country has remained bi-national in its resident population while officially defining itself as a nation-state with its Baltic language the sole official language of the state.

A distinctive feature of language is that it is a collective good; its primary use is to communicate with other people rather than read poetry in private. In Soviet times when Russian was the state language, Russians did not need to learn a Baltic language and Baltic peoples learned Russian. However, since 1991 younger Balts have usually chosen to learn Western languages. For the language of the Russian minority to be accepted as a second official language in parliament today would require the Baltic majorities to abandon their commitment to a nation-state and become a bilingual multi-national state. While this would be a collective good for Russians, for Baltic peoples it would be a collective evil (Hirschman 1970). This has not happened. Estonia and Latvia have made knowledge of the state language a requirement of citizenship for those whose families were not citizens before the Second World War. Since a substantial majority of Russian nationals do not speak the official language, they are legal residents without citizenship.

The application of the Baltic states to join the EU challenged the Union to decide what weight to give to central issues of citizenship and minority rights, since Estonia and Latvia had a far higher proportion of established residents who are not citizens of any member state. EU negotiators had no single, agreed criterion for defining citizenship within member states and human rights, especially where language is concerned, can be defined in many different ways (Gelazis 2003). Since both the EU and NATO wanted to expand their borders to the East and the Baltic states were outstanding examples of having been victimised by the Soviet Union, the politics of the moment created pressures to admit all three Baltic states to the EU in 2004, adding exhortations to accelerate the rate of naturalisation of Russian-speaking non-citizens (Pettai and Zielonka 2003).

While the Baltic states are now in the EU, there remain political questions due to the inconsistency between citizenship and population. First, official records report 'minority' nationalities are 43 per cent of the population of Latvia, 35 per cent of the population of Estonia, and 20 per cent in Lithuania. Second, there is a dichotomous rather than multi-national division of the population in Estonia and Latvia between the titular nationality and Russians.[2] By contrast, the non-titular nationalities in Lithuania are relatively minor: Russians (9 per cent) and Poles (7 per cent). Third, nationality differences are not a residue of historical settlement patterns prior to the modern creation of nation-states, as is the case of Hungarians in contemporary Romania or Catholics in Northern Ireland. The presence of Russian ethnics is a consequence of the Second World War and the Soviet government's post-war shipment of more than a million immigrants there. Fourth, citizenship and language are integrally related in Estonia and Latvia, thus excluding many in the minority from voting. However, they are legal residents with the social welfare rights that go with this and are not threatened with deportation nor do they expect to become refugees (VCIOM 1998).

Whether very striking differences in national identities become a disruptive political problem is itself problematic. It depends on the political and social constructions of identities and interests within and between groups that are indubitably different in language. Theories of nationalism are 'top down' theories that homogenise a population by focusing on a macro construct, the nation or the nation-state. Because nationalism is a collective value, there is a tendency to generalise about the attributes that everyone of a given nationality is expected to share – whether or not there is in fact homogeneity of opinion. This rhetoric is politically convenient for nationalist politicians who wish to maximise the appearance of support. An incidental consequence of nationalist theorising is that those who patently cannot be homogenised to fit the criteria of a nation, such as Russian-born residents in the Baltic states, become an excluded group in an 'ethnic democracy' (Linz and Stepan 1996: chap. 20).

Sociologists and economists take a bottom-up approach in which the individual is the unit of analysis. The aggregation of individuals into groups is a matter of identifying differences within society, between workers, farmers and middle-class people, men and women, or young and old. Individuals in society are seen as having a multiplicity of identities, of which nationality is but one – and that is increasingly seen as contingent rather than fixed, even by official censuses (Prewitt 2005). From such a perspective, a person who is in the minority by one criterion, for example, being a Russian-speaker in a Baltic state, may be in a majority on another attribute, for example, being a woman. From this perspective, differences between individuals and groups may lead to cooperation or exchange. Even if there is a 'war' of the sexes or class 'conflict', such overblown metaphors diminish into insignificance when compared with the realities of armed conflict between nationalities in two established EU member states, Spain and the UK.

Differences between nationalities in the Baltic states have been described as threatening 'a high risk of conflict' about the fundamentals of the regime and of the society, and raise the prospect of the Russian Federation intervening there as a champion of the human rights of its nationals (Tiilikainen 2003: 17).[3] The purpose of this chapter is to examine empirically the extent to which Baltic and Russian nationalities are internally homogeneous or divided about such basic political issues as support for the current political regime or a desire to see a return of Communist rule. Insofar as differences do exist, the chapter tests the extent to which identities – whether within a Baltic nation, Russia or Europe – or interests, whether defined within the state's boundaries or in relation to Europe or Russia, influence support for the current political regime or a desire for regime change. After summarising the recent historical causes of nationality divisions in the Baltic states and reviewing alternative theories of cohesion and cleavage, the chapter analyses data from the New Baltic Barometer survey of Estonia, Latvia and Lithuania; it asks the same questions of representative samples of both titular and Russian-speaking populations in each of the three states. The results show that interests matter more than identities, and good government more than self-government in generating support for the regime.

Changes in states and nationalities

During the twentieth century the Baltic peoples have alternated between periods of living in multi-national and national states. Prior to the First World War the lands were part of multi-national empires ruled from Berlin and St Petersburg. The collapse of these empires led to the creation of Estonia, Latvia and Lithuania as states much closer to the nation-state model officially hailed by the architects of the Versailles peace treaty than were Poland or Czechoslovakia. In the 1930s, 88 per cent of Estonia's population was recorded as Estonian, 84 per cent of the population of what was then Lithuania was Lithuanian, and 77 per cent of the population of Latvia was ethnic Latvian (see Table 17.1).

When Estonia, Latvia and Lithuania gained independence they adopted formally democratic constitutions. The electoral system was that of proportional representation. which offered opportunities to ethnic minorities to gain representation in parliament (Rose and Munro 2003:

Table 17.1 Growth in Russian population of Baltic States, 1934–96

	1934		1959		1989		1996		Change (%)
	N (000)	%	N (000)	%	N (000)	%	N (000)	%	
Baltic									
Estonia	993	88	948	65	963	61	954	65	−23
Latvia	1,467	77	1,298	62	1,388	52	1,378	55	−22
Lithuania	2,418	84	2,151	79	2,924	80	3,023	81	−3
*Russian/Soviet**									
Estonia	93	8	267	22	551	35	482	33	25
Latvia	197	10	648	31	1,118	41	990	40	30
Lithuania	95	3	279	11	393	12	452	12	9
Jews									
Estonia	4	0.5	5	0.5	5	0.3	3	0.2	−0.3
Latvia	93	5	37	2	23	1	11	0.5	−4.5
Lithuania	229	8	25	1	12	0.3	6	0.1	−7.9
Poles									
Latvia	49	3	60	3	60	2	55	2	−1
Lith	86	3	230	9	258	7	258	7	4
Others									
Estonia	21	2	22	2	50	3	41	3	1
Latvia	99	5	56	2	78	3	67	3	−2
Lithuania	42	2	26	1	29	1	25	1	−1

Source: Compiled by the authors from Lauristin and Vihalemm 1997: 305–6.

Note
*Includes Belorussians and Ukrainians.

166, 194, 210). However, democracy did not last. Lithuania succumbed to strongman rule in 1926, and Estonia and Latvia in 1934 (Dellenbrant 1994).

The August 1939 Pact between the Soviet Union and Nazi Germany removed Estonia, Latvia and Lithuania from the list of independent states. The forceful integration of the Baltic peoples into the Soviet Union was accompanied by a wave of deportations, often to the Gulag archipelago. The German invasion of the Soviet Union in 1941 turned many Baltic people into allies of Nazi Germany. Soviet control was restored by the Red Army's advance in the late autumn of 1944. Many Baltic people fled to Germany, Denmark and Sweden. Some joined the armed resistance movement that remained active in opposition to integration in the Soviet Union for almost a decade after the internationally recognised end of the Second World War.

The war and the post-war occupation had a brutal impact on the Baltic peoples. Almost half the families in Estonia, Latvia and Lithuania had a member killed, deported or imprisoned (see Table 17.2). Between the

Table 17.2 Impact of war on Baltic peoples

Q. *During the Second World War and afterwards, many families in this country suffered greatly. Did anyone in your family suffer? (more than one answer accepted)*

	Estonian	Latvians	Lithuanians
	(% of titular nationality)		
Deported	26	29	24
Imprisoned	30	21	16
Executed, perished	24	16	13
None of the above	54	56	63

Q. *If a family member suffered, which force was responsible? (more than one answer accepted)*

	Estonians	Latvians	Lithuanians
	(% of suffering families)		
Soviet	82	74	81
Germans	9	14	8
Both	7	12	6
Other	2	–	5

Source: Centre for the Study of Public Policy (1993). Total interviews: 6,136. For more details, see www.BalticVoices.org.

early 1930s and the late 1950s the absolute number of Estonians in Estonia fell 10 per cent; the number of Latvians in Latvia dropped 12 per cent; and notwithstanding the expansion of Lithuania's border to incorporate Vilnius, the number of Lithuanians fell by 11 per cent. An even worse fate befell Jews, one of the largest minorities in the Baltic states. The Holocaust reduced their number from 326,000 to 67,000 (Lauristin and Vihalemm 1997: 305).

Annexation and population change

Soviet annexation radically changed the composition of the population in Baltic lands. While there had always been some Russians resident in Baltic territories, before the Second World War they were one among a multiplicity of minorities, including Germans, Jews and Poles, and some were refugees from the Soviet regime. After 1945 Moscow adopted an aggressive policy of colonisation. From Moscow's perspective, the Baltic states occupied a 'forward' military position in relation to Western Europe and Scandinavia. Therefore, they received a relatively large influx of Soviet military personnel and became a hub in Soviet post-war economic development. This created a demand for immigrant civilian labour and the relatively higher living standards of the Baltic states made them attractive to Soviet citizens in other republics. In consequence, the percentage of Russians living in Latvia and in Lithuania trebled from the mid 1930s to the late 1950s; and in Estonia it increased two and a half times.

The ethnic composition of the Soviet Union, quite apart from the Baltic Republics, meant that it was not a nation-state in conventional social science terms. Communists defined class divisions as overriding differences of nationality: the object was the progressive creation of a new Soviet man, an achievement to which Jews, Georgians, Armenians and all the other ethnic categories of the Soviet Union were expected to contribute. As Soviet republics, the political administration of Estonia, Latvia and Lithuania was primarily in the hands of people of Baltic nationality, both in state institutions or in local branches of the Communist Party of the Soviet Union (Misiumas and Taagepera 1993). While Soviet nationality policy was complex because of the nominally federal structure of the USSR, the centralised practice of the Communist Party of the Soviet Union emphasised that asserting any national identity inconsistent with loyalty to the Soviet state could be punished as a subversive act.

Independence regained – but not as before

Much to the surprise of Mikhail Gorbachev, his liberalisation of the Soviet regime under the slogans of *glasnost* and *perestroika* in the late 1980s gave an opening to popular movements critical of Soviet domination in the Baltic Republics as well as in the Warsaw Pact countries. Fearing a snowball effect, Gorbachev stalled and tried to repress the independence movement. However, the conflict between Gorbachev and Boris Yeltsin inevitably became a dispute about whether the Soviet Union should be maintained, since Yeltsin's power base was the Russian republic. The Baltic Republics took a lead in asserting a claim to secede from the Soviet Union and when these claims were later advanced by Russian, Ukrainian and Belarus republics this resulted in the break up of the Soviet Union (Lapidus 2004).

Lithuanians reacted to a Soviet attempt to use force against demonstrators and had a relatively smooth path to independence in the absence of serious minority problems (Duvold and Jurkynas 2004). Estonia embraced reform swiftly in a climate often marked by a high level of polarisation along ethnic lines. The authority of the legislature – the Estonian Supreme Soviet – was openly challenged by the creation of a rival political body, including representatives of Estonian expatriates (Lagerspetz and Vogt 2004). Latvia's ethnic composition was potentially divisive, but the Latvian popular front would not have come out on the winning side, if it had not enjoyed the support of a substantial number of ethnic Russians (Smith-Sivertsen 2004).

The post-Soviet independence of Estonia, Latvia and Lithuania is officially cast as a restoration of pre-war states, but it is not a restoration of the *status quo ante.* In place of pre-war authoritarian regimes, there are now competitive elections. The Holocaust eradicated the region's substantial Jewish minorities and Germans were swept out of the Baltic region by the Second World War. Whereas the collapse of the communist bloc led to greater ethnic homogenisation through the achievement of national independence in Slovenia, the Czech Republic and Slovakia, this has not been possible in the Baltic states, for titular nationals and Russians are geographically intermingled, especially in the national capitals. Estonia and Latvia are not bi-national states (see Table 17.1). The proportion of Lithuanians in Lithuania remains roughly the same as in the inter-war era, but the composition of the state is now different. Russians are now the largest minority, Vilnius is no longer ruled from Warsaw, and the Prussian city of Königsberg to the west is incorporated in the Russian Federation as Kaliningrad.

Membership of the EU completes the nationalist strategy of 'returning' to Europe after almost half a century of being subject to alien invaders. Although the economic conditions of the Baltic states place them among the poorest members of the EU, national economies are growing much faster than the pan-Europe average, thus holding out the prospect of catching up with Portugal and Greece, if not with their Nordic neighbours (EBRD 2004). National referendums in each of the Baltic states showed a substantial majority of eligible residents voting in favour of EU membership.

In one critical respect all three countries remain as they were prior to the pact between Nazi Germany and the Soviet Union. Notwithstanding the presence of substantial national minorities and the rise of bi- and multi-culturalism in many Western democracies, their constitutions continue to define them as nation-states rather than multi-national states. Since the ethnic minorities in Lithuania are relatively small and divided in relation to the Lithuanian population, that state has made it possible for all legal residents of the country to become citizens regardless of ethnic background. Faced with national minorities on a scale often found in multi-cultural societies, the Estonian and Latvian governments have insisted on maintaining their nation-state status. This was done by making knowledge of the state language a condition of citizenship. At the time the policy was adopted, this meant that few Russian ethnics could claim citizenship. However, the policy was not a policy of permanent dominance but of assimilation of Russian-speakers who wanted to become citizens of an Estonian or Latvian nation-state, a position consistent with the views of the preponderant groups in both majority and minority nationality groups (Rose 1994). Subsequent liberalisation of standards, accompanied by pressure from the EU and the 'push' on Russians to distance themselves from a troubled homeland as well as the 'pull' of a better future for themselves and their children in Baltic states, has led to a substantial reduction in the proportion of non-citizens.

When the Estonian *Riigikogu* approved the Citizenship Resolution in February 1992, it was automatically granted to pre-1940 citizens and their descendants, irrespective of ethnicity, while Soviet-era immigrants had to undergo a naturalisation process, including a language test, two years of residency and an oath of allegiance (Jurado 2003). This resolution and the subsequent Citizenship Law passed in 1995 effectively created a society with four distinct groups: Estonians who are automatically citizens; Estonian citizens who are Russian by ethnicity; legal residents of Estonia with the citizenship of the Russian Federation or another CIS country; and legal residents, principally Russians, who now have no citizenship. Between 1992 and 2000, 115,000 people obtained citizenship through the naturalisation process (Lagerspetz and Vogt 2004). Subsequent amendments include a provision facilitating the naturalisation of children under the age of 15 whose parents are stateless and have lived in Estonia for at least five years. Concurrently, the entry of Estonia into the EU has also increased the attractiveness of citizenship to Russian ethnics, as it confers an EU passport on Russian ethnics. The proportion of the country's population that hold citizenship has thus increased from just above three-fifths shortly after independence to four-fifths today.

Latvia originally offered citizenship only to citizens before 1940 and their descendants. An initial proposal to naturalise Russians subject to very strict language tests and 16 years of residence failed to become law because of opposition from hard-line nationalists who thought the standards too generous (Smith-Sivertsen 2004). Naturalisation legislation was not enacted until 1994, and began in 1995 under a quota regime designed to keep it below the growth rate of the ethnic Latvian population. Annual application windows for different age groups subsequently replaced the quota regime. In response to pressure from the EU, in 1998 all non-citizens permanently living in Latvia became eligible for naturalisation, provided that they had Latvian language proficiency and paid steep naturalisation fees. These fees were significantly reduced in 2001, so that by December 2002 a total of 59,239 persons had been naturalised, a big increase from the 6,993 individuals naturalised by January 1998. A 1998 referendum also gave children of non-citizens born in Latvia after August 1991 the right to become citizens without further screening. By the end of 2002, almost 1,000 children had obtained Latvian citizenship within this programme and the inclusion of Russians in citizenship continues to grow.

Cohesion and cleavage between and within nationalities

Theories of nationalism tend to be mono-causal; the most important characteristics of society reflect collective characteristics of everyone belonging to a nation. The assumption of homogeneity facilitates macro-sociological generalisation. It is also politically convenient, for the rhetoric of nationalist politics prescribes that everyone with the same nationality ought to endorse the same core set of political values. In a homogeneous nation-state, this implies a great deal of consensus or uniformity, But this proposition can only be maintained by selectively choosing indicators, for example, language use, while ineluctably differentiated dimensions of social life, such as income, gender and party preferences, are ignored.

The homogenising nature of nationalism implies:

> H1: *Members of the same nationality will tend to have common political values.*

This proposition is familiar in consensus theories of democratic political cultures which presuppose a nation-state. Consistent with the nationalist ideology of Baltic peoples, this theory predicts that, for any given indicator, there will 75 to 100 per cent agreement among Estonians, Latvians and Lithuanians to questions about basic political values. The same will be true of Russian-speakers. However, the assumption of homogeneity leaves open whether or not the consensus within each nationality in a multinational state will produce a concurring consensus, as occurs in Switzerland, but is patently lacking in Northern Ireland.

In states with two or more politically mobilised nationalities, the homogenising theory of nationalism becomes a conflict theory.

> H2: *Homogeneity of values within a nationality will cause conflicts about political values between majority and minority nationalities.*

Theories of democracy view its survival as problematic when states have two or more nationalities that could come into violent conflict about the very definition of the state's boundaries (Dahl 1989: 254ff). Insofar as the political mobilisation of individuals into nations is based on exclusive collective goods, then homogeneity within a nationality group will create dissensus between the two nationalities of a bi-national state. Consequences can include political instability, ethnic conflict and even the break up of the state. In Baltic states, language and identity, two primordial national values, have the potential for major conflict. In Estonia and Latvia, the demands of language competence for citizenship has greatly limited the political influence that Russians can wield at the ballot box, inasmuch as those most concerned with maintaining their collective rights as Russians will not have the vote and Russians who have become citizens are most likely to be assimilated. The absence of electoral outlets for frustrations ought to increase the potential for conflict outside conventional institutions. Moreover, in default of a meaningful political arena in

Riga or Tallinn, Russians have the alternative of appealing to Moscow for help.

However, nationality is not the only dimension of social differentiation. It is an axiom of sociology that modern societies are highly differentiated in their economic and social interests. Insofar as politics is about the articulation of competing political demands, then within a modern society:

H3: *Social and economic interests create divisions about political values that cut across nationalities.*

Theories of interest-based cleavages in established democracies emphasise multiple identities of race, religion, social class and urban/rural residence which cut across differences of language and ethnicity (Lipset and Rokkan 1967). The existence of such divisions is contingent, for a nation-state may be homogeneous in terms of nationality, religion, and language; 'only' class and urban/rural differences are inevitably present in all states. The Communist Party of the Soviet Union propagated a homogenising theory of working-class interests as overriding officially recognised but subordinate nationality differences within the Soviet Union.

The European Community was not started because of a common identity among French and Germans or Italians and Belgians. It was founded to advance collective interests in avoiding another European war between different European nationalities and to promote national economic growth. As the EU has expanded, its diversity of nationalities has grown. Today, in an EU of more than 400 million people, the population of every nation-state is a minority; no language is the official language of as much as one-quarter of the Union's population and the majority of participants in EU affairs speak a foreign language when participating in its activities. Many theories of European integration emphasise the need to promote a supra-national European identity to strengthen EU institutions.

For the peoples of the Baltic states:

H4: *Europeanisation offers an alternative or additional layer of national identities and interests.*

Europeanisation can be interpreted in social psychological terms as the development of a European identity that can supplement or substitute for a national identity. The latter possibility is particularly relevant for minorities, whether citizens or not, in the Baltic states. Minorities may view the EU as offering a superior identity, for example, preferring English or French to their state language and seeing their interests better advanced in Brussels or Strasbourg than in their own national capital. If Europeanisation is seen as promoting minority interests, then it may produce a reaction from a majority nationality. On the other hand, if it is seen as offering economic benefits across nationalities, it may produce consensus in pursuit of common interests.

Multiple identities and interests

The conversion of social differences into political cleavages is problematic. Logically, the outcome can take the form of: (i) one cleavage dominates all others; the assumption of theories of conflicts between nationalities or between classes; (ii) two or more cleavages re-enforcing each other, either positively, as in the case of a person being a Texan and an American, or producing conflict, for example, the religion and nationality differences in Northern Ireland; (iii) two or more cleavages exerting cross-pressure, as can happen if national and class identities pull in opposing directions (Lipset 1960: 32; Lijphart 1995: 853–65).

Given that competing hypotheses refer to the bottom-up response of individuals to cues from political leaders and institutions, the appropriate way to assess their relative significance is through survey data. The evidence here comes from the fifth New Baltic Barometer (NBB) survey, which in 2001 interviewed random samples of Estonians, Latvians and Lithuanians in their respective national languages, and in each state also interviewed samples of Russians. (For details of samples and all questions, see Rose 2002b; for comparisons with other EU enlargement countries, see Rose 2002a; for copies of questionnaires and detailed results see www.BalticVoices.org).

Multiple and asymmetrical identities

National identity is but one level in a nested set of territorial identities, ranging from the village to the European level. Self-identification as a Russian or a Soviet citizen provides a link with a foreign state, but multiple identities create the possibility of moderating the gap because people who patently differ in one respect, for example, Latvians and Russians, can share an identity as residents of Riga or as Europeans.

To capture the multiple identities that individuals may hold, the New Baltic Barometer offers respondents a card listing six different choices; in Lithuania a seventh alternative is added, Polish. Everyone is asked to select their first and second choice of identities. In the Baltic states, nearly everyone can readily name two identities (see Table 17.3). Asking for two identities also reveals which identities people regard as having little or no importance.

As expected, an overwhelming majority of Baltic people identify with their nation-state, and very few Russian-speakers do so. While a majority of Russian-speakers endorse a Russian, Soviet or related CIS nationality, the

Table 17.3 Multiple identities in the Baltic states

Q. *With which of the following do you most closely identify yourself? And which do you identify with second?*

	Estonia		Latvia		Lithuania	
	Estonians	Russians	Latvians	Russians	Lithuanians	Russians
	(% naming identity first or second)					
Two identities	94	93	96	90	98	91
Baltic country	83	4	85	7	88	9
Russia, Soviet	2	75	3	62	2	50
City where I live	61	69	70	77	75	69
Region	32	19	28	20	16	18
Europe	11	15	8	11	10	9
Other	3	4	2	6	5	19
Poland	n.a.		n.a.		1	12
Don't know	1	0	1	1	0	1

Source: Centre for the Study of Public Policy (2001). Total number of respondents: 3,133.

proportion doing so varies substantially between five-sixths in Estonia, two-thirds in Latvia and one half in Lithuania. The proportion of Russian-speakers who identify with the former ruling state is lowest in Lithuania because Poles have tended to assimilate to the Russian-speaking community there without adopting a Russian identity.

Big majorities of Russian-speakers do have an identity with a place in the Baltics: the city in which they live. In Latvia and Lithuania more identify with their city of residence than with a CIS country, and so do 72 per cent in Estonia. Moreover, in Latvia an absolute majority of Russian-speakers, 52 per cent, make a civic identity their first choice as against one-third placing a CIS identity first; in Lithuania 45 per cent endorse a civic identity first as against one-quarter giving priority to a CIS identity. In Estonia 32 per cent give an urban identity first, compared to 49 per cent giving priority to a CIS identity. While most Baltic nationals also endorse a civic identification, it is usually as a second choice. Moreover, the meaning of a civic identity differs between the majority and minority nationalities. For Baltic peoples, identification with Tartu, Daugavpils or Kaunas is normally integrated with identification with Estonia, Latvia or Lithuania. However, for Russian-speakers it is a cross-cutting identification as against their CIS nation of origin.

From a legal perspective, membership in the EU is an attribute of states, while for individuals it can be a matter of psychological identity. From a traditional Slavophile perspective, identification with Russia and identification with Europe are mutually exclusive (Neumann 1996). However, for those in a minority nationality, identification with the pan-national idea of Europe could be attractive as conferring a status equal or superior to identification with a less important Baltic nationality. When offered the choice, an average of 11 per cent select a European identity, and this was normally as a second choice. Moreover, there is little difference in the proportion doing so between Russians and Baltic peoples (see Table 17.3).

As theories of ethnic conflict would predict, the territorial identifications of Baltic peoples and Russian-speakers are opposed, for Balts identify with their historic and current state and reject association with almost half a century of Soviet rule, while Russian-speakers, including those born in the Baltic, identify with their historic homeland and very few identify with their country of residence. At the time when entry to the EU was being negotiated, there were insufficient Balts or Russians identifying with Europe for this to influence the collective position of either nationality. The cross-cutting territorial influence on the identity of Russian-speakers comes from the grass roots, the city in which they live.

Identities of interest

While national and religious identities are commonly treated as cultural values, other identities, such as with the working class or middle class, are commonly treated as material interests. Many sociologists besides Marxists emphasise the interest basis of many efforts at nationalist mobilisation or the intertwining of material interests and nationalist appeals, for example, in stipulating a distinctive language requirement for a job in the civil service. Here again, it is an open empirical question whether competing interests tend to re-enforce or cut across differences in nationalities.

In the Baltic states, Russia as well as the EU is of economic and political significance. When the New Baltic Barometer asks people to evaluate the importance of trans-national links, it includes each separately in a list along with four other countries and the EU and Russia are most frequently named as important by all nationality groups. Before any decision had been taken in Brussels or by a national referendum about admission to the EU, majorities regarded EU links as important in 2001 (see Table 17.4). This concurrence is politically more significant than differences of 8 to 20 percentage points in the size of these majorities. When a parallel question is asked about links with Russia, a third to less than half of Baltic nationals think links with Russia are important, whereas half to three-fifths of Russians take this view. Yet here again Russian-speakers are subject to cross-cutting influences, for in all three countries a majority sees links with the EU and with Russia as important. Even though Estonia has a significant common border with Russia, 15 per cent more Russian-speakers see EU links as important than links with the Russian Federation, while in Lithuania the percentage endorsing each link is virtually the same.

The moderating effect of alternative identifications is also provided by an earlier New Baltic Barometer survey that asked how much people had in common with workers and with middle-class people, as well as with

Table 17.4 All nationalities see both the EU and Russia as important

Q. As things now stand, with which of the following do you see our country's future most closely tied up? (respondent can endorse more than one)

	EU (%)	Russia (%)
Estonia		
Estonians	75	34
Russians	67	52
Difference	8	−18
Latvia		
Latvians	72	33
Russians	52	61
Difference	20	−28
Lithuania		
Lithuanians	67	46
Russians	56	58
Difference	11	−12

Source: Centre for the Study of Public Policy (2001). Total number of respondents: 3,133.

defenders of national traditions (see Table 17.5). In all six nationalities, upwards of three-quarters express a sense of common feelings with workers. However, this is not a reflection of political socialisation under Communism, for almost as large a group express common ground with middle-class people too. Of particular relevance here is that upwards of two-thirds do *not* believe that they have a lot in common with defenders of national interests. This implies that nationalists who claim to speak in the name of 'all' Russians are misrepresenting their potential support by a factor of three, and Baltic nationalists who make a similar claim are over-estimating their potential support by two or three times. Electoral mobilisation provides support for this interpretation, for the parties that represent economic interests or make 'catch-all' appeals gain a much larger total vote than parties that emphasise nationalist values (Rose and Munro 2003: chaps 10, 12 and 13).

Interests and performance more important than identities

All residents of post-Communist states have lived under at least two different regimes, palpable evidence that the current political system is not the only one that can govern the society. It also creates conditions for competition between regimes: some people may support the new regime for positive reasons or on the Churchillian grounds that it is the lesser evil to what went before, while others may prefer the old regime (Rose *et al.* 1998: chap. 5). By keeping alive memories of the previous regime under

Table 17.5 Groups promoting a sense of common feeling

Q. People usually feel they have more in common with some groups than others. How much do you have in common with each of the following groups?

	Estonia		Latvia		Lithuania	
	Estonians	Russians	Latvians	Russians	Lithuanians	Russians
	(% with a lot or some things in common)					
Workers	74	77	71	77	65	71
Middle class	66	68	66	66	63	63
Defenders of national traditions	28	34	46	34	32	28

Source: Centre for the Study of Public Policy (1995). Total number of respondents: 4,265. Further details at: www.BalticVoices.org.

Soviet rule, Baltic peoples were able to achieve the restoration of the status quo ante.

Hypotheses 1 and 2 predict that people with a Baltic identity should support the new regime while those with a CIS identity should support a return to a Communist regime. However, hypotheses 3 and 4 propose that social and economic interests and Europe should determine regime support. The New Baltic Barometer includes questions about support for the current and a Communist regime, and it has measures of political performance, such as the trustworthiness or corruption of political institutions, that can be combined in a multiple regression analysis to determine the extent to which there is evidence supporting each approach, net of other influences.

Regime support cuts across nationalities

In the abstract world of democratic theory, governments supply what people want. This is not the history of the Baltic states nor of the Soviet Union. It is also a mistake to describe all post-Soviet regimes as new democracies, for Central Asia regimes are patently dictatorships while new EU member states meet criteria for democratic governance and some post-Communist regimes fall in between (Rose and Shin 2001; www. freedomhouse.org). Moreover, Russians may contest or qualify the term democracy in the Baltic context insofar as Estonian and Latvian citizenship laws deny them the right to vote.

The New Baltic Barometer adopts a positivist approach to measuring regime support: it asks people to evaluate the regime that they now have; the question is placed in context by first requesting an evaluation of the pre-*perestroika* regime. In keeping with the logic of regime competition, respondents are asked to evaluate regimes on a scale that runs from plus 100 to minus 100. Consistent with the Churchill hypothesis that democracy has many faults but is still preferable to any alternative (in the Baltic states, rule by Moscow), this makes it possible to establish a transitive preference between regimes that are viewed as the lesser as against the greater evil. In Estonia, 69 per cent are positive about the new regime, in Latvia 53 per cent and in Lithuania 46 per cent. Within each country, the difference between Balts and Russian-speakers in the percentage approving the new regime is limited. It is six percentage points in Estonia, seven percentage points in Latvia, and four percentage points in Lithuania. Differences about the regime within each nationality are greater than differences between nationalities (see Table 17.6). The standard deviation around the mean is consistently high, ranging between 47 and 55 points on the 201 point scale (see Appendix, 17.A1).

In each Baltic state, multiple regression analysis can explain almost one-quarter of the variance in support for the current regime (see Table 17.7). However, national identities and territorial interests play almost no part in doing so. Being a citizen of a Baltic state does not significantly increase the

Table 17.6 Support for current and communist regimes

Q. Here is a scale for ranking how our system of government works. The top, plus 100, is the best; the bottom, minus 100, the worst. Where on this scale would you put our current system of governing with free elections and many parties?

	Estonia		Latvia		Lithuania	
	Estonians	*Russians*	*Latvians*	*Russians*	*Lithuanians*	*Russians*
	(Percentage)					
Positive	71	65	56	49	48	44
Neutral	10	8	12	9	10	13
Negative	19	27	33	42	42	42
Mean	26	15	7	−4	−3	−10
Standard deviation	43	51	47	49	55	54

Q. Our present system of government is not the only one that this country had. Some people say that we would be better off if the country was governed differently. What do you think? For each point please say whether you strongly agree, somewhat agree, somewhat disagree or strongly disagree.

We should return to communist rule

	Estonia		Latvia		Lithuania	
	Estonians	*Russians*	*Latvians*	*Russians*	*Lithuanians*	*Russians*
Strongly agree	0	3	1	2	2	7
Somewhat agree	2	14	4	9	10	16
Somewhat disagree	20	30	13	35	25	27
Strongly disagree	77	54	82	54	63	50

Source: Centre for the Study of Public Policy (2001). Total number of respondents: 3,133.

Table 17.7 Influences on support for the current regime

	Estonia	*Latvia*	*Lithuania*
Variance explained	23.6%	24.0%	25.7%
	(Significant betas at 0.05)		
Identities			
CIS identity	n.s.	n.s.	n.s
CIS and citizen	n.s.	n.s.	n.s.
European identity	n.s.	n.s.	9
Territorial interests			
Country future tied to Russia	n.s.	n.s.	n.s.
Country future tied to EU	6	n.s.	n.s.
Political performance			
Rate future economic system	25	32	38
Trust political institutions	18	15	8
Respect for human rights	17	8	13
Perceived corruption	−6	−10	−6
Socio-economic characteristics			
Age	−9	−7	−9
Education	n.s.	6	7
Number consumer goods	n.s.	n.s.	n.s.
Gender	n.s.	n.s.	n.s.

Source: Centre for the Study of Public Policy (2001). Total number of respondents: 3,133.
For statistical reasons, the 201-point support for regime scale collapsed to a 21-point scale.

likelihood of a Russian-speaker favouring the current regime, nor does identification with a CIS nation decrease the likelihood of support. Moreover,
people who think the country's future is tied to Russia are no more likely to
reject the current regime than those who do not. In two of the three Baltic
states Europe has no significant influence on support for the current regime.

Political performance drives support for the current regime: all four
performance indicators are substantively and statistically significant in all
the Baltic states. Consistent with hypothesis 3, which emphasises socio-
economic differences, the single most important influence on support for
the regime is a person's expectation of the future of the country's economic system, which is seen as a responsibility of the state. Moreover, the
condition of the economic system creates material wellbeing that is shared
by both Baltic nationals and Russian-speakers. Trust in political institutions is the second most important feature of performances promoting
regime support. Reciprocally, the perception of corruption reduces
support for the regime. Respect for human rights influences the evaluation of both Baltic nationals and Russian-speakers.

The evaluation of political performance is largely independent of individual socio-economic characteristics. Age is the only social characteristic
consistently significant: older people tend to be less supportive of the

regime, a characteristic found across the post-Communist world. Education has a lesser influence in two countries. Not only is gender of no statistical significance, but the same is true of a household's possession of more consumer durable goods such as a car and a video-cassette recorder. The economic influence that counts is the collective state of the economy – and the benefits of economic growth and the costs of inflation affect citizens and non-citizens alike.

Communist regime unappealing to all nationalities

Theories of nationalism predict a widespread rejection of a return to Communist rule, since it was associated with domination by Moscow. However, in the circumstances of bi-national Baltic states, while a big majority of Baltic peoples would be expected to reject a return to a Communist regime, most Russians would take the opposite view, since this is integrally associated with government from Moscow. However, this is not the case. Among all nationalities there is a consensus against a return to Communist rule. The overwhelming opposition of Baltic nationals to a return to Communist rule is matched by 89 per cent of Russian-speakers in Latvia, 84 per cent in Estonia and 77 per cent in Lithuania (see Table 17.7). Moreover, among the minority who would like to see a Communist regime return, there is low expectation of this happening.

Since a big majority reject a return to Communist rule, there is less variance to be explained by multiple regression analysis; it ranges from 11.9 per cent in Estonia to 15.0 per cent in Latvia (see Table 17.8). Within this more limited compass, identification with a CIS country is the most important influence in Estonia and Latvia and significant in Lithuania too. The statistical significance of being a Latvian citizen or having European identification in Lithuania is undermined by the fact that in both cases it tends to boost endorsement of a return to Communist rule. More consistent with theory is that those who see their country's future linked with the EU are less inclined to want a return to Communist rule, and Estonians who see Russia as important for their future are more in favour.

Political performance shows the most influence in predictable directions. In all three Baltic states, those who view the country's economic future positively are less likely to want a return to a Communist regime. Insofar as the new regime is seen as respecting human rights, this increases opposition to a return to Communist rule. Education is a consistently significant substantial influence too: even after controlling for national differences, more educated people are less likely to want a return to Communist authority. The intermittent statistical significance of other influences should be discounted because the direction of influence is not regularly consistent with theory.

Table 17.8 Influences on desire for return of communist regime

	Estonia	Latvia	Lithuania
Variance explained	11.9%	15.0%	14.8%
	(Significant betas at 0.05)		
Identities			
CIS identity	20	16	10
CIS and citizen	n.s.	08	n.s.
European identity	n.s.	n.s.	07
Territorial interests			
Country future tied to Russia	7	n.s.	n.s.
Country future tied to EU	−12	−10	n.s.
Political performance			
Rate future economic system	−6	−7	−26
Respect for human rights	n.s.	−18	−7
Trust political institutions	n.s.	n.s.	9
Perceived corruption	−7	n.s.	n.s.
Socio-economic characteristics			
Education	−8	−15	−10
Age	8	n.s.	−15
Number consumer goods	n.s.	n.s.	−14
Gender	n.s.	n.s.	n.s.

Source: Centre for the Study of Public Policy (2001). Total number of respondents: 3,133.

Implications

The contemporary context and recent history of the Baltic states provide a contextual and theoretical justification for expecting confirmation of hypotheses about national homogeneity and ethnic conflict. However, the above evidence rejects both hypotheses. In most of the regression analyses, the five measures of identity and territorial interests, whether with Russia or with Europe, had no significant influence on support for alternative regimes. Nor is the weakness of these influences an artefact of the particular focus of this chapter. Divisions within each nationality have been greater than differences between nationalities on almost all major political indicators in every New Baltic Barometer survey since 1993 (www.BalticVoices.org). Moreover, where there are big differences they are likely to be non-political, for example, Russian nationals are more likely to speak Russian at home and be married to Russian nationals, and Baltic peoples behave similarly.

European identity has no significant influence on regime attitudes in either Estonia or Latvia, and is of secondary significance in Lithuania. In Estonia and Latvia, the belief that the country's ties lie with Europe achieves statistical significance, but its substantive influence is secondary. In short, social psychological and perceptual theories of the direct influence of Europeanisation on political attitudes are not supported here.

However, the bottom-up evidence of the importance of successful management of the economy by government leaves open the possibility of the indirect influence of Europeanisation. Insofar as entry into the Single European Market is seen as good for Baltic economies, this will boost support for the current regime and depress aspirations for a return to Communism. The potential impact is greatest in Latvia and Lithuania, which have lagged well behind Estonia in making a successful transition from a command economy to a market economy. Yet since 2000, when EU membership became increasingly likely, Latvia and Lithuania have been experiencing rates of economic growth above those for other enlargement countries, not to mention established member states such as France and Germany (EBRD 2004: 38). Insofar as EU membership increases respect for human rights and reduces corruption, this too should increase support for the current regime among all nationalities in the Baltic states.

The influence of political performance is a reminder that politics matters. What governors do influences how they are judged by those whom they govern. Whether people are Baltic or Russian or citizens or non-citizens, individuals are influenced in evaluating regimes by how trustworthy or corrupt are national political institutions, and what the national government's management of the economy does for future economic prospects. From a European perspective it is important to remember that the governors who can directly influence popular attitudes are located in Tallinn, Riga and Vilnius rather than Brussels.

Altogether, the results indicate that Baltic residents, whether titular nationals or ethnic Russians, value good government more than self-government. Given the experience of Soviet times, good government cannot be taken for granted. Moreover, the current standards of government in Latvia and Lithuania leave much to be desired in the eyes of their citizens. On some indicators, the regimes rank below Bulgaria and Romania, countries that were not admitted to EU membership when the Baltic states joined (Rose 2005). Estonia confirms the importance of good government, for while the Russian minority there is very large and has been viewed as a source of trouble because of barriers to citizenship (Linz and Stepan 1996), Russians resident in Estonia are more likely to support their regime than are Latvian and Lithuania citizens. Good government does not mean the end of political disputes for, consistent with hypothesis 3, differences about governance are inherent in politics. What good government produces is a translation of nationality differences, with all their destructive potential, into a constructive evaluation of the necessary responsibilities of government – managing the economy, maintaining human rights, enforcing the law without corruption and earning trust – and allocating political support in accord with what government does.

Appendix

Table 17.A1 Variables in analysis

	Minimum	Maximum	Mean	Std. deviation
Dependent				
Support for current regime	−100 worst	100 best	6.5	49.5
Desire return to communism	1 strongly disagree	4 strongly agree	1.44	0.70
Identities				
CIS identity	0 no	1 yes	0.19	0.39
CIS and citizen	0 no	1 yes	0.14	0.35
European identity	0 no	1 yes	0.10	0.30
Territorial interests				
Country future tied to Russia	0 no	1 yes	0.44	0.50
Country future tied to EU	0 no	1 yes	0.68	0.47
Political performance				
Rate future economic system	−100 worst	100 best	22.0	42.3
Trust political institutions	1 not at all	7 great trust	3.27	1.06
Gov't respects human rights	1 none	4 a lot	2.44	0.78
Perceived corruption	1 few corrupt	3 all corrupt	2.19	0.68
Socio-economic characteristics				
Age	18	95	46	17
Education	1 elementary	4 university	2.42	1.02
Number of consumer goods	0	3	1.71	0.90
Gender	0 male	1 female	0.54	0.50

Source: Centre for the Study of Public Policy (2001). Estonia: 1,008 persons interviewed between 21–30 November 2001 by Saar Poll; Latvia: 1,001 persons interviewed between 5–28 October 2001 by Baltic Data House; Lithuania: 1,124 persons interviewed between 4–8 October 2001 by Vilmorus. Further details: www.BalticVoices.org; Rose 2002b.

18 EU accession and conflict resolution in theory and practice

The case of Cyprus

Nathalie Tocci

The existence and persistence of the Cyprus conflict is characterised by a fundamental reluctance by all the principal parties to create, re-establish or run a unified independent Cyprus in which Greek and Turkish Cypriots would coexist peacefully on the basis of a shared understanding of their political equality. This reluctance has been driven by the parties' understanding of how they could each attain their own objectives of self-determination, individual rights and communal security. Their positions have revolved around a legalistic and modernist discourse of absolute sovereignty, statehood and military power and balance.

Thwarted by these mutually exclusive positions, efforts aimed at inter-communal reconciliation went through an unending series of failures. The conflict emerged between the 1930s and 1950s when the Greek Cypriot community, supported by Greece, articulated its struggle for self-determination in terms of *enosis*, i.e. union with Greece. Unlike other former Ottoman possessions swept by the tide of ethnic nationalism, the Greek Cypriots were faced with the additional obstacle of British colonial rule, adamantly opposed to *enosis*. Thereafter, the Turkish Cypriot community and Turkey mounted a reactive counter-*enosis* campaign, which by the late 1950s found form in the diametrically opposed position of partition (*taksim*). In 1960 a compromise was found. Cyprus would become an independent bi-communal republic. Yet, the Greek Cypriot leadership remained implicitly devoted to *enosis* and by 1963 the bi-communal republic had collapsed. With its breakdown, both the Greek Cypriot and the Turkish Cypriot leaderships lost their already limited commitment to the 1960 agreements, culminating in the 1974 Greek coup in Cyprus and the ensuing Turkish military intervention. The decades that followed witnessed a series of failed negotiations and rejected proposals, as the positions of the parties moved further apart. Both parties articulated their claims in the mutually exclusive language of absolute statehood and exclusive and undivided sovereignty. No third party, other than the UN, actively attempted to alter these perceptions.

Over the course of the 1990s, the European Union (EU) became a principal external determinant of the conflict (Tocci 2004). The Greek

Cypriot Republic of Cyprus (RoC) applied for EU membership in 1990, generating considerable resistance from Turkey and the Turkish Cypriots. Following a positive Commission Opinion in 1993, the Republic embarked on an accession process. At the 1994 Corfu European Council, the Union decided to include Cyprus in the future round of enlargement. In 1998 the RoC launched accession negotiations with the Union. In December 1999, the Helsinki European Council decided that Cyprus could enter the EU despite the persistence of the conflict. Indeed the divided island joined the Union on 1 May 2004.

The impact of the EU on conflict settlement and resolution in Cyprus has two important dimensions. The first is related to the EU framework, into which a unified Cyprus was expected to enter. Within the EU, while remaining fully-fledged states, EU members delegate important competences to 'Brussels'. In turn, within EU institutions, decisions in most domains are taken collectively on the basis of majority rule. The EU framework also allows for the potential mobilisation of the sub-national level of government (Harvie 1994; Scharpf 1994; Hooghe 1996). While the significance of direct forms of communication between sub-national and supranational levels should not be overestimated (e.g. regional representations in Brussels or the Committee of the Regions), constitutional regions can play an important role in the formulation and implementation of EU policy, particularly through state channels (Jeffrey 2000; Keating 2004a). Hence, different levels of government become inter-related and inter-dependent through channels of communication and policy procedures. As such the notion of sovereignty is essentially transformed, and thus seeking self-determination through independence and exclusive sovereignty acquires a fundamentally different meaning.

The EU framework could also impinge on other features of an ethno-political conflict like the one in Cyprus. Transforming the meaning of borders through the liberalisation of the 'four freedoms', protecting individual rights and freedoms while encouraging the respect for cultural and regional specificities, in addition to the evident material benefits gained through accession, could have raised the potential for conflict settlement and resolution (Diez *et al.* 2004). In other words, the prospects of accession could have positively affected the material, identity and security-related aspects of the conflict. A UN official mediating in Cyprus shared this intuition when stating that 'the vast gap that separates the positions of the two sides on the issue of sovereignty could be narrowed by applying EU norms, something that could give Annan a way out of this maze' (*Cyprus Weekly* 2002). But how exactly did the UN Secretary General use the features of the EU framework to craft a peace plan that would be more appealing to the parties?

The second dimension of the role of the EU is related to the impact of the accession process on the domestic parties in the Cyprus conflict. The value of the EU framework for conflict resolution in Cyprus could only translate from potential into actual to the extent that it was appreciated domestically by the main parties to the conflict. Only if the latter viewed the EU framework as a valuable asset for a win–win agreement could accession generate positive incentives for conflict settlement and resolution. Did all the relevant actors in the Cyprus conflict appreciate the value of a settlement within the EU? More specifically, how and through what mechanisms did EU policies impact on the positions of the parties? Did (positive or negative) change occur through EU conditionality or/and were more diffuse and endogenous processes of social learning at work (Borzel and Risse 2000; Checkel 2000; Olsen 2001)?

In Cyprus, the impact of the accession process did not correspond to the professed expectations of the member states and the Commission. On the contrary, the major visible development during the 1990s and early 2000s was the hardening of the parties' positions, and those of Turkey and the Turkish Cypriot side in particular. The specific gains and losses presented to the parties, and the way in which they were presented by EU actors had unintended effects up until late 2001. This was because they played into the discourse of the most nationalist elements in the conflict, legitimising their hardened positions. The tide seemed to reverse by late 2001, and as Cyprus approached the deadline of accession, the 2002–04 peace efforts offered the prospects of a final breakthrough. Yet despite unprecedented international efforts to seal a deal between 2002 and May 2004, the divided Cyprus entered the Union, this time as the result of the Greek Cypriot rejection of the UN proposed peace plan. What explains these unintended effects and what does this say about the strengths and weaknesses of EU foreign policy in the context of enlargement?

This chapter begins by mapping out the key differences between the objectives and bargaining positions of the principal parties to the Cyprus conflict. It then analyses the way in which the EU framework could have helped the parties bridge the gaps that divided them by analysing the way in which the UN-proposed 'Annan Plan' cast a United Republic of Cyprus in the EU. Finally, this chapter examines the impact of the accession process on the conflict by assessing the interaction between the accession process and the incentives for conflict resolution of the principal parties.

The positions of the principal parties in the Cyprus conflict

The main differences between the Greek Cypriot and Turkish Cypriot communities, supported by Greece and Turkey, respectively, can be highlighted by briefly analysing their general national aspirations and their bargaining positions throughout the years of inter-communal talks, particularly since 1974.

The Greek Cypriot community, supported by Greece, sought the reunification of Cyprus and the prevention of northern Cyprus' secession or annexation to Turkey. Within a reunified island, they called for a fair and fully functioning arrangement in terms of territorial distribution and government structures. They insisted on the liberalisation of the 'three free-doms' (of movement, settlement and property), which would allow Greek Cypriots to live and return to their properties in the north. They also demanded security arrangements guaranteeing Cyprus against Turkey.

The Turkish Cypriots sought political equality with and prevention of domination of the larger Greek Cypriot community, the highest degree of self-rule and physical separation from the Greek Cypriots (at least for a limited period in time). They called for Turkey's involvement in Cyprus' security situation, given their underlying mistrust of other foreign involve-ment. However, the Turkish Cypriot people equally rejected integration with Turkey. Other than supporting the Turkish Cypriots, Turkey also had specific concerns that went beyond the welfare of the community. Turkey's understanding of its national security needs led to its pursuit of a balance between the roles of Greece and Turkey in the eastern Mediter-ranean and of a role in Cyprus's security arrangements.

Since 1974 these different yet not necessarily incompatible security, identity and justice objectives of the two communities were articulated through largely contrasting positions over the constitution, territory, rights and freedoms, and security arrangements. The inherent incompati-bility of these positions was primarily due to their elaboration within the prism of absolute and monolithic sovereignty. Both parties believed that if they held absolute sovereignty they would fulfil their underlying needs. Neither party genuinely accepted the logic of federalism. Moreover, as the parties became locked into the logic of negotiations, statehood and sover-eignty became ends in themselves, rather than the possible means to address the underlying aims of the parties. As put by UN Secretary General Kofi Annan:

> in the decades during which it has resisted efforts at settlement, the Cyprus problem has become overlain with legalistic abstractions and artificial labels, which are more and more difficult to disentangle and which appear increasingly removed from the actual needs of both communities.
>
> (UN Secretary General 1999)

Absolutist views of sovereignty led to contrasting positions over consti-tutional matters. The Turkish Cypriots emphasised divided sovereignty as a means to ensure their political equality. In practice, this entailed the establishment of two largely self-governing states, which would delegate limited sovereign powers to a subordinate centre (the 'partnership state'). The centre would be governed by maximum numerical equality in com-munal representation and by unanimity in decision-making. The two con-stituent states would have extensive competences, including the power to conclude international agreements with third states. The leadership believed that only what in substance would be a confederation or at most a loose federation by aggregation (between the two existing constituent states) would ensure political equality between the communities. To the Greek Cypriot side these positions were anathema to their aims. While accepting the concept of a bi-communal and bi-zonal federation, the leadership has insisted on the single and indivisible sovereignty of the Republic. The Greek Cypriot side held that the federation would be established through the disaggregation of the existing (Greek Cypriot) Republic (Chrysostomides 2000). Any other solution, including the establishment of a new state, would have entailed the recognition of the self-declared Turkish Republic of Northern Cyprus. The Greek Cypriot side also formally accepted the idea of political equality between the communities, agreeing to guaranteed quotas of Turkish Cypriots in the executive, in the legislature and in the judiciary. However, bi-communal participation was accepted to the extent that it would reflect the demographic balance and it would not hinder majority rule in executive and legislative decisions. The competences reserved to the two provinces were limited to welfare, religion, personal status, education and culture.

The prism of absolute sovereignty also led to contrasting positions over territory and the 'three freedoms'. The Turkish Cypriot leadership accepted the notion of territorial readjustments but stated that it was only willing to consider a map entitling the Turkish Cypriot state to over 29 per cent of the island's territory. Greater readjustments were rejected on the grounds that they would displace too many Turkish Cypriots and deprive northern Cyprus of crucial agricultural, land and water resources. In other words, the state needed sufficient territory to be economically self-sufficient and thus sustain its sovereignty. The Greek Cypriot side, while accepting the idea of bi-zonality, did not consider the territorial boundary as dividing two sovereign states, but rather as tracing an invisible line within the sovereign federation. As such, that boundary should be grounded on principles of fair distribution, i.e. the demographic balance.[1] Hence, the Greek Cypriots expected a considerable reduction of Turkish Cypriot controlled land from 37 per cent of the island. Figures privately mentioned by Greek Cypriot officials ranged from 28 to 24 per cent of the land.

While accepting the concept of bi-zonality in name, the Greek Cypriot side called for the full respect of individual rights and freedoms. To the Greek Cypriots, in addition to the right of return of all Greek Cypriot displaced persons, the 'three freedoms' of movement, settlement and property should be liberalised throughout the island. This was because the Cypriots, as the ultimate repositories of the single sovereignty of the state, should enjoy equal rights throughout the island. As such, the principle of bi-zonality could be effectively eliminated. The Turkish Cypriots rejected this position, insisting on their separate sovereign self-rule. Cyprus, in their view, was composed of two, not one, sovereign peoples, that would be territorially based in northern and southern Cyprus, respectively. In particular, the leadership objected to the full liberalisation of the freedoms of property and settlement. It argued that property claims should be settled mainly through compensation and property exchange, thus ensuring that the Turkish Cypriots remained a demographic majority in northern Cyprus.

Differing perceptions of security threats articulated within the prism of state sovereignty also led to contrasting positions over external guarantees. To the Turkish Cypriots, within a system of two sovereign entities, Turkey alone could protect the security of the smaller Turkish Cypriot state. The leadership thus supported a retention of the 1959 Treaties of Guarantee and Alliance that provided for unilateral rights of intervention of the three guarantors–Greece, Turkey and the UK – and for the stationing of Greek and Turkish troops on the island. However, Turkey's self-interested strategic calculations were precisely the reason for Greek Cypriot resistance to Turkish Cypriot proposals. The Greek Cypriot side insisted on a demilitarisation of the island, that would include the withdrawal of all foreign troops. There would be no unilateral rights of intervention by foreign powers. On the contrary, there would be international guarantees against foreign interventions in the internal affairs of the independent and sovereign Republic.

The use of the EU framework in the 2004 'Annan Plan'

In view of the approaching deadline of EU accession, when direct talks were re-launched in Cyprus in early 2002, UN mediators elaborated their bridging proposals with the aim of embedding a loose common state agreement within the EU. The resulting Annan Plan was put to separate referenda on the two sides of the island on 24 April 2004. How did UN mediators use the provisions and features of the EU framework to draft a more palatable proposal?

Let us begin by assessing the principal aspects of the 'Annan Plan'.[2] Constitutionally, the Plan adopted several aspects of the Swiss and Belgian federal constitutions. It retained an aura of vagueness regarding questions of state sovereignty and state succession. Sovereignty would be shared, with both the federal and the constituent state levels 'sovereignly' exercising the powers granted to them by the Constitution in a non-hierarchical fashion (Main Articles, articles 2.1 and 2.3; Constitution, article 3.2). The Plan also fudged the question of state succession. Other than stating that Cyprus would enter into a 'new state of affairs', the Plan left the question of state succession unanswered (Main Articles, article 1.1). This seemed to be the only way to square the circle between the mutually exclusive bargaining positions of the parties.

The Constitution envisaged that most powers would be attributed to the constituent states. The common state level would be responsible mainly for foreign relations, monetary policy, federal finance and common state citizenship and immigration. Common state institutions would be marked by effective political equality between the parties. Rather than a presidency (as provided for in the 1960 Constitution and in past UN proposals), there would be a five-year term Presidential Council comprising of nine members (of which three would be Turkish Cypriots), within which there would be a rotating presidency. The Presidential Council would strive to reach decisions by consensus. It would otherwise take decisions by majority vote, provided decisions were supported by at least one member from each constituent state. The common state parliament would be composed of two houses, one representing Greek and Turkish Cypriot citizens and the second representing the two constituent states. Decisions would require the approval of both chambers by simple majority, including one quarter (or two-fifths for specified matters) of voting Senators from each constituent state. The Supreme Court would be represented by an equal number of Greek and Turkish Cypriots and would serve as a dispute-resolving mechanism if common state institutions became deadlocked.

The constitutional aspect was counterbalanced by territorial proposals which provided for a reduction of the northern zone to 28.5 per cent of the land. Territorial readjustments in turn would allow the majority of Greek Cypriot displaced persons to return to their properties under Greek Cypriot rule. Most of the remaining displaced persons would have the right to reinstatement of one-third of the value and one-third of the area of their total property. They would receive compensation for the remaining two-thirds.

In terms of military security, the Greek and Turkish contingents would be reduced to 6,000 troops until 2011, and 3,000 troops until 2018 (or until Turkey's EU membership). Thereafter figures would be scaled down to the figures envisaged in the 1959 Treaty of Alliance with the objective of complete demilitarisation (Main Articles, article 8.1b). A UN peace-keeping force, empowered by a new mandate, would monitor the implementation of the agreement. The 1959 Treaty of Guarantee would remain in force but would be amended so as to allow the three guarantors to protect the constitutional status and territorial integrity not only of the common state, but also of the two constituent states (Main Articles, article 8.1a). The UN Plan further stipulated that Cyprus would not put its territory at the disposal of international military operations (including European Security and Defence operations) without the consent of both constituent states and of both Greece and Turkey until the accession of Turkey (Main Articles, article 8.4; Constitution, article 53).

Turning now specifically to the manner in which the United Cyprus Republic was foreseen to operate within the EU, a key feature of the Plan was its provision regarding Cyprus' participation in EU decision-making. The Annan Plan aimed to make a settlement within the EU more appealing to the sceptical Turkish Cypriot side by endorsing the Belgian model of domestic coordination and policy implementation on EU matters. The Plan stated that:

> constituent states shall participate in the formulation and implementation of policy in external relations and EU affairs on matters within their sphere of competence in accordance with Cooperation agreements modelled on the Belgian example.
>
> (Main Articles, article 2.2)

Thus, as in Belgium, the Plan stated that the various levels of government would need to coordinate their stances in order to reach common positions to be represented at EU level. The Belgian model of domestic coordination is based on the consensus principle whereby each participating entity (i.e. each federal and federated representative) can potentially use its right of veto and thus block the coordination process (Kerremans 2000). As in the case of Belgium, the Annan Plan also stipulated that the implementation of EU laws and regulations would be shared in accordance with the internal division of powers (Constitution, article 19.4). By emulating these aspects of the Belgian model, the Annan Plan enhanced the role of the constituent state level, which would be entitled to exert its powers both within the common state, and, through the UCR, outside it (in Brussels). More precisely, the constituent states could use their constitutionally enshrined rights and competences to play a role beyond the United Cyprus Republic in the formulation and implementation of EU policy. These provisions were highly appreciated by the Turkish Cypriot side, without being resisted by the Greek Cypriot leadership.

However, while the Annan Plan's formulations on domestic coordination on and implementation of EU matters were modelled on the Belgian example, those on representation in EU Councils were rather vague, departing from the Belgian model. Article 19.3 of the Constitution, making use of the possibilities allowed for under article 146 of the Treaty of the EU, stated:

> Cyprus shall be represented in the EU by the federal government in its areas of competence or where a matter predominantly concerns an area of its competence. Where a matter falls predominantly or exclusively into an area of competence of the constituent states, Cyprus *may* be represented either by a federal government or by a constituent state representative, provided the latter is able to commit Cyprus [my italics].

This meant that Cyprus, together with the Belgian, German and Austrian federations, would have belonged to the limited number of member states that can be represented at the EU level by federated entities (Kovziridze

2002). However, unlike Belgium – where in areas of competence of the federated entities the Federation can be only represented in EU Councils by these entities acting as leaders of the Belgian delegation – the Annan Plan merely allowed for the possibility of sub-state representation in EU Councils, without making it mandatory. In this respect the regulations in the Plan resembled the German and Austrian models of representation rather than the Belgian one.

The Annan Plan ensured that the implementation of the EU *acquis communautaire* would not become a hindrance to an agreement. Most of the provisions of the *acquis* would be implemented in EU member Cyprus. This was in line both with the requirements of accession and with Greek Cypriot interests. However, in the 'Draft Act of Adaptation' the Plan set out a number of temporary exemptions to the *acquis*, intended to allay Turkish Cypriot concerns about being overwhelmed by the larger and richer Greek Cypriot community. In terms of the 'three freedoms', there would be restrictions on the freedoms of settlement and property acquisition, to be phased out over 20 years or retained if the Turkish Cypriot state's GDP did not reach 85 per cent of that of the Greek Cypriot state (Draft Act of Adaptation, article 1.1). In another temporary exemption to the *acquis*, residence rights for citizens hailing from the other constituent state would be limited and phased out over 19 years (or until Turkey's EU membership) (Draft Act of Adaptation, article 2). The Turkish Cypriot constituent state could also adopt temporary economic 'safeguard measures' during the first six years of EU membership, if EU internal market laws threatened the economic development of northern Cyprus (Draft Act of Adaptation, article 4.1).

The Draft Act of Adaptation also set out temporary exemptions to the *acquis* that would ensure the greatest possible balance between the rights of Greece and Turkey despite Greece and Cyprus' EU membership and Turkey's temporary exclusion. The retention of equal numbers of Greek and Turkish troops (until Turkey's EU membership), the continuation of the Treaty of Guarantee and the exclusion of Cyprus from possible ESDP operations created a balance in the security and military sphere. In the economic sphere, the Plan stipulated that Cyprus would accord both Greece and Turkey 'most favoured nation' status and apply the rules of the EU–Turkey customs union. The Plan also attempted to retain a balance between Greece and Turkey in the spheres of property acquisition, residence and movement of persons (Draft Act of Adaptation, article 3). For 19 years or until Turkey's EU membership, the right of Greek (Turkish) nationals to reside in Cyprus would be restricted if this figure amounted to more than 5 per cent of the number of resident Greek Cypriot constituent state citizens. The Plan also stated that Greek and Turkish nationals would receive equal treatment in their movements to and from Cyprus. The Plan did not specify whether this entailed Cyprus' non-participation in the Schengen system, or whether additional benefits would be extended to Turkey in Cyprus, despite its non-membership of the EU (and non-inclusion in the EU visa-free list).

The impact of the EU accession process on the principal parties in the conflict

The Annan Plan used many of the provisions of the EU framework to embed a settlement in the EU. But to what extent, and through what mechanisms, were the features of the EU appreciated by the conflicting parties? And what, in turn, was the impact of the accession process on the principal parties to the conflict? When discussing the meaning of the EU dimension in the Cyprus conflict, the starting point is the differentiated interpretation and value of EU accession to the domestic players, who had different interests and different ideological standpoints. The accession process had a dual effect on these domestic players. On the one hand, it has transformed their ideological and bargaining positions. On the other hand, it has been used by the domestic players to legitimise their ideological positions and further their interests.

The EU accession process, particularly in its final stage (which coincided with the latest UN mediation efforts), had diverse effects on the Greek and Turkish Cypriot political elites (Brewin 2000; Diez 2002; Tocci 2002). It induced the more moderate forces in Cyprus to be more active in seeking a solution prior to accession, while it contributed to a covert hardening of the positions of the least flexible forces.

To begin with the Greek Cypriot side, it is important to note that the decision to apply for and pursue EU membership in the early 1990s was linked to the aim of strengthening the Greek Cypriot bargaining position in negotiations. First, the EU accession process and final EU membership would bolster the RoC's status as the only legitimate government on the island, it would further discredit the TRNC, and it would provide the RoC with an additional forum in which to put forward its cause. Second, Cyprus' accession process would increase Greek Cypriot leverage over Turkey both because of an expected rise in EU pressure on Turkey and because of Turkey's own aspirations to join the Union. Third, membership would yield critical security gains to the Greek Cypriots, given the unlikelihood of a Turkish attack on an EU member state. Finally, with the implementation of the *acquis* liberalising the 'four freedoms' (of movement of goods, services, capital and labour), accession would provide a framework for the liberalisation of the 'three freedoms' in Cyprus.

In this context, the EU accession process had diverse effects on the Greek Cypriot political elites. Former President Clerides appeared far more open to compromise in 2002–03 than he had been in 1993, when he ran for and won his first presidency on a bid to reject the UN's federal proposals at the time (the 'Set of Ideas'). Two of the key reasons for this change are deeply connected to the ongoing process of Europeanisation in Cyprus. The EU accession process and the immediate prospect of membership imbued the Greek Cypriot political elites with an increased sense of security. This increased the readiness of the moderate forces to make new concessions (such as accepting Turkey's role in Cyprus' security arrangements or accepting limits on the numbers of Greek Cypriot returnees). In this respect, the lifting of conditionality on the Greek Cypriot side in 1999 (i.e. allowing for the possibility of accession without a settlement being a condition) may have had a positive influence on the positions of the former Greek Cypriot leadership.

Europeansation has also had an indirect effect on Cyprus, through the ongoing Europeanisation of Greece, especially in the realm of foreign policy over the course of two decades of EU membership (Ioakimidis 2002). EU membership aided the transformation of Greek governments both at the level of discourse and mode of operation (e.g. increasingly accepting moderate positions and multilateral decision-making) as well as at the level of interest perception and understanding. In the realm of foreign policy, the former Simitis government made a historic u-turn in the official Greek position towards Turkey. For the first time, a Greek government embraced and acted upon the notion that Greek national interests would be served best through a policy of rapprochement with Turkey and through Turkey's inclusion in the EU. Through contact with Greece as well as with EU institutions, Greek Cypriot elites who had been in power during the process of Cyprus' accession (i.e. the two Clerides Presidencies from 1993–2003) learnt this new logic. In turn, they revised their perceived interests and preferred courses of action. In other words, irrespective of EU policies of conditionality, some Greek Cypriot elites came to moderate their views as a result of a more endogenous process of learning.

To the extent that, by 2002, the Greek Cypriot government was genuinely willing to reach a settlement, the accession deadline may have increased their incentives to clinch an early deal (Wallace 2002). Greek Cypriot officials appreciated that the international and domestic momentum generated during 2002–04 would evaporate post-accession. Hence, despite the greater Greek Cypriot bargaining strength after EU entry, this strength could remain latent probably until Turkey's own uncertain accession prospects became clearer. Furthermore, time could work against the Greek Cypriots, given the trends of Turkish Cypriot emigration from, and Turkish immigration to, the island. The EU 'deadline' may therefore have strengthened the previous administration's determination to settle the conflict.

Yet the same cannot be said of the ensuing Papadopoulous administration. The presidential victory of Tassos Papadopoulous in February 2003 led to a resurfacing of Greek Cypriot nationalism. Having secured EU membership, and aided by the non-committal stance of the New Democracy government in Athens (in power since March 2004), Papadopoulous felt unconstrained in his flat rejection of the Annan Plan in April 2004.

The President was well aware of the stronger Greek Cypriot bargaining position post-accession. In his rejection of the Plan, Papadopoulous evidently felt that he would be able to use his increased bargaining strength to secure a more favourable agreement. Not only would member state Cyprus be able to exert pressure on Turkey by hindering its EU accession course, but it would also be in a stronger position to reject any provisions that contravened the EU *acquis*. In other words, the lifting of conditionality on the Greek Cypriot side hardened the positions of the more nationalist forces. The new leadership that came to power only one year before Cyprus' accession, far from having greater incentives to reach an early solution on the basis of a re-conceptualised understanding of Greek Cypriot interests, preferred to wait, and use its greater strength post-accession to bargain a better deal in future.

The discourse used to criticise the provisions of the Draft Act of Adaptation was particularly interesting. Whereas in the past, uncompromising positions were couched in the language of human rights and majoritarian democracy, the accession process allowed the far more specific and binding language of the *acquis* to legitimise inflexibility. The restrictions to the freedom of settlement and property, and the economic safeguards for the Turkish Cypriots, were criticised for being insufficiently 'EU-ised'.

Turning to the Turkish Cypriots, the EU accession process appeared to have its strongest negative effects between 1993 and 2001. They occurred because the presentation of costs and benefits of EU membership was frequently based on misinformation about the EU or about existing practices within the Union. EU institutions over-emphasised the material benefits of accession, without sufficiently highlighting the means and ways in which the EU framework could have accounted for the identity and security needs of the Turkish Cypriots. On the contrary, the Turkish Cypriots initially viewed many aspects of EU accession as a threat to their identity and security. In turn, although for the Turkish Cypriots accession was conditional on a settlement, up until the turn of the century, the perceived benefits of EU membership were simply not valued enough by the authorities for them to make concessions with a view to finding a solution.

The main incentive offered by the Commission to the Turkish Cypriots was economic (Bahceli 2001). But in a context of international isolation stemming from embargoes and trade restrictions, the offer of conditional economic carrots had an adverse effect. The lure of economic incentives was branded a 'bribe' by several Turkish Cypriot and Turkish officials. They argued that if Europeans had been genuinely concerned about the welfare of the Turkish Cypriots they would not have restricted trade since 1994. The 1994 European Court of Justice ruling, banning the export of products carrying Turkish Cypriot certificates of origin, was interpreted as a deliberate and unethical attempt by 'the EU' to strangle the northern economy and force the Turkish Cypriots into compliance with Greek Cypriot demands.

Furthermore, the perceived zero-sum nature of Greek Cypriot gains from EU membership automatically made the Turkish Cypriot leadership view EU accession as a threat to their identity and security. What made matters worse was that, until late in 2001, EU players failed to convey the message, through an effective and systematic information campaign, that many of these perceived threats were in fact based on serious misconceptions of EU law and policy.

Until late 2001, EU players did little to oppose the view that Cyprus' EU membership would necessitate a strongly centralised state in order to speak with a single voice in the EU. The EU did not inform the Turkish Cypriot side about its framework's potential to blur the distinctions between single and divided sovereignty. On the contrary, several EU decisions, such as the 1994 European Court of Justice ruling, highlighted the significance of recognised statehood. Commission officials also did nothing to discredit the view that bi-zonality within the EU called for a confederal rather than a federal agreement. EU law guarantees freedoms between member states. So a confederal (or a two-state solution) within the EU would not guarantee bi-zonality any more than a federal solution would.

Finally, the debate in northern Cyprus suffered from serious misinformation concerning the implications of membership for relations with Turkey. A Turkish argument made against Cyprus' EU membership was that it would contravene the 1960 provisions granting 'most favoured nation' (MFN) status to the three guarantor powers. However, the joint membership of Cyprus, Greece and Turkey in a customs union (as part of the Turkey–EU customs union) should automatically eliminate these concerns. The Turkish side also argued that EU membership would make any future Turkish security guarantee obsolete and that the EU Rapid Reaction Force (RRF) could be mobilised to expel Turkish troops from Cyprus. Yet the mandate of the RRF was not planned to extend beyond limited peace-keeping tasks. The idea of a hypothetical EU military intervention in Cyprus, against Turkey, was a myth that EU officials for too long failed to invalidate.

Because of these concerns, throughout the 1990s Turkish Cypriots and the TRNC establishment supported EU membership only after a settlement and/or after Turkey's accession. Membership after a settlement in Cyprus would mitigate the potential threats from EU accession, while Cypriot membership together with Turkey would provide additional security guarantees. Thus as Cyprus' accession process went ahead while Turkey's path to the EU was blocked, those Turkish Cypriots who supported EU membership only after Turkey's entry became more reluctant to reach an agreement. To the most nationalist forces in northern Cyprus, moreover, the accession of a divided island was seen as a blessing in disguise, by settling the conflict on the basis of partition.

The mounting pressure on the Turkish Cypriot leader, Rauf Denktaş in

2002–03 suggests that the lure of EU accession did generate important incentives amongst the Turkish Cypriot public. While the President continued to dismiss economic incentives as a cheap bribe designed to turn the people against their government, the appeal of EU membership appeared to be gaining hold amongst the public. The increasing divide between the Turkish Cypriot leadership and the public led to important changes within Turkish Cypriot politics in 2003–04. The results of the December 2003 Turkish Cypriot parliamentary elections led for the first time to the relative victory of the pro-solution and pro-EU CTP (Republican Turkish Party). The views of the new Prime Minister reflected those of the majority of the public who backed the Annan Plan in popular referenda on 24 April 2004.

What led to the changes in the Turkish Cypriot political scene? Economic incentives were an important part of the explanation, particularly in view of the steady deterioration of the Turkish Cypriot economy since 1999. However, what apparently lay at the heart of the public's concern was not simply the fear of poverty accentuated by the allure of EU-generated prosperity. It was rather the fear that economic ills and isolation would lead to their disappearance as a self-governing and well-defined community in northern Cyprus – that the Turkish Cypriots would disappear through emigration. These trends, they thought, would become exacerbated following Cyprus' EU membership, as the Greek Cypriot government would make EU passports available to all Cypriots.

Another consequence of isolation was the increasing dependence on Turkey, which led to a growing sense among the Turkish Cypriot public that they were not democratically governing themselves but were being controlled by Ankara. More and more, they saw poverty and isolation not simply as 'economic' issues but also as security- and identity-related issues. Increasingly, they came to view their self-determination and communal security as depending on a solution and EU membership. In other words, the isolation of Turkish Cypriots increased their desire to accede to the Union, partly as a mechanism for securing democratic self-government in northern Cyprus.

The mobilisation of the Turkish Cypriot opposition and public in support of EU membership in 2002–03 was also linked to the publication of the Annan Plan. The Plan showed how a solution and EU membership could satisfy basic Turkish Cypriot needs. In doing so, it laid to rest many Turkish Cypriot fears about EU membership.

Finally, the prospect of Turkey's EU accession was a critical factor. All Turkish Cypriot pro-solution leaders agree that the mass mobilisation would not have been possible without the launching of Turkey's accession process after the December 1999 Helsinki European Council.[3]

The last crucial dimension of the effects of the EU in Cyprus indeed concerns Turkey. As noted above, the prospect of Turkish accession became clearer after the 1999 Helsinki European Council. This improved the prospects for a settlement, by increasing the value of expected EU benefits to Turkey and raising the credibility of EU conditionality. However, the fundamental Turkish and EU ambivalence about Turkey's EU membership continued to have an adverse affect on mediation efforts until 2004. Those in Turkey who were sceptical of Turkey's EU membership vehemently rejected any link between a Cyprus settlement and Turkey's accession. Nationalists argued that Cyprus was a national security issue, which could not be compromised for the sake of the EU. They relied on Turkish Cypriot 'intransigence' to prevent a settlement in Cyprus, which would erect a further barrier in EU–Turkey relations. This, in turn, would reduce EU pressure on Turkey to embark on difficult reforms, and it would provide an opportunity for it to annex northern Cyprus. Those who instead genuinely favoured Turkey's full membership were far readier to accept the link between a settlement and EU–Turkey relations, and became more willing to modify their Turkish position since Turkey was granted candidate status in December 1999. The coming to power of the AKP (Justice and Development Party) in 2002 led to the clearest change in the rhetoric of Turkey's Cyprus policy. In sharp contrast to previous administrations, the government was willing to acknowledge and act upon the fact that Turkey's accession process was effectively conditional upon a settlement.

Yet even after the 1999 Helsinki European Council, the insufficient credibility of EU policies on Turkey strengthened the arguments of nationalist and eurosceptic forces. Moderates in Turkey accepted that because of Turkey's own political and economic shortcomings, Cyprus would join the EU before Turkey. However, they could not accept that, because of unchangeable features of the Turkish state and society (e.g. culture, religion and geography), the EU would keep Cyprus and Turkey on opposite sides of the European divide. Hence, the more EU attitudes and decisions fed Turkish mistrust of the Union, the less credible the positions of Turkish moderates became and in turn, the less well-disposed Turkey became towards a resolution of the conflict. Throughout 2003, trends in Turkey continued to oscillate for and against the Annan Plan. By February 2004, those in Turkey pushing for an early settlement appeared to gain the upper hand. The government's commitment to the February–April 2004 peace process clearly pointed to a new consensus within the Turkish establishment. This new consensus, while being advocated by the AKP government, was either backed or not forcefully opposed by other segments of the establishment, including the influential military.

This argument suggests that while the 'stick' of Cyprus' accession proved insufficient to generate Turkish willingness to seek a solution, the 'carrot' of Turkey's own accession together with a change in Turkey's domestic political dynamics triggered a shift in Turkey's policies towards Cyprus. A greater Turkish readiness to settle the conflict under the current government has been evident. This has been largely due to the government's unprecedented commitment to EU accession (manifested also by the perseverance in pursuing domestic reforms). It has also been due to the increasing link made by EU actors between EU–Turkey relations and conflict settlement. However, without the more credible EU commitments to Turkey since 1999, and particularly since December 2002, stronger conditionality on Turkey probably would have had a limited effect. In other words, without the carrot of a credible Turkish EU accession process, the stick of Cyprus' accession was more likely to consolidate partition rather than catalyse a settlement on the island. As the carrot became more credible and thus more valuable, the Turkish government shifted position in 2003–04.

Conclusions

The 'Annan Plan' was critical in using much of the potential provided by the EU framework to draft proposals accounting for the basic needs of the principal parties and finding compromises between their mutually exclusive positions based on absolute notions of sovereignty and statehood. This does not entail that a solution within the EU framework could have automatically eliminated all sources of friction and disagreement in Cyprus. Nor do the above arguments intend to underestimate the complexity of operating ethno-federations, within or outside the EU. Yet, the EU framework, with its institutions and policies, could have offered the opportunity to draw on an alternative context within which to forge a win–win settlement, opening the way for the gradual resolution of the conflict. The UN Plan sought to draw on that very opportunity. While not being a perfect plan, it used the possibilities within EU law and drew inspiration from the institutional and constitutional practice of several member states to forge proposals that allowed for a greater sharing of sovereignty, for a stronger assurance of individual rights and for a more effective protection of collective rights and security than past mediation attempts.

But EU policies throughout the 1990s failed to present this potential in Cyprus. On the contrary, several EU decisions generated misperceptions about the role and importance of recognised statehood within the Union. These decisions also fuelled greater mistrust, particularly on the Turkish Cypriot and Turkish sides. This in turn entrenched negotiation stances and bolstered the positions of the least compromising elements on all sides of the conflict. The reasons underlying these unintended effects are linked to the broader limits of EU foreign policy in general and EU policies of conditionality in particular. They are connected to the absence of a clear, consistent and common EU policy, including both an objective concerning the most desirable solution as well as a strategy to contribute to it.

In particular, EU actors paid insufficient attention to the reasons behind the strong Greek Cypriot commitment to join the Union, and the effects that Cyprus–EU relations had on internal Greek Cypriot political dynamics. Political and security interests, specifically related to the conflict, led the Greek Cypriot side to engage in the accession process. These gains were not related to an expectation that the Union would foster the emergence of a post-nationalist Cyprus in which ethnic rivalries would be subsumed. The attraction was that of strengthening the Greek Cypriot national cause against its local enemies. The same can be said of other conflicts and ethno-political issues in Europe. Judy Batt notes how Hungary's support for EU membership has been linked to its national ambitions to unite all Hungarians under a common roof (see Chapter 9). Likewise, John McGarry explains how nationalists in Northern Ireland supported EU membership as a means to erode British sovereignty, reduce the importance of the border with Ireland and internationalise the conflict (Chapter 15). In Cyprus, as the receipt of EU-related benefits was freed from progress in conflict settlement, the accession process reduced the incentives to seek an early agreement by those Greek Cypriot nationalists who sought considerable changes in UN guidelines. Those nationalists had the upper hand in southern Cyprus during the referendum campaign in April 2004.

EU institutions also overplayed the importance of material benefits to the Turkish Cypriots while neglecting their fears about how accession would harm their identity and security. Insufficiently attractive gains and the perceived costs that EU membership could entail thus reduced the Turkish Cypriot leadership's incentives to broker a settlement. Furthermore, the fact that full membership of a divided Cyprus could consolidate partition was viewed as a desirable outcome by the most nationalist forces in northern Cyprus and Turkey. To them, EU conditionality, far from acting as an incentive for a settlement, induced even more uncompromising positions. By 2002–03, the Turkish Cypriot government came under increasing pressure from the public, which instead was more persuaded about the desirability of a settlement within the EU. Indeed when push came to shove during the referendum of 24 April 2004, the majority of Turkish Cypriots voted in favour of the Annan Plan and EU accession.

Finally, and particularly until the turn of the century, perhaps the most serious flaw in EU policy was the absence of a strategy towards Turkey. As a result, EU incentives were insufficiently strong to trigger a change in Turkey's Cyprus policy. Following the Turkish elections in November 2002, the domestic dynamics in the country were seriously altered. A more credible EU accession process, together with the rise to power of a government that appeared to be seriously committed to the goal of membership, altered the internal dynamics in Turkey and brought about a change in state policies towards Cyprus. In other words, EU conditionality towards Turkey ultimately had the desired effect as it interacted with different domestic dynamics. But when these positive effects came into play, they could not, alone, secure an agreement on the island.

Notes

1 Introduction: European integration and the nationalities question

* This volume is based largely on papers that were presented at a conference on 'European Integration and the Nationalities Question', which took place at the European University Institute, Florence, in May of 2004. We express our thanks to the Carnegie Corporation of New York for funding the conference as well as our own research.

1 The last two are not restricted to European states, but both are heavily European in their composition and focus.

2 Settlers are different from immigrant groups, and not just because they are generally not voluntarily admitted. Settlers often come around the same time and from the same place, in significant numbers, and locate in the same region. They tend to strongly think of themselves as a community. Most immigrant groups come as individuals, at different times, from different places, settle in dispersed patterns, albeit sometimes in ghettoes, and, while they may have a view of themselves as a community, e.g. Muslims in France, or Kurds in Germany, are seldom as tightly integrated as settler groups.

3 Note that some academics distinguish between 'minority nations' and 'national minorities', and between the rights that each is entitled to. For Seymour *et al.* (1998), a minority nation is a group without a state, and is entitled to self-determination. A national minority, on the other hand, is a group that lives within a minority nation's homeland, and whose ethnic kin dominate the state. A national minority, in their view, has no right to self-determination, only a right to be fairly integrated in a self-determining unit. This distinction is designed to show that the Québécois have a right to self-determination, but Quebec's Anglophone community have no right to have their regions remain in Canada after Quebec's independence. It is an example of philosophy being informed by, rather than informing, a particular political project.

4 On three occasions within the past few months, one of us has been corrected for using the term minority when speaking about a 'nationality'. The offended people were, respectively, Québécois, Kurds and (south) Ossetians.

5 Virtually all Protestants, however, are unionists (British nationalists).

6 The relevant passage from the 'Discourse on Political Economy' reads:

> If children are brought up in common ... imbued with the laws of the state and the precepts of the general will; if they are taught to respect these above all things; if they are surrounded by examples and objects which constantly remind them of the tender mother who nourishes them, of the love she bears them, of the inestimable benefits they receive from

her, and of the return they owe her, we cannot doubt that they will learn to cherish one another mutually as brothers, to will nothing contrary to the will of society . . . and to become in time defenders and fathers of the country of which they will have been so long the children.

7 Indeed, even those who did not support an eventual European federation hoped for the transcendence of aggressive nationalism. This is one interpretation of Bevan's speech on 22 January 1948, in which he indicated that the British government supported 'the closer consolidation and economic development [of Europe] and eventually . . . the spiritual unity of Europe as a whole' (cited in McKay 1996: 37–8).

8 Most contemporary versions of this line of argument tend to nod in a postmodernist direction, emphasizing the challenge posed to the nation-state model, with its modernist emphasis on unity, sovereignty and consensus, in favour of a post-modernist preference for *dissensus* (diversity without synthesis) (see Kristeva 1995; Bhabha 1990; Ricoeur 1995). However, this view is rarely discussed in the concrete form that is necessary to allow a full assessment of it.

9 With the exception of supporters of political violence, a small minority among Basque nationalists.

10 For a strong statement of this position, see Kymlicka 2001a: 28–9. Not all 'progressives' lambast minority nationalism. There is a tradition on the left that sees minority nationalism as associated with anti-imperialism. Thus, Tom Nairn is insistent that we should support minority nationalism if we think, along democratic and anti-imperialist lines, that people should govern themselves, and alien rule should be resisted (see Nairn 1997: 47–8).

11 This argument is frequently made in terms of allowing multiple layers of compatible identification – local, national and European (see Taylor 1995). For a similar, but much less sympathetic (to nationalism) reading, see Kristeva (1995).

12 This is why Quebec sovereigntists object to the Canadian Charter of Rights and Freedoms, which they identify with Pierre Trudeau's Canadian nation-building agenda. Quebec sovereigntists are not against rights per se, which is how their position is sometimes interpreted. Indeed, the province has its own provincial Charter of Rights and Freedoms, which, while it is a provincial statute and not a constitutional document, has been used to strike down provincial legislation.

13 The latter explain that not only did pressure from the EU lead to a more liberal naturalization regime in Estonia, but also made the Russian minority more willing to apply for citizenship, as this entailed access to a European passport. As a result, the proportion of the country's population that holds citizenship has increased from just above three-fifths shortly after independence to four-fifths currently.

14 Baubock is also pessimistic that Western Europe's practice of granting autonomy to nationalities will lead to the EU endorsing a general right to minority self-government (Chapter 5).

15 Serbia has lost Kosovo *de facto* but not yet *de jure*.

16 While most Eastern European states have now signed and ratified the FCNM, Belgium, France, Greece, Luxembourg and the Netherlands have not done so. See http://conventions.coe.int/Treaty/Commun/ChercheSig.asp?NT=157&CM=2&DF=18/04/02&CL=ENG (accessed 16 September 2005).

17 Concern for the Roma, however, did not seriously affect the accession process. Sasse notes that the EU harshly criticized the candidate countries for their treatment of the Roma, while simultaneously acknowledging that they continued 'to fulfil the Copenhagen criteria'. The EU and the candidate countries, she argues, 'appear to be acting out a charade on Roma policy' (Chapter 4).

2 Europe, the state and the nation

1 A more detailed version of this argument, including cases, is given in Keating (2004a).

3 Evolving basis of European norms of minority rights: rights to culture, participation and autonomy

1 See the issue of the *New Statesman and Society*, 19 June 1992, headlined 'Eurogeddon? The Coming Conflagration in East–Central Europe'.

2 By 'national minorities' I mean groups living on (what they view to be) their historic homeland, but whose homeland (or part of it) has been incorporated into a larger state in which they form a minority. This includes both transborder minorities – i.e. national groups which form the majority in one state, but whose historic homeland extends across what is now an international boundary, so that some members of the group are on the 'wrong' side of the border from their 'kin-state' (e.g. ethnic Hungarians in Romania and Slovakia). It also includes stateless nations – i.e. groups which think of themselves as 'nations' but do not control any state, and whose historic homeland is incorporated into a larger country (e.g. Scots) or divided between two or more countries (e.g. Basques). Some commentators would also include indigenous peoples, like the Sami, into this category, since they too share the characteristic of having their historic homeland incorporated into a larger state. However, most commentators distinguish indigenous peoples from national minorities, partly on the grounds that indigenous peoples have not traditionally understood themselves as 'nations', or engaged in the project of 'nation-building'. I return to these definitional issues below.

3 The EU did set up the European Monitoring Centre on Racism and Xenophobia in 1997, but it has focused primarily on immigrant groups (rather than national minorities), and primarily on member states in the West, not post-communist Europe.

4 See Brett (1993: 157–8). For a detailed discussion of the way various countries try to deny the existence of minorities see Greek Helsinki Monitor (2000) and Dimitras (2004).

5 Since 1966, the UN Human Rights Committee has attempted to re-interpret the Article so as to include certain positive rights, particularly for indigenous peoples, but it has not been interpreted in a way that addresses the positive claims underlying the conflicts in post-communist Europe.

6 For a more detailed elaboration of the way that traditional civil rights principles fail to protect national minorities from grave injustice see Kymlicka (2001c: chap. 4).

7 For example, the UN's Convention on the Protection of the Rights of All Migrant Workers (1990).

8 For example, these norms often allow minorities to submit documents to public authorities in their language, but do not require that they get an answer in their own language.

9 One possible exception to this generalisation is the Roma. Some commentators speculate that issues relating to the Roma could become sources of violence and instability, even though the Roma have not shown an interest in territorial autonomy or in creating their own separate public institutions. European organisations are therefore devoting much time and effort into examining state policies towards the Roma. However, the current FCNM/OSCE norms were not intended to deal with the situation of the Roma. Indeed, the OSCE has recently recommended the adoption of a separate Romani Rights Charter.

10 There is no conceptual or philosophical reason why a right to enjoy one's culture cannot be interpreted in such a robust way as to support claims to territorial autonomy or official language status. Indeed, this is precisely what various 'liberal nationalist' political theorists have done in their writings. The idea of a right to culture is invoked by writers like Yael Tamir and Joseph Raz as the basis for their defence of a right to national self-determination (Margalit and Raz 1990; Tamir 1993). But, politically speaking, there is no chance that such a 'nationalist' reading of a right to culture will be adopted in international law. As I discuss below, the Article 27 right to enjoy one's culture was intended as an alternative to the right of national self-determination.

11 See, for example, Hofmann (2002a: 254–6).

12 It is worth noting that none of the EU states has ratified the 1990 UN Convention on migrant rights.

13 It would be ironic if European norms on the rights of national minorities turned out to be more beneficial to immigrant groups, for whom they were not originally intended, than for the ethnonational groups whose plight generated the call for international norms in the first place.

14 Article 1: 'All peoples have the right of self-determination. By virtue of that right they freely determine their political status and freely pursue their economic, social and cultural development'.

15 My focus here is on groups that demonstrate a desire for TA, as reflected for example in consistently high levels of support for politicians or political parties that campaign for TA. We can call these 'mobilised' national minorities, since their members have demonstrated consistent support for national(ist) goals of autonomy and official language rights. The emergence of such mobilised national minorities is of course the result of political contestation. National minorities do not enter the world with a fully-formed nationalist consciousness: they are constructed by ethnic entrepreneurs and ethnic elites who seek to persuade enough of their members that it makes sense to mobilise politically as a national minority for national goals. There are cases where these attempts to generate a nationalist consciousness amongst the members of a minority have failed. One clear case in Western Europe are the Frisians in the Netherlands. From a historical viewpoint, they have as much claim to be a distinct 'people' as any other ethnonational group in Europe. Yet attempts by Frisian elites to persuade people of Frisian descent, or people living in historic Friesland, that they should support nationalist political objectives have repeatedly failed. This is of course fully acceptable from a liberal point of view. National minorities may have a *right* to claim territorial autonomy, but they certainly have no *duty* to do so. Whether or not a national minority claims territorial autonomy should be determined by the wishes of the majority of its members, as shaped and expressed through free democratic debate and contestation.

My focus here is on how European states deal with those groups that have demonstrated a desire for TA – i.e. in which nationalist political leaders have succeeded in a free and democratic debate in gaining the support of a majority of the members of the group. I am not assuming that such nationalist constructions will (or should) succeed. Their success has to be explained, not simply taken, just as the failure of the nationalists in Friesland has to be explained, rather than taken as somehow normal or natural. My project in this chapter is not to explain the success or failure of particular acts of nationalist construction, but rather to explore how states should respond to the cases of successful mobilisation, in which the members of national minority groups have shown consistently high levels of support for nationalist objectives. It is these cases that are the 'problem' to which European organisations were seeking a solution through the adoption of international norms of minority rights.

16 For a more detailed defence of this claim see Kymlicka (2004).

17 Indeed, the most influential discussion and defence of the international law on indigenous rights accepts that other national groups should also be able to claim rights to internal self-determination (Anaya 1996). For a detailed discussion of the similarities and differences between indigenous peoples and national minorities, see Kymlicka (2001c: chap. 6). It is worth noting that organisations representing one national minority in Eastern Europe – namely, the Crimean Tatars – have explicitly defined themselves as an 'indigenous people' for the purposes of international law.

18 The Hague Recommendations on Education Rights of National Minorities (1996); Oslo Recommendations on Linguistic Rights of National Minorities (1998); Lund Recommendations on Effective Participation of National Minorities (1999).

19 The European Free Alliance, a coalition of minority nationalist parties from various regions of Western Europe (e.g. Catalonia, Scotland, Flanders), proposed that the EU Constitution contain a clause that recognised 'the right of self-government of all those territorial entities in the Union whose citizens have a strong and shared sense of national, linguistic or regional identity'. The proposal was never seriously debated (www.greens-efa.org).

20 I criticise Offe's claim that escalation and proliferation are inherent dangers of TA in Kymlicka (2002).

21 This is one of the factors that contributes to the general 'securitisation' of state–minority relations in post-communist Europe – see Kymlicka (2004). It is interesting to note that even when national minorities in the West are linked by ethnicity to a neighbouring state, they do not today raise fears of disloyalty or security. The French in Switzerland or Belgium are not seen as a fifth-column for France; the Flemish are not seen as a fifth-column for the Netherlands. Even the Germans in Belgium, who have historically collaborated with Germany's aggression against Belgium, are no longer viewed that way. This is testament to the extraordinary success of the EU and NATO in 'desecuritising' ethnic relations in Western Europe.

22 This is particularly true of those countries, like Romania or Turkey, influenced by the French Jacobin tradition. For the strength of this ideology in post-communist Europe see Liebich (2004).

23 Recall that, prior to 1989, the EU tacitly allowed Greece to persecute its minorities, and NATO allowed Turkey to persecute its minorities (Batt and Amato 1998).

24 When Western governments were deciding whether to intervene in Kosovo, Edward Luttwak, an American security expert and media commentator, famously argued that we should 'give war a chance' (Luttwak 1999). 'War is bad', he said, 'but it is important for both sides to learn the hard way that they can't defeat the other, and so accept the need to sit down and negotiate a compromise'. A more modest version of the same idea is defended by Adam Burgess. He says we should 'give assimilation a chance' (Burgess 1999). Assimilationist policies in post-communist Europe might be unpleasant, and might fail, but it is important for states (and dominant groups) to learn the limits of their capacities, and the strength of minority resistance, and so accept the necessity of coming to some settlement with their minorities.

25 For a more detailed discussion of these two tracks see Kymlicka and Opalski (2001: 369–86).

26 It is interesting to note that the draft EU Constitution incorporates all of the 'Copenhagen criteria' except for minority rights. This is a tacit recognition, I suspect, that the 1991 decision to make minority rights a determinant of EU membership was based on a (mis)-reading of events in the early 1990s, not any genuine normative commitment.

27 Chandler (1999: 68). Cf. 'Minorities should not be confronted with the situation that the international community will only respond to their concerns if there is a conflict. Such an approach could easily backfire and generate more conflicts than it resolves. An objective, impartial and non-selective approach to minorities, involving the application of minority standards across the board, must therefore remain a crucial part' (Alfredsson and Turk 1993: 176–7).

28 In all of these cases except Crimea, the minority seized power through an armed uprising. In the case of Crimea, the Ukrainian state barely existed on Crimean territory, and so the Russians did not have to take up arms to overthrow the existing state structure. They simply held an (illegal) referendum on autonomy and then started governing themselves.

29 'The participating States will respect the right of persons belonging to national minorities to effective participation in public affairs, including participation in the affairs relating to the protection and promotion of the identity of such minorities' (OSCE Copenhagen Declaration 1990: Article 35). 'The Parties shall create the conditions necessary for the effective participation of persons belonging to national minorities in cultural, social and economic life and in public affairs, in particular those affecting them' (FCNM 1995: Article 15).

30 Annelies Verstichel argues that the Advisory Committee examining conformity with the FCNM has implicitly adopted a non-retrogression clause regarding autonomy (Verstichel 2002/3). Similarly, Lewis-Anthony argues that the jurisprudence regarding Article 3 of the First Protocol of the European Charter of Human Rights can be extrapolated to protect existing forms of autonomy (Lewis-Anthony 1998). At a more philosophical level, Allen Buchanan argues that there should be international protections for existing forms of TA, but denies that there should be norms supporting claims for TA by groups that do not yet have it (Buchanan 2004).

31 This puts a different light on claims about the 'essentialising' character of minority rights. I noted earlier that many post-modernists and critical theorists have rejected the idea of substantive minority rights to culture or self-determination on the grounds that they prejudge and falsely homogenise the character of the group. Yet in rejecting such claims, they did not intend to be supporting essentialising accounts of the 'nation-state' as a unitary and monolingual state composed of a single people. They hoped that the idea of effective participation could be neutral in the struggle between minority nationalists and nationalising states, and could be implemented without prejudging whether it is a multilingual, multination state or a monolingual, unitary nation-state. Yet it is not clear to me that the idea of effective participation can be implemented without taking a stand on this question. If so, the risk of essentialism arises equally whether we accept or reject claims to internal self-determination. Accepting such claims runs the risk of essentialising our conception of the national minority; rejecting them runs the risk of essentialising our conception of the state. Whichever choice we make, we must therefore put in place safeguards that allow citizens to continually challenge oppressive essentialisms, whether minoritarian or majoritarian. This is a central element of a genuinely *liberal* conception of minority rights.

32 For optimistic views along these lines see Verstichel (2002/03) and Weller (2003).

33 Conversely, several commentators argue that some of the more intractable conflicts in the West, such as Northern Ireland and Cyprus, cannot be resolved by purely domestic procedures and negotiations, and that the international community needs to play a more active role. See the essays in Keating and McGarry (2001b).

34 For a discussion of some of the factors that have helped make these settlements domestically self-sustaining and self-enhancing see Kymlicka (2003).

35 The role of violence is obvious in Northern Ireland, the Basque Country, Cyprus and Corsica, but there were also low-level acts of violence in Quebec and South Tyrol (e.g. bombings of state property like mailboxes or energy pylons). The knowledge that some members of the minority were willing to resort to violence undoubtedly concentrated the mind of the state. As Deets puts it, 'Across Europe, autonomy came out of specific historical and political contexts, and it is far easier to discuss the political calculations and the desire to quell bombing campaigns that went into autonomy decisions than it is to point to a clear acceptance of principles of justice for minorities' (Deets 2002a).

36 However, the case of indigenous peoples shows what can be achieved on these issues through international law where there is a political commitment to do so.

37 Or so I argue in Kymlicka and Opalski (2001).

4 National minorities and EU enlargement: external or domestic incentives for accommodation?

1 This chapter is based on research conducted within the framework of a Leverhulme Research Fellowship. It has also been supported by an LSE STICERD grant and a Jean Monnet Fellowship at the European University Institute, Florence.

2 Non-discrimination as an EU norm is rooted in the Treaties of Maastricht and Amsterdam, the Directives 2000/78/EC and 2000/43/EC and ECJ rulings. Their transposition into national legislation is covered by the third Copenhagen criterion, referring to the adoption of the *acquis*. For a case-by-case overview of the gradual adoption of anti-discrimination norms and legislation, see European Commission, Directorate General (DG) Employment and Social Affairs Unit D.4, *Equality, diversity and enlargement. Report on measures to combat discrimination in acceding and candidate countries*, Luxembourg: European Communities, 2003.

3 Article F TEU stipulated that 'The Union shall respect fundamental rights, as guaranteed by the European Convention for the Protection of Human Rights and Fundamental Freedoms signed in Rome on 4 November 1950 and as they result from the constitutional traditions common to the Member States, as general principles of Community law.' See www.eurotreaties.com/maastrichtec.pdf.

4 For a reminder of the limits of this human rights conditionality, see Bruno de Witte and Gabriel N. Toggenburg (2004: 61–62).

5 After the EU Copenhagen criteria were formulated, but before the accession negotiations began, the Council of Europe's Framework Convention for the Protection of National Minorities (FCNM) of 1995 put in place a complex and legally binding pan-European instrument for the continuous assessment of minority issues. Members (and non-members) of the Council of Europe can choose, however, whether or not to ratify the FCNM.

6 See Chapter 4 of the Document of the Copenhagen Meeting of the Conference on the Human Dimension of the CSCE, 5–29 June 1990: www.osce.org/docs/english/1990-1999/hd/cope90e.htm.

7 See under 'Human Dimension' at www.osce.org/docs/english/1990-1999/summits/paris90e.htm#Anchor-Huma-3228

8 For a discussion of the methodological pitfalls in the study of conditionality, see Hughes *et al.* (2004: chap. 1). For a taxonomy of EU conditionality, see Heather Grabbe (2001: 8(6): 1013–31).

9 Here the author's interviews with 16 Commission officials (DG Enlargement,

DG Justice and Home Affairs, DG External Relations, DG Employment and Social Affairs, Legal Service), conducted in Brussels on 12–13 January 2004 and 19–20 February 2004 have been a valuable source.

10 See europa.eu.int/eur-lex/en/treaties/dat/eu_cons_treaty_en.pdf.

11 See, for example, footnote 3 in the 2002 Regular Report on Bulgaria's progress towards accession, p. 18; europa.eu.int/comm/enlargement/report2002/bu_en.pdf.

12 See europa.eu.int/comm/enlargement/pas/phare/statistics/commit_sector.pdf.

13 The bodies set up under the Europe Agreements, such as the annual meeting of the Association Committee and the Joint Parliamentary Committee provided a limited additional forum for the discussion of political issues (including minority protection).

14 Author's interviews with officials from the Country Desks in DG Enlargement, the Horizontal Co-ordination Unit and the Legal Service, Brussels, 12–13 January 2004. The manual, which was prepared each year by the Horizontal Co-ordination Unit for the Country Desks in advance of the drafting of the Regular Reports, listed the FCNM as an explicit point of reference.

15 'These meetings helped us to get a flavour of the wider process we were part of'; author's interview with a Commission official, formerly Horizontal Co-ordination Unit, DG Enlargement, 13 January 2004.

16 Author's interview with a Commission official, formerly DG Enlargement, 13 January 2004.

17 Ibid.

18 The checklist on minority issues in the Unit's handbook for 2002 included the following: ratification and implementation of the FCNM; the situation of the Roma, ethnic Russians and other minorities; citizenship legislation, rate of naturalisation, stateless children, non-citizens' passports; active policies to integrate minorities; language legislation/language training programmes; professional restrictions; minority-rights ombudsman (if relevant).

19 Author's interview with a Commission official, formerly DG Enlargement, 13 January 2004.

20 Author's interview with a Commission official, Horizontal Co-ordination Unit, DG Enlargement, 13 January 2004.

21 Author's interview with a Commission official, DG Enlargement, Brussels, 12 January 2004.

22 Author's interview with a Commission official, DG Enlargement, Brussels, 13 January 2004.

23 Regular Report on Romania's progress towards accession, 1998 (hereafter referred to as Report on Romania, 1998), p. 12; Report on Romania, 2001, p. 29; Report on Slovakia, 1999, p. 16; Report on Slovakia, 2002, p. 33; Report on Estonia, 2000, p. 20; Report on Estonia, 2001, p. 23.

24 Report on Hungary, 2001, p. 22; Report on Hungary, 2002, p. 30. The Reports are available at europa.eu.int/comm/enlargement/index_en.html.

25 See OJ L68 of 9.3.98, pp. 3–4 and OJ L26 of 2.2.98, pp. 3–4.

26 Report on Latvia, 1998, p. 11.

27 Report on Latvia, 1999, p. 17.

28 Report on Latvia, 2001, p. 26.

29 As a Commission official put it: 'Although the closure of the OSCE missions was not a formal condition, the Commission had a clear interest in it' (author's interview with a Commission official, DG Enlargement, Brussels, 12 January 2004).

30 Report on Latvia, 2002, pp. 30–5.

31 This inherent tension is particularly striking in the Reports on the Czech

Republic, which refer to the construction of a wall in Ušti nad Lábem that physically separates Roma and non-Roma residents. See the Report on the Czech Republic, 1999, pp. 16–17; ibid, 2000, pp. 25–7.

32 Author's interview with a Commission official, DG Enlargement, 13 January 2004.

33 Report on Slovakia, 2000, p. 22; ibid, 2000, p. 31.

34 Report on Bulgaria, 2002, p. 33. Without referring back to this alarmist scenario, the 2003 Report offers a much more optimistic assessment based on more realistic budgetary provisions for a government programme: 'On the whole, initiatives have started to address the situation of the Roma minority', see Report on Bulgaria, 2003, p. 26.

35 Report on Bulgaria, 1999, p. 75.

36 Report on Romania, 2003, p. 30.

37 The following quotes, unless specifically footnoted, are taken from the author's interviews with 7 Commission officials from DG Enlargement (Country Desks and Horizontal Co-ordination Unit) which were conducted in Brussels on 12 and 13 January 2004.

38 Author's interview with an official from the Legal Service, Brussels, 13 January 2004.

39 Author's interview with a Commission official, DG Justice and Home Affairs, 12 January 2004.

40 Author's interview with a Commission official, Horizontal Co-ordination Unit, DG Enlargement, 13 January 2004.

41 France has not even signed it; see conventions.coe.int/Treaty/EN/CadreListe-Traites.htm.

42 Bulgaria, Declaration of 7 May 1999.

43 Estonia, Declaration of 6 January 1997.

44 Poland, Declaration of 20 December 2000.

45 Slovenia, Declaration of 25 March 1998. According to the 1991 census, there were 81,220 Serbo-Croat speakers, and 52,110 Croat speakers, but only 9,240 Hungarian speakers, 4,009 Italian speakers, and 2,847 Romani speakers; see www.ecmi.de/emap/slo_stat.html.

46 Romania, the Czech Republic and Poland have signed, though not yet ratified the ECRML.

47 Slovenia, Declaration of 4 October 2000.

48 Slovakia, Declaration of 5 September 2001.

49 After the introduction of the Regular Reports all of the candidates of CEE formally adopted government programmes to protect or integrate minority groups. According to the 2002 EUMAP, Bulgaria, the Czech Republic, Hungary and Romania are committed to a comprehensive approach to minority protection, by policies to eliminate discrimination and actively promote minority identities. See EUMAP, 2002, p. 25.

50 www.riga.lv/minelres/NationalLegislation/Hungary/Hungary_Minorities_English.htm.

51 Hungary produced a draft anti-discrimination law in the second half of 2003, suggesting a slow uptake of minority-related issues inside the country. Commission officials from DG Employment and DG Enlargement, however, emphasised that the anti-discrimination legislation represents a more comprehensive package than in some other candidate countries and is based on a wider process of consultation (author's interview with a Commission official, DG Enlargement, 20 February 2004 and with a Commission official from the Anti-Discrimination Unit, Fundamental Social Rights and Civil Society, DG Employment and Social Affairs, 20 February 2004).

52 See Deets (2002b: 39)

53 Local self-governments are either set up by the local government or by the initiative of five minority members who gain the support of 100 people in the elections.

54 Deets (2002b: 49).

55 Ibid., p. 50.

56 For a detailed discussion of the 'Status Law' and its challenge to modern notions of territoriality and citizenship, see Brigid Fowler (2002).

57 Report on Hungary, 2001, p. 91; ibid., 2002, p. 122.

58 In the 1996 election this number was as low as about 1,800 votes; see Deets (2002b: 46).

59 Ibid., p. 48.

60 By 1998 Romania was already seen to fulfil the political Copenhagen criteria; see Report on Romania, 1998, p. 12.

61 Ibid., p. 23.

62 The coalition also agreed to sign the European Charter on Regional and Minority Languages and the FCNM.

63 See Slovakia's Law on the Use of Minority Languages (11 July 1999), Article 2(1), 51; www.riga.lv/minelres/NationalLegislation/Slovakia/Slovakia_Minor-Lang_English.htm. The Romanian Law on Local Public Administration (23 April 2001) envisages the same threshold; see www.riga.lv/minelres/National-Legislation/Romania/Romania_LocAdm2001_excerpts_English.htm.

64 For a discussion of the interaction of Slovakia's laws and EU pressures, see Farimah Daftary and Kinga Gál, 'The New Slovak Language Law: internal or external politics', *ECMI Working Paper* no. 8, September 2000: 1–71; see www.ecmi.de/doc/download/working_paper_8.pdf.

65 GVT/COM/INF/OP/I(2001)001 E Slovakia; points 33–36.

66 See www.europa.eu.int/comm/external_relations/see/docs/conditionality_29_april_97.htm.

67 See europa.eu.int/eur-lex/en/treaties/dat/ec_cons_treaty_en.pdf; Council Directive 2000/43/EC of 29 June 2000: OJ L 180, 19.07.2000.

68 For a systematic discussion see Bruno de Witte (forthcoming). For a related discussion of the future of minority protection in a supranational context see also Gabriel von Toggenburg's introduction to the same volume.

69 The Network presents its annual reports as a follow-up to the EU's Regular Reports, in particular in the area of minority rights and non-discrimination; see EU Network of Independent Experts in Fundamental Rights, *Report on the Situation of Fundamental Rights in the European Union and its Member States in 2002*, Luxembourg: European Communities, 2003, p. 21.

70 The Representatives of the Member States, meeting at Head of State or Government level in Brussels on 13 December 2002, agreed to extend its mandate to become a Human Rights Agency; see www.ueitalia2003.it/NR/rdonlyres/7FAB788D-1686-4A44-B977-974CCB70F69B/0/1205_location_EN.pdf. According to a Commission official, this Council decision 'came as a complete surprise to the Commission' and forms part of a 'late-night political deal'; author's interview with a Commission official, DG External Relations, 20 February 2004.

71 'The Union is founded on the values of respect for human dignity, liberty, democracy, equality, the rule of law and respect for human rights. These values are common to the Member States in a society of pluralism, tolerance, justice, solidarity and non-discrimination.'

72 See the text of Article I-2 proposed by the Italian Presidency on 25 November 2003, CIG 52/03.

73 CIG 73/04 (Annex 1), Brussels, 29 April 2004 and CIG 85/04, Brussels, 18 June 2004.

5 Autonomy, power-sharing and common citizenship – principles for accommodating national minorities in Europe

1 Csergö and Goldgeier (2004: 23) have recently suggested another typology of nationalisms in Europe that aims at 'comparing national groups and governments that want to weaken state sovereignties with those that do not'. They therefore classify national minority secessionism and kin-state irredentism as traditional forms of nationalism, while identifying as sub-state and transsovereign nations only those groups and states that forgo political ambitions to change international borders. One should, however, remain aware that both sub-state and transborder nationalist movements can adopt either 'sovereigntist' or 'post-sovereigntist' ideological orientations.

2 Keating's definition of national minorities combines these two elements:

> The latter are groups located territorially within a wider nationality but who do not identify with it, often because they identify with a group elsewhere, including one in another state. They have thus not constituted themselves as a distinct group claiming self-determination.
>
> (Keating 2001a: 5)

The conclusion in the last sentence appears to me questionable. National minorities that identify with a kin-state or a group elsewhere (e.g. the German language group in South Tyrol or the Swedish population of the Åland Islands) may still claim self-determination or self-government and have in fact often done so. The distinction between stateless nations and external national minorities has no obvious implications for the group's desire, capacity or right of self-government.

3 Article 3 of the First Protocol of the European Convention on Human Rights defines a right to free elections 'under conditions which will ensure the free expression of the opinion of the people in the choice of the legislature'. This provision has been interpreted as protecting constitutionally recognised special jurisdictions from being abolished or being stripped of their powers (Lewis-Anthony 1998: 341; Suksi 1998: 360).

4 The horizontal dimension may also include bilateral cooperation between particular units outside the federal framework. This dimension is of particular interest in multinational democracies with several autonomous minorities such as Spain. The Catalan and Basque autonomous communities have experimented with various forms of bilateral cooperation in order to strengthen their hand vis-à-vis the Madrid government.

5 I use the term polity to refer to the institutional structure of a political community. Countries such as France, Romania or Turkey include substantial national minorities but have not institutionalised their political autonomy. These countries can thus be described as multinational societies, but not as multinational polities.

6 This principle of international law is spelled out in Article 1 of The Hague Convention on Certain Questions Relating to the Conflict of Nationality Laws (1930).

7 This is, however, a relatively recent development. In the inter-war German and Austrian republics, federal citizenship was still formally derived from provincial citizenship.

8 For Austria and Germany see Waldrauch and Çinar (2003), Hagedorn (2001).

9 In Canada, the Quebec provincial government promotes Francophone immigration by allocating additional points for French language skills, but does not control naturalisation in the province.

10 In South Tyrol, a bilingualism requirement for civil servants has helped to over-

turn the historic dominance of native Italian speakers in the province's administration.

11 In Belgium and Austria, provincial representation in the federal chamber is proportional to population. The German formula balances both concerns. Each province gets between three and six seats depending on its population size, which means that voters in smaller provinces will still be overrepresented in decisions taken by the federal chamber.

12 Since Romania and Serbia are not members of the EU, this law would also create a large number of EU citizens residing permanently outside the EU territory.

13 In an interesting article, Janos Kis (2001) has argued that political communities living on two sides of an international border should have a right to form joint institutions of self-government. For Kis, supranational integration in Europe may provide an umbrella that permits the realisation of such schemes without raising irritations of the kind caused by the Hungarian Status Law. My objections would, however, also apply within a supranational federation.

14 The Austrian role as an external protector of the South Tyrolean autonomy agreement did not involve an offer of dual citizenship for the German-speaking population. Promoting dual citizenship could have easily upset the autonomy solution by signalling that South Tyroleans still consider themselves as belonging to the Austrian polity.

15 The principle that '[t]he Union shall respect the national identities of its Member States' was first inserted into the Treaty on European Union by the Amsterdam Treaty of 1997.

6 Kin-states protecting national minorities: positive trend or dangerous precedent?

1 As prescribed in paragraph 3 Article 6 of the Constitution of the Republic, see preamble to Act on Hungarians Living in Neighbouring Countries.

2 See preamble to the Act on Hungarians Living in Neighbouring Countries.

3 See Article 20(1) of the Act.

4 Ibid.

5 Aide Memoire of the Republic of Slovakia, May 2001.

6 Letter from H.E. Janos Martonyi, Foreign Minister of Hungary, to H.E. Mircea Geaona, Minister for Foreign Affairs of Romania, 27 June 2001.

7 Statement following the meeting between Croatian Assistant Foreign Minister Nenad Prelog and Tibor Szabo, President of the Office for Hungarian Minorities Abroad and Csaba Lorincz, Deputy State Secretary of the Ministry for Foreign Affairs of Hungary, Budapest, 10 July 2001.

8 See also a 'Statement on the Law on Hungarians Living in Neighbouring Countries' made by the delegation of Ukraine to the OSCE, 28 June 2001, PC. DEL/486/01.

9 See annex 2 outlining 'consultation with neighbouring countries' in the Paper Containing the Position of the Hungarian Government in Relation to the Act on Hungarians Living in Neighbouring Countries, Opinion no. 168/2001, Strasbourg, 21 August 2001.

10 Aide Memoire from the Ministry for Foreign Affairs of Hungary, 23 October 2001.

11 European Commission Regular Report, 13 November 2001, p. 91.

12 See for example, an Aide Memoire of the Slovak Republic to the Bill of the

Republic of Hungary on Hungarians Living in Neighbouring Countries, 13 June 2001 and the Aide Memoire of the Slovak Republic of 29 October 2001.

13 Letter from Prime Minister Nastase to Prime Minister Orban, 14 November 2001.

14 The Romanians insisted on this point, despite the fact that no European institution did and despite the fact that it would seem to discriminate on the basis of ethnicity.

15 Memorandum of Understanding between the Government of the Republic of Hungary and the Government of Romania concerning the Law on Hungarians Living in Neighbouring Countries and issues of bilateral cooperation, 22 December 2001.

16 Letter from Mircea Geoana to Ekeus, 7 January 2002.

17 Ibid.

18 Ibid.

19 Statement of the National Council of the Slovak Republic to the Act on Hungarians Living in Neighbouring Countries, 7 February 2002.

20 Ibid.

21 This was repeated by the Hungarian Ambassador to the OSCE, Dr Istvan Horvath, to a meeting of the Permanent Council on 27 June 2002. See PC.DEL/460/02.

22 UDMR and the ruling PSD have a protocol of cooperation although they are not part of a coalition per se.

23 See para. 16 of the Venice Commission report.

24 Letter from OSCE High Commissioner on National Minorities, Rolf Ekeus, to H.E. Laszlo Kovacs, Minister for Foreign Affairs of Hungary, 7 November 2002.

25 See Concluding Document of the Sixth Meeting of the Hungarian Standing Committee, 17 November 2002.

26 Letter from Gunther Verheugen to Foreign Minister Laszlo Kovacs, 20 January 2001.

27 Letter from OSCE High Commissioner on National Minorities, Rolf Ekeus, to H.E. Laszlo Kovacs, 23 January 2003.

28 Ibid.

29 Note of the Ministry of Foreign Affairs of the Republic of the Slovak Republic to the Ministry of Foreign Affairs of the Republic of Hungary, 29 May 2003.

30 Ibid.

31 Ibid.

32 Para. 1, 'Preferential treatment of national minorities by the kin-state: the case of the Hungarian law of 19 June 2001 on Hungarians Living in Neighbouring Countries ('Magyars')', Resolution 1335, adopted on 25 June 2003 by the Parliamentary Assembly of the Council of Europe.

33 Ibid.: para. 10.

34 For an interesting reflection on terminological problems created by nationhood and statehood, see Jean-Francois Allain (2002: 11–13).

35 Ibid.: para. 11.

36 Ibid.: para. 13.

37 Ibid.: para. 14.

38 Romania, Hungary Sign Agreement on Status Law Implementation, 24 September 2003.

39 President of the Advisory Committee on the Council of Europe Framework Convention for the Protection of National Minorities as well as Professor of International Law at the University of Kiel.

7 Minorities, violence and statehood on the European periphery

1 For a comparison of the origins of wars in the Soviet Union and socialist Yugoslavia, see R. Lukic and A. Lynch (1996) and S. Kaufman (2001).
2 World Bank (1998). An updated account of the economy of Transnistria is at the time of writing being prepared by the International Crisis Group.
3 For analyses of the Transnistrian case in particular, see Stefan Troebst (2003: 1: 437–66) and Vladimir Solonari (2003: 4(2): 411–38).
4 The most complete account of Russian assistance in all these conflicts is Mihai Gribincea (2001).
5 Barometrul opiniei publice din Republica Moldova, Chisinau, March–April, 2002.
6 Author's confidential interview with senior manager of United States assistance programme, Stepanakert, 28 September 2000. Even the OSCE's special representative for Karabakh is based in Tbilisi, Georgia, since placing the office in either the Armenian or the Azerbaijani capital would have been unacceptable to one of the sides.
7 Author's confidential interview with senior official in the United Nations Office for the Coordination of Humanitarian Assistance (UNOCHA), Tbilisi, 29 August 2000.
8 In July 2002, the OSCE put forward a discussion document that argued for the creation of a federation of Moldova and Transnistria. The Moldovan side signalled its acceptance of the idea in principle, but the Transnistrian side was unenthusiastic. In 2003 Russia put forward its own federal plan which was rejected by the Moldovan side.
9 The estimate was as high as 54 per cent for Armenia (see Evgeny Polyakov 2000).

8 The impact of post-communist regime change and European integration on ethnic minorities: the 'special' case of ethnic Germans in Eastern Europe

* In this chapter, I am drawing to a significant extent on previous and current published and unpublished research. Among published research I am relying especially on Wolff (2000c), Wolff and Cordell (2003) and Wolff (2004b). My thanks to both Berghahn Books and Palgrave Macmillan for allowing me to use parts of previously published work in a revised and updated form. I am grateful to Detlef Rein and Hans-Joachim Jansen of the German Ministry of the Interior for providing me with insights from the perspective of the German government and to Uwe Stiemke of the Herman Niermann Foundation for information on his organisation's work with German minorities in Central and Eastern Europe. Special thanks are also due to Karl Cordell for his long-standing collaboration with me on German minorities in Europe and for insightful comments on earlier drafts of this chapter.
1 The so-called Copenhagen criteria for EU membership refer, relatively vaguely, to 'respect for and protection of minorities', but there is an implicit understanding that the minority-rights standards set by the CoE and the OSCE have to be adhered to as well if a country wants to launch a successful membership bid.
2 On the range of institutional designs and their impact on the resolution of self-determination conflicts, see the excellent analysis of Danspeckgruber (2002).
3 On the role of minority-rights issues in the accession process, see Hughes and Sasse (2003); more specifically on Estonia, see Smith (2003); on Latvia, Morris

(2003); on the Czech Republic, Hungary and Poland, Vermeersch (2003, 2004); and on Hungary and Macedonia, see Dutceac (2004).

4 Cyprus, the Czech Republic, Estonia, Hungary, Latvia, Lithuania, Malta, Poland, Slovakia, Slovenia.

5 Bulgaria, Croatia, Romania, Turkey.

6 Germany has concluded such treaties with Czechoslovakia (acceded to by both the Czech and Slovak Republics), Hungary, Poland, Romania and the Soviet Union (acceded to by Russia). In addition, there are a number of bilateral agreements to similar effects, for example, with Estonia, Latvia, Lithuania, Kazakhstan, Kyrgyzstan and Ukraine.

7 For example, during his failed presidential campaign of 2000, Marian Krzaklewski, the chairman of the now defunct *Akcja Wyborcza Solidarno* (Solidarity Electoral Action), made great play of the threat to Polish interests posed by Germany in general and the German expellee organisations in particular. His poor performance with only 15.6 per cent of the vote demonstrated that such atavistic sentiments can only go so far in today's Poland (Cordell and Wolff 2005).

8 For example, in cases of scattered minorities, cultural rather than territorial autonomy may be more opportune and individual classes taught in a minority language may be more reasonable and cost-efficient a measure than entire minority-language schools. On the other hand, subsidies for minority print media and regular airtime on radio and television are not affected by settlement patterns in their effectiveness to enable members of ethnic minorities to preserve, express and develop their distinct identities.

9 There is, of course, the use of sanctions, including the withholding of benefits of membership in international or regional organisations, preferential trading arrangements and other forms of economic cooperation. However, these have been used only in exceptional cases, such as in the former Yugoslavia.

10 Figures on Estonia from Cordell (2002) and on Latvia and Lithuania from German government estimates (Welt 1999a).

11 Interestingly, this law, affecting domestic minority policy, was passed in 1993 after a Government Decree creating the Government Office for Hungarian Minorities Abroad had come into effect the year before.

12 According to Act LXXVII of 1993 on the Rights of National and Ethnic Minorities, any minority has the right to establish a minority municipal government or directly or indirectly formed local minority self-governments in townships, towns or the districts of the capital city, as well as a national minority self-government. Minority self-governments may, among other things, establish and run institutions concerned with culture, education and print and electronic media.

13 The latest available figures are for the financial year of 2000. Then, the Polish government spent almost €3 million out of a budget of €6.5 million on projects in support of the German minority. Since then, the overall budget, however, has decreased.

14 A new census was held in March 2002 but at the time of writing the results had not been made public yet.

15 For a more detailed analysis of this constructivist approach to foreign policy analysis as applied to Germany's *Ostpolitik*, see Cordell and Wolff (2005).

16 A similar case can be made for Slovakia and the defeat of the Meciar government in 1998.

10 From 'full national status' to 'independence' in Europe: the case of Plaid Cymru – the Party of Wales

1 The empirical research on which this chapter is based draws on documentation in the Plaid Cymru Archive, based at the National Library of Wales, Aberystwyth, and interviews conducted with Plaid Cymru representatives between April 2002 and December 2003.

2 Saunders Lewis was Plaid Cymru's president for the period 1926 to 1939, the first having been Lewis Valentine from 1925 to 1926.

3 Plaid's first Parliamentary seat was won by the President, Gwynfor Evans, in the Carmarthen by-election in 1966, and was followed by heartening returns in the Rhondda and Caerphilly by-elections a few years later (Wigley 1992: 78–81). The party's number of MPs in Westminster increased to three in the 1974–79 legislature.

4 On a turnout of 66.7 per cent, the Welsh electorate voted in favour of continued UK membership of the EEC by 66.5 per cent, marginally lower than the 67.2 per cent of the British electorate as a whole who voted in favour of continued membership.

5 The Wales Act 1978 contained a specific requirement that, in the case of the devolution proposals being approved by a Yes vote in favour of devolution, the support of more than 40 per cent of the eligible electorate in Wales was required for the proposals to be implemented. Measured against this criteria, only 11.8 per cent of the eligible Welsh electorate voted Yes in favour of referendum.

6 Draft European manifesto presented by Dafydd Williams to the Bureau of Unrepresented Nations, Paris, 27 January 1979. Plaid Cymru Archive, A66.

7 Interview with the author.

8 For example, Dafydd Elis Thomas, then party president, stood in the North Wales constituency in June 1989, a seat which the party considered it had a realistic chance of winning. The majority of Plaid's candidates in European elections have been members holding senior posts within the party, often sitting on the National Executive Committee.

9 Plaid Cymru Press Release, *Plaid move on Brussels office*, 22 June 1975, Plaid Cymru Archive, M687.

10 Jill Evans was elected as one of Plaid Cymru's MEPs in June 1999, and was re-elected in June 2004.

11 *Western Mail*, 21 September 2000.

12 Senior Plaid Cymru member, interview with the author.

13 The reactions of Labour Welsh Secretary Peter Hain to Plaid Cymru's adoption of independence typified the reactions of Plaid's political opponents to the move: 'Now everybody in Wales knows what Plaid Cymru is about – full blooded separation and independence, which would bankrupt Wales and make us an international laughing stock.' *BBC Wales*, 21 September 2001.

14 As one of the most outspoken critics of 'independence in Europe', the most recent articulation of Dafydd Elis Thomas' alternative governing strategy can be found at: www.epolitix.com/EN/Interviews (16 September 2004).

11 Nations without states in the EU: the Catalan case

1 At the election, the PSC(PSC-PSOE)-CpC obtained 42 seats, corresponding to 31.17 per cent of the vote. Against all predictions, the CiU, with its new leader Artur Mas, managed to obtain 30.93 per cent of the vote, which corresponded to 46 seats. As well as the PSC, it had also lost ten seats when compared to 1999. The key to political change in Catalonia was then in the hands of the

ERC which obtained a record 23 seats corresponding to 16.47 per cent of the vote. In the 1999 election, it had obtained 8.7 per cent of the vote corresponding to 12 seats. The ICV achieved a significant recovery, obtaining nine seats (it had five previously), and the PP obtained 15 seats, three more than in 1999.

2 Convenció Catalana per al debat sobre el futur de la Unió Europea, *80 Propostes per a una nova Europa*, Generalitat de Catalunya, January 2003, pp. 117–18.

3 European Convention. Paper presented by regions with legislative powers within the EU, CONV 321/02, Marienhamm (Åland Islands) Helsinki/Brussels, 4–7 October 2002.

4 Political Declaration of the Constitutional Regions of Bavaria, Catalonia, Scotland, Flanders, North Rhine-Westphalia, Salzburg and Wallonia. Signed in Brussels, 28 May 2001.

12 Scottish autonomy and European integration: the response of Scotland's political parties

1 In Wales, support for devolution was far lower, with only 11.8 per cent of the total electorate in favour of an Assembly.

2 About 80 per cent of Scotland's MPs and MEPs attended meetings.

3 Smith did not, however, suggest that the UK should develop along federal lines to advance Scotland's status in Europe.

4 First Minister of Scotland Jack McConnell proposed the establishment of a 'Subsidiarity Council' in Europe to ensure that EU legislation respects national and regional devolved responsibilities (*The Herald*, 6 January 2002).

5 Scottish Liberal Democrat Party Leader Jim Wallace, quoted in *The Herald*, 7 June 1994.

6 In Wales, the single question of whether the Welsh wished to have an Assembly gained only 50.3 per cent of the overall vote, whilst support for an Assembly in Northern Ireland was high, especially amongst the Catholic population.

7 Felicity Garvie, MSP (SSP), quoted in *The Socialist Voice*, April 2004, p. 2.

8 Alex Neil, MSP (SNP), quoted in *The Scotsman*, 27 September 2003.

9 This suggestion was made by Murdo Fraser MSP during an interview with the author, 6 January 2004.

10 Speech by John Swinney MSP to the Scottish Council of the European Movement, Perth, November 2003.

13 Basque nationalism: sovereignty, independence and European integration

1 Translated by Michael Keating.

2 'Propuesta de Estatuto Político de la Comunidad de Euskadi.' The English version of the proposal is available on the internet: 'Proposal for the Political Statute of the Community of the Basque Country.' www.nuevoestatutodeeuskadi.net/docs/estatutovasco_ing.pdf.

3 Since 1978, the date of approval of the Basque Statute of Autonomy, the PNV has controlled, inside the Basque Government, international and European relations. Therefore, the activity of the Basque Government is an exact reflection of the policy of the PNV.

14 Liberalising Estonia's citizenship policy: the role of the EU, OSCE and Council of Europe

1 In 1991, Estonia's resident population was 1.57 million. Russian-speakers represented approximately 35 per cent of the total. The term 'Russian-speaker' captures the main (i.e. linguistic) cleavage in Estonia's population: besides ethnic Russians, Estonia's non-indigenous population also included ethnic Ukrainians, Belorussians, Tatars, Kazakhs, and others, most of whom adopted Russian as their 'mother tongue'.

2 Russian had been the 'language of inter-ethnic communication' during the Soviet era, giving Estonia's non-indigenous population few incentives to learn the Estonian language (Laitin 1998: 81).

3 The term *norm* is used in this chapter to refer to a generally accepted standard of behaviour. Later I explain that the norms on immigrant naturalisation that I deal with in this chapter were only beginning to gain acceptance among European states in the 1990s.

4 Estonian concessions were particularly rapid in the area of minority education and in issuing residence permits. For a full overview of Estonia's evolving minority policy, see Jurado (2003).

5 See, especially, Birckenbach (1997). Latvian minority policy evolved along very similar lines to that of Estonia, with policy changes in Latvia generally trailing behind those in Estonia. These parallels have to do with the similar historical, geopolitical and demographic background of the two countries (Russian-speakers represented 44 per cent of the total Latvian population in 1989). Estonia and Latvia have also been treated in similar ways by the EU, OSCE and COE – with one important exception: the EU's decision to open membership talks with Latvia in February 2000, two years after Estonia.

6 Distinguishing between indigenous and immigrant minorities was made possible by a prior decision to avoid defining the term 'national minority' in any minority-relevant convention (Chandler 1999: 61–76).

7 Various authors have identified a trend towards liberalisation in the naturalisation policies of European states consistent with the Convention's provisions (Çınar 1994: 64; Checkel 1999: 93–96; Hansen and Weil 2001: 11).

8 Keohane (1984) is a good example of rationalist work on compliance.

9 The cognitivist approach has been treated in depth by Haas (1990).

10 March and Olsen (1999: 311) define this as a 'logic of appropriateness', distinguishable from the 'logic of expected consequences' typical of rationalist theory.

11 Estonia's first coalition government was made up of Fatherland (*Isamaa*), the Estonian National Independence Party (*Eesti Rahvusliku Sõltumatuse Partei*) and the Moderates (*Mõõdukad*).

12 This parliamentary minority should not be confused with Estonia's Russian-speaking minority. Deprived of Estonian citizenship and thus voting rights, the latter had no representatives in the Estonian parliament at this time.

13 The new Centre was also responsible for coordinating language training for school children and for employees seeking professional language qualifications (Language Training Strategy 1998).

14 Figures provided by the Estonian Citizenship and Migration Board (Poleshchuk 2004: 18).

15 The two plus one year residence requirement increased to five plus one; the language test was made more demanding; applicants were now required to pass a separate examination in Estonian on the contents and principles of the Estonian Constitution; and the categories of people denied access to citizenship were expanded, to include those without a steady income (IOM 1996: 90–101).

16 The centrist Coalition Party (*Koonderakond*), which had forged an electoral coalition with the more leftward-leaning Estonian Rural Union (*Eesti Maaliit*) and Centre Party (*Eesti Keskerakond*), won the majority of votes.

17 European Convention on Nationality, Strasbourg, 6 November 1997, Chapter III, Article 6 (2). Accessed online at www.conventions.coe.int/Treaty/en/ Treaties/Html/166.htm.

18 The parliamentary vote on this occasion was 55 to 20 in favour of the bill (*Riigikogu* debate 1998).

19 Author's interview with Sarah Keating, administrative officer at the Modern Language Centre of the COE, DG IV, Strasbourg, 8 March 2000.

20 Author's interview with Leeni Simm, Deputy Director of the National Examination and Qualification Centre, Tallinn, 30 August 2000, Tallinn.

21 The fact that Estonia's citizenship policy continued evolving in a multicultural direction after 1999 is particularly noteworthy as parliamentary elections held on 7 March 1999 brought into government the same coalition of right-of-centre parties which had governed Estonia during the early 1990s, when an exclusionary approach to minorities was the norm.

22 Whilst the success rate amongst those who apply for naturalisation is high, the number of applicants is still worryingly low: after a peak in 1996 (when 22,773 individuals were naturalised), the number of persons receiving citizenship through naturalisation in Estonia has stabilised to about 3,500 a year (Citizenship and Migration Board 2003).

23 The notions of 'securitisation' and 'desecuritisation' are explained in Waever (1995).

24 Treaty Establishing a European Constitution, signed on 18 June 2004 (Article III-229 para. 1).

15 Europe's limits: European integration and conflict management in Northern Ireland

1 Unionists have often argued that nationalism in Northern Ireland draws its strength from the exogenous support offered by the Irish republic's irredentism (McGarry and O'Leary 1995: chap. 3).

2 See Hume (1993: 227). Hume told the SDLP's 1997 party conference that 'Europe through the Single Market has created an economic space where we can grow together... In almost every sector – farming, business, tourism, energy – the main groupings and interests on both sides of the border are calling for a more integrating, harmonised and united approach to marketing, to planning, to taxation, to regulation' (*Irish Times*, 17 November 1997).

3 The theme that Northern Ireland can develop its own regional identity within a regime of 'multi-level governance' is also discussed by Wilson (1997) and by Hodgett and Meehan (2003).

4 Taylor believes that 'increasing European integration has led to the erosion of absolutist conceptions of national sovereignty' while Meehan argues that it is 'difficult to understand' the Good Friday Agreement 'without situating it in a larger European framework and the new definition of sovereignty to which the EU has given birth' (Meehan 2000: 83; Taylor 2001: 45).

5 In the European elections of 1999, of the unionist candidate Ian Paisley's surplus of 22,969, 22,162 were transferred to the other unionist candidate Jim Nicholson, while only 32 went to the nationalist and republican candidate Mitchell McLaughlin. The number is low enough that it can safely be attributed to mistakes or mental disorders. In the 2004 European elections, 450 or 1.17 per cent of the DUP candidate's surplus of 38,441 were transferred across

the ethnonational divide, even though it was a moderate nationalist, Martin Morgan of the SDLP, who was left in the count.

6 As O'Leary and I have argued elsewhere, much of Sinn Fein's increasing popularity within the nationalist bloc can be attributed to its increasing moderation rather than to voters becoming more radical (McGarry 2001b: 126; McGarry and O'Leary 2004: 26). However, as Sinn Fein remains clearly a radical nationalist party, its rise in popularity is difficult to reconcile with the view that traditional national identities are fading.

7 The Opsahl Commission's views are cited approvingly by Taylor (2001).

8 In elections to the European Parliament in 1994 and 1999, the turnout in Northern Ireland was 49.4 and 57 per cent respectively. In the UK the turnout was 36.4 and 24 per cent. While turnout in local government elections in Northern Ireland in the 1990s ranged between 54.7 per cent (1997) and 56.6 per cent (1993), turnout in Britain ranged between 32.5 per cent (Metropolitan Boroughs in 1992) and an unusually high 53.4 per cent (Welsh districts in 1991). All Northern Ireland data are from www.explorers.whyte.com. Data for turnout in European elections in the UK are from www.europarl.eu.int/election/results/uk taux.htm. Data for local government results in Britain are from Rallings and Thrasher (1997: 53).

9 See Whyte, www.explorers.whyte.com. The turnout data do not show any significant trend during the period under review (1973–99). The highest turnout for a local government election between 1973 and 1997 was in 1973 (68.1 per cent). The highest turnout for a Northern Ireland regional election between 1973 and 1998 was in 1998 (68.6 per cent).

10 Post-sovereigntism and post-nationalism are often conflated, but should be distinguished. A post-nationalist disposition suggests that one no longer identifies as a nationalist. A post-sovereigntist disposition suggests that one no longer sees merit in traditional, autarkic, sovereign states. A nationalist might support post-sovereigntism, and my colleague, Michael Keating, argues that many do. See Keating (2001a).

11 For Ahern's comments, see *Irish Times*, 27 November 1998. For Adams's, see *Irish Times*, 20 April 1998. The politically correct reasoning behind their optimism was that the Agreement would make it easier to persuade unionists of the merits of unification, and would be more effective than the previous campaign of violence had been. More important, perhaps, was the popular understanding that the Catholic and nationalist share of the population will, at some point in the foreseeable future, surpass the Protestant and unionist share.

12 Exit polls from the referendum on the agreement in May of 1998 showed that only a bare majority of Unionists voted 'yes'. In the Assembly elections of June 1998, Unionists supporting the accord won 23.9 per cent of the vote and 30 seats while Unionist rejectionists won 24.9 per cent of the vote and 28 seats.

13 The *Irish Times* recounted a Trimble speech to the Northern Ireland Forum in the week after the Agreement was signed:

> Mr. Trimble said the Agreement was a disaster for Sinn Fein and the IRA, and that it strengthened the North's position within the UK. Trimble claimed the alternative was the Anglo-Irish Agreement, and that he had achieved the ending of the Republic's territorial claim and a recognition of the territorial integrity of the UK.
>
> (18 April 1998)

14 As Kennedy argues,

> the experience of working together in the institutions of the Community, particularly at Council of Minister and senior diplomat and official level,

> was slowly transforming the relationship ... The patron–client pattern was dissolved; in the new circumstances British ministers and diplomats could see their Irish counterparts as clever partners in Europe.
>
> (Kennedy 1994: 177)

15 Interestingly, better Anglo-Irish relations cannot be seen as a result of spillover from closer economic cooperation within the EU, as crude neo-functionalist analysis would suggest. Rather, Ireland was more tightly linked to the UK economically in the decades *before* both countries joined the EU, decades in which relations between the two countries were not good and in which there was little or no political cooperation between them. Rather than conforming with neo-functionalist arguments, the improvement in Anglo-Irish relations appear to contradict them. The effect of EU membership for Ireland has been a radical reduction in its dependence on the UK. Whereas the UK took about 75 per cent of Ireland's exports in 1960, by 1997 this share had dropped to approximately 21.4 per cent. Imports dropped from 50 to 30.9 per cent. While Ireland's recent economic miracle is closely tied to foreign direct investment, this is mostly from the US rather than from the UK. Since both countries joined the EU, they have moved apart in other ways. Both had a common currency zone even before European monetary union. Ireland broke with the Sterling zone after joining the EU, and is now, unlike the UK, in the Euro zone.

16 Denis Kennedy, a former head of the EU Commission Office in Belfast, writes that 'without the European Union, it is almost impossible to see how Dublin–London relations could have been transformed as they were between the mid seventies and the mid eighties'. Francesca Lacaita writes that 'without the improvement of British-Irish relationships following the accession of both countries to the EC in 1973, the peace process in Northern Ireland would hardly have been possible'.

17 Two academics have argued that European integration and American involvement in Northern Ireland are related, i.e. America was interested in conflict resolution in Northern Ireland, in part, because of international investment flows and European integration. From this perspective, America's intervention was due to its economic interest in stability in Ireland, which is the location of considerable and increasing American investment, and an important American foothold in the integrating EU (MacGinty 1997; Wilson 1997: 36–7).

18 For the sake of clarity, I am not arguing that Northern Ireland is properly seen as a colony of the UK; the standard republican argument. My point is that substantial sections of the British elite and public have seen it in this way, and that this is seriously at odds with traditional republican arguments.

19 *Atlantic Charter*, 14 August 1941 (www.yale.edu/lawweb/avalon/wwii/atlantic.htm).

20 Ninety-nine per cent (57 per cent of the electorate) supported the continuation of the Union in a poll boycotted by nationalists.

21 This practice, entrenched in the Good Friday Agreement of 1998, was changed by Dublin in 2004, following a referendum. Now, those born in Northern Ireland have a right to citizenship only if they were born to a parent who was eligible for such citizenship. The change, which unhelpfully suggested that the Agreement could be changed unilaterally, was to prevent children born in Northern Ireland 'in transit' from claiming Irish citizenship, something that has become more likely given Ireland's recent economic success.

22 For information on this and several other polls, see McGarry and O'Leary (1995: 114–20).

23 'The British government agree that it is for the people of the island of Ireland

alone, by agreement between the two parts, respectively, to exercise their right of self-determination on the basis of consent, freely and concurrently given, north and south, to bring about a united Ireland, if that is their wish' (cited in McGarry and O'Leary 1995: 409).

24 Mallon exaggerated. The 1998 Agreement was more far-reaching in a number of respects than Sunningdale, including in its provisions for inclusive executive government, treatment of prisoners, policing reform, and a role for the Irish government in Northern Ireland. However, in some ways, including in its name, the Council of Ireland that was proposed in 1973 was a grander body than the North–South Ministerial Council established in 1998.

25 Many in the British state would no doubt accept that unionists are as British as the people of Gibraltar. Just as London has been prepared to cooperate with the Irish republic in the governance of Northern Ireland, it has recently seemed prepared to cooperate with the Spanish government in the governance of Gibraltar.

26 Ironically, the traditional Irish American position, which was based on traditional Irish republicanism, held that the British did want to be in Northern Ireland and would have to be forced out of it.

27 Spain's new socialist government appears more flexible on the question of accommodating Spain's minority nations, but it is not yet clear how far it will go towards meeting their aspirations.

28 Most East European states are at what Ian Lustick describes as a 'hegemonic' stage with respect to abandoning territory, i.e. such an idea is unthinkable (Lustick 1993). NATO's bombing and occupation of Kosovo may have helped some Serbian elites to move beyond the hegemonic stage. This will become clearer in time.

16 Breton identity highlighted by European integration

1 Where the Queen Mary II was built.

2 For example the IFOP investigation of 28–29 June 2004 for '*Ouest-France*' (the first daily in France): 75 per cent of the inhabitants of Loire-Atlantique *département* is in favour of the reunification.

3 In April 2004, the new President of the Breton Region was elected vice-president of the conference.

4 This operates under the aegis of the National Centre of Scientific Research and the National Foundation of Political Science.

5 See Elizabeth Dupoirier (1993: 10).

6 See Political Inter-regional Observatory (2004: 3).

7 The area, which corresponds to the zone of influence of the leading French daily newspaper *Ouest-France*, is usually recognised as corresponding to the administrative regions of Brittany, Pays de Loire and Basse-Normandie.

8 Soon after, in 1994, the Democratic Party of the Peoples of Europe – European Free Alliance, was created, officially made up of a federation of parties.

9 Other movements exist in the following regions: Occitan, Corsica, the Basque Country, Catalonia, Ireland, Galicia, Val d'Aoste, Sardinia, the Asturies, Frioul and Wales.

10 They only generate the equivalent of 2 per cent of the total public budget.

11 Belgium, Holland and Denmark, for example.

12 Associative schools where Breton is taught according to the principle of linguistic immersion from playschool into secondary school.

13 European Bureau of Lesser Used Languages (EBLUL).

17 Baltic identities and interests in a European setting: a bottom-up perspective

1 The research reported herein was made possible by grants from the Tercentenary Fund of the Bank of Sweden to Sten Berglund, Professor of Politics at Orebro University and from the British ESRC to Richard Rose for a study of Diverging Paths of Post-Communist Regimes RES-000-23-0193. It is a revised version of a paper initially presented to the Conference on Nations, Minorities and European Integration at the European University Institute, Florence, 7–8 May 2004. Useful comments were received on an earlier draft from the editors and from Professor Piret Ehin of Tartu University.

2 Throughout this chapter the term 'Russian' refers to people whose family nationality on their Soviet passport was that of a Soviet territory now grouped in the Commonwealth of Independent States (CIS). In fact, the great majority are ethnically Russians and the remainder have a cognate nationality such as Belorussian or Ukraine. Thus, there is no minority problem among Russian-speakers.

3 However, the number of Russians in the Baltic states is far fewer than those living in many other successor states of the Soviet Union, such as Ukraine. Moreover, Russians are relatively indifferent to the Baltic states. When the New Russia Barometer (Rose 2003: 36) asked a nationwide sample of the Russian Federation about the CIS states that they would like to have closer ties with, 77 per cent named Belarus and 73 per cent Ukraine. Latvia (56 per cent) and Estonia and Lithuania (55 per cent each) came at the bottom of the list of 14 former Soviet republics.

18 EU accession and conflict resolution in theory and practice: the case of Cyprus

1 In 1960 the Turkish Cypriots amounted to 18.5 per cent of the population.

2 Five versions of the Plan were presented between November 2002 and March 2004. In what follows I shall concentrate on the fifth and final version of the Plan (UN Secretary General 2004).

3 Interviews with Turkish Cypriot opposition leaders, Nicosia, February 2002 and July 2003.

Bibliography

Alcock, A. (2001) 'From conflict to agreement in Northern Ireland: lessons from Europe', in J. McGarry (ed.) *Northern Ireland and the Divided World*, Oxford: Oxford University Press.

Aldecoa, F. and Keating, M. (eds) (1999) *Paradiplomacy in Action. The Foreign Relations of Subnational Governments*, London and Portland, OR: Frank Cass.

Alfredsson, G. and Turk, D. (1993) 'International mechanisms for the monitoring and protection of minority rights: their advantages, disadvantages and interrelationships', in A. Bloed (ed.) *Monitoring Human Rights in Europe: Comparing International Procedures and Mechanisms*, Norwell MA: Kluwer: 169–86.

Allain, J.-F. (2002) 'Some thoughts on language, the protection of national minorities by their kin-state', *The Protection of National Minorities by Their Kin-State*, European Commission for Democracy through Law, Strasbourg.

Althusius, J. (1603/1995) *Politica. Politics Methodically Set Forth and Illustrated with Sacred and Profane Examples*, edited and translated and with introduction by F.S. Carney, Indianapolis: Liberty Fund.

Altmann, F.-L. (2004) 'Regional economic problems and prospects' in J. Batt (ed.) *The Western Balkans: Moving On*, Chaillot Paper no. 70, Paris: EU Institute for Security Studies.

Anaya, S.J. (1996) *Indigenous Peoples in International Law*, New York: Oxford University Press.

Anderson, J. and Shuttleworth, I. (1992) 'Currency of co-operation', *Fortnight*, 3(12): 18.

Applegate, C. (1999) 'A Europe of regions: reflections on the historiography of subnational places in modern times', *The American Historical Review*, 104(4): 1157–82.

Archibugi, D. and Held, D. (1995) *Cosmopolitan Democracy. An Agenda for a New World Order*, Cambridge: Polity Press.

Arjupin, A. (2000) 'Differences in the rights enjoyed by the inhabitants of the Republic of Estonia, as provided by law', unpublished manuscript by Arjupin, legal consultant for the Legal Information Centre for Human Rights, 1 June, Tallinn.

Ashford, N. (1992) 'The political parties', in S. George (ed.) *Britain and the European Community. The Politics of Semi-Detachment*, Oxford: Clarendon Press.

Azaola, J.M. (1995) 'El PNV y la Unidad Europea', *100 años de Nazionalismo*, Bilbao: El Correo.

Badie, B. (1995) *La fin des territoires. Essai sur le désordre international et sur l'utilité sociale du respect*, Paris: Fayard.

Bahceli, T. (2001) 'The lure of economic prosperity versus ethno-nationalism: Turkish Cypriots, the EU option, and the resolution of ethnic conflict in Cyprus', in M. Keating and J. McGarry (eds) *Minority Nationalism and the Changing International Order*, Oxford: Oxford University Press: 203–22.

Barker, R. (1992) 'Legitimacy in the United Kingdom: Scotland and the Poll Tax', *British Journal of Political Science*, 22(4): 521–33.

Barrington, L.W. (1995) 'The domestic and international consequences of citizenship in the Soviet successor states', *Europe–Asia Studies*, 47(5): 731–63.

—— (1999) 'The making of citizenship policy in the Baltic states', *Georgetown Immigration Law Journal*, 13(2): 159–200.

Batt, J. (2003) '"Fuzzy statehood" versus hard borders: the impact of EU enlargement on Romania and Yugoslavia', in M. Keating and J. Hughes (eds) *The Regional Challenge in Central and Eastern Europe, Territorial Restructuring and European Integration*, Brussels: Presses interuniversitaires européennes/Peter Lang.

—— (2004) 'Minorities, borders and European integration in Southeast Europe: The Hungarians and Serbs compared', Paper presented at Conference on 'Nations, Minorities and European Integration', 7–8 May 2004, European University Institute, Florence.

Batt, J. and Amato, J. (1998) 'Minority rights and EU enlargement to the East', EUI, RSC Policy Paper no. 98/5.

Bauböck, R. (1994) *Transnational Citizenship. Membership and Rights in International Migration*, Aldershot, UK: Edward Elgar.

—— (2003) 'Towards a political theory of migrant transnationalism', *International Migration Review*, 37(3): 700–23.

—— (2004a) 'Paradoxes of self-determination and the right to self-government', in C. Eisgruber and A. Sajo (eds) *Bulwarks of Localism. Human Rights in Context*, Leiden, Netherlands: Brill Academic Publishers.

—— (2004b) 'Territorial or cultural autonomy for national minorities?', in A. Dieckhoff (ed.) *The Politics of Belonging. Nationalism, Liberalism and Pluralism*, Lanham, MD: Lexington Books: 221–58.

—— (2004c) 'Civic citizenship – a new concept for the New Europe', in R. Süssmuth and W. Weidenfeld (eds) *Managing Integration. The European Union's Responsibilities towards Immigrants*, Bertelsmann Stiftung, CD-ROM.

BBC Monitoring Service (2001a) 'Belgrade accepts principle', 6 July.

—— (2001b) 'Hungary sees no reason to change status law, official says', 22 October.

—— (2002) 'MP questions Hungarian premier over use of Nazi term "living space"', 5 February.

Beissinger, M.R. (2002) *Nationalist Mobilization and the Collapse of the Soviet State*, Cambridge: Cambridge University Press.

Benhabib, S. (2002) *The Claims of Culture*, Princeton: Princeton University Press.

Bennie, L., Brand, J. and Mitchell, J. (1997) *How Scotland Votes. Scottish Parties and Elections*, Manchester: Manchester University Press.

Benôit-Rohmer, F. (1996) *The Minority Question in Europe: Texts and Commentary*, Strasbourg: Council of Europe Publishing.

Beran, H. (1984) 'A liberal theory of secession', *Political Studies*, xxxii: 21–31.

Beran, H. (1998) 'A democratic theory of political self-determination for a new world order', in P. Lehning (ed.) *Theories of Secession*, London: Routledge: 32–59.

Berglund, S. and Aarebrot, F. (1997) *The Political History of Eastern Europe: The Struggle between Democracy and Dictatorship*, Cheltenham: Edward Elgar.

Berglund, S., Ekman, J. and Aarebrot, F. (2004) 'The challenge of history in Central and Eastern Europe', in S. Berglund, J. Ekman and F. Aarebrot (eds) *The Handbook of Political Change in Eastern Europe*, Cheltenham: Edward Elgar.

Bew, P., Patterson, H. and Teague, P. (1997) *Between War and Peace: The Political Future of Northern Ireland*, London: Lawrence and Wishart.

Bhabha, H. (ed.) (1990) *Nation and Narration*, London: Routledge.

Bindig, R. (1993) 'Opinion on the Application of the Republic of Estonia for Membership of the Council of Europe', PACE Sub-Committee on Human Rights of the Committee on Legal Affairs and Human Rights, 5 May (Doc. 6824).

Birckenbach, H.-M. (1997) *Preventive Diplomacy through Fact-Finding: How International Organisations Review the Conflict over Citizenship in Estonia and Latvia*, Hamburg: Lit Verlag.

Bloed, A. and Van Dijk, P. (eds) (1999) *Protection of Minority Rights Through Bilateral Treaties*, The Hague: Kluwer Law.

Borzel, T. and Risse, T. (2000) 'When Europe hits home: Europeanisation and domestic change', *European Integration Online Papers*, 4(15): www.eiop.or.at/eiop/texte/2000-015.htm.

Bratinka, M. (1993) 'Report on the application of the Republic of Estonia for membership of the Council of Europe', PACE Political Affairs Committee, 14 April (Doc. 6810).

Bray, Z. (2002) 'Boundaries and identities in Bidasoa-Txingudi on the Franco Spanish frontier', doctoral thesis, European University Institute, Florence.

Brett, R. (1993) 'The human dimension of the CSCE and the CSCE response to minorities', in M.R. Lucas (ed.) *The CSCE in the 1990s: Constructing European Security and Cooperation*, Baden-Baden: Nomos Verlagsgesellschaft: 143–60.

Brewin, C. (2000), *The European Union and Cyprus*, Huntingdon: Eothen.

Broudic, F. (1999) *Qui parle breton aujourd'hui ?*, Brest Brud: Nevez.

Brown, A., McCrone, D. and Paterson, L. (1998) *Politics and Society in Scotland*, Basingstoke: Macmillan Press.

Brown, M.E. (2001) 'The causes of internal conflict', in M.E. Brown, O.R. Coté Jr, S.M. Lynn-Jones, and S.E. Miller (eds) *Nationalism and Ethnic Conflict*, Cambridge, MA: The MIT Press.

Brubaker, R. (1996) *Nationalism Reframed: Nationhood and the National Question in the New Europe*, Cambridge: Cambridge University Press.

Brusis, M. (2003) 'The European Union and inter-ethnic power-sharing arrangements in accession countries', *Journal on Ethnopolitics and Minority Issues in Europe*, 1: 1–20.

Buchanan, A. (1997) 'Theories of secession', *Philosophy and Public Affairs*, 26(1): 31–61.

—— (2003) 'The making and unmaking of boundaries: what liberalism has to say', in A. Buchanan and M. Moore (eds) *States, Nations, and Borders. The Ethics of Making Boundaries*, Cambridge, UK: Cambridge University Press: 231–61.

—— (2004) *Justice, Legitimacy and Self-Determination*, Oxford: Oxford University Press.

Bullman, U. (ed.) (1994) *Die Politik der dritten Ebene. Regionen im Europa der Union,* Baden-Baden: Nomos.

Bunce, V. (1999) *Subversive Institutions: The Design and Destruction of Socialism and the State,* Cambridge: Cambridge University Press.

Burgess, A. (1999) 'Critical reflections on the return of national minority rights to East/West European affairs', in K. Cordell (ed.) *Ethnicity and Democratisation in the New Europe,* London: Routledge: 49–60.

Burns, M. (1996) 'Disturbed spirits: minority rights and the New World Orders, 1919 and the 1990s', in S.F. Wells and P. Bailey-Smith (eds) *New European Orders: 1919 and 1991,* Washington, DC: Woodrow Wilson Center.

Butler D. and Kavanagh, D. (1992) *The British General Election of 1992,* New York: St Martin's Press.

—— (1997) *The British General Election of 1997,* New York: St Martin's Press.

Butler, D. and Kitzinger, U. (1996) *The 1975 Referendum,* 2nd edn, London: Macmillan.

Butt Philip, A. (1975) *The Welsh Question: Nationalism in Welsh Politics 1945–70,* Cardiff: University of Wales Press.

Buzan, B. and Wæver, O. (2003) *Regions and Powers: The Structure of International Security,* Cambridge: Cambridge University Press.

Cabrol, K. (2001) 'The European challenge of devolution in Scotland', Paper presented at the conference 'Diversity, Difference and Democracy: Political Responses to the Challenge of Identity', Jean Monnet Centre for European Studies, University of Wales, 22–25 April.

Cadogan Group (1992) *Northern Limits,* Belfast: Cadogan Group.

Camilleri, J.A. and Falk, J. (1992) *The End of Sovereignty?* Aldershot: Edward Elgar Publishing.

Caminal, M. (2002) *El federalismo pluralista. Del federalismo nacional al federalismo plurinacional,* Barcelona: Paidós.

Capotorti, F. (1991) *Study on the Rights of Persons Belonging to Ethnic, Religious and Linguistic Minorities,* New York: United Nations.

Carens, J.H. (1989), 'Membership and Morality' in R.W. Brubaker (ed.) *Immigration and the Politics of Citizenship in Europe and North America,* Lanham and London: University Press of America.

Cassese, A. (1995) *Self-Determination of Peoples. A Legal Reappraisal,* Cambridge: Cambridge University Press.

Castells, M. (1997) *The Information Age: Economy, Society and Culture,* Vol. 1, *The Power of Identity,* Oxford: Blackwell.

Centre for the Study of Public Policy (1993) *New Baltic Barometer I Survey,* 5 September–12 October, Glasgow: University of Strathclyde.

—— (1995) *New Baltic Barometer II Survey,* Fieldwork 3–17 April, Glasgow: University of Strathclyde.

—— (2001) *New Baltic Barometer V Survey,* Fieldwork 4 October–30 November by Saar Poll, Baltic Institute of Social Science and Vilnorus.

Chandler, D. (1999) 'The OSCE and the internationalisation of national minority rights', in K. Cordell (ed.) *Ethnicity and Democratisation in the New Europe,* London: Routledge: 61–76.

Checkel, J. (2000) 'Social construction and integration', *Journal of European Public Policy,* 6(4): 545–60.

Checkel, J.T. (1999) 'Norms, institutions, and national identity in contemporary Europe', *International Studies Quarterly*, 43: 83–114.

Christiansen, T. (1998) 'Plaid Cymru: dilemmas and ambiguities of Welsh regional nationalism', in L. de Winter and H. Türsan (eds) *Regionalist Parties in Western Europe*, London: Routledge: 125–42.

Chrysostomides, K. (2000) *The Republic of Cyprus: A Study in International Law*, The Hague and London: M. Nijhoff Publishers.

Cigar, N. (2001) *Vojislav Kostunica and Serbia's Future*, London: Saqui Books/The Bosnian Institute.

Çinar, D. (1994) 'From aliens to citizens: a comparative analysis of rules of transition', in R. Bauböck (ed.) *From Aliens to Citizens: Redefining the Status of Immigrants in Europe*, Aldershot, UK: Avebury.

Citizenship and Migration Board (2003) *Yearbook*. Tallinn (at www.mig.ee).

Citron, S. (1987) *Le mythe national*, Paris: Les éditions ouvrières.

Closa, C. (2002) 'La Pluralidad Nacional en un mismo Estado y en la UE', in F. Requejo (ed.) *Democracia y pluralismo nacional*, Barcelona: Ariel.

Cochrane, F. (2001) 'Unsung heroes? The role of peace and conflict resolution organizations in the Northern Ireland Conflict', in J. McGarry (ed.) *Northern Ireland and the Divided World*, Oxford: Oxford University Press.

Cohen, J. (1998) *Conflict Prevention Instruments in the Organisation for Security and Cooperation in Europe,* The Hague: Netherlands Institute of International Relations.

Collectif (1997) *Toute l'histoire de Bretagne*, Morlaix: Skol Vreizh.

—— (1998) *L'espoir breton du XXIè siècle. La Bretagne en âge de réveil*, Spézet: Coop-Breizh.

Connor, W. (1999) 'National self-determination and tomorrow's political map', in A.C. Cairns, J.C. Courtney, P. MacKinnon, H.J. Michelman and D.E. Smith (eds) *Citizenship, Diversity and Pluralism: Canadian and Comparative Perspectives*, Montreal: McGill-Queen's University Press.

Convenció Catalana per al debat sobre el future de la Unió Europea (2003) 80 Propostes per una nova Europa, Barcelona: Generalitat de Catalunya.

Conversi, D. (1997) *The Basques, the Catalans and Spain*, London: Hurst and Company.

Cordell, K. (2002) 'The creation of a "multicultural Estonia" and the decline and disappearance of the last of the Baltic Germans', unpublished paper presented at the International Conference 'Multicultural Estonia' organised by the Integration Foundation of the Ministry of Foreign Affairs of the Republic of Estonia, Tallinn, 24–25 October.

Cordell, K. and Wolff, S. (2005) *The German Question Continued? German–Czech and German–Polish Relations since 1990*, London: Routledge.

Cornwall, M. (1996) 'Minority rights and wrongs in Eastern Europe in the twentieth century', *The Historian*, 50: 16–20.

Council of Europe (COE) (1997) *European Convention on Nationality and Explanatory Report*, Strasbourg: Council of Europe, Document DIR/JUR (97) 6.

Courchene, T.J. (2001) *A State of Minds. Toward a Human Capital Future for Canadians*, Montreal: Institute for Research in Public Policy.

Cox, M. (1997) 'Bringing in the "international": the IRA ceasefire and the end of the Cold War', *International Affairs*, 14(1): 671–93.

Croisat, M. (1995) *Le fédéralisme dans les démocraties contemporaines*, Paris: Monchrestien.

CSCE (1992) 'Helsinki Document: The Challenges of Change', Helsinki, 9–10 July.

Csepeli, G. (1997) *National Identity in Contemporary Hungary*, Boulder, CO: Social Science Monographs.

—— (1998) 'Not known, only felt: representation of national sovereignty in Hungarian society today', in C. Gombar, E. Hankiss, L. Lengyel and G. Virnai (eds) *The Appeal of Sovereignty*, Boulder, Colorado: Social Science Monographs.

Csergö, Z. (2002) 'Beyond ethnic division: majority–minority debate about the post-communist state in Romania and Slovakia', *East European Politics and Societies*, 16(1): 4–5.

Csergö, Z. and Goldgeier, J.M. (2004) 'Nationalist strategies and European integration', *Perspectives on Politics*, 2(1): 21–37.

CTK (2002) 'Slovakia astonished by Hungary linking Status Law to NATO accession', 14 February.

Cyprus Weekly (2002) 'Tough task for Annan', 6 September.

Daftary, F. and Gál, K. (2000) 'The New Slovak Language Law: internal or external politics', *ECMI Working Paper* no. 8, September: 1–71: www.ecmi.de/doc/download/working_paper_8.pdf.

Dahl, R.A. (1989) *Democracy and its Critics*, New Haven: Yale University Press.

—— (2001) *How Democratic is the American Constitution?* New Haven: Yale University Press.

Dahrendorf, R. (1995) 'Preserving prosperity', *New Statesmen and Society*, 13(29): 36–40.

—— (2000) 'La sconfitta della vecchia democrazia', *La Repubblica*, 12 January.

Danspeckgruber, W. (2002) 'Self-determination and regionalisation in contemporary Europe', in W. Danspeckgruber (ed.) *The Self-determination of Peoples: Community, Nation and State in an Interdependent World*, Boulder, CO: Lynne Rienner.

Dauvin, P. (1993) *Constructions et représentations de l'institution régionale. L'exemple breton*. Thèse pour le doctorat d'études politiques. Faculté de droit et de science politique, Université Rennes 1.

Davies, D.H. (1983) *The Welsh Nationalist Party, 1925–1945*, Cardiff: University of Wales Press.

Davies, N. (1997) *Europe. A History*, London: Pimlico.

De Castro, J.L. and Ugalde, A. (2004) *La acción exterior del País Vasco (1980–2003)*, Oñati: Ivap.

De Pablo, S., Mees, L. and Rodríguez Ranz, J.A. (1999/2001) *El péndulo patriótico: Historia del Partido Nacionalista Vasco*, 2 vols, Barcelona: Crítica.

De Winter, L. (1998) 'The Volksunie and the dilemma between policy success and electoral survival in Flanders', in L. de Winter and H. Tursan (eds) *Regionalist Parties in Western Europe*, London: Routledge.

—— (2001) *The Impact of European Integration on Ethnoregionalist Parties*, Working Paper no. 195, Institut de Ciènces Polítiques I Socials, Barcelona.

De Winter, L. and Gomez-Reino Cachafeiro, M. (2002) 'European integration and ethnoregionalist parties', *Party Politics*, 8(4): 483–503.

De Witte, B. (forthcoming) 'The constitutional resources for an EU minority protection policy', in G.N. Toggenburg (ed.) *The Protection of Minorities and the Enlarged Union. The Way Forward*, Budapest: LGI Books.

De Witte, B. and Toggenburg, G.N. (2004) 'Human rights and membership of the

European Union', in S. Peers and A. Ward (eds) *The EU Charter of Fundamental Rights: Law Context and Policy*, Oxford: Hart: 61–2.

Deets, S. (2002a) 'Liberal pluralism: does the West have any to export?', *Journal on Ethnopolitics and Minority Issues in Europe*, 4. Available at: www.ecmi.de/jemie/download/Focus4-2002_Deets.pdf [online version].

—— (2002b) 'Reconsidering East European Minority Policy: Liberal Theory and European Norms', *East European Politics and Societies*, vol. 16/1: 30–53.

Delanty, G. (1996) 'Northern Ireland in a Europe of regions', *Political Quarterly*, 67(2): 127–34.

Dellenbrant, J.-Å. (1994) 'Multi-partyism in the Baltic states', in S. Berglund and J-Å. Dellenbrant (eds) *The New Democracies in Eastern Europe*, Cheltenham: Edward Elgar.

Deutsch, K. (1953) *Nationalism and Social Communication: An Inquiry into the Foundations of Nationality*, Cambridge, MA: Technology Press of the Massachusetts Institute of Technology.

Deutsche Presse Agentur (2001) 'Hungary hails Ukrainian stance on controversial law', 2 August.

Diez, T. (ed.) (2002) *The European Union and the Cyprus Conflict – Modern Conflict, Post Modern Union*, Manchester: Manchester University Press.

Diez, T., Stetter, S. and Albert, M. (2004) 'The EU and the transformation of border conflicts', *EUBorderConf Working Papers*, no. 1, January.

Dimitras, P. (2004) *Recognition of Minorities in Europe: Protecting Rights and Dignity*, London: Minority Rights Group.

Dixon, P. (2000) 'European integration and Irish disunity', in S. Byrne and C. Irvin, (eds) *Reconcilable Differences: Turning Points in Ethnopolitical Conflicts*, West Hartford: Kumarian Press: 174–89.

Dragovic, J. (2004) 'Rethinking Yugoslavia: Serbian intellectuals and the "national question" in historical perspective', *Contemporary European History*, 13(2): 170–84.

Drucker, H. (1977) *Breakaway: The Scottish Labour Party*, Edinburgh: EUSPB.

Druviete, I. (1997) 'Linguistic human rights in the Baltic states', *International Journal of the Sociology of Language*, 127: 161–85.

Dupoirier, E. (1993) 'The Maastricht referendum and the RegDuons', *Review of Administrative Science of the Western Mediterranean*, no. 10.

Durkheim, E. (1973) 'Pacifisme et Patiotisme', translated by N. Layne, *Sociological Inquiry*, 43(2): 99–103.

Dutceac, A. (2004) 'Globalization and ethnic conflict: beyond the liberal–nationalist distinction', *The Global Review of Ethnopolitics*, 3(2): 20–39.

Duvold, Kj. and Jurkynas, M. (2004) 'Lithuania', in S. Berglund, J. Ekman and F. Aarebrot (eds) *The Handbook of Political Change in Eastern Europe*, Cheltenham: Edward Elgar.

ECRE (2002) 'European Council on Refugees and Exiles Country Report 2002: Serbia and Montenegro'. Available at: www.ecre.org.

Edwards, D. (ed.) (1988) *A Claim of Right for Scotland*, Edinburgh: Polygon.

Eisfeld, A. (1993) 'Zwischen Bleiben und Gehen: Die Deutschen in den Nachfolgestaaten der Sowjetunion', *Aus Politik und Zeitgeschichte*, no. 48/1993.

Ekeus, R. (2001) 'Sovereignty, responsibility, and national minorities', Statement by the OSCE High Commissioner on National Minorities, Rolf Ekeus, 26 October, HCNM.GAL/5/01.

Elazar, D. (1987) *Exploring Federalism*, Tuscaloosa, AL: The University of Alabama Press.

Elégoët, F. (2000) *Bretagne, vingtième siècle*, Rennes, France: Université de Bretagne.

Elias, A. (2004) 'A squandered success? The experiences of "Plaid Cymru – the Party of Wales" in the National Assembly of Wales', Paper presented at the colloquium *Les partis régionalistes en Europe*, Université Libre de Bruxelles, 27–28 February.

Emerson, M. and Tocci, N. (2002) *Cyprus as Lighthouse of the Eastern Mediterranean*, Brussels: CEPS.

ESI (European Stability Initiative) (2004) 'The Lausanne Principle: multiethnicity, territory and the future of Kosovo's Serbs', 7 June 2004, Berlin: ESI.

Estebanez, M. (1997) 'The High Commissioner on National Minorities: development of the mandate', in M. Brohe, N. Ronzitti and A. Rosas (eds) *The OSCE in the Maintenance of Peace and Security*, New York: Springer.

European Anti-Capitalist Left (2003), *Statement of the Paris Meeting of the Anti-Capitalist Left*, November.

European Bank for Reconstruction and Development (EBRD) (2004) *Transition Report 2004: Infrastructure*, London: EBRD.

European Commission for Democracy through Law (1996) 'Opinion of the Venice Commission on the Interpretation of Article 11 of the draft protocol to the European Convention on Human Rights appended to Recommendation 1201'.

—— (2001) Report on the Preferential Treatment of National Minorities by their Kin-State, 22 October.

European Convention (2002) Paper presented by regions with legislative powers within the EU, CONV 321/02, Marienhamm (Åland Islands), Helsinki/Brussels.

Evans, G. (2003) 'Will we ever vote for the Euro?' in A. Park, J. Curtice, K. Thomson, L. Jarvis and C. Bromley (eds) *British Social Attitudes. Community and Change Over Two Decades. The 20th Report*, London: Sage Publications.

Faist, T. (2001) 'Dual Citizenship as Overlapping Membership', Willy Brandt Working Paper Series no. 3, IMER, Malmö University.

Fenet, A. (1995), 'L'Europe et les minorités', in A. Fenet (ed.) *Le Droit et les Minorités*, Brussels: Bruylant: 83–195.

Finnemore, M. and Sikkink, K. (1998) 'International norm dynamics and political change', *International Organisation*, 52(4): 887–917.

Fitzmaurice, J. (1999) 'Belgium. A laboratory of federalism', in D. MacIvor (ed.) *The Politics of Multinational States*, Houndmills, UK: Macmillan: 87–106.

Ford, S. (1999) 'OSCE national minority rights in the United States: the limits of conflict resolution', *Suffolk Transnational Law Review*, 23(1): 1–55.

Foundation on Inter-Ethnic Relations (1999) *The Lund Recommendations on the Effective Participation of National Minorities in Public Life and Explanatory Notes*, The Hague.

Fowler, B. (2002) 'Fuzzing citizenship, nationalising political space: a framework for interpreting the Hungarian "Status Law" as a new form of kin-state policy in Central and Eastern Europe', ESRC 'One Europe or Several?' Working Paper no. 40/02, Brighton: University of Sussex.

Fraser, N. and Honneth, A. (2003) *Recognition or Redistribution? A Political-Philosophical Exchange*, London: Verso.

Friedrich, C. (1968) *Trends of Federalism in Theory and Practice*, Praeger: New York.

Fure, J.S. (1997) 'The German–Polish border region: a case of regional integration?', ARENA Working Papers, no. 97/19, Oslo: ARENA Project.

Gagnon, A.G. (2001) 'Le Québec, une nation inscrite au sein d'une démocratie étriquée', in J. McCure and A.G. Gagnon (eds) *Repères en mutation. Identité et citoyenneté dans le Québec contemporain*, Montreal: Québec-Amérique.

Gal, K. (1999) 'Bilateral agreements in Central and Eastern Europe: a new interstate framework for minority protection', Flensburg: European Centre for Minority Issues, Working Paper no. 4.

Gauthier, D. (1994) 'Breaking up: an essay on secession', *Canadian Journal of Philosophy*, 24(3): 357–72.

Gelazis, N.M. (2003) 'The effects of EU conditionality on citizenship policies and the protection of national minorities in the Baltic states', in V. Pettai and J. Zielonka (eds) *The Road to the European Union: Estonia, Latvia and Lithuania*, vol. 2, Manchester: Manchester University Press: 46–74.

Gilbert, G. (2002) 'The burgeoning minority rights jurisprudence of the European Court of Human Rights', *Human Rights Quarterly*, 24(3): 736–80.

Giordan, H. (ed.) (1992) *Les minorités en Europe*, Paris: Droits linguistiques et droits de l'Homme, Edition Kimé.

Glenny, M. (2004) 'The Kosovo question and regional stability', in J. Batt (ed.) *The Western Balkans: Moving On*, Chaillot Paper no. 70, Paris: EU Institute for Security Studies.

Grabbe, H. (2001) 'How does Europeanisation affect CEE governance? Conditionality, diffusion and diversity', *Journal of European Public Policy*, 8(6): 1013–31.

Greek Helsinki Monitor (2000) 'Statement at the OSCE on (Partly or Fully) Unrecognized Minorities in Albania, Bulgaria, France, Greece, Macedonia, Slovenia and Turkey', 24 October, posted on MINELRES.

Gribincea, M. (2001) *The Russian Policy on Military Bases: Georgia and Moldova*, Oradea, Romania: Cogito.

Guelke, A. (1988) *Northern Ireland: The International Dimension*, Dublin: Gill and Macmillan.

Guglielmo, R. (2004) 'Minority protection. Long-term implications of the EU accession process', Paper presented at the Conference on 'Minority Protection and the EU: The Way Forward', European Academy, Bolzano, 30–31 January.

Guibernau, M. (1999) *Nations without States. Political Communities in a Global Age*, Cambridge: Polity Press.

—— (2004) *Catalan Nationalism: Francoism, Transition and Democracy*, London: Routledge.

Gurr, T. (2000) *Peoples versus States: Minorities at risk in the New Century*, Washington, DC: United States Institute of Peace Press.

Haagerup, N. (1984). Report drawn up on behalf of the Political Affairs Committee on the situation in Northern Ireland (Haagerup Report), European Parliament Working Documents 1983–4: 1–1526/83.

Haas, E.B. (1990) *When Knowledge is Power: Three Models of Change in International Organisations*, Berkeley and Oxford: University of California Press.

Hagedorn, H. (2001) 'Föderalismus und die deutsche Staatsangehörigkeit: die Einbürgerungspolitik der Bundesländer', in D. Thränhardt (ed.) *Integrationspolitik in föderalistischen Systemen*, Münster: LIT-Verlag: 91–117.

Hagège, C. (2000) *Halte à la mort des langues*, Paris: Édition Odile Jacob.

Hailbronner, K. and Martin, D. (eds) (2003) *Rights and Duties of Dual Nationals, Evolution and Prospects*, The Hague and New York: Kluwer Law International.

Hansen, R. and Weil, P. (2001) 'Introduction: citizenship, immigration and nationality: towards a convergence in Europe', in R. Hansen and P. Weil (eds) *Towards a European Nationality: Citizenship, Immigration and Nationality in the EU*, Basingstoke, Hampshire and New York: Palgrave.

Hansson, U. (2002) 'The Latvian language legislation and the involvement of the OSCE-HCNM: The developments 2000–2002', *The Global Review of Ethnopolitics*, 2(1): 17–28.

Hart, H.L.A. (1995) *El Concepto de Derecho*, Buenos Aires: Abeledo-Perrot.

Harvie, C. (1994) *The Rise of Regional Europe*, New York: Routledge.

—— (1998) *No Gods and Precious Few Heroes. Twentieth-Century Scotland*, 3rd edn, Edinburgh: Edinburgh University Press.

HCNM (1993) 'Letter to His Excellency Mr Trivimi Velliste Foreign Minister of the Republic of Estonia, by Max van der Stoel', 6 April, Document no. 206/93/L/Rev.

—— (1994) 'Letter to His Excellency Mr Jüri Luik Foreign Minister of the Republic of Estonia, by Max van der Stoel', 9 March, Document no. 3005/94/L.

—— (1997) 'Letter to His Excellency Mr Toomas Hendrik Ilves Minister for Foreign Affairs of the Republic of Estonia, by Max van der Stoel the OSCE High Commissioner on National Minorities', 21 May, Document no. 359/97/L.

Heintze, H.-J. (2000) 'The status of German minorities in bilateral agreements of the Federal Republic', in S. Wolff (ed.) *German Minorities in Europe: Ethnic Identity and Cultural Belonging*, New York and Oxford: Berghahn.

—— (2004) 'Bilateral agreements and their role in the settlement of ethnic conflicts: a case study of German minorities', in U. Schneckener and S. Wolff (eds) *Managing and Settling Ethnic Conflicts*, London: Hurst and New York: Palgrave Macmillan.

Held, D. (2003) 'Cosmopolitanism: taming globalization', in D. Held and A. McGrew (eds) *The Global Transformations Reader*, Cambridge: Polity Press.

Heller, H. (1985) *Teoría del Estrado*, México: Fondo de Cultura Económica.

Henrard, K. (2000) *Devising an Adequate System of Minority Protection*, The Hague, Boston, London: Martinus Nijhoff.

—— (2001) 'The interrelationship between individual human rights, minority rights and the right to self-determination and its importance for the adequate protection of linguistic minorities', *The Global Review of Ethnopolitics*, 1(1): 41–61.

—— (2003) 'Relating human rights, minority rights and self-determination to minority protection', in U. Schneckener and S. Wolff (eds) *Managing and Settling Ethnic Conflicts*, London: Hurst and New York: Palgrave Macmillan.

Hermant, D. (1992) 'Nationalismes et construction européenne', *Cultures et Conflits*, 7: 1–7.

Hesse, K. (1996) 'Constitución y Derecho Constitucional', in AAVV. *Manual de Derecho Constitucional.* IVAP-Marcial Pons.

Hillgruber, C. and Jestaedt, M. (1994) *The European Convention on Human Rights and the Protection of National Minorities*, Cologne: Verlag Wissenschaft und Politik.

Hirschman, A.O. (1970) *Exit, Voice and Loyalty*, Princeton: Princeton University Press.

Hobsbawm, E. (1990) *Nations and Nationalism since 1780*, Cambridge: Cambridge University Press.

Hodgett, S. and Meehan, E. (2003) 'Multilevel governance in the European Union: The case of Northern Ireland', in J. Magione (ed.) *Regional Institutions and Governance in the European Union*, London: Praeger: 135–52.

Hofmann, R. (2002a) 'Protecting the rights of national minorities in Europe: first experiences with the Council of Europe Framework Convention for the Protection of National Minorities', *German Yearbook of International Law*, 44: 237–69.

Hofmann, R. (2002b) 'Preferential treatment of kin minorities and monitoring of the implementation of the Framework Convention for National Minorities', *The Protection of National Minorities by their Kin-State*, European Commission for Democracy through Law, Strasbourg.

Hooghe, L. (1996) *Cohesion Policy and the European Union*, Oxford: Clarendon Press.

Hroch, M. (1985) *Preconditions of National Revival in Europe: A Comparative Analysis of the Social Composition of Patriotic Groups among the Smaller European Nations*, Cambridge: Cambridge University Press.

Hughes, J. and Sasse, G. (2003) 'Monitoring the monitors: EU enlargement conditionality and minority protection in the CEECs', *Journal of Ethnopolitics and Minority Issues in Europe*, 1: 1–36.

Hughes, J., Sasse, G. and Gordon, C. (2003) 'EU enlargement, Europeanisation and the dynamics of regionalisation in the CEECs', in M. Keating and J. Hughes (eds), *The Regional Challenge in Central and Eastern Europe. Territorial Restructuring and European Integration*, Presses interuniversitaires européennes/Peter Lang. Online journal: www.ecmi.de/jemie/; edited under the European Centre for Minority Issues (ECMI), Flensburg, Germany.

—— (2004) *Europeanization and Regionalization in Central and Eastern Europe during the EU's Eastward Enlargement: The Myth of Conditionality*, New York: Palgrave.

Huguenin, J. and Martinat, P. (1998) *Les régions entre l'Etat et l'Europe*, Paris: Le Monde Editions.

Hume, J. (1993) 'A New Ireland in a New Europe', in D. Keogh and M. Haltzel (eds) *Northern Ireland and the Politics of Reconciliation*, Cambridge: Cambridge University Press.

Hungarian Radio (2002) 'Premier to ask Hungarians to rethink as status law talks with Slovakia fail', 27 November.

Ibarretxe, J.J. (2003) 'Propuesta de Estatuto Político de la Comunidad de Euskadi', English version on Internet: 'Proposal for the Political Statute of the Community of the Basque Country', www.nuevoestatutodeeuskadi..net/docs/estatutovasco_ing.pdf.

ICG (International Crisis Group) (2001) 'The wages of sin: confronting Bosnia's Republika Srpska', ICG Balkans Report no. 118, 8 October, Brussels.

—— (2002) 'UNMIK's Kosovo albatross: tackling division in Mitrovica' ICG Balkans Report no. 131, 3 June, Brussels.

—— (2003a) 'A marriage of inconvenience: Montenegro 2003', ICG Balkans Report no. 142, 16 April, Brussels.

—— (2003b) 'Bosnia's nationalist governments: Paddy Ashdown and the paradoxes of state-building', ICG Balkans Report no. 146, 22 July, Brussels.

—— (2004) 'Collapse in Kosovo', ICG Balkans Report no. 155, 22 April, Brussels.

Infodienst Deutsche Aussiedler (2000) 'Besuch des Aussiedlerbeauftragten der

Bundesregierung in Kasachstan und Kyrgystan', Berlin: Bundesministerium des Innern.

—— (2001) '10 Jahre Deutscher Nationaler Rayon Asowo', Berlin: Bundesministerium des Innern.

Ioakimidis, P. (2002) 'The Europeanization of Greece: an overall assessment', in K. Featherstone and G. Kazamias (eds), *Europeanization and the Southern Periphery*, London: Frank Cass.

IOM (1996), 'Citizenship Law of the Republic of Estonia', *Legislative Acts of the CIS and the Baltic States on Citizenship, Migration, and Related Matters*, Moscow and Helsinki: International Organisation for Migration.

Ismailzade, F. (2002) 'The OSCE Minsk Group and the failure of negotiation in the Nagorno-Karabakh conflict,' Caspian Brief no. 23, Cornell Caspian Consulting, April.

Jackson Preece, J. (1998) *National Minorities and the European Nation-States System*, Oxford: Oxford University Press.

Jakobsson Hatay, A. (2001) 'The contribution of European integration to ethnic conflict resolution: the cases of Northern Ireland and Cyprus', *Cyprus Review*, 13(1): 31–57.

Jallon, H. and Mounier, P. (1999) *Les enragés de la République*, Paris: Editions La Découverte.

Jáuregui, G. (1981) *Ideología y estrategia política de ETA: Análisis de su evolución entre 1959 y 1968*, Madrid: Siglo XXI.

—— (1996) *Entre la tragedia y la esperanza: Vasconia ante el nuevo milenio*, Barcelona: Ariel.

—— (1997) *Los nacionalismos minoritarios y la Unión Europea: ¿Utopía o ucronía?*, Barcelona: Ariel.

Jeffrey, C. (2000) 'Sub-national mobilisation and European integration: Does it make any difference?' *Journal of Common Market Studies*, 38(1): 1–23.

Jellinek, G. (1981) *Fragmentos de Estado*, translation of *Uber Staatsfragmente*, Madrid: Civitas.

Jones, R.W. (2000) 'Penblwydd Hapus', *Barn*, July, 8–9.

Jones, T. (1985) *Plaid Cymru and Welsh Politics: 1979–85*, Plaid Cymru Archive.

Jurado, E. (2003) *Complying with European standards of minority protection: Estonia's relations with the European Union, OSCE and Council of Europe*, DPhil thesis, Oriel College, University of Oxford.

Kant, I. (1996) *Practical Philosophy*, Cambridge: Cambridge University Press.

Kaplan, D. (2000) 'Conflict and compromise among borderland identities in Northern Italy', *Tijdschrift voor Economische en Sociale Geografie*, 91(1): 44–60.

Kask, P. (1994) 'National radicalization in Estonia: legislation on citizenship and related issues', *Nationalities Papers*, 22(2): 379–91.

Kaufman, S. (2001) *Modern Hatreds: The Symbolic Politics of Ethnic War*, Ithaca: Cornell University Press.

Kearney, R. (1997) *Postnationalist Ireland. Politics, Culture, Philosophy*, London: Routledge.

Kearney, R. and Wilson, R. (1997) 'Northern Ireland's future as a European region', in R. Kearney (ed.) *Postnationalist Ireland*, London: Routledge.

Keating, M. (1996) *Nations against the State. The New Politics of Nationalism in Quebec, Catalonia and Scotland*, London: Macmillan.

—— (1997) 'Stateless nation-building: Quebec, Catalonia and Scotland in the changing state system', *Nations and Nationalism*, 3 (4): 689–717.

—— (1998) *The New Regionalism in Western Europe. Territorial Restructuring and Political Change*, Aldershot: Edward Elgar.

—— (2001a) *Plurinational Democracy. Stateless Nations in a Post-Sovereignty Era*, Oxford: Oxford University Press.

—— (2001b) 'Nations without states: the accommodation of nationalism in the new state order', in M. Keating and J. McGarry (eds) *Minority Nationalism and Changing International Order*, Oxford: Oxford University Press: 19–43.

—— (2001b) 'Northern Ireland and the Basque Country', in J. McGarry, (ed.) *Northern Ireland and the Divided World: Post-Agreement Northern Ireland in Comparative Perspective*, Oxford: Oxford University Press: 181–208.

—— (2003), 'Regionalization in Central and Eastern Europe. The diffusion of a Western Model?', in M. Keating and J. Hughes (eds) *The Regional Challenge in Central and Eastern Europe. Territorial Restructuring and European Integration*, Paris: Presses interuniversitaires européennes/Peter Lang.

—— (2004a) 'European integration and the nationalities question', *Politics and Society*, 32(3): 367–88.

—— (2004b) 'European integration and the nationalities question', Paper presented at Conference on 'Nations, Minorities and European Integration', 7–8 May, European University Institute, Florence.

Keating, M. and McGarry, J. (2001a) 'Introduction', in M. Keating and J. McGarry (eds) *Minority Nationalism and the Changing International Order*, Oxford: Oxford University Press.

—— (eds) (2001b) *Minority Nationalism and the Changing International Order*, Oxford: Oxford University Press.

Keating, M., Loughlin, J. and Deschouwer, K. (2003) *Culture, Institutions and Economic Development. A Study of Eight European Regions*, Aldershot: Edward Elgar.

Keelan, P. (1989) *Beyond Thatcher – Wales 2000 in a Green Europe*, Cardiff: Plaid Cymru Archive.

Kemp, W. (2001) *Quiet Diplomacy in Action: The OSCE High Commissioner on National Minorities*, The Hague, London and Boston, MA: Kluwer Law International.

—— (2002) 'Applying the nationality principle: handle with care', *Journal on Ethnopolitics and Minority Issues in Europe*, 4. Available at: www.ecmi.de/jemie/download/Focus4-2002_Kemp_Kymlicka.pdf.

Kennedy, D. (1994) 'The European Union and the Northern Ireland question', in B. Barton and P. Roche (eds) *The Northern Ireland Question: Perspectives and Policies*, Aldershot: Avebury.

Keohane, R.O. (1984) *After Hegemony: Cooperation and Discord in the World Political Economy*, Princeton, NJ: Princeton University Press.

Kerremans, B. (2000) 'Determining a European policy in a multi-level setting: the case of specialised co-ordination in Belgium', *Regional and Federal Studies*, 10(1): 36–61.

Kionka, R. (2000) *The International Politics of Estonian Nationality Policy*, unpublished manuscript.

Kis, J. (2001) 'Nation-building and beyond', in W. Kymlicka and M. Opalski, *Can Liberal Pluralism be Exported? Western Political Theory and Ethnic Relations in Eastern Europe*, Oxford: Oxford University Press: 220–42.

Knaus, G. and Cox, M. (2004) 'Bosnia and Hercegovina: Europeanisation by decree?' in J. Batt (ed.) *The Western Balkans: Moving On*, Chaillot Paper no. 70, Paris: EU Institute for Security Studies.

Kovacs, M. (2003) 'Standards of self-determination and standards of minority-rights in the post-communist era: a historical perspective', *Nations and Nationalism* 9(3): 433–50.

Kovziridze, T. (2002) 'Europeanization of federal institutional relationships: hierarchical and interdependent relationship structures in Belgium, Germany and Austria', *Regional and Federal Studies*, 12(3): 128–55.

Kramer, H. (1997) 'The Cyprus problem and European security', *Survival*, 39(3): 16–32.

Kristeva, J. (1995) 'Strangers to ourselves', in R. Kearney (ed.) *States of Mind: Dialogues with Contemporary Thinkers on the European Mind*, Manchester: Manchester University Press.

Kymlicka, W. (1995) *Multicultural Citizenship: A Liberal Theory of Minority Rights*, Oxford: Clarendon Press.

—— (2001a) 'Western political theory and ethnic relations in Eastern Europe', in W. Kymlicka and M. Opalski (eds) *Can Liberal Pluralism Be Exported?*, Oxford: Oxford University Press.

—— (2001b) 'Reply and conclusion', in W. Kymlicka and M. Opalski (eds) *Can Liberal Pluralism Be Exported? Western Political Theory and Ethnic Relations in Eastern Europe*, Oxford: Oxford University Press.

—— (2001c) *Politics in the Vernacular: Nationalism, Multiculturalism and Citizenship*, Oxford: Oxford University Press.

—— (2002) 'The impact of group rights on fear and trust: a response to Offe', *Hagar: International Social Science Review*, 3(1): 19–36.

—— (2003) 'Canadian multiculturalism in historical and comparative perspective', *Constitutional Forum*, 13(1): 1–8.

—— (2004) 'Justice and security in the accommodation of minority nationalism: comparing East and West', in A. Dieckhoff (ed.) *The Politics of Belonging: Nationalism, Liberalism and Pluralism*, New York: Lexington: 127–54.

Kymlicka, W. and Opalski, M. (2001) *Can Liberal Pluralism be Exported? Western Political Theory and Ethnic Relations in Eastern Europe*, Oxford: Oxford University Press.

Kymlicka, W. and Grin, F. (2003) 'Assessing the politics of diversity in transition countries', in F. Daftary and F. Grin (eds) *Nation-building, Ethnicity and Language Politics in Transition Countries*, Budapest: LGI.

Kymlicka, W. and Patten, A. (2003) 'Language rights and political theory: context, issues and approaches', in W. Kymlicka and A. Patten (eds) *Language Rights and Political Theory*, Oxford: Oxford University Press.

Labasse, J. (1991) *L'Europe des régions*, Paris: Flammarion.

Lacaita, F. (2004) 'What Europe for Northern Ireland? European approaches and conflict resolution', Paper presented at the Conference on 'Northern Ireland: A Civil or Uncivil Society?', 25 September, Burwalls Centre for Continuing Education, Bristol, UK.

Lachuer, V. (1998) 'L'Etat face à la langue bretonne – Klask, Klaskerezh Keltiek/Recherche celtique', *Revue du Centre de Recherche sur la Bretagne et les Pays Celtiques*, vol. 4, Rennes, France: Presses Universitaires de Rennes.

Lagerspetz, M. and Vogt, H. (2004) 'Estonia', in S. Berglund, J. Ekman and F. Aarebrot (eds) *The Handbook of Political Change in Eastern Europe*, Cheltenham: Edward Elgar.

Laitin, D. (1998) *Identity in Formation: The Russian-speaking Populations in the Near Abroad*, Ithaca, NY and London: Cornell University Press.

—— (2001) 'National identities in the emerging European state', in M. Keating and J. McGarry (eds) *Minority Nationalism and the Changing International Order*, Oxford: Oxford University Press: 84–113.

Language Training Strategy for the Non-Estonian-Speaking Population, 21 April 1998. Tallinn.

Lapidus, G.W. (2004) 'Transforming the national question' in A. Brown (ed.) *The Demise of Marxism-Leninism in Russia*, Basingstoke: Palgrave Macmillan, 119–77.

Lauristin, M. and Vihalemm, P. (1997) *Return to the Western World*, Tartu: Tartu University Press.

Le Coadic, R. (1997) *L'identité bretonne*, Thèse de sociologie, Université Bretagne Occidentale (Brest).

Le Rhun, P.-Y. (1991) *La Bretagne face à l'Europe et à l'Ile-de-France*, Morlaix: Skol Vreizh.

Le Tellier (sous la dir. De G.) (1998) *L'espoir breton du 21e siècle*, Spézet: Coop-Breizh.

Lewis, S. (1926) *Egwyddorion Cenedlaetholdeb*, Plaid Cymru: Machynlleth.

Lewis-Anthony, S. (1998) 'Autonomy and the Council of Europe – with special reference to the application of Article 3 of the First Protocol of the European Convention on Human Rights', in M. Suksi (ed.) *Autonomy: Applications and Implications*, The Hague: Kluwer: 317–42.

—— (1999) 'Autonomy and the Council of Europe – with special reference to the application of Article 3 of the First Protocol of the European Convention on Human Rights', in M. Suski (ed.) *Autonomy: Applications and Implication*. The Hague: Kluwer Law International: 317–42.

Liberal Party (1975) *The Liberal Programme for Europe*, London: Liberal Party.

Liebich, A. (2004) 'The old and the new: historical dimensions of majority–minority relations in an enlarged Union', presented at ECMI conference on 'An Ever More Diverse Union?', Berlin.

Lijphart, A. (1977) *Democracy in Plural Societies. A Comparative Exploration*, New Haven: Yale University Press.

—— (1995) 'Multiethnic democracy' in S.M. Lipset (ed.) *The Encyclopedia of Democracy*, Washington, DC: CQ Press, vol. 3, 853–65.

Linz, J. and Stepan, A. (1996) *Problems of Democratic Transition and Consolidation*, Baltimore, MD: Johns Hopkins University Press.

Lipset, S.M. (1960) *Political Man*, New York: Doubleday.

Lipsett, S.M. and Rokkan, S. (eds) (1967) *Party Systems and Voter Alignments*, New York: Free Press.

Lukic, R. and Lynch, A. (1996) *Europe from the Balkans to the Urals: The Disintegration of Yugoslavia and the Soviet Union*, Oxford: Oxford University Press for SIPRI.

Lustick, I. (1993) *Unsettled States, Disputed Lands: Britain and Ireland, France and Algeria, Israel and the West Bank-Gaza*, Ithaca, NY: Cornell University Press.

Luttwak, E. (1999) 'Give war a chance', *Foreign Affairs*, 78(4).

Lynch, P. (1995) 'From red to green: the political strategy of Plaid Cymru in the 1980s and 1990s', *Journal of Federal and Regional Studies*, 5(2): 197–210.

—— (1996) *Minority Nationalism and European Integration*, Cardiff: University of Wales Press.

—— (2002) *SNP. The History of the Scottish National Party*, Cardiff: Welsh Academic Press.

Lyne, T. (1990) 'Ireland, Northern Ireland and 1992: the barriers to technocratic anti-partitionism', *Public Administration*. 68(4): 417–33.

MacCormick, N. (1988) 'Unrepentant gradualism', in D. Edwards (ed.) *A Claim of Right for Scotland,* Edinburgh: Polygon.

—— (1993) 'Beyond the sovereign state', *The Modern Law Review*, 56(1).

—— (1999) *Questioning Sovereignty. Law, State and Nation in the European Commonwealth*, Oxford: Oxford University Press.

—— (2003) 'European convention, draft constitution, and stateless nations: What's in it for Wales?' Speech given at the Institute of Welsh Affairs, University of Aberystwyth, 3 November.

MacGinty, R. (1997) 'American influences on the Northern Ireland peace process', *Journal of Conflict Studies*, 43.

Macwhirter, I. (1992) 'The political year in Westminster October 1990–July 1991', *Scottish Government Yearbook*.

McAllister, L. (2001) *Plaid Cymru: The Emergence of a Political Party*, Bridgend: Poetry Wales Press.

McCall, C. (1998) 'Postmodern Europe and the resources of communal identities in Northern Ireland', *European Journal of Political Research*, 33: 389–411.

McCrone, D. (1998) *The Sociology of Nationalism*, London: Routledge.

McGarry, J. (1998) 'Orphans of secession: national pluralism in secessionist regions and post-secessionist states', in M. Moore (ed.) *National Self-Determination and Secession*, Oxford: Oxford University Press: 215–32.

—— (2001a) 'Globalization, European integration and the Northern Ireland conflict', in M. Keating and J. McGarry (eds) *Minority Nationalism and the Changing International Order*, Oxford: Oxford University Press: 295–323.

—— (2001b) 'Northern Ireland, civic nationalism, and the Good Friday Agreement', in J. McGarry (ed.) *Northern Ireland and the Divided World*, Oxford: Oxford University Press: 109–36.

—— (2004) 'The impact of European integration on the Northern Ireland conflict', Paper presented at Conference on 'Nations, Minorities and European Integration', 7–8 May, European University Institute, Florence.

McGarry, J. and O'Leary, B. (1995) *Explaining Northern Ireland: Broken Images*, Oxford: Blackwell.

—— (2004) *The Northern Ireland Conflict: Consociational Engagements*, Oxford: Oxford University Press.

McGarry, J. and Moore, M. (2005) 'Karl Renner, power-sharing and non-territorial autonomy', in E. Nimni (ed.) *National Cultural Autonomy and its Contemporary Critics*, London: Routledge: 74–94.

McIntyre, A. (1998) 'We, the IRA, have failed', *Guardian*, 22 May.

McKay, D. (1996) *Rush to Union. Understanding the European Federal Bargain*, Oxford: Clarendon.

Malinverni, G. (2002) 'La Protection Des Minorities Nationales Par Leur Etat-Parent', in *The Protection of National Minorities by their Kin-State*, European Commission for Democracy through Law, Strasbourg.

March, J.G. and J.P. Olsen (1999) 'The institutional dynamics of international political orders', in P.J. Katzenstein, R.O. Keohane and S.D. Krasner (eds) *Exploration and Contestation in the Study of World Politics*, Cambridge, MA: MIT Press.

Marcus, L.P. (2000) 'The Carpathian Germans', in S. Wolff (ed.) *German Minorities in Europe: Ethnic Identity and Cultural Belonging*, New York and Oxford: Berghahn.

Margalit, A. and Raz, J. (1990) 'National self-determination', *Journal of Philosophy*, 87(9): 439–61.

Martin, D. (1988) *Bringing Common Sense to the Common Market: A Left Agenda for Europe*, London: Fabian Society, Tract no. 525.

Martray, J. and Ollivro, J. (2001) *La Bretagne au cœur du monde nouveau*, Rennes, France: Les Portes du large.

—— (2002) *La Bretagne réunifiée, une véritable région ouverte sur le monde*, Rennes, France: Les Portes du large.

Marx, K. and Engels, F. (2002) *The Communist Manifesto*, London: Penguin.

Mathews, G.E. (1971) *Wales and the Common Market*, Cardiff: Plaid Cymru.

May, S. (2001) *Language and Minority Rights: Ethnicity, Nationalism and the Politics of Language*, London and New York: Longman.

—— (2003) 'Language, nationalism and democracy in Europe', in G. Hogan-Brun and S. Wolff (eds) *Minority Languages in Europe: Frameworks, Status, Prospects*, London: Palgrave Macmillan.

Meehan, E. (1992) 'Citizens are plural', *Fortnight*, 311: 13–14.

—— (2000) ' "Britain's Irish Question: Britain's European Question?" British Irish relations in the context of European Union and the Belfast Agreement', *Review of International Studies*, 26: 83–97.

Merlin, A. (2002) *Regional Initiatives in the South Caucasus*, Geneva: Humanitarian Dialogue, September.

Miall, H. (1992) *New Conflicts in Europe: Prevention and Resolution*, Oxford Research Group, no. 10.

Mill, J.S. (1972) *On Liberty, Utilitarianism, and Considerations on Representative Government*, London: Dent.

Miller, D. (1995) *On Nationality*, Oxford: Clarendon.

—— (2000) *Citizenship and National Identity*, Cambridge: Polity Press.

Minelres (2000) 'New amendments to the Estonian Law on Citizenship'. Available at: www.riga.lv/minelres/archive.htm.

Misiumas, R.J. and Taagepera, R. (1993) *The Baltic States: Years of Dependence 1940–1990*, London: Hurst and Co.: expanded and updated edition.

Mitchell, J. (1996) *Strategies for Self-Government. The Campaigns for a Scottish Parliament*, Edinburgh: Polygon.

Moore, M. (2001) *Ethics of Nationalism*, Oxford: Oxford University Press.

Moravscik, A. (1995) 'Explaining international human rights regimes: liberal theory and Western Europe', *European Journal of International Relations*, 1(2): 157–89.

Morgan, K.O. (1981) *Rebirth of a Nation: Wales 1880–1980*, Oxford: Clarendon Press.

Morris, H.M. (2003) 'EU enlargement and Latvian citizenship policy', *Journal on Ethnopolitics and Minority Issues in Europe*, 1. Available at: www.ecmi.de/jemie/download/Focus1-2003_Morris.pdf.

Morvan, Y. (1997) *Demain, la Bretagne ou la métamorphose du modèle breton*, Rennes, France: Editions Apogée.

MRG (Minority Rights Group) (1997) *World Report on Minorities*, London: Minority Rights Group.

—— (1999) *The Framework Convention for the Protection of National Minorities: A Guide*, London: Minority Rights Group.

Münz, R. and Ohliger, R. (1998) 'Long-distance citizens. Ethnic Germans and their immigration to Germany', in P. Schuck and R. Münz (eds) *Paths to Inclusion. The Integration of Migrants in the United States and Germany*, New York: Berghahn: 155–202.

Murphy, A.B. (1999) 'Rethinking the concept of European identity', in G.H. Herb and D.H. Kaplan (eds) *Nested Identities. Nationalism, Territory, and Scale*, Lanhmam, MD: Rowman and Littlefield.

Murphy, D. (1979) *A Place Apart*, Harmondsworth: Penguin.

Nairn, T. (1997) *Faces of Nationalism: Janus Revisited*, London: Verso: 47–8.

Nelde, P.H. (2000) 'Bilingualism among ethnic Germans in Hungary', in S. Wolff (ed.) *German Minorities in Europe: Ethnic Identity and Cultural Belonging*, New York and Oxford: Berghahn.

Neumann, I.B. (1996) *Russia and the Idea of Europe*, London: Routledge.

News Letter (2004) 'Need to sell Britishness to nationalists', Belfast, 17 May, 5.

Nicolas, M. (1982) *Histoire du mouvement breton*, Paris: Syros.

—— (1986) *Le séparatisme en Bretagne*, Spézet, France: Beltan.

—— (2001) *Bretagne, un destin européen. Ou la Bretagne et le fédéralisme en Europe*, Rennes, France: Presses Universitaires de Rennes.

Nicolas, M. and Pihan, J. (1998) *Les Bretons et la politique. 1958–1988: 30 ans de scrutins en Bretagne*, Rennes, France: Presses Universitaires de Rennes, Institut Culturel de Bretagne.

Nine O'clock (2001) 'Nastase and Orban fail to compromise on Status Law'. Available at: www.nineoclock.ro, accessed 30 July.

O'Leary, B. (1997) 'The Conservative stewardship of Northern Ireland 1979–97. Sound-bottomed contradictions or slow learning?', *Political Studies*, 45(4): 663–76.

—— (2001) 'An iron law of nationalism and federation? A (neo-Diceyian) theory of the necessity of a federal Staatsvolk, and of consociational rescue', *Nations and Nationalism*, 7(3): 273–96.

O'Leary, B. and McGarry, J. (1996) *The Politics of Antagonism: Understanding Northern Ireland*, London: Athlone Press.

O'Leary, B. and Evans, G. (1997) 'Northern Ireland: la fin de siecle, the twilight of the second Protestant Ascendancy and Sinn Fein's second coming', *Parliamentary Affairs*, 50: 672–80.

O'Neill, S. (1999) 'Mutual recognition and the accommodation of national diversity: constitutional justice in Northern Ireland', MS, Queen's University, Belfast.

Offe, C. (1998) '"Homogeneity" and constitutional democracy: coping with identity conflicts with group rights', *Journal of Political Philosophy*, 6(2): 113–41.

—— (2001) 'Political liberalism, group rights and the politics of fear and trust', *Studies in East European Thought*, 53: 167–82.

Ohmae, K. (1995) *The End of the Nation State. The Rise of Regional Economies*, New York: Free Press.

Olgun, E. (2002) 'Some characteristics of the Belgian state that may apply to the New Partnership State of Cyprus', unpublished paper dated 26/06/2002, Brussels.

Ollivro, J. (2000) *La Bretagne en l'an 2000. Diagnostic et tendances prospectives*, Rennes, France: PUR, Collection espace et territoires.

Olsen, J.P. (2001) 'The many faces of Europeanisation', *Arena Working Papers* WP01/2.

Paasi, A. (2002) 'Place and region: regional world and words', *Progress in Human Geography*, 26(6): 802–11.

PACE (1997) Resolution 1117 of Sub-Committee on the Honouring of Obligations and Commitments by Estonia, seventh sitting of the ordinary session, 30 January.

Packer, J. (1996) 'The OSCE and international guarantees of local self-government', in *Local Self-Government, Territorial Integrity, and protection of minorities*, Strasbourg: European Commission for Democracy through Law, Council of Europe Publishing: 250–72

—— (1998) 'Autonomy within the OSCE: the case of Crimea', in M. Suksi (ed.) *Autonomy: Applications and Implications*, The Hague: Kluwer: 295–316.

—— (2000) 'Making international law matter in preventing ethnic conflicts', *New York University Journal of International Law and Politics*, 32(3): 715–24.

—— (2003) 'The practitioner's perspective: minority languages and linguistic minorities in the work of the OSCE High Commissioner on National Minorities', in G. Hogan-Brun and S. Wolff (eds) *Minority Languages in Europe: Frameworks, Status, Prospects*, London: Palgrave Macmillan.

Paladi-Kovacs, A. (1996) *Ethnic Traditions, Classes and Communities*, Budapest: Institute of Ethnology, Hungarian Academy of Science.

Paquin, S. (2001) *La revanche des petites nations. Le Québec, l'Écosse et la Catalogne face à la mondialisation*, Montreal: vlb.

Peeters, P. (1994) 'Federalism: a comparative perspective – Belgium transforms from a unitary to a federal state', in B. de Villers (ed.) *Evaluating Federal Systems*, Dordrecht, Boston, MA, London: Martinus Nijhoff: 194–207.

Pentassuglia, G. (2001) 'The EU and the protection of minorities: the case of Eastern Europe', *European Journal of International Law*, 12(1): 3–38.

—— (2003) *Minorities in International Law*, Strasbourg: Council of Europe Publishing.

Perry, G. (2001) 'Status Law victory', *Budapest Sun*, 5 November.

Pettai, V. (2000a) 'Estonia and Latvia: international influences on citizenship and minority integration,' in A. Pravda and J. Zielonka (eds) *International Influences on Domestic Transition in Central and Eastern Europe*, Oxford: Oxford University Press.

—— (2000b) 'Competing conceptions of multiethnic democracy: debating minority integration in Estonia', Paper presented at the European Consortium for Political Research, 14–19 April, Copenhagen, Denmark.

Pettai, V. and Zielonka, J. (eds) (2003) *The Road to the European Union: Estonia, Latvia and Lithuania*, vol. 2, Manchester: Manchester University Press.

Plaid Cymru (1979) *Plaid Cymru Fights for Wales*, Cardiff: Plaid Cymru.

—— (1981) *Report of the Plaid Cymru Commission of Inquiry*, Cardiff: Plaid Cymru.

—— (1984) *A Voice for Wales in Europe*, Cardiff: Plaid Cymru.

—— (1989) *Wales in Europe. A Community of Communities*, Cardiff: Plaid Cymru.

—— (1995) *A Democratic Wales in a United Europe*, Cardiff: Plaid Cymru.

—— (2004) *Fighting Hard for Wales. A Manifesto for the European Parliament Elections 2004*, Cardiff: Plaid Cymru.

Pogány, I. (2003) 'The impact of EU enlargement on the treatment of national and ethnic minorities in CEE', Paper given at the Workshop 'Implications of Enlargement for the Rule of Law, Democracy and Constitutionalism in Post-Communist Legal Orders', European University Institute, Florence, 28–29 November.

Poleshchuk, V. (2004) 'Non-citizens in Estonia', Legal Information Centre for Human Rights, Report, Tallinn.

Political Inter-regional Observatory (PIO) (2004) 'The regional barometer of 2003. Related to regional synthesis', a study carried out in Brittany, 8–11 September 2003.

Political Declaration of the Constitutional Regions of Bavaria, Catalonia, Scotland, Flanders, North Rhine-Westphalia, Salzburg and Wallonia. Signed in Brussels, 28 May 2001.

Pollock, A. (1993) *A Citizen's Inquiry: The Opsahl Report on Northern Ireland.* Dublin: Lilliput.

Polyakov, E. (2000) *Changing Trade Patterns after Conflict Resolution in the South Caucasus,* Washington, DC: Poverty Reduction and Economic Management Sector Unit, Europe and Central Asia Region World Bank.

Prewitt, K. (2005) 'Racial classification in America', *Daedalus,* 134(1): 5–17.

Prodi, R. (2002) 'The Role of the Regions in building the Europe of tomorrow. Goverance and the Convention; meeting with the Presidents of the Regions, Bellagio, 15 July 2002.

Radaelli, C.M. (2000) 'Whither Europeanization: concept stretching and substantive change', *European Integration online Paper (EioP),* 4(8). Available at: http//ssm.com/abstract=302761.

Rallings, C. and Thrasher, M. (eds) (1997) *Local Elections in Britain,* New York: Routledge.

Rangelov, I. (2001) 'Bulgaria's struggle to make sense of EU human rights criteria', EU Monitoring Accession Program (EUMAP), Open Society Institute, 1 October.

Ratner, S. (2000) 'Does international law matter in preventing ethnic conflicts?' *New York University Journal of International Law and Politics,* 32(3): 591–698.

Raunio, T. (2003) 'Relationships between MEPs and domestic parties: a comparative analysis of regionalist parties', Paper presented at the *ECPR Joint Sessions of Workshops,* Edinburgh, 28 March–2 April.

Report (2000) 'PHARE II: Actions Financed, 1998–2000'. Unpublished document by Ave Härsing, Project Co-ordinator of the EU PHARE Language Training Programme in Estonia.

Republic of Cyprus (1999) *The Cyprus Problem, Historical Review and the Latest Developments,* Information Office, Nicosia.

Requejo, F. (2001) 'Political liberalism in multinational states: the legitimacy of plural and asymmetrical federalism', in A.G. Gagnon and J. Tully (eds) *Multinational Democracies,* Cambridge, UK: Cambridge University Press: 110–32.

RFE/RL (2001a) 'Romania continues attack on Hungarian Status Law', 4 July.

—— (2001b) 'Romania escalates conflict over Status Law', 22 June.

—— (2003) 'Fidesz says cabinet is "hangman of Status Law"', 8 January.

Ricoeur, P. (1995) 'Universality and the power of difference', in R. Kearney (ed.) *States of Mind: Dialogues with Contemporary Thinkers on the European Mind,* Manchester: Manchester University Press.

Riigikogu (1993a) debate on the Bill for the Law establishing Language Requirements for Citizenship, first reading, 20 January.

—— (1993b) debate on the Bill for the Law establishing Language Requirements for Citizenship, second reading, 10 February.

—— (1995) debate on the Bill for the Law on Citizenship, continuation of third reading, 19 January.

—— (1997) debate on the Bill to amend the Aliens Law, continuation of second reading, 24 September.

—— (1998) debate on the Bill to amend the Citizenship Law, third reading, 8 December.

Roberts, H. (1990) 'Sound stupidity: the British party system and the Northern Ireland question', in J. McGarry and B. O'Leary (eds) *The Future of Northern Ireland*, Oxford: Oxford University Press: 100–36.

Roeder, P.G. (2004) *Where Nation-States Come From: Soviet Lessons, Global Implications*, San Diego: University of California at San Diego.

Rose, R. (1994) 'Conflict or compromise in the Baltic states?', *RFE/RL Research Report*, 3(28): 26–35.

—— (2002a) *A Bottom Up Evaluation of Enlargement Countries*, Glasgow: University of Strathclyde Studies in Public Policy no. 364.

—— (2002b) *New Baltic Barometer V: A Pre-enlargement Survey*, Glasgow: University of Strathclyde Studies in Public Policy no. 368.

—— (2003) *New Russia Barometer XI: An End of Term Report*, Glasgow: University of Strathclyde Studies in Public Policy no. 378.

—— (2005) *Are Bulgaria and Romania Up to EU Standards?* Glasgow: University of Strathclyde Studies in Public Policy no. 400.

Rose, R. and Shin, D.C. (2001) 'Democratization backwards: the problem of third-wave democracies', *British Journal of Political Science*, 31(2): 331–54.

Rose, R. and Munro, N. (2003) *Elections and Parties in New European Democracies*, Washington, DC: CQ Press.

Rose, R., Mishler, W. and Haerpfer, C. (1998) *Democracy and Its Alternatives: Understanding Post-Communist Societies*, Oxford: Polity Press and Baltimore, MD: Johns Hopkins University Press.

Roter, P. (1997) 'Towards an international regime relating to the protection of national minorities in Europe', in M. Zagar, B. Jesih and R. Bester (eds) *The Constitutional and Political Regulation of Ethnic Relations and Conflicts*, vol. 2, Ljubljana: Institute for Ethnic Studies.

Rousseau, J.J. (1973) *The Social Contract and Discourses*, trans. G.D.H. Cole, J.H. Brumfitt, John C. Hall London: Everyman.

Rowthorn, B. (1993) 'Foreword', in R. Munck (ed.) *The Irish Economy*, London: Pluto Press.

Ruane, J. and Todd, J. (1996) *The Dynamics of Conflict in Northern Ireland: Power, Conflict and Emancipation*, Cambridge, UK: Cambridge University Press.

Sahlins, P. (1989) *Boundaries: the making of France and Spain in the Pyrenees*, Berkeley, CA: University of California Press.

Salmond, A. and Sturgeon, N. (2004) *A Winning Team*. Online document at: www.salmond-sturgeon.com.

Scharpf, F.W. (1994) 'Community and autonomy: multi-level policy-making in the EU', *Journal of European Public Policy*, 1(1): 219–42.

Scott, A. (1998) *Regions and the World Economy*, Oxford: Oxford University Press.

Scott, J.W. (1999) 'European and North American contexts for cross-border regionalism', *Regional Studies*, 33(13): 605–17.

Scottish Constitutional Convention (1990) *Towards Scotland's Parliament*, Edinburgh: Cosla.

—— (1995) *Scotland's Parliament. Scotland's Right*, Edinburgh: Cosla.

Scottish Executive (2004) *The Scottish Executive's European Strategy*, Edinburgh: Scottish Executive.

Scottish Green Party (2003) *Scotland's Place in the World*, Campaign Manifesto.

Scottish National Party (2004) *Vote for Scotland*, European Parliament Election Manifesto, Edinburgh: SNP.

Scottish Socialist Party (2003) *Another Scotland is possible!* SSP Holyrood Election Campaign Manifesto, Edinburgh: SSP.

Seymour, M., Couture, J. and Nielsen, K. (1998) 'Introduction: questioning the ethnic/civic dichotomy', in J. Couture, K. Nielsen and M. Seymour (eds) *Rethinking Nationalism. Canadian Journal of Philosophy*, 22(Suppl.): 1–61.

Sharp, A. (1996) 'The genie that would not go back into the bottle: national self determination and the legacy of the First World War and the Peace Settlement', in S. Dunn and T.G. Fraser (eds) *Europe and Ethnicity: The First World War and Contemporary Ethnic Conflict*, London: Routledge.

Siedentop, L. (2000) *Democracy in Europe*, London: Allen Lane.

Smith, A. (1995) *Nations and Nationalism in a Global Era*, Cambridge: Polity.

Smith, D. (2002) 'Framing the national question in Central and Eastern Europe. A quadratic nexus?', *The Global Review of Ethnopolitics*, 2(1): 3–16.

—— (2003) 'Minority rights, multiculturalism and EU enlargement: the case of Estonia', *Journal on Ethnopolitics and Minority Issues in Europe*, 1. Available at: www.ecmi.de/jemie/download/Focus1-2003_Smith.pdf.

Smith-Sivertsen, H. (2004) 'Latvia', in S. Berglund, J. Ekman and F. Aarebrot (eds) *The Handbook of Political Change in Eastern Europe*, Cheltenham: Edward Elgar.

Smooha, S. (2001) 'The tenability of partition as a mode of conflict-regulation: comparing Ireland with Palestine – Land of Israel', in J. McGarry (ed.) *Northern Ireland and the Divided World*, Oxford: Oxford University Press: 309–36.

Solonari, V. (2003) 'Creating a "People": a case study in post-Soviet history-writing,' *Kritika*, 4(2), Spring 2003: 411–38.

Stavrinides, Z. (2001) *Greek Cypriot Perceptions on the Cyprus Problem*. Available at: http://website.lineone.net/~acgta/Stavrinides.htm.

Stepan, A. (2001) *Arguing Comparative Politics*, Oxford: Oxford University Press.

Stivachtis, Y.A. (2000) *The Enlargement of the European Union: The Case of Cyprus*, Conference Paper, International Studies Association, 41st Annual Convention, Los Angeles, CA, 14–18 March 2000. Available at: www.cc.columbia.edu/sec/dlc/ciao/isa/sty01/.

Storper, M. (1997) *The Regional World. Territorial Development in a Global Economy*, New York: Guildford.

Suksi, M. (1998) 'Concluding remarks', in M. Suski (ed.) *Autonomy: Applications and Implication*, The Hague: Kluwer Law International: 357–63.

Tamir, Y. (1993) *Liberal Nationalism*, Princeton: Princeton University Press.

Taylor, C. (1995) 'Nations and federations: living among others', in R. Kearney (ed.) *States of Mind: Dialogues with Contemporary Thinkers on the European Mind*, Manchester: Manchester University Press.

Taylor, R. (2001) 'Northern Ireland: consociation or social transformation?', in J. McGarry (ed.) *Northern Ireland and the Divided World*, Oxford: Oxford University Press: 36–52.

Thatcher, M. (1993) *The Downing Street Years*, London: Harper Collins Publishers.

The Economist (1998) 'Anglo-Irish relations: Entente Cordiale', 28 November

—— (2002) 'Viktor Orban, an assertive Hungarian', 2 March, 35.

The Times (2002) 'Spain sees no hope of a solution in 'Irish model', 24 August.

Thiesse, A.-M. (1999) *La création des identités nationales. Europe 18è–20e siècle,* Paris: Seuil.

Thio, L.-A. (2003) 'Developing a "peace and security" approach towards minorities' problems', *International and Comparative Law Quarterly,* 52: 115–50.

Thomas, D.E. (1989) *Strategy Paper for 1989 European Elections,* Cardiff: Plaid Cymru Archive.

Tiilikainen, T. (2003) 'The political implications of the EU's enlargement to the Baltic states', in V. Pettai and J. Zielonka (eds) *The Road to the European Union: Estonia, Latvia and Lithuania,* vol. 2, Manchester: Manchester University Press: 14–28.

Tocci, N. (2002) 'Cyprus and the EU: catalysing crisis or settlement?', *Turkish Studies,* 3(2): 105–38.

—— (2003) 'Self-determination in Cyprus: future options within a European order', in B. Coppieters and R. Sakwa (eds) *Contextualising Secession: Normative Analysis in Comparative Perspective,* Oxford: OUP: 71–96.

—— (2004) *EU Accession Dynamics and Conflict Resolution: Catalysing Peace or Consolidating Partition in Cyprus,* Aldershot: Ashgate.

Troebst, S. (2003) 'We are Transnistrians! Post-Soviet identity management in the Dniester Valley', *Ab Imperio,* 1: 437–66.

Turner, C. (1998) *Plaid Cymru and European Integration. An Empirical Study of Multilevel Governance,* Unpublished PhD thesis, University of Aberystwyth.

Ugalde Zubiri, A. (1996) *La acción exterior del nacionalismo vasco (1890–1939): Historia, pensamiento y relaciones internacionales,* Oñati: IVAP.

Uğur, M. (1999) *The EU and Turkey: An Anchor Credibility Dilemma,* Aldershot: Ashgate.

United Nations Secretary General (1999) *Report of the Secretary General on his Mission of Good Offices in Cyprus,* 22 June, S/1999/707, New York.

—— (2003) *Report of the Secretary General on his Mission of Good Offices in Cyprus,* 7 April.

—— (2004) *The Comprehensive Settlement of the Cyprus Problem.* Available at: www.cyprus-un-plan.org

van der Stoel, M. (1999) *Peace and Stability through Human and Minority Rights: Speeches by the OSCE High Commissioner on National Minorities,* Baden-Baden: Nomos Verlagsgesellschaft.

van Meurs, W. (2002) 'Serbia and Montenegro: one small step for mankind, one giant leap for the Balkans?' CAP Working Paper, March, Munich.

—— (2004) *Moldova Ante Portas: The EU Agendas of Conflict Management and 'Wider Europe',* Munich: Centrum für Angewandte Politikforschung: 4.

VCIOM (1998) *Russians in the Baltic: A 1991 Survey,* Glasgow: University of Strathclyde Studies in Public Policy no. 287.

Venice Commission (European Commission for Democracy through Law) (2001) *Report on the Preferential Treatment of National Minorities by their Kin-State,* CDL-INF 19, Strasbourg: Council of Europe.

Verheugen, G. (2003) 'The European Neighbourhood Initiative: an opportunity for enhanced co-operation EU-Moldova,' speech at the Public Policy Institute, Chisinau, December 5.

Vermeersch, P. (2003) 'EU enlargement and minority rights policies in Central Europe: explaining policy shifts in the Czech Republic, Hungary and Poland',

Journal on Ethnopolitics and Minority Issues in Europe, 1. Availabe at: www.ecmi.de/jemie/download/Focus1-2003_Vermeersch.pdf.

—— (2004) 'Minority policy in Central Europe: exploring the impact of the EU's enlargement strategy', *The Global Review of Ethnopolitics*, 3(2): 3–19.

Verstichel, A. (2002/03) 'Elaborating a catalogue of best practices of effective participation of national minorities', *European Yearbook of Minority Issues*, vol. 2, The Hague: Kluwer Law International.

Vetik, R. (undated) 'Democratic multiculturalism: a new model of national integration', unpublished manuscript.

Visek, R.C. (1997) 'Creating the ethnic electorate through legal restorationism: citizenship rights in Estonia', *Harvard International Law Journal*, 38(2): 326–31.

Vlahutin, R. (2004) 'The Croatian exception', in J. Batt (ed.) *The Western Balkans: Moving On*, Chaillot Paper no. 70, Paris: EU Institute for Security Studies.

Vorontsov, Y. (1994) 'Information on Latvian and Estonian discrimination against the Russian-speaking population,' 19 July, UN Documents A/49/265.

Wæver, O. (1995) 'Securitization and desecuritization', in R.D. Lipschutz (ed.) *On Security*, New York: Columbia University Press.

Waldrauch, H. and Çinar, D. (2003) 'Staatsbürgerschaftspolitik und Einbürgerungspraxis in Österreich' in H. Fassmann and I. Stacher (eds) *Österreichischer Migrations- und Integrationsbericht*, Drava: Klagenfurt: 261–83.

Walker, N. (1996) 'European constitutionalism and European integration', *Public Law*, Summer: 266–90.

Wallace, W. (2002) *Reconciliation in Cyprus: The Window of Opportunity*, Mediterranean Programme Report, EUI, Florence.

Walzer, M. (1983) *Spheres of Justice: A Defense of Pluralism and Equality*, New York: Basic Books.

Weber, E. (1979) *Peasants into Frenchmen: The Modernization of Rural France, 1870–1914*, London: Routledge & Kegan Paul.

Weller, M. (2003) 'Filling the Frame: 5th Anniversary of the Entry into Force of the Framework Convention for the Protection of National Minorities' Conference Report', Strasbourg: Council of Europe, 30–31 October.

Welsh Nation (1983) 'Europe – New deal sought for Wales,' September 1983, p. 1.

Welt, J. (1999a) 'Beauftragter der Bundesregierung für Aussiedlerfragen besucht Litauen und Lettland', Pressemitteilung des Bundesministeriums des Innern, 21 October.

—— (1999b) 'Beauftragter der Bundesregierung für Aussiedlerfragen zieht positive Bilanz seiner Russlandreise', Pressemitteilung des Bundesministeriums des Innern, 10 August.

—— (2000a) 'Humanitäre Hilfen für notleidende Angehörige der deutschen Minderheit in den Staaten der GUS', Pressemitteilung des Bundesministeriums des Innern, 10 May.

—— (2000b) 'Neue russische Regierung unterstützt aktiv die Hilfenpolitik der Bundesregierung für die deutsche Minderheit', Pressemitteilung des Bundesministeriums des Innern, 28 June.

—— (2000c) 'Russland und Deutschland einigen sich auf weitere Unterstützung der Russlanddeutschen', Pressemitteilung des Bundesministeriums des Innern, 29 September.

—— (2002a) 'Benachteiligung der Rumäniendeutschen bei der Bodenrückgabe beseitigt', Pressemitteilung des Bundesministeriums des Innern, 15 March.

—— (2002b) 'Jochen Welt, MdB, begrüßt Ergebnis der 6. Deutsch–Kirgisischen Regierungskommission', Pressemitteilung des Bundesministeriums des Innern, 19 April.

Wheatley, S. (1997) 'Minority rights and political accommodation in the "New" Europe', *European Law Review,* 22(Suppl.): HRC63–81.

Wigley, D. (1992) *O Ddifri,* Caernarfon: Gwasg Gwynedd.

—— (1993) *Dal Ati,* Caernarfon: Gwasg Gwynedd.

—— (2001) *Maen i'r Wal,* Caernarfon: Gwasg Gwynedd.

Wilson, A. (1997) 'From the Beltway to Belfast: the Clinton administration, Sinn Fein, and the Northern Ireland peace process', *New Hibernia Review,* 1(3): 22–39.

Wilson, R. (1997) *Continentally Challenged: Securing Northern Ireland's Place within the European Union,* Belfast: Democratic Dialogue.

Wolff, S. (2000a) 'Changing priorities or changing opportunities? German external minority policy, 1919–1998', in S. Wolff (ed.) *German Minorities in Europe: Ethnic Identity and Cultural Belonging,* New York and Oxford: Berghahn.

—— (2000b) 'German as a minority language: the legislative and policy framework in Europe', in G. Hogan-Brun (ed.) *National Varieties of German Abroad,* Oxford: Peter Lang.

—— (2000c) *German Minorities in Europe: Ethnic Identity and Cultural Belonging,* New York and Oxford: Berghahn.

—— (2001) 'From irredentism to constructive reconciliation? Germany and its minorities in Poland and the Czech Republic', in C. O'Reilly (ed.) *Language, Ethnicity and the State,* Basingstoke: Palgrave Macmillan.

—— (2002a) 'The politics of Homeland. Irredentism and reconciliation in the external minority policies of German Federal governments and expellee organisations', *German Politics,* 11(2): 183–204.

—— (2002b) 'Beyond ethnic politics in Central and Eastern Europe', *Journal on Ethnopolitics and Minority Issues in Europe,* 4. Available at: www.ecmi.de/jemie/download/Focus4-2002_Wolff_Kymlicka.pdf.

—— (2004a) 'The comparative politics of linguistic diversity', in B. de Witte (ed.) *European Law and Linguistic Diversity,* Bologna: Il Molino.

—— (2004b) 'The double-edged sword of post-communist transition and European Union enlargement: German minorities in Central and Eastern Europe and the Former Soviet Union since 1990', in G. Gozzi (ed.) *Human Rights and Minority Rights in Eastern Europe,* Bologna: Il Molino (in Italian).

Wolff, S. and Cordell, K. (2003) 'Ethnic Germans as a language minority in Central and Eastern Europe: legislative and policy frameworks in Poland, Hungary and Romania', in G. Hogan-Brun and S. Wolff (eds) *Minority Languages in Europe: Frameworks, Status, Prospects,* London: Palgrave Macmillan.

Wolff, S. and Hogan-Brun, G. (2003) 'Minority languages in Europe: an introduction to the current debate', in G. Hogan-Brun and S. Wolff (eds) *Minority Languages in Europe: Frameworks, Status, Prospects,* London: Palgrave Macmillan.

World Bank (1998) *Republic of Moldova: Economic Review of the Transnistria Region, June 1998,* Washington, DC: World Bank: 27.

Wright, A. (2000) 'Scotland and the EU: all bark and no bite?', in A. Wright (ed.) *Scotland: the Challenge of Devolution,* Aldershot and Burlington: Ashgate.

Young, I.M. (2000) *Democracy and Inclusion,* Oxford: Oxford University Press.

Zaagman, R. (1999) *Conflict Prevention in the Baltic States: The OSCE High Commissioner on National Minorities in Estonia, Latvia and Lithuania*, ECMI Monograph no. 1, Flensburg: European Centre for Minority Issues.

Zhuryari, O., Surgailis, G. and Prikulis, J. (1994) 'Echo of the Versailles Peace Treaty? Border problems of the Baltic countries, 1920–1993', in P. Joenniemi, and J. Prikulis (eds) *The Foreign Policies of the Baltic Countries: Basic Issues*, Riga: Centre of Baltic-Nordic History and Political Sciences.

Zolotarev, V.A. (ed.) (2000) *Rossiia (SSSR) v lokal'nykh voinakh i voennykh konfliktakh vtoroi poloviny XX veka*, Moscow: Institute of Military History, Russian Ministry of Defence.

Index

Abkhazia 125, 126–35
accession countries: Hungary as 173–4, 177–8; Serbia as 181–4
accession policies, double standards in 72–4; *see also* conditionality strategy; criteria for accession; enlargement
accession process, impact on conflict resolution in Cyprus 330–1, 334–44
Act of Adaptation Cyprus 337–8, 340
Act on Hungarians Living in Neighbouring Countries (2001) 77–8, 82, 97, 185–7; amendments 118–20; blueprint for compromise 115–16; countdown to implementation 110–12; dangerous precedent 109–10; deal with Romania 112–13; fatigue 117–18; internationalising the issue 106–7; kinship and citizenship 120–3; Memorandum of Understanding 112–13, 114–15, 119; new government 114–15; positive trends 107–9; stepping up the pressure 116–17; trouble with the Slovaks 113–14
Agenda 2000 269
AKP (Justice and Development Party, Cyprus) 343
Åland Islands 47, 61, 85, 92, 136
Aliens Law (1998), Estonia 267
Alliance of Free Democrats (SZDSZ), Hungary 114–15
Alliance of Vojvodina Hungarians, Serbia 104
Alliance Party of Northern Ireland 276
Alsace nationalist movements 210
Alto Adige 85, 92; *see also* South Tyrol
Amsterdam Treaty (1997) 67, 212
Anglo-Irish Agreement (1985) 273, 280, 282–3, 286
Anglo-Irish cooperation 280–7
Anglo-Irish Treaty (1921) 283, 287
annexation, Baltic states 312
Armenia 44, 127, 132–5
Association of Language Testers in Europe (ALTE) 270
Association of the Regions of Europe (ARE) 302
asymmetrical identities 318–20
Atlantic Charter (1941) 283–4

Austria: Hungarian minorities in 173; kinship ties with Hungary 105–6
Axis Powers 172, 174
Azerbaijan 127, 129–35

Baltic states: changes in states and nationalities 310–15; cohesion and cleavage within nationalities 315–18; economic interests 317–18, 320–6; identities 318–26; implications of surveys 326–7; importance of interests and performance 321–6; multiple identities and interests 318–20; overview 308–10; population change 312–13; *see also* Estonia; Latvia; Lithuania
Banat area, Romania 159
Basque Country 288; EU constitution 253–7; nationalism and Constitution 241–3; overview 239–40; self-determination 47, 247–57; sovereignty 245–7, 253–7; Spanish Constitution 247–53; status of free association 243–5; *see also* Ibarretxe Proposal
Basque Nationalist Party (PNV) 210, 220, 240
Basque Parliament 249–50, 252
Belgium: model of domestic coordination 336; obstacles to power-sharing 91, 92
bi-zonality, Cyprus 333–8
bilateral relations: Central and Eastern Europe 145–6, 147–8; Poland 156–7
Bishkek protocol 132–3
borders: erosion of 8–10, 13–16; Hungary 171–2, 173, 174, 176–7; Serbia 178, 180–1; transformation of 31–2
Bosnia-Herzegovina (BiH): economic reconstruction 11; Hungarian minorities in 177–8; relations with Serbia 188–9; Serbian minorities in 178, 179
Breton Autonomy Party 297
Breton Democratic Union (UDB) 297–8
Brittany: identity legitimacy system 303–6; institutional alternative proposal 300–3; Maastricht Treaty referendum results 296, 297, 301; new political alliances 297–300; overview 290–1; preferential relationship with Europe 293–7; restored spatial identity 291–3
Brittany Reunified movement 292